Lecture Notes in Computer Science 9203

Commenced Publication in 1973
Founding and Former Series Editors:
Gerhard Goos, Juris Hartmanis, and Jan van Leeuwen

More information about this series at http://www.springer.com/series/7409

Wolfgang Faber · Adrian Paschke (Eds.)

Reasoning Web

Web Logic Rules

11th International Summer School 2015
Berlin, Germany, July 31 – August 4, 2015
Tutorial Lectures

 Springer

Editors
Wolfgang Faber
University of Huddersfield
Huddersfield
UK

Adrian Paschke
FU Berlin Institut für Informatik
Berlin
Germany

ISSN 0302-9743   ISSN 1611-3349   (electronic)
Lecture Notes in Computer Science
ISBN 978-3-319-21767-3   ISBN 978-3-319-21768-0   (eBook)
DOI 10.1007/978-3-319-21768-0

Library of Congress Control Number: 2015944148

LNCS Sublibrary: SL3 – Information Systems and Applications, incl. Internet/Web, and HCI

Printed on acid-free paper

Springer International Publishing AG Switzerland is part of Springer Science+Business Media
(www.springer.com)

Preface

This volume contains tutorial papers prepared for the 11th Reasoning Web Summer School (RW 2015) held from July 31 to August 4, 2015, in Berlin, Germany. The Reasoning Web series of annual summer schools was initiated in 2005 by the European Network of Excellence REWERSE. Since 2005, the school has become the prime educational event in the field of reasoning techniques on the Web, attracting both young and established researchers.

The 2015 edition of the school was organized by the Institute for Computer Science, Freie Universität Berlin, Germany, and the School of Computing and Engineering, University of Huddersfield, UK. As with previous editions, this year's summer school was co-located with the 9th International Conference on Web Reasoning and Rule Systems (RR 2015); this year there was also a collocation with the 9th International Web Rule Symposium (RuleML, four of the lectures are joint with the RuleML programme) and the 25th International Conference on Automated Deduction.

In 2015, the theme of the school was "Web Logic Rules."

The research areas of the Semantic Web and Linked Data have received a lot of attention in academia and industry recently. Since its inception in 2001, the Semantic Web has aimed at enriching the existing Web with meta-data and processing methods, so as to provide Web-based systems with intelligent capabilities such as context-awareness and decision support. Over the years, the Semantic Web vision has been driving many community efforts, which have invested substantial resources in developing vocabularies and ontologies for annotating their resources semantically. Besides ontologies, rules have long been a central part of the Semantic Web framework and are available as one of its fundamental representation tools, with logic serving as a unifying foundation. Linked Data is a related research area that studies how one can make RDF data available on the Web, and interconnect it with other data with the aim of increasing its value for everybody. Many advanced capabilities required by Semantic Web and Linked Data application scenarios call for reasoning. Thus, a perspective centered on the reasoning techniques complementing other research efforts in this area is desirable. The Summer School was devoted to this perspective, and provided insight into the Semantic Web, Linked Data, ontologies, rules, and logic.

The tutorial papers cover the research topics addressed in the lectures by the distinguished invited speakers of the school. They are either in-depth surveys or shorter papers containing references to existing work. These papers have been written as accompanying material for the students of the summer school, to deepen their understanding and to serve as a reference for further detailed study.

We would like to thank everybody who made this event possible. First and foremost, the presenters of the lectures and their co-authors. Secondly, the members of our scientific advisory board (Grigoris Antoniou, Nick Bassiliades, Diego Calvanese, Thomas Eiter, Tim Furche, Pascal Hitzler, and Sebastian Rudolph) and the additional reviewer (Lukas Schweizer). We are thankful for their advice, feedback, and their

timely reviews of the papers. Furthermore, we would like to thank the local organization team at Freie Universität Berlin, in particular Ralph Schäfermeier. We would
also like to thank our sponsors: the *Artificial Intelligence* journal, the Association for
Logic Programming, and Siemens. Last but not least, we would like to thank the team
of RR 2015, Balder ten Cate, Marco Maratea, Alessandra Mileo, Luca Pulina, and
Marco Montali, and the chairs of RuleML 2015, Nick Bassiliades, Georg Gottlob, and
Fariba Sadri, for the great collaboration in putting together all the details of the two
events.

June 2015

Wolfgang Faber
Adrian Paschke

Organization

Chairs

Wolfgang Faber   University of Huddersfield, UK
Adrian Paschke   Freie Universität Berlin, Germany

Scientific Advisory Board

Grigoris Antoniou   University of Huddersfield, UK
Nick Bassiliades   Aristotle University of Thessaloniki, Greece
Diego Calvanese   Free University of Bozen-Bolzano, Italy
Thomas Eiter   Vienna University of Technology, Austria
Tim Furche   University of Oxford, UK
Pascal Hitzler   Wright State University, USA
Sebastian Rudolph   Technische Universität Dresden, Germany

Web Chair

Ralph Schäfermeier   Freie Universität Berlin, Germany

Sponsorship Chair

Marco Maratea   Università di Genova, Italy

Publicity Chair

Luca Pulina   Università di Sassari, Italy

Additional Reviewer

Lukas Schweizer   Technische Universität Dresden, Germany

Sponsors

Artificial Intelligence Journal

Association for Logic Programming

SIEMENS

Siemens

Contents

All About Fuzzy Description Logics
and Applications

Umberto Straccia[(✉)]

ISTI - CNR, Pisa, Italy
straccia@isti.cnr.it
http://www.umbertostraccia.it

Abstract. The aim of this talk is to present a detailed, self-contained and comprehensive account of the state of the art in representing and reasoning with structured fuzzy knowledge. Fuzzy knowledge comes into play whenever one has to deal with concepts for which membership is a matter of degree (e.g., the degree of illness is a function of, among others, the body temperature). Specifically, we address the case of the fuzzy variants of conceptual languages of the OWL 2 family.

1 Introduction

Managing uncertainty and fuzziness is growing in importance in Semantic Web research as recognised by a large number of research efforts in this direction [155,160]. *Semantic Web Languages* (SWL) are the languages used to provide a formal description of concepts, terms, and relationships within a given domain, among which the OWL 2 family of languages is a major player [116]. OWL 2 has its logical grounding in *Description Logics* (DLs) [3] and the main aim of fuzzifying DLs is then to allow dealing with fuzzy concepts occurring in real world applications.

Uncertainty versus Fuzziness. One of the major difficulties, for those unfamiliar on the topic, is to understand the conceptual differences between uncertainty and fuzziness. Specifically, we recall that there has been a long-lasting misunderstanding in the literature of artificial intelligence and uncertainty modelling, regarding the role of probability/possibility theory and vague/fuzzy theory. A clarifying paper is [56]. We recall here the salient concepts.

Uncertainty. Under *uncertainty theory* fall all those approaches in which statements rather than being either true or false, are true or false to some *probability* or *possibility* (for example, "it will rain tomorrow"). That is, a statement is true or false in any world/interpretation, but we are "uncertain" about which world to consider as the right one, and thus we speak about e.g. a probability distribution or a possibility distribution over the worlds. For example, we cannot exactly establish whether it will rain tomorrow or not, due to our *incomplete* knowledge about our world, but we can estimate to which degree this is probable, possible, or necessary.

© Springer International Publishing Switzerland 2015
W. Faber and A. Paschke (Eds.): Reasoning Web 2015, LNCS 9203, pp. 1–31, 2015.
DOI: 10.1007/978-3-319-21768-0_1

To be somewhat more formal, consider a propositional statement (formula) ϕ ("tomorrow it will rain") and a propositional interpretation (world) $\mathcal{I}$. We may see $\mathcal{I}$ as a function mapping propositional formulae into $\{0,1\}$, i.e. $\mathcal{I}(\phi) \in \{0,1\}$. If $\mathcal{I}(\phi) = 1$, denoted also as $\mathcal{I} \models \phi$, then we say that the statement ϕ under $\mathcal{I}$ is true, false otherwise. Now, each interpretation $\mathcal{I}$ depicts some concrete world and, given n propositional letters, there are 2^n possible interpretations. In uncertainty theory, we do not know which interpretation $\mathcal{I}$ is the actual one and we say that we are *uncertain* about which world is the real one that will occur.

To deal with such a situation, one may construct a *probability distribution over the worlds*, that is a function Pr mapping interpretations in $[0,1]$, i.e. $Pr(\mathcal{I}) \in [0,1]$, with $\sum_{\mathcal{I}} Pr(\mathcal{I}) = 1$, where $Pr(\mathcal{I})$ indicates the probability that $\mathcal{I}$ is the actual world under which to interpret the propositional statement at hand. Then, the *probability* of a statement ϕ in Pr, denoted $Pr(\phi)$, is the sum of all $Pr(\mathcal{I})$ such that $\mathcal{I} \models \phi$, i.e.

$$Pr(\phi) = \sum_{\mathcal{I} \models \phi} Pr(\mathcal{I}).$$

Fuzziness. On the other hand, under *fuzzy theory* fall all those approaches in which statements (for example, "heavy rain") are true to some *degree*, which is taken from a truth space (usually $[0,1]$). That is, the convention prescribing that a proposition is either true or false is changed towards graded propositions. For instance, the compatibility of "heavy" in the phrase "heavy rain" is graded and the degree depends on the amount of rain is falling.[1] Often we may find rough definitions about rain types, such as:[2]

Rain. Falling drops of water larger than 0.5 mm in diameter. In forecasts, "rain" usually implies that the rain will fall steadily over a period of time;
Light Rain. Rain falls at the rate of 2.6 mm or less an hour;
Moderate Rain. Rain falls at the rate of 2.7 mm to 7.6 mm an hour;
Heavy Rain. Rain falls at the rate of 7.7 mm an hour or more.

It is evident that such definitions are quite harsh and resemble a bivalent (two-valued) logic: e.g. a precipitation rate of 7.7 mm/h is a heavy rain, while a precipitation rate of 7.6 mm/h is just a moderate rain. This is clearly unsatisfactory, as quite naturally the more rain is falling, the more the sentence "heavy rain" is true and, vice-versa, the less rain is falling the less the sentence is true.

> In other words, this means essentially, that the sentence "heavy rain" is no longer either true or false as in the definition above, but is intrinsically graded.

A more fine grained way to define the various types of rains is illustrated in Fig. 1.

---

[1] More concretely, the intensity of precipitation is expressed in terms of a precipitation rate R: volume flux of precipitation through a horizontal surface, i.e. $m^3/m^2s = ms^{-1}$. It is usually expressed in mm/h.

[2] http://usatoday30.usatoday.com/weather/wds8.htm.

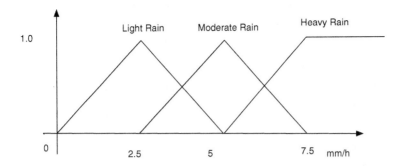

Fig. 1. Light, moderate and heavy rain.

Light rain, moderate rain and heavy rain are called *Fuzzy Sets* in the literature [176] and are characterised by the fact that membership is a matter of degree. Of course, the definition of fuzzy sets is frequently context dependent and subjective: e.g. the definition of heavy rain is quite different from heavy person and the latter may be defined differently among human beings.

From a logical point of view, a propositional interpretation maps a statement ϕ to a truth degree in $[0,1]$, i.e. $\mathcal{I}(\phi) \in [0,1]$. Essentially, we are unable to establish whether a statement is entirely true or false due to the involvement of *vague/fuzzy* concepts, such as "heavy".

Note that all fuzzy statements are truth-functional, that is, the degree of truth of every statement can be calculated from the degrees of truth of its constituents, while uncertain statements cannot always be a function of the uncertainties of their constituents [55]. For the sake of illustrative purpose, an example of truth functional interpretation of propositional statements is as follows:

$$\mathcal{I}(\phi \wedge \psi) = \min(\mathcal{I}(\phi), \mathcal{I}(\psi))$$
$$\mathcal{I}(\phi \vee \psi) = \max(\mathcal{I}(\phi), \mathcal{I}(\psi))$$
$$\mathcal{I}(\neg\phi) \ \ = 1 - \mathcal{I}(\phi).$$

In such a setting one may be interested in the so-called notions of *minimal (resp. maximal) degree of satisfaction* of a statement, i.e. $\min_{\mathcal{I}} \mathcal{I}(\phi)$ (resp. $\max_{\mathcal{I}} \mathcal{I}(\phi)$).

Uncertain Fuzzy Sentences. Let us recap: in a probabilistic setting each statement is either true or false, but there is e.g. a probability distribution telling us how probable each interpretation is, i.e. $\mathcal{I}(\phi) \in \{0,1\}$ and $Pr(\mathcal{I}) \in [0,1]$. In fuzzy theory instead, sentences are graded, i.e. we have $\mathcal{I}(\phi) \in [0,1]$.

A natural question is: can we have sentences combining the two orthogonal concepts? Yes, for instance, "there will be heavy rain tomorrow" is an uncertain fuzzy sentence. Essentially, there is uncertainty about the world we will have tomorrow, and there is fuzziness about the various types of rain we may have tomorrow.

From a logical point of view, we may model uncertain fuzzy sentences in the following way:

- we have a probability distribution over the worlds, i.e. a function Pr mapping interpretations in $[0,1]$, i.e. $Pr(\mathcal{I}) \in [0,1]$, with $\sum_{\mathcal{I}} Pr(\mathcal{I}) = 1$;
- sentences are graded. Specifically, each interpretation is truth functional and maps sentences into $[0,1]$, i.e. $\mathcal{I}(\phi) \in [0,1]$;
- for a sentence ϕ, we are interested in the so-called *expected truth* of ϕ, denoted $ET(\phi)$, namely

$$ET(\phi) = \sum_{\mathcal{I}} Pr(\mathcal{I}) \cdot \mathcal{I}(\phi).$$

Note that if $\mathcal{I}$ is bivalent (that is, $\mathcal{I}(\phi) \in \{0,1\}$) then $ET(\phi) = Pr(\phi)$.

Talk Overview. We present here some salient aspects dealing with fuzzy knowledge in the context of the OWL 2 family of languages, specifically we address fuzzy DLs. We refer the reader to [160] for an extensive presentation concerning fuzzy OWL and other semantic web languages.

In the following, we briefly sketch the basic notions about Fuzzy Sets and Fuzzy Logic, which we require then in the subsequent section about fuzzy DLs.

2   Basics: From Fuzzy Sets to Mathematical Fuzzy Logic

2.1   Fuzzy Sets Basics

The aim of this section is to introduce the basic concepts of fuzzy set theory. To distinguish between fuzzy sets and classical (nonfuzzy) sets, we refer to the latter as *crisp sets*. For an in-depth treatment we refer the reader to, e.g. [54,86].

From Crisp Sets to Fuzzy Sets. To better highlight the conceptual shift from classical sets to fuzzy sets, we start with some basic definitions and well-known properties of classical sets. Let X be a *universal set* containing all possible elements of concern in each particular context. The *power set*, denoted 2^A, of a set $A \subset X$, is the set of subsets of A, i.e., $2^A = \{B \mid B \subseteq A\}$. Often sets are defined by specifying a property satisfied by its members, in the form $A = \{x \mid P(x)\}$, where $P(x)$ is a statement of the form "x has property P" *that is either true or false* for any $x \in X$. Examples of universe X and subsets $A, B \in 2^X$ may be

$$X = \{x \mid x \text{ is a day}\}$$
$$A = \{x \mid x \text{ is a rainy day}\}$$
$$B = \{x \mid x \text{ is a day with precipitation rate } R \geq 7.5\,\text{mm/h}\}.$$

In the above case we have $B \subseteq A \subseteq X$.

The *membership function* of a set $A \subseteq X$, denoted χ_A, is a function mapping elements of X into $\{0,1\}$, i.e. $\chi_A \colon X \to \{0,1\}$, where $\chi_A(x) = 1$ iff $x \in A$. Note that for any sets $A, B \in 2^X$, we have that

$$A \subseteq B \text{ iff } \forall x \in X. \ \chi_A(x) \leq \chi_B(x). \tag{1}$$

The *complement* of a set A is denoted $\bar{A}$, i.e. $\bar{A} = X \setminus A$. Of course, $\forall x \in X$. $\chi_{\bar{A}}(x) = 1 - \chi_A(x)$. In a similar way, we may express set operations of intersection and union via the membership function as follows:

$$\forall x \in X. \ \chi_{A \cap B}(x) = \min(\chi_A(x), \chi_B(x)) \tag{2}$$

$$\forall x \in X. \ \chi_{A \cup B}(x) = \max(\chi_A(x), \chi_B(x)). \tag{3}$$

The *Cartesian product*, $A \times B$, of two sets $A, B \in 2^X$ is defined as $A \times B = \{\langle a, b \rangle \mid a \in A, b \in B\}$. A relation $R \subseteq X \times X$ is *reflexive* if for all $x \in X$ $\chi_R(x, x) = 1$, is *symmetric* if for all $x, y \in X$ $\chi_R(x, y) = \chi_R(y, x)$. The *inverse* of R is defined as function $\chi_{R^{-1}} : X \times X \rightarrow \{0, 1\}$ with membership function $\chi_{R^{-1}}(y, x) = \chi_R(x, y)$.

As defined so far, the membership function of a crisp set A assigns a value of either 1 or 0 to each individual of the universe set and, thus, discriminates between being a member or not being a member of A.

A *fuzzy set* [176] is characterised instead by a membership function $\chi_A : X \rightarrow [0, 1]$, or denoted simply $A : X \rightarrow [0, 1]$. With $\tilde{2}^X$ we denote the *fuzzy power set* over X, i.e. the set of all fuzzy sets over X. For instance, by referring to Fig. 1, the fuzzy set

$$C = \{x \mid x \text{ is a day with } heavy \text{ precipitation rate } R\}$$

is defined via the membership function

$$\chi_C(x) = \begin{cases} 1 & \text{if } R \geq 7.5 \\ (x - 5)/2.5 & \text{if } R \in [5, 7.5) \\ 0 & \text{otherwise.} \end{cases}$$

As pointed out previously, the definition of the membership function may depend on the context and may be subjective. Moreover, also the *shape* of such functions may be quite different. Luckily, the trapezoidal (Fig. 2(a)), the triangular (Fig. 2(b)), the *L*-function (left-shoulder function, Fig. 2(c)), and the *R*-function (right-shoulder function, Fig. 2(d)) are simple, but most frequently used to specify membership degrees.

The usefulness of fuzzy sets depends critically on our capability to construct appropriate membership functions. The problem of constructing meaningful membership functions is a difficult one and we refer the interested reader to, e.g. [86, Chap. 10]. However, one easy and typically satisfactory method to define the membership functions (for a numerical domain) is to uniformly partition the range of, e.g. precipitation rates values (bounded by a minimum and maximum value), into 5 or 7 fuzzy sets using either trapezoidal functions (e.g. as illustrated in Fig. 3), or using triangular functions (as illustrated in Fig. 4). The latter one is the more used one, as it has less parameters.

The standard fuzzy set operations are defined for any $x \in X$ as in Eqs. (2) and (3). Note also that the set inclusion defined as in Eq. (1) is indeed crisp in the sense that either $A \subseteq B$ or $A \not\subseteq B$.

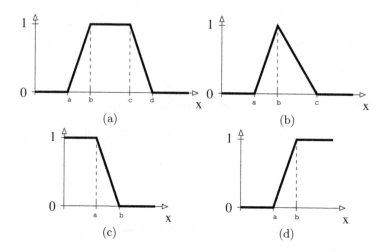

(a)   (b)

(c)   (d)

Fig. 2. (a) Trapezoidal function $trz(a,b,c,d)$; (b) Triangular function $tri(a,b,c)$; (c) L-function $ls(a,b)$; and (d) R-function $rs(a,b)$.

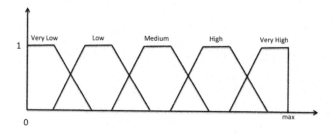

Fig. 3. Fuzzy sets construction using trapezoidal functions.

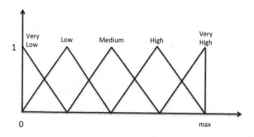

Fig. 4. Fuzzy sets construction using triangular functions.

Norm-Based Fuzzy Set Operations. Standard fuzzy set operations are not the only ones that can be conceived to be suitable to generalise the classical Boolean operations. For each of the three types of operations there is a wide class of plausible fuzzy version. The most notable ones are characterised by the so-called class of *t-norms* $\otimes$ (called *triangular norms*), *t-conorms* $\oplus$ (also called *s-norm*), and *negation* $\ominus$ (see, e.g. [85]). An additional operator is used to define set inclusion (called *implication* $\Rightarrow$). Indeed, the *degree of subsumption* between two fuzzy sets A and B, denoted $A \sqsubseteq B$, is defined as $\inf_{x \in X} A(x) \Rightarrow B(x)$, where $\Rightarrow$ is an implication function.

An important aspect of such functions is that they satisfy some properties that one expects to hold (see Tables 1 and 2). Usually, the implication function $\Rightarrow$ is defined as *r-implication*, that is,

$$a \Rightarrow b = \sup \{c \mid a \otimes c \le b\}.$$

Table 1. Properties for t-norms and s-norms.

Axiom name	T-norm	S-norm
Tautology/Contradiction	$a \otimes 0 = 0$	$a \oplus 1 = 1$
Identity	$a \otimes 1 = a$	$a \oplus 0 = a$
Commutativity	$a \otimes b = b \otimes a$	$a \oplus b = b \oplus a$
Associativity	$(a \otimes b) \otimes c = a \otimes (b \otimes c)$	$(a \oplus b) \oplus c = a \oplus (b \oplus c)$
Monotonicity	if $b \le c$, then $a \otimes b \le a \otimes c$	if $b \le c$, then $a \oplus b \le a \oplus c$

Table 2. Properties for implication and negation functions.

Axiom name	Implication function	Negation function
Tautology/Contradiction	$0 \Rightarrow b = 1,\ a \Rightarrow 1 = 1,\ 1 \Rightarrow 0 = 0$	$\ominus 0 = 1,\ \ominus 1 = 0$
Antitonicity	if $a \le b$, then $a \Rightarrow c \ge b \Rightarrow c$	if $a \le b$, then $\ominus a \ge \ominus b$
Monotonicity	if $b \le c$, then $a \Rightarrow b \le a \Rightarrow c$	

Of course, due to commutativity, $\otimes$ and $\oplus$ are monotone also in the first argument. We say that $\otimes$ is *indempotent* if $a \otimes a = a$, for any $a \in [0,1]$. For any $a \in [0,1]$, we say that a negation function $\ominus$ is *involutive* iff $\ominus \ominus a = a$. Salient negation functions are:

Standard or Łukasiewicz Negation: $\ominus_l a = 1 - a$;
Gödel Negation: $\ominus_g a$ is 1 if $a = 0$, else is 0.

Of course, Łukasiewicz negation is involutive, while Gödel negation is not. Salient t-norm functions are:

Gödel t-norm: $a \otimes_g b = \min(a, b)$;
Bounded Difference or Łukasiewicz t-norm: $a \otimes_l b = \max(0, a + b - 1)$;
Algebraic Product or Product t-norm: $a \otimes_p b = a \cdot b$;
Drastic Product: $a \otimes_d b = \begin{cases} 0 & \text{when } (a,b) \in [0,1[\times [0,1[\\ \min(a,b) & \text{otherwise} \end{cases}$

Salient s-norm functions are:

Gödel s-norm: $a \oplus_g b = \max(a, b)$;
Bounded Sum or Łukasiewicz s-norm: $a \oplus_l b = \min(1, a + b)$;
Algebraic Sum or Product s-norm: $a \oplus_p b = a + b - ab$;
Drastic sum: $a \oplus_d b = \begin{cases} 1 & \text{when } (a, b) \in]0, 1] \times]0, 1] \\ \max(a, b) & \text{otherwise} \end{cases}$

We recall that the following important properties can be shown about t-norms and s-norms.

1. There is the following ordering among t-norms ($\otimes$ is any t-norm):

$$\otimes_d \leq \otimes \leq \otimes_g$$
$$\otimes_d \leq \otimes_l \leq \otimes_p \leq \otimes_g.$$

2. The only idempotent t-norm is $\otimes_g$.
3. The only t-norm satisfying $a \otimes a = 0$ for all $a \in [0, 1[$ is $\otimes_d$.
4. There is the following ordering among s-norms ($\oplus$ is any s-norm):

$$\oplus_g \leq \oplus \leq \oplus_d$$
$$\oplus_g \leq \oplus_p \leq \oplus_l \leq \oplus_d.$$

5. The only idempotent s-norm is $\oplus_g$.
6. The only s-norm satisfying $a \oplus a = 1$ for all $a \in]0, 1]$ is $\oplus_d$.

The *dual s-norm* of $\otimes$ is defined as

$$a \oplus b = 1 - (1 - a) \otimes (1 - b). \tag{4}$$

Some t-norms, s-norms, implication functions, and negation functions are shown in Table 3. One usually distinguishes three different sets of fuzzy set operations (called fuzzy logics), namely, Łukasiewicz, Gödel, and Product logic; the popular Standard Fuzzy Logic (SFL) is a sublogic of Łukasiewicz logic as $\min(a, b) = a \otimes_l (a \Rightarrow_l b)$ and $\max(a, b) = 1 - \min(1 - a, 1 - b)$. The importance of these three logics is due to the Mostert–Shields theorem [114] that states that any continuous t-norm can be obtained as an ordinal sum of these three (see also [67]).

The implication $x \Rightarrow y = \max(1 - x, y)$ is called *Kleene-Dienes implication* in the fuzzy logic literature. Note that we have the following inferences: let $a \geq n$ and $a \Rightarrow b \geq m$. Then, under Kleene-Dienes implication, we infer that if $n > 1 - m$ then $b \geq m$. Under r-implication relative to a t-norm $\otimes$, we infer that $b \geq n \otimes m$.

The *composition* of two fuzzy relations $R_1 \colon X \times X \to [0, 1]$ and $R_2 \colon X \times X \to [0, 1]$ is defined as $(R_1 \circ R_2)(x, z) = \sup_{y \in X} R_1(x, y) \otimes R_2(y, z)$. A fuzzy relation R is *transitive* iff $R(x, z) \geqslant (R \circ R)(x, z)$.

Fuzzy Modifiers. Fuzzy modifiers are an interesting feature of fuzzy set theory. Essentially, a fuzzy modifier, such as `very`, `more_or_less`, and `slightly`, apply to fuzzy sets to change their membership function.

Table 3. Combination functions of various fuzzy logics.

	Łukasiewicz logic	Gödel logic	Product logic	SFL
$a \otimes b$	$\max(a+b-1,0)$	$\min(a,b)$	$a \cdot b$	$\min(a,b)$
$a \oplus b$	$\min(a+b,1)$	$\max(a,b)$	$a+b-a \cdot b$	$\max(a,b)$
$a \Rightarrow b$	$\min(1-a+b,1)$	$\begin{cases} 1 & \text{if } a \leq b \\ b & \text{otherwise} \end{cases}$	$\min(1,b/a)$	$\max(1-a,b)$
$\ominus a$	$1-a$	$\begin{cases} 1 & \text{if } a = 0 \\ 0 & \text{otherwise} \end{cases}$	$\begin{cases} 1 & \text{if } a = 0 \\ 0 & \text{otherwise} \end{cases}$	$1-a$

Table 4. Some additional properties of combination functions of various fuzzy logics.

Property	Łukasiewicz Logic	Gödel Logic	Product Logic	SFL
$x \otimes \ominus x = 0$	+	−	−	−
$x \oplus \ominus x = 1$	+	−	−	−
$x \otimes x = x$	−	+	−	+
$x \oplus x = x$	−	+	−	+
$\ominus \ominus x = x$	+	−	−	+
$x \Rightarrow y = \ominus x \oplus y$	+	−	−	+
$\ominus (x \Rightarrow y) = x \otimes \ominus y$	+	−	−	+
$\ominus (x \otimes y) = \ominus x \oplus \ominus y$	+	+	+	+
$\ominus (x \oplus y) = \ominus x \otimes \ominus y$	+	+	+	+

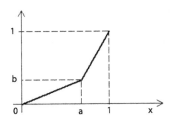

Fig. 5. Linear modifier $lm(a,b)$.

Formally, a *fuzzy modifier* m represents a function

$$f_m \colon [0,1] \to [0,1].$$

For example, we may define $f_{\texttt{very}}(x) = x^2$ and $f_{\texttt{slightly}}(x) = \sqrt{x}$. In this way, we may express the fuzzy set of very heavy rain by applying the modifier *very* to the fuzzy membership function of "heavy rain" i.e.

$$\chi_{\texttt{very heavyrain}}(x) = f_{very}(\chi_{\texttt{heavyrain}}(x)) = (\chi_{\texttt{heavyrain}}(x))^2 = (rs(5,7.5)(x))^2.$$

A typical shape of modifiers is the so-called *linear modifiers*, as illustrated in Fig. 5. Note that such a modifier can be parameterized by means of one parameter c only, i.e. $lm(a,b) = lm(c)$, where $a = c/(c+1)$, $b = 1/(c+1)$.

2.2   Mathematical Fuzzy Logic Basics

Given that the OWL 2 family of languages is grounded on Mathematical Logic, it is quite natural to look at *Mathematical Fuzzy Logic* [67] to get inspiration for a fuzzy logic extensions of the OWL family. So, we recap here briefly that in Mathematical Fuzzy Logic, the convention prescribing that a statement is either true or false is changed and is a matter of degree measured on an ordered scale that is no longer $\{0,1\}$, but $[0,1]$. This degree is called *degree of truth* of the logical statement ϕ in the interpretation $\mathcal{I}$. *Fuzzy statements* have the form $\langle \phi, r \rangle$, where $r \in [0,1]$ (see, e.g. [66,67]) and ϕ is a statement, which encodes that the degree of truth of ϕ is *greater or equal* r. A *fuzzy interpretation* $\mathcal{I}$ maps each basic statement p_i into $[0,1]$ and is then extended inductively to all statements:

$$\begin{aligned}
\mathcal{I}(\phi \wedge \psi) &= \mathcal{I}(\phi) \otimes \mathcal{I}(\psi) \\
\mathcal{I}(\phi \vee \psi) &= \mathcal{I}(\phi) \oplus \mathcal{I}(\psi) \\
\mathcal{I}(\phi \rightarrow \psi) &= \mathcal{I}(\phi) \Rightarrow \mathcal{I}(\psi) \\
\mathcal{I}(\phi \leftrightarrow \psi) &= \mathcal{I}(\phi \rightarrow \psi) \otimes \mathcal{I}(\psi \rightarrow \phi) \\
\mathcal{I}(\neg \phi) &= \ominus \mathcal{I}(\phi) \\
\mathcal{I}(\exists x.\phi) &= \sup_{a \in \Delta^{\mathcal{I}}} \mathcal{I}_x^a(\phi) \\
\mathcal{I}(\forall x.\phi) &= \inf_{a \in \Delta^{\mathcal{I}}} \mathcal{I}_x^a(\phi),
\end{aligned} \tag{5}$$

where $\Delta^{\mathcal{I}}$ is the domain of $\mathcal{I}$, and $\otimes$, $\oplus$, $\Rightarrow$, and $\ominus$ are the *t-norms, t-conorms, implication functions*, a *negation functions* we have seen in the previous section.[3]

One may also consider the following abbreviations:

$$\phi \wedge_g \psi \stackrel{\text{def}}{=} \phi \wedge (\phi \rightarrow \psi) \tag{6}$$

$$\phi \vee_g \psi \stackrel{\text{def}}{=} (\phi \rightarrow \psi) \rightarrow \phi) \wedge_g (\psi \rightarrow \phi) \rightarrow \psi) \tag{7}$$

$$\neg_\otimes \phi \stackrel{\text{def}}{=} \phi \rightarrow 0. \tag{8}$$

In case $\Rightarrow$ is the r-implication based on $\otimes$, then $\wedge_g$ (resp. $\vee_g$) is interpreted as Gödel t-norm (resp. s-norm), while $\neg_\otimes$ is interpreted as the negation function related to $\otimes$.

A fuzzy interpretation $\mathcal{I}$ *satisfies* a fuzzy statement $\langle \phi, r \rangle$, or $\mathcal{I}$ is a *model* of $\langle \phi, r \rangle$, denoted $\mathcal{I} \models \langle \phi, r \rangle$, iff $\mathcal{I}(\phi) \geq r$. We say that $\mathcal{I}$ is a *model* of ϕ if $\mathcal{I}(\phi) = 1$. A *fuzzy knowledge base* (or simply knowledge base, if clear from context) is a set of fuzzy statements and an interpretation $\mathcal{I}$ *satisfies* (is a *model* of) a knowledge base, denoted $\mathcal{I} \models \mathcal{K}$, iff it satisfies each element in it.

We say $\langle \phi, n \rangle$ is a *tight logical consequence* of a set of fuzzy statements $\mathcal{K}$ iff n is the infimum of $\mathcal{I}(\phi)$ subject to all models $\mathcal{I}$ of $\mathcal{K}$. Notice that the latter is

---

[3] The function $\mathcal{I}_x^a$ is as $\mathcal{I}$ except that x is interpreted as a.

equivalent to $n = \sup \{r \mid \mathcal{K} \models \langle \phi, r \rangle\}$. n is called the *best entailment degree* of ϕ w.r.t. $\mathcal{K}$ (denoted $bed(\mathcal{K}, \phi)$), i.e.

$$bed(\mathcal{K}, \phi) = \sup \{r \mid \mathcal{K} \models \langle \phi, r \rangle\}. \tag{9}$$

On the other hand, the *best satisfiability degree* of ϕ w.r.t. $\mathcal{K}$ (denoted $bsd(\mathcal{K}, \phi)$) is

$$bsd(\mathcal{K}, \phi) = \sup_{\mathcal{I}} \{\mathcal{I}(\phi) \mid \mathcal{I} \models \mathcal{K}\}. \tag{10}$$

Of course, the properties of Table 4 immediately translate into equivalence among formulae. For instance, the following equivalences hold (in brackets we indicate the logic for which the equivalences holds)

$$\neg\neg\phi \equiv \phi \quad (\text{Ł})$$
$$\phi \wedge \phi \equiv \phi \quad (G)$$
$$\neg(\phi \wedge \neg\phi) \equiv 1 \quad (\text{Ł}, G, \Pi)$$
$$\phi \vee \neg\phi \equiv 1 \quad (\text{Ł}).$$

Remark 1. Unlike the classical case, in general, we do not have that $\forall x.\phi$ and $\neg\exists x.\neg\phi$ are equivalent. They are equivalent for Łukasiewicz logic and SFL, but are neither equivalent for Gödel nor for Product logic. For instance, under Gödel negation, just consider an interpretation $\mathcal{I}$ with domain $\{a\}$ and $\mathcal{I}(p(a)) = u$, with $0 < u < 1$. Then $\mathcal{I}(\forall x.p(x)) = u$, while $\mathcal{I}(\neg\exists x.\neg p(x)) = 1$ and, thus, $\forall x.p(x) \not\equiv \neg\exists x.\neg p(x)$.

We refer the reader to [160] for an overview of reasoning algorithms for fuzzy propositional and First-Order Logics.

On Witnessed Models. We say that a fuzzy interpretation $\mathcal{I}$ is a *witnessed interpretation* iff

$$\mathcal{I}(\exists x.\phi) = \mathcal{I}_x^a(\phi), \text{ for some } a \in \Delta^{\mathcal{I}} \tag{11}$$
$$\mathcal{I}(\forall x.\phi) = \mathcal{I}_x^a(\phi), \text{ for some } a \in \Delta^{\mathcal{I}}. \tag{12}$$

These equations say that the supremum (resp. infimum) are attained at some point for a witnessed interpretation. Now, unlike the classical case, it may not be true that Eqs. (11) and (12) hold for all $\mathcal{I}$, i.e. $\mathcal{I}$ may not be witnessed. For instance, for $\mathcal{I}$ with domain the natural numbers and $\mathcal{I}_x^n(A(x)) = 1 - 1/n$, we have that $\mathcal{I}(\exists x.A(x)) = \sup_n \mathcal{I}_x^n(A(x)) = \sup_n 1 - 1/n = 1$, while in no point $\mathcal{I}_x^n(A(x))$ is 1. So, $\mathcal{I}$ is not witnessed (the argument for $\forall$ is similar). The following important property can be shown (see, e.g. [67–70]) stating that in Łukasiewicz logic and, thus, in SFL, a fuzzy statement $\langle \phi, r \rangle$ has a witnessed fuzzy model iff it has a fuzzy model. This is not true for Gödel and product logic however. Therefore, for Łukasiewicz logic, we may restrict our attention to witnessed models only. That is, Łukasiewicz has the so-called *witnessed model property* (there is a model iff there is witnessed model). Of course, if the truth space is finite then any fuzzy logic has the witnessed model property as well.

3   Fuzzy Description Logics and OWL 2

We have seen in the previous sections how to "fuzzify" classical sets and FOL. In the latter case, fuzzy statements are of the form $\langle \phi, n \rangle$, where ϕ is a statement and $n \in [0,1]$.

The natural extension to fuzzy DLs [160] consists then in replacing ϕ with appropriate expressions belonging to the DL family of languages, as we will illustrate next.

3.1   Fuzzy DLs

Description Logics (DLs) [3] are the logical counterpart of the family of OWL languages. So, to illustrate the basic concepts of fuzzy OWL, it suffices to show the fuzzy DL case (see [108,160], for a survey). We recap that the basic ingredients are the descriptions of classes, properties, and their instances, such as

- $a{:}C$, such as a:Person $\sqcap$ $\forall$hasChild.Femal, meaning that individual a is an instance of concept/class C (here C is seen as a unary predicate);
- $(a,b){:}R$, such as $(\mathsf{tom}, \mathsf{mary}){:}\mathsf{hasChild}$, meaning that the pair of individuals $\langle a, b \rangle$ is an instance of the property/role R (here R is seen as a binary predicate);
- $C \sqsubseteq D$, such as Person $\sqsubseteq$ $\forall$hasChild.Person, meaning that the class C is a subclass of class D;

So far, several *fuzzy* variants of DLs have been proposed: they can be classified according to

- the description logic resp. ontology language that they generalize [10,15,17, 18,21,53,103–107,109,110,128–130,134,140,146,147,150,154,170,175];
- the allowed fuzzy constructs [14,71,72,77–84,111,157];
- the underlying fuzzy logic [12,13,19,68,69,145,149,152];
- their reasoning algorithms and computational complexity results [4,5,8,9,11, 16,26–36,39,40,117,135,138,139,143,144,148,151,153,161,162,174,178].

We also refer the reader to [160] for a comprehensive survey.

In general, fuzzy DLs allow expressions of the form $\langle a{:}C, n \rangle$, stating that a is an instance of concept/class C with degree at least n, i.e. the FOL formula $C(a)$ is true to degree at least n. Similarly, $\langle C_1 \sqsubseteq C_2, n \rangle$ states a vague subsumption relationships. Informally, $\langle C_1 \sqsubseteq C_2, n \rangle$ dictates that the FOL formula $\forall x.C_1(x) \rightarrow C_2(x)$ is true to degree at least n. Essentially, *fuzzy DLs* are then obtained by interpreting the statements as fuzzy FOL formulae and attaching a weight n to DL statements, thus, defining so *fuzzy DL statements*.

As matter of example, consider the DL $\mathcal{ALC}$ ($\mathcal{A}$ttributive $\mathcal{L}$anguage with $\mathcal{C}$omplement), a major DL representative used to introduce new extensions to DLs: the table below shows its syntax, semantics and provides examples. In the table, a *fuzzy interpretation* $\mathcal{I} = (\Delta^{\mathcal{I}}, \cdot^{\mathcal{I}})$ consists of a nonempty set $\Delta^{\mathcal{I}}$ (the *domain*) and of a *fuzzy interpretation function* $\cdot^{\mathcal{I}}$ that assigns

- to each atomic concept A a function $A^{\mathcal{I}} \colon \Delta^{\mathcal{I}} \to [0,1]$;
- to each abstract role R a function $R^{\mathcal{I}} \colon \Delta^{\mathcal{I}} \times \Delta^{\mathcal{I}} \to [0,1]$;
- to each individual a an element $a^{\mathcal{I}} \in \Delta^{\mathcal{I}}$ such that $a^{\mathcal{I}} \neq b^{\mathcal{I}}$ if $a \neq b$ (unique Name Assumption, UNA).

$C^{\mathcal{I}}$ denotes the membership function of the fuzzy concept C with respect to the fuzzy interpretation $\mathcal{I}$. For $x \in \Delta^{\mathcal{I}}$, $C^{\mathcal{I}}(x)$ gives us the degree of being x an element of the fuzzy concept C under $\mathcal{I}$. Similarly, $R^{\mathcal{I}}$ denotes the membership function of the fuzzy role R with respect to $\mathcal{I}$. For $x, y \in \Delta^{\mathcal{I}}$, $R^{\mathcal{I}}(x,y)$ gives us the degree of being (x,y) an element of the fuzzy role R.

Syntax		Semantics	Example
$C, D \to$	$\top$	$\top(x)$	
	$\bot$	$\bot(x)$	
	A	$A^{\mathcal{I}}(x)$	$Human$
	$C \sqcap D$	$C^{\mathcal{I}}(x) \otimes D^{\mathcal{I}}(x)$	$Human \sqcap Male$
	$C \sqcup D$	$C^{\mathcal{I}}(x) \oplus D^{\mathcal{I}}(x)$	$Nice \sqcup Rich$
	$C \to D$	$C^{\mathcal{I}}(x) \Rightarrow D^{\mathcal{I}}(x)$	$Nice \to Rich$
	$\neg C$	$\neg C^{\mathcal{I}}(x)$	$\neg Meat$
	$\exists R.C$	$\sup_{y \in \Delta^{\mathcal{I}}} R^{\mathcal{I}}(x,y) \otimes C^{\mathcal{I}}(y)$	$\exists has\_child.Blond$
	$\forall R.C$	$\inf_{y \in \Delta^{\mathcal{I}}} R^{\mathcal{I}}(x,y) \Rightarrow C^{\mathcal{I}}(y)$	$\forall has\_child.Human$
$C \sqsubseteq D$		$\inf_{x \in \Delta^{\mathcal{I}}} C^{\mathcal{I}}(x) \Rightarrow D^{\mathcal{I}}(x)$	$Happy\_Father \sqsubseteq Man \sqcap \exists has\_child.Female$
$a{:}C$		$C^{\mathcal{I}}(a^{\mathcal{I}})$	$John{:}Happy\_Father$
$(a,b){:}R$		$R^{\mathcal{I}}(a^{\mathcal{I}}, b^{\mathcal{I}})$	$(John, Mary){:}Loves$

The upper pane describes how *concepts/classes* can be formed, while the lower pane shows the form of *statements/axioms* a knowledge base may be build of. Axioms of the form $C \sqsubseteq D$, called, *General Inclusion Axioms* (GCIs), dictated that the class C is a subclass of the class D, $a{:}C$ dictates that individual a is an instance of class C, while $(a,b){:}R$ states that $\langle a,b \rangle$ is an instance of the binary relation R. The definition $A = C$, is used in place of having both $A \sqsubseteq C$ and $C \sqsubseteq A$, stating that class A is defined to be equivalent to C.

Fuzzy DLs [160] are then obtained by interpreting the statements as fuzzy FOL formulae and attaching a weight n to DL statements, yielding *fuzzy DL statements*, such as $\langle C \sqsubseteq D, n \rangle, \langle a{:}C, n \rangle$ and $\langle (a,b){:}R, n \rangle$. The former is called *fuzzy GCI*, while the latter two are called *fuzzy assertions*.

It is worth noting that one may find in fuzzy DLs also fuzzy statements of the form $\langle \alpha \geqslant n \rangle, \langle \alpha \leqslant n \rangle, \langle \alpha > n \rangle, \langle \alpha < n \rangle$, and $\langle \alpha{=}n \rangle$, stating that the degree of truth of axiom α is bounded by $\bullet n$, where $\bullet \in \{\geqslant, \leqslant, >, <, =\}$. We stick here to the form $\langle \alpha, n \rangle$, i.e. $\langle \alpha \geqslant n \rangle$ only, by reminding that as graded axioms are intended to be produced semi- or automatically, it is hardly conceivable that they may have, e.g. the form $\langle \alpha \leqslant n \rangle, \langle \alpha > n \rangle$ or $\langle \alpha < n \rangle$.

A *fuzzy knowledge base* is a tuple $\mathcal{K} = \langle \mathcal{T}, \mathcal{A} \rangle$, where now fuzzy axioms occur in place of classical DL axioms. $\mathcal{T}, \mathcal{A}$ are called now *fuzzy TBox* (that is a finite set of fuzzy GCIs) and *fuzzy ABox* (that is a finite set of fuzzy assertions), respectively. An interpretation $\mathcal{I}$ is a model of a fuzzy statement $\langle \phi, n \rangle$, denoted $\mathcal{I} \models \langle \phi, n \rangle$ if $\phi^{\mathcal{I}} \geq n$. We say that a fuzzy interpretation $\mathcal{I}$ *satisfies (is a model of)* a fuzzy KB $\mathcal{K} = \langle \mathcal{T}, \mathcal{A} \rangle$ iff it satisfies each element in $\mathcal{A}$ and $\mathcal{T}$. A fuzzy KB $\mathcal{K} = \langle \mathcal{T}, \mathcal{A} \rangle$ *entails* an axiom E, denoted $\mathcal{K} \models E$, iff every model of $\mathcal{K}$ satisfies E. We say that two concepts C and D are *equivalent*, denoted $C \equiv_{\mathcal{K}} D$ iff in evry model $\mathcal{I}$ of $\mathcal{K}$ and for all $x \in \Delta^{\mathcal{I}}$, $C^{\mathcal{I}}(x) = D^{\mathcal{I}}(x)$.

As for the fuzzy FOL case, for concept assertion, role assertion, GCI or role inclusion axiom ϕ, we say that $\langle \phi, n \rangle$ is a *tight logical consequence* of $\mathcal{K}$ iff n is the infimum of $\phi^{\mathcal{I}}$ subject to all models $\mathcal{I}$ of $\mathcal{K}$. Notice that the latter is equivalent to

$$n = \sup\{r \mid \mathcal{K} \models \langle \phi, r \rangle\}.$$

n is called the *best entailment degree* of ϕ w.r.t. $\mathcal{K}$ (denoted $bed(\mathcal{K}, \phi)$), i.e.

$$bed(\mathcal{K}, \phi) = \sup\{r \mid \mathcal{K} \models \langle \phi, r \rangle\}. \tag{13}$$

On the other hand, the *best satisfiability degree* of ϕ w.r.t. $\mathcal{K}$ (denoted $bsd(\mathcal{K}, \phi)$) is

$$bsd(\mathcal{K}, \phi) = \sup_{\mathcal{I}}\{\phi^{\mathcal{I}} \mid \mathcal{I} \models \mathcal{K}\}. \tag{14}$$

For a concept C, we also say that the *best satisfiability degree* of C w.r.t. $\mathcal{K}$ (denoted $bsd(\mathcal{K}, C)$) is

$$bsd(\mathcal{K}, C) = \sup_{\mathcal{I} \models \mathcal{K}} \sup_{x \in \Delta^{\mathcal{I}}} C^{\mathcal{I}}(x).$$

Example 1. Consider the following background knowledge about cars encoded as the fuzzy TBox:

$$Car \sqsubseteq \exists HasPrice.Price$$
$$Sedan \sqsubseteq Car$$
$$Van \sqsubseteq Car$$
$$CheapPrice \sqsubseteq Price$$
$$ModeratePrice \sqsubseteq Price$$
$$ExpensivePrice \sqsubseteq Price$$
$$\langle CheapPrice \sqsubseteq ModeratePrice, 0.7 \rangle$$
$$\langle ModeratePrice \sqsubseteq ExpensivePrice, 0.4 \rangle$$
$$CheapCar = Car \sqcap \exists HasPrice.CheapPrice$$
$$ModerateCar = Car \sqcap \exists HasPrice.ModeratePrice$$
$$ExpensiveCar = Car \sqcap \exists HasPrice.ExpensivePrice$$

Essentially, the vague concepts here are $CheapPrice, ModeratePrice$, and $ExpensivePrice$ and the graded GCIs declare to which extent there is a relationship among them.

The facts about two specific cars a and b are encoded with the following fuzzy ABox $\mathcal{A}$:

$$\langle a{:}Sedan \sqcap \exists HasPrice.CheapPrice, 0.7 \rangle$$
$$\langle b{:}Van \sqcap \exists HasPrice.ModeratePrice, 0.8 \rangle.$$

So, a is a sedan having a cheap price, while b is a van with a moderate price.
Under Gödel semantics it can be shown that

$$\mathcal{K} \models \langle a{:}ModerateCar, 0.7 \rangle$$
$$\mathcal{K} \models \langle b{:}ExpensiveCar, 0.4 \rangle.$$

Informally, in the former case the reasoning is as follows. As a is a sedan (at least to degree 0.7), it is a car (at least to degree 0.7) and, thus, a is a car with a cheap price (at least to degree 0.7). Therefore, by the definition of a cheap car, a is, thus, a cheap car (at least to degree 0.7). In the latter case, as b is a van (at least to degree 0.8), it is a car (at least to degree 0.8) and, thus, b is a car with a moderate price (at least to degree 0.8). Therefore, as a moderate price is to some degree an expensive price, b has, thus, an expensive price (at least to degree $\min(0.8, 0.4) = 0.4$). Eventually, by the definition of expensive car, b is, thus, an expensive car (at least to degree 0.4).

Remark 2. Like for the fuzzy FOL case, for which $\forall$ and $\exists$ are not complementary in general (see Remark 1), also for fuzzy DLs we have that $\forall R.C$ and $\neg \exists R.\neg C$ are not equivalent in general, unlike the classical case. However, they are equivalent under Łukasiewicz logic and SFL.

Remark 3. It is worth noting that, w.l.o.g., an axiom $\langle C \sqsubseteq D, n \rangle$ may be rewritten as $\langle \top \sqsubseteq C \rightarrow D, n \rangle$

Remark 4 (Fuzzy DLs under SFL). [143], which presents fuzzy $\mathcal{ALC}$ under SFL, proposes a slightly different semantics for fuzzy GCIs. In fact, in [143] a fuzzy GCI is of the form $C \sqsubseteq D$ with semantics: $\mathcal{I}$ is a model of $C \sqsubseteq D$ iff for every $x \in \Delta^{\mathcal{I}}$ we have that $C^{\mathcal{I}}(x) \leq D^{\mathcal{I}}(x)$. This is the same of any fuzzy axiom of the form $\langle \top \sqsubseteq C \rightarrow_x D, 1 \rangle$, where $\rightarrow_x$ is an r-implication.

Acyclic Fuzzy Ontologies. *Acyclic fuzzy ontologies* play an important role in fuzzy DLs both as they occur often in practice as well as from a computational complexity point of view. Specifically, let us also introduce a restricted form of TBoxes, i.e. *acyclic* TBoxes. That is, let $\mathcal{T}$ be a TBox in which the GCIs have one of the following form

$$A \sqsubseteq_n C$$
$$A \tilde{\sqsubseteq} C$$
$$A \doteq C,$$

where A is a concept name, C is a concept, and $A \sqsubseteq_n C$ is a shorthand for $\langle \top \sqsubseteq A \rightarrow C, n \rangle$. We call the former two GCIs *primitive* and call the latter *definitional*. We say that A is the head of these axioms and C is the body. Furthermore, we also assume that no concept name A is in the head of more than one axiom. Now, we say that

- concept name A *directly uses* concept name B w.r.t. $\mathcal{T}$, denoted $A \rightarrow_{\mathcal{T}} B$, if A is the head of some axiom $\tau \in \mathcal{T}$ such that B occurs in the body of τ;
- concept name A *uses* concept name B w.r.t. $\mathcal{T}$, denoted $A \rightsquigarrow_{\mathcal{T}} B$, if there exist concept names $A_1, \ldots, A_n$, such that $A_1 = A$, $A_n = B$ and, for every $1 \leq i < n$, it holds that $A_i \rightarrow_{\mathcal{T}} A_{i+1}$.

Eventually, we say that a TBox $\mathcal{T}$ is *cyclic* (*acyclic*) if there is (no) A such that $A \leadsto_\mathcal{T} A$. We say also that a fuzzy TBox is *unfoldable* if it is an acyclic TBox which only contains inclusion axioms of the form $A \tilde{\sqsubseteq} C$ and if there is an $A \tilde{=} C$ then A does not occur in the head of any other axiom.

On Witnessed Models. As for fuzzy FOL, the use of infima (universal quantification $\forall$) and suprema (existential quantification $\exists$) may lead to counterintuitive behaviours (see also, e.g. [67–70]). For instance, consider the concept assertion $\langle a{:}\exists R.A, 1 \rangle$. Consider the interpretation $\mathcal{I}$ with domain $\mathbb{N}$, $a^\mathcal{I} = 1$, and for all $n, m \in \mathbb{N}$

$$A^\mathcal{I}(n) = 1 - \frac{1}{n}$$
$$R^\mathcal{I}(m, n) = 1.$$

Then for any $n \in N$, $R^\mathcal{I}(a^\mathcal{I}, n) \otimes A^\mathcal{I}(n) = A^\mathcal{I}(n) = 1 - \frac{1}{n} < 1$. However,

$$(\exists R.A)^\mathcal{I}(a^\mathcal{I}) = \sup_{n \in \mathbb{N}} R^\mathcal{I}(a^\mathcal{I}, n) \otimes A^\mathcal{I}(n) = \sup_{n \in \mathbb{N}} A^\mathcal{I}(n) = \sup_{n \in \mathbb{N}} 1 - \frac{1}{n} = 1.$$

That is, unlike the crisp case, notwithstanding there is no individual n of the domain of $\mathcal{I}$ satisfying $R^\mathcal{I}(a^\mathcal{I}, n) \otimes A^\mathcal{I}(n) = 1$, still, $\mathcal{I}$ satisfies the assertion $\langle a{:}\exists R.A, 1 \rangle$. Similar arguments apply to all of the expressions involving infima and suprema. While such interpretations may exist in theory, they unlikely may model any practical knowledge representation domain. Therefore, it is customary to restrict the attention to *witnessed models* only.

Eventually, we recall from [7] the following property: in Łukasiewicz logic, thus, in SFL, an acyclic knowledge base $\mathcal{K}$ is satisfiable iff $\mathcal{K}$ has a finite model. This property is not true if we drop the acyclicity condition, i.e., if arbitrary CGIs may occur in the TBox (see [7], Theorem 3.3).

3.2   Salient Language Extensions

One may use additionally some special constructs to enhance the expressivity of fuzzy DLs [14,23,25,146,160] such as fuzzy concrete domains, modifiers and aggregation functions.

Fuzzy Concrete Domains. We rely on [146]. In general, a *fuzzy concrete domain*, also called a *fuzzy datatype theory* $\mathbf{D} = \langle \Delta^\mathbf{D}, \cdot^\mathbf{D} \rangle$ consists of a datatype domain $\Delta^\mathbf{D}$ and a mapping $\cdot^\mathbf{D}$ that assigns to each data value an element of $\Delta^\mathbf{D}$, and assigns to every n-ary datatype predicate d an n-ary fuzzy relation over $\Delta_\mathbf{D}$. More specifically, fuzzy DLs do support unary datatypes only. Therefore, $\cdot^\mathbf{D}$ maps indeed each datatype predicate into a function from $\Delta^\mathbf{D}$ to $[0, 1]$. Typical examples of datatype predicates $\mathbf{d}$ are the well known fuzzy membership functions

$$\mathbf{d} := ls(a, b) \mid rs(a, b) \mid tri(a, b, c) \mid trz(a, b, c, d)$$

and the crisp membership functions

$$\mathbf{d} := \geq_v \ | \ \leq_v \ | \ =_v,$$

where, e.g. $\geq_v$ corresponds to the crisp set of data values that are greater than or equal to the value v.

Concerning roles, a role R is either an *object property* or a *datatype property*. An interpretation maps an *object property* into a function $\Delta^\mathcal{I} \times \Delta^\mathcal{I} \to [0,1]$, while it maps a *datatype property* into a function $\Delta^\mathcal{I} \times \Delta^\mathbf{D} \to \{0,1\}$. A datatype property does not have an inverse, but may be functional.

We also use an alphabet for concrete individuals, denoted v, and extend an interpretation to concrete individuals by mapping them into $\Delta^\mathbf{D}$. As for individuals, we adopt the UNA, i.e., $v_1^\mathcal{I} \neq v_2^\mathcal{I}$ if $v_1 \neq v_2$.

We can now extend concept expressions according to the following syntax:

$$C, D \to \forall T.\mathbf{d} \ | \ \exists T.\mathbf{d},$$

where $\mathbf{d}$ is a datatype and T is a datatype property.

For instance, the definition

$$HeavyRain = Rain \sqcap \exists hasPrecipitationRate.rs(5, 7.5),$$

where the datatype property $hasPrecipitationRate$ has been declared functional, corresponds to our definition of heavy rain seen in Sect. 1.

Modifiers. Fuzzy modifiers (see also [14,52,71–75,169]) such as very and slightly, apply to fuzzy concepts to change their membership function. We recall from Sect. 2.1 that a *fuzzy modifier* m represents a function $f_m : [0,1] \to [0,1]$. Now, we extend the language of fuzzy concept constructors by allowing to apply a modifier m to a concept C or a concrete domain predicate $\mathbf{d}$: i.e.

$$C \to m(C) \ | \ \forall T.m(\mathbf{d}) \ | \ \exists T.m(\mathbf{d})$$

allowing, e.g. to define

$$VeryHeavyRain = Rain \sqcap \exists hasPrecipitationRate.\mathbf{very}(rs(5, 7.5)) \ .$$

From a semantics point of view, we extend fuzzy interpretations in the obvious way

$$m(C)^\mathcal{I}(x) = f_m(C^\mathcal{I}(x))$$
$$m(\mathbf{d})^\mathcal{I}(x) = f_m(\mathbf{d}^\mathbf{D}(x)).$$

Aggregation Operators. Eventually, we may extend fuzzy DLs by allowing *aggregation operators* (such as the mean, median, weighted sum operators) to aggregate concepts, as illustrated, e.g. in [23,24]. Given an n-ary aggregation operator $@ : [0,1]^n \rightarrow [0,1]$, then we extend the language of fuzzy concepts by allowing to apply $@$ to n concepts $C_1, \ldots, C_n$, i.e.

$$C \rightarrow @(C_1, \ldots, C_n)$$

allowing, e.g. to express the concept

$$0.7 \cdot ExpensiveHotel + 0.3 \cdot LuxuriousHotel$$

denoting the fuzzy set of expensive and luxurious hotels, whose membership function is the weighted sum of being an expensive and luxurious hotel.

From a semantics point of view, we extend fuzzy interpretations in the obvious way

$$@(C_1, \ldots, C_n)^{\mathcal{I}}(x) = @(C_1^{\mathcal{I}}(x), \ldots, C_n^{\mathcal{I}}(x)).$$

Applications. Fuzzy set theory and fuzzy logic [176] have proved to be suitable formalisms to handle fuzzy knowledge. Not surprisingly, *fuzzy ontologies* already emerge as useful in several applications, such as information retrieval [2,37,101,166,167,171,177], recommendation systems [38,90,118,173], image interpretation [47–49,113,137,141,142], the Semantic Web and the Internet [44,120,131], ambient intelligence [50,51,100,127], ontology merging [42, 168], matchmaking [1,43,121–125,164,165], decision making [156], summarization [89], robotics [57,58], machine learning [92–99,163] and many others [6,46,59,76,88,91,102,112,119,126,132,157].

3.3   Representing Fuzzy OWL Ontologies in OWL

OWL [115] and its successor OWL 2 [45,116] are standard W3C languages for defining and instantiating Web ontologies whose logical counterpart are classical DLs. So far, several fuzzy extensions of DLs exists and some fuzzy DL reasoners have been implemented, such as FUZZYDL [14], DELOREAN [10], FIRE [60,136], SOFTFACTS [159], *GURDL* [64], *GERDS* [65], *YADLR* [87], *FRESG* [172] and DLMEDIA [158,167].

Not surprisingly, each reasoner uses its own fuzzy DL language for representing fuzzy ontologies and, thus, there is a need for a standard way to represent such information.

A first possibility would be to adopt as a standard one of the fuzzy extensions of the languages OWL and OWL 2 that have been proposed, such as [63,133, 134]. However, as it is not expected that a fuzzy OWL extension will become a W3C proposed standard in the near future, [20,22,25] identifies the syntactic differences that a fuzzy ontology language has to cope with, and proposes to use OWL 2 *itself* to represent fuzzy ontologies. More precisely, [25] uses OWL 2 annotation properties to encode fuzzy $\mathcal{SROIQ}(\mathbf{D})$ [160] ontologies. The use of annotation properties makes it possible *(i)* to use current OWL 2 editors for fuzzy ontology representation, and *(ii)* that OWL 2 reasoners discard the fuzzy part of a fuzzy ontology, producing almost the same results as if it would not exist. In order to support this methodology for fuzzy ontology representation, [25] describes an implementation of a Protégé plug-in to edit fuzzy ontologies and some parsers that translate fuzzy ontologies represented using this methodology into the languages supported by some fuzzy DL reasoners.

Furthermore, the plug-in is integrated with the *fuzzyDL* [61] reasoner [9] and makes it possible to submit queries to it. For the moment, such queries must be expressed using the particular syntax supported by *fuzzyDL*.

We are not going into more detail here and refer the reader to [25] and the FuzzyOWL2 web site [62], from which one may download some fuzzy OWL 2 ontologies as well, such as a fuzzy wine ontology, an ontology for matchmaking, and multi-criteria decision making.

3.4   Reasoning Problems and Algorithms

In fuzzy DLs the following problems are of interest.

Consistency Problem:
  – Is $\mathcal{K}$ satisfiable?
  – Is C coherent, i.e. is $C^{\mathcal{I}}(x) > 0$ for some model $\mathcal{I}$ of $\mathcal{K}$ and $x \in \Delta^{\mathcal{I}}$?
Instance Checking Problem:
  – Does $\mathcal{K} \models \langle a{:}C, n \rangle$ hold?
Subsumption Problem:
  – Does $\mathcal{K} \models \langle C \sqsubseteq D, n \rangle$ hold?
Best Entailment Degree Problem:
  – What is $bed(\mathcal{K}, \phi)$?
Best Satisfiability Degree Problem:
  – What is $bsd(\mathcal{K}, \phi)$?
Instance Retrieval Problem:
  – Compute the set $\{\langle a, n \rangle \mid n = bed(\mathcal{K}, a{:}C)\}$.

Similarly as for the crisp case, all the above problems can be reduced to satisfiability degree problems as long as the below presented reductions are supported by the underlying DL language (if not then specific algorithms have been developed): indeed, we have

Remark 5. (Fuzzy DL problem reductions). The following problem reductions hold:

  – $\mathcal{K}$ is satisfiable iff $bsd(\mathcal{K}, a{:}\bot) > 0$, where a is a new individual.
  – C is coherent w.r.t. $\mathcal{K}$ iff one of the following holds:
     • $\mathcal{K} \cup \{\langle a{:}C{>}0 \rangle\}$ is satisfiable, where a is a new individual;
     • $\mathcal{K} \not\models \langle C \sqsubseteq \bot, 1 \rangle$;
     • $bsd(\mathcal{K}, a{:}C) > 0$, where a is a new individual.
  – $\mathcal{K} \models \langle a{:}C, n \rangle$ iff one of the following holds:
     • $\mathcal{K} \cup \{\langle a{:}C{<}n \rangle\}$ is not satisfiable;
     • $bed(\mathcal{K}, a{:}C) \geq n$.

- $\mathcal{K} \models \langle C \sqsubseteq D, n \rangle$ iff one of the following holds:
  - $\mathcal{K} \cup \{\langle a{:}C \to D{<}n \rangle\}$ is not satisfiable, where a is a new individual;
  - $bed(\mathcal{K}, C \sqsubseteq D) \geq n$.
- We have that

$$bed(\mathcal{K}, \phi) = \min x. \text{ such that } \mathcal{K} \cup \{\langle \phi {\leq} x \rangle\} \text{ satisfiable} \tag{15}$$

$$bsd(\mathcal{K}, \phi) = \max x. \text{ such that } \mathcal{K} \cup \{\langle \phi {\geq} x \rangle\} \text{ satisfiable.} \tag{16}$$

Various reasoning methods have been worked out for fuzzy DLs (see [160]), which can be classified in the following categories:

- *Tableaux* algorithms, extending the tableaux algorithms for classical DLs to the fuzzy case.
- *Tableaux algorithms and optimisation* problems, using a tableaux algorithm to reduce the reasoning to an optimisation problem.
- *Automata*-based algorithms, adopting similar ideas used to prove some results in the classical case.
- *Reduction to classical DLs*, for which existing reasoning algorithms are well-known.
- *Reduction to propositional fuzzy logics*, for which reasoning has been widely studied.

We are not going to detail them here. However, let us point out that recently there have been some unexpected surprises [4,5,7,41]. Reference [7] shows that $\mathcal{ALC}$ with GCIs *(i)* does not have the finite model property under Łukasiewicz Logic or Product Logic, contrary to the classical case; *(ii)* illustrates that some developed algorithms are neither complete not correct; and *(iii)* shows some interesting conditions under which decidability is still guaranteed. References [4, 5] show that knowledge base satisfiability is an undecidable problem for Product Logic. The same holds for Łukasiewicz Logic as well [41]. In case the truth-space is finite and defined a priori, decidability is guaranteed (see, e.g. [12,16,144]).

The generalisation of fuzzy OWL to the case in which an annotation $n \in [0, 1]$ is replaced with an annotation value λ taken from another structure such as a complete lattice has been addressed in [149]. From a computational complexity point of view, similar results hold as for the $[0, 1]$ case [31,33,149]. While [149] provides a decidability result in case the lattice is finite, [31] further improves the decidability result by characterising the computational complexity of KB satisfiability problem for $\mathcal{ALC}$ with GCIs over finite lattices being EXPTIME-complete, as for the crisp variant, while [33] shows that the KB satisfiability problem for $\mathcal{ALC}$ with GCIs over non finite lattices is undecidable.

4   Conclusions

We have provided a "crash course" through fuzzy DLs, by illustrating the basic concepts involved in. For a more in depth presentation, we refer the reader to [160].

References

1. Agarwal, S., Lamparter, S.: Smart: a semantic matchmaking portal for electronic markets. In: CEC 2005: Proceedings of the Seventh IEEE International Conference on E-Commerce Technology (CEC 2005), pp. 405–408. IEEE Computer Society, Washington (2005)
2. Andreasen, T., Bulskov, H.: Conceptual querying through ontologies. Fuzzy Sets Syst. **160**(15), 2159–2172 (2009)
3. Baader, F., Calvanese, D., McGuinness, D., Nardi, D., Patel-Schneider, P.F. (eds.): The Description Logic Handbook: Theory, Implementation, and Applications. Cambridge University Press, Cambridge (2003)
4. Baader, F., Peñaloza, R.: Are fuzzy description logics with general concept inclusion axioms decidable? In: Proceedings of 2011 IEEE International Conference on Fuzzy Systems (Fuzz-IEEE 2011). IEEE Press (2011)
5. Baader, F., Peñaloza, R.: GCIs make reasoning in fuzzy DLs with the product T-norm undecidable. In: Proceedings of the 24th International Workshop on Description Logics (DL-11). CEUR Electronic Workshop Proceedings (2011)
6. Balaj, R., Groza, A.: Detecting influenza epidemics based on real-time semantic analysis of Twitter streams. In: Proceedings of the 3rd International Conference on Modelling and Development of Intelligent Systems (MDIS 2013), pp. 30–39 (2013)
7. Bobillo, F., Bou, F., Straccia, U.: On the failure of the finite model property in some fuzzy description logics. Fuzzy Sets Syst. **172**(1), 1–12 (2011)
8. Bobillo, F., Delgado, M., Gómez-Romero, J.: A crisp representation for fuzzy $\mathcal{SHOIN}$ with fuzzy nominals and general concept inclusions. In: Proceedings of the 2nd Workshop on Uncertainty Reasoning for the Semantic Web (URSW-06), November 2006
9. Bobillo, F., Delgado, M., Gómez-Romero, J.: A crisp representation for fuzzy $\mathcal{SHOIN}$ with fuzzy nominals and general concept inclusions. In: da Costa, P.C.G., d'Amato, C., Fanizzi, N., Laskey, K.B., Laskey, K.J., Lukasiewicz, T., Nickles, M., Pool, M. (eds.) URSW 2005–2007. LNCS (LNAI), vol. 5327, pp. 174–188. Springer, Heidelberg (2008)
10. Bobillo, F., Delgado, M., Gómez-Romero, J.: Delorean: a reasoner for fuzzy OWL 1.1. In: Proceedings of the 4th International Workshop on Uncertainty Reasoning for the Semantic Web (URSW 2008), October 2008, vol. 423. CEUR Workshop Proceedings (2008)
11. Bobillo, F., Delgado, M., Gómez-Romero, J.: Optimizing the crisp representation of the fuzzy description logic $\mathcal{SROIQ}$. In: da Costa, P.C.G., d'Amato, C., Fanizzi, N., Laskey, K.B., Laskey, K.J., Lukasiewicz, T., Nickles, M., Pool, M. (eds.) URSW 2005–2007. LNCS (LNAI), vol. 5327, pp. 189–206. Springer, Heidelberg (2008)
12. Bobillo, F., Delgado, M., Gómez-Romero, J., Straccia, U.: Fuzzy description logics under Gödel semantics. Int. J. Approx. Reason. **50**(3), 494–514 (2009)
13. Bobillo, F., Straccia, U.: A fuzzy description logic with product T-norm. In: Proceedings of the IEEE International Conference on Fuzzy Systems (Fuzz-IEEE-07), pp. 652–657. IEEE Computer Society (2007)
14. Bobillo, F., Straccia, U.: fuzzyDL: an expressive fuzzy description logic reasoner. In: 2008 International Conference on Fuzzy Systems (FUZZ-08), pp. 923–930. IEEE Computer Society (2008)

15. Bobillo, F., Straccia, U.: On qualified cardinality restrictions in fuzzy description logics under Łukasiewicz semantics. In: Magdalena, L., Ojeda-Aciego, M., Luis Verdegay, J. (eds.) Proceedings of the 12th International Conference of Information Processing and Management of Uncertainty in Knowledge-Based Systems (IPMU 2008), June 2008, pp. 1008–1015 (2008)

16. Bobillo, F., Straccia, U.: Towards a crisp representation of fuzzy description logics under Łukasiewicz semantics. In: An, A., Matwin, S., Raś, Z.W., Ślzak, D. (eds.) Foundations of Intelligent Systems. LNCS (LNAI), vol. 4994, pp. 309–318. Springer, Heidelberg (2008)

17. Bobillo, F., Straccia, U.: Extending datatype restrictions in fuzzy description logics. In: Proceedings of the 9th International Conference on Intelligent Systems Design and Applications (ISDA-09), pp. 785–790. IEEE Computer Society (2009)

18. Bobillo, F., Straccia, U.: Fuzzy description logics with fuzzy truth values. In: Carvalho, J.P.B., Dubois, D., Kaymak, U., Sousa, J.M.C. (eds.) Proceedings of the 13th World Congress of the International Fuzzy Systems Association and 6th Conference of the European Society for Fuzzy Logic and Technology (IFSA-EUSFLAT 2009), July 2009, pp. 189–194 (2009)

19. Bobillo, F., Straccia, U.: Fuzzy description logics with general T-norms and datatypes. Fuzzy Sets Syst. **160**(23), 3382–3402 (2009)

20. Bobillo, F., Straccia, U.: An OWL ontology for fuzzy OWL 2. In: Rauch, J., Raś, Z.W., Berka, P., Elomaa, T. (eds.) ISMIS 2009. LNCS, vol. 5722, pp. 151–160. Springer, Heidelberg (2009)

21. Bobillo, F., Straccia, U.: Supporting fuzzy rough sets in fuzzy description logics. In: Sossai, C., Chemello, G. (eds.) ECSQARU 2009. LNCS, vol. 5590, pp. 676–687. Springer, Heidelberg (2009)

22. Bobillo, F., Straccia, U.: Representing fuzzy ontologies in OWL 2. In: Proceedings of the 19th IEEE International Conference on Fuzzy Systems (FUZZ-IEEE 2010), July 2010, pp. 2695–2700. IEEE Press (2010)

23. Bobillo, F., Straccia, U.: Aggregation operators and fuzzy OWL 2. In: Proceedings of the 20th IEEE International Conference on Fuzzy Systems (FUZZ-IEEE 2011), June 2011, pp. 1727–1734. IEEE Press (2011)

24. Bobillo, F., Straccia, U.: Fuzzy ontologies and fuzzy integrals. In: Proceedings of the 11th International Conference on Intelligent Systems Design and Applications (ISDA 2011), November 2011, pp. 1311–1316. IEEE Press (2011)

25. Bobillo, F., Straccia, U.: Fuzzy ontology representation using OWL 2. Int. J. Approx. Reason. **52**, 1073–1094 (2011)

26. Bobillo, F., Straccia, U.: On partitioning-based optimisations in expressive fuzzy description logics. In: Proceedings of the 2015 IEEE International Conference on Fuzzy Systems (FUZZ-IEEE 2015), 2–5 August 2015. IEEE Press (2015)

27. Bobillo, F., Straccia, U.: Optimising fuzzy description logic reasoners with general concept inclusions absorption. Fuzzy Sets Syst. http://www.sciencedirect.com/science/article/pii/S0165011414004850

28. Bonatti, P.A., Tettamanzi, A.G.B.: Some complexity results on fuzzy description logics. In: Di Gesú, V., Masulli, F., Petrosino, A. (eds.) WILF 2003. LNCS (LNAI), vol. 2955, pp. 19–24. Springer, Heidelberg (2006)

29. Borgwardt, S., Distel, F., Peñaloza, R.: How fuzzy is my fuzzy description logic? In: Gramlich, B., Miller, D., Sattler, U. (eds.) IJCAR 2012. LNCS, vol. 7364, pp. 82–96. Springer, Heidelberg (2012)

30. Borgwardt, S., Distel, F., Peñaloza, R.: Non-Gödel negation makes unwitnessed consistency undecidable. In: Proceedings of the 2012 International Workshop on Description Logics (DL-2012), vol. 846. CEUR-WS.org (2012)

31. Borgwardt, S., Peñaloza, R.: Description logics over lattices with multi-valued ontologies. In: Proceedings of the Twenty-Second International Joint Conference on Artificial Intelligence (IJCAI-11), pp. 768–773 (2011)

32. Borgwardt, S., Peñaloza, R.: Finite lattices do not make reasoning in $\mathcal{ALCI}$ harder. In: Proceedings of the 7th International Workshop on Uncertainty Reasoning for the Semantic Web (URSW-11), vol. 778, pp. 51–62. CEUR-WS.org (2011)

33. Borgwardt, S., Peñaloza, R.: Fuzzy ontologies over lattices with T-norms. In: Proceedings of the 24th International Workshop on Description Logics (DL-11). CEUR Electronic Workshop Proceedings (2011)

34. Borgwardt, S., Peñaloza, R.: A tableau algorithm for fuzzy description logics over residuated de morgan lattices. In: Krötzsch, M., Straccia, U. (eds.) RR 2012. LNCS, vol. 7497, pp. 9–24. Springer, Heidelberg (2012)

35. Borgwardt, S., Peñaloza, R.: Undecidability of fuzzy description logics. In: Proceedings of the 13th International Conference on Principles of Knowledge Representation and Reasoning (KR-12), pp. 232–242. AAAI Press, Rome (2012)

36. Bou, F., Cerami, M., Esteva, F.: Finite-valued Łukasiewicz modal logic is PSPACE-complete. In: Proceedings of the 22nd International Joint Conference on Artificial Intelligence (IJCAI-11), pp. 774–779 (2011)

37. Calegari, S., Sanchez, E.: Object-fuzzy concept network: an enrichment of ontologies in semantic information retrieval. J. Am. Soc. Inf. Sci. Technol. **59**(13), 2171–2185 (2008)

38. Carlsson, C., Brunelli, M., Mezei, J.: Decision making with a fuzzy ontology. Soft Comput. **16**(7), 1143–1152 (2012)

39. Cerami, M., Esteva, F., Bou, F.: Decidability of a description logic over infinite-valued product logic. In: Proceedings of the Twelfth International Conference on Principles of Knowledge Representation and Reasoning (KR-10). AAAI Press (2010)

40. Cerami, M., Straccia, U.: On the undecidability of fuzzy description logics with GCIs with Lukasiewicz T-norm. Technical report, Computing Research Repository (2011). Available as CoRR technical report at http://arxiv.org/abs/1107.4212

41. Cerami, M., Straccia, U.: Undecidability of KB satisfiability for Ł-$\mathcal{ALC}$ with GCIs. Unpublished manuscript, July 2011

42. Chen, R.-C., Bau, C.T., Yeh, C.-J.: Merging domain ontologies based on the WordNet system and fuzzy formal concept analysis techniques. Appl. Soft Comput. **11**(2), 1908–1923 (2011)

43. Colucci, S., Di Noia, T., Ragone, A., Ruta, M., Straccia, U., Tinelli, E.: Informative Top-k retrieval for advanced skill management. In: de Virgilio, R., Giunchiglia, F., Tanca, L. (eds.) Semantic Web Information Management, Chap. 19. Springer, Heidelberg (2010)

44. Costa, P.C.G., Laskey, K.B., Lukasiewicz, T.: Uncertainty representation and reasoning in the semantic web. In: Semantic Web Engineering in the Knowledge Society, pp. 315–340. IGI Global (2008)

45. Cuenca-Grau, B., Horrocks, I., Motik, B., Parsia, B., Patel-Schneider, P.F., Sattler, U.: OWL 2: the next step for OWL. J. Web Seman. **6**(4), 309–322 (2008)

46. d'Aquin, M., Lieber, J., Napoli, A.: Towards a semantic portal for oncology using a description logic with fuzzy concrete domains. In: Sanchez, E. (ed.) Fuzzy Logic and the Semantic Web, Capturing Intelligence, pp. 379–393. Elsevier, New York (2006)

47. Dasiopoulou, S., Kompatsiaris, I.: Trends and issues in description logics frameworks for image interpretation. In: Konstantopoulos, S., Perantonis, S., Karkaletsis, V., Spyropoulos, C.D., Vouros, G. (eds.) SETN 2010. LNCS, vol. 6040, pp. 61–70. Springer, Heidelberg (2010)

48. Dasiopoulou, S., Kompatsiaris, I., Strintzis, M.G.: Applying fuzzy DLs in the extraction of image semantics. J. Data Seman. **14**, 105–132 (2009)

49. Dasiopoulou, S., Kompatsiaris, I., Strintzis, M.G.: Investigating fuzzy DLs-based reasoning in semantic image analysis. Multimed. Tools Appl. **49**(1), 167–194 (2010)

50. Díaz-Rodríguez, N., León-Cadahía, O., Pegalajar-Cuéllar, M., Lilius, J., Delgado, M.: Handling real-world context-awareness, uncertainty and vagueness in real-time human activity tracking and recognition with a fuzzy ontology-based hybrid method. Sensors **14**(10), 18131–18171 (2014)

51. Díaz-Rodríguez, N., Pegalajar-Cuéllar, M., Lilius, J., Delgado, M.: A fuzzy ontology for semantic modelling and recognition of human behaviour. Knowl.-Based Syst. **66**, 46–60 (2014)

52. Dinh-Khac, D., Hölldobler, S., Tran, D.-K.: The fuzzy linguistic description logic $\mathcal{ALC}_{FL}$. In: Proceedings of the 11th International Conference on Information Processing and Managment of Uncertainty in Knowledge-Based Systems. IPMU-06, pp. 2096–2103. E.D.K, Paris (2006)

53. Dubois, D., Mengin, J., Prade, H.: Possibilistic uncertainty and fuzzy features in description logic. A preliminary discussion. In: Sanchez, E. (ed.) Capturing Intelligence: Fuzzy Logic and the Semantic Web. Elsevier, New York (2006)

54. Dubois, D., Prade, H.: Fuzzy Sets and Systems. Academic Press, Orlando (1980)

55. Dubois, D., Prade, H.: Can we enforce full compositionality in uncertainty calculi? In: Proceedings of the 12th National Conference on Artificial Intelligence (AAAI-94), Seattle, Washington, pp. 149–154 (1994)

56. Dubois, D., Prade, H.: Possibility theory, probability theory and multiple-valued logics: a clarification. Ann. Math. Artif. Intel. **32**(1–4), 35–66 (2001)

57. Eich, M., Hartanto, R., Kasperski, S., Natarajan, S., Wollenberg, J.: Towards coordinated multirobot missions for lunar sample collection in an unknown environment. J. Field Robot. **31**(1), 35–74 (2014)

58. Eich, T.: An application of fuzzy DL-based semantic perception to soil container classification. In: IEEE International Conference on Technologies for Practical Robot Applications (TePRA-13), pp. 1–6. IEEE Press (2013)

59. Fernández, C.: Understanding image sequences: the role of ontologies in cognitive vision systems. Ph.D. thesis, Universitat Autònoma de Barcelona, Spain (2010)

60. Fire. http://www.image.ece.ntua.gr/~nsimou/FiRE/

61. fuzzyDL. http://www.straccia.info/software/fuzzyDL/fuzzyDL.html

62. Fuzzy OWL 2 web ontology language (2011). ISTI - CNR. http://www.straccia.info/software/FuzzyOWL/

63. Gao, M., Liu, C.: Extending OWL by fuzzy description logic. In: Proceedings of the 17th IEEE International Conference on Tools with Artificial Intelligence (ICTAI-05), pp. 562–567. IEEE Computer Society, Washington (2005)

64. Haarslev, V., Pai, H.-I., Shiri, N.: Optimizing tableau reasoning in ALC extended with uncertainty. In: Proceedings of the 2007 International Workshop on Description Logics (DL-07) (2007)

65. Habiballa, H.: Resolution strategies for fuzzy description logic. In: Proceedings of the 5th Conference of the European Society for Fuzzy Logic and Technology (EUSFLAT-07), vol. 2, pp. 27–36 (2007)

66. Hähnle, R.: Advanced many-valued logics. In: Gabbay, D.M., Guenthner, F. (eds.) Handbook of Philosophical Logic, vol. 2, 2nd edn. Kluwer, Dordrecht (2001)
67. Hájek, P.: Metamathematics of Fuzzy Logic. Kluwer, Dordrecht (1998)
68. Hájek, P.: Making fuzzy description logics more general. Fuzzy Sets Syst. **154**(1), 1–15 (2005)
69. Hájek, P.: What does mathematical fuzzy logic offer to description logic? In: Sanchez, E. (ed.) Fuzzy Logic and the Semantic Web, Capturing Intelligence, Chap. 5, pp. 91–100. Elsevier, New York (2006)
70. Hájek, P.: On witnessed models in fuzzy logic. Math. Logic Q. **53**(1), 66–77 (2007)
71. Hölldobler, S., Khang, T.D., Störr, H.-P.: A fuzzy description logic with hedges as concept modifiers. In: Phuong, N.H., Nguyen, H.T., Ho, N.C., Santiprabhob, P. (eds.) Proceedings InTech/VJFuzzy'2002, pp. 25–34. Institute of Information Technology, Vietnam Center for Natural Science and Technology, Science and Technics Publishing House, Hanoi (2002)
72. Hölldobler, S., Nga, N.H., Khang, T.D.: The fuzzy description logic $\mathcal{ALC}_{FH}$. In: Proceeedings of the International Workshop on Description Logics (DL-05) (2005)
73. Hölldobler, S., Störr, H.-P., Khang, T.D.: The fuzzy description logic $\mathcal{ALC}_{FH}$ with hedge algebras as concept modifiers. J. Adv. Comput. Intel. **7**(3), 294–305 (2003)
74. Hölldobler, S., Störr, H.-P., Khang, T.D.: A fuzzy description logic with hedges and concept modifiers. In: Proceedings of the 10th International Conference on Information Processing and Managment of Uncertainty in Knowledge-Based Systems, IPMU-04 (2004)
75. Hölldobler, S., Störr, H.-P., Khang, T.D.: The subsumption problem of the fuzzy description logic $\mathcal{ALC}_{FH}$. In: Proceedings of the 10th International Conference on Information Processing and Managment of Uncertainty in Knowledge-Based Systems (IPMU-04) (2004)
76. Iglesias, J., Lehmann, J.: Towards integrating fuzzy logic capabilities into an ontology-based inductive logic programming framework. In: Proceedings of the 11th International Conference on Intelligent Systems Design and Applications (ISDA 2011), pp. 1323–1328 (2011)
77. Jiang, Y., Liu, H., Tang, Y., Chen, Q.: Semantic decision making using ontology-based soft sets. Math. Comput. Model. **53**(5–6), 1140–1149 (2011)
78. Jiang, Y., Tang, Y., Chen, Q., Wang, J., Tang, S.: Extending soft sets with description logics. Comput. Math. Appl. **59**(6), 2087–2096 (2010)
79. Jiang, Y., Yong Tang, J., Wang, P.D., Tang, S.: Expressive fuzzy description logics over lattices. Knowl.-Based Syst. **23**, 150–161 (2010)
80. Jiang, Y., Tang, Y., Wang, J., Tang, S.: Reasoning within intuitionistic fuzzy rough description logics. Inf. Sci. **179**, 2362–2378 (2009)
81. Jiang, Y., Tang, Y., Wang, J., Tang, S.: Representation and reasoning of context-dependant knowledge in distributed fuzzy ontologies. Expert Syst. Appl. **37**(8), 6052–6060 (2010)
82. Jiang, Y., Wang, J., Deng, P., Tang, S.: Reasoning within expressive fuzzy rough description logics. Fuzzy Sets Syst. **160**(23), 3403–3424 (2009)
83. Yuncheng Jiang, J., Wang, S.T., Xiao, B.: Reasoning with rough description logics: an approximate concepts approach. Inf. Sci. **179**(5), 600–612 (2009)
84. Kang, D., Xu, B., Lu, J., Li, Y.: Reasoning for a fuzzy description logic with comparison expressions. In: Proceeedings of the International Workshop on Description Logics (DL-06). CEUR Workshop Proceedings (2006)
85. Klement, E.P., Mesiar, R., Pap, E.: Triangular Norms. Trends in Logic - Studia Logica Library. Kluwer Academic Publishers, Dordrecht (2000)

86. Klir, G.J., Yuan, B.: Fuzzy Sets and Fuzzy Logic: Theory and Applications. Prentice-Hall Inc., Upper Saddle River (1995)

87. Konstantopoulos, S., Apostolikas, G.: Fuzzy-DL reasoning over unknown fuzzy degrees. In: Meersman, R., Tari, Z. (eds.) OTM-WS 2007, Part II. LNCS, vol. 4806, pp. 1312–1318. Springer, Heidelberg (2007)

88. Konstantopoulos, S., Karkaletsis, V., Bilidas, D.: An intelligent authoring environment for abstract semantic representations of cultural object descriptions. In: Proceedings of the EACL 2009 Workshop on Language Technology and Resources for Cultural Heritage, Social Sciences, Humanities, and Education (LaTeCHSHELT&R 2009), pp. 10–17 (2009)

89. Lee, C.-S., Jian, Z.-W., Huang, L.-K.: A fuzzy ontology and its application to news summarization. IEEE Trans. Syst. Man Cybern. Part B **35**(5), 859–880 (2005)

90. Lee, C.-S., Wang, M.H., Hagras, H.: A Type-2 fuzzy ontology and its application to personal diabetic-diet recommendation. IEEE Trans. Fuzzy Syst. **18**(2), 374–395 (2010)

91. Letia, I.A., Groza, A.: Modelling imprecise arguments in description logic. Adv. Electr. Comput. Eng. **9**(3), 94–99 (2009)

92. Lisi, F.A., Straccia, U.: A logic-based computational method for the automated induction of fuzzy ontology axioms. Fundamenta Informaticae **124**(4), 503–519 (2013)

93. Lisi, F.A., Straccia, U.: A system for learning GCI axioms in fuzzy description logics. In: Proceedings of the 26th International Workshop on Description Logics (DL-13). CEUR Workshop Proceedings, vol. 1014, pp. 760–778. CEUR-WS.org (2013)

94. Lisi, F.A., Straccia, U.: Can ILP deal with incomplete and vague structured knowledge? In: Muggleton, S.H., Watanabe, H. (eds.) Latest Advances in Inductive Logic Programming, Chap. 21, pp. 199–206. World Scientific, Singapore (2014)

95. Lisi, F.A., Straccia, U.: Learning in description logics with fuzzy concrete domains. Fundamenta Informaticae in press

96. Lisi, F.A., Straccia, U.: An inductive logic programming approach to learning inclusion axioms in fuzzy description logics. In: 26th Italian Conference on Computational Logic (CILC-11). CEUR Electronic Workshop Proceedings, vol. 810, pp. 57–71 (2011)

97. Lisi, F.A., Straccia, U.: Towards learning fuzzy DL inclusion axioms. In: Petrosino, A. (ed.) WILF 2011. LNCS, vol. 6857, pp. 58–66. Springer, Heidelberg (2011)

98. Lisi, F.A., Straccia, U.: Dealing with incompleteness and vagueness in inductive logic programming. In: 28th Italian Conference on Computational Logic (CILC-13). CEUR Electronic Workshop Proceedings, vol. 1068, pp. 179–193 (2013)

99. Lisi, F.A., Straccia, U.: A FOIL-like method for learning under incompleteness and vagueness. In: Zaverucha, G., Santos Costa, V., Paes, A. (eds.) ILP 2013. LNCS, vol. 8812, pp. 123–139. Springer, Heidelberg (2014)

100. Liu, C., Liu, D., Wang, S.: Situation modeling and identifying under uncertainty. In: Proceedings of the 2nd Pacific-Asia Conference on Circuits, Communications and System (PACCS 2010), pp. 296–299 (2010)

101. Liu, C., Liu, D., Wang, S.: Fuzzy geospatial information modeling in geospatial semantic retrieval. Adv. Math. Comput. Meth. **2**(4), 47–53 (2012)

102. Liu, O., Tian, Q., Ma, J.: A fuzzy description logic approach to model management in R&D project selection. In: Proceedings of the 8th Pacific Asia Conference on Information Systems (PACIS-04) (2004)

103. Lukasiewicz, T.: Fuzzy description logic programs under the answer set semantics for the semantic web. In: Second International Conference on Rules and Rule Markup Languages for the Semantic Web (RuleML-06), pp. 89–96. IEEE Computer Society (2006)

104. Lukasiewicz, T.: Fuzzy description logic programs under the answer set semantics for the semantic web. Fundamenta Informaticae **82**(3), 289–310 (2008)

105. Lukasiewicz, T., Straccia, U.: Description logic programs under probabilistic uncertainty and fuzzy vagueness. In: Mellouli, K. (ed.) ECSQARU 2007. LNCS (LNAI), vol. 4724, pp. 187–198. Springer, Heidelberg (2007)

106. Lukasiewicz, T., Straccia, U.: Tightly integrated fuzzy description logic programs under the answer set semantics for the semantic web. In: Marchiori, M., Pan, J.Z., Marie, C.S. (eds.) RR 2007. LNCS, vol. 4524, pp. 289–298. Springer, Heidelberg (2007)

107. Lukasiewicz, T., Straccia, U.: Top-k retrieval in description logic programs under vagueness for the semantic web. In: Prade, H., Subrahmanian, V.S. (eds.) SUM 2007. LNCS (LNAI), vol. 4772, pp. 16–30. Springer, Heidelberg (2007)

108. Lukasiewicz, T., Straccia, U.: Managing uncertainty and vagueness in description logics for the semantic web. J. Web Seman. **6**, 291–308 (2008)

109. Lukasiewicz, T., Straccia, U.: Tightly coupled fuzzy description logic programs under the answer set semantics for the semantic web. Int. J. Seman. Web Inf. Syst. **4**(3), 68–89 (2008)

110. Lukasiewicz, T., Straccia, U.: Description logic programs under probabilistic uncertainty and fuzzy vagueness. Int. J. Approx. Reason. **50**(6), 837–853 (2009)

111. Mailis, T., Stoilos, G., Stamou, G.: Expressive reasoning with horn rules and fuzzy description logics. In: Marchiori, M., Pan, J.Z., Marie, C.S. (eds.) RR 2007. LNCS, vol. 4524, pp. 43–57. Springer, Heidelberg (2007)

112. Martínez-Cruz, C., van der Heide, A., Sánchez, D., Triviño, G.: An approximation to the computational theory of perceptions using ontologies. Expert Syst. Appl. **39**(10), 9494–9503 (2012)

113. Meghini, C., Sebastiani, F., Straccia, U.: A model of multimedia information retrieval. J. ACM **48**(5), 909–970 (2001)

114. Mostert, P.S., Shields, A.L.: On the structure of semigroups on a compact manifold with boundary. Ann. Math. **65**, 117–143 (1957)

115. OWL web ontology language overview. W3C (2004). http://www.w3.org/TR/owl-features/

116. OWL 2 web ontology language document overview. W3C (2009). http://www.w3.org/TR/2009/REC-owl2-overview-20091027/

117. Pan, J.Z., Stamou, G., Stoilos, G., Thomas, E.: Expressive querying over fuzzy DL-Lite ontologies. In: Twentieth International Workshop on Description Logics (2007)

118. Pérez, I.J., Wikström, R., Mezei, J., Carlsson, C., Herrera-Viedma, E.: A new consensus model for group decision making using fuzzy ontology. Soft Comput. **17**(9), 1617–1627 (2013)

119. Quan, T.T., Hui, S.C., Fong, A.C.M., Cao, T.H.: Automatic fuzzy ontology generation for semantic help-desk support. IEEE Trans. Ind. Inf. **2**(3), 155–164 (2006)

120. Quan, T.T., Hui, S.C., Fong, A.C.M., Cao, T.H.: Automatic fuzzy ontology generation for semantic web. IEEE Trans. Knowl. Data Eng. **18**(6), 842–856 (2006)

121. Ragone, A., Straccia, U., Bobillo, F., Di Noia, T., Di Sciascio, E.: Fuzzy bilateral matchmaking in e-marketplaces. In: Lovrek, I., Howlett, R.J., Jain, L.C. (eds.) KES 2008, Part III. LNCS (LNAI), vol. 5179, pp. 293–301. Springer, Heidelberg (2008)

122. Ragone, A., Straccia, U., Di Noia, T., Di Sciascio, E., Donini, F.M.: Extending datalog for matchmaking in P2P e-marketplaces. In: Ceci, M., Malerba, D., Tanca, L. (eds.) 15th Italian Symposium on Advanced Database Systems (SEBD-07), pp. 463–470 (2007)

123. Ragone, A., Straccia, U., Di Noia, T., Di Sciascio, E., Donini, F.M.: Vague knowledge bases for matchmaking in P2P e-marketplaces. In: Franconi, E., Kifer, M., May, W. (eds.) ESWC 2007. LNCS, vol. 4519, pp. 414–428. Springer, Heidelberg (2007)

124. Ragone, A., Straccia, U., Di Noia, T., Di Sciascio, E., Donini, F.M.: Towards a fuzzy logic for automated multi-issue negotiation. In: Hartmann, S., Kern-Isberner, G. (eds.) FoIKS 2008. LNCS, vol. 4932, pp. 381–396. Springer, Heidelberg (2008)

125. Ragone, A., Straccia, U., Di Noia, T., Di Sciascio, E., Donini, F.M.: Fuzzy matchmaking in e-marketplaces of peer entities using datalog. Fuzzy Sets Syst. **160**(2), 251–268 (2009)

126. Rodger, J.A.: A fuzzy linguistic ontology payoff method for aerospace real options valuation. Expert Syst. Appl. **40**(8), 2828–2840 (2013)

127. Rodríguez, N.D., Cuéllar, M.P., Lilius, J., Calvo-Flores, M.D.: A survey on ontologies for human behavior recognition. ACM Comput. Surv. **46**(4), 43:1–43:33 (2014)

128. Sanchez, D., Tettamanzi, A.G.B.: Generalizing quantification in fuzzy description logics. In: Reusch, B. (ed.) Proceedings 8th Fuzzy Days in Dortmund. Springer, Heidelberg (2004)

129. Sánchez, D., Tettamanzi, A.G.B.: Reasoning and quantification in fuzzy description logics. In: Bloch, I., Petrosino, A., Tettamanzi, A.G.B. (eds.) WILF 2005. LNCS (LNAI), vol. 3849, pp. 81–88. Springer, Heidelberg (2006)

130. Sanchez, D., Tettamanzi, A.G.B.: Fuzzy quantification in fuzzy description logics. In: Sanchez, E. (ed.) Capturing Intelligence: Fuzzy Logic and the Semantic Web. Elsevier, New York (2006)

131. Sanchez, E. (ed.): Fuzzy Logic and the Semantic Web. Capturing Intelligence, vol. 1. Elsevier Science, New York (2006)

132. Slavíček, V.: An ontology-driven fuzzy workflow system. In: van Emde Boas, P., Groen, F.C.A., Italiano, G.F., Nawrocki, J., Sack, H. (eds.) SOFSEM 2013. LNCS, vol. 7741, pp. 515–527. Springer, heidelberg (2013)

133. Stoilos, G., Stamou, G., Pan, J.Z.: Fuzzy extensions of OWL: logical properties and reduction to fuzzy description logics. Int. J. Approx. Reason. **51**(6), 656–679 (2010)

134. Stoilos, G., Stamou, G.: Extending fuzzy description logics for the semantic web. In: 3rd International Workshop of OWL: Experiences and Directions (2007)

135. Stoilos, G., Stamou, G., Pan, J., Tzouvaras, V., Horrocks, I.: The fuzzy description logic f-SHIN. In: International Workshop on Uncertainty Reasoning for the Semantic Web (2005)

136. Stoilos, G., Simou, N., Stamou, G., Kollias, S.: Uncertainty and the semantic web. IEEE Intel. Syst. **21**(5), 84–87 (2006)

137. Stoilos, G., Stamou, G., Tzouvaras, V., Pan, J.Z., Horrock, I.: A fuzzy description logic for multimedia knowledge representation. In: Proceedings of the International Workshop on Multimedia and the Semantic Web (2005)

138. Stoilos, G., Stamou, G.B., Pan, J.Z., Tzouvaras, V., Horrocks, I.: Reasoning with very expressive fuzzy description logics. J. Artif. Intel. Res. **30**, 273–320 (2007)

139. Stoilos, G., Straccia, U., Stamou, G., Pan, J.Z.: General concept inclusions in fuzzy description logics. In: Proceedings of the 17th Eureopean Conference on Artificial Intelligence (ECAI-06), pp. 457–461. IOS Press (2006)

140. Straccia, U.: A fuzzy description logic. In: Proceedings of the 15th National Conference on Artificial Intelligence (AAAI-98), Madison, USA, pp. 594–599 (1998)

141. Straccia, U.; Foundations of a logic based approach to multimedia document retrieval. Ph.D. thesis, Department of Computer Science, University of Dortmund, Dortmund, Germany, June 1999

142. Straccia, U.: A framework for the retrieval of multimedia objects based on four-valued fuzzy description logics. In: Crestani, F., Pasi, G. (eds.) Soft Computing in Information Retrieval: Techniques and Applications, pp. 332–357. Physica Verlag (Springer Verlag), Heidelberg (2000)

143. Straccia, U.: Reasoning within fuzzy description logics. J. Artif. Intel. Res. **14**, 137–166 (2001)

144. Straccia, U.: Transforming fuzzy description logics into classical description logics. In: Alferes, J.J., Leite, J. (eds.) JELIA 2004. LNCS (LNAI), vol. 3229, pp. 385–399. Springer, Heidelberg (2004)

145. Straccia, U.: Uncertainty in description logics: a lattice-based approach. In: Proceedings of the 10th International Conference on Information Processing and Managment of Uncertainty in Knowledge-Based Systems (IPMU-04), pp. 251–258 (2004)

146. Straccia, U.: Description logics with fuzzy concrete domains. In: Bachus, F., Jaakkola, T. (eds.) 21st Conference on Uncertainty in Artificial Intelligence (UAI-05), pp. 559–567. AUAI Press, Edinburgh (2005)

147. Straccia, U.: Fuzzy ALC with fuzzy concrete domains. In: Proceeedings of the International Workshop on Description Logics (DL-05), pp. 96–103. CEUR, break Edinburgh (2005)

148. Straccia, U.: Answering vague queries in fuzzy DL-Lite. In: Proceedings of the 11th International Conference on Information Processing and Managment of Uncertainty in Knowledge-Based Systems, IPMU-06, pp. 2238–2245. E.D.K, Paris (2006)

149. Straccia, U.: Description logics over lattices. Int. J. Uncertainty, Fuzziness Knowl.-Based Syst. **14**(1), 1–16 (2006)

150. Straccia, U.: Fuzzy description logic programs. In: Proceedings of the 11th International Conference on Information Processing and Managment of Uncertainty in Knowledge-Based Systems, IPMU-06, pp. 1818–1825. E.D.K, Paris (2006)

151. Straccia, U.: Towards Top-k query answering in description logics: the case of DL-Lite. In: Fisher, M., van der Hoek, W., Konev, B., Lisitsa, A. (eds.) JELIA 2006. LNCS (LNAI), vol. 4160, pp. 439–451. Springer, Heidelberg (2006)

152. Straccia, U.: Uncertainty and description logic programs over lattices. In: Sanche, E. (ed.) Fuzzy Logic and the Semantic Web, Capturing Intelligence, Chap. 7, pp. 115–133. Elsevier, Amsterdam (2006)

153. Straccia, U.: Reasoning in L-$\mathcal{SHIF}$: an expressive fuzzy description logic under łukasiewicz semantics. Technical report TR-2007-10-18, Istituto di Scienza e Tecnologie dell'Informazione, Consiglio Nazionale delle Ricerche, Pisa, Italy (2007)

154. Straccia, U.: Fuzzy description logic programs. In: Marsala, C., Bouchon-Meunier, B., Yager, R.R., Rifqi, M. (eds.) Uncertainty and Intelligent Information Systems, Chap. 29, pp. 405–418. World Scientific, Singapore (2008)

155. Straccia, U.: Managing uncertainty and vagueness in description logics, logic programs and description logic programs. In: Baroglio, C., Bonatti, P.A., Małuszyński, J., Marchiori, M., Polleres, A., Schaffert, S. (eds.) Reasoning Web. LNCS, vol. 5224, pp. 54–103. Springer, Heidelberg (2008)

156. Straccia, U.: Multi criteria decision making in fuzzy description logics: a first step. In: Velásquez, J.D., Ríos, S.A., Howlett, R.J., Jain, L.C. (eds.) KES 2009, Part I. LNCS, vol. 5711, pp. 78–86. Springer, Heidelberg (2009)

157. Straccia, U.: Towards spatial reasoning in fuzzy description logics. In: 2009 IEEE International Conference on Fuzzy Systems (FUZZ-IEEE-09), pp. 512–517. IEEE Computer Society (2009)

158. Straccia, U.: An ontology mediated multimedia information retrieval system. In: Proceedings of the the 40th International Symposium on Multiple-Valued Logic (ISMVL-10), pp. 319–324. IEEE Computer Society (2010)

159. Straccia, U.: Softfacts: a Top-k retrieval engine for ontology mediated access to relational databases. In: Proceedings of the 2010 IEEE International Conference on Systems, Man and Cybernetics (SMC-10), pp. 4115–4122. IEEE Press (2010)

160. Straccia, U.: Foundations of Fuzzy Logic and Semantic Web Languages. CRC Studies in Informatics Series. Chapman & Hall, Boca Raton (2013)

161. Straccia, U., Bobillo, F.: Mixed integer programming, general concept inclusions and fuzzy description logics. In: Proceedings of the 5th Conference of the European Society for Fuzzy Logic and Technology (EUSFLAT-07), University of Ostrava, Ostrava, Czech Republic, vol. 2, pp. 213–220 (2007)

162. Straccia, U., Bobillo, F.: Mixed integer programming, general concept inclusions and fuzzy description logics. Mathw. Soft Comput. **14**(3), 247–259 (2007)

163. Straccia, U., Mucci, M.: pFOIL-DL: learning (fuzzy) $\mathcal{EL}$ concept descriptions from crisp owl data using a probabilistic ensemble estimation. In: Proceedings of the 30th Annual ACM Symposium on Applied Computing (SAC-15), pp. 345–352. ACM, Salamanca (2015)

164. Straccia, U., Tinelli, E., Colucci, S., Di Noia, T., Di Sciascio, E.: Semantic-based Top-k retrieval for competence management. In: Rauch, J., Raś, Z.W., Berka, P., Elomaa, T. (eds.) ISMIS 2009. LNCS, vol. 5722, pp. 473–482. Springer, Heidelberg (2009)

165. Straccia, U., Tinelli, E., Di Noia, T., Di Sciascio, E., Colucci, S.: Top-k retrieval for automated human resource management. In: Proceedings of the 17th Italian Symposium on Advanced Database Systems (SEBD-09), pp. 161–168 (2009)

166. Straccia, U., Visco, G.: DL-Media: an ontology mediated multimedia information retrieval system. In: Proceeedings of the International Workshop on Description Logics (DL-07), vol. 250. CEUR, Insbruck (2007)

167. Straccia, U., Visco, G.: DLMedia: an ontology mediated multimedia information retrieval system. In: Proceedings of the Fourth International Workshop on Uncertainty Reasoning for the Semantic Web (URSW-08), Karlsruhe, Germany, 26 October 2008. CEUR Workshop Proceedings, vol. 423. CEUR-WS.org (2008)

168. Todorov, K., Hudelot, C., Popescu, A., Geibel, P.: Fuzzy ontology alignment using background knowledge. Int. J. Uncertainty, Fuzziness Knowl.-Based Syst. **22**(1), 75–112 (2014)

169. Tresp, C., Molitor, R.: A description logic for vague knowledge. In: Proceedings of the 13th European Conference on Artificial Intelligence (ECAI-98), Brighton (England), August 1998

170. Venetis, T., Stoilos, G., Stamou, G., Kollias, S.: f-DLPs: extending description logic programs with fuzzy sets and fuzzy logic. In: IEEE International Conference on Fuzzy Systems (Fuzz-IEEE 2007) (2007)

171. Wallace, M.: Ontologies and soft computing in flexible querying. Control Cybern. **38**(2), 481–507 (2009)
172. Wang, H., Ma, Z.M., Yin, J.: FRESG: a kind of fuzzy description logic reasoner. In: Bhowmick, S.S., Küng, J., Wagner, R. (eds.) DEXA 2009. LNCS, vol. 5690, pp. 443–450. Springer, Heidelberg (2009)
173. Yaguinuma, C.A., Santos, M.T.P., Camargo, H.A., Reformat, M.: A FML-based hybrid reasoner combining fuzzy ontology and mamdani inference. In: Proceedings of the 22nd IEEE International Conference on Fuzzy Systems (FUZZ-IEEE 2013) (2013)
174. Lu, J., Li, Y., Xu, B., Kang, D.: Discrete tableau algorithms for $\mathcal{SHI}$. In: Proceeedings of the International Workshop on Description Logics (DL-06). CEUR (2006)
175. Yen, J.: Generalizing term subsumption languages to fuzzy logic. In: Proceedings of the 12th International Joint Conference on Artificial Intelligence (IJCAI-91), Sydney, Australia, pp. 472–477 (1991)
176. Zadeh, L.A.: Fuzzy sets. Inf. Control **8**(3), 338–353 (1965)
177. Zhang, L., Yu, Y., Zhou, J., Lin, C., Yang, Y.: An enhanced model for searching in semantic portals. In: WWW 2005: Proceedings of the 14th International Conference on World Wide Web, pp. 453–462. ACM Press, New York (2005)
178. Zhou, Z., Qi, G., Liu, C., Hitzler, P., Mutharaju, R.: Reasoning with fuzzy-$\mathcal{EL}^+$ ontologies using mapreduce. In: 20th European Conference on Artificial Intelligence (ECAI-12), pp. 933–934. IOS Press (2012)

Higher-Order Modal Logics: Automation and Applications

Christoph Benzmüller[1]([✉]) and Bruno Woltzenlogel Paleo[2]

[1] Freie Universität Berlin, Berlin, Germany
c.benzmueller@fu-berlin.de
[2] Vienna University of Technology, Vienna, Austria
bruno@logic.at

Abstract. *These are the lecture notes of a tutorial on higher-order modal logics held at the 11th Reasoning Web Summer School.* After defining the syntax and (possible worlds) semantics of some higher-order modal logics, we show that they can be embedded into classical higher-order logic by systematically lifting the types of propositions, making them depend on a new atomic type for possible worlds. This approach allows several well-established automated and interactive reasoning tools for classical higher-order logic to be applied also to modal higher-order logic problems. Moreover, also meta reasoning about the embedded modal logics becomes possible. Finally, we illustrate how our approach can be useful for reasoning with web logics and expressive ontologies, and we also sketch a possible solution for handling inconsistent data.

1 Introduction and Overview

Expressivity matters. Often problems can be elegantly encoded and solved in expressive higher-order logics, while their encoding and/or solution in (theoretically or practically) less expressive logics is significantly more involved or even condemned to fail. A prominent example that well illustrates this issue for the transition from first-order to higher-order logic is Boolos' *curious inference* [29] (which has been formalized with modern higher-order proof assistants [15]). In higher-order logic there is a short, one page proof, whereas the corresponding first-order proof is intractably long.

Another, more practical example from mathematics is Cantor's theorem (the set of all subsets of A, that is, the power set of A, has a strictly greater cardinality than A itself). In classical higher-order logic Cantor's theorem (surjective version) can be encoded as $\neg \exists F \forall G \exists X . F X = G$. Higher-order theorem provers can solve this problem very efficiently, and their solution includes the detection and application of the diagonalisation argument [8]. In fact, this theorem is today often used as a very first test example for new higher-order theorem provers. Other illustrating examples include McCarthy's checkerboard problem or the fixed point theorem [9].

C. Benzmüller—This work has been supported by the German Research Foundation DFG under grants BE2501/9-1,2 and BE2501/11-1.

W. Faber and A. Paschke (Eds.): Reasoning Web 2015, LNCS 9203, pp. 32–74, 2015.
DOI: 10.1007/978-3-319-21768-0_2

Modal logics [26] extend usual formal logic languages by adding modal operators ($\square$ and $\lozenge$) and are characterized by the *necessitation rule*, according to which $\square A$ is a theorem if A is a theorem, even though $A \supset \square A$ is not necessarily a theorem. Various notions, such as *necessity and possibility*, *obligation and permission*, *knowledge and belief*, and *temporal globality and eventuality*, which are ubiquitous in various application domains, have been formalized with the help of modal operators.

In Philosophy, Gödel's modern version of the ontological argument [43,65] is an interesting example that uses modal operators to express metaphysical necessity and possibility as fundamental notions. In knowledge representation, higher-order logic's expressivity is well-suited to automate meta-logical reasoning about distinct formalisms, such as description logics and modal logics, establishing and verifying correspondence results between them; and, furthermore, some ontologies, such as SUMO [58], could benefit from a reformalisation using modal operators.

Despite the importance of modal logics, general automated reasoning support for them is still not as well-developed as for classical logics. Deduction tools for modal logics are often limited to propositional, quantifier-free fragments or tailored to particular modal logics and their applications; first-order automated deduction techniques based on tableaux, sequent calculi and connection calculi have only recently been generalized and implemented in a few new provers able to directly cope with modalities [17,55].

Another approach is the embedding of first-order and even higher-order modal logics (HOML) into classical higher-order logics (HOL) [20,21], for which a range of robust and increasingly effective automated theorem provers has been recently developed [12,28,30,48,50,54].

The embedding approach is flexible, because various modal logics (even with multiple modalities or varying/cumulative domain quantifiers) can be easily supported by stating their characteristic axioms. Moreover, the approach is relatively simple to implement, because it does not require any modification in the source code of the higher-order prover. The prover can be used as is, and only the input files provided to the prover must be specially encoded (using lifted versions of connectives and logical constants instead of the usual ones). Furthermore, the efficacy and efficiency of the embedding approach has been confirmed in philosophical benchmarks such as Gödel's ontological argument and some of its variants [13,19,24,56]. These qualities make embedding a convenient approach for *automated* and *interactive* reasoning with propositional and quantified modal logics and possibly many other prominent non-classical logics such as hybrid logics and paraconsistent logics.

In these lecture notes, the syntax and semantics of higher-order logics and higher-order modal logics are introduced and the embedding approach is explained. Then some of the motivating applications described above are explored in greater detail.

2   Higher-Order Modal Logic: Syntax and Semantic

In this section a higher-order modal logic (HOML) is defined by extending a higher-order logic (HOL) with the modal operator $\Box$. An appropriate notion of semantics for HOML is obtained by adapting Henkin semantics for HOL (cf. [39, 45]). The presentation in this section is borrowed from [19], which adapts [7,53].

HOML is a typed logic. More precisely, it is based on Church's simple types. Below only two base types are assumed, but other base types could be easily added.

Definition 1. *The set T of simple types is freely generated from the set of basic types $\{o, \mu\}$ (o stands for Booleans and μ for individuals) using the function type constructor $\to$. We may avoid parentheses, and $\alpha \to \alpha \to \alpha$ then stands for $(\alpha \to (\alpha \to \alpha))$, that is, function types associate to the right.*

The syntax of the HOML language is given below.

Definition 2. *The grammar for HOML is:*

$$s, t \quad ::= \quad p_\alpha \mid X_\alpha \mid (\lambda X_\alpha \cdot s_\beta)_{\alpha \to \beta} \mid (s_{\alpha \to \beta} t_\alpha)_\beta \mid (\neg_{o \to o} s_o)_o \mid$$
$$((\vee_{o \to o \to o} s_o) t_o)_o \mid (\forall_{(\alpha \to o) \to o}(\lambda X_\alpha \cdot s_o))_o \mid (\Box_{o \to o} s_o)_o$$

where $\alpha, \beta \in T$. p_α denotes typed constants and X_α typed variables (distinct from p_α). Complex typed terms are constructed via abstraction and application. The type of each term is given as a subscript. Terms s_o of type o are called formulas. The logical connectives of choice are $\neg_{o \to o}$, $\vee_{o \to o \to o}$, $\forall_{(\alpha \to o) \to o}$ (for $\alpha \in T$), and $\Box_{o \to o}$. Type subscripts may be dropped if irrelevant or obvious. Similarly, parentheses may be avoided. Binder notation $\forall X_\alpha s_o$ is used as shorthand for $\forall_{(\alpha \to o) \to o}(\lambda X_\alpha \cdot s_o)$, and infix notation $s \vee t$ is employed instead of $((\vee s) t)$. From the above connectives, other logical connectives, such as $\top$, $\bot$, $\wedge$, $\supset$, $\equiv$, $\exists$, and $\Diamond$, can be defined in the usual way.

Substitution and λ-conversion are defined as usual.

Definition 3. Substitution *of a term A_α for a variable X_α in a term B_β is denoted by $[A/X]B$. Since we consider α-conversion implicitly, we assume the bound variables of B avoid variable capture.*

Definition 4. *Two common relations on terms are given by β-reduction and η-reduction. A β-redex has the form $(\lambda X.s)t$ and β-reduces to $[t/X]s$. An η-redex has the form $(\lambda X.sX)$ where variable X is not free in s; it η-reduces to s. We write $s =_\beta t$ to mean s can be converted to t by a series of β-reductions and expansions. Similarly, $s = beta_\eta t$ means s can be converted to t using both β and η. For each $s_\alpha \in HOML$ there is a unique β-normal form and a unique $\beta\eta$-normal form.*

As a first step towards defining a semantics for HOML, frame structures are introduced. Variables, constants and terms of HOML will subsequently be identified with objects provided in a frame.

Definition 5. *A frame D is a collection $\{D_\alpha\}_{\alpha\in T}$ of nonempty sets D_α, such that $D_o = \{T, F\}$ (for truth and falsehood). The $D_{\alpha\to\beta}$ are collections of functions mapping D_α into D_β.*

Starting from a frame, the notion of a HOML model structure is introduced.

Definition 6. *A model for HOML is a quadruple $M = \langle W, R, D, \{I_w\}_{w\in W}\rangle$, where W is a set of worlds (or states), R is an accessibility relation between the worlds in W, D is a frame, and for each $w \in W$, $\{I_w\}_{w\in W}$ is a family of typed interpretation functions mapping constant symbols p_α to appropriate elements of D_α, called the denotation of p_α in world w (the logical connectives $\neg$, $\vee$, $\forall$, and $\square$ are always given the standard denotations, see below). Moreover, it is assumed that the domains $D_{\alpha\to\alpha\to o}$ contain the respective identity relations on objects of type α (to overcome the extensionality issue discussed in [6]).*

Variable assignments are a technical aid for the subsequent definition of an interpretation function $\|.\|^{M,g,w}$ for HOML terms. This interpretation function is parametric over a model M, a variable assignment g and a possible world w.

Definition 7. *A variable assignment g maps variables X_α to elements in D_α. $g[d/W]$ denotes the assignment that is identical to g, except for variable W, which is now mapped to d.*

Definition 8. *The value $\|s_\alpha\|^{M,g,w}$ of a HOML term s_α on a model $M = \langle W, R, D, \{I_w\}_{w\in W}\rangle$ in a world $w \in W$ under variable assignment g is an element $d \in D_\alpha$ defined in the following way:*

1. $\|p_\alpha\|^{M,g,w} = I_w(p_\alpha)$
2. $\|X_\alpha\|^{M,g,w} = g(X_\alpha)$
3. $\|(s_{\alpha\to\beta}\, t_\alpha)_\beta\|^{M,g,w} = \|s_{\alpha\to\beta}\|^{M,g,w}(\|t_\alpha\|^{M,g,w})$
4. $\|(\lambda X_\alpha \bullet s_\beta)_{\alpha\to\beta}\|^{M,g,w} =$ *the function f from D_α to D_β such that $f(d) = \|s_\beta\|^{M,g[d/X_\alpha],w}$ for all $d \in D_\alpha$*
5. $\|(\neg_{o\to o}\, s_o)_o\|^{M,g,w} = T$ *if and only if* $\|s_o\|^{M,g,w} = F$
6. $\|((\vee_{o\to o\to o}\, s_o)\, t_o)_o\|^{M,g,w} = T$ *if and only if* $\|s_o\|^{M,g,w} = T$ *or* $\|t_o\|^{M,g,w} = T$
7. $\|(\forall_{(\alpha\to o)\to o}(\lambda X_\alpha \bullet s_o))_o\|^{M,g,w} = T$ *if and only if for all $d \in D_\alpha$ we have* $\|s_o\|^{M,g[d/X_\alpha],w} = T$
8. $\|(\square_{o\to o}\, s_o)_o\|^{M,g,w} = T$ *if and only if for all $v \in W$ with wRv we have* $\|s_o\|^{M,g,v} = T$

Standard semantics does not allow a complete mechanization of HOML. For this reason, Henkin style semantics is introduced here and assumed in the remainder. Henkin semantics allows a complete mechanization of HOML (at least in theory).

Definition 9. *A model $M = \langle W, R, D, \{I_w\}_{w\in W}\rangle$ is called a standard model if and only if for all $\alpha, \beta \in T$ we have $D_{\alpha\to\beta} = \{f \mid f : D_\alpha \longrightarrow D_\beta\}$. In a Henkin model function spaces are not necessarily full. Instead it is only required that $D_{\alpha\to\beta} \subseteq \{f \mid f : D_\alpha \longrightarrow D_\beta\}$ (for all $\alpha, \beta \in T$) and that the valuation function $\|\cdot\|^{M,g,w}$ from above is total (i.e., every term denotes). Any standard model is obviously also a Henkin model. We consider Henkin models in the remainder.*

Truth in a model, validity in a model M and general validity are defined as usual.

Definition 10. *A formula s_o is true in model M for world w under assignment g if and only if $\|s_o\|^{M,g,w} = T$; this is also denoted as $M, g, w \models s_o$. A formula s_o is called valid in M if and only if $M, g, w \models s_o$ for all $w \in W$ and all assignments g. Finally, a formula s_o is called valid, which we denote by $\models s_o$, if and only if s_o is valid for all M.*

The definitions above introduce higher-order modal logic K. In order to obtain logics KB, KD, S4 and S5, for example, respective conditions on accessibility relation R are postulated: R is a symmetric relation in logic KB, and it is an equivalence relation in logic S5. If these restriction apply, we use the notations $\models^{KB}$ and $\models^{S5}$. In a similar way we may introduce further logics between K and S5, such as KD, S4, KD45, etc.

   An important issue for quantified modal logics is whether constant domain or varying domain semantics is considered. The definitions above assume constant domains. An adaptation to varying or cumulative domains is straightforward (cf. [37]).

3   Semantic Embedding in Classical Higher-Order Logic

A crucial aspect of modal logics [26] is that the so-called *necessitation rule* allows $\Box A$ to be derived if A is a theorem, but $A \supset \Box A$ is not necessarily a theorem. Naive attempts to define the modal operators $\Box$ and $\Diamond$ may easily be unsound in this respect. To avoid this issue, the *possible world semantics* of modal logics can be explicitly embedded into HOL [20, 21].

   The embedding technique described in this section is related to labeling techniques [38]. However, the expressiveness of HOL can be exploited in order to encode the labels within the logical language itself. HOML is embedded into HOL by systematically lifting the types of propositions, making them depend on a new atomic type for possible worlds. This approach allows several well-established automated and interactive reasoning tools for HOL to be applied also to HOML problems. Moreover, also meta reasoning about the embedded modal logics becomes possible [14]. The presentation in this section is adapted from [17, 19].

3.1   Classical Higher-Order Logic: Syntax and Semantic

HOL is easily obtained from HOML by removing the modal operator $\Box$ from the grammar, and by dropping the set of possible worlds W and the accessibility relation R from the definition of a model. Nevertheless, we explicitly state the most relevant definitions for the particular notion of HOL as employed in this paper. One reason is that we do want to carefully distinguish the HOL and HOML languages in the remainder (we use boldface fonts for HOL and standard fonts for HOML). There is also a subtle, but harmless, difference in the HOL language defined here in comparison to the language in standard presentations: here three base types are employed, whereas usually only two base types are considered. The third base type plays a crucial role in our embedding of HOML in HOL.

Definition 11. *The set T of simple types freely generated from a set of basic types $\{o, \mu, \iota\}$ using the function type constructor $\rightarrow$. o is the type of Booleans, μ is the type of individuals, and ι is the type of possible worlds below. As before we may avoid parentheses.*

Definition 12. *The grammar for higher-order logic HOL is:*

$$s, t \quad ::= \quad p_\alpha \mid X_\alpha \mid (\lambda X_\alpha \cdot s_\beta)_{\alpha \rightarrow \beta} \mid (s_{\alpha \rightarrow \beta}\, t_\alpha)_\beta \mid \neg_{o \rightarrow o}\, s_o \mid$$
$$((\vee_{o \rightarrow o \rightarrow o}\, s_o)\, t_o) \mid \forall_{(\alpha \rightarrow o) \rightarrow o}(\lambda X_\alpha \cdot s_o)$$

where $\alpha, \beta \in T$. The text from Definition 2 analogously applies, except that we do not consider the modal connectives $\square$ and $\Diamond$.

The definitions for substitution (Definition 3), β- and η-reduction (Definition 4), frame (Definition 5), and assignment (Definition 7) remain unchanged.

Definition 13. *A model for HOL is a tuple $M = \langle D, I \rangle$, where D is a frame, and I is a family of typed interpretation functions mapping constant symbols p_α to appropriate elements of D_α, called the denotation of p_α (the logical connectives $\neg$, $\vee$, and $\forall$ are always given the standard denotations, see below). Moreover, we assume that the domains $D_{\alpha \rightarrow \alpha \rightarrow o}$ contain the respective identity relations.*

Definition 14. *The value $\|s_\alpha\|^{M,g}$ of a HOL term s_α on a model $M = \langle D, I \rangle$ under assignment g is an element $d \in D_\alpha$ defined in the following way:*

1. $\|p_\alpha\|^{M,g} = I(p_\alpha)$
2. $\|X_\alpha\|^{M,g} = g(X_\alpha)$
3. $\|(s_{\alpha \rightarrow \beta}\, t_\alpha)_\beta\|^{M,g} = \|s_{\alpha \rightarrow \beta}\|^{M,g}(\|t_\alpha\|^{M,g})$
4. $\|(\lambda X_\alpha \cdot s_\beta)_{\alpha \rightarrow \beta}\|^{M,g} =$ *the function f from D_α to D_β such that $f(d) = \|s_\beta\|^{M,g[d/X_\alpha]}$ for all $d \in D_\alpha$*
5. $\|(\neg_{o \rightarrow o}\, s_o)_o\|^{M,g} = T$ *if and only if* $\|s_o\|^{M,g} = F$
6. $\|((\vee_{o \rightarrow o \rightarrow o}\, s_o)\, t_o)_o\|^{M,g} = T$ *if and only if* $\|s_o\|^{M,g} = T$ *or* $\|t_o\|^{M,g} = T$
7. $\|(\forall_{(\alpha \rightarrow o) \rightarrow o}(\lambda X_\alpha \cdot s_o))_o\|^{M,g} = T$ *if and only if for all $d \in D_\alpha$ we have* $\|s_o\|^{M,g[d/X_\alpha]} = T$

The definition for standard and Henkin models (Definition 9), and for truth in a model, validity, etc. (Definition 10) are adapted in the obvious way, and we use the notation $M, g \models s_o$, $\models s_o$. Moreover, we write $\Gamma \models \Delta$ (for sets of formulas Γ and Δ) if and only if there is a model $M = \langle D, I \rangle$ and an assignment g such that $M, g \models s_o$ for all $s_o \in \Gamma$ and $M, g \models t_o$ for at least one $t_o \in \Delta$. As for HOML, we assume Henkin semantics in the remainder.

3.2 Semantic Embedding

Before we now present the embedding of HOML in HOL a clarifying remark concerning flexible and rigid constant symbols is required.

Remark 1. In Definition 6, constants are assumed to be *flexible*, because their interpretations may depend on worlds. A constant p_α is said to be *rigid* if it has the same interpretation in all worlds (i.e. there exists $d \in D_\alpha$ such that for all worlds w, $I_w(p_\alpha) = d$). For the sake of simplicity, we assume from now on (except in Sect. 5.4) that for every type α different from o, all constant symbols p_α are rigid. With this assumption, we may work with a non-world-indexed interpretation function I for types different from o. Clearly, I is then chosen so that $I(p_\alpha) = I_w(p_\alpha)$ for all w and for all p_α.

The encoding of HOML in HOL is simple: we identify HOML formulas of type o with certain HOL formulas (predicates) of type $\iota \to o$. The HOL type $\iota \to o$ is abbreviated in the remainder as σ.

Definition 15. *We define for each HOML type $\alpha \in T$ the associated raised HOL type $\lceil \alpha \rceil$ as follows:*

$$\lceil \mu \rceil = \mu$$
$$\lceil o \rceil = \sigma = \iota \to o$$
$$\lceil \alpha \to \beta \rceil = \lceil \alpha \rceil \to \lceil \beta \rceil$$

Hence, all HOML terms are rigid, except for those of type o.

Definition 16. *HOML terms s_α are associated with type-raised HOL terms $\lceil s_\alpha \rceil$ in the following way:*

$$\lceil p_\alpha \rceil = p_{\lceil \alpha \rceil}$$
$$\lceil X_\alpha \rceil = X_{\lceil \alpha \rceil}$$
$$\lceil (s_{\alpha \to \beta}\, t_\alpha) \rceil = (\lceil s_{\alpha \to \beta} \rceil\, \lceil t_\alpha \rceil)$$
$$\lceil (\lambda X_\alpha . s_\beta) \rceil = (\lambda \lceil X_\alpha \rceil . \lceil s_\beta \rceil)$$
$$\lceil (\neg_{o \to o}\, s_o) \rceil = (\dot\neg_{\sigma \to \sigma}\, \lceil s_\alpha \rceil)$$
$$\lceil ((\vee_{o \to o \to o}\, s_o)\, t_o) \rceil = ((\dot\vee_{\sigma \to \sigma \to \sigma}\, \lceil s_\alpha \rceil)\, \lceil t_\alpha \rceil)$$
$$\lceil ((\forall_{(\alpha \to o) \to o}\, (\lambda X_\alpha . s_\beta)) \rceil = (\dot\forall_{(\alpha \to \sigma) \to \sigma}\, (\lambda \lceil X_\alpha \rceil . \lceil s_\beta \rceil))$$
$$\lceil (\Box_{o \to o}\, s_o) \rceil = (\dot\Box_{\sigma \to \sigma}\, \lceil s_\alpha \rceil)$$

where $\dot\neg, \dot\vee, \dot\forall$, and $\dot\Box$ are the type-raised modal HOL connectives *associated with the corresponding modal HOML connectives. They are defined as follows (where $r_{\iota \to \iota \to o}$ is a new constant symbol in HOL associated with the accessibility relation R of HOML):*

$$\dot\neg_{\sigma \to \sigma} = \lambda s_\sigma . \lambda W_\iota . \neg (s\, W)$$
$$\dot\vee_{\sigma \to \sigma \to \sigma} = \lambda s_\sigma . \lambda t_\sigma . \lambda W_\iota . s\, W \vee t\, W$$

$$\dot{\forall}_{(\alpha\to\sigma)\to\sigma} = \lambda s_{\alpha\to\sigma}.\lambda W_\iota.\forall X_\alpha.\, s\, X\, W$$

$$\dot{\square}_{\sigma\to\sigma} = \lambda s_\sigma.\lambda W_\iota.\forall V_\iota.\neg(r_{\iota\to\iota\to o}\, W\, V) \vee s\, V$$

As before, we write $\dot{\forall} X_\alpha.\, s_\sigma$ *as shorthand for* $\dot{\forall}_{(\alpha\to\sigma)\to\sigma}(\lambda X_\alpha\, s_\sigma)$. *Further operators, such as* $\dot{\top}$, $\dot{\perp}$, $\dot{\wedge}$, $\dot{\supset}$, $\dot{\equiv}$, $\dot{\Diamond}$, *and* $\dot{\exists}$ *(*$\dot{\exists} X_\alpha.\, s_\sigma$ *is used as shorthand for* $\dot{\exists}_{(\alpha\to\sigma)\to\sigma}(\lambda X_\alpha.\, s_\sigma)$) *can now be easily defined. Moreover, we can define further modal operators, such as the difference modality* **D***, the global modality* **E***, nominals with* **!***, and the* **@** *operator (cf. [21]). The above equations can be treated as abbreviations in HOL theorem provers. Alternatively, they can be stated as axioms where* = *is either Leibniz equality or primitive equality (if additionally provided in the HOL grammar, as is the case for most modern HOL provers).*

As a consequence of the above embedding we can express HOML proof problems elegantly in the type-raised syntax of HOL. By rewriting or expanding definitions, we can reduce these representations to corresponding statements containing only the basic HOL connectives $\neg_{o\to o}$, $\vee_{o\to o\to o}$, and $\forall_{(\alpha\to o)\to o}$.

Example 1. The HOML formula $\square\,\exists P_{\mu\to o}.\, P\, a_\mu$ is associated with the type raised HOL formula $\dot{\square}\,\dot{\exists} P_{\mu\to\sigma}.\, P\, a_\mu$, which rewrites into the following $\beta\eta$-normal HOL term of type σ

$$\lambda W_\iota.\forall V_\iota.\neg(r\, W\, V) \vee \neg\forall P_{\mu\to\sigma}.\neg(P\, a_\mu\, V)$$

Next, we define validity of type-raised modal HOL propositions s_σ in the obvious way: s_σ is valid if and only if for all possible worlds w_ι we have $w_\iota \in s_\sigma$, that is, if and only if $(s_\sigma\, w_\iota)$ holds.

Definition 17. Validity *is modeled as an abbreviation for the following λ-term:*

$$valid = \lambda s_{\iota\to o}\forall W_\iota.\, s\, W$$

(alternatively, we could define validity simply as $\forall_{(\iota\to o)\to o}$). *Instead of* **valid** s_σ *we also use the notation* $[s_\sigma]$.

Example 2. We analyze whether the type raised modal HOL formula $\dot{\square}\,\dot{\exists} P_{\mu\to\sigma}.(P\, a_\mu)$ is valid or not. For this, we formalize the HOL proof problem $[\dot{\square}\,\dot{\exists} P_{\mu-\to\sigma}.(P\, a_\mu)]$, which expands into $\forall W_\iota.\forall V_\iota.\neg(r\, W\, V) \vee \neg\forall P_{\mu\to\sigma}.\neg(P\, a_\mu\, V)$. It is easy to check that this term is valid in Henkin semantics: put $P = \lambda X_\mu \lambda Y_\iota.\top$.

3.3   Soundness and Completeness

Theorem 1. (Soundness and Completeness). *For all HOML formulas s_o we have:*

$$\models s_o \quad \text{if and only if} \quad \models [\lceil s_o \rceil]$$

Proof sketch: *The proof adapts the ideas presented in [21]. By contraposition it is sufficient to show $\not\models s_o$ if and only if $\not\models [\lceil s_o \rceil]$, that is, $\|s_o\|^{M,g,w}$ (for some HOML model M, assignment g, and w) if and only if $\|\forall W_\iota. \lceil s_o \rceil W\|^{M,g}$ (for some HOL model M and assignment g) if and only if $\|\lceil s_o \rceil W\|^{M,g[w/W]}$ (for some M, g, and w). We easily get the proof by choosing the obvious correspondences between D and D, W and D_ι, I and I, g and g, R and $r_{\iota\rightarrow\iota\rightarrow o}$, and w and w.* □

From Theorem 1 we, for example, get the following corollaries:

$$\models^{KB} s_o \quad \text{if and only if} \quad (\textbf{symmetric } r_{\iota\rightarrow\iota\rightarrow o}) \models [\lceil s_o \rceil]$$

$$\models^{S5} s_o \quad \text{if and only if} \quad (\textbf{equiv-rel } r_{\iota\rightarrow\iota\rightarrow o}) \models [\lceil s_o \rceil]$$

where **symmetric** and **equiv-rel** are defined in an obvious way. Analogous corollaries can be stated for other normal modal logics including, for example, KD and S4.

3.4   Logic Variations

The semantics of a higher-order modal logic depends on subtle and often implicit assumptions. In the following two subsubsections, we explicitly discuss which assumptions have been made in the previous sections and how different choices would lead to different higher-order modal logics.

Constant, Varying and Cumulative Domains. In the previous sections we have focused on quantification over *constant domains*, which assumes that all individuals in D_μ actually exist in all worlds. Alternatively, quantified modal logics may also use quantification over *varying domains*, which assumes that the subset of individuals actually existing in a world w may depend on w.

Techniques for handling varying domain quantification in the embedding of first-order modal logics in HOL have been outlined in [17], and they can be extended to higher-order modal logics as well. For this, the following modifications are required:

1. The definition of $\overset{.}{\forall}$ (for type $(\mu \rightarrow \sigma) \rightarrow \sigma$, which encodes first-order quantification, is modified as follows: $\overset{.}{\forall} = \lambda s_{\mu\rightarrow\sigma}.\lambda w_\iota.\forall x_\mu.\textbf{ExistsInW } x \, w \supset s \, x \, w$, where the relation $\textbf{ExistsInW}_{\mu\rightarrow\iota\rightarrow o}$ (for 'Exists in world') relates individuals with worlds. The sets $\{x \mid \textbf{ExistsInW } x \, w\}$ are the possibly varying individual domains associated with the worlds w.
2. A non-emptiness axiom for these individual domains is added: $\forall w_\iota \exists x_\mu \textbf{ExistsInW } x \, w$.
3. For each individual constant symbol c in the proof problem an axiom $\forall w_\iota. \textbf{ExistsInW } c \, w$ is postulated; these axioms enforce the designation of c in the individual domain of each world w. Analogous designation axioms are required for function symbols.

Modifications 1–3 adapt the HOL approach to varying domains. For the special case of *cumulative domains*, in which the varying domains are assumed to be increasing along the accessibility relation r, an additional modification is needed:

4. The axiom $\forall x_\mu.\forall v_\iota.\forall w_\iota.\text{ExistsInW}\,x\,v \land r\,v\,w \Rightarrow \text{ExistsInW}\,x\,w$ is added.

If we were using a richer higher-order logic with not only simple types but also dependent types, we could achieve varying domains without using existence predicates, by making the type of individuals depend on worlds.

Rigidity and Flexibility. In the previous sections, it is assumed that all terms (except terms of boolean type) are *rigid*: independent of the world. The alternative option of *flexible* terms can be easily handled by type-raising. For example, a flexible HOML constant symbol kingOfFrance$_\mu$ would be mapped to a type-raised (and thus world-dependent) HOL constant symbol **kingOfFrance**$_{\iota \to \mu}$. Higher-order modal logics with flexible terms may, for example, be useful for dealing with certain kinds of inconsistency, as discussed in Sect. 5.4.

4 Reasoning Tools for Higher-Order Modal Logic

The above approach to automate HOML in HOL can be employed in combination with any ATP system that is sound and (possibly) complete for HOL with Henkin semantics. The embeddings approach is particularly simple to implement, because it does not require any modification in the source code of the HOL prover.

4.1 TPTP thf0-compliant Reasoning Tools

An encoding of second-order modal logic KB in HOL using the concrete TPTP thf0-syntax[1] [71] is exemplarily provided in Fig. 1.[2] The lifted modal connectives $\dot{\neg}, \dot{\lor}, \dot{\land}, \dot{\supset}, \dot{\Box}, \dot{\Diamond}, \dot{\forall}$ and $\dot{\exists}$ are in this representation called mnot, mor, mand, mimplies, mbox, mdia, mforall and mexists. Since thf0 does not support polymorphism, a generic modeling of mforall and mexists is not possible here and concrete instances of these quantifiers for individuals and sets of individuals (properties) are provided instead. Of course, further copies of these definitions could be added and adapted in order to obtain quantifiers for higher-types.

---

[1] thf stands for *typed higher-order form* and it refers to a family of syntax formats for higher-order logic. So far only the fully developed thf0 format, for simple type theory, is in practical use.

[2] In thf0, which is a concrete syntax for HOL, $i and $o represent the HOL base types i and o (Booleans). $i>$o encodes a function (predicate) type. Predicate application, as in $A(X, W)$, is encoded as ((A@X)@W) or simply as (A@X@W), i.e., function/predicate application is represented by @; universal quantification and λ-abstraction as in $\lambda A_{i \to o} \forall W_i (A\,W)$ and are represented as in ^[X:$ i>$ o]:![W:$ i]:(A@W); comments begin with %.

The given set of axioms turns any `thf0`-compliant HOL-ATP in a reasoning tool for second-order modal logic KB. Examples for `thf0`-compliant provers are LEO-II [12], Satallax [30], Isabelle [54], agsyHOL [50], HOLyHammer [48], cocATP and Nitpick [28]. Nitpick is specialized in (counter-)model finding. The other systems are in the first place theorem provers, although Satallax and LEO-II may occasionally also find countermodels for given non-valid conjectures.

The `thf0`-encoding from Fig. 1 has been applied and tested with the provers LEO-II, Satallax and Nitpick in the context of our work on the ontological

```
1   %----The base type $i (already built-in) stands here for worlds and
2   %----mu for individuals; $o (also built-in) is the type of Booleans
3   thf(mu_type,type,(mu:$tType)).
4   %----Reserved constant r for accessibility relation
5   thf(r,type,(r:$i>$i>$o)).
6   %----Modal logic operators not, or, and, implies, box, diamond
7   thf(mnot_type,type,(mnot:($i>$o)>$i>$o)).
8   thf(mnot,definition,(mnot = (^[A:$i>$o,W:$i]:~(A@W)))).
9   thf(mor_type,type,(mor:($i>$o)>($i>$o)>$i>$o)).
10  thf(mor,definition,(mor = (^[A:$i>$o,Psi:$i>$o,W:$i]:((A@W)|(Psi@W))))).
11  thf(mand_type,type,(mand:($i>$o)>($i>$o)>$i>$o)).
12  thf(mand,definition,(mand = (^[A:$i>$o,Psi:$i>$o,W:$i]:((A@W)&(Psi@W))))).
13  thf(mimplies_type,type,(mimplies:($i>$o)>($i>$o)>$i>$o)).
14  thf(mimplies,definition,(
15      mimplies = (^[A:$i>$o,Psi:$i>$o,W:$i]:((A@W)&(Psi@W))))).
16  thf(mbox_type,type,(mbox:($i>$i>$o)>($i>$o)>$i>$o)).
17  thf(mbox,definition,(mbox = (^[A:$i>$o,W:$i]:![V:$i]:(~(r@W@V)|(A@V))))).
18  thf(mdia_type,type,(mdia:($i>$i>$o)>($i>$o)>$i>$o)).
19  thf(mdia,definition,(mdia = (^[A:$i>$o,W:$i]:?[V:$i]:((r@W@V)&(A@V))))).
20  %----Quantifiers (constant domains) for individuals and propositions
21  thf(mforall_ind_type,type,(mforall_ind:(mu>$i>$o)>$i>$o)).
22  thf(mforall_ind,definition,(
23      mforall_ind = (^[A:mu>$i>$o,W:$i]:![X:mu]:(A@X@W)))).
24  thf(mforall_indset_type,type,(mforall_indset:((mu>$i>$o)>$i>$o)>$i>$o)).
25  thf(mforall_indset,definition,(
26      mforall_indset = (^[A:(mu>$i>$o)>$i>$o,W:$i]:![X:mu>$i>$o]:(A@X@W)))).
27  thf(mexists_ind_type,type,(mexists_ind:(mu>$i>$o)>$i>$o)).
28  thf(mexists_ind,definition,(
29      mexists_ind = (^[A:mu>$i>$o,W:$i]:?[X:mu]:(A@X@W)))).
30  thf(mexists_indset_type,type,(mexists_indset:((mu>$i>$o)>$i>$o)>$i>$o)).
31  thf(mexists_indset,definition,(
32      mexists_indset = (^[A:(mu>$i>$o)>$i>$o,W:$i]:?[X:mu>$i>$o]:(A@X@W)))).
33  %----Definition of validity (grounding of lifted modal formulas)
34  thf(v_type,type,(v:($i>$o)>$o)).
35  thf(mvalid,definition,(v = (^[A:$i>$o]:![W:$i]:(A@W)))).
36  %----Properties of accessibility relations: symmetry
37  thf(msymmetric_type,type,(msymmetric:($i>$i>$o)>$o)).
38  thf(msymmetric,definition,(
39      msymmetric = (^[R:$i>$i>$o]:![S:$i,T:$i]:((R@S@T)=>(R@T@S))))).
40  %----Here we work with logic KB, i.e., we postulate symmetry for r
41  thf(sym,axiom,(msymmetric@r)).
```

Fig. 1. HOL encoding of second-order modal logic KB in `thf0`-syntax. Modal formulas are mapped to HOL predicates (with type $i>$o); type $i now stands for possible worlds. The modal connectives ¬ (mnot), ∨ (mor) and □ (mbox), universal quantification for individuals (mall_ind) and for sets of individuals (mall_indset) are introduced in lines 7–18. Validity of lifted modal formulas is defined in the standard way (lines 20–21). Symmetry of accessibility relation r is postulated in lines 23–26. Hence, second-order KB is realized here; for logic K the symmetry axiom can be dropped.

```
1    %------------------------------------------------------------------------
2    %----Axioms for Quantified Modal Logic KB.
3    include('Quantified_KB.ax').
4    %------------------------------------------------------------------------
5    %----constant symbol for positive: p
6    thf(p_tp,type,( p: ( mu > $i > $o ) > $i > $o )).
7
8    %----constant symbol for God-like: g
9    thf(g_tp,type,( g: mu > $i > $o )).
10
11   %----constant symbol for essence: ess
12   thf(ess_tp,type,( ess: ( mu > $i > $o ) > mu > $i > $o )).
13
14   %----constant symbol for necessary existence: ne
15   thf(ne_tp,type,( ne: mu > $i > $o )).
16
17   %----D1: A God-like being possesses all positive properties.
18   thf(defD1,definition, (
19       g = ( ^ [X: mu] :
20               ( mforall_indset
21                 @ ^ [Phi: mu > $i > $o] :
22                     ( mimplies @ ( p @ Phi ) @ ( Phi @ X ) ) ) ) )).
23
24   %----C: Possibly, God exists. (Proved before)
25   thf(corC,axiom,
26       ( v
27       @ ( mdia
28         @ ( mexists_ind
29           @ ^ [X: mu] :
30               ( g @ X ) ) ) )).
31
32   %----T2: Being God-like is an essence of any God-like being. (Proved before)
33   thf(thmT2,axiom,
34       ( v
35       @ ( mforall_ind
36         @ ^ [X: mu] :
37             ( mimplies @ ( g @ X ) @ ( ess @ g @ X ) ) ) )).
38
39   %----D3: Necessary existence of an individual is the necessary
40   %----exemplification of all its essences
41   thf(defD3,definition, (
42       ne = ( ^ [X: mu] :
43               ( mforall_indset
44                 @ ^ [Phi: mu > $i > $o] :
45                     ( mimplies @ ( ess @ Phi @ X )
46                     @ ( mbox
47                       @ ( mexists_ind
48                         @ ^ [Y: mu] :
49                             ( Phi @ Y ) ) ) ) ) ) )).
50
51   %----A5: Necessary existence is positive.
52   thf(axA5,axiom, ( v @ ( p @ ne ) )).
53
54   %----T3: Necessarily God exists.
55   thf(thmT3,conjecture,
56       ( v
57       @ ( mbox
58         @ ( mexists_ind
59           @ ^ [X: mu] :
60               ( g @ X ) ) ) )).
61
```

Fig. 2. TPTP thf0-encoding of theorem T3 in Scott's adaptation (see also Fig. 11) of Gödel's ontological argument [19,65].

argument for the existence of God [19]; more on this study will be provided in Sect. 5.3. Figure 2 presents a most prominent proof problem from these studies in thf0-syntax. In Fig. 2 an improved (but more spacious) formatting is employed; such a formatting can easily be obtained with the help of the TPTP2X or TPTP4X tools of Sutcliffe's SystemOnTPTP infrastructure [70].

In the context of first-order modal logic (FML) theorem proving, the FMLtoHOL tool [23] has been developed, which converts problems in FML, formulated in qmf-syntax [63] (which extends the TPTP fol-syntax [70] with operators #box and #dia), into HOL problems in thf0-syntax. FMLtoHOL automatically transforms constant domain FML problems in corresponding HOL problems [21]. The tool has been extended to also support varying and cumulative domains. At present FMLtoHOL supports modal logics from $L := \{K,K4,D,D4,T,S4,S5\}$.

The FMLtoHOL tool has been exemplarily applied in combination with a meta-prover for HOL. This meta-prover exploits the SystemOnTPTP infrastructure [70] and sequentially schedules the HOL reasoners LEO-II, Satallax, Isabelle, agsyHOL and Nitpick. The system has been evaluated with respect to 580 benchmark problems in the QMLTP library [63]. As a side contribution, the complete translation of the QMLTP library (for all logics in L, all different domain conditions, and both options as explained in (C)) into HOL (resp. thf0) resulted in $7 \times 3 \times 2 \times 580 = 24360$ new problems.[3]

Experiments [23] show that the FMLtoHOL approach to automate FMLs is very competitive. Regarding the combined performance (number of proved or refuted problems) the HOL approach performed best in this study.

4.2   Interactive Proof Assistants – Isabelle

The TPTP THF embedding of HOML is very useful for flexible proof automation of HOML with off-the-shelf HOL-ATPs. Unfortunately, however, it is not particularly well suited for enabling user interaction at an intuitive abstraction level. In this subsection we therefore briefly illustrate how the embedding of HOML can be encoded and exploited in the interactive proof assistant Isabelle/HOL. A very useful tool of Isabelle/HOL is Sledgehammer [27], which connects the Isabelle core system with external ATPs, including remote calls to the LEO-II and Satallax provers running at the SystemOnTPTP infrastructure in Miami.

An embedding of HOML with constant domain semantics in Isabelle/HOL is presented in the upper part of Fig. 3, which displays the content of an Isabelle theory file named QML.thy.[4] Note that in the definition of mforall and mexists a type variable 'a is used. Thus, in contrast to the non-polymorphic TPTP THF encoding of second-order modal logic from above, polymoprhic quantifiers are introduced here to obtain full HOML. Additional quantifiers for varying domains can easily be added, this is illustrated in the lower part of Fig. 3.[5]

---

[3] The 3480 problems for logic S4 can be download from http://christoph-benzmueller. de/papers/THF-S4-ALL.zip.

[4] See file QML.thy available at https://github.com/FormalTheology/GoedelGod/blob/ master/Formalizations/Isabelle/.

[5] See file QML_var.thy at the github url from above.

An obvious advantage of Isabelle is its comparably good notation support in the user interface. The connectives `mnot, mor, mand, mimplies, mbox, mdia, mforall` and `mexists` are displayed here as m¬, m∨, m∧, m→, □, ◊, ∀ and ∃.

Figure 4 exemplarily displays the development of Gödel's ontological argument (in Scott's version, cf. Fig. 11) in Isabelle/HOL. Varying domain quantifiers for individuals are employed in this particular encoding; see e.g. the occurrence of ∀e in Axiom A2 and the occurrence of ∃e in Theorem T3. Note that the second-order quantifier ∀, as used for instance in T1, is a constant domain quantifier. Hence, we here illustrate the flexibility of the embeddings approach, in which we can even easily mix different types of quantifiers. Note that proofs in Fig. 4 are fully automatic; here Isabelle's Metis prover is used. However, Metis has to be called here with the appropriate assumptions. When using Sledgehammer instead, for example, in combination with LEO-II, Satallax or other ATPs, the respective assumptions can be avoided in the Sledgehammer call and will be automatically determined.

4.3 Interactive Proof Assistants – Coq

We have already seen how the embedding approach is flexible and effective for *fully automated* reasoning. However, one may wonder whether the embedding approach is adequate also for intuitive *interactive* reasoning, when the user proves theorems by interacting with a proof assistant such as Coq. In this section, we study this question, and show that the answer is positive.

One major concern is whether the embedding could be a disturbance to the user. Fortunately, by using Coq's Ltac tactic language, we are able to define intuitive new tactics that hide the technical details of the embedding from the user. The resulting infra-structure for modal reasoning within Coq provides a user experience where modalities can be handled transparently and straightforwardly. Therefore, a user with basic knowledge of modal logics and Coq's tactics should be able to use (and extend) our implementation with no excessive overhead. It should be straightforward to analogously implement respective tactics in other interactive proof assistants, including Isabelle/HOL.

As before, the first step in the shallow embedding of modal logics is the declaration of a type for worlds. Modal propositions are then not of type `Prop` but of a lifted type o that depends on possible worlds (o corresponds to σ in the Isabelle/HOL encoding from before):

```
Parameter i: Type. (* Type for worlds *)
Parameter u: Type. (* Type for individuals *)
Definition o := i -> Prop. (* Type of modal propositions *)
```

Possible worlds are connected by an accessibility relation, which can be represented in Coq by a parameter r, as follows:

```
Parameter r: i -> i -> Prop. (* Accessibility relation for worlds *)
```

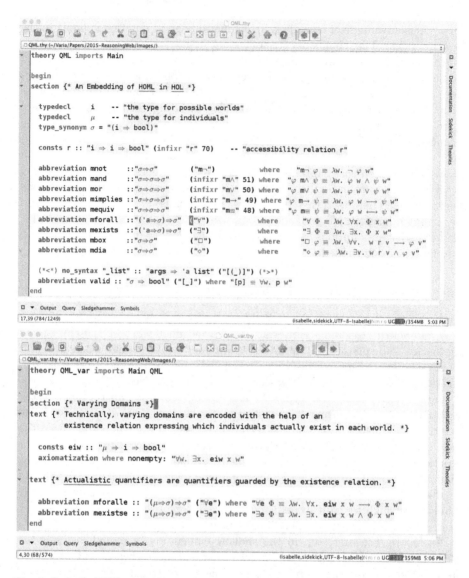

Fig. 3. Isabelle/HOL embedding of HOML K (above), and the subsequent extension of this theory by varying domain quantifiers ∀e and ∃e for individuals.

As before, all modal connectives are simply lifted versions of the usual logical connectives. Notations are used to allow the modal connectives to be used as similarly as possible to the usual connectives. As before, the prefix "m" is used to distinguish the modal connectives: if ⊙ is a connective on type Prop, m⊙ is a connective on the lifted type o of modal propositions.

```
Definition mnot (p: o)(w: i) := ~ (p w).
Notation"m~ p" := (mnot p) (at level 74, right associativity).

Definition mand (p q:o)(w: i) := (p w) /\ (q w).
Notation "p m/\ q" := (mand p q) (at level 79, right associativity).

Definition mor (p q:o)(w: i) := (p w) \/ (q w).
Notation "p m\/ q" := (mor p q) (at level 79, right associativity).

Definition mimplies (p q:o)(w:i) := (p w) -> (q w).
Notation "p m-> q" := (mimplies p q) (at level 99, right associativity).

Definition mequiv (p q:o)(w:i) := (p w) <-> (q w).
Notation "p m<-> q" := (mequiv p q) (at level 99, right associativity).

Definition mequal (x y: u)(w: i) := x = y.
Notation "x m= y" := (mequal x y) (at level 99, right associativity).
```

Fig. 4. Scott's version of Gödel's ontological argument encoded and proved in Isabelle/HOL. Varying domain quantifiers for individuals are mixed with constant domain quantifiers for properties of individuals.

Likewise, modal quantifiers are lifted versions of the usual quantifiers. Coq's type system with dependent types is particularly helpful here. The modal quantifiers A and E are defined as depending on a type t. Therefore, they can quantify over variables of any type. Moreover, the curly brackets indicate that t is an implicit argument that can be inferred by Coq's type inference mechanism. This allows notations[6] (i.e. mforall and mexists) that mimic the notations for Coq's usual quantifiers (i.e. forall and exists).

```
Definition A {t: Type}(p: t -> o)(w: i) := forall x, p x w.
Notation "'mforall' x , p" := (A (fun x => p))
  (at level 200, x ident, right associativity) : type_scope.
Notation "'mforall' x : t , p" := (A (fun x:t => p))
  (at level 200, x ident, right associativity,
    format "'[' 'mforall' '/' x : t ,'/' p ']'")
  : type_scope.

Definition E {t: Type}(p: t -> o)(w: i) := exists x, p x w.
Notation "'mexists' x , p" := (E (fun x => p))
  (at level 200, x ident, right associativity) : type_scope.
Notation "'mexists' x : t , p" := (E (fun x:t => p))
  (at level 200, x ident, right associativity,
    format "'[' 'mexists' '/' x : t ,'/' p ']'")
  : type_scope.
```

The modal operators ◊ (*possibly*) and □ (*necessarily*) are defined accordingly to their meanings in the possible world semantics. □p holds at a world w iff p holds in every world w_1 reachable from w. ◊p holds at world w iff p holds in some world w_1 reachable from w.

```
Definition box (p: o) := fun w => forall w1, (r w w1) -> (p w1).
Definition dia (p: o) := fun w => exists w1, (r w w1) /\ (p w1).
```

A modal proposition is valid iff it holds in every possible world. This notion of modal validity is encoded by the following defined predicate:

```
Definition V (p: o) := forall w, p w.
```

To prove a modal proposition p (of type o) within Coq, the proposition (V p) (of type Prop) should be proved instead. To increase the transparency of the embedding to the user, the following notation is provided, allowing [p] to be written instead of (V p).

```
Notation "[ p ]" := (V p).
```

Interactive theorem proving in Coq, and likewise in other interactive proof assistants, is usually done with tactics, imperative commands that reduce the theorem to be proven (i.e. the goal) to simpler subgoals, in a bottom-up manner. The simplest tactics can be regarded as rules of a natural deduction calculus[7]

---

[6] The keyword **fun** indicates a lambda abstraction: fun x => p (or fun x:t => p) denotes the function $\lambda x : t.p$, which takes an argument x (of type t) and returns p.

[7] The underlying proof system of Coq (the Calculus of Inductive Constructions (CIC) [57]) is actually more sophisticated and minimalistic than the calculus shown in Fig. 5. But the calculus shown here suffices for the purposes of this tutorial. This calculus is classical, because of the double negation elimination rule. Although CIC is intuitionistic, it can be made classical by importing Coq's classical library, which adds the axiom of the *excluded middle* and the double negation elimination lemma.

(e.g. as those shown in Fig. 5). For example: the `intro` tactic can be used to apply the introduction rules for implication and for the universal quantifier; the `apply` tactic corresponds to the elimination rules for implication and for the universal quantifier; `split` performs conjunction introduction; `exists` can be used for existential quantifier introduction and `destruct` for its elimination.

To maximally preserve user intuition in interactive modal logic theorem proving, the embedding via the possible world semantics should be as transparent as possible to the user. Fortunately, the basic Coq tactics described above automatically unfold the shallowest modal definition in the goal. Therefore, they can be used with modal connectives and quantifiers just as they are used with the usual connectives and quantifiers. The situation for the new modal operators, on the other hand, is not as simple, unfortunately.

Since the modal operators are, in our embedding, essentially just abbreviations for quantifiers guarded by reachability conditions, the typical tactics for quantifiers can be used, in principle. However, this exposes the user to the technicalities of the embedding, requiring him to deal with possible worlds and

---

$$\frac{\bot}{A} \perp_E \qquad \frac{B}{A \supset B} \supset_I \qquad \frac{\overset{\displaystyle \overline{A}^{\,n}}{\vdots}\ B}{A \supset B} \supset_I^n \qquad \frac{A \quad A \supset B}{B} \supset_E$$

$$\frac{\neg\neg A}{A} \neg\neg_E \qquad \frac{A \quad B}{A \wedge B} \wedge_I \qquad \frac{A \wedge B}{A} \wedge_{E_1} \qquad \frac{A \wedge B}{B} \wedge_{E_2}$$

$$\frac{A \vee B \quad \overset{\overline{A}}{\overset{\vdots}{C}} \quad \overset{\overline{B}}{\overset{\vdots}{C}}}{C} \vee_E \qquad \frac{A}{A \vee B} \vee_{I_1} \qquad \frac{B}{A \vee B} \vee_{I_2}$$

$$\frac{A[\alpha]}{\forall x_\tau . A[x]} \forall_I \qquad \frac{\forall x_\tau . A[x]}{A[t]} \forall_E$$

$$\frac{A[t]}{\exists x_\tau . A[x]} \exists_I \qquad \frac{\exists x_\tau . A[x] \quad \overset{\overline{A[\alpha]}}{\overset{\vdots}{C}}}{C} \exists_E$$

α must respect the usual *eigen-variable conditions*.

$\neg A$ is an abbreviation for $A \supset \bot$.

Rules for $\alpha\beta\eta$-equality and axioms (or rules) for extensionality are omitted here since they are not important for the rest of the tutorial. For a full, sound and Henkin-complete, classical higher-order natural deduction calculus, see [16].

Fig. 5. Rules of a (classical) natural deduction calculus

their reachability explicitly. In order to obtain transparency also for the modal operators, we can implement the following specialized tactics using Coq's Ltac language.

When applied to a goal of the form ((box p) w0), the tactic box_i will introduce a fresh new world w and then introduce the assumption that w is reachable from w0. The new goal will be (p w).

```
Ltac box_i := let w := fresh "w" in let R := fresh "R"
              in (intro w at top; intro R at top).
```

If the hypothesis H is of the form ((box p) w0) and the goal is of the form (q w), the tactic box_e H H1 creates a new hypothesis H1: (p w). The tactic box_elim H w1 H1 is an auxiliary tactic for box_e. It creates a new hypothesis H1: (p w1), for any given world w1, not necessarily the goal's world w. It is also responsible for automatically trying (by assumption) to solve the reachability guard conditions, releasing the user from this burden.

```
Ltac box_elim H w1 H1 := match type of H with
    ((box ?p) ?w) => cut (p w1);
                     [intros H1 | (apply (H w1); try assumption)] end.

Ltac box_e H H1:= match goal with | [ |- (_ ?w) ] => box_elim H w H1 end.
```

If the hypothesis H is of the form ((dia p) w0), the tactic dia_e H generates a new hypothesis H: (p w) for a fresh new world w reachable from w0.

```
Ltac dia_e H := let w := fresh "w" in let R := fresh "R" in
                (destruct H as [w [R H]]; move w at top; move R at top).
```

The tactic dia_i w transforms a goal of the form ((dia p) w0) into the simpler goal (p w) and automatically tries to solve the guard condition that w must be reachable from w0.

```
Ltac dia_i w := (exists w; split; [assumption | idtac]).
```

If the new modal tactics above are regarded from a natural deduction point of view, they correspond to the inference rules shown in Fig. 6. Because of this correspondence and the Henkin-completeness of the modal natural deduction calculus[8], the tactics allow the user to prove any valid modal formula without having to unfold the definitions of the modal operators.

The labels that name boxes in the inference rules of Fig. 6 are precisely the worlds that annotate goals and hypotheses in Coq with the modal embedding. A hypothesis of the form (p w), where p is a modal proposition of type o and w is a world of type i indicates that p is an assumption created inside a box with name w.

---

[8] The natural deduction calculus with the rules from Figs. 5 and 6 is sound and complete relatively to the calculus of Fig. 5 extended with a necessitation rule and the modal axiom K [67]. Starting from a sound and Henkin-complete natural deduction calculus for classical higher-order logic (cf. Fig. 5), the additional modal rules in Fig. 6 make it sound and Henkin-complete for the rigid higher-order modal logic **K**.

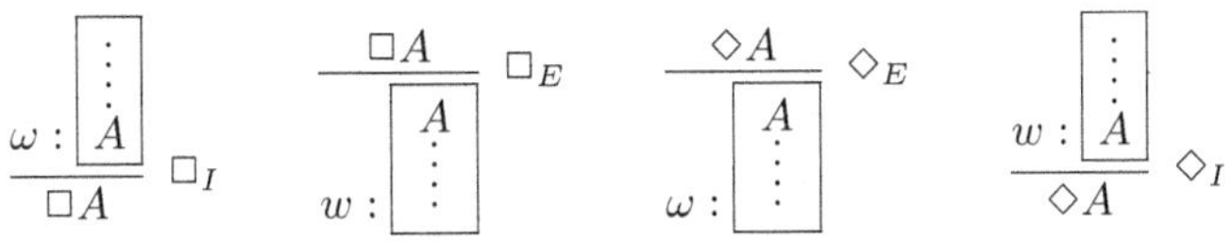

eigen-box condition:
$\Box_I$ and $\Diamond_E$ are *strong* modal rules:
ω must be a fresh name for the box they access
(in analogy to the eigen-variable condition for strong quantifier rules).
Every box must be accessed by *exactly one* strong modal inference.

boxed assumption condition:
assumptions should be discharged within the box where they are created.

Fig. 6. Rules for modal operators

Finally, the tactic mv, standing for *modal validity*, replaces a goal of the form
[p] (or equivalently (V p)) by a goal of the form (p w) for a fresh arbitrary
world w.

```
Ltac mv := match goal with [|- (V _)] => intro end.
```

In order to illustrate the tactics described above, we show Coq proofs for two
simple but useful modal lemmas. The first lemma resembles modus ponens, but
with formulas under the scope of modal operators.

```
Lemma mp_dia:
  [mforall p, mforall q, (dia p) m-> (box (p m-> q)) m-> (dia q)].
Proof. mv.
intros p q H1 H2. dia_e H1. dia_i w0. box_e H2 H3. apply H3. exact H1.
Qed.
```

The proof of this lemma is displayed as a natural deduction proof in Fig. 7.
As expected, Coq's basic tactics (e.g. intros and apply) work without modification. The intros p q H1 H2 tactic application corresponds to the universal
quantifier and implication introduction inferences in the bottom of the proof. The
apply H3 tactic application corresponds to the implication elimination inference.
The $\Diamond_E$, $\Diamond_I$ and $\Box_E$ inferences correspond, respectively, to the dia_e H1, dia_i
w0 and box_e H2 H3 tactic applications. The internal box named w_0 is accessed
by exactly one strong modal inference, namely $\Diamond_E$.

The same lemma could be proved without the new modal tactics, as shown
below. But this is clearly disadvantageous, for several reasons: the proof script
becomes longer; the definitions of modal operators must be unfolded, either
explicitly (as done below) or implicitly in the user's mind; tactic applications
dealing with modal operators cannot be easily distinguished from tactic applications dealing with quantifiers; and hypotheses about the reachability of worlds
(e.g. R1 below) must be handled explicitly. In summary, without the modal tactics, a convenient and intuitive correspondence between proof scripts and modal
natural deduction proofs would be missing.

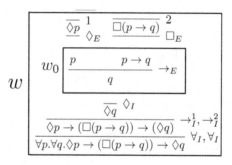

Fig. 7. Natural deduction proof of `mp_dia`

```
Lemma mp_dia_alternative:
  [mforall p, mforall q, (dia p) m-> (box (p m-> q)) m-> (dia q)].
Proof. mv.
intros p q H1 H2. unfold dia. unfold dia in H1. unfold box in H2.
destruct H1 as [w0 [R1 H1]]. exists w0. split.
  exact R1.
  apply H2.
    exact R1.
    exact H1.
Qed.
```

The second useful lemma allows negations to be pushed inside modalities, and again the modal tactics allow this to be proved conveniently and elegantly.

```
Lemma not_dia_box_not: [mforall p, (m~ (dia p)) m-> (box (m~ p))].
Proof. mv.
intro p. intro H. box_i. intro H2. apply H. dia_i w0. exact H2.
Qed.
```

The embedding and the new tactics allow convenient interactive reasoning for modal logic **K** within `Coq`. The axiom K is easily derivable:

```
Theorem K:
  [ mforall p, mforall q, (box (p m-> q)) m-> (box p) m-> (box q) ].
Proof. mv.
intros p q H1 H2. box_i. box_e H1 H3. apply H3. box_e H2 H4. exact H4.
Qed.
```

For other modal logics beyond **K**, their frame conditions, which constrain the reachability relation, must be stated as `Coq` axioms.

```
Axiom reflexivity: forall w, r w w.
```

```
Axiom transitivity: forall w1 w2 w3, (r w1 w2) -> (r w2 w3) -> (r w1 w3).
```

```
Axiom symmetry: forall w1 w2, (r w1 w2) -> (r w2 w1).
```

Hilbert-style modal logic axioms, such as for example T, can be easily derived from their corresponding frame conditions:

```
Theorem T: [ mforall p, (box p) m-> p ].
Proof. mv.
intro p. intro H. box_e H H1. exact H1. apply reflexivity.
Qed.
```

In a strong modal logic such as **S5** (which requires all three frame conditions specified above), sequences of modal operators can be collapsed to a single modal operator. One such collapsing principle is specified and proven below. By applying it iteratively, any sequence $\Diamond \ldots \Diamond \Box p$ could be collapsed to $\Box p$.

```
Theorem dia_box_to_box: [ mforall p, (dia (box p)) m-> (box p) ].
Proof. mv.
intros p H1. dia_e H1. box_i. box_e H1 H2. exact H2. eapply transitivity.
  apply symmetry. exact R.
  exact R0.
Qed.
```

It should be easily possible to analogously define corresponding HOML tactics within other interactive proof assistants, including Isabelle/HOL.

5   Applications

Propositional and quantified modal logics have (potential) applications in various fields, including, for instance, philosophy, verification, artificial intelligence agent technologies, law and linguistics (cf. [26] and the references therein). Therefore, the techniques described in these lecture notes – convenient embeddings for leveraging higher-order automated theorem provers and proof assistants for reasoning within and about modal logics – may serve as a starting point for many interesting projects, as illustrated in the following subsections.

5.1   Description Logics

Given that the embeddings approach can handle higher-order modal logics it is not surprising that the approach is also applicable to prominent description logics. For example, an Isabelle/HOL embedding of the prominent description logic ALC [11], see Fig. 8, is presented in Fig. 9. Note in particular the close correspondence between the embeddings of the ALC connectives and their corresponding semantical characterisations in Fig. 8.

Moreover, in Fig. 9 we present a simple reasoning example. Here we are interested to check whether the concept ($\exists$married Human) subsumes the concept HappyMan which is defined in the displayed TBox as HappyMan $\doteq$ Human $\sqcap$ ~Female $\sqcap$ ($\exists married$ Doctor) $\sqcap$ ($\forall$hasChild(Doctor $\sqcup$ Professor))

In Fig. 10 we exemplarily prove the soundness of the standard ALC tableau rules, and we also show the correspondence between ALC and the propositional modal logic K. Note that in the embedding of propositional modal logic we here work with generic box and diamond operators which receive as first argument their accessibility relation r (of course, we could have done this also in the previous sections of these lecture notes). Apparently, from the perspective of the embeddings approach, the correspondence between ALC and propositional modal logic K becomes entirely trivial, essentially just a syntax variation. And this is exactly what the relationship between the two logics actually is.

Syntax	Semantics	Description	Example
A	$A^I \subseteq \Delta^I$	atomic concept	Human, Female, ...
r	$r^I \subseteq \Delta^I \times \Delta^I$	binary relation	married, ...
$\bot$	$\emptyset$	empty concept	
$\top$	Δ^I	universal concept	
$\sim A$	$\Delta^I \setminus A^I$	complement	$\sim$ Female
$A \sqcup B$	$A^I \cup B^I$	disjunktion	Female $\sqcup$ Male
$A \sqcap B$	$A^I \cap B^I$	conjunction	Female $\sqcap$ Human
$\exists r\ C$	$\{x\mid\exists y.r^I(x,y) \wedge C^I(y)\}$	existential role restriction	$\exists$married Female
$\forall r\ C$	$\{x\mid\forall y.r^I(x,y) \to C^I(y)\}$	universal role restriction	$\forall$ married Female
$A \sqsubseteq B$	$A^I \subseteq B^I$	B subsumes A	Doctor $\sqsubseteq$ Human
$A \doteq B$	$A^I \sqsubseteq B^I$ and $B^I \sqsubseteq A^I$	A defined by B	Parent $\doteq$ Human $\sqcap$ $\exists$hasChild Human

Fig. 8. Description logic ALC

5.2   Expressive Ontologies and Context

The study of notions of context has a long history in philosophy, linguistics, and artificial intelligence. In artificial intelligence, a major motivation has been to resolve the problem of generality of computer programs as identified by McCarthy [51]. The generality aspect of context scrutinizes flexible combinations (nestings) of contexts in combination with rich context descriptions. Giunchiglia [40] additionally emphasizes the locality aspect and the need for structured representations of knowledge. The locality aspect is particularly important for large knowledge bases, where the challenge is to effectively identify and access information that is relevant within a given reasoning context.

Different approaches to formalizing and mechanizing context have been proposed in the last decades. Many of these are outlined in the literature [1,3,66]. McCarthy [52] has pioneered the modeling of contexts as first class objects (in first-order logic) and he introduced the predicate *ist*. For example, in his approach the expression *ist(context_of("Ben's Knowledge"), likes(Sue, Bill))* encodes that proposition Sue likes Bill is true in the context of Ben's knowledge. A motivation for McCarthy's approach is actually to avoid modal logics (here for the modeling of Ben's knowledge). His line of research has been followed by a number of researchers, including, for example, Guha (who has put contexts into Cyc), Buvac and Mason [31,44]. Also Giunchiglia and Serafini [41] avoid modal logics and propose the use of so called multilanguage systems. They show various equivalence results to common modal logics, but they also discuss several properties of multilanguage systems not supported in modal logics.

All of the above approaches avoid a higher-order perspective on context. However, we think that a solid higher-order perspective on context can be very valuable for various reasons. On the theory side the twist between formalisms based on modal logic and formalisms based on first-order logic seems to dissolve,

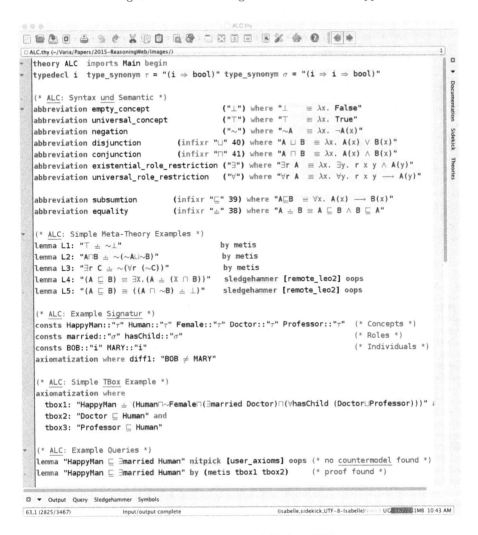

Fig. 9. Embedding of ALC in HOL

since both modal logics (and other non-classical logics) and first-order logics are just natural fragments of HOL. Moreover, modal (and other) contexts can be elegantly combined and nested in HOL, so that a flexible solution to McCarthy's generality problem appears in reach. Also the locality aspect can be addressed. The means for this is provided by relevance filtering and premise selection [4, 49].

Expressive ontologies such as the Suggested Upper Merged Ontology SUMO [58] or CYC [62] already contain a small but significant number of higher-order representations, cf. [22]. Most importantly, they employ embedded formulas (formulas at term positions), and these constructs are in fact used for modeling contexts as proposed by McCarthy, including temporal, epistemic, or doxastic contexts. The basic idea for modeling such contexts, for example, in

Fig. 10. Various meta-results on ALC in HOL

SUMO is simple. A statement like *(loves Bill Mary)* is restricted, for instance, to the year 2009 by wrapping it (at subterm level) into respective context information:

$$(holdsDuring \ (YearFn \ 2009) \ (loves \ Bill \ Mary))$$

Similarly, the statement can be put into an epistemic or doxastic context:

$$(knows/believes \ Ben \ (loves \ Bill \ Mary))$$

Moreover, contexts can be flexibly combined and the embedded formulas may be complex:

$(believes\ Bill\ (knows\ Ben\ (forall(?X)\ ((woman?X) => (loves\ Bill\ ?X))))$

The similarity to McCarthy's approach is obvious.

Another higher-order construct used in SUMO is the set (or class) constructor *KappaFn*. It takes two arguments, a variable and a formula, and returns the set (or class) of things that satisfy the formula. Moreover, SUMO allows the use of relation and function variables.

A crucial requirement in the context of SUMO and similar expressive ontologies thus is to support flexible context reasoning in combination with other first-order and even higher-order reasoning aspects. A particular challenge thereby is to appropriately handle modal contexts, since their naive treatment may easily lead to incorrect respectively unintuitive reasoning results. As a solution we propose to encode SUMO axioms as axioms in HOML and to apply the embeddings approach to automate reasoning for SUMO. We will outline this proposal in the remainder of this section.

To illustrate the reasoning with modal contexts in SUMO we consider an example. In this example we want to answer query (C1) from axiom (A1):

$$(holdsDuring\ (YearFn\ 2009)\ (and(likes\ Mary\ Bill)\ (likes\ Sue\ Bill))) \quad \text{(A1)}$$

$$(holdsDuring\ (YearFn\ 2009)\ (likes\ ?X\ Bill)) \quad \text{(C1)}$$

The challenge is to reason about the embedded formulas within the temporal context $(holdsDuring\ (YearFn\ 2009)\ ...)$. In our example, the embedded formula in the query does not match the embedded formula in the premise, however, it is inferable from it. The first-order quoting technique for reasoning with such embedded formulas presented by Pease and Sutcliffe [59], which encodes embedded formulas as strings, fails for this query. There are possible further "tricks" though which could eventually be applied. For example, we could split axiom (A1) in a pre-processing step into *(holdsDuring (YearFn 2009) (likes Mary Bill))* and *(holds-During (YearFn 2009) (likes Sue Bill))*. However, such simple tricks quickly reach their limits when considering more involved embedded reasoning problems. The following modification of our example illustrates the challenge:

$$(holdsDuring\ ?Y\ (likes\ Mary\ Bill)) \quad \text{(A2)}$$

$$(holdsDuring\ (YearFn\ 2009)\ (forall\ (?X)(=>(likes\ Mary\ ?X)\ (likes\ Sue\ ?X)))) \quad \text{(A3)}$$

$$(holdsDuring\ (YearFn\ ?Y\ )\ (likes\ Sue\ ?X)) \quad \text{(C2)}$$

The embedded quantified formula in this example well illustrates that the reasoning tasks may quickly become non-trivial for approaches based on translations to first-order logic.

In the above examples we have (silently) assumed that the semantics of the logic underlying SUMO is a classical, bivalent logic, meaning that Boolean extensionality (BE) is valid:

$$(<=> \; (<=> \; ?P \; ?Q) \; (equal \; ?P \; ?Q)) \qquad \text{(BE)}$$

The left to right direction of (BE) says that there are not more than two truth values, respectively that whenever two formulas A and B can be shown equivalent then their denotations must be the same, namely either *true* or *false*. Once we have established equivalence between formulas A and B in a bivalent logic, then, in any formula C in this logic, we may substitute occurrences of A by B (and vice versa). The important aspect is that this principle not only applies to occurrences of A or B at formula level but also to occurrences at term level. For example, (*and* (*likes Mary Bill*) (*likes Sue Bill*)) and (*and* (*likes Sue Bill*) (*likes Mary Bill*)) are obviously equivalent, and hence, by Boolean extensionality, they have identical denotations. Thus, they can always be substituted by each other, also at the term level positions as in this situation:

$$(holdsDuring \; (YearFn \; 2009) \; (and \; (likes \; Mary \; Bill) \; (likes \; Sue \; Bill))) \qquad \text{(A4)}$$

$$(holdsDuring \; (YearFn \; 2009) \; (and \; (likes \; Sue \; Bill) \; (likes \; Mary \; Bill))) \qquad \text{(C3)}$$

Boolean extensionality seems fine for the particular temporal contexts of our previous examples. In fact, these examples have been chosen to raise the impression that Boolean extensionality is generally a natural and useful requirement for SUMO and similar ontologies. However, as we will show next, it quickly leads to counterintuitive inferences in other modal contexts. We illustrate this for epistemic and doxastic contexts. Assume that in given, concrete situation (ABox) we have:

$$(knows \; Chris \; (equal \; Chris \; Chris)) \qquad \text{(A5)}$$

$$(likes \; Mary \; Bill) \qquad \text{(A6)}$$

$$(knows \; Chris \; (forall \; (?X) \; (=> \; (likes \; Mary \; ?X) \; (likes \; Sue \; ?X))) \qquad \text{(A7)}$$

$$(knows \; Chris \; (likes \; Sue \; Bill)) \qquad \text{(C4)}$$

Assuming Boolean extensionality, the query (C4) follows from Axioms (A5)-(A7), even though we have not explicitly stated the fact (*knows Chris* (*likes Mary Bill*)). Intuitively, however, assuming that Chris actually knows that Mary likes Bill seems mandatory for enabling the proof of the query. Hence, we here (re-)discover a well known issue: modalities have to be treated with great care in classical, bivalent logics.

A solution to this problem is to model SUMO's modal operators as proper modalities in HOML respectively in HOL via our embedding approach. That is, instead of translating SUMO directly into classical logic we propose to translate SUMO into HOML respectively HOL. This enables the mapping of epistemic contexts like $(knows\,Peter\ \langle whatever\rangle)$ or doxastic contexts like $(believes\,Peter\ \langle whatever\rangle)$ to proper modalities in modal logic like $\Box_{Knowledge\,Peter}\ \langle whatever\rangle$ and $\Box_{Believes\,Peter}\ \langle whatever\rangle$. The need for quantifiers and for multiple modalities is obvious from our examples so far. We may add respective axioms in order to appropriately characterize the modalities we obtain and to specify their interaction. For example, to appropriately characterize $\Box_{Knowledge\,Peter}$ as an epistemic modality we may use the S5 axioms and to characterize $\Box_{Believes\,Peter}$ as a doxastic modality we may use the S45 axioms. Moreover, an inclusion axiom between Peter's knowledge and Peter's beliefs can be added. Alternatively, we may postulate corresponding conditions for the respective accessibility relations, cf. the symmetry condition in lines 37–14 in Fig. 1 for logic KB.

We illustrate the approach with the above example. In order to capture the ABox-like status of these axioms, we introduce a fresh constant symbol cw (of world type i) to represent the current situation (as current world). The SUMO axioms (A5)-(A7) and the query (C4) are now mapped to[9]

$$(\Box_{Knowledge\,Chris}(equal\,Chris\,Chris))\ cw) \tag{A5}$$

$$((likes\ Mary\ Bill)\ cw) \tag{A6}$$

$$((\Box_{Knowledge\,Chris})(forall(?X)(=> (likes\ Mary\ ?X)\ (likes\ Sue\ ?X)))\ cw) \tag{A7}$$

$$((\Box_{Knowledge\,Chris})(likes\ Sue\ Bill)\ cw) \tag{C4}$$

Moreover, appropriate axioms need to be generated and added for each epistemic and doxastic modal operator. For example, for the epistemic modality $\Box_{Knowledge\,Chris}$ the following S5 axioms can be added. Since these axioms are supposed to be valid in all situations (TBox-like information), they are stated with the validity operator $[.]$.

$$[\forall \phi_{\mu \to o}\centerdot \Box_{Knowledge\,Chris}\,\phi \supset \phi]$$
$$[\forall \phi_{\mu \to o}\centerdot \Diamond_{Knowledge\,Chris}\,\phi \supset \Box_{Knowledge\,Chris}\,\Diamond_{Knowledge\,Chris}\,\phi]$$

Alternatively, we may simply postulate reflexivity and seriality for the accessibility relation $Knowledge\,Chris$.

Subsequently the above problem can be expanded in the embeddings approach into a proper HOL encoding, and then HOL reasoners can be applied for proving or refuting it. In fact, the mapped example in HOML is not valid and HOL-ATPs are able to detect a counter model, which is what we wanted to achieve. However, if we replace (A6) by $(\Box_{Knowledge\,Chris}\ (likes\ Mary\ Bill)\ cw)$, then the problem can be quickly proved.

Note that the sketched approach scales for other modal operators in SUMO besides *knows* and *believes*. Most importantly, it even supports their flexible combination and bridge rules can be easily postulated.

---

[9] More elegantly, we could employ an $@_{cw}$-operator; for example, (A6) would then be encoded as $@_{cw}(likes\,Mary\,Bill)$ (see also Sect. 5.4).

5.3   Metaphysics

In this subsection we illustrate the use of the embeddings approach for the formalization and verification of Scott's version [65] of Gödel's ontological argument for God's existence [13,19]; cf. Fig. 11. This proof was chosen mainly for two reasons. Firstly, it requires not only modal operators, but also higher-order quantification. Therefore, it is beyond the reach of specialized propositional and first-order (modal) theorem provers. Secondly, this argument addresses an ancient problem in Philosophy and Metaphysics, which has nevertheless received a lot of attention in the last 15 years, because of the discovery of the modal collapse [68,69]. This proof lies in the center of a vast and largely unexplored application domain for automated and interactive theorem provers.

Attempts to prove the existence (or non-existence) of God by means of abstract ontological arguments are an old tradition in philosophy and theology. Gödel's proof [42] is a modern culmination of this tradition, following particularly the footsteps of Leibniz. Various slightly different versions of axioms and definitions have been considered by Gödel and by several philosophers who commented on his proof (cf. [2,5,33,36,69]).

Thanks to the embedding approach, Gödel's theorem stating God's necessary existence was automatically proven from his five axioms using fully automated higher-order theorem provers [13,19].

The respective encodings and the results of a series of recent experiments with LEO-II (version 1.6.2), Satallax (version 2.7), and Nitpick (version 2013) are provided in Fig. 12. The first row marked with T1, for example, shows that theorem T1 follows from axioms A2 and A1 (where only the ⊃-direction is needed); LEO-II and Satallax confirm this in 0.1 s. The experiments have been carried out w.r.t. the logics K and/or KB, and w.r.t. constant (const) and varying (vary) domain semantics for the domains of individuals. The exact dependencies (available axioms and definitions) are displayed for each single problem. The results of the prover calls are given in seconds. '—' means timeout. 'THM', 'CSA', 'SAT', and 'UNS' are the reported result statuses; they stand for 'Theorem', 'CounterSatisfiable', 'Satisfiable', and 'Unsatisfiable', respectively. The experiments were executed remotely using calls to LEO-II, Satallax, and Nitpick installed at Sutcliffe's SystemOnTPTP infrastructure [70] at the University of Miami, which comprises of standard 2.80 GHz computers with 1 GB memory. An example problem from these experiments has been presented in Fig. 2.

Several interesting and partly novel findings have been discovered by the HOL-ATPs, including:

1. The axioms and definitions from Fig. 11 are consistent (cf. CO in Fig. 12).
2. Logic K is sufficient for proving T1, C and T2.
3. For proving the final theorem T3, logic KB is sufficient (and for K a countermodel is reported). This is highly relevant since several philosophers have criticized Gödel's argument for the use of logic S5.
4. Only for T3 the HOL-ATPs still fail to produce a proof directly from the axioms; thus, T3 remains an interesting benchmark problem; T1, C, and T2 are rather trivial for HOL-ATPs.

A1 Either a property or its negation is positive, but not both:

$$\forall\phi[P(\neg\phi) \equiv \neg P(\phi)]$$

A2 A property necessarily implied by a positive property is positive:

$$\forall\phi\forall\psi[(P(\phi) \wedge \Box\forall x[\phi(x) \supset \psi(x)]) \supset P(\psi)]$$

T1 Positive properties are possibly exemplified:

$$\forall\phi[P(\phi) \supset \Diamond\exists x\phi(x)]$$

D1 A *God-like* being possesses all positive properties:

$$G(x) \equiv \forall\phi[P(\phi) \supset \phi(x)]$$

A3 The property of being God-like is positive:

$$P(G)$$

C   Possibly, God exists:

$$\Diamond\exists x G(x)$$

A4 Positive properties are necessarily positive:

$$\forall\phi[P(\phi) \supset \Box\, P(\phi)]$$

D2 An *essence* of an individual is a property possessed by it and necessarily implying any of its properties:

$$\phi \ ess. \ x \equiv \phi(x) \wedge \forall\psi(\psi(x) \supset \Box\forall y(\phi(y) \supset \psi(y)))$$

T2 Being God-like is an essence of any God-like being:

$$\forall x[G(x) \supset G \ ess. \ x]$$

D3 *Necessary existence* of an individ. is the necessary exemplification of all its essences:

$$NE(x) \equiv \forall\phi[\phi \ ess. \ x \supset \Box\exists y\phi(y)]$$

A5 Necessary existence is a positive property:

$$P(NE)$$

T3 Necessarily, God exists:

$$\Box\exists x G(x)$$

Fig. 11. Scott's version of Gödel's ontological argument [65].

5. Gödel's original version of the proof [43], which omits conjunct $\phi(x)$ in the definition of *essence* (cf. D2'), seems inconsistent (cf. the failed consistency check for CO' in Fig. 12). As far as we are aware of, this is a new result.

HOL encoding	dependencies	logic	status	LEO-II const/vary	Satallax const/vary	Nitpick const/vary
A1 $[\dot{\forall}\phi_{\mu\to\sigma}\bullet P_{(\mu\to\sigma)\to\sigma}(\lambda X_\mu\bullet\dot{\neg}(\phi X)) \doteq \dot{\neg}(p\phi)]$						
A2 $[\dot{\forall}\phi_{\mu\to\sigma}\bullet\dot{\forall}\psi_{\mu\to\sigma}\bullet(P_{(\mu\to\sigma)\to\sigma}\phi \wedge \Box\dot{\forall}X_\mu\bullet(\phi X \supset \psi X)) \supset p\psi]$						
T1 $[\dot{\forall}\phi_{\mu\to\sigma}\bullet P_{(\mu\to\sigma)\to\sigma}\phi \supset \Diamond\dot{\exists}X_\mu\bullet\phi X]$	A1($\supset$), A2	K	THM	0.1/0.1	0.0/0.0	—/—
	A1, A2	K	THM	0.1/0.1	0.0/5.2	—/—
D1 $g_{\mu\to\sigma} = \lambda X_\mu\bullet\dot{\forall}\phi_{\mu\to\sigma}\bullet P_{(\mu\to\sigma)\to\sigma}\phi \supset \phi X$						
A3 $[P_{(\mu\to\sigma)\to\sigma} g_{\mu\to\sigma}]$						
C $[\Diamond\dot{\exists}X_\mu\bullet g_{\mu\to\sigma}X]$	T1, D1, A3	K	THM	0.0/0.0	0.0/0.0	—/—
	A1, A2, D1, A3	K	THM	0.0/0.0	5.2/31.3	—/—
A4 $[\dot{\forall}\phi_{\mu\to\sigma}\bullet P_{(\mu\to\sigma)\to\sigma}\phi \supset \Box p\phi]$						
D2 $\mathrm{ess}_{(\mu\to\sigma)\to\mu\to\sigma} = \lambda\phi_{\mu\to\sigma}\bullet\lambda X_\mu\bullet\phi X \wedge \dot{\forall}\psi_{\mu\to\sigma}\bullet(\psi X \supset \Box\dot{\forall}Y_\mu\bullet(\phi Y \supset \psi Y))$						
T2 $[\dot{\forall}X_\mu\bullet g_{\mu\to\sigma}X \supset (\mathrm{ess}_{(\mu\to\sigma)\to\mu\to\sigma}gX)]$	A1, D1, A4, D2	K	THM	19.1/18.3	0.0/0.0	—/—
	A1, A2, D1, A3, A4, D2	K	THM	12.9/14.0	0.0/0.0	—/—
D3 $\mathrm{NE}_{\mu\to\sigma} = \lambda X_\mu\bullet\dot{\forall}\phi_{\mu\to\sigma}\bullet(\mathrm{ess}\,\phi X \supset \Box\dot{\exists}Y_\mu\bullet\phi Y)$						
A5 $[P_{(\mu\to\sigma)\to\sigma}\mathrm{NE}_{\mu\to\sigma}]$						
T3 $[\Box\dot{\exists}X_\mu\bullet g_{\mu\to\sigma}X]$	D1, C, T2, D3, A5	K	CSA	—/—	—/—	3.8/6.2
	A1, A2, D1, A3, A4, D2, D3, A5	K	CSA	—/—	—/—	8.2/7.5
	D1, C, T2, D3, A5	KB	THM	0.0/0.1	0.1/5.3	—/—
	A1, A2, D1, A3, A4, D2, D3, A5	KB	THM	—/—	—/—	—/—
MC $[s_\sigma \supset \Box s_\sigma]$	D2, T2, T3	KB	THM	17.9/—	3.3/3.2	—/—
	A1, A2, D1, A3, A4, D2, D3, A5	KB	THM	—/—	—/—	—/—
FG $[\dot{\forall}\phi_{\mu\to\sigma}\bullet\dot{\forall}X_\mu\bullet(g_{\mu\to\sigma}X \supset (\dot{\neg}(P_{(\mu\to\sigma)\to\sigma}\phi) \supset \dot{\neg}(\phi X)))]$	A1, D1	KB	THM	16.5/—	0.0/0.0	—/—
	A1, A2, D1, A3, A4, D2, D3, A5	KB	THM	12.8/15.1	0.0/5.4	—/—
MT $[\dot{\forall}X_\mu\bullet\dot{\forall}Y_\mu\bullet(g_{\mu\to\sigma}X \supset (g_{\mu\to\sigma}Y \supset X \doteq Y))]$	D1, FG	KB	THM	—/—	0.0/3.3	—/—
	A1, A2, D1, A3, A4, D2, D3, A5	KB	THM	—/—	—/—	—/—
CO $\emptyset$ (no goal, check for consistency)	A1, A2, D1, A3, A4, D2, D3, A5	KB	SAT	—/—	—/—	7.3/7.4
D2' $\mathrm{ess}_{(\mu\to\sigma)\to\mu\to\sigma} = \lambda\phi_{\mu\to\sigma}\bullet\lambda X_\mu\bullet\dot{\forall}\psi_{\mu\to\sigma}\bullet(\psi X \supset \Box\dot{\forall}Y_\mu\bullet(\phi Y \supset \psi Y))$						
CO' $\emptyset$ (no goal, check for consistency)	A1($\supset$), A2, D2', D3, A5	KB	UNS	7.5/7.8	—/—	—/—
	A1, A2, D1, A3, A4, D2', D3, A5	KB	UNS	—/—	—/—	—/—

Fig. 12. HOL encodings and experiment results for the ontological argument from Fig. 11.

6. Gödel's axioms imply what is called the modal collapse (cf. MC in Fig. 12) $\phi \supset \Box\phi$, that is, contingent truth implies necessary truth (which can even be interpreted as an argument against free will; cf. [69]). MC is probably the most fundamental criticism put forward against Gödel's argument.

7. All of the above findings hold for both constant domain semantics and varying domain semantics (for the domain of individuals).

The above findings, in particular (7), illustrate that the modal reasoning framework described here has a great potential towards a flexible support system for *computational theoretical philosophy*. In fact, Gödel's ontological argument has been verified and even automated not only for one particular setting of logic parameters, but these logic parameters have been varied and the validity of the argument has been reconfirmed (or falsified, cf. D2' and CO') for the modified setting. Moreover, our framework is not restricted to a particular theorem proving system, but has been fruitfully employed with some of the most prominent automated theorem provers available to date. A semi-automatic verification of Gödel's argument was also realized in `Isabelle`, with partial automation via Sledgehammer, Nitpick and Metis (see Figs. 3 and 4) [18].

When a fully automatic or semi-automatic verification is performed, the formal proof structure is hidden and may not correspond to the informal structure of the argument. In order to verify the exact argument in all detail, a fully interactive and fine-grained formalization is needed. We show and discuss such a formalization in Coq (version 8.4pl5) below. In contrast to the formalization in Isabelle [18], the formalization in Coq used no automation. This was a deliberate choice, mainly because it allowed a qualitative evaluation of the convenience of the embedding approach for *interactive* theorem proving.

The formalization shown below aims at being as similar as possible to Dana Scott's version of the proof [65]. The formulation and numbering of axioms, definitions and theorems is the same as in Scott's notes. Even the Coq proof scripts follow precisely all the steps in Scott's notes. Scott's assertions are emphasized below with comments. Furthermore, the deliberate preference for simple tactics (mostly *intro*, *apply* and the modal tactics described in Sect. 4.3) results in proof scripts that closely correspond to common natural deduction proofs.

Gödel's proof requires Coq's classical logic libraries as well as the Modal library developed by us and described in Sect. 4.3.

```
Require Import Coq.Logic.Classical Coq.Logic.Classical_Pred_Type Modal.
```

In Scott's notes, classicality occurs in uses of the principle of proof by contradiction. In order to clearly indicate where classical logic is needed in the proof scripts, a simple tactic that simulates proof by contradiction was created:

```
Ltac proof_by_contradiction H := apply NNPP; intro H.
```

Gödel's theory has a single higher-order constant, Positive, which ought to hold for properties considered *positive* in a moral sense.

```
(* Constant predicate that distinguishes positive properties *)
Parameter Positive: (u -> o) -> o.
```

God is defined as a being possessing all positive properties, and five axioms are stated to characterize positivity. The first part of the proof culminates in corollary1 and establishes that God's existence is possible.

```
(* Axiom A1 (divided into two directions):
   either a property or its negation is positive, but not both *)
Axiom axiom1a :
  [ mforall p, (Positive (fun x: u => m~(p x))) m-> (m~ (Positive p)) ].

Axiom axiom1b :
  [ mforall p, (m~ (Positive p)) m-> (Positive (fun x: u => m~ (p x))) ].

(* Axiom A2:
   a property necessarily implied by a positive property is positive *)
Axiom axiom2: [ mforall p, mforall q,
  Positive p m/\ (box (mforall x, (p x) m-> (q x) )) m-> Positive q ].

(* Theorem T1: positive properties are possibly exemplified *)
Theorem theorem1: [ mforall p, (Positive p) m-> (dia (mexists x, p x) ].
Proof. mv.
intro p. intro H1. proof_by_contradiction H2. apply not_dia_box_not in H2.
assert (H3: ((box (mforall x, m~ (p x))) w)). (* Scott *)
  box_i. intro x. assert (H4: ((m~ (mexists x : u, p x)) w0)).
    box_e H2 G2. exact G2.
    clear H2 R H1 w. intro H5. apply H4. exists x. exact H5.
  assert (H6: ((box (mforall x, (p x) m-> m~ (x m= x))) w)). (* Scott *)
    box_i. intro x. intros H7 H8. box_elim H3 w0 G3. eapply G3. exact H7.
    assert (H9: ((Positive (fun x => m~ (x m= x))) w)). (* Scott *)
      apply (axiom2 w p (fun x => m~ (x m= x))). split.
```

```
         exact H1.
         exact H6.
      assert (H10: ((box (mforall x, (p x) m-> (x m= x))) w)). (* Scott *)
        box_i. intros x H11. reflexivity.
        assert (H11 : ((Positive (fun x => (x m= x))) w)). (* Scott *)
          apply (axiom2 w p (fun x => x m= x )). split.
            exact H1.
            exact H10.
          apply axiom1a in H9. contradiction.
Qed.

(* Definition D1:
   God: a God-like being possesses all positive properties *)
Definition G(x: u) := mforall p, (Positive p) m-> (p x).

(* Axiom A3: the property of being God-like is positive *)
Axiom axiom3: [ Positive G ].

(* Corollary C1: possibly, God exists *)
Theorem corollary1: [ dia (mexists x, G x) ].
Proof. mv. apply theorem1. apply axiom3. Qed.
```

The second part of the proof consists in showing that if God's existence is possible then it must be necessary (lemma2). The controversial **S5** principle dia_box_to_box is used.

```
(* Axiom A4: positive properties are necessarily positive *)
Axiom axiom4: [ mforall p, (Positive p) m-> box (Positive p) ].

(* Definition D2:
   essence: an essence of an individual is a property possessed by it
   and necessarily implying any of its properties *)
Definition Essence(p: u -> o)(x: u) :=
   (p x) m/\ mforall q, ((q x) m-> box (mforall y, (p y) m-> (q y))).
Notation"p 'ess' x" := (Essence p x) (at level 69).

(* Theorem T2: being God-like is an essence of any God-like being *)
Theorem theorem2: [ mforall x, (G x) m-> (G ess x) ].
Proof. mv. intro g. intro H1. unfold Essence. split.
  exact H1.
  intro q. intro H2. assert (H3: ((Positive q) w)).
    proof_by_contradiction H4. unfold G in H1. apply axiom1b in H4.
    apply H1 in H4. contradiction.

    cut (box (Positive q) w). (* Scott *)
      apply K. box_i. intro H5. intro y. intro H6.
      unfold G in H6. apply (H6 q). exact H5.

      apply axiom4. exact H3.
Qed.

(* Definition D3:
   necessary existence: necessary existence of an individual
   is the necessary exemplification of all its essences *)
Definition NE(x: u) := mforall p, (p ess x) m-> box (mexists y, (p y)).

(* Axiom A5: necessary existence is a positive property *)
Axiom axiom5: [ Positive NE ].

Lemma lemma1: [ (mexists z, (G z)) m-> box (mexists x, (G x)) ].
Proof. mv.
intro H1. destruct H1 as [g H2]. cut ((G ess g) w). (* Scott *)
  assert (H3: (NE g w)).        (* Scott *)
    unfold G in H2. apply (H2 NE). apply axiom5.
    unfold NE in H3. apply H3.
  apply theorem2. exact H2.
```

```
Qed.

Lemma lemma2: [ dia (mexists z, (G z)) m-> box (mexists x, (G x)) ].
Proof. mv.
intro H. cut (dia (box (mexists x, G x)) w).  (* Scott *)
  apply dia_box_to_box.
  apply (mp_dia w (mexists z, G z)).
    exact H.
    box_i. apply lemma1.
Qed.

(* Theorem T3: necessarily, a God exists *)
Theorem theorem3: [ box (mexists x, (G x)) ].
Proof. mv. apply lemma2. apply corollary1. Qed.

(* Corollary C2: There exists a god *)
Theorem corollary2: [ mexists x, (G x) ].
Proof. mv. apply T. apply theorem3. Qed.
```

5.4   Paraconsistent Reasoning Through Higher-Order Hybrid Logics

Inconsistencies pose a significant challenge to proper reasoning in the web. It is well-known that classical logic validates the *principle of explosion*, according to which every proposition follows from a contradiction (*ex contractione quodlibet*). Hence, any inconsistency in the vast knowledge available in the web, no matter how tiny, insignificant, unreliable, exceptional or irrelevant it is to our query, would render classical reasoners useless.

Several approaches have been proposed to overcome this challenge. The diversity of approaches reflects the large variety of kinds of inconsistency that we can encounter. For example, contradictory pieces of information may be due to errors made by ourselves; or they may merely express divergent opinions from other sources. Or perhaps two statements may contradict one another because one of them expresses a general rule that is not always applicable, while the other describes an exception to the rule. If we adhered to dialetheism, contradictions in a theory could even be taken to reflect actual contradictions in models where statement could be simultaneously true and false. Depending on the situation, we may wish to, for instance, *revise* the data (i.e. our *beliefs*) [60,64], do *default reasoning* preferring exceptions to general rules, simply ignore contradictions when they are *irrelevant* [35,61] to the reasoning task at hand, or use non-classical *paraconsistent logics* that block the principle of explosion [25,34,72].

In this section we informally sketch a logic that is adequate for applications where data originates from different independent sources, which are assumed to be separately consistent but possibly mutually inconsistent. Such a scenario is common in the web, where we must do the best reasoning we can despite the limited control over the information provided by (often not fully trusted) data sources. The basic idea of this logic goes back to the modal *discussive logics* of Jaskowski [46,47], in which the fact that a participant/source claims p is expressed by $\Diamond p$. These logics exhibit a paraconsistent behavior in the following sense: if two participants make contradictory claims such as q and $\neg q$, an arbitrary proposition r is not implied, because $\Diamond q \wedge \Diamond \neg q \supset r$ is not valid. Jaskowski's logics assume the modal axiom T ($\Box p \supset p$), which in this context expresses the fact that a proposition holds if all participants unanimously claim it.

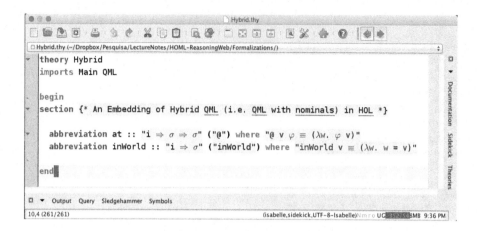

Fig. 13. Higher-order hybrid logics

In Jaskowski's Discussive logics each participant/source is a distinct possible world. Their main limitation is the impossibility of referring to each participant/source/world explicitly, because $\Diamond$ and $\Box$ are the only available modalities. A problematic consequence of this parsimony is, for instance, the lack of modus ponens relative to the claims of a single participant: if a participant claims p and later claims $p \supset q$, these claims are formalized as $\Diamond p$ and $\Diamond(p \supset q)$; but then, unfortunately, $\Diamond q$ cannot be deduced. Discussive logics try to remedy this problem in ways (cf. [10]) that may seem unnatural and unnecessary after the advent of hybrid logics, which extend modal logics with nominals and the @ modality. In a hybrid discussive logic, as proposed here, the claims p and $p \supset q$ by a participant j could be formalized as $@_j p$ and $@_j(p \supset q)$. Hence, information about who claimed what is preserved. Furthermore, the @ modality gives greater flexibility and control over which sources/participants to trust. In addition to trusting the consensus ($\Box p \supset p$), it becomes possible to declare that a particular source s is trusted, by stating that ($@_s p \supset p$).

With the embedding approach, it is trivial to define nominals and the @ modality, because worlds are already syntactically explicit. This is shown in Fig. 13.

Note that we have in fact already employed the @ modality in Sect. 5.2 in the axioms (A5)-(A7) and conjecture (C4).

Once we have a higher-order hybrid modal logic at our disposal, we assign each information source to a different world, and we may reason explicitly about inconsistencies between the information sources. This is shown in Fig. 14. The fact that Nitpick finds a counter-model for the principle of explosion demonstrates that this logic is paraconsistent.

Figure 15 shows a toy example of reasoning with two sources of information, the TV channels *CNN* and *Russia Today* (*RT*), which disagree with each other about the qualities of the president of Russia. If we simply believed everything that we hear from CNN and RT, our beliefs would be inconsistent. The hybrid

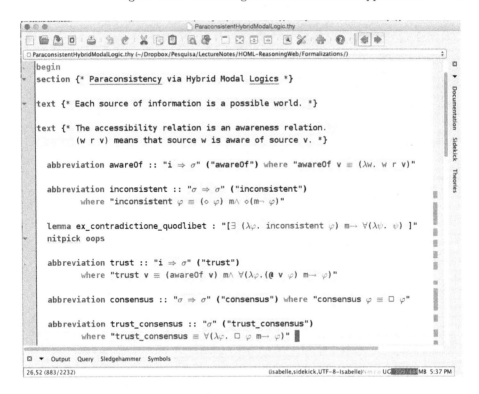

Fig. 14. Paraconsistency

modal logic proposed here allow us to be skeptikal about our information sources and possibly choose which source we would like to trust.

Distinct sources of information may disagree not only on the propositional level but also on their understanding of properties and individuals. Consider, for example, a model with two worlds: m (Mars) and e (Earth); and consider whether the sentence $\Box blue^\star(sky^\star)$ ("necessarily the sky is blue") is true in this model. From an external absolute perspective, the sky is assumed to be $blue^\star$ in Earth and $red^\star$ in Mars, and therefore, if $blue^\star$ were considered to be a *rigid property* (equal to the absolute notion of "blue", so that $blue^\star = blue^\star$), the sentence would be clearly false, because the sky is not $blue^\star$ in Mars. However, if $blue^\star$ were considered to be a *flexible property* (i.e. depending on worlds), the sentence would be ambiguous. In fact, also $sky^\star$ refers to a different thing in each world and hence it could also be considered as a *flexible individual* dependent on worlds. These ambiguities become clear when we try to translate the sentence to classical higher-order logic and they are resolved when we opt for one of the following four possible translations:

A: $\forall\, w\ w'.(rww') \supset (((blue^\star\ w')(sky^\star\ w'))\ w')$
B: $\forall\, w\ w'.(rww') \supset (((blue^\star\ w)(sky^\star\ w'))\ w')$
C: $\forall\, w\ w'.(rww') \supset (((blue^\star\ w')(sky^\star\ w))\ w')$
D: $\forall\, w\ w'.(rww') \supset (((blue^\star\ w)(sky^\star\ w))\ w')$

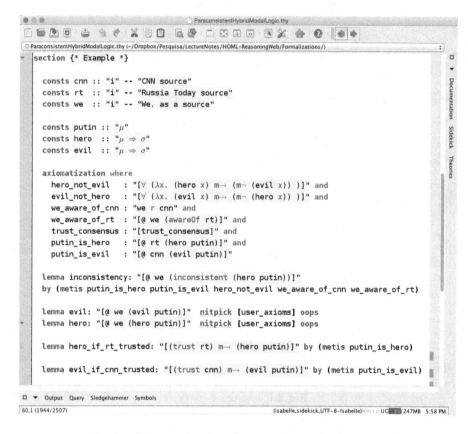

Fig. 15. An example of conflicting sources of information

These translations differ on the world that is taken for grounding flexible constants (e.g. *blue*⋆ and *sky*⋆) under the scope of modal operators. Translation A, for example, grounds the flexible constants on the world w' introduced by the modal operator, while translation D grounds them on the current world w. If the Martian understanding of *blue*⋆ is equal to the absolute notion of *red* (i.e. (*blue*⋆ m) = *red*) (and, likewise for Earth, (*blue*⋆ e) = *blue*), then translation A would be true.

Flexible constants (properties or individuals) may be useful for reasoning with many knowledge bases (e.g. in description logics or expressive ontologies such as SUMO) having overlapping names for concepts or objects. Merely merging these knowledge bases could easily lead to inconsistencies (e.g. with the sky being both blue, according to the Earthling knowledge base, and not blue, according to the Martian knowledge base). Instead, embedding these knowledge bases into a higher-order hybrid logic, with each knowledge base occupying a separate world and flexible constants used for conflicting concepts and objects, provides a simple and safe alternative to avoid inconsistencies.

The language of quantified modal logic defined in Sect. 2 does not allow the user to specify on which world a flexible property or object should be grounded. There is also no way for flexible and rigid properties/objects to be used together. The semantic embedding described in Sect. 3.2 assumes that they are all rigid. An alternative would be to assume that they are flexible and ground them on the world introduced by the closest modal operator (e.g. as in translation A). Fitting [36] discusses yet another possibility, at least for certain kinds of properties introduced by higher-order quantifiers: they are grounded to the world where they were introduced (i.e. a modal formula such as $\exists\psi.\Box\psi(c)$ (where c is assumed to be a rigid constant) would be translated[10] as $\forall w.\exists\psi.\forall w'.(r\ w\ w') \supset (\psi w)(c)$, and not as $\forall w.\exists\psi.\forall w'.(r\ w\ w') \supset (\psi w')(c)$ because w is the world having scope over the existential quantifier introducing ψ).

Instead of being content with the language of higher-order modal logic from Sect. 3.2 and then choosing either the rigid translation or some flexible translation, an even more interesting possibility, whose details remain for future work, would be to enrich the language of higher-order quantified modal logic, in order to empower the user to conveniently specify how flexible terms should be grounded. What currently prevents this is that the worlds implicitly introduced by modal operators are hidden. Therefore, one approach would be to enrich the language with modal operators that explicitly expose the introduced worlds. The four alternative disambiguations of $\Box blue^{\star}(sky^{\star})$ discussed above, for example, could then be written as follows in the enriched language:

A: $\Box_{w'}\, blue^{w'}(sky^{w'})$
B: $\Box_{w'}\, blue^{w}(sky^{w'})$
C: $\Box_{w'}\, blue^{w'}(sky^{w})$
D: $\Box_{w'}\, blue^{w}(sky^{w})$

where w would be the current world, by convention.

With embeddings, enriching the language in this manner is easy, as shown in Figs. 16 and 17.

Another approach would be to use a nameless bound variable notation [32] for worlds, as follows:

A: $\Box blue^{0}(sky^{0})$
B: $\Box blue^{1}(sky^{0})$
C: $\Box blue^{0}(sky^{1})$
D: $\Box blue^{1}(sky^{1})$

where the superscript indices are de-Bruijn indices indicating the nameless bound world that should be used for grounding.

Achieving such nameless notation in Isabelle is made possible by the advanced feature of syntax translations, as exemplified in the formalization of Hoare Logic [73].

---

[10] Fitting [36] (pp. 83ff) actually does not use a translation to higher-order logic, where worlds become part of the syntax. But what he does, using his style of syntax (which distinguishes extensional and intensional types), is essentially analogous to the translation described here.

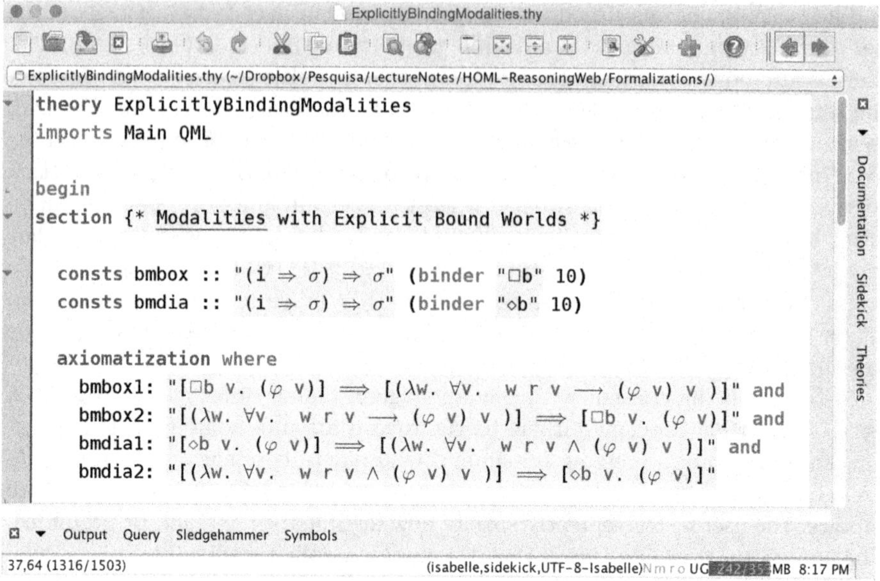

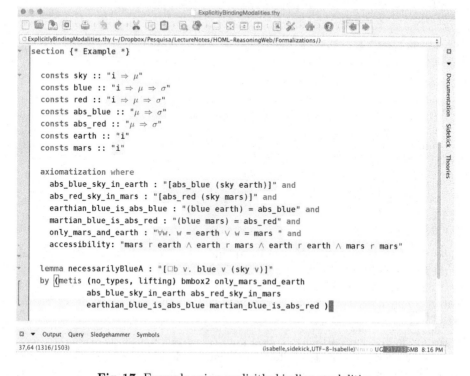

Fig. 16. Explicitly binding modalities

Fig. 17. Example using explicitly binding modalities

6   Conclusion

In these lecture notes, we have explained the latest developments in automated reasoning for higher-order modal logics. We have also surveyed recent and potential applications of such expressive logics. This is a vast and exciting direction of research, which has become possible by the high degree of maturity achieved by current higher-order theorem provers and proof assistants.

Acknowledgments. We would like to thank João Marcos for consistently useful discussions about discussive logics and paraconsistency. Various persons have contributed or positively influenced this line of research in the past, including, Larry Paulson, Chad Brown, Geoff Sutcliffe, and Jasmin Blanchette.

References

1. Web semantics: Science, services and agents on the world wide web, special issue on reasoning with context in the semantic web, vol. 12–13, pp. 1–160 (2012)
2. Adams, R.M.: Introductory Note to *1970. In: Feferman, S., et al. (eds.) Kurt Gödel, Collected Works, vol. III. Oxford University Press, New York (1995)
3. Akman, V., Surav, M.: Steps toward formalizing context. AI Mag. **17**(3), 55–72 (1996)
4. Alama, J., Heskes, T., Kühlwein, D., Tsivtsivadze, E., Urban, J.: Premise selection for mathematics by corpus analysis and kernel methods. J. Autom. Reasoning **52**(2), 191–213 (2014)
5. Anderson, A.C., Gettings, M.: Gödel's ontological proof revisited. In: Hájek, P. (ed.) Gödel '96: Logical foundations of mathematics, computer science and physics. Lecture Notes in Logic, vol. 6, pp. 167–172. Springer, Berlin (1996)
6. Andrews, P.B.: General models and extensionality. J. Symb. Logic **37**(2), 395–397 (1972)
7. Andrews, P.B.: Church's type theory. In: Zalta, E.N. (ed.), The Stanford Encyclopedia of Philosophy. Spring 2014 edition, 2014
8. Andrews, P.B., Miller, D.A.: Eve Longini Cohen, and Frank Pfenning. Automating higher-order logic. In: Bledsoe, W.W., Loveland, D.W., et al., Automated Theorem Proving: After 25 Years, vol. 29 of Contemporary Mathematics series, pp. 169–192. American Mathematical Society (1984)
9. Andrews, P.B., Bishop, M.: On sets, types, fixed points, and checkerboards. In: Miglioli, P., Moscato, U., Mundici, D., Ornaghi, D. (eds.) Theorem Proving with Analytic Tableaux and Related Methods. LNCS, vol. 1071, pp. 1–15. Springer, Heidelberg (1996)
10. Marcos, J.: Modality and paraconsistency. The Logica Yearbook, pp. 213–222 (2005)
11. Baader, F., Calvanese, D., McGuinness, D.L., Nardi, D., Patel-Schneider, P.F. (eds.): The Description Logic Handbook: Theory, Implementation, and Applications. Cambridge University Press, New York (2003)
12. Benzmüller, C., Theiss, F., Paulson, L., Fietzke, A.: LEO-II - a cooperative automatic theorem prover for higher-order logic. In: Proceedings of IJCAR 2008, number 5195 in LNAI, pp. 162–170. Springer, Berlin (2008)

13. Benzmüller, C., Woltzenlogel Paleo, B.: Formalization, Mechanization and Automation of Gödel's Proof of God's Existence. arXiv:1308.4526 (2013)
14. Benzmüller, C.: Verifying the modal logic cube is an easy task (for higher-order automated reasoners). In: Siegler, S., Wasser, N. (eds.) Walther Festschrift. LNCS, vol. 6463, pp. 117–128. Springer, Heidelberg (2010)
15. Benzmüller, C., Brown, C.: The curious inference of Boolos in MIZAR and OMEGA. In: Matuszewski, R., Zalewska, A. (eds.) From Insight to Proof - Festschrift in Honour of Andrzej Trybulec. Studies in Logic, Grammar, and Rhetoric, vol. 10(23), pp. 299–388. The University of Bialystok, Polen (2007)
16. Benzmüller, C., Brown, C.E., Kohlhase, M.: Higher-order semantics and extensionality. J. Symb. Logic 69(4), 1027–1088 (2004)
17. Benzmüller, C., Otten, J., Raths, T.: Implementing and evaluating provers for first-order modal logics. In: Raedt, L.D., Bessiere, C., Dubois, D., Doherty, P., Frasconi, P., Heintz, F., Lucas, P. (eds.), ECAI 2012, Frontiers in Artificial Intelligence and Applications, vol. 242, pp. 163–168. IOS Press, Montpellier (2012)
18. Benzmüller, C., Woltzenlogel Paleo, B.: Gödel's God in Isabelle/HOL. Arch. Formal Proofs, 2013 (2013)
19. Benzmüller, C., Woltzenlogel Paleo, B.: Automating Gödel's ontological proof of God's existence with higher-order automated theorem provers. In: Schaub, T., Friedrich, G., O'Sullivan, B., (eds.), ECAI 2014, Frontiers in Artificial Intelligence and Applications, vol. 263, pp. 93–98, IOS Press (2014)
20. Benzmüller, C., Paulson, L.: Exploring properties of normal multimodal logics in simple type theory with LEO-II. In: Benzmüller, C., Brown, C., Siekmann, J., Statman, R. (eds.), Reasoning in Simple Type Theory – Festschrift in Honor of Peter B. Andrews on His 70th Birthday, Studies in Logic, Mathematical Logic and Foundations, pp. 386–406, College Publications (2008)
21. Benzmüller, C., Paulson, L.: Quantified multimodal logics in simple type theory. Logic Univers. (Spec. Issue Multimodal Logics) 7(1), 7–20 (2013)
22. Benzmüller, C., Pease, A.: Higher-order aspects and context in SUMO. J. Web Seman. (Spec. Issue Reasoning with context in the Semant. Web) 12–13, 104–117 (2012)
23. Benzmüller, Christoph, Raths, Thomas: HOL based first-order modal logic provers. In: McMillan, Ken, Middeldorp, Aart, Voronkov, Andrei (eds.) LPAR-19 2013. LNCS, vol. 8312, pp. 127–136. Springer, Heidelberg (2013)
24. Benzmüller, C., Weber, L., Woltzenlogel Paleo, B.: Computer-assisted analysis of the Anderson-Hájek ontological controversy. In: Silvestre, R.S., Béziau, J.-Y. (eds.), Handbook of the 1st World Congress on Logic and Religion, Joao Pessoa, Brasil (2015)
25. Beziau, J.Y., Carnielli, W., Gabbay, D.: Handbook of Paraconsistency. College Publications, London (2007)
26. Blackburn, P., van Benthem, J.F.A.K., Wolter, F.: Handbook of Modal Logic, Volume 3 (Studies in Logic and Practical Reasoning). Elsevier Science Inc., New York (2006)
27. Blanchette, J.C., Böhme, S., Paulson, L.C.: Extending Sledgehammer with SMT solvers. J. Autom. Reasoning 51(1), 109–128 (2013)
28. Blanchette, Jasmin Christian, Nipkow, Tobias: Nitpick: A counterexample generator for higher-order logic based on a relational model finder. In: Kaufmann, Matt, Paulson, Lawrence C. (eds.) ITP 2010. LNCS, vol. 6172, pp. 131–146. Springer, Heidelberg (2010)
29. Boolos, G.: A curious inference. J. Philos. Logic 16, 1–12 (1987)

30. Brown, C.E.: Satallax: An automated higher-order prover. In: Gramlich, B., Miller, D., Sattler, U. (eds.) Automated Reasoning. LNCS, vol. 7364, pp. 111–117. Springer, Heidelberg (2012)
31. Bucav, S., Buvac, V., Mason, I.A.: Metamathematics of contexts. Fundamenta Informaticae **23**(3), 263–301 (1995)
32. Charguéraud, A.: The locally nameless representation. J. Autom. Reasoning **49**(3), 363–408 (2012)
33. Corazzon, R.: Contemporary bibliography on ontological arguments. http://www.ontology.co/biblio/ontological-proof-contemporary-biblio.htm
34. da Costa, N.C.A., Alves, E.H.: Semantical analysis of the calculi cn. Notre Dame J. Formal Logic **18**(4), 621–630 (1977)
35. Dunn, J.M., Restall, G.: Relevance logic. Handbook of Philosophical Logic **6**, 1–136 (2002)
36. Fitting, M.: Types, Tableaux and Gödel's God, Kluwer (2002)
37. Fitting, M., Mendelsohn, R.L.: First-Order Modal Logic. Synthese Library. Kluwer, Netherlands (1998)
38. Gabbay, D.M.: Labelled Deductive Systems. Clarendon Press, Oxford (1996)
39. Gallin, D.: Intensional and Higher-Order Modal Logic. North Holland, New York (1975)
40. Giunchiglia, F.: Contextual reasoning. Epistemologia (Special Issue on Languages and Machines) **16**, 345–364 (1993)
41. Giunchiglia, F., Serafini, L.: Multilanguage hierarchical logics or: How we can do without modal logics. Artif. Intell. **65**(1), 29–70 (1994)
42. Gödel, K.: Collected Works, Unpublished Essays and Letters. Ontological Proof, pp. 65–85. Oxford University Press, Oxford (1970)
43. Gödel, K.: Appx.A: Notes in Kurt Gödel's Hand. In: [70], pp. 144–145 (2004)
44. Guha, R.V.: Context: A Formalization and Some Applications. Ph.D. thesis, Stanford University (1991)
45. Henkin, L.: Completeness in the theory of types. J. Symb. Logic **15**(2), 81–91 (1950)
46. Jaśkowski, S.: Rachunek zdań dla systemów dedukcyjnych sprzecznych. Stud. Soc. Scientiarun Torunesis **1**(5), 55–77 (1948)
47. Jaśkowski, S.: Propositional calculus for contradictory deductive systems. Stud. Logica. **24**, 143–157 (1969)
48. Kaliszyk, C., Urban, J.: Hol(y)hammer: online ATP service for HOL light. Math. Comput. Sci. **9**(1), 5–22 (2015)
49. Kaliszyk, C., Urban, J.: Learning-assisted theorem proving with millions of lemmas. J. Symb. Comput. **69**, 109–128 (2015)
50. Lindblad, F.: agsyHOL website. https://github.com/frelindb/agsyHOL
51. McCarthy, J.: Generality in artificial intelligence. Commun. ACM **30**(12), 1030–1035 (1987)
52. McCarthy, J.: Notes on formalizing context. In: Proceedings of IJCAI 1993, pp. 555–562 (1993)
53. Muskens, R.: Higher order modal logic. In: Blackburn, P., et al. (eds.) Handbook of Modal Logic, pp. 621–653. Elsevier, Dordrecht (2006)
54. Nipkow, T., Paulson, L.C., Wenzel, M.: Isabelle/HOL: A Proof Assistant for Higher-Order Logic. LNCS, vol. 2283. Springer, Berlin (2002)
55. Otten, J.: Mleancop: A connection prover for first-order modal logic. In: Demri, S., Kapur, D., Weidenbach, C. (eds.) Automated Reasoning. LNCS, vol. 8562, pp. 269–276. Springer, Switzerland (2014)

56. Woltzenlogel Paleo, B., Benzmüller, C.: Formal theology repository. (https://github.com/FormalTheology/GoedelGod)
57. Paulin-Mohring, C.: Introduction to the calculus of inductive constructions. In: Delahaye, D., Woltzenlogel Paleo, B. (eds.), All about Proofs, Proofs for All, Mathematical Logic and Foundations. College Publications, London (2015)
58. Pease, A.: Ontology: A Practical Guide. Articulate Software Press, Angwin (2011)
59. Pease, A., Sutcliffe, G.: First order reasoning on a large ontology. In: Sutcliffe, G., Urban, J., Schulz, S. (eds.), Proceedings of the CADE-21 Workshop on Empirically Successful Automated Reasoning in Large Theories (ESARLT), CEUR Workshop Proceedings, vol. 257, CEUR-WS.org (2007)
60. Priest, G.: Paraconsistent belief revision. Theoria **67**, 214–228 (2001)
61. Priest, G., Sylvan, R.: Simplified semantics for basic relevant logics. J. Philos. Logic (1992)
62. Ramachandran, D., Reagan, P., Goolsbey, K.: First-orderized ResearchCyc: Expressivity and efficiency in a common-sense ontology. In: Shvaiko P. (ed.), Papers from the AAAI Workshop on Contexts and Ontologies: Theory, Practice and Applications, Pittsburgh, Pennsylvania, USA, 2005. Technical report WS-05-01 published by The AAAI Press, Menlo Park, California, July 2005
63. Raths, Thomas, Otten, Jens: The QMLTP problem library for first-order modal logics. In: Gramlich, Bernhard, Miller, Dale, Sattler, Uli (eds.) IJCAR 2012. LNCS, vol. 7364, pp. 454–461. Springer, Heidelberg (2012)
64. Restall, G., Slaney, J.: Realistic belief revision. In: Proceedings of the Second World Conference in the Fundamentals of Artificial Intelligence, pp. 367–378 (1995)
65. Scott, D.: Appx.B: Notes in Dana Scott's Hand. In: [70], pp. 145–146 (2004)
66. Serafini, L., Bouquet, P.: Comparing formal theories of context in AI. Artif. Intell. **155**, 41–67 (2004)
67. Siders, A., Woltzenlogel Paleo, B.: A variant of Gödel's ontological proof in a natural deduction calculus. (github.com/FormalTheology/GoedelGod/blob/master/Papers/InProgress/NaturalDeduction/GodProof-ND.pdf?raw=true)
68. Sobel, J.H.: Gödel's ontological proof. In On Being and Saying. Essays for Richard Cartwright, pp. 241–261, MIT Press (1987)
69. Sobel, J.H.: Logic and Theism: Arguments for and Against Beliefs in God. Cambridge University Press, Cambridge (2004)
70. Sutcliffe, G.: The TPTP problem library and associated infrastructure. J. Autom. Reasoning **43**(4), 337–362 (2009)
71. Sutcliffe, G., Benzmüller, C.: Automated reasoning in higher-order logic using the TPTP THF infrastructure. J. Formalized Reasoning **3**(1), 1–27 (2010)
72. Tanaka, K.: Three schools of paraconsistency. The Australas. J. Logic **1**, 28–42 (2003)
73. Wenzel, M.: Hoare logic in isabelle. http://isabelle.in.tum.de/dist/library/HOL/HOL-Isar_Examples/Hoare.html

Web Stream Reasoning: From Data Streams to Actionable Knowledge

Alessandra Mileo[✉]

Insight Centre for Data Analytics, National University of Ireland, Galway, Ireland
alessandra.mileo@insight-centre.org

Abstract. A fast growing torrent of data is being created by companies, social networks, mobile phones, smart homes, public transport vehicles, healthcare devices, and other modern infrastructures. Being able to unlock the potential hidden in this torrent of data would open unprecedented opportunities to improve our daily lives that were not possible before. Advances in the Internet of Things (IoT), Semantic Web and Linked Data research and standardization have already established formats and technologies for representing, sharing and re-using (dynamic) knowledge on the Web. However, transforming data into actionable knowledge requires to cater for (i) automatic mechanisms to discover and integrate heterogeneous data streams on the fly and extract patterns for applications to use, (ii) concepts and algorithms for context and quality-aware integration of semantic data streams, and (iii) the ability to synthesize domain-driven commonsense knowledge (and answers derived from it) with expressive inference that can capture decision analytics in a scalable way. In the first part of this lecture we will characterize the main approaches to stream processing for the Web of Data, showing how data quality and context can guide semantic integration. In the second part of this lecture we will focus on rule-based Web Stream Reasoning and illustrate how scalability and uncertainty issues can be addressed in a rule-based approach. We will discuss new challenges and opportunities in Web Stream Reasoning, briefly considering economical and societal impact in real application scenarios in a smart city context, and we will conclude by providing a brief overview of ongoing research and standardization activities in this area.

Keywords: Stream reasoning · Continuous query processing · Quality of information · Logic programming · Semantic web · Inductive logic reasoning

1 Introduction

The Semantic Web and the growing interests in linking data for sharing, re-use, and understanding has started to intersect with the domain of *Big Data* [38].

This research has been partially supported by Science Foundation Ireland (SFI) under grant No. SFI/12/RC/2289 and EU FP7 CityPulse Project under grant No.603095. http://www.ict-citypulse.eu.

W. Faber and A. Paschke (Eds.): Reasoning Web 2015, LNCS 9203, pp. 75–87, 2015.
DOI: 10.1007/978-3-319-21768-0_3

To be successful and efficient in this joint space, we must consider the impact of the volume, variety, and velocity of data on the Web similarly to the Big Data world. The use of RDF as the common data model helped in dealing with the *variety* of information, while various software technologies – such as advanced RDF triplestores – are handling the *volume* of already available data. However, the problem of *velocity*, i.e., frequently produced and *streamed* data still presents some open challenges [10, 11].

Applications that can process streaming data incrementally are required for sensor networks and the Internet of Things (IoT), Smart Grids, Smart Cities, health care and assisted living, security, social network analysis, financial planning, etc. In these domains it is not only necessary to *make sense* of the data very quickly but also to do so in the context of "static" background knowledge such as planning goals, plans, capacities and physical layouts. These real-world requirements necessitate to move the processing paradigms for vast amounts of data from the current batch-like approaches (e.g., distributed and parallel computing with MapReduce) towards processing of data streams and stream reasoning in near-real-time.

Advances on Semantic Web & Linked Data research and standards have already provided formats and technologies for representing and sharing knowledge on the Web. In the last few years, Semantic Web technologies such as RDF, OWL, SPARQL have provided mechanisms and related engines for continuously querying semantic data streams [5, 7, 22] and for semantic complex event processing [2, 20, 21]. Despite their potentials for dealing with data that changes in high volume at high frequency, these solutions can not properly deal with the noisy and imprecise nature of data in dynamic domains such as those mentioned earlier in this section, which are characterized by incomplete information, uncertainty, inconsistencies, preferences and qualitative optimization.

Dealing with these characteristics of dynamic information requires complex reasoning capabilities such as the ability of managing defaults, common-sense, preferences, recursion, and non-determinism which might be required for more expressive reasoning tasks. Logic-based non-monotonic reasoners can perform such computationally intensive tasks but available solutions are suitable for data that changes in low volumes at low frequency and therefore their applicability is limited.

This lecture will characterize IoT Intelligence solutions based on their scalability and expressivity, and will explore their synergies and potentials to be used as a pipeline for scalable and expressive Web Stream Reasoning. Approaches and techniques to handle uncertainty and context-driven information integration will also be presented.

The remainder of the material is structured as follows: Sect. 2 identifies the IoT Intelligence layers considering their expressivity and scalability based on the underlying semantics of existing systems. Section 3 provides some pointers and principles for RDF stream processing and Semantic Complex Event Processing, touching upon quality-aware information integration. Section 4 focuses on the non-monotonic reasoning layer and discusses the latest directions in this area, including hybrid mechanisms where non-monotonic logics and inductive reasoning are combined to deal with uncertainty. Section 5 concludes by presenting recent developments on formal generalizations and standards.

2   IoT Intelligence Layers

Scenarios and requirements for Stream Reasoning have been presented in [27] considering applications for smart grids and smart cities, health monitoring, social media and logistics among others. If we consider existing approaches and solutions for transforming IoT data produced as web streams into knowledge, we can characterize them into three main layers based on the expressivity of the reasoning tasks they support. The conceptual representation of these layers is indicated in Fig. 1. Several interesting approaches are flourishing, which try to extend existing systems for web stream reasoning with cross-layer features. However, we argue existing solutions can be associated to one of these conceptual layer:

Stream Query Processing Layer: This layer includes systems which rely on SPARQL extensions to deal with streaming data. In principle they support all the features and operators of SPARQL 1.1, although implementations might vary, and they have the ability to process and semantically integrate static and dynamic Linked Data.

Example 1. Let us consider data about taxis in a smart city (inspired by the last DEBS Grand Challenge[1] based on NYC open data). Finding the most frequent routes, the most profitable pick-up or drop-off point, the neighborhoods in which pick-up/drop-off increased, or comparing taxi rides with areas served with public transportation are all examples of stream query processing, where dynamic data streams about taxi rides, and static linked data about bus routes or GeoNames need to be semantically integrated.

Semantic Complex Event Processing (SCEP) Layer: Systems in this layer aim at combining stream query processing with operators for complex event pattern detection. These approaches are mostly based on rules for pattern detection using logical operators, and go beyond the current support provided by stream query processing engines to the SPARQL 1.1 semantics. Approaches and systems for semantic complex event processing have leveraged engines for stream query processing and complex event processing in combination, in order to achieve better trade-offs when it comes to expressivity vs. scalability.

Example 2. Let us consider a Social Sensing scenario where we aim at detecting some specific patterns in the interactions among people. In order to detect the most active subjects (e.g. subjects that have been in more than 10 interactions in the last half an hour) stream query processing with aggregates would be enough. But if we want to detect whenever two subjects have moved from one

---

[1] http://www.debs2015.org/call-grand-challenge.html.

room X to another room Y, maybe counting how many times this happened for two specific rooms or for two specific subjects, or finding all the sequences of rooms $< X, Y >$ for which the counting is higher than a threshold, then we fall into complex event processing and need to make sure certain operators are supported: we need to keep track of the status of certain events (i.e. a subject being with another subject and moving from a room to another) and identify sequences and repetitions of such events.

Stream Reasoning Layer: This layer is concerned with approaches to producing new logical conclusions from a given set of input facts, by applying a set of rules. It is the more expressive and less explored layer of web stream reasoning, and it includes approaches that are able to deal with uncertainty, non-monotonicity, defaults and common sense inference. In this lecture we consider rule-based approaches to non-monotonic stream reasoning and presents some principles and directions in this area.

Example 3. Let us consider a geo-fencing scenario similar to the one described in [28]. People wear RFID tags and move around a building or an area such as an airport or a shopping mall, equipped with RFID readers producing streams of position information. Within the area, we have defined "geo-fences", i.e., virtual perimeter for a real-world area which are used to mark particular spaces as "off-limits". Rule-based inference that considers conflicts, non-monotonicity, and uncertainty are required to detect when a particular area is at risk and what are the different ways somebody could breach the geo-fence. When we introduce noise in the sensory input, and constraints based on adjacency of certain areas, conflicts can be detected and noise needs to be filtered out. This can be done with rule-based approach by encoding optimization (e.g. minimizing the error) or by using probabilistic approaches to rule-based inference.

Cross-Layer Processing: Recent approaches attempt to improve scalability by relying on systems from the underlying layers to filter and aggregate sensor data into events or complex events, and then use results of this pre-processing to perform complex inference. For example, few approaches have combined SCEP systems with production rules systems [32, 36], although they often trade expressiveness for response time. Relying on underlying mechanisms for Strem Query Processing in order to filter relevant data has also been considered as a way to reduce the size of the input for the more expressive layers, as in the combination with Stream Query Processing and Answer Set Programming [28].

In this lecture we are mainly concerned with the following requirements from real world applications:

– **Expressivity:** Deduction processes aim at deriving knowledge from data, and the underlying semantics dictates how complex and expressive an inference language is; application scenarios that require to deal with default knowledge, preferential and probabilistic rules, non-determinisms and recursion require more expressive stream reasoning formalisms that are sitting at the top layer of IoT Intelligence, identified as Layer 3 in Fig. 1;

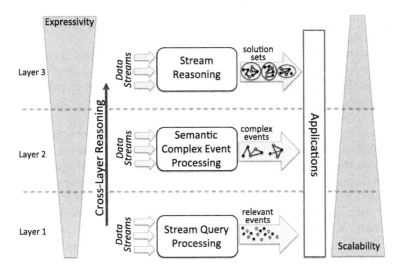

Fig. 1. IoT intelligence layers

- **Efficiency:** Some real world applications demand for low latency processing and require a timely response; this can be challenging with high volumes of incoming data, since it requires to design solutions that can achieve low latency and high throughput, possibly sacrificing expressivity;
- **Quality-Aware Stream Processing:** When it comes to application and services, quality constraints and requirements might vary; being able to identify the quality of a stream, being it part of input data or resulting from a processing step, Quality of Information (QoI) can play a crucial role not only in providing better solutions but also in solving inconsistencies and conflicts;
- **Uncertainty Management:** IoT data can be incomplete, contradictory and noisy, which requires to deal with uncertainty and approximation without loosing structural and causal connections between data and event streams.

These requirements have been only partially addressed in existing systems across the three layers. As part of this lecture, we will provide an overview of to what extent existing approaches to IoT Intelligence meet these requirements, and this will help identifying the gaps in existing solutions for Web Stream Reasoning[2].

3   RDF Stream Processing

The ability to process RDF streams requires to adapt the RDF data model to capture data items that flow continuously over time, forming unbounded sequences of data. To date several stream processing engines have been proposed for processing RDF streams as Linked Data and the semantic web community

---

[2] Slides will be available for download from http://www.streamreasoning.org/events/.

has been active in this area, defining vocabularies and languages to represent and process RDF streams.

As a consequence, more and more semantic data streams have appeared on the open, loosely governed and heterogeneous Web environment, increasing dramatically the potentials for observable events to be captured and processed. This attracted the attention of the CEP community and the Semantic Web community to join forces towards bridging this semantic gap.

Advances in Semantic Web and Linked Data research and standardization have established formats and technologies for representing, sharing and re-using knowledge on the Web, including streaming data such as social content and the Internet of Things [33]. As a result, the Web of Data is today overwhelmed with events, which has contributed to an unprecedented shift in the quantity and quality of dynamic information enabling complex knowledge to be linked and available for processing.

Acknowledging the need of semantics for better interpretation of such a massive amount of events, the Semantic Web community has moved towards Semantic Complex Event Processing (or SCEP) which uses ontological models to filter, aggregate and interpret complex events based on their semantic correlation. Beyond the continuous identification of complex semantic events via query processing, the need for more expressive rules to enhance reasoning capabilities in transforming events to actionable knowledge has also been recently investigated, as well as the introduction of mechanisms to deal with noisy data by using quality-aware complex event processing.

In the remainder of this section we will provide a quick overview and a few pointers on RDF stream processing and quality-aware event composition.

3.1   Linked Streams Data Processing

As Linked Data facilitates the data integration process among heterogenous collections, Linked Stream Data has the same goal with respect to data streams. Considering streams as another form of Linked Data bridges the gap between dynamic and static data sources, and makes it possible to query and integrate them in a single framework.

Stream query processing is under active research for several years in Database as well as in the Semantic Web community [5,8,22,25] and interesting solutions have been proposed to process static and dynamic structured data via continuous queries [5–7,22].

Unlike query processing for linked datasets which is mostly pull-based and one-time only, in Linked Stream Data processing new data items are produced continuously, the data is often valid only during a time window, and it is continually pushed to the query processor. Queries are continuous, i.e., they are registered once and then are evaluated continuously over time against the changing dataset. The results of a continuous query are updated as new data appears. We refer the reader to [23] for an overview of Linked Stream Data processing, which highlights basic requirements, language syntax and semantics, different processing methods and the advantages and disadvantages of existing approaches.

3.2 Semantic Complex Event Processing (SCEP)

The combination of Complex Event Processing (CEP) and semantic technologies plays a key role in enabling IoT Intelligence in such a way to improve flexibility and expressivity of current Linked Stream Data processing. There is a need to cater for available background knowledge when detecting and responding to complex events, motivated in many application scenarios where it is important to seamlessly integrate changes into CEP systems, translating events, patterns and reactions into operations in a declarative way.

Semantic Complex Event Processing (SCEP) [9,34] started in recent years, and a number of systems exist [1,2,20,21]. These systems support operators that are not natively implemented in Linked Stream Data processing engines, such as the ability to detect complex event patterns as sequences, temporally ordered events and repetitions. Unlike stream query processing systems, SCEP engines do not have the ability to process structured streams as Linked Data, but they support background knowledge and some form of (monotonic) reasoning.

For these reasons, in the scope of this lecture we position them in a different layer and we separate them from non-monotonic reasoning approaches, which we will be investigating more in details in Sect. 4.

Rule-based SCEP has been investigated in the last decade, with a growing scientific community that is also active in standardization activities. This includes initiatives around RuleML and reaction rules [32] as well as Prolog-based approaches for processing complex events [31]. We invite the readers to consult surveys and tutorials on SCEP available at http://wiki.ruleml.org/index.php/Reaction_RuleML.

3.3 Quality-Aware SCEP

SCEP has been proved to be efficient for processing streams with high frequency and complex query semantics. Recent developments in Internet-of-Things (IoT) and Smart City applications bring new challenges to conventional SCEP systems, e.g., incorporating heterogeneous event sources, formats or event stream processing engines. Moreover, there is a need to explore automatic ways to recover the system from erroneous states, and to discover and compose event streams according to application requirements and constraints. Solving this problem often boils down to automatically discover what streaming sources can best answer complex event requests and identify which event source should be considered to match specific quality requirements from users and applications.

Non-functional properties, e.g.: quality-of-service (QoS) properties, can play a pivotal role in guiding such selection if used as dimensions for finding the optimal event service composition plan that provides the best available results. Existing publish/subscribe based event systems and middleware use proprietary event advertisement and subscription formats (which leads to silo architectures) and provide limited supports for non-functional requirements related to event subscriptions [26].

To address these issues, a body of work has been proposed that integrates SCEP systems with Service Oriented Architecture (SOA) [15]. This approach directly addresses the problem of dealing with data quality of streams and uses it not only to provide the best available semantic complex event plan, but also to support the engineering side of practical deployments by helping to plan what performance parameters work best under a given input load.

4   Web Stream Reasoning

Stream Reasoning for the (Semantic) Web is mainly concerned with the ability to deal with the imperfect nature of web streams, so that inference algorithms can be successfully applied to a variety of real-world applications. As mentioned in Sect. 1, streaming sources can sometimes behave erratically and generate incomplete and noisy data. Without proper mechanisms, stream reasoning systems can then be caught up in attempting to deal with situations involving conflicting knowledge (e.g. temperature sensors providing a value of $20C$ and fire detectors alerting of a fire). Even worse, a system can end up failing when it enters an undecidable reasoning state due to contradiction or non-determinism. This happens when there are several possible conclusions or solutions as a result of given observations, or when there is no outcome satisfying all given constraints. For example each traffic light in a crossing can be red, yellow or green in different combinations, and there are constraints on synchronization between them; similarly, there are different possible paths for going form A to B and there might be constraints and preferences on time, distance, CO2 intake, safety of the road etc. that determine which solution is best. Non-monotonic formalisms can help dealing with logical contradiction, incompleteness and non-determinisms in stream reasoning by embracing incomplete and noisy streams and presenting results as a set of plausible (possibly ranked) solutions. This leads to a system which is more robust and expressive than any current stream reasoning implementation for the (Semantic) Web. As a result, Non-Monotonic Reasoning (NMR) techniques for (Semantic) Web Streams can be seen as having high potential impact in a variety of real-world applications.

The ability of dealing with incomplete and noisy input streams is one of the capabilities induced by non-monotonicity, but providing support for dealing with conflicts, defaults, qualitative preferences, constraints, and non-determinism requires computationally intensive reasoning.

A few approaches have been investigated that aims at supporting NMR for big data. The prominent categories of such approaches rely on either the Well-Founded Semantics (WFS) and defeasible reasoning, or the Stable Model Semantics and Answer Set Programming (ASP). Given the complexity of NMR reasoning over streams, cross-layer approaches that leverage processing at different level of complexity is recently being investigated. In what follows we briefly summarize the approaches in each of these categories, that will be covered in this lecture.

4.1 Large-Scale Defeasible Reasoning with MapReduce

Authors in [3,35] focus on distributed methods for non-monotonic rule-based reasoning. Their current works perform parallel defeasible reasoning under the assumption of stratification which imposed a severe limitation considering the range of allowed rule set. Also, they focus on optimization of WFS computation based on MapReduce. Despite these approaches might have computational advantages over the more complex ASP-based approaches, the implementation based on MapReduce makes them suitable for embarrassingly parallel problems but not for problems with exponential complexity. Additionally, the available implementations based on MapReduce do not natively support stream processing concepts such as time-decay model and sliding window, making it less intuitive to specify problems in terms of stream reasoning tasks. We will briefly illustrate the core idea behind these approaches.

4.2 Web Stream Reasoning with Answer Set Programming

Developments on the Datalog side are evolving in this directions, and extensions of Datalog towards the logic paradigm of Answer Set Programming (ASP) [4,17,24] have been implementing these reasoning capabilities which can go far beyond the capabilities of existing query engines. Logic programming dialects like Datalog with negation, covered by ASP, are viewed as a natural basis for the Semantic Web rule layer [13], but the full expressivity of ASP introduces new challenges concerning the trade-off between expressivity and scalability, especially in a streaming scenario. Therefore, when dealing with NMR approaches based on ASP, particular attention should be given to the scalability of such systems. The development of stream reasoning systems based on the Stable Model Semantics focuses on extending the well established declarative complex reasoning framework of ASP with dynamic data. M. Gebser et al. [16] proposed modeling approaches for continuous stream reasoning based on reactive ASP, utilizing time-decaying logic programs to capture sliding window data in a natural way. This is a first step towards gearing ASP to continuous reasoning tasks. However, these approaches still mainly process on low changing data and relatively smaller data sizes. Do et al. [12] also utilize ASP in their stream reasoning system and the approach is based on the DLV engine [14], which does not deal with continuous and window-based reasoning over data stream within the reasoner.

4.3 Cross-Layer Web Stream Reasoning with ASP

NMR for Semantic Web Streams has only started to be investigated in recent years and no commercial systems beyond a few small-scale research prototypes exist. There is little scientific work which tries to capitalize on the synergies between stream query processing and stream reasoning and there is a quickly growing demand for software solutions that can efficiently process web streams and perform complex reasoning tasks on noisy and incomplete input. A similar approach is proposed in [28], where the authors present the StreamRule framework as a combination of linked stream data processing and NMR in ASP.

In this lecture we will mostly focus on ASP-based approaches to NMR, relying on existing solvers that support stream processing features and uncertainty management via rule learning. As mentioned earlier in this section, ASP-based approaches are computationally more expensive than parallel approaches based on defeasible reasoning, but they are suitable for problems with exponential complexity. We will investigate a new line of research that leverages cross-layer processing of streams, combining approaches across the three layers of Fig. 1. Our main assumption is that we can efficiently perform NMR by utilizing approaches from both stream processing and stream reasoning, when combined correctly under a common and sound model. Focusing on NMR methods, we will explore approaches and open challenges for web stream reasoning which rely on the synergies between RDF stream processing and rule-based inference. The two main directions we will consider in this lecture are:

- Combined approaches that rely on web stream reasoning layers at lower complexity to reduce the size of the input and increase scalability at the higher levels [18,28];
- Hybrid approaches to uncertainty management, which combine declarative non-monotonic reasoning with inductive inference and learning [29,30].

We will provide an overview of prototypical tools and showcase how they can be used in a smart city context[3].

5   Conclusive Remarks

In this lecture we provide an overview of Web Stream Reasoning, considered as the application of reasoning techniques to help deriving actionable knowledge from web data streams. Stream reasoning is an unexplored yet high impact research area and encompasses a series of new multidisciplinary approach that can provide the abstractions, foundations, methods, and tools required to integrate data streams, semantic representations, complex events, and reasoning systems [37].

A variety of concrete applications highlight clearly the need for scalable web stream reasoning and the importance of characterizing the expressivity vs. scalability trade-off to tackle the efficiency and expressivity challenges. Approaches that incrementally filter, process and aggregate web streams to enable higher level inference are in their infancy and they are only one possible direction to address such challenges. Even though IoT intelligence in modern applications often requires expressive and scalable languages and methods for web stream reasoning, current approaches rely on different underlying formalisms which require the use of an external reasoner and expensive mapping and synchronization between the different layers, with consequent negative impact on scalability.

---

[3] http://www.ict-citypulse.eu.

Promising research activities are ongoing to address these challenges. Some of them worth mentioning include the DHSR project[4] and the W3C RDF Stream Processing Working Group (RSP WG)[5]. The DHSR project aims at providing a strong model-based semantic foundation to distributed heterogeneous stream reasoning. RSP WG standardization activities are fostering the semantic community to define a common and extensible core model for RDF stream processing, envisioning an ecosystem of streaming and static RDF data sources whose data can be combined through standard models, languages and protocols. Relevant research is being carried forward in the context of the EU FP7 project CityPulse, where mechanisms for adaptive RDF stream processing and dynamic data-driven heuristics for scalable NMR over streams are being investigated [19].

References

1. Anicic, D., Fodor, P., Rudolph, S., Stojanovic. N.: ET-SPARQL: a unified language for event processing and stream reasoning. In: Proceedings of the 20th WWW Conference, pp. 635–644, ACM (2011)
2. Anicic, D., Rudolph, S., Fodor, P., Stojanovic, N.: Stream reasoning and complex event processing in etalis. Semant. Web **3**(4), 397–407 (2011)
3. Antoniou, G., Batsakis, S., Tachmazidis, I.: Large-scale reasoning with (semantic) data. In: Proceedings of the 4th International Conference on Web Intelligence, Mining and Semantics (WIMS 2014), p. 1, ACM (2014)
4. Baral, C.: Knowledge Representation Reasoning and Declarative Problem Solving. Cambridge University Press, Cambridge (2003)
5. Barbieri, D.F., Braga, D., Ceri, S., Valle, E.D., Grossniklaus, M.: Querying rdf streams with C-SPARQL. SIGMOD Rec. **39**(1), 20–26 (2010)
6. Bolles, Andre, Grawunder, Marco, Jacobi, Jonas: Streaming SPARQL - Extending SPARQL to process data streams. In: Bechhofer, Sean, Hauswirth, Manfred, Hoffmann, Jörg, Koubarakis, Manolis (eds.) ESWC 2008. LNCS, vol. 5021, pp. 448–462. Springer, Heidelberg (2008)
7. Calbimonte, J., Jeung, H., Corcho, Ó., Aberer, K.: Enabling query technologies for the semantic sensor web. Int. J. Semant. Web Inf. Syst. **8**(1), 43–63 (2012)
8. Carney, D., Çetintemel, U., Cherniack, M., Convey, C., Lee, S., Seidman, G., Stonebraker, M., Tatbul, N., Zdonik, S.: Monitoring streams: a new class of data management applications. In: VLDB 2002, pp. 215–226, VLDB Endowment (2002)
9. Della Valle, E., Ceri, S., Barbieri, D.F., Braga, D., Campi, A.: A First Step Towards Stream Reasoning. In: Domingue, J., Fensel, D., Traverso, P. (eds.) FIS 2008. LNCS, vol. 5468, pp. 72–81. Springer, Heidelberg (2009)
10. Della Valle, E., Ceri, S., van Harmelen, F., Fensel, D.: It's a streaming world! reasoning upon rapidly changing information. IEEE Intell. Syst. **24**(6), 83–89 (2009)
11. Della Valle, E., Schlobach, S., Krötzsch, M., Bozzon, A., Ceri, S., Horrocks, I.: Order matters! harnessing a world of orderings for reasoning over massive data. J. Semant. Web **4**(2), 219–231 (2012)
12. Do, Thang M., Loke, Seng W., Liu, Fei: Answer set programming for stream reasoning. In: Butz, Cory, Lingras, Pawan (eds.) Canadian AI 2011. LNCS, vol. 6657, pp. 104–109. Springer, Heidelberg (2011)

---

[4] http://www.kr.tuwien.ac.at/research/projects/dhsr/.
[5] https://www.w3.org/community/rsp/.

13. Eiter, T., Ianni, G., Polleres, A., Schindlauer, R., Tompits, H.: Reasoning with rules and ontologies. In: Barahona, P., Bry, F., Franconi, E., Henze, N., Sattler, U. (eds.) Reasoning Web 2006. LNCS, vol. 4126, pp. 93–127. Springer, Heidelberg (2006)

14. Eiter, T., Ianni, G., Schindlauer, R., Tompits, H.: Dlv-hex: Dealing with semantic web under answer-set programming. In: The Proceedings of the 4th International Semantic Web Conference (2005)

15. Gao, F., Curry, E., Ali, M.I., Bhiri, S., Mileo, A.: QoS-Aware complex event service composition and optimization using genetic algorithms. In: Franch, X., Ghose, A.K., Lewis, G.A., Bhiri, S. (eds.) ICSOC 2014. LNCS, vol. 8831, pp. 386–393. Springer, Heidelberg (2014)

16. Gebser, M., Grote, T., Kaminski, R., Obermeier, P., Sabuncu, O., Schaub, T.: Answer set programming for stream reasoning (2013). CoRR abs/1301.1392

17. Gelfond, M., Lifschitz, V.: The stable model semantics for logic programming. In: Proceedings of the 5th International Conference on Logic Programming, vol. 161 (1988)

18. Germano, S., Pham, T.-L., Mileo, A.: Web stream reasoning in practice: on the expressivity vs. scalability tradeoff. In: Web Reasoning and Rule Systems - 9th International Conference, RR 2014, Berlin, Germany, 5–6 August 2015, page to appear. Proceedings (2015)

19. W. S. R. in Practice: on the Expressivity vs. Scalability tradeoff. Stefano germano and thu-le pham and alessandra mkileo. In: Web Reasoning and Rule Systems - 9th International Conference, RR 2015, Berlin, Germany, 4–5 August 2015, page to appear. Proceedings (2015)

20. Komazec, S., Cerri, D., Fensel, D.: Sparkwave: continuous schema-enhanced pattern matching over rdf data streams. In: Proceedings of the 6th ACM International Conference on Distributed Event-Based Systems, pp.58–68, ACM (2012)

21. Lanzanasto, N., Komazec, S., Toma, I.: Reasoning over real time data streams (2012). http://www.envision-project.eu/wp-content/uploads/2012/11/D4-8_v1-0.pdf

22. Le-Phuoc, D., Dao-Tran, M., Xavier Parreira, J., Hauswirth, M.: A native and adaptive approach for unified processing of linked streams and linked data. In: Aroyo, L., Welty, C., Alani, H., Taylor, J., Bernstein, A., Kagal, L., Noy, N., Blomqvist, E. (eds.) ISWC 2011, Part I. LNCS, vol. 7031, pp. 370–388. Springer, Heidelberg (2011)

23. Le-Phuoc, D., Xavier Parreira, J., Hauswirth, M.: Linked stream data processing. In: Eiter, T., Krennwallner, T. (eds.) Reasoning Web 2012. LNCS, vol. 7487, pp. 245–289. Springer, Heidelberg (2012)

24. Lifschitz, V.: Answer set programming and plan generation. AI **138**(1), 39–54 (2002)

25. Madden, S., Shah, M., Hellerstein, J.M., Raman, V.: Continuously adaptive continuous queries over streams. In: 2002 ACM SIGMOD International Conference on Management of Data, pp. 49–60, ACM, New York (2002)

26. Mahambre, S.P., Kumar, M., Bellur, U.: A taxonomy of qos-aware, adaptive event-dissemination middleware. IEEE Internet Comput. **11**(4), 35–44 (2007)

27. Margara, A., Urbani, J., van Harmelen, F., Bal, H.: Streaming the web: Reasoning over dynamic data. Web Semant.: Sci. Serv. Agents World Wide Web **25**, 24–44 (2014)

28. Mileo, A., Abdelrahman, A., Policarpio, S., Hauswirth, M.: StreamRule: A non-monotonic stream reasoning system for the semantic web. In: Faber, W., Lembo, D. (eds.) RR 2013. LNCS, vol. 7994, pp. 247–252. Springer, Heidelberg (2013)

29. Nickles, M., Mileo, A.: Probabilistic inductive logic programming based on answer set programming (2014). CoRR abs/1405.0720

30. Nickles, M., Mileo, A.: Web stream reasoning using probabilistic answer set programming. In: Kontchakov, R., Mugnier, M.-L. (eds.) RR 2014. LNCS, vol. 8741, pp. 197–205. Springer, Heidelberg (2014)

31. Paschke, A.: Rules and logic programming for the web. In: Polleres, A., d'Amato, C., Arenas, M., Handschuh, S., Kroner, P., Ossowski, S., Patel-Schneider, P. (eds.) Reasoning Web 2011. LNCS, vol. 6848, pp. 326–381. Springer, Heidelberg (2011)

32. Paschke, A., Boley, H.: Rule responder: Rule-based agents for the semant. pragmatic web. Int. J. Artif. Intell. Tools **20**(6), 1043–1081 (2011)

33. Sheth, A., Henson, C., Sahoo, S.S.: Semantic sensor web. IEEE Internet Comput. **12**(4), 78–83 (2008)

34. Stuckenschmidt, H., Ceri, S., Della Valle, E., Van Harmelen, F., di Milano, P.: Towards expressive stream reasoning. In: Proceedings of the Dagstuhl Seminar on Semantic Aspects of Sensor Networks (2010)

35. Tachmazidis, I., Antoniou, G., Faber, W.: Efficient computation of the well-founded semantics over big data (2014). CoRR abs/1405.2590

36. Teymourian, K., Rohde, M., Paschke, A.: Fusion of background knowledge and streams of events. In: Proceedings of the 6th ACM International Conference on Distributed Event-Based Systems, DEBS 2012, pp. 302–313. ACM, New York (2012)

37. Valle, E.D., Ceri, S., Harmelen, F.V., Fensel, D.: It's a streaming world! reasoning upon rapidly changing information. IEEE Intell. Syst. **24**(6), 83–89 (2009)

38. Zaino, J.: Big data and the semantic web: Their paths will cross. http://semanticweb.com/big-data-and-the-semantic-web-their-paths-will-cross_b32027

Recommender Systems and Linked Open Data

Tommaso Di Noia[1](✉) and Vito Claudio Ostuni[2]

[1] SisInf Lab, Polytechnic University of Bari, Via Orabona 4, 70125 Bari, Italy
`tommaso.dinoia@poliba.it`
[2] Pandora Media Inc., 2101 Webster Street, Oakland, CA 9461, USA
`vostuni@pandora.com`

Abstract. The World Wide Web is moving from a Web of hyper-linked documents to a Web of linked data. Thanks to the Semantic Web technological stack and to the more recent `Linked Open Data` (`LOD`) initiative, a vast amount of RDF data have been published in freely accessible datasets connected with each other to form the so called `LOD` cloud. As of today, we have tons of RDF data available in the Web of Data, but only a few applications really exploit their potential power. The availability of such data is for sure an opportunity to feed personalized information access tools such as recommender systems. We present an overview on recommender systems and we sketch how to use `Linked Open Data` to build a new generation of semantics-aware recommendation engines.

1 Introduction

The recent emergence of social networks and pervasive mobile devices has contributed to the publication of a massive amount of information on the Web. We entered into an era of Information Overload: more information is produced than what we can really consume and process. Just to have an idea of what it means in practice, we know[1] that in just one minute about 694,445 searches are performed on Google, more than 6,600 pictures are uploaded on Flickr, about 13,000 hours of music streaming is done by the personalized Internet radio provider Pandora and so on.

Potentially, such enormous and heterogeneous collection of information allows users to find anything they may be looking for. However, in practice humans cannot process so much information without the assistance of any automatic filtering tool. Recommender Systems (RSs) [49] are a family of information filtering tools which have proven to be valuable means in assisting users to find, in a personalized manner, what is relevant for them in such overflowing complex information spaces. They provide users with personalized access to large collections of resources. On the one hand in the last twenty years we have assisted to the proliferation of this new kind of information filtering tools, namely recommender systems, which have proven to be very useful in supporting users in dealing with everyday decision making tasks in complex scenarios. Examples

---

[1] http://www.go-gulf.com/blog/60-seconds/.

© Springer International Publishing Switzerland 2015
W. Faber and A. Paschke (Eds.): Reasoning Web 2015, LNCS 9203, pp. 88–113, 2015.
DOI: 10.1007/978-3-319-21768-0_4

of such tasks are buying a product, looking for an accommodation or choosing the right movie to watch, just to cite few examples. On the other hand in the same temporal period we have also observed a shift from a Web conceived exclusively for humans to a Web of Data where information is made available also for machines.

Together with the appearing of social networks and Internet-enabled mobile devices, the Web has moved from a Web of hyper-linked Documents to one where both documents and data are linked. Thanks to the Semantic Web spread and to the more recent **Linked Open Data** (**LOD**) initiative, a vast amount of structured semantic data have been published in freely accessible datasets. More and more semantic data are published following the **Linked Data** [10] principles, that enable to set up links between objects in different data sources by connecting information in a single global data space: the **Web of Data**.

The matter in question is how to leverage the progresses made in the LOD field for improving that of recommender systems and vice versa. Here we see how the semantics encoded in the Linked Open Data can be used for improving traditional recommender systems. Actually, it is particularly interesting also to notice that such techniques can be used the other way around.

In this paper we introduce all the notions and elements needed to build and evaluate the effectiveness of a RS which leverages the data accessible in the LOD cloud. In the next section, we briefly review the recommendation problem and then in Sect. 3 we describe some basic metrics to evaluate the performance of a recommendation engine. In Sect. 4 we discuss on how to exploit the knowledge encoded in the Linked Open Data cloud to design a semantics-aware recommender system while in Sect. 5 we present some relevant related work.

2   Recommender Systems

Recommender Systems (**RSs**) are software tools and techniques providing suggestions for items to be of use to a user [49]. Such suggestions can relate to different decision-making processes, such as what users to connect to in a social network, what product to buy, what music to listen to, or what movie to watch. Products, music, movies are all examples of items in specific recommendation scenarios. Nowadays, almost every online service has a recommendation feature. Pandora[2], Netflix[3], Linkedin[4] and many others use recommendation functionalities in their systems to engage the users and offer them a better service.

The main aim of RSs is to help users in satisfying their information needs when dealing with huge information spaces. To achieve this, RSs try to select the subset of items which best match the users' preferences and tastes. Among the several definitions given in the literature, we report the one proposed by [15] which says: *the recommender system term indicates any system that produces individualized recommendations as output or has the effect of guiding the user*

---

[2] http://www.pandora.com/.

[3] http://www.netflix.com.

[4] http://www.linkedin.com.

Fig. 1. Example of Information Overload scenario.

in a personalized way to interesting or useful objects in a large space of possible options.

In Fig. 1 an example of typical Information Overload scenario is depicted where the user is exposed to a set of movies and does not know which one to select. If we contextualize this example to real situations where the user is overwhelmed with thousands/millions of items, then it is easy to imagine that it is very hard for her to make the right choice without any assistance.

In principle, the primary aim of both recommendation systems and search systems is to satisfy users' information needs. Nonetheless, there are quite a few fundamental differences between the two technologies. Towards the end of 2006, Jeffrey O'Brien, a Fortune writer, talking about recommender systems on the Web, quoted[5] *"The Web, they say, is leaving the era of search and entering one of discovery. What's the difference? Search is what you do when you're looking for something. Discovery is when something wonderful that you didn't know existed, or didn't know how to ask for, finds you"*. Compared to search systems, recommender systems provide the possibility for users to discover new resources that they may have not initially thought about, without the necessity of formulating their needs explicitly.

2.1 The Recommendation Problem

A formal formulation of the recommendation problem has been given in [2] and it is defined as follows. Let U represent the set of users and I the set of items in the system. Potentially, both sets can be very large. Let $f : U \times I \to R$, where R is a totally ordered set, be a utility function measuring the usefulness of item $i \in I$ for user $u \in U$. Then, the recommendation problem consists in finding for each user u such item $i^{max,u} \in I$ maximizing the utility function f. More formally, this corresponds to the following:

$$\forall u \in U, \ i^{max,u} = \arg\max_{i \in I} f(u, i)$$

---

[5] http://archive.fortune.com/magazines/fortune/fortune_archive/2006/11/27/8394347/index.htm.

Typically, the utility of an item is represented by a rating, which indicates how a particular user liked a particular item. The central problem of recommender systems is that the utility is not defined on the whole $U \times I$ space, but only a subset of it is actually available. For each user only a portion of her ratings is known. Hence, the main task of the system concerns the estimation of the utility function from the available data. Once the utility function is obtained it can be used to predict unknown values and recommendations are eventually generated by selecting for each user the best N items with highest utility (*top-N* recommendation list).

2.2   Users, Items and Ratings

As described in the formal definition of the recommendation problem, at the base of each RS there are three main essential elements which are: **users**, **items** and **ratings**. Usually such information are represented all together by means of a user-item ratings matrix. Such ratings matrix consists of a table where each row represents a user, each column represents a specific item, and each entry represents the rating given by the user to the particular item. Usually, such matrix results very sparse in practice because users rate only a small portion of items. Figure 2 shows an example of user-item ratings matrix in a movie RS where users express their preferences to the items (movies) by using a five points rating scale. The items with a question mark (unknown rating) are unseen for the corresponding user.

Users. Users are those actors of the system who are provided with recommendations. Users can be represented in different ways depending on the recommendation techniques used to compute recommendations. In order to provide personalized recommendations the system has to model and maintain information about their preferences. In a content-based RS users' preferences can be represented in a more transparent way by means of attribute/term vectors in a heuristic-based approach, by means of a model in a model-based approach or by means of knowledge representation tools (ontologies, rules, etc.).

Items. Item is the general term used to denote the resource the system recommends to users. Items may be characterized by their complexity and their value or utility [49]. Examples of items with low complexity and value are: news, Web pages, books, movies. While examples of more complex and higher value items can range from mobile phones, laptops to financial services, jobs and travels. Depending on the system and the recommendation technique the item content can be more or less structured and complex. It can range from just a numeric ID in a collaborative filtering system a to a a bag of keywords or set of attribute value pairs in a content-based system till to an ontology-based description in systems using a domain ontology.

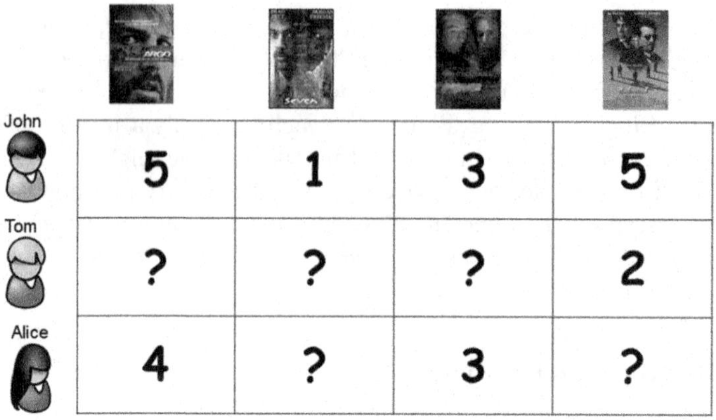

Fig. 2. Example of user-item ratings matrix in a movie recommendation scenario.

Ratings. The most important thing RSs rely on is the availability of up to date information about users' preferences in the form of users' feedback. Depending on the way such information is collected, users' feedback can be classified as **explicit** or **implicit**. In the former case feedback come in the form of ratings. The user is asked to provide her opinion about an item on a rating scale which can be either numerical (e.g. 1–5 stars) or ordinal (strongly agree, agree, neutral, disagree, strongly disagree) or also binary (like/dislike). Although the explicit feedback case is more common in literature mostly due to the availability of many datasets with ratings, in practice is more common the case where the system gathers implicit feedback from the user. A system can infer the user preferences by monitoring user's behaviour without any bother to the user.

From Rating Prediction to Ranking. In the formulation of the recommendation problem given above the system is mainly seen as a predictive system in the way that the main goal is to accurately predict ratings. Such problem is known as the **rating prediction task**. However, the ultimate goal of the system in most situations is to provide the user with a ranked list of recommendations, namely **top-N recommendations**. As pointed out by [20] in many commercial systems, the *best bet* recommendations are shown, but the predicted rating values are not. This is usually referred to as a **top-N recommendation task**, where the goal of the recommender system is to find a few specific items which are supposed to be most appealing to the user. Other researchers [47] have refereed to such task also using a different terminology, namely **item recommendation task**, that is the task of predicting a personalized ranking on a set of items.

2.3   Recommendation Techniques

Depending on the the way the utility function is estimated and the availability of additional data about the characteristics of items for example, there are different types of recommendation techniques. The main two are: collaborative filtering and content-based. Besides these two, there also other approaches such as knowledge-based, demographic and community-based just to cite a few. A complete list of techniques is given in [16] and in [49]. An important class of recommender systems which are often used in real systems are the hybrid recommenders [15] which combine different strategies to improve their separate performance and obtain higher recommendation quality.

Collaborative Filtering Recommendation. Collaborative Filtering is the process of filtering or evaluating items using the opinions of other people [52]. In this approach personalized recommendations for a target user are generated using opinions of users having similar tastes to those of the target user [48]. The main assumption in this approach is that users with similar preferences in the past will have similar preferences in the future.

Differently from any other technique the only input data that CF-RSs need is the user-item ratings matrix. Figure 3 shows a simple example of collaborative filtering case corresponding to the user-item ratings ratings matrix depicted in Fig. 2. If we consider Alice as target user, as said before, recommendations are generated considering the ratings given by other users with similar tastes. In this particular case, both John and Alice have similar tastes because they both rated similarly Argo and Righteous Kill. The system can exploit John's ratings for estimating Alice's unknown ratings. The basic intuition behind this method is that since John really likes Heat then also Alice may like it.

According to [12] there are two main types of collaborative filtering methods: memory-based and model-based. Memory-based CF uses a particular type of

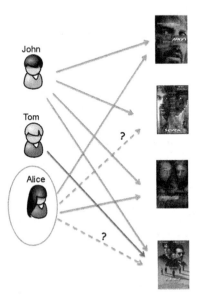

Fig. 3. Illustration of a CF-based recommender system.

Machine Learning methods that is the nearest neighborhood (k-NN) algorithm. The main property of such approach is that it does not require any preliminary model building phase because predictions are made by aggregating the ratings of the closest neighbours. On the contrary, model-based techniques first learn a predictive model which is eventually used to make predictions.

Memory-based approaches can be classified either in user-based or item-based. The user-based approach consists of predicting the relevance of an item for the target user by a linear combination of her neighbour's ratings, weighted by the similarity between the target user and such neighbours. One of the first implementation of such approach is the one presented in [48] which considers the rating deviations from the user's and neighbour's rating means $(\bar{r}_u)$. Prediction for the active user u and target item i is computed as:

$$r_{u,i} = \bar{r}_u + \frac{\sum_{j=1}^{K}(r_{u_j,i} - \bar{r}_u) \cdot w_{u,u_j}}{\sum_{j=1}^{|U|} w_{u,u_j}}$$

where K is the number of neighbors for user u and w_{u,u_j} is the similarity weight between the active user u and neighbor u_j defined by the Pearson correlation coefficient:

$$w_{u,u_j} = \frac{\sum_i (r_{u,i} - \bar{r}_u) \cdot (r_{u_j,i} - \bar{r}_{u_j})}{\sqrt{\sum_{i=1}(r_{u,i} - \bar{r}_u)^2} \cdot \sqrt{\sum_{i=1}(r_{u_j,i} - \bar{r}_{u_j})^2}}$$

For a more detailed list of similarity measures and aggregation function please refer to [2]. The item-based CF approach bases on the usage of the same correlation-based or cosine-based techniques to compute similarities between items instead of users. The idea is to derive a notion of item similarity from user rating or purchase behavior and recommend items similar to those the user has already said they like. In [23] such idea has been applied to compute *top-N* item recommendations in e-commerce scenarios.

While at the beginning most of the research in this area focused on memory-based approaches, in the last years more attention has been paid to model-based techniques. In particular mode after the Netflix competition which showed that model-based techniques have higher accuracy [32]. The most adopted model-based approaches are the matrix factorization or latent factor models [33] which apply some form of dimensionality reduction on the user item ratings matrix to map both users and items into a joint lower dimensional latent factor space.

Even if collaborative filtering is the most widely adopted approach it can suffer from different drawbacks. First of all, to work properly it needs enough rating data to find meaningful correlations among items or users. This is main known as sparsity or cold-start problem [53]. In relation to that, there are two specific issues which are the new user and new item problem. When a new user enters the system till she has not rated a sufficient number of items the system is unable to compute reliable similarities with other users. When a new item is added to the catalog there is no way to recommend it before till no ratings about it are obtained. A typical way to tackle such cold-start problems is to combine collaborative-filtering with content-based approaches. Another problem of CF is the so called `Grey sheep problem`, that is the inability of the system to properly treat users with very unusual preferences since the system is unable to find other similar users.

Content-Based Recommendation. Content-based RSs recommend an item to a user based upon a description of the item and a profile of the user's interests [46]. Briefly, the basic process performed by a content-based recommender consists in matching up the attributes of a user profile in which preferences and interests are stored, with the attributes of a content object (item) [36].

Differently from collaborative filtering, such recommendation approach relies on the availability of content features describing the items. Such features can be extracted from unstructured or semi-structured item descriptions by using proper Natural Language Processing (NLP) techniques or can be obtained from structured data as the case of tabular data in a relational database. A high level architecture of a content-based RS is presented in [36] (Fig. 5).

Figure 4 shows an example of content-based approach with reference to the user `Alice`. As we can see, differently from the CF case in this approach movies are provided with attributes, such as actors, genres, etc. The other difference is that only the target user is considered in the recommendation process. The basic intuition behind this approach is that since `Alice` likes `Argo` she might like `Heat` because they both belong to the `Drama` genre.

There are two main content-based recommendation approaches: *heuristic-based* or *model-based*.

Approaches using heuristic functions have their roots in Information Retrieval and Information Filtering. Items are recommended based on a comparison between their content and a user profile. The idea is to represent both items and users using typical IR techniques [6], e.g. vectors of terms, and compute a match between their representations. The user profile consists in a vector of terms built from the analysis of the items liked by the user. A typical approach is to use the Vector Space Model (VSM) [5] where items and user profiles can be represented as weighted vectors computed using the *tf-idf* formula [5]. The match

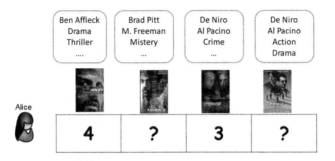

Fig. 4. Illustration of a content-based RS.

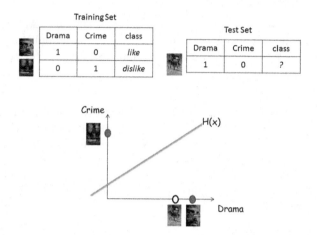

Fig. 5. Example of model-based CB-RS.

between items and user profile vectors can be computed using cosine similarity and eventually the most similar items to the user profile are recommended.

Model-based approaches [45] use Machine Learning techniques to learn a model of the user's preferences by analyzing the content characteristics of items the user rated. Specifically, a regression or classification model is learnt from a collection of items for which past user's ratings are available. The training set consists of item feature vectors labelled with ratings. Eventually, such learnt user model can be used for estimating the unknown ratings. This process is usually done for each user separately.

Differently from the heuristic-based case where the user model can be seen as an explicit representation of the user preferences (a vector containing the most preferred terms by the user), in this case the user profile is represented as a function obtained by means of an inductive learning process. Such function can be a complete black box or have a more interpretable form depending on the machine learning algorithm adopted.

A possible limitation of model-based approaches with respect heuristic-based ones is that the learning algorithm does not build a model with acceptable accuracy until it sees a relatively large number of examples (e.g. 50) [61].

Content-based methods can have several limitations. Maybe the main one is the `content overspecialization` which consists in the incapability of the system to recommend relevant items which are different to the ones the user already knows. Related to the previous issue, there is also the `portfolio effect` problem consisting in the redundancy and low diversity among the items in the recommendation lists.

Another limitation affecting CB systems is the `limited content analysis`. The quality of CB recommendations depends on the vailability and quality of features extracted from the items content.

For a complete and detailed description of content-based techniques for recommendations please refer to [36,46].

Knowledge-Based Recommandation. Both collaborative and content-based approaches work very well for all those domains where we have a user with an interaction history with the system. This is the case for instance of movies, books or music. Actually, there are some domains where it is quite difficult to have the user interacting with the system over the time. We may think of a student who wants to enroll at university or someone looking for a house to buy. In both cases it is unlikely that the users interact with the corresponding systems many times. Nevertheless, the information overload problem holds also in these situations and the help of a RS is highly desirable. A recommender system should guide the user through the set of possible choices by guessing or explicitly asking for her preferences. By combining its knowledge on the user desires and the one on the specific domain, the system selects a ranked list of items to be shown to the user. These classes of applications are classified as knowledge-based recommender systems [26].

Such systems are very often also referred to as *conversational* recommender systems [14]. Indeed, the user's preferences are elicited during her interaction with the system that may in turn ask her explicit questions regarding some characteristics of the item she is looking for. All these user requirements may vary in importance going from strict/hard to soft/graded requirements. Moreover, they can be updated while the user interplays with the application. Besides these user-generated constraints, as stated before, the system may also be aware of other constraint that are specific of the knowledge domain such as "**if** *the house has a big garden* **then** *it cannot be in the city center*".

We basically have two main types of knowledge-based recommender systems: *case-based* [13] and *constraint-based* [19,24,62] depending on the approach adopted in the representation and reasoning with user requirements and domain knowledge.

Hybrid Recommendation. The main idea behind hybrid recommender systems is to combine two or more classes of algorithms in order to mitigate the weaknesses of the individual approaches and obtain better recommendation quality. In [15] a taxonomy of several hybridization schemes is given which consists in the following list:

- Weighted: the scores provided by the individual recommenders are combined using a linear combination or a voting scheme;
- Switching: a special case of the previous type considering binary weights such that one recommender is turned on and the others are turned off;
- Mixed: recommendations generated from several recommenders are presented together at the same time by means of certain ranking or combination strategy;
- Feature combination: the features used by different recommenders are integrated and combined into a single data source, which is finally used by a single recommender;
- Cascade: the recommendation is performed as a sequential process where each recommender refines the recommendations given by the previous one;

- Feature augmentation: the output from one recommender is used as an additional input feature for other recommender;
- Meta-level: the model generated by one recommender is used as the input for another recommender.

Most common example of hybridization is the combination of collaborative and content strategies for mitigating CF limitations such as cold start and sparsity.

Semantics-Aware Recommendation. One of the main limitation of traditional content-based approaches is that they completely ignore the semantics associated to the item attributes because they rely on keyword-based representations. Keyword-based approaches to user profiling are unable to capture the semantics of user interests [22] because they are primarily driven by a string matching operation which suffers from problems of *polysemy*, the presence of multiple meanings for one term, and *synonymy*, multiple terms having the same meaning.

Furthermore, such textual approaches are incapable of capturing more complex relationships among objects at a deeper semantic level based on the inherent properties associated with these objects [21]. For example let us consider two generic movies $m1$ and $m2$, which have $a1$ and $a2$ as directors, respectively. Let make the case that even if the two movies have different directors $a1$ and $a2$, those directors have however many things in common such as they both were born in the same country and they both won a particular award. It is reasonable to assume that if a user likes $m1$ because of $a1$ then she might like with a certain degree $m2$ because $a2$ is similar to $a1$. In this case, an approach based on keyword matching would fail because the two values for the attribute director are different. When considering plain keyword representations possible relations among structured objects are completely missed. The system needs a better representation of the items content.

As described in [36] **semantic analysis** and its integration in personalization models is one of the most innovative and interesting approaches proposed in literature to solve those problems. The key idea is the adoption of knowledge bases for annotating items and representing profiles in order to obtain a *"semantic"* interpretation of the user information needs.

The core idea behind Semantics-aware Recommender Systems then, is to use ontological knowledge to describe items in order to have a deeper and more structured representation of their content.

The availability of additional semantic knowledge can allow the system to go beyond the simple keyword matching. Common-sense and domain-specific knowledge may be useful to give some meaning to the content of items, thus helping to generate more informative features than "plain" attributes [56]. Example of semantics-aware RSs can be any content-based or hybrid recommender where items are described by means of domain ontologies.

It is easy to see that depending on the addressed domain, we may build a semantics-aware RS that falls either in the content-based category or in the knowledge-based one.

3   Recommender Systems Evaluation

Several different recommendation approaches have been proposed in the last years. Generally, some of those different approaches can perform differently depending on the domain and on the task or other conditions such as sparseness of the ratings matrix. Clearly identifying the best algorithm for a given purpose has proven challenging, in part because researchers disagree on which attributes should be measured, and on which metrics should be used for each attribute [29]. Due to different reasons, the evaluation of recommender systems is inherently difficult to perform. For example different algorithms may be better or worse on different data sets or they may have different evaluation goals depending on the task. Furthermore, based on the adopted evaluation strategy, results may vary considerably.

An extensive review of evaluation metrics and techniques is provided in [29].

3.1   Metrics and Protocols

The most common aspect of recommendation quality measured in offline experimentations is **accuracy**. The literature on recommender systems typically distinguishes between two ways of measuring recommendation accuracy [59] which can be reconducted to two different main tasks which are rating prediction and ranking or *top-N* recommendations. Most of the evaluation methodologies adopted to asses the performances of recommendation systems are derived from the well established methodologies developed in the Information Retrieval field. This is particularly true when the system is used for *top-N* recommendation tasks. As reported in [7] although there are many commonalities between IR and recommendation systems there are also important differences to take into consideration. Two of the most significant ones regard the nature and the availability of relevance information about items. While in IR the relevance of a document with respect to a query is objective and is assessed by domain experts, in the RS field each user has her personal relevance for items which is determined by her ratings. Furthermore, in IR there is almost complete knowledge about such relevance information. This is not true at all for RSs because the system has knowledge only about a small portion of ratings for each user.

This latter aspect is crucial when evaluating ranking accuracy because some assumptions about the unknown ratings must be done. In [59] the authors argue that the main difference between the evaluation of the rating prediction and ranking tasks consists in how the training and test data are considered. They say that rating prediction is concerned with only the observed ratings, while ranking typically accounts for all items in the collection, whether the user has rated them or not. Hence, they present two protocols for evaluating ranking accuracy: **all unrated items** and **rated test-items**. The all unrated items protocol consists in creating a *top-N* recommendation list for each user by predicting a score for every item not rated by that particular user, whether the item appears in the user test set or not. Then, performance metrics are computed comparing recommendation lists with test data. The main assumption in this methodology is that all the *unrated items* are considered to be *irrelevant* for the user with the effect of underestimating real recommendation quality. However, the authors of [59] argue that since the user-experience in *top-N* recommendation applications depends on the ranking of all items, this is a better evaluation methodology than the rated test-items one where only rated test items are considered for generating the *top-N* list. In fact, this latter method is the one adopted in evaluating the rating prediction task by using error based metrics.

Accuracy Metrics. Traditionally, the most popular metrics to measure the accuracy in the rating prediction task are error based metrics such as `Root Mean Squared Error (RMSE)` and `Mean Absolute Error (MAE)`. The main goal in the rating prediction task is to predict the rating value that a user would assign to an item. Then the evaluation consists in predicting ratings $\hat{r}_{u,i}$ for a test set TS of user-item pairs (u, i) for which the true ratings $r_{u,i}$ are known.

$$\text{MAE} = \frac{1}{|TS|} \sum_{(u,i)\in TS} |\hat{r_{u,i}} - r_{u,i}| \qquad (1)$$

$$\text{RMSE} = \sqrt{\frac{1}{|TS|} \sum_{(u,i)\in TS} (\hat{r_{u,i}} - r_{u,i})^2} \qquad (2)$$

Such error based metrics can be useful for measuring rating prediction accuracy. Despite the large adoption of error metrics in the past several recent studies [9,20] have demonstrated that the accurate prediction of ratings does not imply the best *top-N* ranking of items. In case one wants to use such metrics for measuring the accuracy of *top-N* recommendations the main limitation of such metrics is that they do not make any distinction between the errors made on the high rated items and the errors made for the rest of the items.

More appropriate measures for evaluating *top-N* recommendation accuracy are precision-oriented metrics which take into account the ranked list of items. Examples of such metrics are `Precision`, `Recall` and `Normalized Discounted Cumulative Gain`. They are usually computed considering incremental list sizes, that is considering items up to a given ranking position (N). Typical values for N are 1, 5, 10, 25, 50, 100.

Precision and recall are binary metrics in the sense that they require binary rating data. Hence, we need to distinguish between relevant and not relevant items for the user. For example in a 5 points ratings scale, 4 and 5 ratings may be considered as relevant. In case of implicit feedback with unary rating data instead, all rated items can be considered as relevant.

Precision@N for user u $(P_u@n)$ is computed as the fraction of *top-N* recommended items appearing in the user test set and which are relevant for the user, while Recall@N $(R_u@N)$ is computed as the ratio of *top-N* recommended items appearing in the user test set which are also relevant to the number of relevant items in the user test set.

$$P_u@N = \frac{|L_u(N) \cap TS_u^+|}{n} \qquad (3)$$

$$R_u@N = \frac{|L_u(N) \cap TS_u^+|}{|TS_u^+|} \qquad (4)$$

where TS_u^+ is the set of relevant test items for u and $L_u(N)$ the ranked recommendation list up to position N. Both metrics are inversely related, typically an improvement in recall produces a decrease in precision.

Differently from precision and recall, the normalized discounted cumulative gain nDCG metric takes into account both relevance and rank position. Denoting with $r_{u,k}$ the rating given by user u to the item in position k in the top-N list, then nDCG@N for u can be defined as:

$$\text{nDCG@N} = \frac{1}{\text{IDCG@N}} \sum_{k=1}^{n} \frac{2^{r_{u,k}} - 1}{\log_2(1 + k)} \qquad (5)$$

where $IDCG@N$ indicates the score obtained by an ideal or perfect ranking of $L_u(N)$ and acts as normalization factor. When using the `all unrated items` protocol for those items with no rating in the test set a fixed default value can be assumed as suggested in [59].

Other Metrics. As pointed out by [39], the most accurate recommendations according to the standard metrics are sometimes not the recommendations that are most useful to users. Many researchers in the past proposed several metrics to measure the quality of the system from different perspectives. For example, an algorithm may provide very accurate recommendations but only for a small proportion of users or recommend only too popular items.

Some important qualities which have considered in literature besides accuracy regard the the ability of the system to compute *diverse* and *novel* suggestions. The novelty of a piece of information generally refers to how different it is with respect to *"what has been previously seen"*, by a specific user, or by a community as a whole. A possible way to compute recommendation novelty is to look at the popularity distribution of items. The `Entropy-Based Novelty` (EBN) [8] expresses the ability of a recommender system to suggest less popular items, i.e. items not known by a wide number of users. In particular, for each user's recommendation list $L_u(N)$, the novelty is computed as:

$$EBN_u@N = - \sum_{i \in L_u(N)} p_i \cdot \log_2 p_i$$

where:

$$p_i = \frac{|\{u \in U \mid i \text{ is relevant to } u\}|}{|U|}$$

In such formulation the lower $EBN_u@N$, the better the novelty. A broader discussion of novelty metrics is given in [60]. The aim of diversity metrics instead is to measure how diverse is the recommendation list. A well adopted diversity metric to measure the degree of diversification of the recommendation list is the `Intra-List Diversity` (ILD) [64].

Other important qualities of a system are catalog and user coverage. User coverage is the proportion of users to whom the system can recommend items. Catalog coverage is the percentage of the available items that are effectively recommended. A metric for measuring catalog coverage or equivalently, aggregate diversity [1], is the diversity-in-top-N metric presented in [1].

$$ADiv@N = \frac{|\bigcup_{u \in U} L_u(N)|}{|I|}$$

Low values of aggregated diversity indicate that all users are being recommended almost the same few items. This corresponds to a low level of personalization of the system.

4   Linked Open Data for Recommender Systems

Nowadays the Web of Data represents a huge repository of different kinds of knowledge spanning from sedimentary-one such as encyclopedic, linguistic, common-sense and so on, to real-time one such as data streams, events, etc. Several works on ontological or semantics-aware recommender systems have been proposed in the past before the LOD initiative was officially launched [3,17,22,40,41,55,56,63]. Most of them exploit item's ontological knowledge to boost collaborative filtering systems or to build better content-based ones. Such approaches have been shown to be particularly effective in solving some drawbacks of pure collaborative methods such as cold start and data sparsity, two well known problems in the recommender systems world. However, we argue that those approaches are not particularly suited for working with LOD datasets and new techniques are required for properly incorporating LOD into RSs and effectively exploiting their semantics.

We recognize two main reasons why new approaches are needed. The first reason is that those ontological recommendation algorithms developed before the LOD initiative referred principally to the usage of specific domain ontologies and taxonomies. LOD datasets have the peculiarity of being published according to the Semantic Web technologies and of using a graph-based data model. Such aspects require specific models and paradigms for their effective usage and incorporation into recommender systems.

Past works on ontology-based RSs base on the usage of taxonomies, controlled vocabulary and limited domain ontologies. With the advent of LOD new interesting possibilities appear for realizing better recommendation applications. The main advantages of using LOD for content-based and hybrid recommender systems can be summarized as:

- Availability of a great amount of multi-domain and ontological knowledge freely available for feeding the system;
- Semantic Web standards and technologies to retrieve the required data and hence no need for content analysis tasks for obtaining a structured representation of the items content;
- The ontological and relational nature of the data allows the system to analyze item descriptions at a semantic level.

Table 1. Datasets by domain.

Domain	Datasets
Government	183
Publications	96
Life sciences	83
User-generated content	48
Cross-domain	41
Media	22
Geographic	21
Social web	520

Multi-domain Knowledge. Depending on the dataset, there is the availability of multi-relational data related to different domains. We can get data about geographic locations, music, movies, art, people, facts, and general common-sense knowledge (see Table 1 [54]). If we consider encyclopedic datasets such as DBpedia [34] or Freebase [11], we have access to a huge amount of factual knowledge referring to a variety of topics. As pointed out by [56] factual and common sense knowledge bases can provide the system with the "cultural" background knowledge needed to compute an accurate content analysis. Another important advantage of datasets as DBpedia is their multi-lingual nature which grants the development of cross-language applications [43].

Standardized Access to Data. The usage of Linked Open Data datasets to retrieve information related to an item eases the pre-processing steps performed by the *Content Analyzer* [36] – the module of a CB-RS in charge of extracting relevant information from item descriptions – since the data is already structured in an ontological way and represented by using Semantic Web standards.

LOD datasets can be queried by means of their respective SPARQL endpoints. For DBpedia, it allows anyone to ask complex queries about any topic available in Wikipedia. For example, we can obtain information about which actors starred in the movie *Pulp Fiction* via a simple SPARQL query:

```
PREFIX dbpedia: <http://dbpedia.org/resource/>
PREFIX dbpedia-owl: <http://dbpedia.org/ontology/>
SELECT ?actor WHERE {
      dbpedia:Pulp_Fiction dbpedia-owl:starring ?actor.
}
```

Starting from the previous query we see how to extract rich data related to a specific resource/item as well as to a bunch of them. Given the URI corresponding to an item, it is possible for instance to extract the associated sub-graph by performing various SPARQL queries using a breadth-first search strategy up to a limited depth.

Semantic Analysis. The main advantage of using LOD is the availability of well structured graph-based item descriptions. In fact, items are connected to entities by means of semantic relations. Such entities are classified in more or less complex classes. The semantics of those classes and relations is described by means of ontologies. For example if we consider the resource dbpedia:Bruce_Willis in DBpedia, it is instance of the class dbpedia-owl:Person which in turn is sub-class of dbpedia-owl:Agent. In such ontology it is also defined the semantics of properties. For example the property dbpedia-owl:starring which connects dbpedia:Pulp_Fiction to dbpedia:Bruce_Willis has domain dbpedia-owl:Work and range dbpedia-owl:Actor which is sub-class of dbpedia-owl:Person.

Thanks to the semantic relations among entities the system can perform a deeper semantic analysis of the item content. In a keyword-based representation the system is limited to compute the syntactic match between keywords. Instead, thanks to the availability of semantic entities the system can potentially detect complex associations between the user profile and the items.

4.1   Feeding Recommender Systems with LOD

There are several aspects to consider in order to effectively incorporate LOD in recommendation applications. Ultimately, the goal is to provide the system with background knowledge about the domain of interest in the form of a knowledge graph. In Fig. 6 we show a high level architecture of a component in charge of retrieving portions of the LOD graph regarding the items in the system which are used to form the knowledge graph. Such component consists of two main modules: the Item Linker and the Item Graph Analyzer.

Item Linker. The Item Linker addresses the task of linking the items in the system with the corresponding resources in the LOD knowledge bases. The aim of such component is bridging the gap between between the items in the catalog and LOD. We have hypothesized two main ways for performing the linking task: Direct Item Linking, Item Description Linking. This module takes as input any dataset in the LOD cloud and the list of items in the catalog with associated side information, if available, and returns either the mapping between items and URIs or the set of URIs found in each item description, depending on the way the task is performed.

Direct Item Linking. This approach is the more straightforward way for accessing LOD datasets. However, it requires that items have to be LOD resources, otherwise it cannot be used.

Item Description Linking. This approach bases on the exploitation of side information about the items such as textual descriptions or attributes. Such information can be used as input for entity linking tools in order to have access to LOD resources and link them to the item. Specifically, entity linking is the task

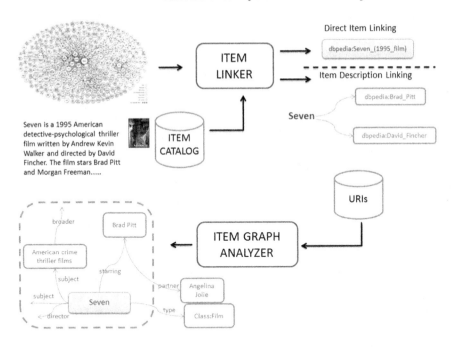

Fig. 6. High-level architecture for feeding RSs with LOD.

of linking the entity mentioned in the text with the corresponding real world
entity in the existing knowledge base [57].

Item Graph Analyzer. This module is responsible of the extraction from the
knowledge base of a descriptive and informative subgraph for each item, that
is a set of RDF triples somehow related to the item resource. Eventually, all the
extracted portions of LOD can be merged to obtain a specific knowledge graph
representative of the domain of interest covered by the recommender. It takes
as input the list of items URI returned by the Item Linker and returns a set of
RDF triples for each item.

Performing some SPARQL queries for obtaining a set of RDF triples related
to the item is an easy task, however extracting an informative and compact
subgraph descriptive of the item is not. Potentially, each item resource may
be connected to a big portion of the LOD graph. However, not all entities and
relations may be informative and descriptive of the item content. Moreover, too
much information may be problematic to handle.

After all, the main advantage of using LOD is that data are structured in an
ontological way. Hence, one can consider specific classes and/or properties for
extracting the subgraph of interest. The problem is how to use such information
about classes and properties. Some properties can be very useful for a particular
task and not for others. For example, the dbpedia-owl:country property can
be useful in a location-based service, but maybe it is not in a movie recommen-

dation system. Speaking about classes, in a single domain recommender, class information is not that informative. For example in a movie recommender we can omit to consider the `Movie` class as feature because it would represent redundant information (all items – movies – are instances of the same class). Conversely, in a cross-domain system classes and relations among them may be very useful.

Several strategies to select a relevant subset of RDF triples for each item may be considered and adopted. One strategy can be to manually define a set of properties or sequences of properties by using some domain knowledge. One can automatically obtain a set of `object properties` related to the domain of interest by performing a `SPARQL` query like the following:

```
PREFIX dbpedia: <http://dbpedia.org/resource/>
PREFIX dbpedia-owl: <http://dbpedia.org/ontology/>
PREFIX owl: <http://www.w3.org/2002/07/owl#>
SELECT distinct(?p) where{
    ?s ?p ?o.
    ?s rdf:type dbpedia-owl:Film.
    ?p rdf:type owl:ObjectProperty.
}
```

4.2 Which Classes of RSs?

Due to the very rich and structured knowledge layer represented in the data available in the LOD cloud we may think to build different classes of recommender systems with respect to the ones introduced in Sect. 2. In particular we are allowed to build:

- *heuristic-based* content-based recommender systems;
- *model-based* content-based recommender systems;
- *hybrid* recommender systems;
- *knowledge-based* recommender systems.

4.3 Evaluating LOD-based RSs

There are many datasets available for the evaluation of recommender systems. However, such datasets are not appropriate for evaluating LOD-based recommendation algorithms because they do not contains links to URIs. In order to evaluate LOD-based RSs we can use three datasets belonging to three different domains which are movies, music and book. These datasets contain mappings between items (movies, artists, books) and their corresponding DBpedia URIs. The mappings for the datasets is available at http://sisinflab.poliba.it/semanticweb/lod/recsys/datasets/. In the following we describe the main characteristics of the three datasets.

Movielens. This dataset is based on the `MovieLens` 1M dataset[6] released by the GroupLens research group. The original dataset contains 1,000,209 1–5 stars ratings given by 6,040 users to 3,883 movies. We found a valid mapping for 3,148 out of the all movies.

LibraryThing. The second dataset is derived from the `LibraryThing`[7] dataset[8]. This dataset is related to the book domain and contains 7,112 users, 37,231 books and 626,000 ratings ranging from 1 to 10. In this case we found a match for 8,170 books.

LastFM. While the first two datasets contain explicit feedback data, this third dataset is based on implicit feedback consisting of user-artist listening data. This dataset comes from recent initiatives on information heterogeneity and fusion in recommender systems[9] [18]. It has been built on top of the `Last.fm` music system[10]. The original dataset contains 1,892 users, 17,632 artists and 92,834 relations between a user and a listened artist together with their corresponding listening counts. For this dataset we found a match for 9,490 out of a total of 17,632 artists.

5 Related Work

Many researches in the past have proposed different ways of using domain ontologies and taxonomies to improve the quality of conventional RSs.

In [37] the authors presented a content-based filtering approach wherein user and item profiles are described in terms of concepts belonging to a domain taxonomy. Specifically, the user profile is built by aggregating the concepts of items preferred by the user. The computation of the matching between user and item profiles base on a similarity function able to exploit the hierarchical taxonomy structure. They propose different possible matches between user and item such as exact or partial and different match scores depending also on the hierarchical distance between concepts. Such approach can be seen as a particular case of heuristic-based content recommendation technique where items are described using a domain taxonomy.

In [40] the authors describe an approach for ontological user profiling and an application of such approach for building a research paper recommendation system. In such system both research papers and user profiles are described in terms of topics organized in taxonomy. Each time the user browses a paper, the related topics are added to his profile together with the broader topics in the taxonomy. Those broader topics however just receive a smaller portion of the original topics.

---

[6] http://www.grouplens.org/node/73.
[7] http://www.librarything.com.
[8] http://www.macle.nl/tud/LT/.
[9] http://ir.ii.uam.es/hetrec2011/datasets.html.
[10] http://www.lastfm.com.

In this way also general topics were added to the user profile in order to have a deeper content representation. Recommendations were eventually computed considering the correlation between the user's topics of interest and papers classified to those topics. In [41] the authors present a semantically enhanced collaborative filtering approach where structured semantic knowledge about items is used in conjunction with user-item ratings to create a combined similarity measure for item comparisons. Taxonomic information is used in [63] to represents the user's interest in categories of products. Consequently, user similarity is determined by common interests in categories and not by common interests in items. In [3] the authors present an approach that infers user preferences from rating data using an item ontology. The system collaboratively generates recommendations using the ontology and infers preferences during similarity computation. Another hybrid ontological recommendation system is proposed in [17] where user preferences and item features are described by semantic concepts to obtain users' clusters corresponding to implicit *Communities of Interest.*

A semantic content-collaborative hybrid recommender is presented in [22] which computes similarities between users relying on their content-based profiles. The particularity of such work is the usage of sense-based user profiles instead of keyword-based ones. Such semantic profiles are obtained by integrating machine learning algorithms for text categorization with a word sense disambiguation strategy based exclusively on the lexical knowledge stored in WordNet. Most of the presented works used ontologies to compute better user-user or item-item similarities in memory-based collaborative filtering approaches. However little work has been done in exploiting ontologies for computing model-based recommendations. A detailed description of recommendation techniques based on ontological filtering is given in [30,36].

In the last few years with the availability of Linked Open Data a new class of recommender systems has emerged which can be named as LOD-based recommender systems. This new typology of recommendation methods is attracting increasingly interest in both the communities of Semantic Web and Recommender Systems.

Most of the proposed works regarding this topic tried to reuse and adapt some of the ideas presented in the context of ontological RSs to LOD datasets which have their own characteristics, while others proposed new approaches specifically suited for working with Linked Data technologies and others proposed new applications of recommendation technologies for Linked Data. In what follows we review the most significant contributions.

One of the first approaches that exploits Linked Open Data for building recommender systems is [28]. Here the authors, for the first time propose a recommender system fed by Linked Open Data. In [27] the authors present a knowledge-based framework leveraging DBpedia for computing cross-domain recommendations. In [35] the authors propose a graph-based recommendation approach utilizing model- and memory-based link prediction methods. In [38] LOD datasets are used for personalized exploratory search using a spreading activation method. They use a spreading activation method with the purpose of finding semantic relatedness between items belonging to different domains. *dbrec* [44] is a music content-based recommender system leveraging the DBpedia dataset. They define the *Linked Data Semantic Distance* in order to find semantic distances between resources and then compute recommendations.

A full SPARQL-based recommendation engine named RecSPARQL is presented in [4]. The proposed tool extends the syntax and semantics of SPARQL to enable a generic and flexible way for collaborative filtering and content-based recommendations over arbitrary RDF graphs. The authors of [58] propose an approach for topic suggestions based on some proximity measures defined on the top of the DBpedia graph.

In [31] the authors present an event recommendation system based on linked data and user diversity. A semantic-aware extension of the SVD++ model, named SemanticSVD++, is presented in n [50]. It incorporates semantic categories of items into the model. The model is able also to consider the evolution over time of user's preferences. In [51] the authors improve their previous work for dealing with cold-start items by introducing a vertex kernel for getting knowledge about the unrated semantic categories starting from those categories which are known. Another interesting direction about the usage of LOD for content-based RSs is explored in [42] where the authors present Contextual eVSM, a content-based context-aware recommendation framework that adopts a semantic representation based on distributional models and entity linking techniques. In particular entity linking is used to detect entities in free text and map them to LOD.

Finally, in [25] the authors propose the usage of recommendation techniques for providing personalized access to Linked Data. The proposed recommendation method is a user-user collaborative filtering recommender wherein the similarity between the users takes into account the commonalities and informativeness of the resources instead of treating resources as plain identifiers.

References

1. Adomavicius, G., Kwon, Y.: Improving aggregate recommendation diversity using ranking-based techniques. IEEE Trans. Knowl. Data Eng. **24**(5), 896–911 (2012)
2. Adomavicius, G., Tuzhilin, A.: Toward the next generation of recommender systems: a survey of the state-of-the-art and possible extensions. IEEE Trans. Knowl. Data Eng. **17**(6), 734–749 (2005)
3. Anand, S.S., Kearney, P., Shapcott, M.: Generating semantically enriched user profiles for web personalization. ACM Trans. Internet Technol. **7**(4), October 2007
4. Ayala, V.A.A., Przyjaciel-Zablocki, M., Hornung, T., Schätzle, A., Lausen, G.: Extending SPARQL for recommendations. In: Proceedings of Semantic Web Information Management on Semantic Web Information Management, SWIM 2014, pp. 1:1–1:8. ACM, New York (2014)
5. Baeza-Yates, R.A., Ribeiro-Neto, B.: Modern Information Retrieval: The Concepts and Technology behind Search. Addison-Wesley Professional, Boston (2011)
6. Balabanović, M., Shoham, Y.: Fab: Content-based, collaborative recommendation. Commun. ACM **40**(3), 66–72 (1997)

7. Bellogín, A.: Performance prediction and evaluation in recommender systems: an information retrieval perspective. Ph.D. thesis, Escuela Politécnica Superior Departamento de Ingeniería Informática (2012)
8. Bellogín, A., Cantador, I., Castells, P.: A study of heterogeneity in recommendations for a social music service. In: Proceedings of the 1st International Workshop on Information Heterogeneity and Fusion in Recommender Systems, HetRec 2010, pp. 1–8. ACM, New York (2010)
9. Bellogin, A., Castells, P., Cantador, I.: Precision-oriented evaluation of recommender systems: an algorithmic comparison. In: Proceedings of the Fifth ACM Conference on Recommender Systems, RecSys 2011, pp. 333–336. ACM, New York (2011)
10. Bizer, C., Heath, T., Berners-Lee, T.: Linked data - the story so far. Int. J. Semant. Web Inf. Syst 5(3), 1–22 (2009)
11. Bollacker, K., Evans, C., Paritosh, P., Sturge, T., Taylor, J.: Freebase: a collaboratively created graph database for structuring human knowledge. In: Proceedings of the 2008 ACM SIGMOD International Conference on Management of Data, SIGMOD 2008, pp. 1247–1250. ACM, New York (2008)
12. Breese, J.S., Heckerman, D., Kadie, C.: Empirical analysis of predictive algorithms for collaborative filtering. In: Proceedings of the Fourteenth Conference on Uncertainty in Artificial Intelligence, UAI 1998, pp. 43–52 (1998)
13. Bridge, D., Göker, M.H., McGinty, L., Smyth, B.: Case-based recommender systems. Knowl. Eng. Rev. 20(3), 315–320 (2005)
14. Burke, R.: Knowledge-based recommender systems. In: Kent, A. (ed.) Encyclopedia of Library and Information Science, vol. 69, pp. 181–201. CRC Press, Boca Raton (2000)
15. Burke, R.D.: Hybrid recommender systems: survey and experiments. User Model. User-Adapt. Interact. 12(4), 331–370 (2002)
16. Burke, R.: Hybrid web recommender systems. In: Brusilovsky, P., Kobsa, A., Nejdl, W. (eds.) Adaptive Web 2007. LNCS, vol. 4321, pp. 377–408. Springer, Heidelberg (2007)
17. Cantador, I., Bellogín, A., Castells, P.: A multilayer ontology-based hybrid recommendation model. AI Commun. Special Issue Recomm. Syst. 21(2—-3), 203–210 (2008)
18. Cantador, I., Brusilovsky, P., Kuflik, T.: 2nd workshop on information heterogeneity and fusion in recommender systems (hetrec 2011). In: Proceedings of the 5th ACM Conference on Recommender systems, RecSys 2011. ACM, New York (2011)
19. Colucci, S., Di Noia, T., Di Sciascio, E., Donini, F.M., Ragone, A.: Knowledge elicitation for query refinement in a semantic-enabled e-marketplace. In: Proceedings of the 7th International Conference on Electronic Commerce, ICEC 2005, pp. 685–691. ACM, New York (2005)
20. Cremonesi, P., Koren, Y., Turrin, R.: Performance of recommender algorithms on Top-N recommendation tasks. In: Proceedings of the Fourth ACM Conference on Recommender Systems, RecSys 2010, pp. 39–46. ACM, New York (2010)
21. Dai, H., Mobasher, B.: A road map to more effective web personalization: integrating domain knowledge with web usage mining. In: Proceedings of the International Conference on Internet Computing, IC 2003, Las Vegas, Nevada, USA, 23–26 June 2003, vol. 1, pp. 58–64 (2003)
22. Degemmis, M., Lops, P., Semeraro, G.: A content-collaborative recommender that exploits wordnet-based user profiles for neighborhood formation. User Model. User-Adapt. Inter. 17(3), 217–255 (2007)

23. Deshpande, M., Karypis, G.: Item-based Top-N recommendation algorithms. ACM Trans. Inf. Syst. **22**(1), 143–177 (2004)
24. Di Noia, T., Di Sciascio, E., Donini, F.M.: Semantic matchmaking as non-monotonic reasoning: a description logic approach. J. Artif. Int. Res. **29**(1), 269–307 (2007)
25. Dojchinovski, M., Vitvar, T.: Personalised access to linked data. In: Janowicz, K., Schlobach, S., Lambrix, P., Hyvönen, E. (eds.) EKAW 2014. LNCS, vol. 8876, pp. 121–136. Springer, Heidelberg (2014)
26. Felfernig, A., Burke, R.: Constraint-based recommender systems: technologies and research issues. In: Proceedings of the 10th International Conference on Electronic Commerce, ICEC 2008, pp. 3:1–3:10. ACM, New York (2008)
27. Fernández-Tobías, I., Cantador, I., Kaminskas, M., Ricci, F.: A generic semantic-based framework for cross-domain recommendation. In: Proceedings of the 2nd International Workshop on Information Heterogeneity and Fusion in Recommender Systems, HetRec 2011, pp. 25–32. ACM, New York (2011)
28. Heitmann, B., Hayes, C.: Using linked data to build open, collaborative recommender systems. Linked data meets artificial intelligence. In: AAAI Spring Symposium (2010)
29. Herlocker, J.L., Konstan, J.A., Terveen, L.G., Riedl, J.T.: Evaluating collaborative filtering recommender systems. ACM Trans. Inf. Syst. **22**(1), 5–53 (2004)
30. Jannach, D., Zanker, M., Felfernig, A., Friedrich, G.: Recommender systems and the next-generation web. In: Recommender Systems, pp. 253–288. Cambridge University Press, Cambridge (2010)
31. Khrouf, H., Troncy, R.: Hybrid event recommendation using linked data and user diversity. In: Proceedings of the 7th ACM Conference on Recommender Systems, RecSys 2013, pp. 185–192. ACM, New York (2013)
32. Koren, Y.: Factorization meets the neighborhood: a multifaceted collaborative filtering model. In: Proceedings of the 14th ACM SIGKDD International Conference on Knowledge Discovery and Data Mining, KDD 2008, pp. 426–434. ACM, New York (2008)
33. Koren, Y., Bell, R., Volinsky, C.: Matrix factorization techniques for recommender systems. Computer **42**(8), 30–37 (2009)
34. Lehmann, J., Isele, R., Jakob, M., Jentzsch, A., Kontokostas, D., Mendes, P.N., Hellmann, S., Morsey, M., van Kleef, P., Auer, S., Bizer, C.: DBpedia - a large-scale, multilingual knowledge base extracted from wikipedia. Semant. Web J. **6**(2), 167–195 (2015)
35. Lommatzsch, A., Plumbaum, T., Albayrak, S.: A linked dataverse knows better: boosting recommendation quality using semantic knowledge. In: Proceedings of the 5th International Conference on Advances in Semantic Processing, pp. 97–103. IARIA, Wilmington (2011)
36. Lops, P., Gemmis, M., Semeraro, G.: Content-based recommender systems: state of the art and trends. In: Ricci, F., Rokach, L., Shapira, B., Kantor, P.B. (eds.) Recommender Systems Handbook, pp. 73–105. Springer, USA (2011)
37. Maidel, V., Shoval, P., Shapira, B., Taieb-Maimon, M.: Evaluation of an ontology-content based filtering method for a personalized newspaper. In: Proceedings of the 2008 ACM Conference on Recommender Systems, RecSys 2008, Lausanne, Switzerland, 23–25 October 2008, pp. 91–98 (2008)
38. Marie, N., Corby, O., Gandon, F., Ribière, M.: Composite interests' exploration thanks to on-the-fly linked data spreading activation. In: Proceedings of the 24th ACM Conference on Hypertext and Social Media, HT 2013, pp. 31–40. ACM, New York (2013)

39. McNee, S.M., Riedl, J., Konstan, J.A.: Being accurate is not enough: how accuracy metrics have hurt recommender systems. In: CHI 2006 Extended Abstracts on Human Factors in Computing Systems, CHI EA 2006, pp. 1097–1101. ACM, New York (2006)

40. Middleton, S.E., Shadbolt, N.R., De Roure, D.C.: Ontological user profiling in recommender systems. ACM Trans. Inf. Syst. **22**, 54–88 (2004)

41. Mobasher, B., Jin, X., Zhou, Y.: Semantically enhanced collaborative filtering on the web. In: Berendt, B., Hotho, A., Mladenič, D., van Someren, M., Spiliopoulou, M., Stumme, G. (eds.) EWMF 2003. LNCS (LNAI), vol. 3209, pp. 57–76. Springer, Heidelberg (2004)

42. Musto, C., Semeraro, G., Lops, P., de Gemmis, M.: Combining distributional semantics and entity linking for context-aware content-based recommendation. In: Dimitrova, V., Kuflik, T., Chin, D., Ricci, F., Dolog, P., Houben, G.-J. (eds.) UMAP 2014. LNCS, vol. 8538, pp. 381–392. Springer, Heidelberg (2014)

43. Narducci, F., Palmonari, M., Semeraro, G.: Cross-language semantic retrieval and linking of E-Gov services. In: Alani, H., Kagal, L., Fokoue, A., Groth, P., Biemann, C., Parreira, J.X., Aroyo, L., Noy, N., Welty, C., Janowicz, K. (eds.) ISWC 2013, Part II. LNCS, vol. 8219, pp. 130–145. Springer, Heidelberg (2013)

44. Passant, A.: Measuring semantic distance on linking data and using it for resources recommendations. In: Proceedings of the AAAI Spring Symposium "Linked Data Meets Artificial Intelligence", vol. 3 (2010)

45. Pazzani, M., Billsus, D.: Learning and revising user profiles: the identification ofinteresting web sites. Mach. Learn. **27**(3), 313–331 (1997)

46. Pazzani, M.J., Billsus, D.: Content-based recommendation systems. In: Brusilovsky, P., Kobsa, A., Nejdl, W. (eds.) Adaptive Web 2007. LNCS, vol. 4321, pp. 325–341. Springer, Heidelberg (2007)

47. Rendle, S., Freudenthaler, C., Gantner, Z., Schmidt-Thieme, L.: BPR: bayesian personalized ranking from implicit feedback. In: Proceedings of the Twenty-Fifth Conference on Uncertainty in Artificial Intelligence, UAI 2009, pp. 452–461. AUAI Press, Arlington (2009)

48. Resnick, P., Iacovou, N., Suchak, M., Bergstrom, P., Riedl, J.: Grouplens: an open architecture for collaborative filtering of netnews. In: CSCW 1994, Proceedings of the Conference on Computer Supported Cooperative Work, Chapel Hill, NC, USA, 22–26 October 1994, pp. 175–186 (1994)

49. Ricci, F., Rokach, L., Shapira, B., Kantor, P.B. (eds.): Recommender Systems Handbook. Springer, USA (2011)

50. Rowe, M.: SemanticSVD++: incorporating semantic taste evolution for predicting ratings. In: 2014 IEEE/WIC/ACM International Conferences on Web Intelligence, WI 2014 (2014)

51. Rowe, M.: Transferring semantic categories with vertex kernels: recommendations with SemanticSVD++. In: Mika, P., Tudorache, T., Bernstein, A., Welty, C., Knoblock, C., Vrandečić, D., Groth, P., Noy, N., Janowicz, K., Goble, C. (eds.) ISWC 2014, Part I. LNCS, vol. 8796, pp. 341–356. Springer, Heidelberg (2014)

52. Schafer, J.B., Frankowski, D., Herlocker, J., Sen, S.: Collaborative filtering recommender systems. In: Brusilovsky, P., Kobsa, A., Nejdl, W. (eds.) Adaptive Web 2007. LNCS, vol. 4321, pp. 291–324. Springer, Heidelberg (2007)

53. Schein, A.I., Popescul, A., Ungar, L.H., Pennock, D.M.: Methods and metrics for cold-start recommendations. In: Proceedings of the 25th Annual International ACM SIGIR Conference on Research and Development in Information Retrieval, SIGIR 2002, pp. 253–260. ACM, New York (2002)

54. Schmachtenberg, M., Bizer, C., Paulheim, H.: Adoption of the linked data best practices in different topical domains. In: Mika, P., Tudorache, T., Bernstein, A., Welty, C., Knoblock, C., Vrandečić, D., Groth, P., Noy, N., Janowicz, K., Goble, C. (eds.) ISWC 2014, Part I. LNCS, vol. 8796, pp. 245–260. Springer, Heidelberg (2014)

55. Semeraro, G., Degemmis, M., Lops, P., Basile, P.: Combining learning and word sense disambiguation for intelligent user profiling. In: IJCAI 2007, Proceedings of the 20th International Joint Conference on Artificial Intelligence, Hyderabad, India, 6–12 January 2007, pp. 2856–2861 (2007)

56. Semeraro, G., Lops, P., Basile, P., de Gemmis, M.: Knowledge infusion into content-based recommender systems. In: Proceedings of the Third ACM Conference on Recommender Systems, RecSys 2009, pp. 301–304, ACM, New York (2009)

57. Shen, W., Wang, J., Luo, P., Wang, M.: Linden: linking named entities with knowledge base via semantic knowledge. In: Proceedings of the 21st International Conference on World Wide Web, WWW 2012, pp. 449–458. ACM, New York (2012)

58. Stankovic, M., Breitfuss, W., Laublet, P.: Linked-data based suggestion of relevant topics. In: Proceedings of the 7th International Conference on Semantic Systems, I-Semantics 2011, pp. 49–55. ACM, New York (2011)

59. Steck, H.: Evaluation of recommendations: rating-prediction and ranking. In: RecSys, pp. 213–220 (2013)

60. Vargas, S., Castells, P.: Rank and relevance in novelty and diversity metrics for recommender systems. In: Proceedings of the Fifth ACM Conference on Recommender Systems, RecSys 2011, pp. 109–116. ACM, New York (2011)

61. Webb, G.I., Pazzani, M.J., Billsus, D.: Machine learning for user modeling. User Model. User-Adap. Inter. **11**(1–2), 19–29 (2001)

62. Zanker, M., Jessenitschnig, M., Schmid, W.: Preference reasoning with soft constraints in constraint-based recommender systems. Constraints **15**(4), 574–595 (2010)

63. Ziegler, C.-N., Lausen, G., Schmidt-Thieme, L.: Taxonomy-driven computation of product recommendations. In: Proceedings of the Thirteenth ACM International Conference on Information And Knowledge Management, CIKM 2004, pp. 406–415. ACM, New York (2004)

64. Ziegler, C.-N., McNee, S.M., Konstan, J.A., Lausen, G.: Improving recommendation lists through topic diversification. In: Proceedings of the 14th International Conference on World Wide Web, WWW 2005, pp. 22–32. ACM, New York (2005)

PSOA RuleML: Integrated Object-Relational Data and Rules

Harold Boley[⊠]

Faculty of Computer Science, University of New Brunswick, Fredericton, Canada
harold.boley@unb.ca

Abstract. Object-relational combinations are reviewed with a focus on the integrated Positional-Slotted, Object-Applicative (PSOA) RuleML. PSOA RuleML permits a predicate application (atom) to be without or with an Object IDentifier (OID) – typed by the predicate as its class – and, orthogonally, the predicate's arguments to be positional, slotted, or combined. This enables six uses of atoms, which are systematically developed employing examples in presentation syntaxes derived from RuleML/POSL and RIF-BLD, and visualized in Scratch Grailog. These atoms, asserted as facts, are retrieved by object-relational look-in queries. On top of such facts, PSOA rules and their inferential querying are explored, e.g. permitting F-logic-like frames derived from relational joins. A use case of bidirectional SQL-PSOA-SPARQL transformation (schema/ontology mapping) is shown. Objectification and the presentation plus (XML-)serialization syntaxes of PSOA RuleML are described. The first-order model-theoretic semantics is formalized, blending (OID-over-)slot distribution, as in RIF, with integrated psoa terms, as in RuleML. The PSOATransRun implementation is surveyed, translating PSOA RuleML to TPTP (PSOA2TPTP) or Prolog (PSOA2Prolog).

1 Introduction

Data has recently obtained the status of what might be called "raw and processed material for all endeavors". In analogy to the many distinctions for materials (e.g., concerning, 'externally', their cost and logistics, and, 'internally', their plasticity and reactivity), both external and internal distinctions can also be made in the realm of (complex) data. External distinctions for data include "proprietary vs. *open*" (e.g., on an intranet vs. on the Internet, particularly the Web) and, orthogonally, "siloed vs. *linked*", with two popular choices in italics.[1] Internal distinctions include a couple that is often described by the contrasting data paradigms of *relations* (below: "predicate-centered, positional" data), e.g. in the SQL-queried Deep Web, vs. *graphs* (below: "object-centered, slotted" data), e.g. in the SPARQL-queried Semantic Web.

This divide has also led to separate relational and graph rule paradigms that capture knowledge for processing the data (e.g., for inferencing/reasoning

---

[1] http://en.wikipedia.org/wiki/Linked_open_data.

© Springer International Publishing Switzerland 2015
W. Faber and A. Paschke (Eds.): Reasoning Web 2015, LNCS 9203, pp. 114–150, 2015.
DOI: 10.1007/978-3-319-21768-0_5

with them). Projects involving both relations and graphs are thus impeded by the paradigm boundaries, from modeling to implementation. These boundaries can be bridged or even dissolved by languages combining the relational and graph paradigms for data as well as rules:

- A heterogeneous combination (an amalgamation), as in F-logic [1] and RIF [2], allows atomic formulas in the separated relational and graph language paradigms for data as well as rules, possibly mixed within the same rule.
- The homogeneous combination (an integration) Positional-Slotted, Object-Applicative (PSOA) RuleML [3][2] blends the atomic relational and graph formulas themselves into a uniform kind of atom, allowing language-internal transformation of data as well as rules.

In PSOA RuleML, data, i.e. ground (variable-less) facts, include (table-row-like) relational atoms without an Object IDentifier (OID) and with positional arguments vs. (graph-node-like) graph atoms with an OID and slotted arguments (for the node's outgoing labeled edges). What we call 'slots' is often called 'attributes', 'properties', or 'roles'. Each PSOA slot can have one or more values. Rules (implications) can use non-ground (variable-containing) versions of all of the above atoms anywhere in their conditions (bodies) and conclusions (heads).

Generally, the relational vs. graph distinction can be based on two orthogonal dimensions, creating a system of four quadrants. Expanding one of the dimensions, the object-relational integration in PSOA RuleML is achieved by permitting an atom to be predicate-centered (without an OID) or object-centered[3] (with an OID) – every OID being typed by the predicate as its class – and, orthogonally, the predicate's arguments to be positional (a sequence), slotted (a bag of pairs), or both (a positional-plus-slotted combination). The resulting positional-slotted object-applicative (**psoa**)[4] atoms can be used in six ways, as in this *psoa table* (quadrants 1. to 4. expanded by combined options 5. and 6.):

	predicate-centered	object-centered
positional	1. relationships	2. shelves
slotted	3. pairships	4. frames
positional+slotted	5. relpairships	6. shelframes

Of the six options, positional data are widely used under names like 'tuples', 'vectors', 'lists', and (1-dimensional) 'arrays' (mostly 1.). Likewise, slotted data

---

[2] http://wiki.ruleml.org/index.php/PSOA_RuleML.

[3] With 'object-*centered*' rather than 'object-*oriented*' atoms we refer to atoms that have a typed OID described by slots and/or positional arguments. Object-Oriented Programming (OOP) usually only employs descriptive slots but not positional arguments; on the other hand, OOP allows the *re-assignment* of slot fillers (instance variables) while object-centered modeling – as its declarative core – only allows the *refinement* of non-ground slot fillers and – in PSOA RuleML – positional arguments.

[4] We use the upper-cased "PSOA" as a qualifier for the language and the lower-cased "psoa" for its terms.

include 'objects', 'records', 'maps', and 'property lists' (usually 4.). All six are illustrated with variations of the family-example atoms from [3,4][5]:

1. Predicate-centered, positional atoms (relationships), without an OID and with an – ordered – sequence of arguments, e.g. a $Husb \times Wife$ relationship `family(Joe Sue)`.
2. Object-centered, positional atoms (shelves), with an OID and with a sequence of arguments, e.g. `inst1#family(Joe Sue)` with `family`-typed OID `inst1`.
3. Predicate-centered, slotted atoms (pairships), without an OID and with an – unordered – multi-set of slots (each a pair of a slot name and a slot filler), e.g. `family(husb->Joe wife->Sue)` or `family(wife->Sue husb->Joe)`.
4. Object-centered, slotted atoms (frames), with an OID and with a multi-set of slots, e.g. `inst1#family(husb->Joe wife->Sue)` or commuted (as in 3.).
5. Predicate-centered, positional+slotted atoms (relpairships), without an OID and with both a sequence of arguments and a multi-set of slots, e.g. a 3-slot, 2-argument atom `family(child->Pete dog->Fido dog->Toby Joe Sue)`.
6. Object-centered, positional+slotted atoms (shelframes), with an OID and with both an argument sequence and a slot multi-set, e.g. an `inst1`-identified atom (cf. 5.) `inst1#family(child->Pete dog->Fido dog->Toby Joe Sue)`.

The original family-example rule from [3] illustrates one combination of these six uses of psoa atoms in conditions and conclusions: Its predicate-centered, positional atoms in the condition (1.) derive a predicate-centered, slotted atom in the conclusion (3.). The following family-rule variant illustrates a conjunction of two predicate-centered, positional atoms – a relational join – deriving an object-centered, slotted atom (4.) – an F-logic-like frame – with the application of a fresh function name, `famid`, to `?Hu` and `?Wi` denoting the OID dependent on them but not on `?Ch` (in this preview, free variables are assumed to be universal):

```
famid(?Hu ?Wi)#family(husb->?Hu wife->?Wi child->?Ch) :-
                        And(married(?Hu ?Wi) kid(?Wi ?Ch))
```

With its OID function, this rule crosses from Datalog to Horn-logic expressivity.

PSOA RuleML is a (head-existential-)extended Horn-logic language (with equality) that systematizes the variety of RIF-BLD terms[6] by generalizing its positional and slotted ("named-argument") terms as well as its frame and membership terms. It can be extended in various ways, e.g. with Negation As Failure (NAF), augmenting RuleML's MYNG configurator [5] for the syntax and adapting the RIF-FLD-specified NAF dialects for the semantics. Conversely, PSOA RuleML is being developed as a module that is pluggable into larger (RuleML) logic languages, thus making them likewise object-relational (cf. Sect. 6).

---

[5] http://wiki.ruleml.org/index.php/Grailog#Family_Example.
[6] http://www.w3.org/TR/rif-bld/#Terms.

This paper gives a tutorial-style overview of PSOA RuleML, spanning from conceptual foundation, to data model, to fact and rule querying, to use case, to syntax, to semantics, to implementation. Specifically, the paper:

- visualizes all psoa terms in Grailog, where (n-ary) directed hyperarcs [4] – of directed hypergraphs – are used for positional terms, and (binary) directed arcs – of directed 'graphs' in the narrow sense – are used for slotted terms;
- uses ('functional') *terms* p(...) with a predicate symbol p, taking them as atomic *formulas* as in Relfun, HiLog, and RIF, which – along with equality – is a basis for universal functional-logic programming as in Curry [6];
- is about instance frames (frame atoms) and other psoa atoms employed as queries and facts, as well as about rules having frames etc. as their conditions and/or conclusions; it is not about (signature) declarations, as e.g. for frames in F-logic; however, integrity rules can be defined over arbitrary psoa terms, as e.g. for relationships in Dexter [7];
- uses ordinary constants as Object IDentifiers, which can logically connect (distributed) frames and other psoa atoms describing the same OID, e.g. after disassembling (slotributing) a frame into its smallest (RDF-triple-like) single-slot parts at compile- or interpretation/run-time;
- uses class membership *oid* ∈ *class* (written RIF-like: *oid#class*) as the 'backbone' of (typed) frames etc., where a missing *oid* is provided by the system (e.g. as a Skolem constant or existential variable) and the absence of *class* typing is expressed by the Top class, specifying the root of the class hierarchy;
- is only about (monotonically) deriving new frames etc., and does not go into negation (as failure) or into frame retraction or updating, although the latter operations can again use OIDs to refer to frames (cf. N3 [8]);
- focuses on an SQL-SPARQL interoperation use case about (sub)addresses (Sect. 5), while other use cases are about clinical intelligence [9], music albums[7], and geospatial rules [10][8].

This section introduced object-relational combinations, focused on the PSOA RuleML integration. Next, the paper develops the PSOA data model with a systematically varied example in presentation syntaxes derived from RuleML/POSL and RIF-BLD, and in a neat Grailog visualization syntax. Subsequently, such ground atoms are asserted as ground facts and queried by ground or non-ground atoms, followed by a non-ground OID-existential PSOA fact and its querying. Based on similar facts, PSOA rules and their querying are being explored. The paper then shows a use case of bidirectional SQL-PSOA-SPARQL transformation (schema/ontology mapping). It continues with defining objectification as well as the presentation and serialization syntaxes of PSOA RuleML. Next, it formalizes the model-theoretic semantics, blending (OID-over-)slot distribution, as in RIF, with integrated psoa terms, as in RuleML. Finally, the paper surveys the PSOATransRun implementation, translating PSOA RuleML knowledge bases and queries to TPTP (PSOA2TPTP) or Prolog (PSOA2Prolog).

---

[7] http://www.cs.unb.ca/~boley/papers/MusicAlbumKB.txt.
[8] http://wiki.ruleml.org/index.php/Geospatial_Rules.

2   Grailog-Visualized Data Model of PSOA RuleML

The data model of PSOA RuleML, based on a long tradition of similar distinctions in the space of data, is structured by the two main (orthogonal) dimensions of "predicate-centered vs. object-centered" and "positional vs. slotted". These dimensions permit a more precise terminology than is possible, e.g., with JSON's array vs. object distinction [11][9], which (in spite of JSON's "object" notion) corresponds only to our "positional vs. slotted" dimension.

Our data model will be intuitively explained through a corresponding PSOA RuleML subset of Grailog [4][10] extended with *branch lines*, for multiple, 'split-out' (hyper)arcs, and using the novel *Scratch Grailog* visualization, which emphasizes connecting lines (rather than surrounding boxes). In logical languages, data are conceived as ground (variable-free) facts often given in a (symbolic) presentation syntax. We will use Grailog "skewer figures"[11] as a corresponding (graphical) visualization syntax for PSOA facts integrating relations and objects. Our (Scratch) Grailog figures will visualize the connectivity within a set of *label-nodes*,[12] where color coding will show the correspondence to the symbolic facts. The following subsections will visualize the PSOA RuleML systematics in Sect. 1 of six uses of facts from n-ary relationships, to frames, to integrated object-relational atoms. While the focus will be on single-tuple atoms, the generalization to multi-tuple atoms will be exemplified in Sects. 2.1 and 2.2. Throughout, we will vary a running 'betweenness' example for illustration.

2.1   Predicate-Centered, Positional Atoms (Relationships)

Predicate-centered, positional atoms (often called *relationships*) represent n-ary positional information ($n \geq 0$), i.e. the left-to-right-ordered connection of n arguments into a tuple, where the kind of tuple is represented by a relation name applied to the arguments. In Grailog, each relationship becomes a *directed hyperarc* (directed hyperedge),[13] which is depicted as an arrow shaft starting at the labelnode for the relation name or at a branch line, cutting through the labelnodes for the n-1 initial arguments in the order they occur, and ending with an arrow head at the labelnode for the nth argument. Labelnodes for relation names as well as for arguments can be shared by several hyperarcs.

The sample Grailog figures, right below, visualize 3-ary relational betweenness with hyperarcs (connecting four labelnodes) for two relationships applying the relation name betweenRel, in blue, to three individuals (geographic entities)

---

[9] http://wiki.ruleml.org/index.php/RuleML_in_JSON.

[10] http://wiki.ruleml.org/index.php/Grailog.

[11] The usual "stick figures" for directed graphs – connecting pairs of nodes with arrows – are generalized to "skewer figures" for directed hypergraphs – each (bendable) skewer holding arbitrarily many nodes together in a totally ordered fashion.

[12] A labelnode can be used as a label (relation) or as a node (argument).

[13] In the following, "hyperarc" will be used as an abbreviation for "directed hyperarc".

as arguments, in red. The variant without branch lines can be seen as a shortcut for the variant with branch lines, shown here in preparation for extensions.[14]

The corresponding relational PSOA facts in POSL-like [12][15] and RIF-like Presentation syntax, further below, employ traditional parenthesized relation applications. Here, the POSL-vs.-RIF difference is only in the use of separator (comma vs. white-space) and terminator (period vs. newline) symbols.[16]

Grailog-Style Visualization Syntax (Without Branch Lines):

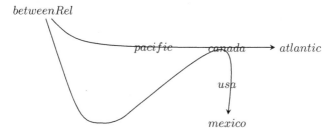

Grailog-Style Visualization Syntax (With Branch Lines):

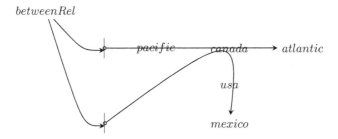

POSL-like Presentation Syntax:

    betweenRel(pacific, canada, atlantic).
    betweenRel(canada, usa,   mexico).

RIF-like Presentation Syntax:

    betweenRel(pacific canada atlantic)
    betweenRel(canada usa   mexico)

Notice that the relation name *betweenRel* as well as the argument *canada* are shared by the two hyperarcs but become copied in the two facts.

The alternative sample Grailog figure, right below, is a visualization that extends the two above vertical branch lines such that they meet, obtaining a single branch line, and uses a single unary *betweenRel* hyperarc pointing to it.

---

[14] Branch lines permit multiple attachment points for visualizing multiple tuples [3], exemplified below, as well as (multiple) slots, to be introduced in Sect. 2.3.

[15] The POsitional-SLotted language started integrating positional and slotted syntaxes: http://ruleml.org/submission/ruleml-shortation.html.

[16] This is partly due to the RIF-like Presentation syntax used here being somewhat simplified w.r.t. the one used by PSOA RuleML tools: in particular, the "_" prefix is omitted from local constants, except for system-generated ones.

Likewise, also as for relational tables (e.g., in SQL), the multiple copies of the relation name can be avoided in the PSOA RuleML facts. The corresponding relational psoa term, further below, replaces the two separate facts for the same relation with a single multi-tuple (specifically, double-tuple) fact.

Grailog-Style Visualization Syntax (With Branch Line):

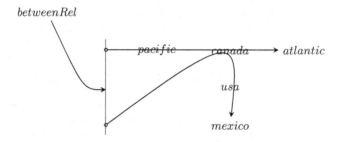

POSL-like Presentation Syntax:
> betweenRel(pacific, canada, atlantic; canada, usa, mexico).

RIF-like Presentation Syntax:
> betweenRel([pacific canada atlantic] [canada usa mexico])

For the frequent case of n-ary relations with of $n = 1$, needed in the next subsection, hyperarcs (connecting two labelnodes) point from the relation labelnode or branch line directly to the only argument labelnode.[17]

2.2   Object-Centered, Positional Atoms (Shelves)

Object-centered, positional atoms (here called *shelves*) describe an OID with n positional arguments ($n \geq 0$). A shelf thus endows an n-tuple with an OID, typed by the relation/class, keeping the positional representation of n-ary relationships in Sect. 2.1.

The sample Grailog figure, right below (objectifying the variant with branch lines in Sect. 2.1), visualizes two OIDs, $a1$ and $a2$, in orange, typed by the relation/class name *betweenObjRel*, in blue, and two 3-tuples with the three individuals as arguments, in red. The corresponding psoa term facts, further below, employ syntaxes augmenting with OIDs the parenthesized relation-application syntaxes for the three positional arguments from the relationship: The POSL-like version specifies the OID at the beginning of the argument sequence, where a hat/caret/circumflex ("^") sign – think of it as a 'property/slot insertion' character – is used as an infix separating the OID from the slots. The RIF-like version specifies the OID along with its typing relation/class, where a hash ("#") sign – think of it as a 'set/class membership' character ("∈") – is used as an infix separating the OID from the relation/class.

---

[17] For the infrequent case of $n = 0$, not needed in this paper, hyperarcs ('connecting' one labelnode) degenerate to an outgoing arrow head attached to the relation labelnode or branch line.

Grailog-Style Visualization Syntax:

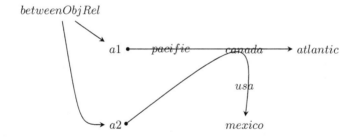

POSL-like Presentation Syntax:
    betweenObjRel(a1^pacific, canada, atlantic).
    betweenObjRel(a2^canada, usa,   mexico).

RIF-like Presentation Syntax:
    a1#betweenObjRel(pacific   canada   atlantic)
    a2#betweenObjRel(canada   usa   mexico)

This shelf version is like the relational version in Sect. 2.1 in that it keeps the three positional arguments for both hyperarcs. It is like the frame version in Sect. 2.4 in that it introduces two relation/class-typed OIDs.

Notice that the use of the same OID for multiple facts/hyperarcs is allowed, e.g. replacing the two above OIDs, a1 and a2, with a single OID, a0.

POSL-like Presentation Syntax:
    betweenObjRel(a0^pacific, canada, atlantic).
    betweenObjRel(a0^canada, usa,   mexico).

RIF-like Presentation Syntax:
    a0#betweenObjRel(pacific   canada   atlantic)
    a0#betweenObjRel(canada   usa   mexico)

Similarly as in Sect. 2.1, these can be merged into a single multi-tuple (specifically, double-tuple) fact.[18]

---

[18] Such merging of tuples – and (later) slots – centered on the same OID is called 'centralization'. It constructs one object-identified psoa term from a given set of equally identified psoa terms. Centralization will be assumed when illustrating the proof-theoretic semantics in Sects. 3 and 4. It is the inverse of tupribution – and slotribution – to be introduced in Sect. 7. Harvesting the set of all psoa terms with a fixed OID from a distributed network – e.g. published on the Web – can use techniques analogous to finding all RDF triples having a fixed resource as their subject (cf. http://www.w3.org/wiki/TaskForces/CommunityProjects/LinkingOpenData/SemanticWebSearchEngines). This is a nontrivial task, since such OIDs and resources normally are not dereferenceable locators themselves but occur within documents at other locators (although, ideally, those documents have filename extensions like .ruleml and .rdf, respectively).

POSL-like Presentation Syntax:

betweenObjRel(a0ˆpacific, canada, atlantic; canada, usa, mexico).

RIF-like Presentation Syntax:

a0#betweenObjRel([pacific canada atlantic] [canada usa mexico])

The corresponding Grailog-style visualization syntax could likewise keep the two a0 nodes separate, e.g. for layout purposes, or merge them into a single a0 node with a single unary *betweenObjRel* hyperarc pointing to it.

2.3 Predicate-Centered, Slotted Atoms (Pairships)

Predicate-centered, slotted atoms (here called *pairships*)[19] apply a relation/class to n non-positional attribute-value pairs (often called *slots*) (n $\geq$ 0). In Grailog, a pairship is depicted as a relation/class node pointing, with a unary hyperarc, to a branch line having n outgoing circle-shaft slot arrows, each using a label for the attribute and a target node for the value. The order in which slot arrows emanate from a branch line is immaterial (like for arrows emanating from a node, as in Sect. 2.4).

The sample Grailog figure, right below (re-representing the same information as the version in Sect. 2.1), visualizes 3-slot betweenness of two pairships that apply the relation name *betweenObj*, in blue, to a branch line for three slots, with labels *outer1*, *inner*, and *outer2*, in magenta, targeting three individuals as values, in red. The corresponding pairship facts, further below, employ syntaxes modifying the relationship syntax of Sect. 2.1: In both the POSL- and RIF-like versions, a 'dash-greater' right-arrow ("->") sign – think of it as a 'has value/filler' character ("→") – is used as an infix separating a slot attribute (name) and value (filler). As in Grailog, the order in which slots occur in an atom is immaterial. In *lexicographic normal form*, slots are ordered alphabetically according to, primarily, their names and, secondarily, their fillers.

Grailog-Style Visualization Syntax:

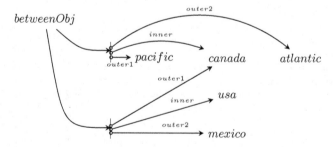

POSL-like Presentation Syntax:

betweenObj(outer1->pacific; inner->canada; outer2->atlantic).
betweenObj(outer1->canada; inner->usa;   outer2->mexico).

---

[19] In RIF called "named-argument terms" [2].

RIF-like Presentation Syntax:

betweenObj(outer1->pacific   inner->canada outer2->atlantic)
betweenObj(outer1->canada inner->usa   outer2->mexico)

The following correspondences lead from the relational version in Sect. 2.1 to the current version: The three positional arguments become the values (fillers) of three non-positional slots with attributes (names) outer1, inner, and outer2. The shared betweenRel becomes the shared betweenObj. The shared argument canada becomes a shared value (filler).

As a second sample, the Grailog figure, right below, visualizes two pairships that apply the relation name, *betweenObjRel*, in blue, to two slots, with labels *orient*ation and *dim*ension[20], targeting three new individuals, as values, in red. The corresponding pairship facts, further below, employ the pairship syntaxes from above.

Grailog-Style Visualization Syntax:

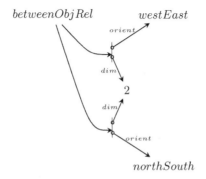

POSL-like Presentation Syntax:

betweenObjRel(dim->2; orient->westEast).
betweenObjRel(dim->2; orient->northSouth).

RIF-like Presentation Syntax:

betweenObjRel(dim->2 orient->westEast)
betweenObjRel(dim->2 orient->northSouth)

This version is like the pairship version above but represents new information.

2.4 Object-Centered, Slotted Atoms (Frames)

Object-centered, slotted atoms (often called *frames*) describe an OID with n non-positional attribute-value pairs (often called *slots*) (n≥0), where the kind of object is represented by a class name typing the OID. In Grailog, a frame is depicted as a typing relation/class node pointing, with a unary hyperarc, to

---

[20] The figure's representation of dimension = 2 indicates that this betweenness is relative to a 2D plane (rather than, say, to a 3D sphere).

a central OID node having n outgoing bullet-shaft (OID-marking) slot arrows, each using a label for the attribute and a target node for the value. A frame can thus be seen as a pairship (as in Sect. 2.3) enriched by an OID that results from expanding the branch line to an entire OID box, and from filling the (empty) circles of outgoing arrow shafts so they become (solid) bullets.

The sample Grailog figure, right below (OID-enriching the first figure in Sect. 2.3), visualizes object-centered 3-slot betweenness with central nodes, $b1$ and $b2$, in orange, for the OIDs of two frames typed by the relation name *betweenObj*, in blue, and three slots, with labels *outer1*, *inner*, and *outer2*, in magenta, targeting three individuals as values, in red. The corresponding psoa frame facts, further below, employ syntaxes enriching the pairship syntaxes.

Grailog-Style Visualization Syntax:

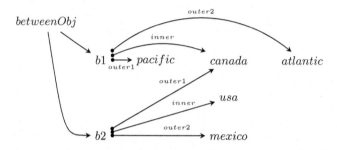

POSL-like Presentation Syntax:

        betweenObj(b1^outer1->pacific; inner->canada; outer2->atlantic).
        betweenObj(b2^outer1->canada; inner->usa;   outer2->mexico).

RIF-like Presentation Syntax:

        b1#betweenObj(outer1->pacific inner->canada outer2->atlantic)
        b2#betweenObj(outer1->canada inner->usa   outer2->mexico)

The following correspondences lead from the relational version in Sect. 2.1 to the current version, complementing both of their characteristics: (1) The anonymous relationships become frames with OIDs b1 and b2. (2) The three positional arguments become the values (fillers) of three slots with attributes (names) outer1, inner, and outer2. Moreover, the shared betweenRel becomes the shared betweenObj. The shared argument canada becomes a shared value (filler).

As a second sample, the Grailog figure, right below (OID-enriching the second pairship figure of Sect. 2.3), again visualizes the two OIDs of Sect. 2.2, $a1$ and $a2$, in orange, typed by their relation/class name, *betweenObjRel*, in blue, but now described by two slots, with labels *orient* and *dim*, targeting three individuals, as values, in red. The corresponding frame facts, further below, employ the frame syntaxes from above.

Grailog-Style Visualization Syntax:

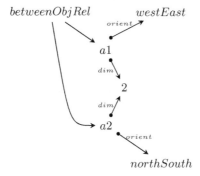

POSL-like Presentation Syntax:

betweenObjRel(a1ˆdim->2; orient->westEast).
betweenObjRel(a2ˆdim->2; orient->northSouth).

RIF-like Presentation Syntax:

a1#betweenObjRel(dim->2 orient->westEast)
a2#betweenObjRel(dim->2 orient->northSouth)

This version is like the frame version above but introduces new information describing its OIDs.

2.5   Predicate-Centered, Positional+Slotted Atoms (Relpairships)

Predicate-centered, positional+slotted atoms (here called *relpairships*) blend the relationships of Sect. 2.1 and pairships of Sect. 2.3 as follows. A branch line typed by the relation/class is shared for a relationship and a pairship. The branch line has an outgoing circle-shaft hyperarc arrow for the relationship part's tuple and outgoing circle-shaft slot arrows for the pairship part's slots. The order between the hyperarc arrow and the slot arrows emanating from a branch line is immaterial (like for arrows emanating from a node, as in Sect. 2.6).

The sample Grailog figure, right below, visualizes two relpairships, each composed of a relationship (as the variant with branch lines in Sect. 2.1) and a pairship (as in Sect. 2.3). The relationship parts use two branch lines, typed by the relation/class name *betweenObjRel*, in blue, and two 3-tuples with the three individuals as arguments, in red. The pairship parts use the same two branch lines, additionally having two slots each, with labels *orient* and *dim*, and targeting three further individuals, as values, in red. The corresponding relpairship facts, further below, employ an integrated syntax blending the three positional arguments from the relationship and the two slots from the pairship. As in Grailog, the order between the tuple of positional arguments and the multi-set of slots occurring in an atom is immaterial. In *left-slot normal form*, the multi-set of slots precedes the tuple. In *right-slot normal form*, it follows the tuple. These normal forms can be combined with the lexicographic normal form of Sect. 2.3 to, respectively, *lexicographic left-slot normal form* and *lexicographic right-slot normal form.* Here we use left-slot normal form, because it directly corresponds to the Grailog figures, while earlier papers have used right-slot normal form.

Grailog-Style Visualization Syntax:

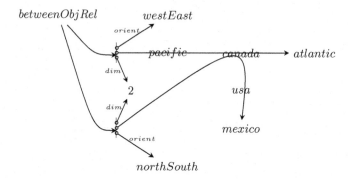

POSL-like Presentation Syntax:

betweenObjRel(dim->2; orient->westEast;   pacific, canada, atlantic).
betweenObjRel(dim->2; orient->northSouth; canada, usa,   mexico).

RIF-like Presentation Syntax:

betweenObjRel(dim->2 orient->westEast   pacific canada atlantic)
betweenObjRel(dim->2 orient->northSouth canada usa   mexico)

This version is a 'disjoint union' of the second pairship version in Sect. 2.3 and the relationship version in Sect. 2.1, 'plugging together' their information over the same branch lines. The graphical overlay thus becomes a logical conjunction, as expected.

2.6   Object-Centered, Positional+Slotted Atoms (Shelframes)

Object-centered, positional+slotted atoms (here called *shelframes*) blend the shelves of Sect. 2.2 and frames of Sect. 2.4 as follows. An OID typed by the relation/class is shared for a shelf and a frame. The OID is described with both the shelf's tuple and the frame's slots. Equivalently, a shelframe can be seen as a relpairship (as in Sect. 2.5) enriched by an OID.

The sample Grailog figure, right below, visualizes two shelframes, each composed of a shelf (as in Sect. 2.2) and a frame (as the second version in Sect. 2.4). They can also be seen as OID enrichments of the relpairships in Sect. 2.5. The shelf parts center on two OIDs, *a*1 and *a*2, in orange, typed by the relation/-class name *betweenObjRel*, in blue, and two 3-tuples with the three individuals as arguments, in red. The frame parts center on the same two OIDs, additionally describing each with two slots, having labels *orient* and *dim*, and targeting three further individuals, as values, in red. The corresponding shelframe facts, further below, employ an integrated syntax blending the three positional shelf arguments and the two frame slots.

Grailog-Style Visualization Syntax:

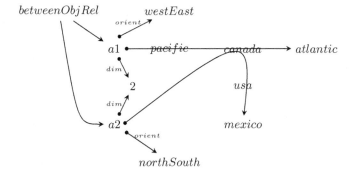

POSL-like Presentation Syntax:

betweenObjRel(a1^dim->2; orient->westEast;   pacific, canada, atlantic).
betweenObjRel(a2^dim->2; orient->northSouth; canada, usa,   mexico).

RIF-like Presentation Syntax:

a1#betweenObjRel(dim->2 orient->westEast   pacific canada atlantic)
a2#betweenObjRel(dim->2 orient->northSouth canada usa   mexico)

This version is a 'disjoint union' of the second frame version in Sect. 2.4 and the shelf version in Sect. 2.6, 'plugging together' their information over the same OIDs. The graphical overlay thus becomes a logical conjunction, as expected.

3   PSOA Facts for Look-in Querying

The Grailog data model of PSOA RuleML in Sect. 2 will serve as the foundation for PSOA RuleML fact querying discussed in the current section, which – along with rule querying in the next section – will illustrate PSOA RuleML's proof-theoretic semantics in preparation for the model-theoretic semantics discussed in Sect. 7.

We will introduce the notion of 'look-in' querying, which generalizes look-up querying by 'looking' for psoa query terms 'in' asserted psoa fact terms. The below definitions of 'equal to' and 'part of' for psoa fact and query terms can be understood in terms of their graph counterparts: For graph equality and parthood, the attachment order of hyperarcs and slot arrows is immaterial; this can be easily gleaned from the relevant sample visualizations in Sect. 2. These definitions correspond to slotribution and tupribution in the model-theoretic semantics of Sect. 7, Definition 5, "Psoa formula", and in the transformational semantics of Sect. 8: The proof-theoretic check that a query term is 'part of' a fact term becomes the model-theoretic/transformational reformulation of the query term into a conjunction of a membership term and single-slot plus single-tuple terms against the likewise reformulated fact term.

Two elementary binary relations between arbitrary psoa terms are defined:

- A psoa term t_1 is *equal to* a psoa term t_2 if t_1 and t_2 can be made (syntactically) identical by renaming any (universally or existentially) bound variables, omitting any duplicate slots (entire pairs) and argument tuples (entire sequences), and reordering any slots and argument tuples in t_1 and in t_2.
- A psoa term t_1 is *part of* a psoa term t_2 if t_1 is equal to a version of t_2 that omits zero or more slots and/or entire argument tuples from t_2. A psoa term t_1 is *proper part of* a psoa term t_2 if t_1 is part of t_2 and t_1 is not equal to t_2.

A set of PSOA ground atoms, e.g. as visualized in Sect. 2, can be asserted as ground facts in a Knowledge Base (KB) and then be queried by ground or non-ground atoms, some of which will succeed while others will fail. This exemplifies a basic notion of the proof-theoretic semantics with positive (success) and negative (fail) entailment tests, KB $\vdash$ q and KB $\nvdash$ q, respectively. Look-in ground and non-ground querying will be defined below, where the former is a special case of the latter.

Look-in Ground Querying: Consider a ground KB k and a ground query q. k $\vdash$ q (resp., k $\nvdash$ q) iff there exists (resp., does not exist) a ground fact g in k such that q is part of g.

Since positional+slotted atoms include both positional and slotted atoms, we will focus on them in the following, i.e. on Sects. 2.5 and 2.6. Also, we will use the (RIF-like) symbolic presentation syntax only, hence color will be omitted.

For example, consider the following ground atom from Sect. 2.6, asserted as a double-slot, single-tuple ground fact in a single-fact sample KB:

```
a2#betweenObjRel(dim->2 orient->northSouth canada usa mexico)
```

This ground atom can be retrieved by issuing an identical ground atom as a ground query (special case of 'equal to'), yielding a success message; it cannot be retrieved by issuing a ground query that is not part of the ground fact, e.g. one that expects `alaska` in place of `canada`, yielding a failure message; it can again be retrieved when commuting ('equal to' as 'non-proper part of') or omitting slots and/or tuples ('proper part of'), but not when commuting the positional arguments or adding/deleting some of them within a tuple, or when inserting slots and/or tuples, or when using a different OID:

```
a2#betweenObjRel(dim->2 orient->northSouth [canada usa mexico])
success   % Desugared positional arguments with square brackets for tuple

a2#betweenObjRel(dim->2 orient->northSouth canada usa mexico)
success   % Syntactic-sugar version is identical to fact

a2#betweenObjRel(dim->2 orient->northSouth alaska usa mexico)
fail      % Different constant in same position of tuple

a2#betweenObjRel(orient->northSouth dim->2 canada usa mexico)
success   % Commuted two slots
```

```
a2#betweenObjRel(canada usa mexico dim->2 orient->northSouth)
success    % Swapped both slots with entire tuple

a2#betweenObjRel(dim->2 canada usa mexico orient->northSouth)
success    % Swapped one slot with entire tuple

a2#betweenObjRel(orient->northSouth canada usa mexico)
success    % Omitted one slot (query is proper part of fact)

a2#betweenObjRel(canada usa mexico orient->northSouth)
success    % Omitted one slot and swapped other slot with entire tuple

a2#betweenObjRel(canada usa mexico)
successs   % Omitted both slots

a2#betweenObjRel(dim->2 orient->northSouth)
success    % Omitted entire tuple

a2#betweenObjRel(orient->northSouth)
success    % Omitted entire tuple and one slot

a2#betweenObjRel()
success    % Omitted entire tuple and both slots

a2#betweenObjRel(dim->2 orient->northSouth usa canada mexico)
fail       % Commuted positional arguments of tuple

a2#betweenObjRel(dim->2 orient->northSouth alaska canada usa mexico)
fail       % Added element to tuple

a2#betweenObjRel(dim->3 orient->northSouth canada usa mexico)
fail       % Different filler for one slot

a2#betweenObjRel(dim->2 orient->northSouth start->1867 canada usa mexico)
fail       % Inserted slot

a2#betweenObjRel(dim->2 orient->northSouth
                 [canada usa mexico] [estonia latvia lithuania])
fail       % Inserted tuple

a2#betweenObjRel(dim->2 orient->northSouth usa mexico)
fail       % Deleted positional argument of tuple

a2#betweenObjRel(usa mexico)
fail       % Deleted positional argument of tuple

a1#betweenObjRel(dim->2 orient->northSouth canada usa mexico)
fail       % Different OID
```

```
betweenObjRel(dim->2 orient->northSouth canada usa mexico)
success     % Omitted OID
```

Apart from the OID-sensitive final two ground queries, all of the above ground queries work the same when omitting the OID specification, "a2#", both from the ground fact and from these queries; hence they also cover Sect. 2.5. The success of the final ground query, without an OID, against the ground fact with an OID is due to objectification to be further discussed in Sect. 6.

The ground atom can also be retrieved by issuing a non-ground query,[21] using non-ground/ground matching, by first 'grounding' the query by consistently substituting all query variables with corresponding ground subterms (remembering these variable bindings for the answer) and then doing retrieval with the ground query as for look-in ground querying above.

Look-in Non-ground Querying: Consider a ground KB k and a non-ground query q. $k \vdash q$ (resp., $k \not\vdash q$) iff there exist (resp., do not exist) a ground fact g in k and a substitution s such that s applied to q gives q' and q' is part of g.

For example, given the above sample KB, the following non-ground queries succeed with the variable bindings shown (for which success is understood, where variables are marked by a "?" prefix) or fail without a variable binding:

```
a2#betweenObjRel(dim->2 orient->northSouth ?X usa mexico)
?X = canada

a2#betweenObjRel(dim->2 orient->northSouth ?X usa ?Z)
?X = canada
?Z = mexico

a2#betweenObjRel(dim->2 orient->northSouth ?X usa ?X)
fail        % No consistent positional-argument substitution possible

a2#betweenObjRel(dim->2 orient->?V canada usa mexico)
?V = northSouth

a2#betweenObjRel(dim->?U orient->?V canada usa mexico)
?U = 2
?V = northSouth

a2#betweenObjRel(dim->?U orient->?U canada usa mexico)
fail        % No consistent slot-filler substitution possible

a2#betweenObjRel(orient->?V canada usa mexico)
?V = northSouth

a2#betweenObjRel(?S->2 orient->northSouth canada usa mexico)
?S = dim    % Slot-name variable bound to slot name
```

---

[21] As usual in Logic Programming, a non-ground query is understood to have existential quantification for all free variables. For basic LP terminology and notions see [13].

```
a2#betweenObjRel(?S->2 ?T->northSouth canada usa mexico)
?S = dim
?T = orient

a2#betweenObjRel(?S->2 ?S->northSouth canada usa mexico)
fail      % No consistent slot-name substitution possible

?I#betweenObjRel(dim->2 orient->northSouth canada usa mexico)
?I = a2   % OID variable bound to OID

?I#betweenObjRel(canada usa mexico)
?I = a2
```

KBs containing non-ground facts are implicit in KBs of rules (specifically, with empty bodies) to be discussed in Sect. 4. As an example, consider a single-fact sample KB containing the following non-ground atom modifying the one from Sect. 2.6, asserted as an *OID-existential fact* stating:
"Every ?M is in an ?O-identified `betweenObjRel` relationship – with dimension = 2 and orientation = north-to-south – of the North Pole, ?M, and the South Pole."[22]

```
Forall ?M (
   Exists ?O ( ?O#betweenObjRel(dim->2 orient->northSouth
                                northPole ?M southPole)   )
            )
```

While the earlier ground fact has an OID constant, a2, the current non-ground fact has an OID variable, ?O, that is existentially quantified in the scope of a universal variable, ?M: For each ?M binding, there is a dependent ?O binding.

This non-ground fact can be retrieved by ground queries as follows, using ground/non-ground matching:

```
a2#betweenObjRel(dim->2 orient->northSouth northPole usa southPole)
fail      % Existential fact does not assert specific OID

a1#betweenObjRel(dim->2 orient->northSouth northPole usa southPole)
fail      % Existential fact does not assert specific OID

?#betweenObjRel(dim->2 orient->northSouth northPole usa southPole)
success

?#betweenObjRel(dim->2 orient->northSouth northPole eu southPole)
success

?#betweenObjRel(dim->2 orient->northSouth northPole usa eu southPole)
fail      % Too many elements in query tuple
```

---

[22] Betweenness with dimension = 2 for geographical entities assumes some projection of the globe to a 2D coordinate system.

```
betweenObjRel(dim->2 orient->northSouth northPole usa southPole)
success
```

The first and second queries, employing respective constants, a2 and a1, in the
OID position, fail since the corresponding Exists variable ?O of the fact does not
need to denote them nor any named constant. In the third and fourth queries,
the anonymous OID variable "?" causes binding-free success because it unifies
with ?O but prevents the creation of a (named-)variable binding.

The non-ground fact can also be retrieved by non-ground queries as follows,
using non-ground/non-ground unification:

```
a2#betweenObjRel(dim->2 orient->northSouth ?X usa southPole)
?X = northPole

a2#betweenObjRel(dim->2 orient->northSouth ?X usa ?Z)
?X = northPole
?Z = southPole

a2#betweenObjRel(dim->2 orient->northSouth ?X usa ?X)
fail      % No consistent positional-argument substitution possible

?I#betweenObjRel(dim->2 orient->northSouth northPole usa southPole)
?I = skolem1(usa)

?I#betweenObjRel(northPole usa southPole)
?I = skolem2(usa)
```

In the fourth query, the OID query variable ?I is successfully bound to a Skolem
function application, skolem1(usa), generated from the Exists by the PSOA-
TransRun system. Similarly, in the fifth query.

4   PSOA Rules for Inferential Querying

PSOA RuleML fact querying can be done interactively by the user, as presented
in Sect. 3, but fact – and rule – querying can also take place in the conditions of
PSOA RuleML rules, as will be discussed in the current section. Using rules, the
user's interactive querying becomes inferential. Rule querying is realized by resolution [13], which employs unification for consistent instantiation – ultimately,
grounding – of a (possibly non-ground) query and the (possibly non-ground)
conclusion of the rule to be applied to it. In PSOA RuleML, after grounding,
the query must be checked to be 'part of' the rule conclusion in the sense defined
in Sect. 3. For the PSOA sublanguage using only single-tuple psoa terms, this
is similar to POSL's [12] unification involving queries that have anonymous rest
slots ("!?"), as implemented in OO jDREW [14][23].

---

[23] http://www.jdrew.org/oojdrew/.

As we have seen, commuting of positional arguments is not supported by fact querying – and it would not make sense for arbitrary pairs of such arguments of relations like betweenObjRel. However, it is possible to use rule definition and querying to selectively specify derivable properties such as the commutativity (symmetry) of certain arguments, e.g. the two outer arguments of betweenObjRel. We define a rule whose derived symmetric tuples are identified by the OID symm(?O), depending, via a function symm, on the orignal tuples, identified by the OID ?O. Following our fact reproduced from Sects. 2.6 and 3, the rule states:

"For every ?Out1, ?In, ?Out2, and ?O, a symm(?O)-identified betweenObjRel relationship – with orientation south-to-north – of ?Out2, ?In, and ?Out1 holds if an ?O-identified betweenObjRel relationship – with orientation north-to-south – of ?Out1, ?In, and ?Out2 holds."

```
a2#betweenObjRel(dim->2 orient->northSouth canada usa mexico)
```

```
Forall ?Out1 ?In ?Out2 ?O (
  symm(?O)#betweenObjRel(orient->southNorth ?Out2 ?In ?Out1) :-
    ?O#betweenObjRel(orient->northSouth ?Out1 ?In ?Out2)
                    )
```

The 'colon-dash' (":-") sign – think of it as an 'if' symbol (a kind of "←") – separates the conclusion from the condition of a rule.

In order to prevent recursive rules, e.g. for commutativity, from repeatedly undoing and redoing their own derivation results, flag-like slots such as the orientation slot come in handy. On backward reasoning for query answering with our above rule, the slot filler will be switched from southNorth in the conclusion to northSouth in the condition, preventing recursive rule application. When this condition is posed as a new query, only our fact will be applicable, terminating rule derivation after one step.

This (non-ground) rule and ground fact can be used for the derivation of ground and non-ground queries as follows (intermediate derivation steps are traced using indentation):

```
symm(a2)#betweenObjRel(dim->2 orient->southNorth mexico usa canada)
fail      % Query is not part of grounded rule conclusion

symm(a2)#betweenObjRel(orient->southNorth mexico usa canada)
  a2#betweenObjRel(orient->northSouth canada usa mexico)
success   % Query is identical to grounded rule conclusion

symm(a2)#betweenObjRel(orient->southNorth mexico usa ?X)
  a2#betweenObjRel(orient->northSouth ?X usa mexico)
?X = canada

?I#betweenObjRel(orient->southNorth mexico usa ?X)
  a2#betweenObjRel(orient->northSouth ?X usa mexico)
?I = symm(a2)
?X = canada
```

```
?I#betweenObjRel(orient->southNorth ?Z usa ?X)
  a2#betweenObjRel(orient->northSouth ?X usa ?Z)
?I = symm(a2)
?X = canada
?Z = mexico

?I#betweenObjRel(orient->southNorth ?X usa ?X)
  a2#betweenObjRel(orient->northSouth ?X usa ?X)
fail      % No consistent positional-argument substitution possible

symm(?J)#betweenObjRel(orient->?V mexico usa canada)
  a2#betweenObjRel(orient->northSouth canada usa mexico)
?J = a2
?V = southNorth
```

Another rule can be used to derive new frames, specifically `GeoUnit` frames. Following our recurring fact, the rule states:
"For every ?Out1, ?In, ?Out2, and ?O, an ?In-identified `GeoUnit` relationship – with northern neighbor ?Out1 and southern neighbor ?Out2 – holds if an ?O-identified `betweenObjRel` relationship – with orientation north-to-south – of ?Out1, ?In, and ?Out2 holds."

```
a2#betweenObjRel(dim->2 orient->northSouth canada usa mexico)

Forall ?Out1 ?In ?Out2 ?O (
  ?In#GeoUnit(neighborNorth->?Out1 neighborSouth->?Out2) :-
    ?O#betweenObjRel(orient->northSouth ?Out1 ?In ?Out2)
                          )
```

This rule and fact can be used for the derivation of ground and non-ground queries as follows (where the final query asks: "Which GeoUnit ?I has Canada as its northern neighbor?"):

```
usa#GeoUnit(neighborNorth->canada neighborSouth->mexico)
  ?O#betweenObjRel(orient->northSouth canada usa mexico)
success   % Query is identical to grounded rule conclusion

usa#GeoUnit(neighborSouth->mexico neighborNorth->canada)
  ?O#betweenObjRel(orient->northSouth canada usa mexico)
success   % Query is equal to grounded rule conclusion

usa#GeoUnit(neighborNorth->canada neighborSouth->?OutX)
  ?O#betweenObjRel(orient->northSouth canada usa ?OutX)
?OutX = mexico

usa#GeoUnit(neighborNorth->canada)
  ?O#betweenObjRel(orient->northSouth canada usa ?Out2)
success   % Query is proper part of grounded rule conclusion

mexico#GeoUnit(neighborNorth->canada)
```

```
  ?O#betweenObjRel(orient->northSouth canada mexico ?Out2)
fail      % OID cannot be proved to be in inner position

?I#GeoUnit(neighborNorth->canada)
  ?O#betweenObjRel(orient->northSouth canada ?I ?Out2)
?I = usa
```

While the first three queries specify both the `neighborNorth` and `neighborSouth` slots (albeit the third uses a free filler variable, `?OutX`), the remaining queries specify only the `neighborNorth` slot. In the subsequent derivation, the omission of the `neighborSouth` slot, hence of a fixed value for its filler, amounts to keeping that filler open as a free variable, `?Out2`.

Let us finally proceed to an *OID-(head-)existential rule*, which can be used to derive new psoa terms, specifically `compassRose` psoa terms. Following our recurring fact and an analogous one, the rule states:
"For every `?Out1`, `?Out2`, `?Out3`, `?Out4`, `?In`, `?O1`, and `?O2`, an existentially quantified `?O`-identified `compassRose` relationship – with western, northern, eastern, and southern values `?Out1`, `?Out2`, `?Out3`, and `?Out4`, respectively – holds of `?In` if a conjunction of an `?O1`-identified `betweenObjRel` relationship – with orientation north-to-south – of `?Out1`, `?In`, and `?Out2` holds, and an `?O2`-identified `betweenObjRel` relationship – with orientation west-to-east – of `?Out3`, `?In`, and `?Out4` holds."

```
a2#betweenObjRel(dim->2 orient->northSouth canada usa mexico)
a3#betweenObjRel(dim->2 orient->westEast pacific usa atlantic)

Forall ?Out1 ?Out2 ?Out3 ?Out4 ?In ?O1 ?O2 (
  Exists ?O (
    ?O#compassRose(west->?Out3 north->?Out1 east->?Out4 south->?Out2 ?In)
        )                                                        :-
      And(?O1#betweenObjRel(orient->northSouth ?Out1 ?In ?Out2)
          ?O2#betweenObjRel(orient->westEast   ?Out3 ?In ?Out4))
                            )
```

The rule conclusion uses four slots representing the cardinal compass directions, `?Out1` through `?Out4`, and a single 'positional' argument, `?In`, representing the rose center. The rule condition uses an explicit `And` conjunction for `?In`-intersecting `northSouth`- and `westEast`-oriented `betweenObjRel` relationship queries. While the first rule of this section employs a user-provided (Skolem-like) function, `symm`, for the conclusion OID, the current rule wraps the entire conclusion (head) into an existential (`Exists`) scope for the OID variable `?O`. However, our PSOATransRun implementation of this (head-)existential rule transforms the `Exists` into a system-provided Skolem function, depending on the enclosing universal variables including the condition OIDs `?O1` and `?O2`.

This rule and the two facts can be used for the derivation of ground and non-ground queries as follows:

```
a4#compassRose(west->pacific north->canada east->atlantic south->mexico usa)
fail      % Existential rule does not assert specific OID
```

```
?#compassRose(west->pacific north->canada east->atlantic south->mexico usa)
   And(a2#betweenObjRel(orient->northSouth canada  usa mexico)
        a3#betweenObjRel(orient->westEast   pacific usa atlantic))
success    % Left-slot normal query is identical to grounded rule conclusion

?#compassRose(usa west->pacific north->canada east->atlantic south->mexico)
   And(a2#betweenObjRel(orient->northSouth canada  usa mexico)
        a3#betweenObjRel(orient->westEast   pacific usa atlantic))
success    % Right-slot normal query is equal to grounded rule conclusion

?#compassRose(south->mexico west->pacific)
   And(a2#betweenObjRel(orient->northSouth ?Out1   ?In mexico)
        a3#betweenObjRel(orient->westEast   pacific ?In ?Out4))
success    % Query is proper part of grounded rule conclusion

?I#compassRose(west->pacific north->canada east->atlantic south->mexico usa)
   And(a2#betweenObjRel(orient->northSouth canada  usa mexico)
        a3#betweenObjRel(orient->westEast   pacific usa atlantic))
?I = skolem3(canada mexico pacific atlantic usa a2 a3)

?I#compassRose(west->?W north->?N east->?E south->?S ?C)
   And(a2#betweenObjRel(orient->northSouth ?N ?C ?S)
        a3#betweenObjRel(orient->westEast   ?W ?C ?E))
?I = skolem4(canada mexico pacific atlantic usa a2 a3)
?W = pacific
?N = canada
?E = atlantic
?S = mexico
?C = usa
```

The first query, while employing a new constant, a4, in the OID position, fails since the corresponding Exists variable ?O of the rule does not need to denote it nor any named constant. In the second to fourth queries, the anonymous OID variable "?" causes binding-free success because it unifies with ?O but prevents the creation of a (named-)variable binding. In the fifth query, the OID query variable ?I is successfully bound to a Skolem function application, skolem3(... a2 a3), generated from the Exists by the PSOATransRun system. Similarly, in the sixth query, which is maximally non-ground, except for its fixed compassRose relation/class.

5   SQL-PSOA-SPARQL Interoperation Use Case

Suppose you are working on a project using SQL queries over relational data and then proceeding to SPARQL queries over graph data to be used as a metadata repository. Or, vice versa, on a project complementing SPARQL with SQL for querying an evolving mass-data store. Or, on a project using SQL and SPARQL from the beginning. In all of these projects, object-relational interoperability issues may arise.

This section explains a use case on bidirectional SQL-PSOA-SPARQL transformation (schema/ontology mapping) for interoperability. The pivotal transformation between the relational and object-centered paradigms is expressed in a language-internal manner within PSOA RuleML itself.

The use case represents addresses as (flat) relational facts and as – subaddress-containing – (nested) object-centered facts, as shown for the Seminaris address below.[24] The OID-conclusion direction of implication from the relational to the object-centered (frame) paradigm is given as the first rule below; the OID-condition direction from the object-centered (frame) to the relational paradigm is given as the second rule:

```
addressRel("Seminaris" "Takustr. 39" "14195 Berlin") % relational fact

r1#addressObj(name->"Seminaris"                       % object-centered fact
              place->r2#placeObj(street->"Takustr. 39"
                                 town->"14195 Berlin"))

Forall ?Name ?Street ?Town (                          % OID-conclusion rule
  Exists ?O1 ?O2 ( ?O1#addressObj(name->?Name
                                  place->?O2#placeObj(street->?Street
                                                      town->?Town)) )   :-
    addressRel(?Name ?Street ?Town)
                                 )

Forall ?Name ?Street ?Town ?O1 ?O2 (                  % OID-condition rule
    addressRel(?Name ?Street ?Town)    :-
      ?O1#addressObj(name->?Name
                     place->?O2#placeObj(street->?Street
                                         town->?Town))
                                 )
```

While these rules define the most cross-paradigmatic cases, versions for the intermediate psoa terms could also be defined, e.g. for shelves and pairships.

Besides directly retrieving the relational fact, the OID-condition rule and the object-centered fact can be used for the derivation of relational queries as follows (corresponding to the RDF-to-RDB data mapping direction [16]):

```
addressRel("Seminaris" ?S "14195 Berlin")

  ?O1#addressObj(name->"Seminaris"
                 place->?O2#placeObj(street->?S
                                     town->"14195 Berlin"))

?S = "Takustr. 39"
```

Besides directly retrieving the object-centered fact, the OID-conclusion rule and the relational fact can be used for the derivation of object-centered queries as follows (corresponding to the RDB-to-RDF data mapping direction [17]):

---

[24] Earlier (flat and nested) positional versions have been used to explain XML-to-XML transformation (http://www.cs.unb.ca/~boley/cs6795swt/cs6795swt-XML.pdf). Later, a similar use case was employed to demonstrate SPINMap for RDF-to-RDF transformation [15].

```
?O1#addressObj(name->"Seminaris"
                place->?O2#placeObj(street->?S
                                    town->"14195 Berlin"))

  addressRel("Seminaris" ?S "14195 Berlin")

?O1 = skolem5("Seminaris" "Takustr. 39" "14195 Berlin")
?O2 = skolem6("Seminaris" "Takustr. 39" "14195 Berlin")
?S = "Takustr. 39"
```

If the object-centered PSOA RuleML fact is replaced by corresponding RDF triple facts, the OID-condition PSOA RuleML rule can also be used for the language-internal transformation of SQL-like queries to SPARQL-like queries as follows ('neutral' column headings Col$i$, with $1 \leq i \leq 3$, are used to avoid providing slot-name-like information, thus keeping SQL purely positional):[25]

```
EXISTS                                                          -- SQL
 (SELECT * FROM addressRel
  WHERE Col1='Seminaris' AND Col2='Wikingerufer 7' AND Col3='14195 Berlin')

  addressRel("Seminaris" "Wikingerufer 7" "14195 Berlin")        % PSOA

  ?O1#addressObj(name->"Seminaris"                               % PSOA
                place->?O2#placeObj(street->"Wikingerufer 7"
                                    town->"14195 Berlin"))

  ASK {?O1 rdf:type addressObj. ?O1 name "Seminaris".            # SPARQL
                        ?O1 place ?O2.
        ?O2 rdf:type placeObj. ?O2 street "Wikingerufer 7".
                        ?O2 town "14195 Berlin".}

fail      % Wrong street


EXISTS                                                          -- SQL
 (SELECT * FROM addressRel
  WHERE Col1='Seminaris' AND Col2='Takustr. 39' AND Col3='14195 Berlin')

  addressRel("Seminaris" "Takustr. 39" "14195 Berlin")           % PSOA

  ?O1#addressObj(name->"Seminaris"                               % PSOA
                place->?O2#placeObj(street->"Takustr. 39"
                                    town->"14195 Berlin"))

  ASK {?O1 rdf:type addressObj. ?O1 name "Seminaris".            # SPARQL
                        ?O1 place ?O2.
```

---

[25] Alternatively, given column headings like Name, Street, and Town, the input conversion for PSOA could skip the relationship addressRel("Seminaris" "Wikingerufer 7" "14195 Berlin"), but generate a pairship addressRel(name->"Seminaris" street->"Wikingerufer 7" town->"14195 Berlin"), already closer to the level of frames and SPARQL.

```
           ?02 rdf:type placeObj. ?02 street "Takustr. 39".
                              ?02 town "14195 Berlin".}
```

```
success
```

```
SELECT * FROM addressRel                                    -- SQL
WHERE Col1='Seminaris'
```

```
  addressRel("Seminaris" ?S ?T)                             % PSOA
```

```
  ?01#addressObj(name->"Seminaris"                          % PSOA
              place->?02#placeObj(street->?S
                                  town->?T))
```

```
  SELECT ?S ?T                                              # SPARQL
  WHERE {?01 rdf:type addressObj. ?01 name "Seminaris".
                                  ?01 place ?02.
          ?02 rdf:type placeObj. ?02 street ?S.
                                  ?02 town ?T.}
```

```
?S = "Takustr. 39"
?T = "14195 Berlin"
```

The paradigm-crossing translation step is thus done by the OID-condition rule completely within PSOA RuleML, starting at SQL queries "lifted" to PSOA and ending at SPARQL queries "dropped" from PSOA.[26] Bridging the paradigm chasm from relations to objects constitutes one direction of PSOA RuleML's interoperation capability.

In the other direction, if the relational PSOA RuleML fact is replaced by a corresponding SQL table row, the OID-conclusion PSOA RuleML rule can be used for the language-internal transformation of SPARQL-like queries to SQL-like queries as follows:

```
ASK {?01 rdf:type addressObj. ?01 name "Seminaris".        # SPARQL
                              ?01 place ?02.
        ?02 rdf:type placeObj. ?02 street "Wikingerufer 7".
                              ?02 town "14195 Berlin".}
```

```
  ?01#addressObj(name->"Seminaris"                          % PSOA
              place->?02#placeObj(street->"Wikingerufer 7"
                                  town->"14195 Berlin"))
```

```
  addressRel("Seminaris" "Wikingerufer 7" "14195 Berlin")   % PSOA
```

```
EXISTS                                                      -- SQL
(SELECT * FROM addressRel
  WHERE Col1='Seminaris' AND Col2='Wikingerufer 7' AND Col3='14195 Berlin')
```

---

[26] The "lift" and "drop" terminology for conversions at the input and output interfaces has been introduced in http://yosemiteproject.org, and is related to the "lifting" and "lowering" terminology of http://www.w3.org/TR/sawsdl/#schemaMapping.

```
fail      % Wrong street
```

```
ASK {?O1 rdf:type addressObj. ?O1 name "Seminaris".          # SPARQL
                      ?O1 place ?O2.
    ?O2 rdf:type placeObj. ?O2 street "Takustr. 39".
                      ?O2 town "14195 Berlin".}
```

```
  ?O1#addressObj(name->"Seminaris"                           % PSOA
              place->?O2#placeObj(street->"Takustr. 39"
                                  town->"14195 Berlin"))
```

```
  addressRel("Seminaris" "Takustr. 39" "14195 Berlin")       % PSOA
```

```
EXISTS                                                       -- SQL
  (SELECT * FROM addressRel
   WHERE Col1='Seminaris' AND Col2='Takustr. 39' AND Col3='14195 Berlin')
```

```
success
```

```
SELECT ?S ?T                                                 # SPARQL
WHERE {?O1 rdf:type addressObj. ?O1 name "Seminaris".
                      ?O1 place ?O2.
    ?O2 rdf:type placeObj. ?O2 street ?S.
                      ?O2 town ?T.}
```

```
  ?O1#addressObj(name->"Seminaris"                           % PSOA
              place->?O2#placeObj(street->?S
                                  town->?T))
```

```
  addressRel("Seminaris" ?S ?T)                              % PSOA
  SELECT * FROM addressRel                                   -- SQL
  WHERE Col1='Seminaris'
```

```
?S = "Takustr. 39"
?T = "14195 Berlin"
```

The reach of the PSOA-internal transformation can be increased at the
PSOA/SPARQL interfaces. First, 'unnested' PSOA intermediaries are introduced as follows, where the placeObj frame is extracted into a conjunction,
leaving behind a copy of its OID variable ?O2:

```
And(?O1#addressObj(name->"Seminaris"
                   place->?O2)
    ?O2#placeObj(street->?S
                 town->?T))
```

These are then used to split the above 'unnesting' PSOA-to-SPARQL transformations and 'nesting' SPARQL-to-PSOA transformations into unnesting/nest-
ing PSOA-to-PSOA transformations and clerical PSOA/SPARQL conversions.

Besides for interoperation, the transformation into unnested sublanguages can also be used for the implementation of nested PSOA RuleML.

6 PSOA RuleML Syntax

The (RIF-like) presentation and (RuleML/XML) serialization syntaxes of PSOA RuleML will be discussed in this section. First, the objectification of the OID-less subset of (atomic and rule) psoa formulas in presentation syntax is introduced. Second, variants of the OID-containing superset of (atomic) psoa formulas in presentation syntax are illustrated, while details (e.g., on the variety of constants such as document-local vs. Web-IRI-global) are specified in [3]. Third, versions of PSOA RuleML serialization syntax are considered.

Object Identifier Assumption: An atomic formula (predicate application) without an OID is assumed to be a shorthand for this formula with an implicit OID, which is made syntactically explicit by objectification (see below) before the atomic formula is endowed with semantics (cf. Sect. 7). Since RIF does not make the OID assumption, it has to separately specify the semantics of its OID-less subset, mainly for "named-argument terms" (pairships).

Objectification Algorithm: This may be seen as mapping the three rows of the psoa table in Sect. 1 to their 2nd ("object-centered") column. Basically, while a ground fact can be given a fixed OID (that the user neglected to provide), a non-ground fact or rule conclusion needs an OID for each grounding.

These formulas, when OID-less, are *objectified* by syntactic transformation: *The OID of a ground fact is a new constant generated by the 'new local constant' (a stand-alone "_", corresponding to "_#" in [18]), where each occurrence of "_" denotes a distinct name, not occurring elsewhere (i.e., a Skolem constant); the OID of a non-ground fact or of an atomic formula in a rule conclusion, $f(...)$, is a new, existentially scoped variable $?i$, resulting in* **Exists** $?i$ $(?i\#f(...))$; *the OID of any other atomic formula, including in a rule condition (also usable as a query), is a new variable generated by the 'anonymous variable' (a standalone "?").*

In our PSOATransRun implementation (cf. Sect. 8), the objectification algorithm is realized as an ANTLR tree walker. Objectification transforms the three uses of psoa facts in Sects. 2.1, 2.3, and 2.5 to, respectively, the three uses in Sects. 2.2, 2.4, and 2.6.

For example, the relational fact `betweenRel(pacific canada atlantic)` in Sect. 2.1 is objectified to a shelf version like the $a1$-identified shelf fact in Sect. 2.2, `_#betweenRel(pacific canada atlantic)`, and – if `_1` is the first new constant from `_1, _2, ...`– to `_1#betweenRel(pacific canada atlantic)`. The query `betweenRel(?X canada ?Z)` is syntactically transformed to the query `?#betweenRel(?X canada ?Z)`, i.e. – if `?1` is the first new variable in `?1, ?2, ...`– to `?1#betweenRel(?X canada ?Z)`. Posed against the fact, it succeeds, with variable bindings `?1 = _1`, `?X = pacific`, and `?Z = atlantic`.

For the general case of *(arbitrary) psoa terms* in [3], k slots and m tuples are permitted (k $\geq$ 0, m $\geq$ 0), with tuple i having length n_i ($1 \leq i \leq$ m, $n_i \geq 0$), where we use both the left-slot and right-slot normal forms of Sect. 2.5 (after objectification):

left-slot $\texttt{o\#f(p_1\text{->}v_1 \ldots p_k\text{->}v_k \ [t_{1,1} \ldots t_{1,n_1}] \ldots [t_{m,1} \ldots t_{m,n_m}])}$
right-slot $\texttt{o\#f([t_{1,1} \ldots t_{1,n_1}] \ldots [t_{m,1} \ldots t_{m,n_m}] \ p_1\text{->}v_1 \ldots p_k\text{->}v_k)}$

We distinguish three cases (explained here for the left-slot normal form):

m > 1 For *multi-tuple psoa terms*, square brackets are necessary (see above).
m = 1 For *single-tuple psoa terms*, focused in this paper, square brackets can be omitted (see `Positional+Slotted` and `Positional` below).
m = 0 For *tuple-less psoa terms*, frames arise (see `Slotted` and `Member` below).

Color coding shows syntactic variants for the cases m = 1 and k = m = 0 (single-tuple brackets and zero-argument parentheses are optional):

```
Positional+Slotted: o#f(p₁->v₁ ... pₖ->vₖ  [t₁ ... tₙ])
Positional:         o#f(                    [t₁ ... tₙ])
Slotted:            o#f(p₁->v₁ ... pₖ->vₖ)
Member:             o#f()
```

An EBNF Grammar for the (RIF-like) presentation syntax of PSOA RuleML can be found in [3], Sect. 2.5.

Regarding the XML serialization syntax, PSOA RuleML is integrated with the earlier RuleML family as follows. We start with a pure PSOA version of the Hornlog RuleML sublanguage of the Deliberation RuleML subfamily of RuleML. We then proceed to a PSOA version extended with "positional rests" from Hornlog RuleML. We finally give a Hornlog RuleML version extended with multiple tuples from PSOA RuleML. Other sublanguages of Deliberation RuleML can also be complemented by pure and extended PSOA versions and be given multiple tuples. Similarly, for the Reaction RuleML subfamily of RuleML. The schema specification of PSOA RuleML/XML in MYNG can reflect these versions in a modular fashion.

The **pure PSOA** version of a multi-tuple psoa atom augments the content of the RuleML `<Atom>` node element[27] with `<Tuple>` node elements, different from RuleML's `<Plex>` and RIF's `<List>` elements. The above left-slot normal form results in the following XML serialization, where the primed meta-variables p_i', v_i', and $t_{i,j}'$ indicate recursive XML serializations of their above presentation-syntax versions (the `style` attribute uses the value `"distribution"` to specify built-in slotribution and tupribution):

```
<Atom style="distribution">
  <oid><Ind>o</Ind></oid><op><Rel>f</Rel></op>
  <slot>p′₁ v′₁</slot> ... <slot>p′ₖ v′ₖ</slot>
  <Tuple>t′₁,₁ ... t′₁,ₙ₁</Tuple> ... <Tuple>t′ₘ,₁ ... t′ₘ,ₙₘ</Tuple>
</Atom>
```

---

[27] For an example-based introduction to the basic tags of Deliberation RuleML see http://ruleml.org/papers/Primer.

The **extended PSOA** version refines the above serialization by using an optional `<repo>` edge element from Hornlog RuleML (in POSL-like presentation syntax corresponding to a "|" infix) to specify a "positional rest" *within* a tuple (on the level of the entire atom, the `style` attribute still specifies `"distribution"`):

```
<Atom style="distribution">
  <oid><Ind>o</Ind></oid><op><Rel>f</Rel></op>
  <slot>p'₁ v'₁</slot>...<slot>p'ₖ v'ₖ</slot>
  <Tuple>t'₁,₁ ... t'₁,ₙ₁<repo>rp'₁</repo></Tuple>...
                  <Tuple>t'ₘ,₁ ... t'ₘ,ₙₘ<repo>rp'ₘ</repo></Tuple>
</Atom>
```

Conversely, Hornlog RuleML can be generalized to **multiple tuples** from PSOA RuleML without specifying PSOA's built-in tupribution, instead using a new optional `<retu>` edge to specify the "rest of tuples", i.e. *further* tuples. Combined with Hornlog RuleML's optional `<resl>` edge (in POSL-like presentation syntax corresponding to a "!" infix) for the "rest of slots", i.e. for *further* slots – hence without specifying built-in slotribution either – the following XML serialization is obtained (as in Hornlog RuleML, no `style` attribute is required):

```
<Atom>
  <oid><Ind>o</Ind></oid><op><Rel>f</Rel></op>
  <slot>p'₁ v'₁</slot>...<slot>p'ₖ v'ₖ</slot>
  <resl>rs'</resl>
  <Tuple>t'₁,₁ ... t'₁,ₙ₁<repo>rp'₁</repo></Tuple>...
                  <Tuple>t'ₘ,₁ ... t'ₘ,ₙₘ<repo>rp'ₘ</repo></Tuple>
  <retu>rt'</retu>
</Atom>
```

When the three above serializations are re-specialized to a single-tuple psoa atom (i.e., for m = 1), the `<Tuple>` ... `</Tuple>` wrapper can be just omitted.

7 PSOA RuleML Semantics

The traces given in Sects. 3, 4, and 5 exemplify PSOA RuleML's proof-theoretic semantics using backward reasoning directly for the PSOA sources (queries, facts, and rules). PSOA RuleML's model-theoretic semantics also involves transformations on the sources, either as a preparatory step (objectification) or as restrictions on truth valuation (slotribution and tupribution).

In the following, key parts of the semantics definitions from [3] are presented for **objectified multi-tuple psoa terms in right-slot normal form**.

Truth valuation of PSOA RuleML formulas is defined as a mapping $TVal_{\mathcal{I}}$ in two steps: 1. A mapping I generically bundles various mappings from the semantic structure, $\mathcal{I}$; I maps a formula to an element of the domain D. 2. A mapping I_{truth} takes such a domain element to the set of truth values, TV.

Definition 4, case 3, as part of a **semantic structure**, introduces the total mapping I_{psoa}:

I_{psoa} maps D to total functions that have the general form $D_{ind} \times$ SetOfFiniteBags(D^*_{ind}) $\times$ SetOfFiniteBags($D_{ind} \times D_{ind}$) $\to D$. This mapping interprets psoa terms, uniformly combining positional, slotted, and frame terms, as well as class memberships. An argument d $\in D$ of I_{psoa} uniformly represents the function or predicate symbol of positional terms and slotted terms, and the object class of frame terms, as well as the class of memberships. An element o $\in D_{ind}$ of the resulting total functions represents an object of class d, which is described with two bags.

- A finite bag of finite tuples $\{<t_{1,1}, ..., t_{1,n_1}>, ..., <t_{m,1}, ..., t_{m,n_m}>\}$ $\in$ SetOfFiniteBags(D^*_{ind}), possibly empty, represents positional information. Here D^*_{ind} is the set of all finite tuples over the domain D_{ind}.
- A finite bag of attribute-value pairs $\{<a1,v1>, ..., <ak,vk>\}$ $\in$ SetOfFiniteBags($D_{ind} \times D_{ind}$), possibly empty, represents slotted information.

The generic recursive mapping I is defined from terms to their subterms and ultimately to D, for the case of psoa terms using I_{psoa}:

I(o#f([$t_{1,1}$ ... t_{1,n_1}] ... [$t_{m,1}$ ... t_{m,n_m}] a_1->v_1 ... a_k->v_k)) =
$I_{psoa}(I(f))(I(o)$,
$\quad \{<I(t_{1,1}), ..., I(t_{1,n_1})>, ..., <I(t_{m,1}), ..., I(t_{m,n_m})>\}$,
$\quad \{<I(a_1), I(v_1)>, ..., <I(a_k), I(v_k)>\})$

When, as in the below Definition 5, case 3, I is applied to a psoa term, its total function is obtained from I_{psoa} applied to the recursively interpreted class argument f. The application of the resulting total function to the recursively interpreted other parts of a psoa term denotes the term's interpretation in term's interpretation in D. PSOA RuleML's use of the class f, rather than the OID o, for the I_{psoa} argument is justified by the class being always user-controlled for psoa terms, even if 'defaulted' to the 'catch-all' total function obtained from I_{psoa} applied to the interpretation $\top$ of the root class Top. On the other hand, the OID o – which in RIF-BLD is used for the I_{frame} argument – need not be user-controlled in PSOA but can be system-generated via objectification, e.g. as an existential variable or a (Skolem) constant, so is not suited to obtain the total function for a psoa term.

Definition 5, cases 3 and 8, recursively define truth valuation $TVal_{\mathcal{I}}$ for psoa formulas and rule implications, based on the above I and on a mapping I_{truth} from D to TV:

Psoa formula:
$TVal_{\mathcal{I}}$(o#f([$t_{1,1}$ ... t_{1,n_1}] ... [$t_{m,1}$ ... t_{m,n_m}] a_1->v_1 ... a_k->v_k)) =
$I_{truth}(I$(o#f([$t_{1,1}$ ... t_{1,n_1}] ... [$t_{m,1}$...t_{m,n_m}] a_1->v_1 ... a_k->v_k))).

Since the formula consists of an object-typing membership, a bag of tuples representing a conjunction of all the object-centered tuples (*tupribution*), and a bag of slots representing a conjunction of all the object-centered slots (*slotribution*), the following restriction is used, where m $\geq$ 0 and k $\geq$ 0:

– $TVal_{\mathcal{I}}(\text{o\#f}([\text{t}_{1,1}...\text{t}_{1,n_1}]...[\text{t}_{m,1}...\text{t}_{m,n_m}]\ \text{a}_1\text{->v}_1...\ \text{a}_k\text{->v}_k)) = \text{t}$
if and only if
$TVal_{\mathcal{I}}(\text{o\#f}) =$
$TVal_{\mathcal{I}}(\text{o\#Top}([\text{t}_{1,1}...\text{t}_{1,n_1}])) = ... = TVal_{\mathcal{I}}(\text{o\#Top}([\text{t}_{m,1}...\text{t}_{m,n_m}])) =$
$TVal_{\mathcal{I}}(\text{o\#Top}(\text{a}_1\text{->v}_1)) = ... = TVal_{\mathcal{I}}(\text{o\#Top}(\text{a}_k\text{->v}_k)) =$
t.

Observe that on the right-hand side of the "if and only if" there are $1+m+k$ subformulas splitting the left-hand side into an object membership, m object-centered positional formulas, each associating the object with a tuple, and k object-centered slotted formulas, i.e. 'triples', each associating the object with an attribute-value pair. All parts on both sides of the "if and only if" are centered on the object o, which connects the subformulas on the right-hand side (the first subformula providing the o-member class f, the remaining $m+k$ ones using the root class Top).

For the root class, Top, and all $\text{o} \in D$, $TVal_{\mathcal{I}}(\text{o\#Top}) = \text{t}$.

To ensure that all members of a subclass are also members of its superclasses, i.e., o#f and f##g imply o#g, the following restriction is imposed:

– For all o, f, g $\in$ D, if $TVal_{\mathcal{I}}(\text{o\#f}) = TVal_{\mathcal{I}}(\text{f\#\#g}) = \text{t}$ then $TVal_{\mathcal{I}}(\text{o\#g}) = \text{t}$.

Rule implication:

– $TVal_{\mathcal{I}}(conclusion :\text{-} condition) = \text{t}$, if either $TVal_{\mathcal{I}}(conclusion) = \text{t}$ or $TVal_{\mathcal{I}}(condition) = \text{f}$.
– $TVal_{\mathcal{I}}(conclusion :\text{-} condition) = \text{f}$ otherwise.

To exemplify the transformations, let us reconsider the GeoUnit KB of Sect. 4, focussing on the rule. Objectification acts as an identity transformation on this input rule, since the psoa atoms in both its condition and conclusion already have OIDs (two different variables, ?O and ?In). Slotribution and tupribution, however, transform the rule such that both its condition and conclusion become a conjunction linked by their OID variable. At that point, the psoa atoms have become minimal (three single-slot frames and one single-tuple shelf), so repeated slotribution and tupribution act as identity transformations on that output rule, which – also insensitive to objectification – is a fixpoint for these transformations. Adding a 'centralization' back arrow for the inverse of slotribution/tupribution, we obtain a bidirectional transformation scheme:

```
a2#betweenObjRel(dim->2 orient->northSouth canada usa mexico)
```

```
Forall ?Out1 ?In ?Out2 ?O (
  ?In#GeoUnit(neighborNorth->?Out1 neighborSouth->?Out2)  :-
    ?O#betweenObjRel(orient->northSouth ?Out1 ?In ?Out2)
                       )
```

$$\begin{array}{c}\text{slotribution/tupribution}\\ \rightleftarrows \\ \text{centralization}\end{array}$$

```
And(a2#betweenObjRel
    a2#Top(dim->2)
    a2#Top(orient->northSouth)
    a2#Top(canada usa mexico))

Forall ?Out1 ?In ?Out2 ?O (
  And(?In#GeoUnit
      ?In#Top(neighborNorth->?Out1)
      ?In#Top(neighborSouth->?Out2)) :-
    And(?O#betweenObjRel
        ?O#Top(orient->northSouth)
        ?O#Top(?Out1 ?In ?Out2))
                      )
```

While slotribution and tupribution of psoa terms is built into the semantics, namely into the above Definition 5, case 3, these transformations can also be performed statically, as pre-processing steps.

8 PSOA RuleML Implementation

In order to support reasoning in PSOA RuleML, we have implemented PSOA-TransRun as an open-source framework system, generally referred to as PSOA-TransRun[*translation, runtime*], with a pair of subsystems plugged in as parameters [3,19,20].[28] The *translation* subsystem is a chain of translators mapping a KB and queries from PSOA RuleML to an intermediate language. The *runtime* subsystem executes KB queries in the intermediate language and extracts the results. Our focus has been on translators, reusing the targeted runtime systems as 'black boxes'. For the intermediate languages we have chosen the first-order subset, TPTP-FOF, of TPTP [21][29] and the Horn-logic subset of ISO Prolog [22]. Since these are also standard languages, their translation subsystems of PSOATransRun serve both for PSOA RuleML implementation and interoperation [20].

The chain targeting TPTP requires fewer translation steps since TPTP systems, being first-order-logic provers, directly accommodate the extra expressivity of PSOA (particularly, head existentials introduced by objectification). The chain targeting ISO Prolog requires more translation steps since ISO Prolog has the lower expressivity of Horn logic (particularly, requiring head existentials to be translated to Skolem function applications). Both translator chains start with parsing PSOA RuleML's (RIF-like) presentation syntax into Abstract Syntax Trees (ASTs). They then perform their transformation steps on AST representations of the PSOA sources, using slotribution/tupribution-introduced 'primitive' PSOA RuleML constructs, namely membership terms, slot terms, and tuple terms. Finally, they map the finished AST representations to TPTP

---

[28] http://wiki.ruleml.org/index.php/PSOA_RuleML#Implementation.

[29] TPTP-FOF is also targeted by http://wiki.ruleml.org/index.php/TPTP_RuleML.

or ISO Prolog presentation syntax as the intermediate languages – over distinguished predicates `memterm`, `sloterm`, and `tupterm` defined by TPTP or Prolog clauses – to be executed by the respective runtime systems. The translators are written in Java 1.6 and ANTLR v3[30].

The following subsections will survey our two implemented PSOATransRun instantiations, the parameterized PSOATransRun[PSOA2TPTP, VampirePrime] and PSOATransRun[PSOA2Prolog, XSBProlog].

We have also implemented the PSOA RuleML API [23][31], which uses JAXB to parse PSOA RuleML/XML syntax into abstract syntax objects, and translates these into PSOA RuleML's RIF-like presentation syntax.

8.1 With PSOA2TPTP to VampirePrime

The PSOATransRun[PSOA2TPTP, VampirePrime] instantiation [19][32], realized by Gen Zou and Reuben Peter-Paul with guidance from the author and Alexandre Riazanov, combines the PSOA2TPTP translator and the VampirePrime runtime system. The runtime system consists of the C++-implemented VampirePrime, accessed through Java.

PSOA2TPTP performs objectification (cf. Sect. 6) as well as slotribution and tupribution (cf. Sect. 7). PSOA2TPTP then maps the transformation result to TPTP.

VampirePrime[33] is an open-source first-order reasoner. KBs and queries in the intermediate TPTP language can also be run on other TPTP systems that allow extracting answers (variable bindings) from successful results.

This PSOA2TPTP instantiation is available online[34] for interactive exploration, with documentation in the above-linked RuleML Wiki page. The sample PSOA KB textbox, pre-filled by the system, shows the easy transcription of our (RIF-like) presentation-syntax examples into executable PSOA RuleML: According to the EBNF referenced in Sect. 6, the PSOA syntax is completed by a `Document`/`Group` wrapper for KBs and the "_" prefix for local constants.

8.2 With PSOA2Prolog to XSB Prolog

The PSOATransRun[PSOA2Prolog, XSBProlog] instantiation [20][35], realized by Gen Zou with guidance from the author, combines the PSOA2Prolog translator and the XSB Prolog runtime system. The runtime system consists of the C++-implemented XSB Prolog, accessed via a Java API[36].

---

[30] http://www.antlr.org.
[31] https://github.com/sadnanalmanir/PSOARuleML-API.
[32] http://psoa2tptp.googlecode.com.
[33] http://riazanov.webs.com/software.htm.
[34] http://psoa-ruleml.rhcloud.com.
[35] http://psoa.ruleml.org/transrun/0.7/local/.
[36] http://interprolog.com.

PSOA2Prolog augments the translation chain of PSOA2TPTP in Sect. 8.1 and performs a different target mapping. PSOA2Prolog is composed of a source-to-source normalizer followed by a mapper to a pure Prolog (Horn logic) subset of the ISO Prolog subset of XSB Prolog. The normalizer is composed of five transformation layers, namely objectification, Skolemization, slotribution/tupribution, flattening, as well as rule splitting. Each layer is a self-contained component that can be reused for processing PSOA KBs in other applications. The mapper performs a recursive transformation from the normalization result to Prolog clauses.

XSB Prolog[37] is a fast Prolog engine, which we use for processing a pure ISO Prolog subset. While this ISO Prolog subset can also be run on other Prolog engines, XSB Prolog is targeted because it enables tabling, supporting both termination and efficiency. XSB Prolog executes queries over KBs in the intermediate Prolog language, and the PSOATransRun framework system performs answer extraction.

9   Conclusions

The integrated object-relational data and rules of PSOA RuleML enable a novel approach to semantic modeling and analysis based on positional-slotted, object-applicative terms. PSOA RuleML's data model visualized in Grailog provides the logical foundation and visual intuition via the psoa-table systematics of six uses of psoa atoms in queries and facts as well as conditions and conclusions of rules. PSOA RuleML allows direct (look-in and inferential) querying over heterogeneous data sets. Moreover, PSOA RuleML serves as an intermediate language for bidirectional query transformation, e.g. between SQL and SPARQL. The syntax and semantics capture the essence of PSOA RuleML's object-relational integration. Two implemented open-source PSOA-TransRun instantiations, one also usable online, allow rapid PSOA RuleML prototyping. Besides the PSOA RuleML test cases on the RuleML Wiki, there are PSOA RuleML use cases such as MusicAlbumKB and GeospatialRules. The latter started with a Datalog$^+$ rulebase for the Region Connection Calculus (RCC) [10] and is being expanded into a Hornlog$^+$-like rulebase over psoa-generalized RCC atoms. Future PSOA RuleML applications are envisioned for data querying and interchange in the domains of biomedicine, finance, and social media.

Acknowledgements. Many thanks go to Gen Zou for helpful discussions on multiple drafts of this paper and for spearheading the PSOATransRun implementation. I want to thank Tara Athan, Sadnan Al Manir, Alexandre Riazanov, and Robert Kirby for reviewing earlier partial versions. I extend my thanks to Michael Genesereth, Sudhir Agarwal, Abhijeet Mohapatra, and Eric Kao for comments on a PSOA RuleML presentation in the Computational Logic Seminar, and to Michael Genesereth and the entire Stanford Logic Group for hosting my research stay. My thankfulness goes to Richard

---

[37] http://xsb.sourceforge.net.

Waldinger for comments at various occasions, and for hosting my recent SRI visits. The 11th Reasoning Web Summer School (RW 2015) reviewer and organizers are thanked for early feedback and for running this event. NSERC is thanked for its support through Discovery Grants.

References

1. Kifer, M., Lausen, G., Wu, J.: Logical foundations of object-oriented and frame-based languages. J. ACM **42**(4), 741–843 (1995)
2. Boley, H., Kifer, M.: RIF Basic Logic Dialect (2nd edn), February 2013 W3C Recommendation. http://www.w3.org/TR/rif-bld
3. Boley, H.: A RIF-Style Semantics for RuleML-Integrated Positional-Slotted, Object-Applicative Rules. In: Bassiliades, N., Governatori, G., Paschke, A. (eds.) RuleML 2011 - Europe. LNCS, vol. 6826, pp. 194–211. Springer, Heidelberg (2011)
4. Boley, H.: Grailog 1.0: Graph-Logic Visualization of Ontologies and Rules. In: Morgenstern, L., Stefaneas, P., Lévy, F., Wyner, A., Paschke, A. (eds.) RuleML 2013. LNCS, vol. 8035, pp. 52–67. Springer, Heidelberg (2013)
5. Athan, T., Boley, H.: The MYNG 1.01 Suite for Deliberation RuleML 1.01: Taming the Language Lattice. In: Patkos, T., Wyner, A., Giurca, A., (eds.). Proceedings of the RuleML 2014 Challenge, at the 8th International Web Rule Symposium, Prague, Czech Republic, Volume 1211 of CEUR, August 2014
6. Hanus (ed.), M.: Curry: An Integrated Functional Logic Language (Vers. 0.8.3). http://www-ps.informatik.uni-kiel.de/currywiki/_media/documentation/report. pdf (February 2014)
7. Agarwal, S., Mohapatra, P., Genesereth, M., Boley, H.: Rule-based exploration of structured data in the browser. In: Bassiliades, N., et al. (eds.) RuleML 2015. LNCS, vol. 9202, pp. 161–175. Springer, Heidelberg (2015)
8. Berners-Lee, T., Connolly, D., Kagal, L., Scharf, Y., Hendler, J.: N3Logic: a logical framework for the world wide web. Theor. Pract. Logic Program. (TPLP) **8**(3), 249–269 (2008)
9. Riazanov, A., Rose, G.W., Klein, A., Forster, A.J., Baker, C.J.O., Shaban-Nejad, A., Buckeridge, D.L.: Towards clinical intelligence with SADI semantic web services: a case study with hospital-acquired infections data. In: Proceedings of the 4th International Workshop on Semantic Web Applications and Tools for the Life Sciences, SWAT4LS 2011, pp. 106–113. ACM New York (2012)
10. Zou, G.: GeospatialRules: A Datalog+ RuleML Rulebase for Geospatial Reasoning. In: Patkos, T., Wyner, A., Giurca, A. (eds.) Challenge+DC@RuleML. Volume 1211 of CEUR Workshop Proceedings., CEUR-WS.org (2014)
11. Crockford, D.: Introducing JSON (May 2009) Format home page. http://json.org
12. Boley, H.: Integrating positional and slotted knowledge on the semantic web. J. Emerg. Technol. Web Intell. **4**(2), 343–353 (2010)
13. Lloyd, J.W.: Foundations of Logic Programming, 2nd edn. Springer, New York (1987)
14. Ball, M., Boley, H., Hirtle, D., Mei, J., Spencer, B.: The OO jDREW reference implementation of RuleML. In: Adi, A., Stoutenburg, S., Tabet, S. (eds.) RuleML 2005. LNCS, vol. 3791, pp. 218–223. Springer, Heidelberg (2005)
15. Knublauch, H.: SPINMap: SPARQL-based Ontology Mapping with a Graphical Notation (April 2011) Composing the Semantic Web: A tool developer's blog on ontology development for the Semantic Web and beyond, http://composing-the-semantic-web.blogspot.ca/2011/04/spinmap-sparql-based-ontology-mapping.html

16. Brunnbauer, M.: RDF2RDB - convert RDF data to relational databases (2012). http://www.netestate.de/en/software-development/rdf2rdb/
17. Das, S., Sundara, S., Cyganiak, R.: R2RML: RDB to RDF mapping language. World Wide Web Consortium, Recommendation REC-r2rml-20120927 (September 2012)
18. Yang, G., Kifer, M.: Reasoning about Anonymous Resources and Meta Statements. In: Spaccapietra, Stefano, March, Sal, Aberer, Karl (eds.) Journal on Data Semantics I. LNCS, vol. 2800, pp. 69–97. Springer, Heidelberg (2003)
19. Zou, G., Peter-Paul, R., Boley, H., Riazanov, A.: PSOA2TPTP: a reference translator for interoperating PSOA RuleML with TPTP reasoners. In: Bikakis, A., Giurca, A. (eds.) RuleML 2012. LNCS, vol. 7438, pp. 264–279. Springer, Heidelberg (2012)
20. Zou, G., Boley, H.: PSOA2Prolog: object-relational rule interoperation and implementation by translation from PSOA RuleML to ISO prolog. In: Bassiliades, N., et al. (eds.) Rule Technologies: Foundations, Tools, and Applications. LNCS, vol. 9202, pp. 176–192. Springer, Heidelberg (2015)
21. Sutcliffe, G.: The TPTP problem library and associated infrastructure. J. Autom. Reasoning **43**(4), 337–362 (2009)
22. ISO/IEC 13211-1: Prolog - part 1: General core (1995)
23. Al Manir, M.S., Riazanov, A., Boley, H., Baker, C.J.O.: PSOA RuleML API: a tool for processing abstract and concrete syntaxes. In: Bikakis, A., Giurca, A. (eds.) RuleML 2012. LNCS, vol. 7438, pp. 280–288. Springer, Heidelberg (2012)

LegalRuleML:
Design Principles and Foundations

Tara Athan[1], Guido Governatori[2]([✉]), Monica Palmirani[3],
Adrian Paschke[4], and Adam Wyner[5]

[1] Athan Services, West Lafayette, USA
[2] NICTA Queensland, Brisbane, Australia
`guido.governatori@nicta.com.au`
[3] CIRSFID, University of Bologna, Bologna, Italy
[4] Corporate Semantic Web, Freie Universitat, Berlin, Germany
[5] University of Aberdeen, Aberdeen, UK

Abstract. This tutorial presents the principles of the OASIS Legal-
RuleML applied to the legal domain and discusses why, how, and when
LegalRuleML is well-suited for modelling norms. To provide a framework
of reference, we present a comprehensive list of requirements for devising rule interchange languages that capture the peculiarities of legal rule
modelling in support of legal reasoning. The tutorial comprises syntactic,
semantic, and pragmatic foundations, a LegalRuleML primer, as well as
use case examples from the legal domain.

Keywords: LegalRuleML · RuleML · Legal rule modelling · Meta
model

1 Introduction

The objective of the LegalRuleML Technical Committee (TC) is to extend
RuleML with formal features specific to legal norms, guidelines, policies and
reasoning; that is, the TC defines a standard (expressed with XML-schema and
Relax NG) that is able to represent the particularities of the legal normative rules
with a rich, articulated, and meaningful markup language. The features are:

- defeasibility of rules and defeasible logic;
- deontic operators (e.g., obligations, permissions, prohibitions, rights);
- semantic management of negation;
- temporal management of rules and temporality in rules;
- classification of norms (i.e., constitutive, prescriptive);
- jurisdiction of norms;
- isomorphism between rules and natural language normative provisions;

G. Governatori—NICTA is funded by the Australian Government through the
Department of Communications and the Australian Research Council through the
ICT Centre of Excellence Program.

© Springer International Publishing Switzerland 2015
W. Faber and A. Paschke (Eds.): Reasoning Web 2015, LNCS 9203, pp. 151–188, 2015.
DOI: 10.1007/978-3-319-21768-0_6

– identification of parts of the norms (e.g., bearer, conditions);
– authorial tracking of rules.

Some matters are out of the scope of the TC and LegalRuleML such as specifications of core or domain legal ontologies. For the full motivation for LegalRuleML and its relationships with other approaches the reader is referred to [5,30].

The main principles of LegalRuleML are as follows.

Multiple Semantic Annotations: A legal rule may have multiple semantic annotations, where these annotations represent different legal interpretations. Each such annotation appears in a separate annotation collection as internal or external metadata. A range of parameters provide the interpretation with respect to provenance, applicable jurisdiction, logical interpretation of the rule, and others.

Tracking the LegalRuleML Creators: As part of the provenance information, a LegalRuleML document or any of its fragments can be associated with its creators. This is important to establish the authority and trust of the knowledge base and annotations. Among the creators of the document can be the authors of the text, knowledge base, and annotations, as well as the publisher of the document.

Linking Rules and Provisions: LegalRuleML includes a mechanism, based on IRI, that allows many to many (N:M) relationships among the rules and the textual provisions: multiple rules are embedded in the same provision, several provisions contribute to the same rule. This mechanism may be managed in the metadata collections, permitting extensible management, avoiding redundancy in the IRI definition, and avoiding errors in the associations.

Temporal Management: LegalRuleML's universe of discourse contains a variety of entities: provisions, rules, applications of rules, references to text, and references to physical entities. All of these entities exist and change in time; their histories interact in complicated ways. Legal RuleML represents these temporal issues in unambiguous fashion. In particular, a rule has parameters which can vary over time, such as its status (e.g., strict, defeasible, defeater), its validity (e.g., repealed, annulled, suspended), and its jurisdiction (e.g., only in EU, only in US). In addition, a rule has temporal aspects such as internal constituency of the action, the time of assertion of the rule, the efficacy, enforcement, and so on.

Formal Ontology Reference: LegalRuleML is independent from any legal ontology and logic framework. However it includes a mechanism, based on IRIs, for pointing to reusable classes of a specified external ontology.

LegalRuleML is Based on RuleML: LegalRuleML reuses and extends concepts and syntax of RuleML wherever possible, and also adds novel annotations. RuleML includes Reaction RuleML.

Mapping: LegalRuleML is mappable to RDF triples for Linked Data reuse.

2 Functionalities

Specifically, LegalRuleML facilitates the following functionalities.

(F1) Supports modelling different types of rules. There are constitutive rules, which define concepts or institutional actions that are recognised as such by virtue of the defining rules (e.g. the legal definition of "transfer property ownership"); and there are prescriptive rules, which regulate actions or the outcome of actions by making them obligatory, permitted, or prohibited.

(F2) Represents normative effects. There are many normative effects that follow from applying rules, such as obligations, permissions, prohibitions, and more articulated effects. Rules are also required to regulate methods for detecting violations of the law and to determine the normative effects triggered by norm violations, such as reparative obligations, which are meant to repair or compensate violations. These constructions can give rise to very complex rule dependencies, because the violation of a single rule can activate other (reparative) rules, which in turn, in case of their violation, refer to other rules, and so forth.

(F3) Implements defeasibility [13,31,34]. In the law, where the antecedent of a rule is satisfied by the facts of a case (or via other rules), the conclusion of the rule presumably, but not necessarily, holds. The defeasibility of legal rules consists of the means to identify exceptions and conflicts along with mechanisms to resolve conflicts.

(F4) Implements isomorphism [7]. To ease validation and maintenance, there should be a one-to-one correspondence between collections of rules in the formal model and the units of (controlled) natural language text that express the rules in the original legal sources, such as sections of legislation.

(F5) Alternatives: often legal documents are left ambiguous on purpose to capture open–ended aspects of the domain they are intended to regulate. At the same time legal documents are meant to be interpreted by end users. This means that there are cases where multiple (and incompatible) interpretations of the same textual source are possible. LegalRuleML offers mechanisms to specify such interpretations and to select one of them based on the relevant context.

(F6) Manages rule reification [13]. Rules are objects with properties, such as Jurisdiction, Authority, Temporal attributes [21,22,29]. These elements are necessary to enable effective legal reasoning.

3 Criteria of Good Language Design

The syntax design should follow from semantic intuitions from the subject matter domain - labelling entities, properties, and relations as well as some of the type constraints amongst them that guide how the labels are combined and used.

Criteria of Good Language Design are:

- Minimality, which requires that the language provides only a small set of needed language constructs, i.e., the same meaning cannot be expressed by different language constructs.

- Referential transparency, which means that the same language construct always expresses the same semantics regardless of the context in which it is used.
- Orthogonality, where language constructs are independent of each other, thus permitting their systematic combination.
- Pattern-based design, where design patterns are a distillation of common wisdom in organizing the structural parts, the grammar and the constraints of a language. Some of them are listed in [9] and as XML Patterns[1]. Inside of LegalRuleML we introduce five design patterns.
- Meta-model based, where the meta-model for a language, also called the abstract syntax, defines the vocabulary for describing the language, including syntactic categories.

LegalRuleML was designed based on such principles. In particular its vocabulary is inspired by terms from the legal domain, which then facilitates its use by users familiar with the domain.

The LegalRuleML meta-model captures the common meaning of domain terms as understood in the legal field, formalizes the connections among the various concepts and their representation in the language, and provides an RDF-based abstract syntax. RDFS [8] is used to define the LegalRuleML metamodel, and graphs of the RDFS schemas accompany the following discussions about the domain concepts.[2]

4   Modelling Norms

According to scholars of legal theory [34], norms can be represented by rules with the form

$$\text{if } A_1, ..., A_n \text{ then } C$$

where $A_1, \ldots, A_n$ are the pre-conditions of the norm, C is the effect of the norm, and *if ... then ...* is a normative conditional, which are generally defeasible and do not correspond to the if-then material implication of propositional logic. Norms are meant to provide general principles, but at the same time they can express exceptions to the principle. It is well understood in Legal Theory [14,34] that, typically, there are different types of "normative conditionals", but in general normative conditionals are defeasible. Defeasibility is the property that a conclusion is open in principle to revision in case more evidence to the contrary is provided. Defeasible reasoning is in contrast to monotonic reasoning of propositional logic, where no revision is possible. In addition, defeasible reasoning allows reasoning in the face of contradictions, which gives rise to *ex false quodlibet* in propositional logic. One application of defeasible reasoning is the ability to model exceptions in a simple and natural way.

---

[1] http://www.xmlpatterns.com/.

[2] https://tools.oasis-open.org/version-control/browse/wsvn/legalruleml/trunk/schemas/rdfs/#_trunk_schemas_rdfs_.

4.1   Defeasibility

The first use of defeasible rules is to capture conflicting rules/norms without making the resulting set of rules inconsistent. Given that $\neg expression$ means the negation of *expression*, the following two rules conclude with the negation of each other

$$body_1 \Rightarrow head$$
$$body_2 \Rightarrow \neg head$$

Without defeasibile rules, rules with conclusions that are negations of each other could give rise, should $body_1$ and $body_2$ both hold, to a contradiction, i.e., *head* and $\neg head$, and consequently *ex falso quodlibet*. Instead, defeasible reasoning is sceptical; that is, in case of a conflict such as the above, it refrains from taking any of the two conclusions, unless there are mechanisms to solve the conflict (see the discussion below on the superiority relation). Notice that an application of this is to model exceptions. Exceptions limit the applicability of basic norms/rules, for example:

$$body \Rightarrow head$$
$$body, exception\_condition \Rightarrow \neg head$$

In this case, the second rule is more specific than the first, and thus it forms an exception to the first, i.e., a case where the rule has extra conditions that encode the exception, blocking the conclusion of the first rule. Often, exceptions in defeasible reasoning can be simply encoded as

$$body \Rightarrow head$$
$$exception\_condition \Rightarrow \neg head$$

In the definition of rules as normative conditionals made up of preconditions and effect, we can see a rule as a binary relationship between the set of preconditions (or body or antecedent) of the rule, and the (legal) effect (head or conclusion) of the rule. Formally, a rule can be defined by the following signature:

$$body \times head$$

We can then investigate the nature of such a relationship. Given two sets, we have the following seven possible relationships describing the "strength" of the connections between the body and the head of a rule:

$$body \text{ always } head$$
$$body \text{ sometimes } head$$
$$body \text{ not complement } head$$
$$body \text{ no relationship } head$$
$$body \text{ always complement } head$$
$$body \text{ sometimes complement } head$$
$$body \text{ not } head$$

In defeasible logic we can represent the relationships using the following formal-isation of rules (rule types):

$$body \rightarrow head$$
$$body \Rightarrow head$$
$$body \rightsquigarrow head$$
$$body \rightarrow \neg head$$
$$body \Rightarrow \neg head$$
$$body \rightsquigarrow \neg head$$

There is no need to have a rule for the case where there is no relationship between the head and the body. The following table summarises the relationships, the notation used for them, and the strength of the relationship.[3]

body always *head*	$body \rightarrow head$	Strict rule
body sometimes *head*	$body \Rightarrow head$	Defeasible rule
body not complement *head*	$body \rightsquigarrow head$	Defeater
body no relationship *head*		
body always complement *head*	$body \rightarrow \neg head$	Strict rule
body sometimes complement *head*	$body \Rightarrow \neg head$	Defeasible rule
body not *head*	$body \rightsquigarrow \neg head$	Defeater

The meaning of the different types of rules is as follows:

For a *strict rule body* $\rightarrow$ *head* the interpretation is that every time the body holds then the head holds.

For a *defeasible rule body* $\Rightarrow$ *head* the reading is when the body holds, then, typically, the head holds. Alternatively we can say that the head holds when the body does unless there are reasons to assert that the head does not hold. This captures that it is possible to have exceptions to the rule/norm, and it is possible to have prescriptions for the opposite conclusion.

For a *defeater body* $\rightsquigarrow$ *head* the intuition is as follows: defeaters are rules that cannot establish that the head holds. Instead they can be use to specify that the opposite conclusion does not hold. In argumentation two types of defeaters are recognized: defeaters used when an argument attacks the preconditions of another argument (or rule); other defeaters used when there is no relationship between the premises of an argument (preconditions of a rule or body) and the conclusion of the argument (effect of the rule or head).

Given the possibility to have conflicting rules, i.e., rules with opposite or contradictory heads, we have, for example

$$body_1 \Rightarrow head$$
$$body_2 \Rightarrow \neg head$$

Systems for defeasible reasoning include mechanisms to solve such conflicts. Dif-ferent methods to solve conflicts have been proposed: *specificity*, *salience*, and

---

[3] The syntax presented here is based on Defeasible Logic, see [4,27].

a *preference relation*. According to specificity, in case of a conflict between two rules, the most specific rule prevails over the less specific one, where a rule is more specific if its body subsumes the body of the other rule. For salience, each rule has an attached salience or weight, where in case of a conflict between two rules, the one with the greatest salience or weight prevails over the other. A preference relation (also known as superiority relation) defines a binary relation over rules, where an element of the relation states the relative strength between two rules. Thus, in case of a conflict between two rules, if the preference relation is defined over such rules, the strongest of the two rules wins over the other.

Various researchers have taken different views on such methods. Specificity corresponds to the well know legal principle of *lex specialis*. [32] argues that specificity is not always appropriate for legal reasoning and that there are other well understood legal principles such as *lex superior* and *lex posterior* that apply instead. [32] cites cases in which the *lex specialis* principle might not be the one used to solve the conflict, for example, a more specific article from a local council regulation might not override a less specific constitutional norm. [32] proposes to use a dynamic preference relation to handle conflicting rules. The preference relation is dynamic in the sense that it is possible to argue about which instances of the relation hold and under which circumstances. [3] proposes that instances of the superiority relation appear in the head of rules, namely:

$$body \Rightarrow superiority$$

where *superiority* is a statement with the form

$$r_1 > r_2$$

where r_1 and r_2 are rule identifiers.

Reference [12] proposes Carneades as a rule-based argumentation system suitable for legal reasoning which uses weights attached to the arguments (rules) to solve conflicts and to define proof standards. [17] shows how to use the weights to generate an equivalent preference relation, and, consequently, how to capture the proposed proof standards. In addition, [17] shows that there are situations where a preference relation cannot be captured by using weights on the rules.

To handle defeasibility, LegalRuleML has to capture the superiority relation and the strength of rules. For the superiority relation, LegalRuleML offers the element `<Overrides>`, which defines a relationship of superiority `cs2` overrides `cs1`, where `cs2` and `cs1` are Legal Statement identifiers.[4] These elements are included through `hasQualification` roles.

```
<lrml:hasQualification>
  <lrml:Overrides over="#cs1" under="#cs2"/>
</lrml:hasQualification>
```

For the representation of the strength of rules, LegalRuleML has two options:

The first is to include it in a `<Context>` element, where a `<Context>` specifies a context in which the rule is applied:

---

[4] LegalRuleML defines a Legal Statement as an expression of a Legal Rule or a part of a Legal Rule where a Legal Rule is a formal representation of a Legal Norm.

```
<lrml:Context key="ruleInfo2">
  <lrml:appliesStrength iri="deovo:defeasible2"/>
  <lrml:toStatement keyref="#cs1"/>
</lrml:Context>
```

The second (and optional) way to express the qualification of the rule is directly inside of the rule, through a `hasStrength` role. The difference is that `<Context>` localises the strength of a rule, while `hasStrength` in effect relates the strength to the rule in all contexts:

```
<lrml:hasStrength>
  <lrml:Defeater key="str4"/>
</lrml:hasStrength>
```

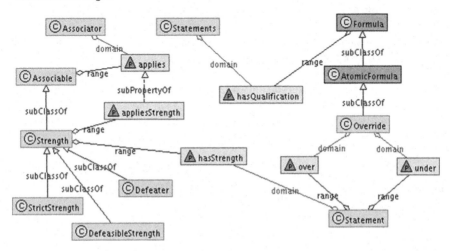

Fig. 1. Partial Metamodel for Defeasible Concepts. LegalRuleML and RuleML classes are labelled with a 'C' in a circle, LegalRuleML properties with a 'P' in a triangle. The Formula and AtomicFormula classes are imported from RuleML.

4.2   Constitutive and Prescriptive Norms

As we have discussed, a Legal Rule can be seen as binary relationship between its antecedent (a set of formulas, encoding the pre-conditions of a norm, represented in LegalRuleML by a formula, where multiple pre-conditions are joined by some logical connective) and its conclusion (the effect of the norm, represented by a formula). It is possible to have different types of relations. In the previous section, we examined one such aspect: the strength of the link between the antecedent and the conclusion. Similarly, we can explore a second aspect, namely what type of effect follows from the pre-condition of a norm. In Legal Theory norms are classified mostly in two main categories: constitutive norms and prescriptive norms, which will be then represented as constitutive rules (also

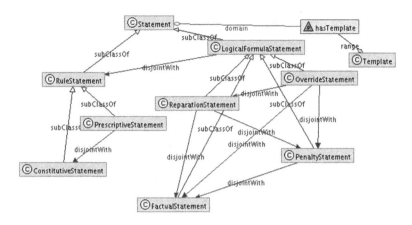

Fig. 2. Partial Metamodel for Statement Subclasses.

known as *counts-as rules*) and prescriptive rules.[5] The (partial) meta-model for the notions described in this section is depicted in Fig. 2.

The function of constitutive norms is to define and create so called institutional facts [36], where an institutional fact is how a particular concept is understood in a specific institution. Thus, constitutive rules provide definitions of the terms and concepts used in a jurisdiction. On the other hand, prescriptive rules dictate the obligations, prohibitions, permissions, etc. of a legal system, along with the conditions under which the obligations, prohibitions, permissions, etc. hold. LegalRuleML uses deontic operators to capture such notions (see Sect. 4.3). Deontic operators are meant to qualify formulas. A Deontic operator takes as its argument a formula and returns a formula. For example, given the (atomic) formula *PayInvoice(guido)*, meaning 'Guido pays the invoice', and the deontic operator [OBL] (for obligation), the application of the deontic operator to the formula generates the new (deontic) formula [OBL]*PayInvoice(guido)*, meaning that "it is obligatory that Guido pays the invoice".

The following is the LegalRuleML format for prescriptive rules. Notice, that in LegalRuleML, legal rules are captured by the broader class of Statement and the `hasTemplate` property links a prescriptive or constitutive statement (see Fig. 2 for the different types of statements available in LegalRuleML) to its template, a fragment of RuleML syntax with root `ruleml:Rule` that denotes a class of rules.

```
<lrml:PrescriptiveStatement key="ps1">
  <lrml:hasTemplate>
    <ruleml:Rule key=":key1">
      <lrml:hasStrength>
        strength of the rule
      </lrml:hasStrength>
      <ruleml:if>
```

---

[5] Reference [14] identify more types of norms/rules. However, most of them can be reduced to the two types described here insofar as the distinction is not on structure of the rules but it depends on the meaning of the content (specific effect) of the rules, while keeping the same logical format.

```
        formula, including deontic formula
      </ruleml:if>
      <ruleml:then>
        <lrml:SuborderList>
          list of deontic formulas
        </lrml:SuborderList>
      </ruleml:then>
    </ruleml:Rule>
  </lrml:hasTemplate>
</lrml:PrescriptiveStatement>
```

The difference between constitutive rules and prescriptive rules is in the content of
the head, where the head of a prescriptive rule is a list of deontic formulas which
is called a suborder list (see Sect. 4.3 below), and represented in LegalRuleML by
the `<lrml:Suborder>` element. Syntactically, a suborder list of one element can be
rendered in LegalRuleML as just the element. Prescriptive and constitutive rules
can have deontic formulas in their set of preconditions (antecedent or body). The
conclusion (head) of a constitutive rule cannot be a deontic formula, nor can it be
a compound formula that contains a deontic formula.

```
<lrml:ConstitutiveStatement key="ps1">
  <ruleml:Rule key=":key1">
    <lrml:hasStrength>
      strength of the rule
    </lrml:hasStrength>
    <ruleml:if>
        formula, including deontic formula
    </ruleml:if>
    <ruleml:then>
        non-deontic formula
    </ruleml:then>
  </ruleml:Rule>
</lrml:ConstitutiveStatement>
```

4.3   Deontic

One of the functions of norms is to regulate the behaviour of their subjects by
imposing constraints on what the subjects can or cannot do, what situations are
deemed legal, and which ones are considered to be illegal. There is an important difference between the constraints imposed by norms and other types of
constraints. Typically a constraint means that the situation described by the
constraint cannot occur. For example, the constraint A means that if $\neg A$ (the
negation of A, that is, the opposite of A) occurs, then we have a contradiction,
or in other terms, we have an impossible situation. Norms, on the other hand,
can be violated. Namely, given a norm that imposes the constraint A, yet we
have a situation where $\neg A$, we do not have a contradiction, but rather a violation, or in other terms we have a situation that is classified as "illegal". From
a logical point of view, we cannot represent the constraint imposed by a norm
simply by A, since the conjunction of A and $\neg A$ is a contradiction. Thus we need
a mechanism to identify the constraints imposed by norms. This mechanism is
provided by modal operators, in particular, deontic operators.

Modal and Deontic Operators. Modal logic is an extension of classical logic with modal operators. A modal operator applies to a proposition to create a new proposition. The meaning of a modal operator is to "qualify" the truth of the proposition that the operator applies to. The basic modal operators are those of *necessity* and *possibility*. Accordingly, given a proposition p expressing, for example that "the snow is white" and the necessity modal operator [NEC], [NEC]p is the proposition expressing that "necessarily the snow is white". Typically, the necessity and possibility operators are the dual of each other, namely:

$$[NEC]p \equiv \neg[POS]\neg p$$
$$[POS]p \equiv \neg[NEC]\neg p$$

The modal operators have received different interpretations: for example, necessity can be understood as logical necessity, physical necessity, epistemic necessity (knowledge), doxastic necessity (belief), temporal necessity (e.g., always in the future), deontic necessity (obligatory), and many more.

In the context of normative reasoning and representation of norms the focus is on the concepts of deontic necessity and deontic possibility. These two correspond to the notions of Obligation, and Permission. In addition, we consider the notion of Prohibition, which corresponds to the operator of deontic impossibility. For something to be "deontically necessary" means that it holds in all situations deemed legal; similarly something is "deontically possible" if there is at least one legal state where it holds. Finally, "deontically impossible" indicates that something does not hold in any legal state. More specifically a legal state is a state where there are no violations. Thus LegalRuleML defines Obligation as a Deontic Specification[6] for a state, an act, or a course of action to which a Bearer is legally bound, and which, if it is not achieved or performed, results in a violation; similarly a Prohibition is a Deontic Specification for a state, an act, or a course of action to which a Bearer is legally bound, and which, if it is achieved or performed, results in a violation. A Permission is a Deontic Specification indicating that the Bearer has no Obligation or Prohibition to the contrary.

We will use [OBL] for the modal/deontic operator of Obligation, [PERM] for Permission, and [FOR] for Prohibition (or Forbidden).

Standard deontic logic assumes the following relationships between the operators:

$$[OBL]p \equiv \neg[PERM]\neg p$$

If p is obligatory, then its opposite, $\neg p$, is not permitted.

$$[FOR]p \equiv [OBL]\neg p$$

If p is forbidden then its opposite is Obligatory. Alternatively, a Prohibition can be understood as Obligation of the negation.

The following is an example of mathematical statement of a Prescriptive Rule:

$$p_1, \ldots, p_n, [DEON_1]p_{n+1}, \ldots, [DEON_m]p_{n+m} \Rightarrow [DEON]q$$

---

[6] Deontic Specification is the class that includes the various deontic notions used in LegalRuleML.

The antecedent, $p_1, \ldots, p_n, [\text{DEON}_1]p_{n+1}, \ldots, [\text{DEON}_m]p_{n+m}$, conditions the applicability of the norm in the consequent $[\text{DEON}]q$; that is, when the antecedent conditions are met, then the consequent is the *deontic* effect of them. Thus, given the antecedent, the rule implies $[\text{DEON}]q$.

The operators of Obligation, Prohibition and Permission are typically considered the basic ones, but further refinements are possible, for example, two types of permissions have been discussed in the literature on deontic logic: *weak permission* (or *negative permission*) and *strong permission* (or *positive permission*). Weak permission corresponds to the idea that some A is permitted if $\neg A$ is not provable as mandatory. In other words, something is allowed by a code only when it is not prohibited by that code [38]. The concept of strong permission is more complicated, as it amounts to the idea that some A is permitted by a code if and only if such a code explicitly states that A is permitted, typically as an exception to the prohibition of A or the obligation of its contrary, i.e., $\neg A$. It follows that a strong permission is not derived from the absence of a prohibition, but is explicitly formulated in a permissive (prescriptive) norm [2]. An example of an explicit permissive norm is manifested by a "U-turn permitted" sign exposed at a traffic light, which derogates the (general) prohibition to U-turn at traffic lights.

Refinements of the concept of obligation have been proposed as well. For example it is possible to distinguish between *achievement* and *maintenance* obligations, where an *achievement* obligation is an obligation that is fulfilled if what the obligation prescribes holds at least once in the period when the obligation holds, while a *maintenance* obligation must be obeyed for all the instants when it holds (see [18] for a classification of obligations).

LegalRuleML is neutral about the different subclasses of the deontic operators; to this end LegalRuleML is equipped with a mechanism to point to the semantics of various Deontic Specifications in a document. The first mechanism is provided by the `iri` attribute of a Deontic Specification for example:

```
<lrml:Obligation
    key="oblig1"
    iri="http://example.org/deontic/vocab#achievementobligation">
    ...
</lrml:Obligation>
```

The second alternative is to use an **Association** to link a Deontic Specification to its meaning using the **applyModality** element, namely:

```
<lrml:Association>
  <lrml:appliesModality
      iri="http://example.org/deontic/vocab#maintenanaceobligation"/>
  <lrml:toTarget keyref="#oblig101"/>
</lrml:Association>'
```

Furthermore, Obligations, Prohibitions and Permissions in LegalRuleML are directed operators [24], thus they have parties (e.g. Bearer), specifying, for example, who is the subject of an Obligation or who is the beneficiary of a Permission.

```
<lrml:Obligation iri="http://example.org/deontic/vocab#obl1">
  <ruleml:slot>
    <lrml:Bearer iri="http://example.org/deontic/vocab#oblBearer"/>
```

```
    <ruleml:Ind>Y</ruleml:Ind>
  </ruleml:slot>
  <ruleml:Atom key=":atom2">
    <ruleml:Rel iri="#rel2"/>
    <ruleml:Ind>X</ruleml:Ind>
  </ruleml:Atom>
</lrml:Obligation>
```

Violation, Suborder, Penalty and Reparation. Obligations can be violated; according to some legal scholars, the possibility of being violated can be used to define an obligation. A violation means that the content of the obligation has not been met. It is important to notice that a violation does not result in an inconsistency. A violation is, basically, a situation where we have

$$([OBL]p) \text{ and } \neg p$$

One of the characteristics of norms is that having violated them, a penalty can be introduced to compensate for the violation, where a penalty is typically a Deontic Specification. To model this feature of norms and legal reasoning [20] introduced what is called here a suborder list, and [16] showed how to combine them with defeasible reasoning for the modelling of (business) contracts. As we have mentioned above, a suborder list is a list of deontic formulas, e.g., formulas of the form [D]A, where [D] is one of [OBL] (Obligation), [FOR] (Prohibition, or forbidden), [PERM] (Permission) and [RIGHT] (Right). Syntactically, a suborder list of one element can be rendered in LegalRuleML as just the element. To illustrate the meaning of suborder lists, consider the following example:

$$[OBL]A, [OBL]B, [FOR]C, [PERM]D$$

The expression means that A is obligatory, but if it is violated, i.e., we have its opposite $\neg A$, then the obligation comes into force to compensate for the violation of [OBL]A with [OBL]B. If also this Obligation of B is violated, then we have [FOR]C, the Prohibition of C. At this stage, if we have a Violation of such a Prohibition, i.e., we have C, then the Permission of D kicks in. Obligations and Prohibitions should not be preceded by Permissions and Rights in a suborder list, for the semantics of suborder lists is such that an element holds in the list only if all the elements that precede it in the list have been violated. It is not possible to have a Violation of a Permission, so it cannot serve a purpose in the suborder list. Accordingly, an element following a permission in a suborder list would never hold. See [19] for a full discussion on the issue of permissions and suborder lists. [16,20] also discuss mechanisms to combine the suborder lists from different rules. For example, given the rules

$$body \Rightarrow [OBL]A$$
$$\neg A \Rightarrow [OBL]B$$

Here the body of the second rule is the negation of the content of the obligation in the head of the first rule. It is possible to merge the two rules above in the following rule

$$body \Rightarrow [OBL]A, [OBL]B$$

stating that one compensates for the violation of the obligation of A with the obligation of B. This suggests that suborder lists provide a simple and convenient mechanism to model penalties. It is not uncommon for a legal text (e.g., a contract) to include sections about penalties, where one penalty is provided as compensation for many norms. To model this and to maintain the isomorphism between a source and its formalisation, LegalRuleML includes a <PenaltyStatement> element, the scope of which is to represent a statement of a penalty as a suborder list (including the trivial non-empty list of a single element).

```
<lrml:PenaltyStatement key="pen1">
  <lrml:SuborderList>
    list of deontic formulas
  </lrml:SuborderList>
</lrml:PenaltyStatement>
```

LegalRuleML not only models penalties, but aims to connect the penalty statement with the corresponding Reparation element:

```
<lrml:Reparation key="rep1">
  <lrml:appliesPenalty keyref="#pen1"/>
  <lrml:toPrescriptiveStatement keyref="#ps1"/>
</lrml:Reparation>
```

With the temporal model of LegalRuleML (see Sect. 5.4), we can model a unique prescriptive statement (e.g., a prohibition) and several penalties that are updated over time according to the modifications of the law. Dynamically, the legal reasoner can point out the correct penalty according to the time of the crime (e.g., an obligation to pay statutory damage \$500 in 2000, \$750 in 2006, \$1000 in 2010).

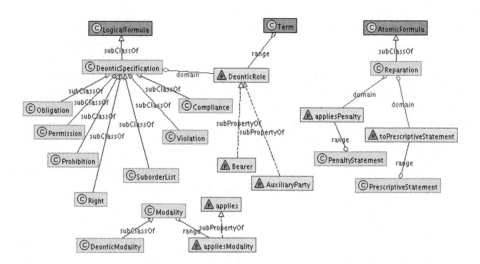

Fig. 3. Partial Metamodel for Deontic Concepts. LogicalFormula, Term and Atomic-Formula classes are imported from RuleML.

4.4 Alternatives

In the legal interpretation theory [37] norms are interpreted by the judges in order to apply them to the concrete cases. Sometime the legal interpretation theories conflict and diverge from each other [11,23,33]. Linguistic elements are added to this also for different reasons such as jurisdiction (e.g., national and regional level) or for competences (e.g., civil or criminal court). The practice of law over time has developed its own catalogue of *hermeneutical principles*, a range of techniques to interpret the law, such as catalogued and discussed in [35]. In addition, in Linguistics, issues about interpretation have long been of central concern (see among others [10,26]), where the need for interpretation arises given that the meanings (broadly construed) of "linguistic signs", (e.g., words, sentences, and discourses), can vary depending on participants, context, purpose, and other parameters. Interpretation is, then, giving the meaning of the linguistic signs for a given set of parameters.

LegalRuleML endeavours not to account for how different interpretations arise, but to provide a mechanism to record and represent them. We have four different templates:

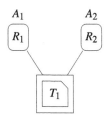

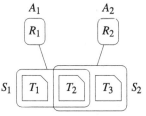

Case 1: Same legal provision(s), T_1, and different alternatives (A_1 and A_2).

Case 2: Different alternatives (A_1 and A_2) that share one or more pieces of text, T_2, but others are not shared (T_1 and T_3).

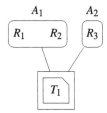

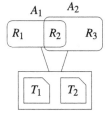

Case 3: Different alternatives (A_1 and A_2) sharing the same legal provision(s) (T_1), but embedding different rules (R_1 and R_2 for A_1 and R_3 for A_1).

Case 4: Different alternatives that share the same legal provision(s), but one or more rules are in common (e.g., R_2).

The element `<lrml:Alternatives>` permits to express all these interpretation templates. The following LegalRuleML fragments illustrate how to represent the four cases above (the first case shows the normalized serialization, while the rest show the compact serialization).

Case 1:

```
<lrml:Alternatives key="alt1">
  <lrml:fromLegalSources>
    <lrml:LegalSources>
      <lrml:hasLegalSource keyref="#ref1"/>
    </lrml:LegalSources>
  </lrml:fromLegalSources>
  <lrml:hasAlternative keyref="#ps1"/>
  <lrml:hasAlternative keyref="#ps2"/>
</lrml:Alternatives>
```

Case 2:

```
<lrml:Alternatives key="alt2">
  <lrml:LegalSources>
    <lrml:hasLegalSource keyref="#ref1"/>
    <lrml:hasLegalSource keyref="#ref2"/>
  </lrml:LegalSources>
  <lrml:hasAlternative keyref="#ps1"/>
  <lrml:hasAlternative keyref="#ps2"/>
</lrml:Alternatives>
```

Case 3:

```
<lrml:Alternatives key="alt3">
  <lrml:LegalSources>
    <lrml:hasLegalSource keyref="#ref1"/>
  </lrml:LegalSources>
  <lrml:hasAlternative keyref="#ss1"/>
  <lrml:hasAlternative keyref="#ss2"/>
</lrml:Alternatives>

<lrml:Statements key="ss1">
  <lrml:ConstitutiveStatement keyref="#ps1"/>
  <lrml:ConstitutiveStatement keyref="#ps2"/>
</lrml:Statements>

<lrml:Statements key="ss2">
  <lrml:ConstitutiveStatement keyref="#ps3"/>
</lrml:Statements>
```

Case 4:

```
<lrml:Alternatives key="alt3">
  <lrml:LegalSources>
    <lrml:hasLegalSource keyref="#ref1"/>
    <lrml:hasLegalSource keyref="#ref2"/>
  </lrml:LegalSources>
  <lrml:hasAlternative keyref="#ss1"/>
  <lrml:hasAlternative keyref="#ss2"/>
</lrml:Alternatives>

<lrml:Statements key="ss1">
  <lrml:ConstitutiveStatement
      keyref="#ps1"/>
  <lrml:ConstitutiveStatement
```

```
    keyref="#ps2"/>
</lrml:Statements>

<lrml:Statements key="ss2">
  <lrml:ConstitutiveStatement
      keyref="#ps1"/>
  <lrml:ConstitutiveStatement
      keyref="#ps3"/>
</lrml:Statements>
```

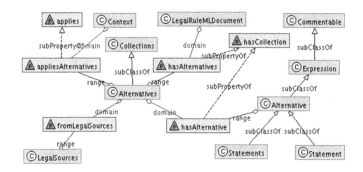

Fig. 4. Partial Metamodel for Alternatives Concepts.

A possible use of the LegalRuleML alternatives mechanism is in legal disputes where the alternatives can be used to model the (different) interpretations of a piece of legislation by the parties involved in the dispute; a comprehensive illustration of this is provided in Sect. 8 based on [6].

5   Meta Data of the Norms

5.1   Sources and Isomorphism

For legal rule modelling, it is important to maintain the connection between the formal norms and the legally binding textual statements that express the norms for several reasons. Legal knowledge engineers and end users should know and be able to track the textual source of the formal representation. Furthermore, because the legal text is the only legally binding element, the connection between text and the rule(s) (or fragment of rule) guarantees the provenance, authoritativeness, and authenticity of the rules modelled by the legal knowledge engineer. In addition, legal experts (judges, lawyers, legal operators) request a mechanism to connect text and rules for legibility and validation of the rules. Finally, because the legal sources of rules change over time, the formal rules need to be updated according to the textual changes; as there is usually no automatic mechanism to correlate and track modifications to rules, the connection between text and rules helps to do so. For these reasons LegalRuleML includes a mechanism for managing this connection, which is called "isomorphism" in the AI & Law community. The mechanism must support a fine granularity (rules, fragments of rules, atoms, fragments of atoms connected with provisions, fragments of provisions, letters, numbers, paragraphs, sentences, and words) as well as to represent temporal modifications. LegalRuleML dedicates two collections (`<lrml:References>`, `<lrml:LegalSources>`) to annotate the original legal sources. In Sect. 6 the mechanism for creating an N:M relationship with rules (e.g., many rules associated with one textual provision; many legal source fragments for one rule) will be described.

`<lrml:References>` is the collection dedicated to record non-IRI based identifier sources, and the attribute `refIDSystemName` is able to annotate the naming convention used. In the following example we refer to the Akoma Ntoso relative IRI of the section 504 of the US Code, following the naming convention of the XML-schema in Akoma Ntoso[7]:

```
<lrml:References refType="http://example.legalruleml.org/lrml#LegalSource">
  <lrml:Reference
      refersTo="ref1"
      refID="/akn/us/act/uscode/eng@/main#title17-chp5-sec504-clsa-lst1-pnt1"
      refIDSystemName="AkomaNtoso3.0-2015-04-16"/>
</lrml:References>
```

`<lrml:LegalSource>` is the construct dedicated to record the IRI based identifier sources. The following example define the source of the U.S. Code, section 504, paragraph 1, title 17 published in the Cornell University portal http://www.law.cornell.edu/:

```
<lrml:LegalSources>
  <lrml:LegalSource
    key="ref2"
    sameAs="http://www.law.cornell.edu/uscode/text/17/504#psection-1"/>
  </lrml:LegalSource>
</lrml:LegalSources>
```

The list of the resources connected with the legal rules that are modelled in a LegalRuleML document are defined once in the first part of the XML file. This minimizes redundant definitions of the resources and avoids errors. As we see later, using the attribute value specified in @key, rules (or fragments of a rule) can be connected to References or LegalSources. The `<lrml:Association>` construct links LegalSources and References with rules (or fragment of rule), thus implementing the N:M relationship.

---

[7] Akoma Ntoso is an XML vocabulary for representing legal, legislative, parliamentary and judiciary documents in a structured and semantic manner. Akoma Ntoso is managed by the LegalDocML TC of OASIS. https://www.oasis-open.org/committees/tc_home.php?wg_abbrev=legaldocml.

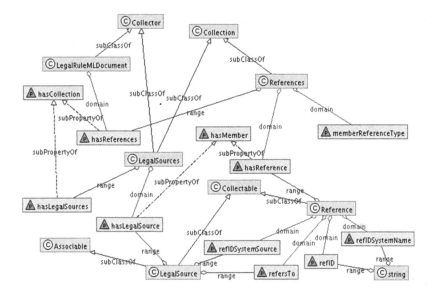

Fig. 5. Metamodel for LegalSource concepts.

5.2 Jurisdiction and Authority

The Jurisdiction element is a geographic area or subject-matter over which an
Authority applies its legal power. It annotates the legal rules that are applicable
to a given region (e.g., the rules applicable only in the United States of America
in contrast to other countries in the world).

```
<lrml:Jurisdictions>
  <lrml:Jurisdiction key="us"
    sameAs="http://example.org/jurisdiction#unitedStatesOfAmerica"/>
</lrml:Jurisdictions>
```

We can use Jurisdiction also to specify a limited subject-matter, for instance,
legal rules which are applicable only to the executive departments.

```
<lrml:Jurisdictions>
  <lrml:Jurisdiction key="exd"
    sameAs="http://example.org/jurisdiction#executiveDepartments"/>
</lrml:Jurisdictions>
```

Similarly, authority qualifies the rules with respect to the authenticity of the
provenance of the formal model. Authority is a person or organization with the
power to create, endorse, or enforce Legal Norms.

```
<lrml:Authorities>
  <lrml:Authority key="congress"
    sameAs="unibo:organization.owl#congress">
    <lrml:hasType iri="lrmlv:Legislature"/>
  </lrml:Authority>
</lrm:Authorities>
```

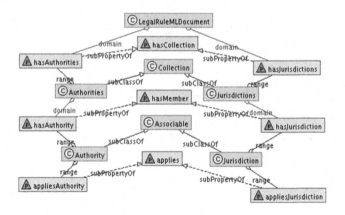

Fig. 6. Metamodel for authority and jurisdiction metadata concepts.

5.3 Agent, Figure, Role

An Agent is an entity that acts or has the capability to act. An Agent could be a physical person, a database, or a bot; for this reason we have the sub-element `<lrml:hasType>` that expresses the category of agent.

```
<lrml:Agents>
  <lrml:Agent key="mp"
    sameAs="http:example.org/agents#MonicaPalmirani">
    <lrml:hasType iri="http://example.org/types#Person"/>
  </lrml:Agent>
  <lrml:Agent key="ta"
    sameAs="http://example.org/agents#TaraAthan"/>
</lrml:Agents>
```

The Agent usually is the author of the rule model and he/she/it can act in a particular function (e.g., as senator). A Figure in LegalRuleML is an instantiation of a function by an Actor, and an Actor could be an Agent or a Figure.

```
<lrml:Figures>
  <lrml:hasMemberType
    iri="http://example.org/figure-types#LegislativeFigure"/>
  <lrml:Figure key="fs">
    <lrml:hasFunction iri="http://example.org/functions#Senator"/>
    <lrml:hasActor keyref="#ta"/>
  </lrml:Figure>
</lrml:Figures>
```

In the end we associate the Actor that fills a Role (using `<lrml:filledBy>`) for a particular rule.

```
<lrml:Roles>
  <lrml:Role key="role1" iri="http://example.org/roles#author">
    <lrml:filledBy keyref="#mp"/>
    <lrml:filledBy keyref="#ta"/>
    <lrml:forExpression keyref="#rule1a"/>
  </lrml:Role>
  <lrml:Role key="role2" iri="http://example.org/roles#author">
    <lrml:filledBy keyref="#mp"/>
    <lrml:forExpression keyref="#atom2a"/>
    <lrml:forExpression keyref="#atom2b"/>
  </lrml:Role>
</lrml:Roles>
```

Using this mechanism we can filter all the rules modelled by a particular Actor when he/she/it acts as a particular figure; for instance, we can filter for all the rules modelled by President Obama when he is acting as chief executive and not as the commander-in-chief of the United States Armed Forces.

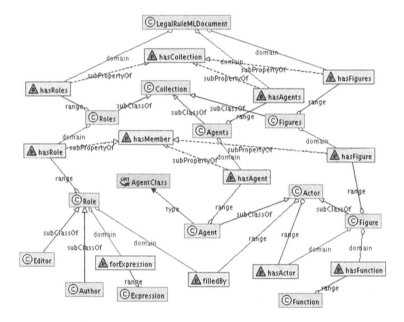

Fig. 7. Partial metamodel for agent, figure and role metadata concepts. AgentClass is imported as URI from dublin core.

5.4   Time and Events

Legal texts are often amended as a society or judicial system evolves. Norms and rules are valid in a particular interval of time and with respect to three main legal axes: when they come into force (entry or enforceability), when they effect the intended or desired result (efficacy), and when they apply (applicability). In this section, we model the external temporal dimensions of the norms (e.g., when the norm is valid) and not the temporal dimensions of the complex events that are the content of the textual provision (e.g., when a person is to present a tax application). Therefore, we only model the intervals and temporal parameters that define the period of validity of the rules. Moreover, in keeping with the sources, it is important to link the temporal parameters to any part of a rule (e.g., atom, rel, ind, if, then, etc.) with a very fine granularity. The following fragment shows the definition of the instant time using the <ruleml:Time> element wrapped by the <lrml:Times> collection element:

```
<lrml:Times>
  <ruleml:Time key="t1">
    <ruleml:Data xsi:type="xs:dateTime">
      1978-01-01T01:01:00.0Z
    </ruleml:Data>
  </ruleml:Time>
  <ruleml:Time key="t2">
    <ruleml:Data xsi:type="xs:dateTime">
      1989-03-01T01:01:00.0Z
    </ruleml:Data>
  </ruleml:Time>
</lrml:Times>
```

The time instants are combined in intervals according with the legal temporal characteristics, e.g. enforceability, efficacy, applicability. In the following case the tblock1 defines the interval $[t_1, t_2]$ of efficacy.

```
<lrml:TemporalCharacteristics key="tblock1">
  <lrml:TemporalCharacteristic key="e1-b">
    <lrml:forStatus iri="lrmlv:Efficacious"/>
    <lrml:hasStatusDevelopment iri="lrmlv:Starts"/>
    <lrml:atTime keyref="#t1"/>
  </lrml:TemporalCharacteristic>
  <lrml:TemporalCharacteristic key="e1-e">
    <lrml:forStatus iri="lrmlv:Efficacious"/>
    <lrml:hasStatusDevelopment iri="lrmlv:Ends"/>
    <lrml:atTime keyref="#t2"/>
  </lrml:TemporalCharacteristic>
</lrml:TemporalCharacteristics>
```

After this definition of the time interval or instant, it is possible to associate them to the legal sources using the <lrml:Association> element or the <lrml:Context> element (see Sect. 6) for associating the temporal parameters with any part of the rule formalization.

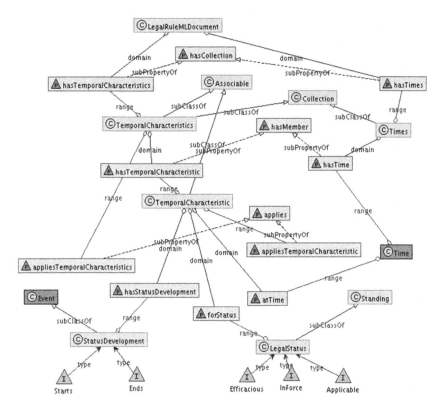

Fig. 8. Partial Metamodel for Temporal Metadata Concepts. Individuals are represented by triangular icons with the letter 'I'. Event and Time classes are imported from RuleML.

6 Association and Context

6.1 Association

To avoid redundancy, we have the element `<Association>` which can be used to group meta information referring to several rules or portions of them. In the following example we have two associations inside of the collection element `<Associations>`. The first `<Association>` applies the temporal parameters of tblock1 to the prescriptive statements 1 and 2. In the second one authority and jurisdiction properties are applied to prescriptive statements 1 and 3:

```
<lrml:Associations key="sourceBlock1">
  <lrml:Association>
    <lrml:appliesTemporalCharacteristics keyref="#tblock1"/>
    <lrml:toTarget keyref="#ps1"/>
    <lrml:toTarget keyref="#ps2"/>
  </lrml:Association>
  <lrml:Association>
    <lrml:appliesAuthority keyref="ex:#congress"/>
    <lrml:appliesJurisdiction keyref="ex:#us"/>
    <lrml:toTarget keyref="#ps1"/>
    <lrml:toTarget keyref="#ps3"/>
```

```
    </lrml:Association>
  </lrml:Associations>
```

This LegalRuleML language construct permits a large flexibility without replicating the information and so maintains the XML representation neatly, cleanly, compactly, and with fewer redundancies and errors. The parameters that we can associate are:

```
<lrml:appliesModality iri="deovo:obl"/>
```

for expressing modality;

```
<lrml:appliesSource keyref="#sec504-clsc-pnt1"/>
```

for connecting LegalSources or References;

```
<lrml:appliesTemporalCharacteristics keyref="#tblock1"/>
```

for connecting temporal parameters;

```
<lrml:appliesStrength iri="lrmlv:Defeasible"/>
```

for qualifying the strength of a rule according to the defeasibility categorization;

```
<lrml:appliesAuthority keyref="authorities:congress"/>
```

for assigning the authority of the editor of the rule;

```
<lrml:appliesJurisdiction keyref="jurisdictions:us"/>
```

for assigning the jurisdiction to a rule.

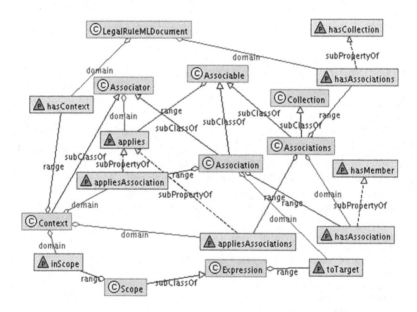

Fig. 9. Partial metamodel for context concepts.

6.2   Context

A rule may be differently interpreted according to a variety of parameters associated with a particular situation. For instance, sometimes an alternative interpretation of a textual source of a rule (and its associated formalisation) is associated with a jurisdiction, e.g., regional, national, or international levels, meaning that in one jurisdiction, the rule is interpreted one way, while in another jurisdiction, it is interpreted in another way. Similarly, temporal parameters (e.g., efficacy, enforceability) can change over time due to the normative modifications, and these changes can also affect the strength of the norms.

To represent such parameters, we introduce the `<lrml:Context>` element, which permits the description of all the characteristics that are linked to a particular rule (e.g., `rule1`) using the operator `<applies*>`, substituting the * with different relationships (see Sect. 6.1). Additionally to the previous relationships we add also the following:

```
<lrml:appliesAssociations keyref="#assoc1"/>
<lrml:appliesAlternatives keyref="#alt2"/>
```

The mechanism combines the relationships and the target rules, and it acts as a bridge between metadata and rules or fragments of them. The following example shows rules `rule1` and `rule4` connected with a LegalSource section 504, point 2, under the authority of Congress, valid in the jurisdiction of the USA, associated with the association `#assoc1` and constrained by the alternatives represented in `#alt2`.

```
<lrml:Context key="ruleInfo4" hasCreationDate="#t1">
  <lrml:appliesSource keyref="#sec504-clsc-pnt2"/>
  <lrml:appliesTemporalCharacteristics keyref="#tblock1"/>
  <lrml:appliesStrength iri="lrmlv:Defeater"/>
  <lrml:appliesAuthority keyref="authorities:congress"/>
  <lrml:appliesJurisdiction keyref="jurisdictions:us"/>
  <lrml:appliesAssociations keyref="#assoc1"/>
  <lrml:appliesAlternatives keyref="#alt2"/>
  <lrml:inScope keyref="#rule1"/>
  <lrml:inScope keyref="#rule4"/>
</lrml:Context>
```

7   Concrete XML-based Syntax Design

The concrete XML-based syntax for LegalRuleML was designed based on the principles in Sect. 3, as well as certain design principles that are specific to XML-based syntaxes.

7.1   XML Elements vs. Attributes

A common design decision for XML-based languages is whether to use an XML element or an attribute to represent a particular abstract syntactic feature. General guidelines are:

– If the information in question could be itself marked up with elements, put it in an element, because attributes cannot contain such complex content;
– If the information is suitable for attribute form (i.e., not complex), but could end up as multiple attributes of the same name on the same element, use child elements instead, avoiding list datatypes for attributes;
– If the information is required to be in a standard XML schema attribute type such as ID, IDREF, ENTITY, KEYREF, use an attribute;
– If the information should not be normalized for white space, use elements (XML processors normalize attributes in ways that can change the raw text of the attribute value.).

Additional general markup conventions developed in RuleML are adopted in LegalRuleML, providing common principles for the merged language hierarchy.

7.2   Node and Edge Elements

There is a distinction between *type* (also called *node*) elements and *role* (also called *edge*) elements, the element name of the former starting with an upper case letter, and the latter with a lower case letter. Node elements correspond to classes of the metamodel while edge elements correspond to relationships between members of these classes. Edge elements correspond, in general, to "object" properties in the metamodel, where the range is a subclass of `rdfs:Resource`. Node elements alternate with edge elements, forming a bipartite pattern, often called a striped syntax (e.g., the striped RDF/XML syntax).

7.3   Specialization of Language Constructs with Attributes and Header Elements

Main XML elements are used for representing general language constructs as recursive trees while XML attributes and nonrecursive *header* elements are used for distinguishing specializations of a given main element. (Attributes are also used for rendering names that are IRIs, as in RDF.) Syntactic and semantic variation can thus be achieved by different attribute values and header elements rather than requiring a different element name. Consider the case of M general language constructs, all of which may be specialized by P attributes, each with N predefined values. With this approach, a vocabulary of size $M + N * (P + 1)$ is able to express $M * N^P$ specialized language constructs. In practice, not all specializing components are appropriate for all general language constructs, so the actual reduction of vocabulary is not as dramatic as the example, but still significant.

7.4   Generic Elements

In addition to predefined values, a number of RuleML and LegalRuleML attributes are allowed values which are IRIs, providing extension points for user-defined syntactic and semantic variation. A *generic* element is a main element whose semantics is underspecified unless an attached attribute or header element provides a predefined value or an IRI pointer to a user-defined semantics (e.g., `<Obligation>` is a generic deontic operator.) In contrast, non-generic main elements have either a fixed semantics (e.g., `<References>`), or a default semantics specified by a profile reference which may be modified through the use of semantic variant attributes (e.g., `<ruleml:And>`).

7.5 Normalized and Compact Serialization

In many cases, edge elements are redundant because they could be reconstructed based on the type or position of the parent and child node elements. RuleML syntax allows such edges to be optionally skipped, called the *stripe-skipped* serialization. LegalRuleML syntax allows the two extreme cases - either no edges are skipped in the document (the *normalized* serialization) or all skippable edges in the document are omitted (the *compact* seralization). The normalized serialization may be reconstructed from a document in stripe-skipped or compact serialization by applying the *normalizer* XSLT transformation.

7.6 Design Patterns

Inside of LegalRuleML we employ five well-known design patterns:

- *container*, which is a structure of elements having independent existence (e.g., `<Context>` can include several `<Association>` sub-elements);
- *collection*, a subpattern of container that is in the form of a list of elements of the same type (e.g., `<Roles>` that is a sequence of `<Role>` elements);
- *recursive element* (e.g., `<Obligation>` can include other `<Obligation>` elements);
- *marker*, an element that uses attribute `@sameAs` for identifying a source, e.g.,
    ```
    <lrml:LegalSource key="sec504-clsa-pnt1"
        sameAs="UScode:title17-chp5-sec504-clsa-lst1-pnt1"/>
    ```
- *composite* elements that are made up of different dependent parts, (e.g., a rule `<Rule>` consists of an antecedent `<if>` and conclusion `<then>`).

7.7 IRI References, CURIES, and the Xsd:ID Datatype

Syntactic labels are attached to fragments of LegalRuleML syntax with the `@key` attribute, and are referenced with `@keyref`. On LegalRuleML elements, the datatype of `@key` values is `xsd:ID`, as is used in HTML for same-document references, while the datatype of `@keyref` is either an IRI reference (`xsd:anyURI`) or a CURIE [1].

The names of elements and attributes in the XML syntax of LegalRuleML are inspired by terms from the legal domain, which then facilitates the use by users familiar with this domain. The LegalRuleML meta-model captures the common meaning of such terms as understood in the legal field and provides an IRI for each metamodel term within the LegalRuleML metamodel namespace.

These IRIs may be used whenever it is appropriate to refer to a "resource", in the sense of RDF, including as values of LegalRuleML attributes.

The element names of the LegalRuleML XML-based syntax are qualified names, and all LegalRuleML attributes are unqualified.[8] An XSLT transformation has been defined that converts a LegalRuleML document in the XML-based syntax into RDF that employs the LegalRuleML metamodel vocabulary[9].

In the following section we illustrate the connections among the various concepts and their representation in the language.

8   Examples

We use a fragment of the US Code, Title 17, sec. 504, point (c) on copyright infringement for presenting how LegalRuleML can model complex legal norms in elegant way. Section 504 was modified seven times over several years. However only three versions are relevant in our scenario: (i) the version entered into force at Oct. 19, 1976; (ii) the version entered into force at Oct. 31, 1988; (iii) the version entered into force at Dec. 9, 1999 that is valid till today. The original version is:

17 USC Sec. 504
(c) Statutory Damages.
(1) Except as provided by clause (2) of this subsection, the copyright owner may elect, at any time before final judgement is rendered, to recover, instead of actual damages and profits, an award of statutory damages for all infringements involved in the action, with respect to any one work, for which any one infringer is liable individually, or for which any two or more infringers are liable jointly and severally, in a sum of not less than $250 or more than $10,000 as the court considers just. For the purposes of this subsection, all the parts of a compilation or derivative work constitute one work.
(2) In a case where the copyright owner sustains the burden of proving, and the court finds that infringement was committed willfully, the court in its discretion may increase the award of statutory damages to a sum of not more than $50,000. In a case where the infringer sustains the burden of proving, and the court finds, that such infringer was not aware and had no reason to believe that his or her acts constituted an infringement of copyright, the court in its discretion may reduce the award of statutory damages to a sum of not less than $100.

The Copyright Act establishes conditions to protect various types of intellectual property or work, by preventing, in general, the use of such works without a license and by providing exceptions to the general provision.

---

[8] Certain qualified attributes in external namespaces are imported into LegalRuleML.
[9] https://tools.oasis-open.org/version-control/browse/wsvn/legalruleml/trunk/schemas/xslt/triplifyMerger-ids.xsl.

For the purpose of this tutorial, the conditions can be paraphrased using the following prescriptive rule:

R1: if a piece of work is covered by copyright, then it is forbidden to use it.

and its companion constitutive rule

C1: an infringer is defined as somebody who used a piece of work when it was forbidden to use it.

The provisions in Section 504 can now be paraphrased as follows:

- R2: if the copyright owner claims statutory damages then the penalty for the infringer is to pay statutory damages of between \$250 and \$10,000.
- R3: if the copyright owner sustains the burden of proof and the infringer infringes copyright willfully then the penalty for the infringer is to pay statutory damages of between \$250 and \$50,000.
- R4: if the infringer sustains the burden of proof and the infringer infringes NOT willfully then the penalty for the infringer is to pay statutory damages of between \$100 and \$10,000.
- Defeasability: $R4 > R3 > R2$.

Over time the penalties change as follow:

	Statutory Damages			
Interval of efficacy of the norm	min	max	Willfully	Not Willfully
[1976-10-19, 1995-03-01[	\$250	\$10,000	\$50,000	\$100
[1995-03-01, 2001-02-01[	\$500	\$20,000	\$100,000	\$200
[2001-02-01, ∞ [	\$750	\$30,000	\$150,000	\$200

The prescriptive rule that represents the first case is the following:[10]

```
<lrml:PrescriptiveStatement key="ps2-tblock1">
  <ruleml:Rule key=":rule2-tblock1" closure="universal">
    <ruleml:if>
      <ruleml:And>
        <ruleml:Atom keyref=":rule0-ruleml-Atom1"/>
        <ruleml:Atom key=":rule2-tblock1-ruleml-Atom1">
          <ruleml:Rel iri="glevo:claimStatutoryDamages">
            claims statutory damages
          </ruleml:Rel>
          <ruleml:Var type="lovo:copyrightOwner">X</ruleml:Var>
        </ruleml:Atom>
      </ruleml:And>
    </ruleml:if>
    <ruleml:then>
      <lrml:Reparation keyref="#rep1-tblock1"/>
    </ruleml:then>
  </ruleml:Rule>
</lrml:PrescriptiveStatement>
```

---

[10] The full LegalRuleML representation of section 504 is available from https://tools. oasis-open.org/version-control/browse/wsvn/legalruleml/trunk/examples/tutorial/ USC_17_504_context.lrml.

The `<lrml:Reparation keyref="#rep1-tblock1"/>` is a reference to the following fragment of code that connects `penalty1` related to the time `tblock1` with the prescriptive rule that is violated:

```
<lrml:Reparation key="rep1-tblock1">
  <lrml:appliesPenalty keyref="#penalty1-tblock1"/>
  <lrml:toPrescriptiveStatement keyref="#ps1"/>
</lrml:Reparation>
```

Finally the penalty is modelled as follows to represent the range of the sanction:

```
<lrml:PenaltyStatement key="penalty1-tblock1">
  <lrml:Obligation key="penalty1-tblock1-obl1">
    <ruleml:slot>
      <lrml:Bearer iri="deovo:oblBearer"/>
      <ruleml:Var>Y</ruleml:Var>
    </ruleml:slot>
    <ruleml:slot>
      <lrml:AuxiliaryParty iri="deovo:auxParty"/>
      <ruleml:Var>X</ruleml:Var>
    </ruleml:slot>
    <ruleml:Atom key=":penalty1-tblock1-obl1-axm1">
      <ruleml:Rel iri="lovo:payStatutoryDamages"/>
      <ruleml:slot>
        <ruleml:Ind iri="lovo:payMin"/>
        <ruleml:Ind>$250</ruleml:Ind>
      </ruleml:slot>
      <ruleml:slot>
        <ruleml:Ind iri="lovo:payMax"/>
        <ruleml:Ind>$10,000</ruleml:Ind>
      </ruleml:slot>
    </ruleml:Atom>
  </lrml:Obligation>
</lrml:PenaltyStatement>
```

As a further illustration of the LegalRuleML modelling capabilities we propose a real life case (taken from the Italian legal system and jurisprudence, originally discussed in [15]) depending on multiple (alternative) interpretation of a norm, and we show possible formalisations of the case and the interpretations. We are going to use the formal representations to illustrate the LegalRuleML mechanisms to cope with the phenomenon of multiple interpretations. The case is based on a dispute of Art. 1, Comma 2, Law 379/1990. The article recites.

> The benefit referred to in comma 1 shall be paid in an amount equal 80 per cent of five-twelfths of the income earned and reported for tax purposes by the freelancer in the second year preceding the year of application.[11]

The case 18/96, Bologna Tribunal, Imola Section, concerns the interpretation of the conjunction in *the income earned **and** reported for tax purposes. . . .*

---

[11] L'indennità di cui al comma 1 viene corrisposta in misura pari all'80 per cento di cinque dodicesimi del reddito percepito e denunciato ai fini fiscali dalla libera professionista nel secondo anno precedente a quello della domanda.

A fundamental and unalienable principle of legal language is its close connection with natural language; in particular, the interpretation of a textual provision should be the ordinary meaning conveyed by the text of the provision taking into account its context in the act in which it appears and the purpose or object underlying the act. For example, in the Italian legal systems this connection is prescribed by Article 12 of the Preleggi, Italian Civil Code, stating.

> In applying a statute, the interpreter should not attribute to it a meaning different from that made evident by the proper meaning of the words and by their connection, as well as by the intention of the law maker.[12]

Accordingly, the literal interpretation of the norm is given by the rule

$$earned(x, y - 2) \wedge reported(x, y - 2) \Rightarrow \left[\text{OBL}_{bearer=employer}^{auxiliary=freelancer}\right] paybenefit(f(x), y) \quad (1)$$

The arguments of the predicates *earned* and *reported* are the income x earned/reported in the year in the second argument $(y - 2)$. Similarly for *paybenefit* where the function f encodes the computation of the value of the benefit based on the value of the income x. However, according to the Italian taxation legislation in force at the time of the dispute the income received in one year is reported for tax purpose the year after the year it has been earned. Thus, for example, the income earned in 1995 is reported in 1996. This principle can be formulated as follows:

$$earned(x, y) \rightarrow reported(x, y + 1) \quad (2)$$
$$reported(x, y) \rightarrow earned(x, y - 1) \quad (3)$$

Consider now the *Income* constant obtained by applying the Russell's definite description operator (ι) on the conjunction in the left-hand side of (1).

$$Income = \iota x(earned(x, y) \wedge reported(x, y)) \quad (4)$$

The conclusion is that the constant *Income* is not denoting, i.e., the interpretation of *Income* is $\emptyset$, thus there is no income "entity" that is earned and reported in one and the same year. Hence, the left hand side of the rule in (1) never holds, and the rule never fires, against the intentions of the legislator.

Based on the textual provision two possible interpretations are possible: in the first interpretation the temporal expression "in the second year preceding the year of application" refers to the income earned in the second year preceding the application, while in the second interpretation it refers to the income reported for tax purposed in the second year preceding the application. For example, for an application in year 1998, the first interpretation bases the computation on

---

[12] Nell'applicare la legge non si può ad essa attribuire altro senso che quello fatto palese dal significato proprio delle parole secondo la connessione di esse, e dalla intenzione del legislatore.

the income earned in 1996 (and reported in 1997), while for the second interpretation, the value of the benefit is computed starting from the income reported in 1996 (and earned in 1995). Accordingly, the first interpretation, the interpretation proposed by the freelancer in the case, can be formalised by the rule

$$earned(x, y - 2) \Rightarrow \left[\mathrm{OBL}^{auxiliary=freelancer}_{bearer=employer}\right] paybenefit(f(x), y) \qquad (5)$$

Similarly the second interpretation, the interpretation proposed by the employer, can be represented by the rule[13]

$$reported(x, y - 2) \Rightarrow \left[\mathrm{OBL}^{auxiliary=freelancer}_{bearer=employer}\right] paybenefit(f(x), y) \qquad (6)$$

The task of the Judge was to decide which of the two interpretations has to be used for the application of the norm. In the case the Judge argued in favour of the interpretation advanced by the freelancer.

We presented three possible interpretations of the norm, the literal interpretation, the interpretation of the freelancer and the interpretation of the employer. Here we are going to present the LegalRuleML fragments required to encode the formalisations corresponding to the three interpretations. The formalisations of these three statements can be represented as prescriptive rules which are encoded by <lrml:PrescriptiveStatement> elements in LegalRuleML, each containing one <ruleml:Rule> Template. The following fragment corresponds to the literal interpretation, i.e., (1)

```
<lrml:PrescriptiveStatement key="literal">
  <ruleml:Rule closure="universal" key=":literal-template">
    <ruleml:if>
      <ruleml:And>
        <ruleml:Atom key=":atom-earned">
          <ruleml:Rel iri="lovo:earned"/>
          <ruleml:Var>income</ruleml:Var>
          <ruleml:Expr>
            <ruleml:Fun iri="glevo:subtract"/>
            <ruleml:Var>year</ruleml:Var>
            <ruleml:Data xsi:type="xs:integer">2</ruleml:Data>
          </ruleml:Expr>
        </ruleml:Atom>
        <ruleml:Atom key=":atom-reported">
          <ruleml:Rel iri="lovo:reported"/>
          <ruleml:Var>income</ruleml:Var>
          <ruleml:Expr>
            <ruleml:Fun iri="glevo:subtract"/>
            <ruleml:Var>year</ruleml:Var>
            <ruleml:Data xsi:type="xs:integer">2</ruleml:Data>
          </ruleml:Expr>
        </ruleml:Atom>
      </ruleml:And>
```

[13] Alternatively, we could use $earned(x, y - 3) \Rightarrow \left[\mathrm{OBL}^{auxiliary=freelancer}_{bearer=employer}\right] paybenefit(f(x))$, while, from a formal point of view, it is semantically equivalent to (6) it is less close in meaning to the textual provision than its counterpart: the temporal reference in the argument would "third year preceding the year of the application".

```
    </ruleml:if>
    <ruleml:then>
      <lrml:Obligation key="obl-paybenefit">
        <ruleml:slot>
          <lrml:Bearer/>
          <ruleml:Var>Employer</ruleml:Var>
        </ruleml:slot>
        <ruleml:slot>
          <lrml:AuxiliaryParty/>
          <ruleml:Var>Freelancer</ruleml:Var>
        </ruleml:slot>
        <ruleml:Atom>
          <ruleml:Rel iri="lovo:paybenefit"/>
          <ruleml:Expr>
            <ruleml:Fun iri="glevo:80_percent_of_five-twelfths_of"/>
            <ruleml:Var>income</ruleml:Var>
          </ruleml:Expr>
          <ruleml:Var>year</ruleml:Var>
        </ruleml:Atom>
      </lrml:Obligation>
    </ruleml:then>
  </ruleml:Rule>
</lrml:PrescriptiveStatement>
```

Since LegalRuleML is built on top of RuleML we can reuse all RuleML facilities, in particular we can use `<ruleml:Expr>` and `<ruleml:Fun>` to encode the computation of the benefit to be paid to the freelancer.

The next snippet captures the interpretation of the freelancer, i.e., (5).

```
<lrml:PrescriptiveStatement key="freelancer">
  <ruleml:Rule closure="universal" key=":freelancer-template">
    <ruleml:if>
      <ruleml:Atom keyref=":atom-earned"/>
    </ruleml:if>
    <ruleml:then>
      <lrml:Obligation keyref="#obl-paybenefit"/>
    </ruleml:then>
  </ruleml:Rule>
</lrml:PrescriptiveStatement>
```

Notice that inside this statement we can use `keyref`s to refer to the elements already defined in the statement corresponding to the literal interpretation. Similar considerations apply to the statement modelling (6), the employer's interpretation, below.

```
<lrml:PrescriptiveStatement key="employer">
  <ruleml:Rule closure="universal" key=":employer-template">
    <ruleml:if>
      <ruleml:Atom keyref=":atom-reported"/>
    </ruleml:if>
      <ruleml:then>
        <lrml:Obligation keyref="#keyobl-paybenefit"/>
      </ruleml:then>
  </ruleml:Rule>
</lrml:PrescriptiveStatement>
```

The following LegalRuleML Constitutive Statement represents the principle expressed in (2), that earned income will be reported in the following year. Because a Constitutive Statement defines concepts and does not prescribe behaviours, the consequent of its `<ruleml:Rule>` Template does not contain deontic operators.

```
<lrml:ConstitutiveStatement key="tax1">
 <ruleml:Rule closure="universal">
   <ruleml:if>
     <ruleml:Atom>
       <ruleml:Rel iri="lovo:earned"/>
       <ruleml:Var>income</ruleml:Var>
       <ruleml:Var>year</ruleml:Var>
     </ruleml:Atom>
   </ruleml:if>
   <ruleml:then>
     <ruleml:Atom>
       <ruleml:Rel iri="lovo:reported"/>
       <ruleml:Var>income</ruleml:Var>
       <ruleml:Expr key=":year+1">
         <ruleml:Fun iri="glevo:add"/>
         <ruleml:Var>year</ruleml:Var>
         <ruleml:Data xsi:type="xs:integer">1</ruleml:Data>
       </ruleml:Expr>
     </ruleml:Atom>
   </ruleml:then>
 </ruleml:Rule>
</lrml:ConstitutiveStatement>
```

Similarly, the following fragment represents the principle that reported income was earned in the previous year, as expressed in (3).

```
<lrml:ConstitutiveStatement key="tax2">
 <ruleml:Rule closure="universal">
   <ruleml:if>
     <ruleml:Atom>
       <ruleml:Rel iri="lovo:reported"/>
       <ruleml:Var>income</ruleml:Var>
       <ruleml:Var>year</ruleml:Var>
     </ruleml:Atom>
   </ruleml:if>
   <ruleml:then>
     <ruleml:Atom>
       <ruleml:Rel iri="lovo:earned"/>
       <ruleml:Var>income</ruleml:Var>
       <ruleml:Expr key=":year-1">
         <ruleml:Fun iri="glevo:subtract"/>
         <ruleml:Var>year</ruleml:Var>
         <ruleml:Data xsi:type="xs:integer">1</ruleml:Data>
       </ruleml:Expr>
     </ruleml:Atom>
   </ruleml:then>
 </ruleml:Rule>
</lrml:ConstitutiveStatement>
```

After the renderings of the alternative interpretations and the relationships between the predicates *earned* and *reported* given by the three constitutive rules, we have to specify that they are mutually exclusive formalisation of the same norm. This can be achieved by the following Alternatives element that represents a mutually-exclusive collection of renderings of the Legal Norms from the Legal Source #ls1. The `<lrml:LegalSource>` with key #ls1, not shown in the text, contains the references to the actual text of the norm.

```
<lrml:Alternatives key="maternity-alts">
  <lrml:Comment> These alternatives are mutually
     incompatible formalizations of the same legal source: keyref="#ls1".
  </lrml:Comment>
  <lrml:hasAlternative keyref="#literal" />
  <lrml:hasAlternative keyref="#freelancer" />
  <lrml:hasAlternative keyref="#employer" />
</lrml:Alternatives>
```

A `<lrml:Context>` element is used to render a collection of Associations, e.g. the Association of a Legal Source with a rendering of it as a LegalRuleML Statement, or to constrain other Contexts with respect to Alternatives. The following Context establishes a constraint that at most one of the Alternatives from the collection #maternity-alts may be selected by each Context:

```
<lrml:Context key="maternity-alts-ctxt">
  <lrml:appliesAssociations keyref="#asn-alts"/>
  <lrml:appliesAlternatives keyref="#maternity-alts"/>
</lrml:Context>
```

The Context metadata, e.g. authorship, source, authority, temporal and jurisdictional properties, are specified in an external (to the Context) Association element with identifier asn-alts, not shown in the paper, which is referenced using keyref. Similarly other Context elements (also not shown in the paper) are given with the metadata about the authors of the various Statements. This permits to establish the provenance of the interpretations.

In the following fragment, a particular Alternative – that proposed by the freelancer – is selected, leading to the generation of the corresponding `<ruleml:Rule>` from the rule Template :freelancer-template.

```
<lrml:Context key="adjudication">
  <lrml:appliesAssociation keyref="#asn-adjudication"/>
  <lrml:inScope keyref="#freelancer"/>
</lrml:Context>
```

Unlike the first Context element, this one contains an `<lrml:inScope>` element. Such Contexts render interpretations that select one or more Statements as their scope of interpretation. When a Context is processed for presentation or inference, Legal Rules[14] are generated from the `<ruleml:Rule>` Templates of in-scope Statements, annotated and optionally modified semantically by the Associations of the Context.

---

[14] In this paper, we focus on Prescriptive and Constitutive Statements, which always lead to generated Legal Rules. However, in the general case, e.g. `<lrml:FactualStatement>`, something other than a Legal Rule may be generated when a Statement is in scope.

In this example the external Association `asn-adjudication` links the metadata for the adjudication of the case with a particular rendering of the norm, the rendering `freelancer`, corresponding to the interpretation proposed by the freelancer and confirmed by the judge[15].

9   Conclusion

The tutorial introduces LegalRuleML, a markup up language with a rich set of features and vocabulary. The language is guided by design principles and illustrated with some examples. LegalRuleML is intended to model legal rules and to facilitate reasoning with them by fulfilling the most important requirements in the legal domain such as the use of deontic operators, defeasible logic, and temporal parameters along with the qualification of the norms (e.g., constitutive, prescriptive, reparation, penalty) and the connection between legal sources and metadata of the rules. In addition to an XML syntax, LegalRuleML provides a methodology for analysing legal texts and for formally representing norms. LegalRuleML permits the representation of alternative interpretations of the same part of legal text, adhering to legal practice. The <lrml:Association> structure helps to compose different properties and to connect such compositions with rules or fragment of rules (e.g., Atom). The metamodel of LegalRuleML is the main pillar of the vocabulary design, helping to guide consistent modelling over time and allowing the language to evolve and be extended. However, sometimes LegalRuleML is too verbose, flexible, or detailed, making it difficult to properly manually manage the markup. The flexibility the XML-schema is especially difficult, for it does not impose some conceptual constraints that are important for the analysis. For these reasons, some tools are now emerging to help legal knowledge engineers, who many not be familiar with XML or RDF principles, to correctly apply LegalRuleML. Other tools can be applied to LegalRuleML representations and reason with them. RAWE is a web editor that supports a legal knowledge engineer to model norms starting from the original legal text [28]. SPINdle is a legal reasoner that implements defeasible reasoning and the temporal reasoning [25]. PROVA is an open-source rule language that can be used by LegalRuleML to manage the temporal parameters and to integrate with Reaction RuleML (https://prova.ws/). There are also tools provided in the LegalRuleML OASIS repository to serialize RDF files in favour of the Semantic Web linked open data model. Considering these tools, the application of LegalRuleML is promising; it is well supported by a robust design, a firm basis in legal theory, a sound XML syntax, and illustrations of how the language is applied.

---

[15] The full example is available from https://tools.oasis-open.org/version-control/browse/wsvn/legalruleml/trunk/examples/approved/maternity_alternatives_compact. lrml.

References

1. Adida, B., Birbeck, M., McCarron, S., Herman, I.: RDFa core 1.1 - third edition. http://www.w3.org/TR/rdfa-core/#s_curies
2. Alchourrón, C.E., Bulygin, E.: Permission and permissive norms. In: Krawietz, W., et al. (eds.) Theorie der Normen, pp. 349–371. Duncker & Humblot, Berlin (1984)
3. Antoniou, G.: Defeasible logic with dynamic priorities. Int. J. Intell. Syst. **19**(5), 463–472 (2004)
4. Antoniou, G., Billington, D., Governatori, G., Maher, M.J.: Representation results for defeasible logic. ACM Trans. Comput. Logic **2**(2), 255–287 (2001)
5. Athan, T., Boley, H., Governatori, G., Palmirani, M., Paschke, A., Wyner, A.: OASIS LegalRuleML. In: Proceedings of the Fourteenth International Conference on Artificial Intelligence and Law, pp. 3–12, New York (2013)
6. Athan, T., Governatori, G., Palmirani, M., Paschke, A., Wyner, A.: Legal interpretations in LegalRuleML. In: Villata, S., Peroni, S., Palmirani, M. (eds.) Proceedings of the Semantic Web for the Law and Second Jurix Doctoral Consortium Workshops (SW4LAW+JURIX-DC 2014). CEUR Workshop Proceedings, vol. 1296, CEUR-WS.org (2014)
7. Bench-Capon, T., Coenen, F.P.: Isomorphism and legal knowledge based systems. Artif. Intell. Law **1**(1), 65–86 (1992)
8. Brickley, D., Guha, R.V.: RDF schema 1.1. http://www.w3.org/TR/rdf-schema/
9. Dattolo, A., Di Iorio, A., Duca, S., Feliziani, A.A., Vitali, F.: Structural patterns for descriptive documents. In: Baresi, L., Fraternali, P., Houben, G.-J. (eds.) ICWE 2007. LNCS, vol. 4607, pp. 421–426. Springer, Heidelberg (2007)
10. de Saussure, F.: Cours de Linguistique Générale. Payot, Lausanne (1916)
11. Dworkin, R.: The model of rules I. In Taking Rights Seriously. Harvard University Presss, Cambridge, MA (1977)
12. Gordon, T., Prakken, H., Walton, D.: The Carneades model of argument and burden of proof. Artif. Intell. **171**, 875–896 (2007)
13. Gordon, T.F.: The Pleadings Game-An Artificial Intelligence Model of Procedural Justice. Springer, New York (1995)
14. Gordon, T.F., Governatori, G., Rotolo, A.: Rules and norms: Requirements for rule interchange languages in the legal domain. In: Governatori, G., Hall, J., Paschke, A. (eds.) RuleML 2009. LNCS, vol. 5858, pp. 282–296. Springer, Heidelberg (2009)
15. Governatori, G.: Un modello formale per il ragionamento giuridico. Ph.D. thesis, CIRFID, Università di Bologna (1997)
16. Governatori, G.: Representing business contracts in RuleML. Int. J. Coop. Inf. Syst. **14**(2–3), 181–216 (2005)
17. Governatori, G.: On the relationship between Carneades and defeasible logic. In: van Engers, T. (ed.) Proceedings of the 13th International Conference on Artificial Intelligence and Law (ICAIL 2011), pp. 31–40. ACM Press (2011)
18. Governatori, G.: Business process compliance: An abstract normative framework. IT Inf. Technol. **55**(6), 231–238 (2013)
19. Governatori, G., Olivieri, F., Rotolo, A., Scannapieco, S.: Computing strong and weak permissions in defeasible logic. J. Philos. Logic **42**(6), 799–829 (2013)
20. Governatori, G., Rotolo, A.: Logic of violations: A Gentzen system for reasoning with contrary-to-duty obligations. Australas. J. Logic **4**, 193–215 (2006)
21. Governatori, G., Rotolo, A.: Changing legal systems: legal abrogations and annulments in defeasible logic. Logic J. IGPL **18**(1), 157–194 (2010)

22. Governatori, G., Rotolo, A., Sartor, G.: Temporalised normative positions in defeasible logic. In: Proceedings of the 10th International Conference on Artificial Intelligence and Law (ICAIL 2005), pp. 25–34. ACM (2005)
23. Hart, H.: The Concept of Law, 2nd edn. Clarendon Press, Oxford (1994)
24. Herrestad, H., Krogh, C.: Obligations directed from bearers to counterparts. In: Proceedings of the Fifth International Conference on Artificial Intelligence and Law (ICAIL 1995), pp. 210–218 (1995)
25. Lam, H.-P., Governatori, G.: The making of SPINdle. In: Governatori, G., Hall, J., Paschke, A. (eds.) RuleML 2009. LNCS, vol. 5858, pp. 315–322. Springer, Heidelberg (2009)
26. Lappin, S. (ed.): The Handbook of Contemporary Semantic Theory. Blackwell Publishers, Cambridge (1997)
27. Nute, D.: Handbook of Logic in Artificial Intelligence and Logic Programming, volume 3, chapter Defeasible Logic, pp. 353–395. Oxford University Press, Oxford, 1994
28. Palmirani, M., Cervone, L., Bujor, O., Chiappetta, M.: RAWE: an editor for rule markup of legal texts. In: Fodor, P., Roman, D., Anicic, D., Wyner, D., Palmirani, M., Sottara, D., Lévy, F. (eds.) Joint Proceedings of the 7th International Rule Challenge, the Special Track on Human Language Technology and the 3rd RuleML Doctoral Consortium. CEUR Workshop Proceedings, Seattle, USA, 11–13 July 2013, vol. 1004, CEUR-WS.org (2013)
29. Palmirani, M., Governatori, G., Contissa, G.: Temporal dimensions in rules modelling. In: Winkels, R. (ed.) JURIX. Frontiers in Artificial Intelligence and Applications, vol. 223, pp. 159–162. IOS Press, Amsterdam (2010)
30. Palmirani, M., Governatori, G., Rotolo, A., Tabet, S., Boley, H., Paschke, A.: LegalRuleML: XML-based rules and norms. In: Palmirani, M. (ed.) RuleML - America 2011. LNCS, vol. 7018, pp. 298–312. Springer, Heidelberg (2011)
31. Prakken, H., Sartor, G.: A dialectical model of assessing conflicting argument in legal reasoning. Artif. Intell. Law 4(3–4), 331–368 (1996)
32. Prakken, H., Sartor, G.: Argument-based extended logic programming with defeasible priorities. J. Appl. Non Class. Logics 7(1), 25–75 (1997)
33. Raz, J.: Between authority and interpretation: on the theory of law and practical reason. Oxford University Press, Oxford (2009)
34. Sartor, G.: Legal reasoning: A cognitive approach to the law. In: Pattaro, E., Rottleuthner, H., Shiner, R.A., Peczenik, A., Sartor, G. (eds.) A Treatise of Legal Philosophy and General Jurisprudence, vol. 5. Springer, Berlin (2005)
35. Scalia, A., Garner, B.A.: Reading Law: The Interpretation of Legal Texts. West, Minneapolis (2012)
36. Searle, J.R.: The Construction of Social Reality. The Free Press, New York (1996)
37. Nicos Stavropoulos. Legal interpretivism. In Edward N. Zalta, editor, The Stanford Encyclopedia of Philosophy. Summer 2014 edition (2014)
38. Georg Henrik von Wright: Norm and action: A logical inquiry. Routledge and Kegan Paul, London (1963)

The Power of Semantic Rules in Rulelog: Fundamentals and Recent Progress (Extended Abstract of Tutorial Presentation)

Benjamin N. Grosof[✉], Michael Kifer, and Paul Fodor

Coherent Knowledge Systems, LLC., Mercer Island, USA
benjamin.grosof@coherentknowledge.com

1 Introduction

In this tutorial, we provide a comprehensive and up-to-date introduction to the fundamental concepts and recent progress in the area of Rulelog, a leading approach to semantic rules knowledge representation and reasoning. Rulelog is expressively powerful, computationally affordable, and has capable efficient implementations. A large subset of Rulelog is in draft as an industry standard[1] to be submitted to RuleML[2] and W3C[3] as a dialect of Rule Interchange Format (RIF) [2,3].

2 Rulelog Logical Language and Capabilities

Rulelog extends well-founded declarative logic programs (LP) with:

- Strong meta-reasoning, including higher-order syntax (Hilog) [4], reification [20], and rule ids (within the logical language).
- Explanations of inferences [1].
- Efficient higher-order defaults, including "argumentation theories" [17,18].
- Flexible probabilistic reasoning, including distribution semantics [14], evidential probability [13], and tight integration with inductive machine learning are key areas of recent technology progress and ongoing R&D.
- Bounded rationality, including restraint—a "control knob" to ensure that the computational complexity of inference is worst-case polynomial time [1,7].
- "Omni-directional" disjunction and existential quantifiers in the rule heads [9].
- Object-orientation and frame syntax [12], which subsumes RDF triples.
- Sound tight integration of first-order-logic ontologies including OWL and several other lesser features, including aggregation operators and integrity constraints.

We will cover many of these features in the tutorial.

---

[1] http://ruleml.org/rif/rulelog/rif/RIF-Rulelog.html.
[2] http://www.ruleml.org.
[3] http://www.w3.org.

W. Faber and A. Paschke (Eds.): Reasoning Web 2015, LNCS 9203, pp. 189–192, 2015.
DOI: 10.1007/978-3-319-21768-0_7

3   Rulelog Implementation Techniques

Implementation techniques for Rulelog inferencing include transformational compilations and extensions of *tabling* algorithms from logic programming. "Tabling" here means smart caching of subgoals and conclusions together with incremental revision of the cached conclusions when facts or rules are dynamically added or deleted [15,16]. "Tabling" is thus a mixture of backward-direction and forward-direction inferencing. There are both open-source and commercial tools for Rulelog that vary in their range of expressive completeness and of user convenience. They are interoperable with databases and spreadsheets, and complement inductive machine learning and natural language processing techniques. The most complete system today for Rulelog is Ergo[4], a commercial platform suite from Coherent Knowledge Systems[5]. Flora-2[6], an open source system, implements a significant subset of Rulelog reasoning [11,19,21].

4   Textual Rulelog

Time permitting, we will discuss "Textual" Rulelog, in which Rulelog is rendered in a natural language, such as English. ErgoText is a commercial realization of this approach. Using Rulelog to interpret and generate English is a key area of ongoing research and development [9].

5   Applications

Using Ergo, we will illustrate the various applications of the Rulelog technology in a wide range of tasks and domains in business, government, and science. We will tour areas of recent applications progress, which include: legal/policy compliance, e.g., in financial services; education/tutoring; and e-commerce marketing [5,6,8,10].

6   Additional Tutorial Material

Previous, longer but now less up-to-date, tutorials on Rulelog were given at our earlier tutorial at AAAI-13 [7].

References

1. Andersen, C., Benyo, B., Calejo, M., Dean, M., Fodor, P., Grosof, B.N., Kifer, M., Liang, S., Swift, T.: Advanced knowledge base debugging for rulelog. In: Joint Proceedings of the 7th International Rule Challenge, the Special Track on Human Language Technology and the 3rd RuleML Doctoral Consortium, Seattle, USA, July 11–13, 2013 (2013). http://ceur-ws.org/Vol-1004/paper8.pdf

---

[4] http://coherentknowledge.com/ergo-suite-platform-technology/.

[5] http://coherentknowledge.com.

[6] http://flora.sourceforge.net.

2. Boley, H., Kifer, M.: RIF Basic logic dialect, February 2013. http://www.w3.org/TR/rif-bld/, W3C Recommendation. http://www.w3.org/TR/rif-bld/
3. Boley, H., Kifer, M.: RIF Framework for logic dialects, February 2013. http://www.w3.org/TR/rif-fld/, W3C Recommendation. http://www.w3.org/TR/rif-fld/
4. Chen, W., Kifer, M., Warren, D.: HiLog: a foundation for higher-order logic programming. J. Logic Program. **15**(3), 187–230 (1993)
5. Fibo technology summit at semtechbiz: Financial industry and sem tech leaders discuss ontology evaluation tools, flora-2's potential, and more, July 2013. http://www.dataversity.net/fibo-technology-summit-at-semtechbiz-financial-industry-and-sem-tech-leaders-discuss-ontology-evaluation-tools-flora-2s-potential-and-more/
6. Grosof, B., Dean, M., Kifer, M.: Semantic web rules: Fundamentals, applications, and standards, tutorial presented at AAAI-2013, July 2013. http://silk.semwebcentral.org/
7. Grosof, B., Swift, T.: Radial restraint: a semantically clean approach to bounded rationality for logic programs. In: AAAI Conference on Artificial Intelligence. AAAI (2013)
8. Grosof, B.N., Burstein, M.H., Dean, M., Andersen, C., Benyo, B., Ferguson, W., Inclezan, D., Shapiro, R.: A SILK graphical UI for defeasible reasoning, with a biology causal process example. In: Palmirani, M., Shafiq, M.O., Francesconi, E., Vitali, F. (eds.) Proceedings of the RuleML-2010 Challenge, at the 4th International Web Rule Symposium, Washington, DC, USA, October, 21–23, 2010. CEUR Workshop Proceedings, vol. 649. CEUR-WS.org (2010). http://ceur-ws.org/Vol-649/paper12.pdf
9. Grosof, B.N.: Rapid text-based authoring of defeasible higher-order logic formulas, via textual logic and rulelog. In: Morgenstern, L., Stefaneas, P., Lévy, F., Wyner, A., Paschke, A. (eds.) RuleML 2013. LNCS, vol. 8035, pp. 2–11. Springer, Heidelberg (2013). http://dx.doi.org/10.1007/978-3-642-39617-5_2
10. Grosof, B.: Making very expressive rules practical in logic and text, November 2013. invited talk. http://coherentknowledge.com/wp-content/uploads/2013/05/DecisionCamp2013-talk-v7-1-BNG.pdf
11. Kifer, M.: Flora-2: an object-oriented knowledge base language. The Flora-2 Web Site (2015). http://flora.sourceforge.net
12. Kifer, M., Lausen, G., Wu, J.: Logical foundations of object-oriented and frame-based languages. J. ACM **42**, 741–843 (1995)
13. Kyburg, H., Teng, C.: Uncertain Inference. Cambridge University Press, Cambridge (2001)
14. Riguzzi, F., Swift, T.: Well-definedness and efficient inference for probabilistic logic programming under the distribution semantics. Theor. Pract. Logic Program. **13**(2), 279–302 (2013)
15. Swift, T., Warren, D.S.: XSB: extending the power of prolog using tabling. Theor. Pract. Logic Program. (TPLP) **12**(1–2), 157–187 (2012)
16. Swift, T.: Incremental tabling in support of knowledge representation and reasoning. TPLP **14**(4–5), 553–567 (2014). http://dx.doi.org/10.1017/S1471068414000209
17. Wan, H., Grosof, B., Kifer, M., Fodor, P., Liang, S.: Logic programming with defaults and argumentation theories. In: Hill, P.M., Warren, D.S. (eds.) ICLP 2009. LNCS, vol. 5649, pp. 432–448. Springer, Heidelberg (2009)
18. Wan, H., Kifer, M., Grosof, B.: Defeasibility in answer set programs with defaults and argumentation rules. Semant. Web J. **5**, 81–98 (2014)

19. Yang, G., Kifer, M.: FLORA: implementing an efficient DOOD system using a tabling logic engine. In: Palamidessi, C., et al. (eds.) CL 2000. LNCS (LNAI), vol. 1861, p. 1078. Springer, Heidelberg (2000)
20. Yang, G., Kifer, M.: Reasoning about anonymous resources and meta statements on the semantic web. In: Spaccapietra, S., March, S., Aberer, K. (eds.) Journal on Data Semantics I. LNCS, vol. 2800, pp. 69–97. Springer, Heidelberg (2003)
21. Yang, G., Kifer, M., Zhao, C.: $\mathcal{F}$LORA-2: a rule-based knowedge representation and inference infrastructure for the semantic web. In: Meersman, R., Schmidt, D.C. (eds.) CoopIS/DOA/ODBASE 2003. LNCS, vol. 2888, pp. 671–688. Springer, Heidelberg (2003)

Recent Advances in Datalog±

Georg Gottlob[1], Michael Morak[2]([✉]), and Andreas Pieris[2]

[1] Department of Computer Science, University of Oxford, Oxford, UK
georg.gottlob@cs.ox.ac.uk
[2] Institute of Information Systems, Vienna University of Technology, Vienna, Austria
{morak,pieris}@dbai.tuwien.ac.at

Abstract. This tutorial, which is a continuation of the tutorial "Datalog and Its Extensions for Semantic Web Databases" presented in the Reasoning Web 2012 Summer School, discusses recent advances in the Datalog± family of languages for knowledge representation and reasoning. These languages extend plain Datalog with key modeling features such as existential quantification (signified by the "+" symbol), and at the same time apply syntactic restrictions to achieve decidability of ontological reasoning and, in some relevant cases, also tractability (signified by the symbol "−"). In this tutorial, we first introduce the main Datalog± languages that are based on the well-known notion of guardedness. Then, we discuss how these languages can be extended with important features such as disjunction and default negation.

1 Introduction

Data and knowledge based systems have been playing a dominant role in computer science since the 70 s when organizations massively adopted them to support their business operations and decision making activities. Yet, in the last decade, such systems became even more popular as data and knowledge turn out to be an intrinsic part of every individual and collective activity in our society. In this setting, a major problem is to represent information in such a way that software programs can access it and act as if they really understand its semantics. On the one hand, initiatives such as the semantic web defined languages like RDF(S) and OWL to support the creation of semantically annotated data, enabling ontological querying and reasoning. On the other hand, the Linked Open Data (LOD) community produced very large amounts of semantically enriched data that enabled a multitude of data-driven semantic web applications. The need for efficient processing of semantic data stimulated several research initiatives addressing data management problems such as representation, storage and querying.

The present tutorial, which is actually a continuation of the tutorial "Datalog and Its Extensions for Semantic Web Databases" presented in the Reasoning Web 2012 Summer School [29], is intended for people familiar with the basics of database and semantic web technologies who want to explore the connection between modeling languages used in these fields, and their practical adoption for knowledge representation and data management purposes in more depth.

© Springer International Publishing Switzerland 2015
W. Faber and A. Paschke (Eds.): Reasoning Web 2015, LNCS 9203, pp. 193–217, 2015.
DOI: 10.1007/978-3-319-21768-0_8

1.1 A Bit of History

The data management problems we are facing today are not completely new. As an example, in the late 70 s, Datalog [1,19] emerged as a prominent language from logic programming [32]. The term Datalog was coined by David Maier and reflects the intention of devising a counterpart of Prolog—the most prominent rule-based formalism in computer science—for data processing. While Prolog is undecidable in general, if we consider the program as fixed, Datalog enjoys tractable reasoning complexity w.r.t. the size of the input database. Datalog's original aim was to be used as an expressive language for querying relational data; in fact, it adds *recursion* to the relational algebra, and therefore goes beyond the expressive power of classical *select-project-join* queries. Recursion is still important today for reasoning over complex paths in graph-like data which is abundant, for example, in the context of social networks and the semantic web.

Applications of Datalog include reasoning about semi-structured data, data integration, routing, security policy management, enterprise decision automation and many others. As a consequence, Datalog has evolved into a first-class formalism with efficient implementations such as DLV [23] and Clingo [25]. On the other hand, since Datalog rules are a representation of clauses in the function-free Horn fragment of *first-order logic (FOL)*, Datalog revealed itself relevant also for semantic web applications such as ontological modeling and reasoning.

Example 1. Consider, as an example, the following Datalog rules expressing the knowledge that every female and every male is a person.

$$person(X) \leftarrow female(X) \qquad person(X) \leftarrow male(X).$$

Intuitively, to construct the set of all persons, we need to take into account the union of all females and males. In other words, some objects can be inferred to be persons, even without stating this fact explicitly. Datalog also provides a natural solution to some fundamental reasoning problems, such as the computation of the *transitive closure* of a binary relation, and is thus adequate for reasoning about graph reachability or connectedness. The rules

$$ancestor(X, Y) \leftarrow parent(X, Y)$$
$$ancestor(X, Z) \leftarrow parent(X, Y), ancestor(Y, Z)$$

express the ancestor relation between persons. Notice that in the last rule the predicate *ancestor* occurs in both sides of $\leftarrow$, which is an example of a recursive definition that is not possible in relational algebra.   □

From the other side, ontology languages for the semantic web were also designed to be able to express ontological information as the one above. In this setting, *ontologies* written in *ontology languages* are intended to describe and structure complex web resources, making them readily available for manipulation by automated agents. The different ontology languages of the semantic web are based on the family of *description logics (DLs)* [6] which, in turn, are decidable fragments of FOL equipped with a convenient syntax.

DLs model a domain of interest in terms of *concepts* and *roles*, where concepts are interpreted as sets of individuals (i.e., constants), and roles as binary relations over them. A DL knowledge base $\mathcal{K} = (\mathcal{T}, \mathcal{A})$ consists of a *TBox* $\mathcal{T}$ and an *ABox* $\mathcal{A}$. The TBox $\mathcal{T}$ consists of axioms, where the most common axioms are statements of inclusion $(\alpha \sqsubseteq \beta)$ between pairs of concepts or roles. The ABox $\mathcal{A}$ is a set of facts about the participation of individuals in concepts and roles. In database terms, an ABox can be seen as a (possibly incomplete) relational database with unary and binary relations only, while a TBox is a set of expressive integrity constraints over the data.

As an example, consider the DL called $\mathcal{SHIF}$, which has most of the features of the OWL languages. $\mathcal{SHIF}$ concepts are built by applying *concept constructors* on roles and other concepts. We use letters A, B, C for concept names and R, S for role names. A $\mathcal{SHIF}$ ABox $\mathcal{A}$ consists of ground atomic formulae of the form $R(a, b)$ and $A(a)$, where R is a role and A is a concept. A $\mathcal{SHIF}$ TBox $\mathcal{T}$ consists of axioms of one of the following forms:

(1) $A \sqcap B \sqsubseteq C$ is a concept inclusion. The complex concept $A \sqcap B$ stands for intersection of A and B, and the whole axiom states that each object that is both A and B is also C. This axiom translates into the FOL formula $\forall X\ p_A(X) \wedge p_B(X) \rightarrow p_C(X)$, where the predicates p_A, p_B, and p_C represent the FOL predicates corresponding to the concept (resp., role) names. As an example, the axiom Parent $\sqcap$ Male $\sqsubseteq$ Father can express the knowledge that male parents are fathers.

(2) $A \sqsubseteq B \sqcup C$ is another form of concept inclusion, stating that each object that is A must also be B or C. The axiom can be written as the FOL formula $\forall X\ p_A(X) \rightarrow p_B(X) \vee p_C(X)$. As an example, the axiom Person $\sqsubseteq$ Female $\sqcup$ Male states that every person must be female or male.

(3) $A \sqsubseteq \forall R.B$ is an inclusion employing on the right hand side a complex concept $\forall R.B$, denoting the set of all the objects such that all R "neighbors" are B, and is captured by $\forall X \forall Y p_R(X, Y) \rightarrow p_B(Y)$. The whole axiom translates into the first-order logic formula $\forall X \forall Y p_A(X) \wedge p_R(X, Y) \rightarrow p_B(Y)$. An example of this axiom could be MetalDevice $\sqsubseteq \forall$hasPart.Metal stating that all parts of a metal device are made of metal.

(4) $A \sqsubseteq \exists R.B$ is an inclusion employing yet another kind of complex concept $\exists R.B$ on the right. $\exists R.B$ denotes the set of objects that have an R "neighbor" that is B, and is captured by $\forall X \exists Y\ p_R(X, Y) \wedge p_B(Y)$. The full axiom translates into the formula $\forall X\ p_A(X) \rightarrow \exists Y\ p_R(X, Y) \wedge p_B(Y)$. For example, we can use Student $\sqsubseteq \exists$attends.Course to express the requirement that each student must attend at least one course.

(5) $A \sqsubseteq\ \leqslant 1\,R.B$ restricts the number of R "neighbors" of type B that A can have, and can make parts of R functional (functionality constraints are common integrity constraints in databases). The axiom says that each object that is A can be related via the role R to at most one object that is B. This axiom translates into the formula $\forall X \forall Y_1 \forall Y_2\ p_A(X) \wedge p_R(X, Y_1) \wedge p_B(Y_1) \wedge p_R(X, Y_2) \wedge p_B(Y_2) \rightarrow Y_1 = Y_2$. An example of this axiom could be Person $\sqsubseteq\ \leqslant 1$ hasIdSocialSecNum, stating that a person can have at most one social security number.

(6) An axiom A **disj** B states disjointness between concepts A and B, e.g., Student **disj** Professor states that students and professors are disjoint sets. The axiom translates into the formula $\forall X\ p_A(X) \wedge p_B(X) \rightarrow \bot$.

(7) $R \sqsubseteq S$ expresses the inclusion of R in S, e.g., brotherOf $\sqsubseteq$ relativeOf captures the knowledge that brothers are relatives. This axiom translates into the formula $\forall X \forall Y\ p_R(X,Y) \rightarrow p_S(X,Y)$ of first-order logic.

(8) An axiom R **inv** S allows to define *inverse* roles, and is translated into first-order logic as $\forall X \forall Y\ p_R(X,Y) \leftrightarrow p_S(Y,X)$. For example, a is *child* of b iff b is a *parent* of a. This can be expressed as parentOf **inv** childOf.

(9) Finally, the axiom **trans**(R) expresses transitivity of the role R, and is translated into the formula $\forall X \forall Y \forall Z\ p_R(X,Y) \wedge p_R(Y,Z) \rightarrow p_R(X,Z)$.

Example 2. Consider the Datalog rules of Example 1. The same can be (rather succinctly) expressed in DL syntax as

$$\text{Female} \sqsubseteq \text{Person} \tag{1}$$

$$\text{Male} \sqsubseteq \text{Person} \tag{2}$$

$$\text{parentOf} \sqsubseteq \text{ancestorOf} \tag{3}$$

$$\textbf{trans}\,(\text{ancestorOf}) \tag{4}$$

where (1,2) are *concept inclusions*, (3) is a *role inclusion*, and (4) states that the role *ancestor* is transitive.   □

Datalog and DLs have several commonalities but also significant differences which need to be reconciled in order to make them interoperable in semantic web applications as also noticed in [35]. Differences include disjunction and existential quantification in DL ontologies, as well as the different assumptions underlying the semantics of the languages (e.g., open vs closed-world assumption). Table 1 shows a partial translation of $\mathcal{SHIF}$ into Datalog. As it can be seen, some expressions have no Datalog counterpart.

(1) An axiom $A \sqsubseteq B \sqcup C$ expresses disjunctive information and thus cannot be directly expressed in plain Datalog. One possibility is to employ, bearing the computational cost, *disjunctive* Datalog, which does support rules of the form $p_B(X) \vee p_C(X) \leftarrow p_A(X)$ [22].

(2) Notice that the translation of a functional constraint $A \sqsubseteq\ \leqslant 1\,R.B$ into first-order logic involves the equality predicate. Due to the slight semantic differences between DLs and Datalog, equality is treated differently in the two settings. For instance, in contrast to Datalog, DLs do not employ the so-called *unique name assumption (UNA)*. Different constants are treated as different domain objects by the Datalog semantics, yet a pair of constants may denote the same object in the standard semantics of first-order logic (and therefore DLs).

(3) A disjointness constraint A **disj** B can cause inconsistency of an ontology. E.g., the ontology $\mathcal{K} = \langle \mathcal{A}, \mathcal{T} \rangle$, where $\mathcal{A} = \{\text{Blue}(ball), \text{Red}(ball)\}$ and $\mathcal{T} = \{\text{Red } \textbf{disj } \text{Blue}\}$, is inconsistent, i.e., the first-order theory underlying

Table 1. From the DL $\mathcal{SHIF}$ to Datalog

$$A \sqcap B \sqsubseteq C \quad\rightsquigarrow\quad p_C(X) \leftarrow p_A(X), p_B(X)$$
$$A \sqsubseteq B \sqcup C \quad\rightsquigarrow\quad \text{N/A}$$
$$A \sqsubseteq \forall R.B \quad\rightsquigarrow\quad p_B(Y) \leftarrow p_A(X), p_R(X,Y)$$
$$A \sqsubseteq \exists R.B \quad\rightsquigarrow\quad \text{N/A}$$
$$A \sqsubseteq \leqslant 1\, R.B \quad\rightsquigarrow\quad \text{N/A}$$
$$R \sqsubseteq S \quad\rightsquigarrow\quad p_S(X,Y) \leftarrow p_R(X,Y)$$
$$A \text{ disj } B \quad\rightsquigarrow\quad \text{N/A}$$
$$R \text{ inv } S \quad\rightsquigarrow\quad p_S(X,Y) \leftrightarrow p_R(Y,X)$$
$$\mathbf{trans}(R) \quad\rightsquigarrow\quad p_R(X,Z) \leftarrow p_R(X,Y), p_R(Y,Z)$$
$$R(a,b) \quad\rightsquigarrow\quad p_R(a,b) \leftarrow$$
$$A(b) \quad\rightsquigarrow\quad p_A(b) \leftarrow$$

$\mathcal{K}$ is unsatisfiable. Unfortunately, plain Datalog does not have inconsistent programs and thus a satisfiability-preserving translation for disjointness constraints is not possible, in general.

(4) The axiom $A \sqsubseteq \exists R.B$, whose translation into first-order logic involves existential quantification, exposes a crucial difference between Datalog and DLs. Datalog was designed and intended for reasoning over finite databases, under the assumption that only the objects explicitly mentioned in the database exist. In contrast, DL-based ontologies support existential quantification, and are thus able to refer to objects that are not explicitly named in the ontology.

1.2 Research Challenges

We note that existential quantification and disjunction play an important role in knowledge representation. They are in fact necessary to represent important constructs of common ontology languages. Adding existential quantification to Datalog is the most interesting and relevant extension. Unfortunately, a naive extension of Datalog with existential quantified variables in the head is undecidable [10], and thus our task is non-trivial. We will try to identify meaningful fragments of Datalog with existential variables in the head that (i) have sufficient expressiveness for the above applications, but still retain the decidability of reasoning, and (ii) can be enriched with disjunction without sacrificing decidability. Notice that the obtained formalisms are actually members of Datalog$^{\pm}$, that is, a recently introduced family of knowledge representation languages [13].

Due to the existential quantification, correct and terminating reasoning algorithms require to develop methods for reasoning about infinite structures without explicitly building them. In the area of DLs and modal logic, decidability, algorithms and complexity results have been shown for various logics that do not exhibit finite models. Most of these fragments allow for only a limited number of variables (often two), and impose some form of *guardedness*, which can be roughly understood as a syntactically restricted form of quantification that only allows to talk about relations between objects that are close to each other in a structure, and results in regular models that are conveniently similar to trees. While guardedness is of course a limitation, it is often claimed to be a robust reason for decidability [30]. Furthermore, there is wide evidence suggesting that guardedness is not overly restrictive for many knowledge representation problems, and it is implicitly or explicitly present in many of the popular languages. Inspired by the above considerations, we will present guarded extensions of Datalog as a solution to our problems.

Remark. The problem of adding existentially quantified variables in Datalog was the main subject of the tutorial "Datalog and Its Extensions for Semantic Web Databases" presented in the Reasoning Web 2012 Summer School [29]. The main subject of the present tutorial is to understand how the guarded-based languages discussed in [29] can be enriched with disjunction, which, as discussed above, is a crucial feature for knowledge representation purposes.

1.3   Roadmap

In Sect. 2, we provide some preliminary notions about relational databases and queries. Syntax and semantics of Datalog is presented in Sect. 3, while syntax and semantics of Datalog$^{\exists,\vee}$, that is, the extension of Datalog with existential quantification and disjunction, is presented in Sect. 4. In Sect. 5, we focus on guarded Datalog$^{\exists,\vee}$, and we give an overview of the complexity results on query answering. A similar complexity overview is given for a key subclass of guarded Datalog$^{\exists,\vee}$, called linear Datalog$^{\exists,\vee}$, in Sect. 6. Finally, Sect. 7 collects several useful pointers to further reading material, and in particular to works that investigate the extension of Datalog$^{\exists}$ with default negation, a useful modeling feature that goes beyond DLs and Datalog$^{\exists,\vee}$.

2   Preliminaries

In this section, we briefly recall some basics on relational databases, homomorphisms and (Boolean) conjunctive queries.

2.1   Relational Databases

Let $\mathbf{C}$, $\mathbf{N}$ and $\mathbf{V}$ be pairwise disjoint infinite countably sets. The elements of $\mathbf{C}$ are called *constants* (constitute the normal domain of a database), the elements of $\mathbf{N}$ are called *(labeled) nulls* (used as placeholders for unknown values, and thus can be also seen as (globally) existentially quantified variables), and the elements of $\mathbf{V}$ are called *(regular) variables* (used in queries and dependencies). A fixed lexicographic order is assumed on $\mathbf{C} \cup \mathbf{N}$, such that every value in $\mathbf{N}$ follows all those in $\mathbf{C}$. We denote by $\mathbf{X}$ sequences (or sets) of variables $X_1, \ldots, X_k$. Throughout, let $[n] = \{1, \ldots, n\}$, for every integer $n \geqslant 1$.

A *relational schema* $\mathcal{R}$ (or simply *schema*) is a set of *relational symbols* (or *predicates*), each with its associated arity. A *position* $p[i]$, in a schema $\mathcal{R}$, is identified by a predicate $p \in \mathcal{R}$ and its i-th argument. A *term* t is a constant ($t \in \mathbf{C}$), labeled null ($t \in \mathbf{N}$), or variable ($t \in \mathbf{V}$). An *atomic formula* (or simply *atom*) has the form $p(t_1, \ldots, t_n)$, where p is an n-ary predicate, and $t_1, \ldots, t_n$ are terms. For an atom $\underline{a}$, we denote as $dom(\underline{a})$ and $var(\underline{a})$ the set of its terms and the set of its variables, respectively. These notations naturally extend to sets of atoms. For convenience, usually conjunctions and disjunctions of atoms are treated as sets of atoms. A *relational instance* (or simply *instance*) I for a schema $\mathcal{R}$ is a (possibly infinite) set of atoms of the form $p(\mathbf{t})$, where p is an n-ary predicate of $\mathcal{R}$, and $\mathbf{t}$ is an n-tuple of constants and nulls. A *database* D is a finite instance where only constants occur. Whenever an instance I is treated as a logical formula, in fact it is the formula $\exists \mathbf{X} (\bigwedge_{\underline{a} \in I} I)$, where $\mathbf{X}$ contains a variable X_z for each null z in I.

2.2 Homomorphisms

A *substitution* from a set of symbols S to a set of symbols S' is a function $h : S \to S'$ defined as follows: $\emptyset$ is a substitution (empty substitution), and if h is a substitution, then $h \cup \{s \to s'\}$ is a substitution, where $s \in S$ and $s' \in S'$. If $s \to s' \in h$, then we write $h(s) = s'$. The *restriction* of h to $T \subseteq S$, denoted $h_{|T}$, is the substitution $h' = \{t \to h(t) \mid t \in T\}$. A *homomorphism* from a set of atoms A to a set of atoms A' is a substitution $h : \mathbf{C} \cup \mathbf{N} \cup \mathbf{V} \to \mathbf{C} \cup \mathbf{N} \cup \mathbf{V}$ such that: *(i)* if $t \in \mathbf{C}$, then $h(t) = t$; and *(ii)* if $p(t_1, \ldots, t_n) \in A$, then $h(p(t_1, \ldots, t_n)) = p(h(t_1), \ldots, h(t_n)) \in A'$.

2.3 Conjunctive Queries

A *conjunctive query (CQ)* q over a schema $\mathcal{R}$ is a first-order formula $\exists \mathbf{Y}(\varphi(\mathbf{X}, \mathbf{Y}))$, where φ is a conjunction of atoms over $\mathcal{R}$ with variables from $\mathbf{X} \cup \mathbf{Y} \subset \mathbf{V}$, and possibly constants of $\mathbf{C}$. The *arity* of q is defined as the cardinality of $\mathbf{X}$, i.e., the number of free variables occurring in $\exists \mathbf{Y}(\varphi(\mathbf{X}, \mathbf{Y}))$. A 0-ary CQ is called *Boolean CQ (BCQ)*. An n-ary *union of conjunctive queries (UCQ)* over $\mathcal{R}$ is a disjunction of a finite number of n-ary CQs over $\mathcal{R}$. By abuse of notation, sometimes we consider a UCQ as set of CQs. The *answer* to an n-ary CQ $q = \exists \mathbf{Y}(\varphi(\mathbf{X}, \mathbf{Y}))$ over an instance I, denoted $q(I)$, is the set of all tuples of constants $\mathbf{t} \in \mathbf{C}^n$ for which there exists a homomorphism h such that $h(\varphi(\mathbf{X}, \mathbf{Y})) \subseteq I$ and $h(\mathbf{X}) = \mathbf{t}$. A BCQ has only the empty tuple as possible answer, in which case it is said to have a positive answer. Formally, a BCQ has a *positive* answer over I, written as $I \models q$, if $q(I) \neq \emptyset$. The answer to an n-ary UCQ Q over an instance I, denoted $Q(I)$, is the set of n-tuples $\bigcup_{q \in Q} q(I)$. The answer to a union of BCQs over I is positive, written as $I \models Q$, if $Q(I) \neq \emptyset$.

3   Datalog: Syntax and Semantics

Datalog (see, e.g., [1,19]) has been used as a paradigmatic database programming and query language for over three decades. While it is rarely used directly as a query language in corporate application contexts, Datalog has influenced the development of popular query languages such as SQL, whose newer versions allow one to express recursive queries.

3.1 Syntax

A *Datalog rule* ρ is an expression of the form

$$\underline{a}_0 \leftarrow \underline{a}_1, \ldots, \underline{a}_n,$$

where $n \geqslant 0$, $\underline{a}_0, \ldots, \underline{a}_n$ are atoms over a relational schema which contain constants of $\mathbf{C}$ and variables of $\mathbf{V}$, and each variable occurring in $\underline{a}_0$ must appear in at least one of $\underline{a}_1, \ldots, \underline{a}_n$. The atom $\underline{a}_0$ is called the *head*, denoted $head(\rho)$, while the set of atoms $\{\underline{a}_1, \ldots, \underline{a}_n\}$ is called the *body*, denoted $body(\rho)$. In other terms, a Datalog rule is a function-free Horn clause. A *Datalog program* P is a finite set of Datalog rules. An *extensional* predicate is a predicate that does not occur in the head of any rule of P, while an *intensional* predicate is a predicate that occurs in the head of some rule of P. The *extensional (database) schema* of P, denoted $EDB(P)$, consists of all the extensional predicates of P, whose values are given via an input database, while the *intensional schema* of P, denoted $IDB(P)$, consists of all the intensional predicates of P, whose values are computed by the program. The schema of P, written $SCH(P)$, is the set of predicates $EDB(P) \cup IDB(P)$. As we shall see, the semantics of a Datalog program is a mapping from databases for $EDB(P)$ to databases for $IDB(P)$.

Example 3. Consider the Datalog program P_{graph} consisting of

$$sp\_reachable(X) \leftarrow sp\_node(X)$$
$$sp\_reachable(Y) \leftarrow edge(X,Y), sp\_reachable(X),$$

which takes as input EDB a directed graph given by a binary *edge* relation, plus a set of special nodes of this graph given by a unary relation *sp_node*. Clearly,

$$EDB(P_{graph}) = \{edge, sp\_node\} \text{ and } IDB(P_{graph}) = \{sp\_reachable\}.$$

The above (recursive) program computes the set *sp_reachable* of all vertices in the graph that are reachable from special nodes.   □

3.2 Semantics

An interesting and elegant property of Datalog is the fact the there are three different but equivalent approaches to defining its semantics: a *model-theoretic* approach where the Datalog rules are considered as logical sentences asserting a property of the desired result, a *fixpoint* approach where the semantics are defined as a particular solution of a fixpoint equation, and a *proof-theoretic* approach which is based on obtaining proofs of facts. In the sequel, we discuss the fixpoint semantics; for details on the other approaches we refer the interested reader to [1, Chap. 12].

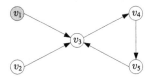

Fig. 1. Directed graph for Example 4.

Fixpoint Semantics. The fixpoint semantics of Datalog programs relies on an operator called the *immediate consequence operator*, which produces new facts starting from known facts. The *semantics* of P on an input database D, denoted $P(D)$, is defined as the smallest solution of a fixpoint equation involving that operator.

Let P be a Datalog program and D a database for $SCH(P)$. A fact $\underline{a}$ is an immediate consequence for D and P if either $\underline{a} \in D$, or there exists a rule $\underline{a}_0 \leftarrow \underline{a}_1, \ldots, \underline{a}_n$ in P and a homomorphism h such that $h(\{\underline{a}_1, \ldots, \underline{a}_n\}) \subseteq D$ and $\underline{a} = h(\underline{a}_0)$. The immediate consequence operator of P, denoted T_P, is the mapping from databases for $SCH(P)$ to databases for $SCH(P)$ defined as follows: for each database D, $T_P(D) = \{\underline{a} \mid \underline{a}\text{ is an immediate consequence for }D\text{ and }P\}$. We write $T_P^i(D)$ for the result obtained by applying T_P i times starting from D. Formally, $T_P^0(D) = D$ and $T_P^{i+1}(D) = T_P(T_P^i(D))$; let $T_P^\omega(D) = \bigcup_{i \geq 0} T_P^i(D)$. From the fact that $D \subseteq T_P(D)$ and the monotonicity of T_P, it is clear that $T_P^i(D) \subseteq T_P^{i+1}(D)$, for each $i \geq 0$. It is well-known that for a Datalog program P and a database D for $EDB(P)$, $T_P^\omega(D)$ is the minimum fixpoint of T_P containing D. Interestingly, $T_P^\omega(D)$ can be obtained by applying T_P finitely many times. More precisely, given a Datalog program P, for each database D there exists an integer k_D (which depends on D) such that $T_P^\omega(D) = T_P^{k_D}(D)$. The semantics of P on D is defined as $T_P^\omega(D)$.

Example 4. Consider the program P_{graph} given in Example 3, and the database

$$D = \{edge(v_1, v_3), edge(v_2, v_3), edge(v_3, v_4),$$
$$edge(v_4, v_5), edge(v_5, v_3), sp\_node(v_1)\}$$

for the schema $EDB(P_{graph})$; the graph G encoded by D is depicted in Fig. 1, where the special node is shaded. Clearly,

$$T_{P_{graph}}(D) = D \cup \{sp\_reachable(v_1)\}$$
$$T_{P_{graph}}^2(D) = T_{P_{graph}}(D) \cup \{sp\_reachable(v_3)\}$$
$$T_{P_{graph}}^3(D) = T_{P_{graph}}^2(D) \cup \{sp\_reachable(v_4)\}$$
$$T_{P_{graph}}^4(D) = T_{P_{graph}}^3(D) \cup \{sp\_reachable(v_5)\}$$
$$T_{P_{graph}}^5(D) = T_{P_{graph}}^4(D).$$

Hence, $P_{graph}(D) = T_P^\omega(D) = T_P^4(D)$.   □

3.3   Query Answering Under Datalog

Consider a Datalog program P and a database D for $EDB(P)$. Given an n-ary CQ $q = \exists \mathbf{Y}(\varphi(\mathbf{X}, \mathbf{Y}))$ over $SCH(P)$, the answer to q w.r.t. P and D is the set of n-tuples $\{\mathbf{t} \mid \mathbf{t} \in q(P(D))\}$. The complexity of deciding whether a tuple of constants belongs to the answer of q w.r.t. P and D is PTime-complete in data complexity, and ExpTime-complete in combined complexity. Recall that the data complexity is calculated by considering only the database as part of the input, while the combined complexity is calculated by taking, apart from the database, also the query and the program as part of the input. For more details on the complexity of Datalog see, e.g., [29].

4   Datalog$^{\exists,\vee}$: Syntax and Semantics

Datalog was designed and intended for reasoning over finite databases, assuming that only the values explicitly mentioned in the extensional database exist. For ontological reasoning, however, it would be desirable that an extended version of Datalog could be able to express the existence of certain values that are not necessarily from the EDB domain. This can be achieved by allowing existentially quantified variables in rule heads. Another key feature for representing ontologies, which is not expressible by Datalog rules, is disjunction that allows for non-deterministic reasoning.

Example 5. As said, ontology languages are based on DLs. Such formalisms can express, for instance, (i) each parent of a parent is a grandparent of a human, and vice versa; and (ii) each human is male or female, and vice versa. This is captured by the following axioms:

$$\exists\mathsf{parentOf.isparent} \equiv \exists\mathsf{grandparentOf.human}$$
$$\mathsf{human} \equiv \mathsf{male} \sqcup \mathsf{female}.$$

In an appropriate extended version of Datalog, the same can be expressed as:

$$\exists Z \, grandparentOf(X, Z) \leftarrow parentOf(X, Y), isparent(Y)$$
$$human(Y) \leftarrow grandparentOf(X, Y)$$
$$\exists Z \, parentOf(X, Z) \leftarrow grandparentOf(X, Y), human(Y)$$
$$isparent(Y) \leftarrow parentOf(X, Y)$$
$$male(X) \vee female(X) \leftarrow human(X)$$
$$human(X) \leftarrow male(X)$$
$$human(X) \leftarrow female(X).$$

Observe that all the predicates occurring in the above program appear both in the body and in the head of some rule. Therefore, in the desired extended version of Datalog, we no longer require the distinction between extensional and intensional predicates. □

Recently a family of Datalog-based languages, called Datalog$^{\pm}$, which is a new framework for tractable ontology querying, has been introduced [14]. The precise aim of Datalog$^{\pm}$ is to extend Datalog with key modeling features, while preserving not only decidability but also tractability of query answering in data complexity. The feature of existential quantification has been extensively discussed in the tutorial paper [29] presented in the Reasoning Web 2012 Summer School. As said, the present paper is a continuation of [29], where the feature of existential quantification together with the feature of disjunction are considered.

4.1 Syntax

A *Datalog$^{\exists,\vee}$ rule* ρ is an expression of the form

$$\gamma_1 \vee \ldots \vee \gamma_m \leftarrow \underline{a}_1, \ldots, \underline{a}_n,$$

where $\underline{a}_1, \ldots, \underline{a}_n$ are atoms over a relational schema that contain constants of $\mathbf{C}$ and variables of $\mathbf{V}$, and, for each $i \in [m]$, γ_i is an expression $\exists Y_1^i \ldots \exists Y_{m_i}^i \underline{b}_i$, where $m_i \geqslant 0$, $\{Y_1^i, \ldots, Y_{m_i}^i\} \subset \mathbf{V}$, $(\{Y_1^i, \ldots, Y_{m_i}^i\} \cap var(\{\underline{a}_1, \ldots, \underline{a}_n\})) = \emptyset$, and $\underline{b}_i$ is an atom that contains constants of $\mathbf{C}$ and variables of $(\{Y_1^i, \ldots, Y_{m_i}^i\} \cup var(\{\underline{a}_1, \ldots, \underline{a}_n\}))$. The expression $\gamma_1 \vee \ldots \vee \gamma_m$ is called the *head*, denoted $head(\rho)$, while the set of atoms $\{\underline{a}_1, \ldots, \underline{a}_n\}$ is called the *body*, denoted $body(\rho)$. A *Datalog$^{\exists,\vee}$ program* P is a finite set of Datalog$^{\exists,\vee}$ rules. The schema of P, written $SCH(P)$, is the set of predicates occurring in P. Notice that $SCH(P)$ is not partitioned, as in plain Datalog programs, into extensional and intensional predicates. Obviously, the program given in Example 5 is a Datalog$^{\exists,\vee}$ program.

4.2 Semantics

To define the semantics of Datalog$^{\exists,\vee}$ we follow an approach similar to the fixpoint semantics of Datalog programs, i.e., given a Datalog$^{\exists,\vee}$ program P and an input database D, $P(D)$ is defined as the least fixpoint of a monotonic operator. This can be achieved by exploiting the *disjunctive chase* introduced in [21], that is, an extension of the well-known chase procedure. Each disjunctive chase step "branches" out several instances, each satisfying one of the disjuncts of the Datalog$^{\exists,\vee}$ rule that is applied, and thus the result of the disjunctive chase is, in general, a set of instances (and not a single instance as that of the classical chase). The disjunctive chase works on an instance through the so-called (disjunctive) chase rule:

Chase Rule. Consider an instance I, and a Datalog$^{\exists,\vee}$ rule ρ of the form

$$\gamma_1 \vee \ldots \vee \gamma_m \leftarrow \underline{a}_1, \ldots, \underline{a}_n$$

as define above. We say that ρ is *applicable* to I if there exists a homomorphism h such that $h(body(\rho)) \subseteq I$, and the result of applying ρ to I with h is the set $\{I_1, \ldots, I_m\}$, where $I_i = I \cup h'(\gamma_i)$, for each $i \in [m]$, and $h' \supseteq h$ is such that $h'(Y)$ is a "fresh" null not occurring in I, and following lexicographically all those in I, for each $Y \in \{Y_1^i, \ldots, Y_{m_i}^i\}$. For such an application, which defines a single *chase step*, we write $I\langle \rho, h \rangle \{I_1, \ldots, I_m\}$.

A *disjunctive chase tree* of a database D and a Datalog$^{\exists,\vee}$ program P is a (possibly infinite) tree such that the root is D, and for every node I, assuming that $\{I_1, \ldots, I_m\}$ are the children of I, there exists $\rho \in P$ and a homomorphism h such that $I\langle\rho, h\rangle\{I_1, \ldots, I_m\}$. The disjunctive chase algorithm for D and P consists of an exhaustive application of chase steps in a *fair fashion*, which leads to a disjunctive chase tree T of D and P; let $chase(D, P)$ be the set $\{I | I$ is a leaf of $T\}$. Notice that each leaf of T is well-defined as the least fixpoint of a monotonic operator. The semantics of P and D, denoted $P(D)$, is defined as the set of instances $chase(D, P)$.

4.3   Query Answering Under Datalog$^{\exists,\vee}$

Consider a Datalog$^{\exists,\vee}$ program P and a database D for $SCH(P)$. Given an n-ary CQ $q = \exists\mathbf{Y}(\varphi(\mathbf{X}, \mathbf{Y}))$ over $SCH(P)$, the answer to q w.r.t. P and D, denoted $q(P, D)$, is the set of n-tuples $\{\mathbf{t} \mid \mathbf{t} \in q(I), \text{for each } I \in P(D)\}$. The query answering problem under Datalog$^{\exists,\vee}$, called CQ-ANSWERING, is defined as follows: given a database D, a Datalog$^{\exists,\vee}$ program P, an n-ary CQ q, and a tuple $\mathbf{t} \in \mathbf{C}^n$, decide whether $\mathbf{t} \in q(P, D)$.

At this point, one may observe that, in contrast to plain Datalog, the instance $P(D)$ is not unique since the result of the chase of D and P depends on the order that the rules of P are executed. In other words, different chase sequences may yield different results. However, $P(D)$ is unique up to homomorphic equivalence; implicit in [21]. More precisely, assuming that C_1 and C_2 are possible results of the chase of D and P, the following hold: (i) for each instance $I \in C_2$, there exists an instance $J \in C_1$ and a homomorphism h such that $h(J) \subseteq I$; and (ii) for each instance $I \in C_1$, there exists an instance $J \in C_2$ and a homomorphism h such that $h(J) \subseteq I$. This immediately implies that

$$\{\mathbf{t} \mid \mathbf{t} \in q(I), \text{for each } I \in C_1\} \;=\; \{\mathbf{t} \mid \mathbf{t} \in q(I), \text{for each } I \in C_2\}$$

and therefore, for CQ answering purposes, $P(D)$ is unique.

4.4   The Challenge of Infinity

Recall that for a Datalog program P and an input database D, $P(D)$ is finite and it is always possible to construct it. In fact, the fixpoint semantics of Datalog programs provide an efficient (w.r.t. the size of the data) algorithm, based on the immediate consequence operator, which constructs $P(D)$. Unfortunately, the situation changes dramatically if P is a Datalog$^{\exists,\vee}$ program. Due to the existentially quantified variables in rule heads, $P(D)$ may consist of infinitely many instances of infinite size, and is thus not explicitly computable. It is an easy exercise to verify that this is the case for the database $\{p(a, b)\}$, and the program consisting of the rules

$$\exists Z\, p(Y, Z) \leftarrow p(X, Y) \quad \text{and} \quad s(X) \vee s(Y) \leftarrow p(X, Y).$$

This is not surprising since query answering is undecidable even if we focus on Datalog$^\exists$ programs; implicit in [10]. Worse than that, undecidability holds even if both the program and the query are fixed, and only the database is given as input [12]. It is thus necessary to identify meaningful fragments of Datalog$^{\exists,\vee}$ for which query answering is decidable, and also tractable in data complexity. In what follows we discuss such fragments of Datalog$^{\exists,\vee}$ that are based on the well-known notion of guardedness.

5 Guarded Datalog$^{\exists,\vee}$

Guardedness, proposed by Andréka et al. [4], is a well-known restriction of first-order logic that ensures decidability of satisfiability, i.e., the problem of deciding whether a first-order theory has at least one model. Inspired by the guarded fragment of first-order logic, guarded Datalog$^\exists$ has been proposed in [12], and can be naturally extended to guarded Datalog$^{\exists,\vee}$. A *guarded Datalog$^{\exists,\vee}$* rule ρ is a Datalog$^{\exists,\vee}$ rule, where at least one atom $\underline{a} \in body(\rho)$ contains all the variables occurring in $body(\rho)$, i.e., $var(\underline{a}) = var(body(\rho))$. The rightmost such atom is called the *guard* of ρ. A *guarded Datalog$^{\exists,\vee}$ program* P is a finite set of guarded Datalog$^{\exists,\vee}$ rules. It is straightforward to verify that the Datalog$^{\exists,\vee}$ program given in Example 5 is guarded.

The decidability of CQ-ANSWERING under guarded Datalog$^{\exists,\vee}$ follows from the fact that the result of the chase of a database w.r.t. to a guarded Datalog$^\exists$ program has finite treewidth, i.e., is a treelike structure; for more details we refer the reader to [12]. The complexity of CQ-ANSWERING under guarded Datalog$^{\exists,\vee}$ programs has been investigated in [11], while the complexity of the same problem when the input query is an atomic query, i.e., a single atom, has been investigated in [28]. In the case of atomic queries the problem is dubbed CQ$_1$-ANSWERING. In what follows, we first focus in Sect. 5.1 on arbitrary conjunctive queries, and then we proceed in Sect. 5.2 with atomic queries.

5.1 Arbitrary Conjunctive Queries

Combined Complexity. Let us first focus on the combined complexity of our problem, and recall the following result established in [11]:

Theorem 1. CQ-ANSWERING *under guarded Datalog$^{\exists,\vee}$ is* 2EXPTIME-*complete in the combined complexity.*

The upper bound is obtained by first relating our problem to the problem of querying a first-order sentence, and then provide a polynomial time reduction to the problem of query answering under the guarded fragment of first-order logic, which is in 2EXPTIME [9]. Consider a database D, a Datalog$^{\exists,\vee}$ program P, an n-ary CQ q, and a tuple $\mathbf{t} \in \mathbf{C}^n$. The problem of deciding whether $\mathbf{t}$ belongs to the answer of q w.r.t. P and D is tantamount to the problem of deciding whether the first-order sentence $(D \wedge \Sigma_P)$ entails $q(\mathbf{t})$, where Σ_P is obtained by associating to each rule

$$\bigvee_{i\in[m]} \exists Y_1^i \ldots \exists Y_{m_i}^i \, \underline{b}_i \ \leftarrow \ \underline{a}_1, \ldots, \underline{a}_n$$

occurring in P, with $var(body(\rho)) = \{X_1, \ldots, X_k\}$, the first-order sentence

$$\forall X_1 \ldots \forall X_k \left(\underline{a}_1 \wedge \ldots \wedge \underline{a}_n \ \rightarrow \ \bigvee_{i\in[m]} \exists Y_1^i \ldots \exists Y_{m_i}^i \, \underline{b}_i \right).$$

It remains to show that $(D \wedge \Sigma_P)$ falls in the guarded fragment of first-order logic. Recall that this logic, introduced in [4], is a collection of first-order formulas with some syntactic restrictions in the quantification pattern, which is analogous to the relativized nature of modal logic. Formally, the *guarded fragment of first-order logic (GFO)* is the smallest set of formulas over a schema $\mathcal{R}$

1. containing all atomic $\mathcal{R}$-formulas;
2. closed under the logical connectives $\neg$, $\wedge$, $\vee$, $\rightarrow$; and
3. if $\underline{a}$ is an $\mathcal{R}$-atom or an equality atom containing all the variables of $\mathbf{X} \cup \mathbf{Y}$, and φ is a GFO formula with free variables contained in $(\mathbf{X} \cup \mathbf{Y})$, then

$$\forall \mathbf{X} \, (\underline{a} \rightarrow \varphi) \qquad \text{and} \qquad \exists \mathbf{X} \, (\underline{a} \wedge \varphi)$$

are GFO formulas as well.

It is not difficult to show that $(D \wedge \Sigma_P)$ is a GFO sentence. Assume, for example, that in P we have the rule $\exists Z \, s(X, Z) \leftarrow p(X, Y), t(Y)$, where $p(X, Y)$ is the guard, which in turn implies that in Σ_P we have the sentence $\forall X \forall Y (p(X, Y) \wedge s(Y) \rightarrow \exists Z \, t(X, Z))$. The latter can be rewritten as the GFO sentence

$$\forall X \forall Y (p(X, Y) \rightarrow (s(Y) \rightarrow \exists Z \, t(X, Z))).$$

By following the same approach, every sentence of Σ_P can be equivalently rewritten as a GFO sentence, and obtain $\hat{\Sigma}_P$. Since $(D \wedge \hat{\Sigma}_P)$ is a GFO sentence, the desired upper bound follows.

The argument for the lower bound is a little more complex. We can show that it is possible to simulate an alternating Turing machine that uses exponential space — it is well-known that alternating ExpSpace equals 2ExpTime [20]. We will give here a rough idea of the proof techniques needed to achieve this. First, we need a way to generate a sequence of configurations, where each such configuration is represented by 2^n null values. Secondly, we need a way to compare the same cell of two subsequent configurations. With these two conditions fulfilled, we can simulate an alternating Turing machine which uses exponential space as follows: for each configuration, guess a state and the head position; for each cell in the configuration, guess the tape content; compare two adjacent cells in a configuration to the same two cells in the subsequent configuration and check, using a query, whether the transition function is violated. Note that the query will thus be true iff the transition function is violated (i.e., when we make a wrong guess). The only case where the query is false is if there is a model that represents a valid, accepting configuration of the Turing machine. In order to describe in more detail how this can be done, let us fix some notation.

The proof is in fact by a reduction from the non-acceptance problem of an alternating exponential space Turing machine M on the empty input. Let $M = (S, \Lambda, \delta, s_0)$, where $S = S_\forall \uplus S_\exists \uplus \{s_a\} \uplus \{s_r\}$ is a finite set of states partitioned into universal states, existential states, an accepting state and a rejecting state, $\Lambda = \{0, 1, \sqcup\}$ is the tape alphabet with $\sqcup$ being the blank symbol, $\delta : S \times \Lambda \rightarrow (S \times \Lambda \times \{-1, +1\})^2$ is the transition function, and $s_0 \in S$ is the initial state. We assume that M is well-behaved and never tries to read beyond its tape boundaries, always halts, and uses exactly 2^n tape cells. Furthermore, we assume that a rejecting configuration does not have a subsequent configuration, while an accepting configuration has only itself as a subsequent configuration. Finally, we assume that $s_0 \in S_\exists$, and also that every universal configuration is followed by two existential configurations and vice versa. The above assumptions can be made, without sacrificing the generality of our proof, since the non-acceptance problem of M remains 2ExpTime-hard.

In order to represent configurations of the Turing machine M, we will use atoms of the form $conf[s](b_1, \ldots, b_n, a, h, t, p, n_1, n_2)$, where $s \in S$ is the state of the encoded configuration and is part of the predicate, $(b_1, \ldots, b_n) \in \{0, 1\}^n$ is an integer from $\{0, \ldots, 2^n - 1\}$ in binary notation which represents the index of the encoded cell with a be its content, $h \in \{0, 1\}$ and $h = 1$ iff the cursor of M is at the encoded cell, and t, p, n_1 and n_2 represent the current (t for this), the previous and the next two configurations, respectively. E.g., assuming that $n = 3$, $conf[s](1, 0, 1, \sqcup, 1, z_1, z_2, z_3, z_4)$, where $\{z_1, \ldots, z_4\} \subset \mathbf{N}$, says that the state of the configuration z_1 (nulls are used to represent configurations) is s, the fifth cell contains the blank symbol, the cursor is at the fifth cell, the previous configuration of z_1 is z_2, and the next two configurations of z_1 are z_3 and z_4.

The first step, generating trees of subsequent configurations, can easily be achieved using the following rules: for each $s \in S_\forall$,

$$\bigvee_{(s_1, s_2) \in S \times S} \exists N_3 \ldots \exists N_6 \; conf_0[s_1](N_1, T, N_3, N_4), conf_0[s_2](N_2, T, N_5, N_6)$$

$$\leftarrow conf_0[s](T, P, N_1, N_2)$$

and for each $s \in S_\exists$,

$$\bigvee_{s' \in S} \bigvee_{i \in \{1,2\}} \exists N_3 \exists N_4 \; conf_0[s'](N_i, T, N_3, N_4) \leftarrow conf_0[s](T, P, N_1, N_2).$$

Note that T, P, N_1 and N_2 stand for this configuration, previous configuration and the next two configurations, respectively.

Next, in order to generate the tape cells, we need to generate every binary number of length n, as previously discussed. For $0 < i < n$, the rule:

$$conf_i[s](X_1, \ldots, X_{i-1}, 0, T, P, N_1, N_2), conf_i[s](X_1, \ldots, X_{i-1}, 0, T, P, N_1, N_2)$$

$$\leftarrow conf_{i-1}[s](X_1, \ldots, X_{i-1}, T, P, N_1, N_2)$$

generates, from a binary number of length $i-1$ both following binary numbers of length i. It follows immediately that $conf_n$-type atoms will represent all possible binary numbers of length n as desired. Finally, with a simple rule we rename $conf_n$ to $conf$, in order to get rid of some tedious notation.

We now need to guess the tape content. The following rule, for each $s \in S$:

$$\bigvee_{a \in \{0,1,\sqcup\}} conf[s](X_1, \ldots, X_n, a, H, T, P, N_1, N_2)$$

$$\leftarrow conf_n[s](X_1, \ldots, X_n, H, T, P, N_1, N_2)$$

takes care of this. In a similar, but slightly more complicated fashion, the position of the head can be guessed, and we end up with atoms of the form

$$conf[s](b_1, \ldots, b_n, a, h, t, p, n_1, n_2)$$

as desired. It thus only remains to check whether the sequence of configurations guessed by our rules indeed represent a valid configuration of our Turing machine.

As discussed we will check the opposite: Our query should be true whenever there is an error. In order to achieve this, we need to compare the same tape cell in two subsequent configurations. But now, finding the same tape cell is easy: Two atoms of the form $conf[s](b_1, \ldots, b_n, a, h, t, p, n_1, n_2)$ represent the same tape cell, if they agree on their $b_1, \ldots, b_n$ bits. Therefore, we will simply take the set of all possible transitions not compatible with the transition function, and construct a query checking for this error. For example, when a change from 1 to 0 under the head is not allowed in (universal) state s, the relevant query could simply be as follows:

$$conf[s](X_1, X_2, X_3, 1, 1, T, P, N_1, N_2) \land conf[s'](X_1, X_2, X_3, 0, 0, N_1, T, N_3, N_4)$$

Note that, for brevity, we have skipped the existential quantifiers. Omitting some small details, it can be seen that a disjunction of such queries representing all invalid transitions now fulfils our requirement: The query is false iff we can guess a valid computation of the Turing machine M, which, by construction of M can only be an accepting computation. We thus have our lower bound as desired. Notice that we originally wanted to state this lower bound for CQs, but we have constructed a union of CQs. This is not a problem, as the following lemma shows:

Lemma 1. *Consider a Datalog$^{\exists,\lor}$ program P, a database D for $SCH(P)$, and an n-ary UCQ Q over $SCH(P)$. A Datalog$^{\exists,\lor}$ program P', a database D' for $SCH(P')$, and an n-ary CQ q over $SCH(P')$ can be constructed in polynomial time such that $Q(P, D) = q(P', D')$.*

Let us give an intuitive explanation of how the transformation from UCQs to CQs works: Each predicate p of the underlying schema is replaced with a new predicate p' with arity $arity(p) + 1$. This extra position holds a marker, either t (for *true*) or f (for *false*). Every database atom gets the value t at this new position, which implies that is a valid atom. Moreover, each rule is extended so that it simply propagates this position unaltered to the head. A copy of each CQ in the given UCQ is added to the database (variables are replaced by new distinct constants) with f at the new position. Clearly, every CQ in the given UCQ trivially maps to the database, with f at the new position. However, all the valid atoms, i.e., the atoms that can be derived by the chase for D and P, have t at the new position. We can now replace disjunctions in the UCQ by conjunctions (and thus convert the UCQ into a CQ), and just check that for at least one query its new position maps to t. This can simply be done by adding to the database atoms of the form $or(\cdot, \cdot, \cdot)$ encoding the logical or, connecting all the subqueries of the original UCQ via such or predicates, and stating that the end result must be t. This concludes the proof sketch of Theorem 5.

Note that the above proof sketch uses unbounded predicate arity and a set of rules that depends on the size of the Turing machine M. In [11], it was shown however, that the same lower bound even holds if only a fixed set of rules using only unary and binary predicates are used. The complexity in this case jumps from NP in case of guarded Datalog$^\exists$ to 2ExpTime when disjunction is allowed, which serves to show that disjunction is indeed a very powerful construct.

Data Complexity. Having seen the results for the combined complexity, let us turn our attention to the case were both the query and the set of rules is fixed, and only the database is considered as input, and recall the following result established in [11]:

Theorem 2. CQ-Answering *under guarded Datalog$^{\exists, \vee}$ is* co-NP*-complete in the data complexity.*

As for the combined complexity, the corresponding upper bound is obtained by exploiting results on query answering under GFO formulas, which was shown to be feasible in co-NP in the data complexity [9]. As we have previously seen, every guarded Datalog$^{\exists, \vee}$ program can be equivalently rewritten as a GFO sentence. Thus, the result in [9] carries over to our CQ-Answering problem.

Regarding the lower bound, it is well known that CQ-Answering under guarded Datalog$^{\exists, \vee}$ is co-NP-hard in data complexity, as shown in [17, Theorem 4.5]; in fact, this result shows that CQ-Answering under a Description Logic TBox with a single axiom of the form $A_1 \sqsubseteq A_2 \sqcup A_3$, where each A_i is an atomic concept, which in turn is equivalent to the rule $A_2(X) \vee A_3(X) \leftarrow A_1(X)$, is co-NP-hard in the data complexity. Such a rule is clearly a guarded Datalog$^{\exists, \vee}$ rule, and thus the result carries over directly to our CQ-Answering problem.

5.2   Atomic Queries

Combined Complexity. It is clear that, as an atomic query is simply a special case of an arbitrary conjunctive query, the 2ExpTime upper bound immediately applies to atomic queries. Interestingly, with minor modifications, we can also show that the lower bound discussed above, can also be suitably adapted to give the corresponding lower bound even for atomic queries. Note that in the original proof idea, we construct CQs that only contain two or three atoms, and where almost all variables are joined. Let us recall the example given in Sect. 5.1, for a universal state s:

$$conf[s](X_1, X_2, X_3, 1, 1, T, P, N_1, N_2) \wedge conf[s'](X_1, X_2, X_3, 0, 0, N_1, T, N_3, N_4)$$

Note that only P, N_3 and N_4 do not participate in a join. The idea is to project these variables out, so that each atom in the query contains the same variables. This can be done by using the following three rules:

$$conf_P[s](X_1, \ldots, X_n, C, H, T, P) \leftarrow conf[s](X_1, \ldots, X_n, C, H, T, P, N_1, N_2)$$
$$conf_L[s](X_1, \ldots, X_n, C, H, T, N_1) \leftarrow conf[s](X_1, \ldots, X_n, C, H, T, P, N_1, N_2)$$
$$conf_R[s](X_1, \ldots, X_n, C, H, T, N_2) \leftarrow conf[s](X_1, \ldots, X_n, C, H, T, P, N_1, N_2).$$

Note that P, L and R stand for previous, next left, and next right configuration, respectively. We can now rewrite our query to look as follows:

$$conf_x[s](X_1, X_2, X_3, 1, yes, T, N) \wedge conf_P[s'](X_1, X_2, X_3, 0, no, N, T).$$

where $x \in \{L, R\}$. Observe that each atom in the query contains all the variables, and it can now simply be added as a guarded rule:

$$error \leftarrow conf_x[s](X_1, X_2, X_3, 1, yes, T, N) \wedge conf_P[s'](X_1, X_2, X_3, 0, no, N, T).$$

In general, this process can be applied to any query from our original UCQ. Once all the sub-queries are added as rules, we now need a query that checks whether there is a rule whose rule-body is true (i.e., where the sub-query is true). This can now be done with an atomic query that simply asks for the propositional atom *error*. Therefore, for guarded Datalog$^{\exists,\vee}$ rules, the combined complexity remains unchanged:

Theorem 3. CQ$_1$-ANSWERING *under guarded Datalog$^{\exists,\vee}$ is 2ExpTime-comp. in the combined complexity.*

Data Complexity. Let us now have a look at the data complexity of atomic query answering under guarded Datalog$^{\exists,\vee}$. As with the combined complexity, for guarded Datalog$^{\exists,\vee}$ rules, the data complexity of answering atomic queries remains the same as in the general case.

The upper bound clearly carries over, while the lower bound follows from a result in [2] where they show that the co-NP-complete problem 3-UNSAT, that is, unsatisfiability of propositional formulas in 3-DNF, can be reduced to a fixed guarded Datalog$^{\exists,\vee}$ program via a so-called metainterpreter. The principle is simple: Store each clause in the database, and then, using the metainterpreter written using guarded Datalog$^{\exists,\vee}$ rules, assign truth values to every literal in every clause. Finally, a rule checks for errors in the truth assignment (i.e., whether some clause becomes true) and derives a propositional atom *error*, if this is the case. Now, one only needs to check the atomic query *error*, which is false iff the input 3-DNF formula is unsatisfiable. We thus have the following:

Theorem 4. CQ$_1$-ANSWERING *under guarded Datalog$^{\exists,\vee}$ is co-NP-complete in the data complexity.*

6   Linear Datalog$^{\exists,\vee}$

In this section, we focus on a key subclass of guarded Datalog$^{\exists,\vee}$, called linear Datalog$^{\exists,\vee}$, which further restricts the rules by allowing only one body-atom in rules (which is automatically a guard). As for guarded Datalog$^{\exists,\vee}$, we first focus in Sect. 6.1 on arbitrary conjunctive queries, and then we proceed in Sect. 6.2 with atomic queries.

6.1   Arbitrary Conjunctive Queries

Surprisingly, in the case of linear Datalog$^{\exists,\vee}$, which clearly is a much weaker subset of guarded Datalog$^{\exists,\vee}$, the (combined and data) complexity of query answering remains unchanged, as the following theorem, established in [11], states:

Theorem 5. CQ-ANSWERING *under linear Datalog$^{\exists,\vee}$ is* 2EXPTIME*-complete in the combined complexity, and* CO-NP*-complete in the data complexity.*

In case of the combined complexity, clearly the upper bound can be inherited, as it holds for a more general language, that is, guarded Datalog$^{\exists,\vee}$. For the lower bound, by carefully inspecting the construction of our 2EXPTIME lower bound construction for guarded Datalog$^{\exists,\vee}$, it becomes apparent that in fact only linear rules were used there. It turns out that it is indeed the case that the whole reduction can be achieved using only linear Datalog$^{\exists,\vee}$ rules. Therefore the 2EXPTIME-hardness proof also applies to the current setting, and the completeness result follows.

In case of the data complexity, the CO-NP upper bound can again be inherited from guarded Datalog$^{\exists,\vee}$, and the corresponding lower bound holds for only one rule of the form $A_2(X) \vee A_3(X) \leftarrow A_1(X)$, which is clearly linear. We therefore obtain the CO-NP-completeness result.

6.2   Atomic Queries

Although under guarded Datalog$^{\exists,\vee}$ answering atomic queries does not reduce the complexity of the problem, under linear Datalog$^{\exists,\vee}$ answering atomic queries does result in a reduction in complexity when compared to arbitrary CQs. This holds for both the combined and the data complexity, and in the latter case we even have a case where the problem is tractable. Note that until now, all upper bounds were obtained by reductions to query answering under the guarded fragment of first-order logic, a well-known and well-studied expressive logic. However, for linear Datalog$^{\exists,\vee}$ rules and atomic queries, this is unfortunately not possible, as we do not obtain tight upper bounds. More refined techniques are thus needed. We will start with an investigation of the combined complexity, and then proceed to the data complexity.

Combined Complexity. We recall the following result established in [28]:

Theorem 6. CQ_1-ANSWERING *under linear Datalog*$^{\exists,\vee}$ *is* EXPTIME-*complete in the combined complexity.*

The desired upper bound is obtained by reducing our problem to the problem of deciding whether a proof-tree exists, that is, a tree structure that encodes the finite part of each model of the given database w.r.t. the given set of linear Datalog$^{\exists,\vee}$ rules due to which the query is entailed, and then exhibit an alternating algorithm for deciding whether such a structure exists. Let us give some more details about proof-trees.

Due to linearity, in order to entail an atomic query in a given model, there needs to be a sequence of atoms, starting from a single database atom, along a sequence of linear rules where the head of the previous rule always satisfies the body of the next, such that the last head atom matches the query. For answering atomic queries, we may in fact focus our attention on a single database atom. Intuitively, derivations from separate database atoms cannot interact with each other, because the body of linear rules is a single atom. Thus, the chase derives a separate sub-model for each atom in the database. A model is thus simply a combination of one possible sub-model from each database atom. Consequently, if there does not exist a database atom where all its possible sub-models entail the query, it is always possible to construct a model where the query is not entailed (simply pick only sub-models that do not entail the query). Formally, the above argument gives us the following auxiliary result:

Lemma 2. *Consider a linear Datalog*$^{\exists,\vee}$ *program* P, *database* D *for* $SCH(P)$, *an* n-*ary atomic query* q *over* $SCH(P)$, *and a tuple* $\mathbf{t} \in \mathbf{C}^n$. *Then,* $\mathbf{t} \in q(P, D)$ *iff there exists* $\underline{a} \in D$ *such that* $\mathbf{t} \in q(P, \{\underline{a}\})$.

Using the above result, we know that we can focus on a single database atom (say $\underline{a} \in D$), for query answering. Towards developing an algorithm, we need to be able to represent the finite initial part of all the models derived from atom $\underline{a}$, that is responsible for the entailment of the query. The formal construct used to do this is called a *proof-tree*. This is a tree where each node is an atom, the root is atom $\underline{a}$ and each edge is labeled with a linear rule, such that the parent node maps to the body of the rule, and one head disjunct maps to the child node. Further, if the rule has n disjuncts in the head, there must be n children, one mapping to each disjunct.

Example 6. Consider the linear Datalog$^{\exists,\vee}$ program consisting of the rules

$$\rho_1 : r(Y, X) \leftarrow p(X, Y) \qquad \rho_2 : p(X, Y) \vee t(X, X) \leftarrow r(X, Y)$$
$$\rho_3 : p(X, Y) \leftarrow t(X, Y) \qquad \rho_4 : \exists Z\, s(Y, Z) \leftarrow r(X, Y).$$

Possible proof-trees from the atom $r(a, b)$ w.r.t. P are shown in Fig. 2. $\square$

As can be seen from the above example, a proof-tree intuitively represents all the choices made via disjunctive rules, combined in one structure. If we can

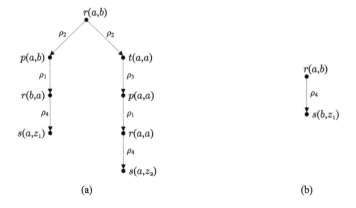

Fig. 2. Possible proof-trees from $r(a,b)$ w.r.t. Σ.

find a proof-tree where each leaf node can be homomorphically mapped to a given atomic query q, then we say the proof-tree is valid for q. In particular, in the above example, proof-tree (a) is valid w.r.t. the atomic (Boolean) queries $\exists X\, s(a,X)$ and $\exists X \exists Y\, s(X,Y)$, while proof-tree (b) is valid w.r.t. $\exists X\, s(b,X)$ and w.r.t. $\exists X \exists Y\, s(X,Y)$.

Given an n-ary atomic query q and a tuple $\mathbf{t} \in \mathbf{C}^n$, it is clear that if such a valid proof-tree from some atom $\underline{a}$ w.r.t. a linear Datalog$^{\exists,\vee}$ program P and $q(\mathbf{t})$ exists, then $\mathbf{t} \in q(P, \{\underline{a}\})$. In fact, in [28] it is shown, via an intricate argument involving skolemization of the rules of P, that also the other direction holds. Thus, atomic query answering is equivalent to deciding whether a proof-tree exists. The latter, as shown in [28], can be achieved via an alternating algorithm that builds the branches of a proof-tree in parallel computations. Each step of this algorithm uses polynomial space, and since alternating polynomial space coincides with exponential time, we obtain the desired upper bound.

The corresponding lower bound is an adaptation of a proof in [18], where it is implicitly shown that atomic query answering under (non-disjunctive) inclusion dependencies, a sub-language of linear Datalog$^{\exists}$ is PSPACE-hard, via simulation of a correspondingly space-bounded Turing machine. Using the same techniques employed in Sect. 5.1, the proof can be straightforwardly extended to simulate an alternating Turing machine using polynomial space, when disjunction is allowed (i.e., when we use linear Datalog$^{\exists,\vee}$ rules). Details can be found in [28].

Data Complexity. Let us now turn to the case where the set of rules is fixed, and thus the atomic query is also fixed, and recall the following result from [28]:

Theorem 7. CQ$_1$-ANSWERING *under linear Datalog*$^{\exists,\vee}$ *is in* AC$_0$ *in the data complexity.*

The above tractability result is shown by establishing that the problem under consideration is first-order rewritable, i.e., it can be reduced to the problem of evaluating a first-order query over a database. Notice that first-order rewritability was first introduced in the context of description logics [16]. Consider a linear Datalog$^{\exists,\vee}$ program P, an n-ary atomic query q over $SCH(P)$, and a tuple $\mathbf{t} \in \mathbf{C}^n$. Let C be the constants occurring in $q(\mathbf{t})$, and $N = \{z_1, \ldots, z_m\}$ be a set of nulls, where m is the maximum arity over all predicates of $SCH(P)$. Let $base(q(\mathbf{t}), P)$ be the set of all atoms that can be formed using terms of $(C \cup N)$ and predicates of $SCH(P)$. Let $B = \{\underline{b} \mid \underline{b} \in base(q(\mathbf{t}), P) \text{ and } \mathbf{t} \in q(P, \{\underline{b}\})\}$, and μ be a renaming substitution that maps each $z \in N$ into a distinct variable $X_z \in \mathbf{V}$. We define the first-order query q_P as $\bigvee_{\underline{b} \in B} \exists X_{z_1} \ldots \exists X_{z_m} \mu(\underline{b})$. In fact, q_P is a UCQs, where each disjunct is an atomic query. It is easy to see that $|B| \leq r \cdot (2m)^m$, where r is the number of predicates of $SCH(P)$. Since, as discussed above, CQ_1-ANSWERING under linear Datalog$^{\exists,\vee}$ is feasible in exponential time, we conclude that the set B, and thus the query q_P, can be constructed in exponential time. It can be shown that q_P is a sound and complete rewriting: for every database D, $\mathbf{t} \in q(P, D)$ iff $D \models q_P$. Intuitively, q_P contains, by construction, all possible images of atoms that will make $q(\mathbf{t})$ true. Thus, if we find an atom in our database that matches such an image, we can safely conclude that $\mathbf{t} \in q(P, D)$. Conversely, if we do not find such a match, we can conclude that the database does not contain any atom that will satisfy $q(\mathbf{t})$ w.r.t. P, which in turn implies that $\mathbf{t} \notin q(P, D)$. Note that as we are in the data complexity case, the original query q and the program P are fixed. Thus, query q_P can be constructed in constant time. Since, as shown by [36], the evaluation of first-order queries is feasible in AC_0 in data complexity, and since a union of atomic queries is clearly a first-order formula, the claim follows.

7   Further Reading

7.1   Disjunction

Apart from guarded and linear Datalog$^{\exists}$, several other classes of guarded-based Datalog$^{\exists}$ programs have been investigated. More precisely,

- The class of *weakly-guarded* programs, an extension of guarded programs where the guard atom must cover only the body-variables that occur at *affected positions*, i.e., positions at which a null value can appear during the construction of the chase, has been investigated in [12];
- The class of *frontier-guarded* programs, an extension of guarded programs where the guard atom must contain only the *frontier*, i.e., the set of variables that appear both in the body and the head, has been studied in [7]; and
- The class of *weakly-frontier-guarded* programs, which extends both weak-guardedness and frontier-guardedness, has been studied in [7].

The addition of disjunction to the above guarded-based formalisms has been considered in [11]. CQ-ANSWERING under weakly-(frontier-)guarded Datalog$^{\exists,\vee}$ is 2ExpTime-complete in the combined complexity, and ExpTime-complete in the data complexity; the same holds even if we focus on atomic queries.

Now, in the case of frontier-guarded Datalog$^{\exists,\vee}$, both CQ-ANSWERING and CQ$_1$-ANSWERING are 2ExpTime-complete in the combined complexity, and co-NP-complete in the data complexity, i.e., frontier-guarded Datalog$^{\exists,\vee}$ and guarded Datalog$^{\exists,\vee}$ have the same combined and data complexity. Note that in [11] more refined complexity metrics have also been investigated. In particular, apart from the combined and the data complexity, also the settings where (i) the arity of the underlying schema is bounded by an integer constant, and (ii) the given program is fixed, have been studied.

A class of Datalog$^\exists$ programs, which is inherently different than the guarded-based formalisms discussed so far, is *sticky Datalog$^\exists$* [15]. Although query answering under this formalism is decidable, and actually tractable in data complexity, the situation changes dramatically once we add disjunction. It is known that query answering under sticky Datalog$^{\exists,\vee}$ is undecidable, even when the program and the query are fixed; for the details see [34].

7.2   Default Negation

Another interesting modeling feature, which cannot be expressed using Datalog$^{\exists,\vee}$ rules, is *default negation*. Adding negation to known decidable Datalog$^\exists$ languages is an intriguing new problem that has given rise to a flourishing research activity over the last few years. A short discussion on existing approaches to enrich Datalog$^\exists$ with default negation follows:

- **Stratified Negation.** Stratified negation for guarded Datalog$^\exists$ was investigated in [13], and extended to the more expressive formalism of weakly-guarded Datalog$^\exists$ in [5]. Stratified negation is well-behaved in the sense that its addition does not sacrifice decidability, and the complexity remains the same. However, stratified negation is limited, and this has motivated the investigation of more expressive types of negation, namely well-founded and stable model negation.

- **Well-Founded Negation.** Two different variants of the well-founded semantics (WFS) for guarded Datalog$^\exists$ were considered in [27,31]. The version of [31] studies the standard WFS for logic programming with function symbols, where the unique name assumption (UNA) is assumed: different Skolem terms are not unifiable. The second variant, called equality-friendly WFS [27], does not use the UNA. The standard WFS for sticky Datalog$^\exists$ has been recently investigated in [3].

- **Stable Model Negation.** Negation under the stable model semantics for (weakly-)guarded Datalog$^\exists$ was investigated in [26], while for sticky Datalog$^\exists$ was recently studied in [3]. In [8,33], acyclicity and stratification conditions are proposed for Datalog$^\exists$ with negation, which identify languages that have finite and/or unique stable models. The FDNC programs in [24] combine default negation and function symbols; decidability is obtained by restricting the structure of rules to one of seven predefined forms. One of the crucial conditions that FDNC programs must satisfy is similar to guardedness.

Acknowledgements. This research has received support from the EPSRC Programme Grant EP/M025268/ "VADA: Value Added Data Systems – Principles and Architecture", and the Austrian Science Fund (FWF), project Y698 "Decodyn".

References

1. Abiteboul, S., Hull, R., Vianu, V.: Foundations of Databases. Addison-Wesley, Boston (1995)
2. Alviano, M., Faber, W., Leone, N., Manna, M.: Disjunctive datalog with existential quantifiers: Semantics, decidability, and complexity issues. TPLP **12**(4–5), 701–718 (2012)
3. Alviano, M., Pieris, A.: Default negation for non-guarded existential rules. In: PODS (2015, to appear)
4. Andréka, H., Németi, I., van Benthem, J.: Modal languages and bounded fragments of predicate logic. J. Philos. Logic **27**(3), 217–274 (1998)
5. Arenas, M., Gottlob, G., Pieris, A.: Expressive languages for querying the semantic web. In: PODS, pp. 14–26 (2014)
6. Baader, F., Calvanese, D., McGuinness, D.L., Nardi, D., Patel-Schneider, P.F. (eds.): The Description Logic Handbook: Theory, Implementation, and Applications. Cambridge University Press, Cambridge (2003)
7. Baget, J.F., Leclère, M., Mugnier, M.L., Salvat, E.: On rules with existential variables: Walking the decidability line. Artif. Intell. **175**(9–10), 1620–1654 (2011)
8. Baget, J., Garreau, F., Mugnier, M., Rocher, S.: Extending acyclicity notions for existential rules. In: ECAI, pp. 39–44 (2014)
9. Bárány, V., Gottlob, G., Otto, M.: Querying the guarded fragment. Log. Meth. Comput. Sci. **10**(2) (2014)
10. Beeri, C., Vardi, M.Y.: The implication problem for data dependencies. In: ICALP, pp. 73–85 (1981)
11. Bourhis, P., Morak, M., Pieris, A.: The impact of disjunction on query answering under guarded-based existential rules. In: IJCAI (2013)
12. Calì, A., Gottlob, G., Kifer, M.: Taming the infinite chase: Query answering under expressive relational constraints. J. Artif. Intell. Res. **48**, 115–174 (2013)
13. Calì, A., Gottlob, G., Lukasiewicz, T.: A general datalog-based framework for tractable query answering over ontologies. J. Web Sem. **14**, 57–83 (2012)
14. Calì, A., Gottlob, G., Lukasiewicz, T., Marnette, B., Pieris, A.: Datalog$^{\pm}$: A family of logical knowledge representation and query languages for new applications. In: LICS, pp. 228–242 (2010)
15. Calì, A., Gottlob, G., Pieris, A.: Towards more expressive ontology languages: The query answering problem. Artif. Intell. **193**, 87–128 (2012)
16. Calvanese, D., De Giacomo, G., Lembo, D., Lenzerini, M., Rosati, R.: Tractable reasoning and efficient query answering in description logics: The DL-Lite family. J. Autom. Reasoning **39**(3), 385–429 (2007)
17. Calvanese, D., De Giacomo, G., Lembo, D., Lenzerini, M., Rosati, R.: Data complexity of query answering in description logics. Artif. Intell. **195**, 335–360 (2013)
18. Casanova, M.A., Fagin, R., Papadimitriou, C.H.: Inclusion dependencies and their interaction with functional dependencies. J. Comput. Syst. Sci. **28**(1), 29–59 (1984)
19. Ceri, S., Gottlob, G., Tanca, L.: Logic Programming and Databases. Springer, Heidelberg (1990)
20. Chandra, A.K., Kozen, D., Stockmeyer, L.J.: Alternation. J. ACM **28**(1), 114–133 (1981)

21. Deutsch, A., Tannen, V.: Reformulation of XML queries and constraints. In: Calvanese, D., Lenzerini, M., Motwani, R. (eds.) ICDT 2003. LNCS, vol. 2572, pp. 225–238. Springer, Heidelberg (2002)
22. Eiter, T., Gottlob, G., Mannila, H.: Disjunctive datalog. ACM Trans. Database Syst. **22**(3), 364–418 (1997)
23. Eiter, T., Leone, N., Mateis, C., Pfeifer, G., Scarcello, F.: A deductive system for non-monotonic reasoning. In: LPNMR, pp. 364–375 (1997)
24. Eiter, T., Simkus, M.: FDNC: decidable nonmonotonic disjunctive logic programs with function symbols. ACM Trans. Comput. Log., **11**(2) (2010)
25. Gebser, M., Kaufmann, B., Kaminski, R., Ostrowski, M., Schaub, T., Schneider, M.T.: Potassco: The potsdam answer set solving collection. AI Commun. **24**(2), 107–124 (2011)
26. Gottlob, G., Hernich, A., Kupke, C., Lukasiewicz, T.: Stable model semantics for guarded existential rules and description logics. In: KR
27. Gottlob, G., Hernich, A., Kupke, C., Lukasiewicz, T.: Equality-friendly well-founded semantics and applications to description logics. In: AAAI (2012)
28. Gottlob, G., Manna, M., Morak, M., Pieris, A.: On the complexity of ontological reasoning under disjunctive existential rules. In: Rovan, B., Sassone, V., Widmayer, P. (eds.) MFCS 2012. LNCS, vol. 7464, pp. 1–18. Springer, Heidelberg (2012)
29. Gottlob, G., Orsi, G., Pieris, A., Šimkus, M.: Datalog and its extensions for semantic web databases. In: Eiter, T., Krennwallner, T. (eds.) Reasoning Web 2012. LNCS, vol. 7487, pp. 54–77. Springer, Heidelberg (2012)
30. Grädel, E.: On the restraining power of guards. J. Symbolic Logic **64**(4), 1719–1742 (1999)
31. Hernich, A., Kupke, C., Lukasiewicz, T., Gottlob, G.: Well-founded semantics for extended datalog and ontological reasoning. In: PODS, pp. 225–236 (2013)
32. Lloyd, J.W.: Foundations of Logic Programming. Springer, New York (1987)
33. Magka, D., Krötzsch, M., Horrocks, I.: Computing stable models for nonmonotonic existential rules. In: IJCAI (2013)
34. Morak, M.: The Impact of Disjunction on Reasoning under Existential Rules. Ph.D. Thesis, University of Oxford, Oxford, Oxfordshire, UK (2015)
35. Patel-Schneider, P.F., Horrocks, I.: A comparison of two modelling paradigms in the semantic web. J. Web Sem. **5**(4), 240–250 (2007)
36. Vardi, M.Y.: On the complexity of bounded-variable queries. In: PODS, pp. 266–276 (1995)

Ontology-Mediated Query Answering
with Data-Tractable Description Logics

Meghyn Bienvenu[1]([✉]) and Magdalena Ortiz[2]([✉])

[1] LRI - CNRS and Université Paris Sud, Orsay, France
`meghyn@lri.fr`
[2] Institute of Information Systems, Vienna University of Technology, Vienna, Austria
`ortiz@kr.tuwien.ac.at`

Abstract. Recent years have seen an increasing interest in ontology-mediated query answering, in which the semantic knowledge provided by an ontology is exploited when querying data. Adding an ontology has several advantages (e.g. simplifying query formulation, integrating data from different sources, providing more complete answers to queries), but it also makes the query answering task more difficult. In this chapter, we give a brief introduction to ontology-mediated query answering using description logic (DL) ontologies. Our focus will be on DLs for which query answering scales polynomially in the size of the data, as these are best suited for applications requiring large amounts of data. We will describe the challenges that arise when evaluating different natural types of queries in the presence of such ontologies, and we will present algorithmic solutions based upon two key concepts, namely, query rewriting and saturation. We conclude the chapter with an overview of recent results and active areas of ongoing research.

1 Introduction

Since the seminal works in the field [50,53,110,144], there has been steadily growing interest in *ontology-mediated query answering* (OMQA), in which the semantic knowledge provided by an ontology is exploited when querying data. Adding an ontology has several advantages. First, by providing an enriched vocabulary that closely matches users' conceptualization of the application domain, an ontology makes it easier for users to formulate their queries. Moreover, the ontology can be used to integrate different data sources through a single conceptual model, facilitating access to them in a uniform and transparent way. Finally, OMQA can provide users with more complete answers to their queries, by taking into account not only the facts explicitly stored in the data, but also facts that are implicit consequences of the data and the domain knowledge. Unfortunately, enriching data with domain knowledge also has a downside: it makes the

This work has been supported by ANR project PAGODA (ANR-12-JS02-007-01) and the Austrian Science Fund (FWF) project T515.

W. Faber and A. Paschke (Eds.): Reasoning Web 2015, LNCS 9203, pp. 218–307, 2015.
DOI: 10.1007/978-3-319-21768-0_9

query answering task significantly more difficult, both conceptually and algorithmically. The specific challenges that arise depend upon which languages are used for expressing the query and the ontological knowledge.

In this chapter, we consider ontologies formulated using *description logics (DLs)*, which are a family of decidable fragments of classical first-order predicate logic that are often used for knowledge representation and reasoning. DLs are arguably the most popular formalisms for representing ontological knowledge nowadays, notably providing the logical underpinnings for the W3C-standardized OWL web ontology languages [170]. There are a multitude of different DLs of varying expressivity, ranging from very simple to highly expressive. Significant research efforts have been devoted to understanding the computational complexity of different reasoning tasks, including the query answering tasks that are the focus of this chapter. The resulting complexity landscape can be used to select the most appropriate DL for a given application. In the case of OMQA applications involving large amounts of data, this complexity analysis has revealed *Horn DLs* – so named because they are expressible in the Horn fragment of first-order logic – as especially relevant, as query answering in the presence of Horn DL ontologies can be performed in polynomial time in the size of the data, for some important types of queries. Prominent Horn DLs include the logics of the DL-Lite and $\mathcal{EL}$ families, which are the basis of the OWL profiles known as OWL 2 QL and OWL 2 EL [159].

This chapter is organized as follows. We begin in Sect. 2 by recalling the syntax and semantics of description logic knowledge bases and introducing some popular Horn DLs. In Sect. 3, we formally introduce the problem of ontology-mediated query answering and compare it to the closely related problem of querying relational databases. We also explain how we will measure the complexity of query answering and briefly introduce the two main algorithmic techniques (*query rewriting* and *saturation*) that underlie most of the querying algorithms that have been proposed for Horn DL ontologies. The following three sections are devoted to different query languages: *instance queries* in Sect. 4, *conjunctive queries* in Sect. 5, and *navigational queries* in Sect. 6. In each of these sections, we will illustrate the kinds of natural queries that can be expressed in the query languages, describe the challenges that arise when evaluating them in the presence of ontologies, present algorithmic solutions involving query rewriting and/or saturation, and summarize what is known about the complexity of the query answering task for different DLs. In Sect. 7, we show the difficulties that arise when querying DL knowledge bases using more expressive query languages involving negation or recursion. The final section of this chapter provides an overview of recent work on OMQA and areas of ongoing research.

This chapter aims to provide a relatively detailed introduction to the area of ontology-mediated query answering with Horn DL ontologies. We chose to focus on Horn DLs in order to showcase the versatility of query rewriting and saturation techniques for handling a variety of different types of queries, including navigational queries that have only recently been considered for OMQA. Although we briefly discuss results and techniques for non-Horn DLs and try to give a relatively complete picture of the complexity landscape, the present chapter should by no means be considered a comprehensive survey of the field. For a detailed treatment of OMQA as it relates to more expressive DLs, we refer to [163,168] and references therein. For introductions to OMQA that focus on DL-Lite and the corresponding OWL 2 QL profile and provide more details on the use of database systems, we direct readers to the tutorials [48,128].

2   Horn Description Logics

In this section, we give a short introduction to description logics and how they are used for describing ontological knowledge. We try to keep it concise, since extensive introductory texts on the topic have been published elsewhere. Readers less familiar with DLs may find useful the long and detailed introductions in [190], and in the first part of [168], or the short basic overview in [137].

2.1   Description Logic Basics

In description logics, a domain of interest is described using a *DL vocabulary* consisting of three countably infinite, pairwise disjoint sets of symbols:

- the set N_C of *concept names*, to capture *classes* of objects
- the set N_R of *role names*, to capture *binary relations* between objects
- the set N_I of *individual names* (often abbreviated to *individuals*), to refer to specific individual objects.

Note that a DL vocabulary can be seen as a restricted first-order logic (FO) vocabulary containing only unary predicates (concept names), binary predicates (role names), and constants (individual names).

From a DL vocabulary, we can build expressions that reflect the knowledge about our domain. In general, we use two kinds of statements:

- *Terminological axioms* specify general properties of concepts and roles, and constrain the way *all* objects in the domain can participate in the different concepts and roles.
- *Assertions* are facts about *specific* objects in the domain, that is, they assert that an individual participates in some concept, or that some role holds between a pair of individuals.

Each DL offers a different syntax for the terminological axioms and different combinations of *concept constructors* and *role constructors* that allow us to build *complex concept and roles* from the symbols in the vocabulary. Table 1 summarizes some DL concept and role constructors, as well as the most common forms of axioms and assertions.

As the inverse role constructor occurs in many of the DLs considered in this chapter, we introduce some dedicated notation and terminology. We use $N_R^\pm$ to denote the set $N_R \cup \{r^- \mid r \in N_R\}$ and use the generic term *role* to refer to elements of $N_R^\pm$. We define the *inverse* $\mathsf{inv}(R)$ of a role as follows: if R is a role name $r \in N_R$, then $\mathsf{inv}(R) = r^-$, and if R is of the form r^-, then $\mathsf{inv}(R) = r$.

Table 1. Syntax and semantics of DL concept and role constructors, TBox axioms, and ABox assertions. Here a, b denote individual names, A denotes a concept name, $C_{(i)}$ denotes a (complex) concept, $r \in \mathsf{N_R}$ denotes a role name, R denotes a role, and $m \in \mathbb{N}$ denotes a natural number.

Name	Syntax	Semantics	
Top concept	$\top$	$\Delta^{\mathcal{I}}$	CONCEPTS
Bottom concept	$\bot$	$\emptyset$	
Nominal	$\{a\}$	$\{a^{\mathcal{I}}\}$	
Negation	$\neg C$	$\Delta^{\mathcal{I}} \setminus C^{\mathcal{I}}$	
Conjunction	$C_1 \sqcap C_2$	$C_1{}^{\mathcal{I}} \cap C_2{}^{\mathcal{I}}$	
Disjunction	$C_1 \sqcup C_2$	$C_1{}^{\mathcal{I}} \cup C_2{}^{\mathcal{I}}$	
Existential restriction	$\exists R.C$	$\{d_1 \mid \text{there exists } (d_1, d_2) \in R^{\mathcal{I}} \text{ with } d_2 \in C^{\mathcal{I}}\}$	
Universal restriction	$\forall R.C$	$\{d_1 \mid d_2 \in C^{\mathcal{I}} \text{ for all } (d_1, d_2) \in R^{\mathcal{I}}\}$	
(Qualified) number restrictions	$\geqslant m\, R.C$	$\{d_1 \mid m \leq \left|\{d_2 \mid (d_1, d_2) \in R^{\mathcal{I}} \text{ and } d_2 \in C^{\mathcal{I}}\}\right|\}$	
	$\leqslant m\, R.C$	$\{d_1 \mid m \geq \left|\{d_2 \mid (d_1, d_2) \in R^{\mathcal{I}} \text{ and } d_2 \in C^{\mathcal{I}}\}\right|\}$	
Inverse	r^-	$\{(d_2, d_1) \mid (d_1, d_2) \in r^{\mathcal{I}}\}$	ROLES
Role negation	$\neg R$	$(\Delta^{\mathcal{I}} \times \Delta^{\mathcal{I}}) \setminus R^{\mathcal{I}}$	
Concept inclusion	$C \sqsubseteq D$	$C^{\mathcal{I}} \subseteq D^{\mathcal{I}}$	TBOX AXIOMS
Role inclusion	$R \sqsubseteq S$	$R^{\mathcal{I}} \subseteq S^{\mathcal{I}}$	
Transitivity axiom	$\mathsf{trans}(R)$	$R^{\mathcal{I}} \circ R^{\mathcal{I}} \subseteq R^{\mathcal{I}}$	
Concept assertion	$A(a)$	$a^{\mathcal{I}} \in A^{\mathcal{I}}$	ABOX ASSERTIONS
Role assertion	$r(a, b)$	$(a^{\mathcal{I}}, b^{\mathcal{I}}) \in R^{\mathcal{I}}$	

Definition 1. *A* TBox *is a finite set of terminological axioms and an* ABox *is a finite set of assertions. A* knowledge base (KB) *$\mathcal{K} = (\mathcal{T}, \mathcal{A})$ is composed of a TBox $\mathcal{T}$ and an ABox $\mathcal{A}$.*

A signature *is a set of concept and role names, and the* signature of a TBox $\mathcal{T}$, *written* $\mathsf{sig}(\mathcal{T})$, *is the set of concept names and role names that occur in $\mathcal{T}$. Signatures of ABoxes and KBs are defined and denoted analogously. Finally, for a given signature Σ, we say that an ABox $\mathcal{A}$ is a Σ-ABox if $\mathsf{sig}(\mathcal{A}) \subseteq \Sigma$.*

Example 1. For the examples in this chapter, we will consider the domain of food, dishes and menus offered by restaurants. The vocabulary we use to model this domain contains concept names for food items, like IceCream or Meat, and for more general types of food, such as vegetarian-friendly options (VegFriendly) or spicy dishes (SpicyDish). We also use concept names for notions like Restaurant, Menu and Dish. The role name hasIngredient is used to relate dishes and their ingredients, and contains is a generalization (or *superrole*) of hasIngredient that can also relate foods with components (such as lactose or gluten) that would not typically be considered as ingredients. The role name hasCourse relates menus to the dishes they contain as courses, and we may also have specialized versions of this role like hasDessert and hasMain. We can also use role names to say that a restaurant offers some menu, or that it serves a dish. For individuals that represent specific menus, dishes, and restaurants, we use italic, lower-case letters.

With this vocabulary in place, we can write ABox assertions such as:

offers(r, m)	hasMain(m, p_1)	PenneArrabiata(p_1)
hasDessert(m, d_1)	IceCream(d_1)	serves(r, p_2)
PizzaCalabrese(p_2)	serves(r, d_2)	Tiramisu(d_2)

which intuitively express that some restaurant (r) offers a menu (m) with penne arrabiata and ice cream, and it also serves pizza calabrese and tiramisu.

We give some examples of TBox axioms that express general knowledge about this domain. Here $C \equiv D$ is shorthand for the pair of axioms $C \sqsubseteq D$ and $D \sqsubseteq C$.

$$\exists \mathsf{hasCourse}.\top \sqsubseteq \mathsf{Menu} \tag{1}$$

$$\exists \mathsf{hasCourse}^-.\top \sqsubseteq \mathsf{Dish} \tag{2}$$

$$\mathsf{hasDessert} \sqsubseteq \mathsf{hasCourse} \tag{3}$$

$$\mathsf{hasMain} \sqsubseteq \mathsf{hasCourse} \tag{4}$$

$$\mathsf{Menu} \sqsubseteq {\leqslant} 1\,\mathsf{hasMain}.\top \tag{5}$$

$$\mathsf{FullMenu} \equiv {\geqslant} 3\,\mathsf{hasCourse}.\top \tag{6}$$

$$\mathsf{PizzaCalabrese} \sqsubseteq \mathsf{Pizza} \sqcap \exists \mathsf{hasIngredient}.\mathsf{PizzaDough} \tag{7}$$

$$\mathsf{PenneArrabiata} \sqsubseteq \exists \mathsf{hasIngredient}.\mathsf{Pasta} \tag{8}$$

$$\mathsf{PizzaDough} \sqcup \mathsf{Tiramisu} \sqcup \mathsf{Pasta} \sqsubseteq \exists \mathsf{contains}.\mathsf{Gluten} \tag{9}$$

$$\mathsf{GlutenFree} \equiv \forall \mathsf{contains}.\neg \mathsf{Gluten} \tag{10}$$

$$\mathsf{hasIngredient} \sqsubseteq \mathsf{contains} \tag{11}$$

$$\mathsf{trans}(\mathsf{contains}) \tag{12}$$

The concept inclusions (1) and (2) state respectively that the domain of hasCourse consists of menus, and its range consists of dishes. The role inclusions (3) and (4) express that hasDessert and hasMain are specializations (or *subroles*) of the role hasCourse, since desserts and mains are types of courses. Concept inclusion (5) stipulates that a menu can only have one main course. The axiom (6) defines full menus as menus that have at least three courses. Axiom (7) states that pizza calabrese is a kind of pizza that has as ingredient pizza dough. The following axiom (8) says that penne arriabiata has pasta as an ingredient. In (9), it is stated that pizza dough, tiramisu and pasta all contain gluten, and (10) defines the gluten-free as the class of entities not containing gluten. The role inclusion (11) expresses that hasIngredient is a subrole of contains, and (12) asserts the transitivity of the relation contains. ▲

There are a wide range of DLs offering different shapes of axioms and different concept and role constructors. For example, the well-known description logic $\mathcal{ALC}$ allows only for concept inclusions $C \sqsubseteq D$ as TBox axioms, where C and

D are complex concepts built using negation, conjunction, disjunction, existential restrictions, and universal restrictions, from the *atomic concepts* that include concept names, top and bottom. The DL $\mathcal{S}$ extends $\mathcal{ALC}$ with transitivity axioms. The presence of additional constructors or axiom types is denoted by additional letters in the name of the logics. For example, the letter $\mathcal{H}$ denotes the presence of role inclusions in the TBox. The letter $\mathcal{I}$ denotes that inverse roles can be used as a role constructor in the TBox axioms, $\mathcal{O}$ denotes the presence of nominals as a concept constructor, and $\mathcal{Q}$ denotes the presence of qualified number restrictions. In this way, we obtain a large number of different DLs like $\mathcal{ALCI}$, $\mathcal{ALCHQ}$, $\mathcal{SHIQ}$, $\mathcal{SHOIQ}$, and so on[1]. We note that the knowledge base in Example 1 is a $\mathcal{SHIQ}$ knowledge base.

Before moving on to the semantics of DLs, a small remark is in order concerning the syntax of ABox assertions. For a DL $\mathcal{L}$, an $\mathcal{L}$ ABox is sometimes defined as a set of assertions of the forms $C(a)$ and $R(a, b)$, where C and R are *possibly complex* concepts and roles in $\mathcal{L}$. In this chapter, for simplicity, ABox assertions take the forms $A(a)$ and $r(a, b)$ only, independently of the DL in question. For our purposes, this simplification is without any loss of generality. Indeed, it is well known that complex assertions $C(a)$ can be replaced by assertions $A_C(a)$ for a fresh concept name A_C, provided that $A_C \sqsubseteq C$ is added to the TBox. Role assertions $r^-(a, b)$ can be replaced by $r(b, a)$, and as inverses are the only role constructor in almost all DLs we consider (the only exception is DL-Lite, discussed further), this is the only kind of complex assertions that could occur. It will be clear from what follows that these transformations preserve the semantics of KBs and that they have no impact on the computational complexity of any of the reasoning and query answering problems we consider.

2.2   Semantics

The semantics of DLs is defined using the notion of interpretations.

Definition 2 (Interpretation, Models). *An interpretation $\mathcal{I}$ is a pair $(\Delta^{\mathcal{I}}, \cdot^{\mathcal{I}})$ where $\Delta^{\mathcal{I}}$ is a non-empty set called the* domain, *and $\cdot^{\mathcal{I}}$ is an interpretation function that maps:*

- *each concept name $A \in \mathsf{N_C}$ to a set $A^{\mathcal{I}} \subseteq \Delta^{\mathcal{I}}$,*
- *$r \in \mathsf{N_R}$ to a set of pairs $r^{\mathcal{I}} \subseteq \Delta^{\mathcal{I}} \times \Delta^{\mathcal{I}}$, and*
- *each individual $a \in \mathsf{N_I}$ to some $a^{\mathcal{I}} \in \Delta^{\mathcal{I}}$, in such a way that $a^{\mathcal{I}} \neq b^{\mathcal{I}}$ whenever $a \neq b$.*

The interpretation function is extended to complex concept and roles as specified in the upper right portion of Table 1.

---

[1] The order of the letters is irrelevant, although some orderings are more frequent in the literature than others, e.g., $\mathcal{SHIQ}$, vs. $\mathcal{SHQI}$. We also point out that some DLs impose additional restrictions, for example, restricting the interaction of number restrictions and transitive roles in $\mathcal{SHIQ}$ and $\mathcal{SHOIQ}$.

Note that this is essentially the traditional notion of interpretation from first-order logic, but restricted to unary and binary predicates, and constants.

Using interpretations, we can define the notions of models, satisfiability, and entailment. The *satisfaction* $\mathcal{I} \models \xi$ of a TBox axiom or ABox assertion ξ in an interpretation $\mathcal{I}$ is defined in the lower right part of Table 1. An interpretation $\mathcal{I}$ is called a *model of a TBox* $\mathcal{T}$, written $\mathcal{I} \models \mathcal{T}$, if $\mathcal{I} \models \xi$ for every axiom ξ in $\mathcal{T}$. Similarly, $\mathcal{I}$ is a *model of an ABox* $\mathcal{A}$, written $\mathcal{I} \models \mathcal{A}$, if $\mathcal{I} \models \xi$ for every assertion ξ in $\mathcal{A}$. If both $\mathcal{I} \models \mathcal{T}$ and $\mathcal{I} \models \mathcal{A}$, then we call $\mathcal{I}$ a *model of the KB* $\mathcal{K} = (\mathcal{T}, \mathcal{A})$, and we write $\mathcal{I} \models (\mathcal{T}, \mathcal{A})$ (or, $\mathcal{I} \models \mathcal{K}$). We call a KB $\mathcal{K}$ *satisfiable* (or *consistent*) if it has at least one model. Entailment is defined in the expected way: a TBox axiom or ABox assertion ξ is said to be *entailed* from a KB $\mathcal{K}$ (in symbols: $\mathcal{K} \models \xi$) if $\mathcal{I} \models \xi$ for every model $\mathcal{I}$ of $\mathcal{K}$. We can also define the corresponding notions of entailment w.r.t. TBoxes and ABoxes: $\mathcal{T} \models \xi$ if $(\mathcal{T}, \emptyset) \models \xi$, and $\mathcal{A} \models \xi$ if $(\emptyset, \mathcal{A}) \models \xi$.

Remark 1. Note that, by definition, interpretations give meaning to all the symbols in the infinite vocabulary $\mathsf{N_C} \cup \mathsf{N_R} \cup \mathsf{N_I}$. Alternatively, interpretations can be defined for a possibly finite signature that contains all the relevant symbols, including the signature of the KB at hand. Since the interpretation of all symbols not occurring in a KB or query is irrelevant to their satisfaction, both semantics are equivalent. Moreover, in definitions and examples, we will allow interpretations to be (finitely) specified for the relevant signature only, and disregard the interpretation of all irrelevant symbols.

Remark 2. Observe that in Definition 2 we require distinct constants to be interpreted as different objects in $\Delta^{\mathcal{I}}$. That is, we make the *unique name assumption* *(UNA)*. This assumption is sometimes made in DLs, and sometimes not. We have chosen to adopt the UNA because it is closer to the intended semantics of ABoxes as data repositories, and hence more natural for the OMQA setting we consider. We should emphasize that *this assumption is not central to the results and techniques presented in this chapter*, which are valid both with or without the UNA. It can be noted however that there do exist cases, not covered in this chapter, in which the complexity of query answering depends on whether the UNA is adopted (see e.g., [10]).

2.3 Some Popular Horn Description Logics

In this chapter, we focus on a specific class of DLs known as *Horn DLs*, whose core feature is that they are incapable of expressing any form of disjunction. This lack of disjunction means that Horn DL knowledge bases can be translated into the Horn fragment of first-order logic.

We first introduce two important sub-families of Horn DLs based upon the 'lightweight' logics DL-Lite and $\mathcal{EL}$, which support efficient reasoning at the cost of limited expressiveness.

DL-Lite Family. The constructors available in the different DLs of the DL-Lite family were selected in order to express the main features present in conceptual and data models, like ISA-relations between classes, class disjointness, domain and range restrictions on roles, functionality constraints, and mandatory (non-)participation constraints. This makes (large fragments of) the formalisms used in databases and software engineering, like entity-relationship and UML class diagrams, expressible as DL-Lite knowledge bases. At the same time, the DL-Lite family (first proposed in [50,52]) was designed to support efficient reasoning in data-oriented applications, even in the presence of large amounts of data. Due to their carefully tailored expressivity and good computational properties, DLs of the DL-Lite family have become extremely popular as ontology languages. This can be witnessed by the recent inclusion of the OWL 2 QL profile [159], based upon DL-Lite, in the latest version of the OWL standard.

In the DL-Lite family, there are no universal restrictions, and existential restrictions can only be of the form $\exists R.\top$ and are thus abbreviated to $\exists R$. The basic DL-Lite dialect, sometimes denoted DL-Lite$_{core}$, only allows *concept inclusions* of the forms $B_1 \sqsubseteq B_2$ and $B_1 \sqsubseteq \neg B_2$, where each B_i is either a concept name or an existential restriction $\exists R$ with $R \in \mathsf{N}_\mathsf{R}^\pm$. We note that *negative concept inclusions* of the form $B_1 \sqsubseteq \neg B_2$ can also be written as *(concept) disjointness constraints* $B_1 \sqcap B_2 \sqsubseteq \bot$; both syntaxes are widely used. Axioms of the form $\exists r \sqsubseteq B$ are often called *domain restrictions*, since they enforce that the domain of role r is contained in the concept B; similarly, axioms of the form $\exists r^- \sqsubseteq B$ are called *range restrictions*. In DL-Lite, it is also common to allow negative concept and role assertions $\neg B(a)$ and $\neg R(a, b)$ in the ABox. We do not allow them explicitly here, since $\neg B(a)$ can be simulated using an assertion $\bar{B}(a)$ for a fresh concept name $\bar{B}(a)$, and adding $\bar{B} \sqsubseteq \neg B$ to the TBox. Likewise, $\neg R(a, b)$ can be simulated via $\bar{R}(a, b)$ and $\bar{R} \sqsubseteq \neg R$, where $\bar{R}$ fresh role name.

One of the most popular dialects of DL-Lite is DL-Lite$_\mathcal{R}$, which additionally allows for role inclusions of the forms $R \sqsubseteq S$ and $R \sqsubseteq \neg S$, where $R, S \in \mathsf{N}_\mathsf{R}^\pm$. We will focus on DL-Lite$_\mathcal{R}$ when discussing the DL-Lite family in this chapter. Another prominent dialect of DL-Lite is DL-Lite$_\mathcal{F}$, which extends DL-Lite by allowing axioms of the form $(\mathsf{funct}\ P)$, which are just an abbreviation of $\top \sqsubseteq\ \leqslant 1\ R.\top$. There are a great many other DL-Lite dialects that have been considered, see [10] for a detailed discussion.

Example 2. Among the axioms in Example 1, only (1) and (2) are expressible in the core dialect of DL-Lite. They would usually be written as follows:

$$\exists\mathsf{hasCourse} \sqsubseteq \mathsf{Menu} \qquad \exists\mathsf{hasCourse}^- \sqsubseteq \mathsf{Dish}$$

In DL-Lite$_\mathcal{R}$, we can also have (3), (4) and (11), and we can simulate (7) using an additional role name hasIngredientPizzaDough as follows:

$$\mathsf{PizzaCalabrese} \sqsubseteq \mathsf{Pizza}$$
$$\mathsf{PizzaCalabrese} \sqsubseteq \exists\mathsf{hasIngredientPizzaDough}$$
$$\exists\mathsf{hasIngredientPizzaDough}^- \sqsubseteq \mathsf{PizzaDough}$$
$$\mathsf{hasIngredientPizzaDough} \sqsubseteq \mathsf{hasIngredient}$$

We can simulate the existential restrictions in the right-hand-side of axioms (8) and (9) in a similar fashion, and replace the axiom with disjunction on the left-hand side by three axioms, each with one concept name. However, we cannot express qualified existential restrictions on the left-hand side of axioms, nor number restrictions as in (5) and (6), universal restrictions as in (10), or transitivity axioms.

In DL-Lite$_\mathcal{F}$, we have a restricted form of number restrictions, and we can express (5) using func(hasMain).   ▲

$\mathcal{EL}$ **Family.** Like DL-Lite, the $\mathcal{EL}$ description logic offers tractable reasoning at the cost of limited expressivity. The constructors offered by $\mathcal{EL}$ and its extensions [19] make them particularly well suited for medical and life science terminologies. Several important large-scale ontologies are written using DLs of the $\mathcal{EL}$ family, including the Gene Ontology [205], the NCI thesaurus [199] (a cancer ontology), and most notably, SNOMED CT, a comprehensive medical ontology[2] that is used by the health-care systems of several countries (including the US and UK).

$\mathcal{EL}$ is the fragment of $\mathcal{ALC}$ that allows for arbitrary use of concept conjunction and existential restrictions, but no negation, concept disjunction, or universal restrictions. Atomic concepts consist of concept names and $\top$, but do not include $\bot$. As $\mathcal{EL}$ cannot express any form of contradictory or negative information, $\mathcal{EL}$ KBs are trivially satisfiable. In order to be able to express disjointness of concepts, it is common to extend $\mathcal{EL}$ by allowing $\bot$ as an atomic concept. The resulting DL, which has essentially the same computational properties as plain $\mathcal{EL}$ [19], is usually denoted $\mathcal{EL}_\bot$.

Like $\mathcal{ALC}$, $\mathcal{EL}$ and $\mathcal{EL}_\bot$ can be extended with the additional features from Table 1 to obtain DLs like $\mathcal{ELH}, \mathcal{ELHO}, \mathcal{ELI}_\bot, \mathcal{ELHI}_\bot$, etc. Some additions, like role hierarchies, have no impact on the positive computational properties of $\mathcal{EL}$ and $\mathcal{EL}_\bot$, while others, like inverse roles, significantly increase the complexity of reasoning. A detailed discussion of the complexity of reasoning in $\mathcal{EL}$ and extensions can be found in [19,20].

The OWL 2 EL profile [159] is based on the $\mathcal{EL}$ family, and in particular on a DL sometimes called $\mathcal{ELRO}^+$, which is in turn a variant of $\mathcal{EL}^{++}$ [19]. Both of these languages extend $\mathcal{ELH}_\bot$ with additional features like nominals and *complex role inclusion axioms* of the form $r_1 \cdot \ldots \cdot r_n \sqsubseteq r$, which intuitively mean that the pairs of objects in the composition of the r_i also belong to r. In particular, transitivity can be expressed using axioms of the form $r \cdot r \sqsubseteq r$. $\mathcal{ELRO}^+$ also allows range restrictions (without allowing inverses in general). We do not consider these logics in detail here, but we remark that OWL 2 EL corresponds to the so-called *regular* fragment of $\mathcal{ELRO}^+$, which imposes a regularity condition on the complex role inclusions to ensure that the set $\{r_1 \cdot \ldots \cdot r_n \mid \mathcal{T} \models r_1 \cdot \ldots \cdot r_n \sqsubseteq r\}$ of role chains implying a role name r can be represented using a finite automaton.

Example 3. Of the TBox axioms in the example, (1), (7), and (8), are all in the core $\mathcal{EL}$, while (9) can be split into three $\mathcal{EL}$ axioms. $\mathcal{ELH}$ can also express (3),

---

[2] http://www.ihtsdo.org/snomed-ct.

Table 2. Syntax of normalized Horn KBs. $\checkmark(conds)$ means that only axioms satisfying *conds* are allowed for the form in question. Here $A_{(i)}$ and B denote atomic concepts from $\mathsf{N_C} \cup \{\top\}$, while R and S are from $\mathsf{N_R} \cup \{r^- \mid r \in \mathsf{N_R}\}$.

TBox axioms	DL-Lite$_\mathcal{R}$	$\mathcal{EL}$	$\mathcal{ELHI}_\perp$	Horn-$\mathcal{SHIQ}$
$A_1 \sqcap \cdots \sqcap A_n \sqsubseteq B$	$\checkmark(n=1)$	$\checkmark$	$\checkmark$	$\checkmark$
$A_1 \sqcap \cdots \sqcap A_n \sqsubseteq \perp$	$\checkmark(n=2)$		$\checkmark$	$\checkmark$
$A \sqsubseteq \exists R.B$	$\checkmark(B=\top)$	$\checkmark(R \in \mathsf{N_R})$	$\checkmark$	$\checkmark$
$\exists R.B \sqsubseteq A$	$\checkmark(B=\top)$	$\checkmark(R \in \mathsf{N_R})$	$\checkmark$	$\checkmark$
$A \sqsubseteq {\leqslant}1\,R.B$				$\checkmark$
$A \sqsubseteq {\geqslant}m\,R.B$				$\checkmark$
$R \sqsubseteq S$	$\checkmark$		$\checkmark$	$\checkmark$
$R \sqsubseteq \neg S$	$\checkmark$			
$\mathsf{trans}(R)$				$\checkmark$
ABox assertions				
$A(a)$	$\checkmark$	$\checkmark$	$\checkmark$	$\checkmark$
$r(a,b)$	$\checkmark$	$\checkmark$	$\checkmark$	$\checkmark$

(4) and (11). The axiom restricting the range of hasCourse is expressible in $\mathcal{ELI}$ and $\mathcal{ELRO}^+$. The inclusion GlutenFree $\sqsubseteq$ $\forall$contains.$\neg$Gluten can be equivalently expressed in $\mathcal{ELI}_\perp$ as

$$\text{Gluten} \sqcap \exists\text{contains}^-.\text{GlutenFree} \sqsubseteq \perp$$

However, the other direction, $\forall$contains.$\neg$Gluten$\sqsubseteq$ GlutenFree is not expressible in any DL of the $\mathcal{EL}$ family. The transitivity axiom (12) is expressible in (regular) $\mathcal{ELRO}^+$ and $\mathcal{EL}^{++}$.   ▲

It is sometimes convenient to assume that $\mathcal{EL}$ and $\mathcal{ELHI}_\perp$ TBoxes are in a normal form that only allows axioms of the forms indicated in Table 2. It is well known that TBoxes can be efficiently transformed into this normal form by introducing fresh concept names. For the sake of comparison, we have also included in the table the syntax of DL-Lite$_\mathcal{R}$, assuming a similar normalization. We introduce another important Horn DL, called Horn-$\mathcal{SHIQ}$, that is not part of the DL-Lite or $\mathcal{EL}$ families.

Horn-$\mathcal{SHIQ}$. The description logic Horn-$\mathcal{SHIQ}$ is the disjunction-free fragment of the well-known DL $\mathcal{SHIQ}$. It supports many of the expressive features of $\mathcal{SHIQ}$, like transitivity and number restrictions, but as we will see later, it is better behaved computationally. The formal definition of Horn-$\mathcal{SHIQ}$ syntax is rather complicated, since fully eliminating disjunction requires taking into account complex interactions between constructors, and in particular, which sub-formulas occur implicitly under the scope of negation. The full definition can be found in [136]. Here we instead give only the definition of *normalized* TBoxes, which allow for axioms of all the forms listed in Table 2 except for $R \sqsubseteq \neg S$.[3] Additionally, in a (Horn-)$\mathcal{SHIQ}$ TBox $\mathcal{T}$, all roles R occurring in a number restriction $\geqslant n \, R.C$ or $\leqslant n \, R.C$ must be *simple*, which means that there does not exist a role S such that $\mathsf{trans}(S) \in \mathcal{T}$ and $\mathcal{T} \models S \sqsubseteq R$. We note that axioms of the form $A \sqsubseteq \forall R.B$ are usually allowed in Horn-$\mathcal{SHIQ}$. We have omitted them from our syntax, but they can be equivalently expressed as $\exists \mathsf{inv}(R).A \sqsubseteq B$.

Example 4. Most of the axioms in our example TBox are expressible in Horn-$\mathcal{SHIQ}$, with the exception of axioms (6) and (10), for which we can only express one half of the stated equivalences:

$$\mathsf{FullMenu} \sqsubseteq \geqslant 3 \, \mathsf{hasCourse}.\top \tag{6$'$}$$

$$\exists \mathsf{contains}^-.\mathsf{GlutenFree} \sqcap \mathsf{Gluten} \sqsubseteq \bot \tag{10$'$}$$

The other halves of (6) and (10)

$$\forall \mathsf{contains}.\neg \mathsf{Gluten} \sqsubseteq \mathsf{GlutenFree} \qquad \geqslant 3 \, \mathsf{hasCourse}.\top \sqsubseteq \mathsf{FullMenu}$$

cannot be expressed in Horn-$\mathcal{SHIQ}$, nor in any other Horn DL.   ▲

Horn Logics and Universal Models. We have mentioned that the main distinguishing feature of Horn DLs is that they can be viewed as subsets of the well-known Horn fragment of first-order logic. Semantically, the crucial property this ensures is that, for every satisfiable KB $\mathcal{K}$, there exists a *universal* model of $\mathcal{K}$ that can be homomorphically embedded into any other model. Intuitively, this model satisfies all the constraints expressed by $\mathcal{K}$ in the minimal, most general way, and it witnesses all entailments. We will present later in the chapter a concrete way of constructing such a model and explain how it can be exploited for answering different kinds of queries.

Unfortunately, this crucial property is lost in non-Horn DLs, which provide means of expressing disjunctive knowledge. The complexity results we will discuss in this chapter illustrate how the lack of a universal model has a negative impact on the complexity of reasoning.

Example 5. Consider the KB consisting of one ABox assertion and two TBox axioms:

$$\mathsf{PastaDish}(d) \qquad \mathsf{PastaDish} \sqsubseteq \mathsf{Dish} \qquad \mathsf{PastaDish} \sqsubseteq \exists \mathsf{hasIngredient}.\mathsf{Pasta}$$

The following interpretation, with $\Delta^{\mathcal{I}} = \{o_d, o_p\}$, is a model of this KB:

$$\begin{aligned} d^{\mathcal{I}} &= o_d & \mathsf{hasIngredient}^{\mathcal{I}} &= \{(o_d, o_p)\} & \mathsf{PastaDish}^{\mathcal{I}} &= \{o_d\} \\ \mathsf{Dish}^{\mathcal{I}} &= \{o_d\} & \mathsf{Pasta}^{\mathcal{I}} &= \{o_p\} \end{aligned}$$

---

[3] $\mathcal{SHIQ}$ does not support negative role inclusions. These could be added at no computational cost, and they are expressible in extensions of $\mathcal{SHIQ}$ for which reasoning has the same complexity, like $\mathcal{ZIQ}$ [57] and the *simple* fragment of $\mathcal{SRIQ}$ [109].

This model is universal: every model of the KB contains an object interpreting d as an instance of Dish and PastaDish, related via hasIngredient to some object that is an instance of Pasta. This is the minimal structure that needs to be present in an interpretation for it to be a model of the KB.

Now suppose we add the axiom Pasta $\sqsubseteq$ freshPasta $\sqcup$ driedPasta. We exhibit two interpretations $\mathcal{I}_1$ and $\mathcal{I}_2$, with the same domain as $\mathcal{I}$, which are both models of the extended KB:

$$\text{hasIngredient}^{\mathcal{I}_1} = \{(o_d, o_p)\} \qquad \text{PastaDish}^{\mathcal{I}_1} = \{o_d\} \qquad \text{freshPasta}^{\mathcal{I}_1} = \{o_p\}$$
$$\text{Dish}^{\mathcal{I}_1} = \{o_d\} \qquad\qquad\quad \text{Pasta}^{\mathcal{I}_1} = \{o_p\} \qquad\quad \text{driedPasta}^{\mathcal{I}_1} = \emptyset$$

$$\text{hasIngredient}^{\mathcal{I}_2} = \{(o_d, o_p)\} \qquad \text{PastaDish}^{\mathcal{I}_2} = \{o_d\} \qquad \text{freshPasta}^{\mathcal{I}_1} = \emptyset$$
$$\text{Dish}^{\mathcal{I}_2} = \{o_d\} \qquad\qquad\quad \text{Pasta}^{\mathcal{I}_2} = \{o_p\} \qquad\quad \text{driedPasta}^{\mathcal{I}_2} = \{o_p\}$$

Observe that $\mathcal{I}_1$ is not (homomorphically) contained in $\mathcal{I}_2$, and $\mathcal{I}_2$ is not (homomorphically) contained in $\mathcal{I}_1$, which shows that there is no universal model of this KB. ▲

3 Ontology-Mediated Query Answering

In this section, we will formally define the problem of ontology-mediated query answering, discuss how the complexity of this task can be measured, and introduce two key algorithmic techniques for OMQA. This will lay the necessary foundations for later sections, in which we will present concrete algorithms and complexity results for different query languages and DLs.

As ontology-mediated query answering is closely related to the more well-studied problem of querying relational databases, the first part of this section will recall some key notions from databases and discuss the important differences between the two settings.

3.1 Databases and ABoxes

Recall from the preceding section that in description logics, data is stored in the ABox as a set of assertions of the forms $A(a)$ and $r(a, b)$, where A is a concept name, r a role name, and a, b are individuals. From the first-order logic point of view, ABox assertions are simply *facts* built from unary and binary relation symbols and constants. ABoxes provide an *incomplete description* of the considered application domain, in the sense that everything stated in the ABox is assumed to be true, but facts which are not present in the ABox are not assumed to be false. This is known as the *open-world assumption* and is a desirable property in our setting as it allows us to leave the truth of some facts unspecified and to be able to infer new pieces of information from the explicit information asserted in ABox and TBox.

Relational databases constitute one of the most common ways of storing data in modern information systems. *Relational database instances* (which we will often abbreviate to databases) can be defined similarly to ABoxes as finite sets of facts $P(a_1, \ldots, a_n)$, where P is a relation symbol of arity $n \geq 0$. In addition to allowing facts of arbitrary arity, databases differ from ABoxes in another important respect: they are interpreted under the *closed-world assumption*, meaning that all facts that are contained in the database are assumed true and those that are absent are *assumed to be false*. Concretely, this means that every database instance $\mathcal{D}$ corresponds to the *unique first-order interpretation* $\mathcal{I}_\mathcal{D}$ whose domain $\Delta^{\mathcal{I}_\mathcal{D}}$ contains all constants appearing in $\mathcal{D}$ and which interprets every relation symbol P as $\{ \boldsymbol{a} \mid P(\boldsymbol{a}) \in D \}$ and every constant as itself.

Remark 3. Databases make the *standard names assumption*, which consists in interpreting constants as themselves. Note that this is strictly stronger than the unique names assumption discussed in Sect. 2.1.

The next example illustrates the difference between ABoxes and databases.

Example 6. Let $\mathcal{D}$ and $\mathcal{A}_1$ be respectively the database and ABox corresponding to the following set of facts (assertions):

$$\mathsf{Cake}(d_1) \quad \mathsf{IceCream}(d_2) \quad \mathsf{Dessert}(d_3) \quad \mathsf{hasDessert}(m, d_4)$$

The database $\mathcal{D}$ corresponds to the interpretation $\mathcal{I}_\mathcal{D}$ defined as follows:

- $\Delta^{\mathcal{I}_\mathcal{D}} = \{m, d_1, d_2, d_3, d_4\}$
- $\mathsf{Cake}^{\mathcal{I}_\mathcal{D}} = \{d_1\}$
- $\mathsf{IceCream}^{\mathcal{I}_\mathcal{D}} = \{d_2\}$
- $\mathsf{Dessert}^{\mathcal{I}_\mathcal{D}} = \{d_3\}$
- $\mathsf{hasDessert}^{\mathcal{I}_\mathcal{D}} = \{(m, d_4)\}$
- $c^{\mathcal{I}_\mathcal{D}} = c$ for every $c \in \{m, d_1, d_2, d_3, d_4\}$

According to the interpretation $\mathcal{I}_D$, there are five entities (m, d_1, d_2, d_3, d_4), and only d_3 belongs to $\mathsf{Dessert}$.

The interpretation $\mathcal{I}_\mathcal{D}$ is a model of the ABox $\mathcal{A}_1$, but $\mathcal{A}_1$ has (infinitely) many other models, including the interpretation $\mathcal{J}$ defined as follows[4]:

- $\Delta^{\mathcal{I}_\mathcal{D}} = \{m, m', d_1, d_2, d_3, d_4, d_7, e, f_4, g\}$
- $\mathsf{Cake}^{\mathcal{I}_\mathcal{D}} = \{d_1, d_3, e\}$
- $\mathsf{IceCream}^{\mathcal{I}_\mathcal{D}} = \{d_2, f_4\}$
- $\mathsf{Dessert}^{\mathcal{I}_\mathcal{D}} = \{d_1, d_2, d_3, d_4, e, f_4\}$
- $\mathsf{hasDessert}^{\mathcal{I}_\mathcal{D}} = \{(m, d_4), (m', d_3)\}$
- $c^{\mathcal{I}_\mathcal{D}} = c$ for every $c \in \{m, d_1, d_2, d_3, d_4\}$

The interpretation $\mathcal{J}$ contains additional domain elements that are not explicitly mentioned in $\mathcal{A}_1$, and it also makes true some assertions that are not present in $\mathcal{A}_1$. For example, there are now six entities (including the ABox individuals d_1, d_2, d_3, and d_4) that belong to the class $\mathsf{Dessert}$. Since some models of $\mathcal{A}_1$ state that d_1 is a dessert, and others do not, the truth of this assertion is left undefined by $\mathcal{A}_1$. However, if we add a TBox containing the information that all cakes are desserts ($\mathsf{Cake} \sqsubseteq \mathsf{Dessert}$), then this will eliminate some of the models and allow us to infer that d_1 is a dessert.   ▲

---

[4] Note that for simplicity, and to facilitate the comparison with $\mathcal{I}_D$, the interpretation $\mathcal{J}$ interprets individuals as themselves. However, we could instead have chosen domain elements distinct from the individual names.

3.2   Querying Databases

Queries provide the means of accessing the data stored in database instances. There are several different query languages that have been proposed for relational databases, each providing a formal syntax for constructing queries and a semantics that defines the result of evaluating a query on a given database. Formally, the semantics of a query q specifies for every database $\mathcal{D}$ the set $\mathsf{ans}(q, \mathcal{D})$ of *answers of q over $\mathcal{D}$*, where the answers take the form of tuples of constants from $\mathcal{D}$. Since databases correspond to interpretations, we can alternatively view database queries as *mappings from interpretations to tuples of domain elements*. Note that although databases correspond to finite interpretations, it is typically straightforward to extend the semantics of queries to arbitrary interpretations, and so we may assume that ans is defined for all interpretations, finite or infinite. Thus, for the purposes of this chapter, a query q of arity $n \geq 0$ associates with every interpretation $\mathcal{I}$ a subset $\mathsf{ans}(q, \mathcal{I}) \subseteq (\Delta^{\mathcal{I}})^n$. Note that when $n = 0$, the query q is called *Boolean*, and $\mathsf{ans}(q, \mathcal{I})$ can take one of two values: the empty tuple $()$ (meaning q holds in $\mathcal{I}$) or $\emptyset$ (q does not hold).

We introduce next two specific database query languages that will play an important role in this chapter, namely, first-order queries and Datalog queries.

First-Order Queries. A common way of specifying queries is to use formulas from some logic, with first-order logic being the standard choice. A *first-order (FO) query* is a first-order formula built from relational atoms $P(t_1, \ldots, t_n)$ and equality atoms $t_1 = t_2$ (with each t_i a constant or variable) using the Boolean connectives $(\vee, \wedge, \neg, \rightarrow)$ and universal and existential quantifiers $(\forall x, \exists x)$. The free variables of FO queries will be called *answer variables*, and the *arity* of an FO query is defined as its number of answer variables. Given an interpretation $\mathcal{I}$, an FO query φ with answer variables $(x_1, \ldots, x_n)$, and a tuple $(e_1, \ldots, e_n)$ of elements from $\Delta^{\mathcal{I}}$, we use $\mathcal{I} \models \varphi[(x_1, \ldots, x_n) \mapsto (e_1, \ldots, e_n)]$ to denote that the FO formula φ is satisfied in $\mathcal{I}$ under the variable assignment that maps each x_i to e_i. The semantics of an FO query φ with answer variables $\boldsymbol{x} = (x_1, \ldots, x_n)$ is defined using this notion of satisfaction:

$$\mathsf{ans}(q, \mathcal{I}) = \{\, \boldsymbol{e} = (e_1, \ldots, e_n) \in (\Delta^{\mathcal{I}})^n \mid \mathcal{I} \models \varphi[\boldsymbol{x} \mapsto \boldsymbol{e}]\,\}$$

An FO query φ is called *domain independent* if $\mathsf{ans}(\varphi, \mathcal{I}) = \mathsf{ans}(\varphi, \mathcal{J})$ for every pair of interpretations $\mathcal{I}, \mathcal{J}$ such that $\cdot^{\mathcal{I}} = \cdot^{\mathcal{J}}$, i.e., $\mathcal{I}$ and $\mathcal{J}$ interpret all predicate and constant symbols identically.

We remark that domain-independent first-order queries provide the logical underpinnings of SQL, which is the most widely used query language in commercial database systems. Every domain independent first-order query can be translated into an equivalent SQL query, which means that such queries can be evaluated using standard relational database management systems.

Remark 4. Unless stated otherwise, all first-order queries considered in this chapter are domain independent.

Datalog Queries. Datalog is a rule-based formalism that originated from work on logic programming and has been extensively studied within the database community as a powerful language for expressing recursive queries (see e.g. [66] and Chaps. 12–13 of [1]). A *Datalog rule* takes the form

$$P_n(\boldsymbol{t_n}) \leftarrow P_1(\boldsymbol{t_1}), \ldots, P_{n-1}(\boldsymbol{t_{n-1}})$$

where each $P_i(\boldsymbol{t_i})$ is a relational atom. We call $P_n(\boldsymbol{t_n})$ the *head* of the rule and $P_1(\boldsymbol{t_1}), \ldots, P_{n-1}(\boldsymbol{t_{n-1}})$ the rule *body*. Datalog rules are required to satisfy the following *safety condition*: every variable that appears in the rule head must also occur in one of the atoms of the rule body. A *Datalog program* consists of a finite set of Datalog rules, and a *Datalog query* is a pair (Π, Q) where Π is a Datalog program and Q is a relation symbol that appears in Π.

Every Datalog rule can be viewed as a first-order sentence[5]: simply reverse the direction of the implication symbol, take the conjunction of the body atoms, and quantify universally over all variables. For example, consider the following Datalog rule and its corresponding FO sentence:

$$Q(v, u) \leftarrow P(v, x), T(x, u, w) \qquad \rightsquigarrow \qquad \forall x u v w \ (P(v, x) \wedge T(x, u, w)) \rightarrow Q(v, u)$$

We will say that a first-order interpretation $\mathcal{I}$ is a *model of a Datalog rule* if $\mathcal{I}$ is a model of the corresponding FO sentence, and we call $\mathcal{I}$ a *model of a Datalog program* Π just in the case that $\mathcal{I}$ is a model of every rule in Π.

Recall that we view sets of facts as interpretations, hence the semantics of a Datalog program is defined relative to a given interpretation that corresponds to an (extensional) database. Given an interpretation $\mathcal{J}$ and a Datalog program Π, we will call an interpretation $\mathcal{I}$ a *minimal model of Π relative to $\mathcal{J}$* just in the case that the following conditions hold:

1. $\Delta^{\mathcal{I}} = \Delta^{\mathcal{J}}$
2. $c^{\mathcal{I}} = c^{\mathcal{J}}$ for every constant c
3. $\mathcal{I}$ is a model of Π
4. for every other interpretation $\mathcal{I}'$ that satisfies the three preceding conditions, we have that $P^{\mathcal{I}} \subseteq P^{\mathcal{I}'}$ for every relation symbol P.

In fact, it can be shown that for every interpretation $\mathcal{J}$ and Datalog program Π there is a *unique minimal model* of Π relative to $\mathcal{I}$. Using the minimal model, we may define the semantics of Datalog queries as follows:

$$\mathsf{ans}((\Pi, Q), \mathcal{I}) = Q^{\mathcal{J}} \qquad \text{where } \mathcal{I} \text{ is the minimal model of } \Pi \text{ relative to } \mathcal{J}$$

Remark 5. Datalog queries can also be given a *procedural semantics*, in which the minimal model is computed by an exhaustive application of the Datalog rules starting from the initial set of facts in the database (or the initial relations in the interpretation).

---

[5] More precisely, Datalog rules correspond to function-free *Horn clauses*.

3.3   Querying Description Logic Knowledge Bases

In principle, any query language defined for databases can be used to query description logic knowledge bases. From the syntactic point of view, the only difference is that in place of arbitrary relation symbols, we will use concept and role names. It is less obvious how to lift the semantics of queries to DL knowledge bases, as DL KBs typically have multiple models, whereas the semantics of queries only states how to obtain answers from a single interpretation. The solution is to adopt so-called certain answer semantics[6], in which we consider those answers that hold with respect to each of the KB's models. The intuition is that since we do not know which of the KB's models provides the correct description of the application domain, we can only be confident in those answers that can be obtained from *every* model of the KB.

Definition 3 (Certain Answers). *Let* $\mathcal{K} = (\mathcal{T}, \mathcal{A})$ *be a DL KB, and let* q *be an n-ary query. The set* $\mathsf{cert}(q, \mathcal{K})$ *of certain answers to* q *over* $\mathcal{K}$ *is defined as follows:*

$$\{(a_1, \ldots, a_n) \in \mathsf{Ind}(\mathcal{A})^n \mid (a_1^{\mathcal{I}}, \ldots, a_n^{\mathcal{I}}) \in \mathsf{ans}(q, \mathcal{I}) \text{ for every } \mathcal{I} \in \mathsf{Mods}(\mathcal{K})\}$$

Remark 6. Observe that certain answers are defined as *tuples of individuals*, rather than tuples of domain elements. This distinction is important since we do not make the standard names assumption, and so an individual may be mapped to different elements in different models of the KB.

Remark 7. If we consider Boolean FO queries, then certain answer semantics corresponds to *logical entailment*. Indeed, the DL KB can be expressed as a FO theory, and the problem is to determine whether the query (an FO sentence) holds in every model of the KB. By contrast, the evaluation of Boolean FO queries over databases corresponds to *model checking*, since we need to check whether the query (FO sentence) holds w.r.t. to a given FO interpretation. It is well known that logical entailment is more difficult than model checking, and so it is no surprise that ontology-mediated query answering is a more challenging computational task than query answering in databases.

We illustrate the notion of certain answers on an example.

Example 7. We consider the KB $\mathcal{K}_1$ consisting of the 'dessert' ABox $\mathcal{A}_1$ from Example 6 and the following TBox $\mathcal{T}_1$:

$$\mathsf{Cake} \sqsubseteq \mathsf{Dessert} \quad \mathsf{IceCream} \sqsubseteq \mathsf{Dessert} \quad \mathsf{hasDessert} \sqsubseteq \mathsf{hasCourse}$$

$$\exists \mathsf{hasCourse} \sqsubseteq \mathsf{Menu} \quad \exists \mathsf{hasDessert}^- \sqsubseteq \mathsf{Dessert}$$

Suppose that we are interested in finding all desserts, i.e., we wish to find all certain answers to the query $q_1 = \mathsf{Dessert}(x)$. Since there are five individuals in the ABox, there are five potential certain answers. We argue that four of them are indeed certain answers:

---

[6] The certain answer semantics is also used in other contexts, such as incomplete databases [112], data integration [142], and data exchange [6].

- $d_1 \in \text{cert}(q, \mathcal{K}_1)$, since $\text{Cake}(d_1) \in \mathcal{A}_1$ and $\text{Cake} \sqsubseteq \text{Dessert} \in \mathcal{T}_1$, and so we must have $d_1^\mathcal{I} \in \text{Dessert}^\mathcal{I}$ for every model $\mathcal{I}$ of $\mathcal{K}_1$
- $d_2 \in \text{cert}(q_1, \mathcal{K}_1)$, since $\text{IceCream}(d_2) \in \mathcal{A}_1$ and $\text{IceCream} \sqsubseteq \text{Dessert} \in \mathcal{T}_1$
- $d_3 \in \text{cert}(q_1, \mathcal{K}_1)$, since $\text{Dessert}(d_3)$ appears explicitly in $\mathcal{A}_1$
- $d_4 \in \text{cert}(q_1, \mathcal{K}_1)$, since $\text{hasDessert}(m, d_4) \in \mathcal{A}_1$ and $\text{hasDessert}^- \sqsubseteq \text{Dessert} \in \mathcal{T}_1$

The fifth individual, m, is not a certain answer to q_1 w.r.t. $\mathcal{K}_1$. To see why, let us extend the interpretation $\mathcal{J}$ from Example 6 by setting:

- $\text{hasCourse}^\mathcal{J} = \{(m, d_4), (m, g), (m', d_3), (m', g)\}$
- $\text{Menu}^\mathcal{J} = \{m, m'\}$

It can be verified that $\mathcal{J}$ is a model of $\mathcal{K}_1$, yet $m^\mathcal{J} = m$ does not belong to $\text{Dessert}^\mathcal{J}$.   ▲

In this chapter, our main focus will be on the problem of ontology-mediated query answering, which will consist in computing the certain answers of queries over a DL KB. We will be particularly interested in understanding how the complexity of this task varies depending on the query language and description logic considered. For the purposes of analyzing the complexity of ontology-mediated query answering, we will recast OMQA as a decision problem[7]:

PROBLEM:	$\mathcal{Q}$ answering in $\mathcal{L}$ (with $\mathcal{Q}$ a query language and $\mathcal{L}$ a DL)
INPUT:	An n-ary query $q \in \mathcal{Q}$, an ABox $\mathcal{A}$, a TBox $\mathcal{T}$ formulated in $\mathcal{L}$, and a tuple $\boldsymbol{a} \in \text{Ind}(\mathcal{A})^n$
QUESTION:	Does $\boldsymbol{a}$ belong to $\text{cert}(q, (\mathcal{T}, \mathcal{A}))$?

To solve the problem of $\mathcal{Q}$ answering in $\mathcal{L}$, we must devise a *decision procedure*, that is, an algorithm that satisfies the following three requirements:

- Termination: the procedure is guaranteed to halt on any input
- Soundness: if the procedure returns 'yes', then $\boldsymbol{a} \in \text{cert}(q, \mathcal{K})$
- Completeness: if $\boldsymbol{a} \in \text{cert}(q, \mathcal{K})$, then the procedure returns 'yes'

We remark that if we have such a decision procedure, then we can use it to solve the original task of computing all certain answers. Indeed, we can enumerate all tuples of the same arity as the query, and for each, we can use the decision procedure to check whether or not the tuple is a certain answer.

According to certain answer semantics, if we pose an n-ary query q to an unsatisfiable KB $\mathcal{K}$, then every n-tuples of individuals from $\mathcal{K}$ is a certain answer, and so we will answer 'yes' for every tuple. Thus, query answering is trivial when the KB is unsatisfiable. It follows that to obtain a decision procedure for $\mathcal{Q}$ answering in $\mathcal{L}$, it suffices to provide decision procedures for the following two problems: (i) satisfiability of $\mathcal{L}$ KBs, and (ii) $\mathcal{Q}$ answering over *satisfiable* $\mathcal{L}$ KBs.

---

[7] We recall that a *decision problem* (alternatively known as a recognition problem) is a problem with a yes-or-no answer.

3.4   Complexity of Query Answering

We have seen in the previous subsection how the problem of ontology-mediated query answering can be formulated as a decision problem. Database query evaluation can be similarly recast as a decision problem: we are given as input a query q, database $\mathcal{D}$, and tuple of constants $\boldsymbol{a}$, and the problem is to decide whether $\boldsymbol{a} \in \mathsf{cert}(q, \mathcal{I}_{\mathcal{D}})$. When we speak of the complexity of OMQA or database query evaluation, we will always mean the complexity of these decision problems. In what follows, we assume that we have a function $|\cdot|$ that assigns to each of the objects (queries, TBoxes, ABoxes, databases, tuples) appearing in the input a natural number corresponding to the *size* of the object, e.g. the length of its string representation according to some suitable encoding. For example, $|\mathcal{T}|$ will denote the size of TBox $\mathcal{T}$.

The complexity of decision problems can be measured in different ways, depending on which inputs we choose to count and which we treat as fixed. When analyzing the complexity of query answering, there are two commonly considered complexity measures [209]:

- *Combined complexity* is measured as a function of the *size of the whole input*, that is, $|q| + |\mathcal{T}| + |\mathcal{A}| + |\boldsymbol{a}|$ in the case of OMQA and $|q| + |\mathcal{D}| + |\boldsymbol{a}|$ in the case of database query evaluation[8].
- *Data complexity* is with respect to the *size of the data*, that is, $|\mathcal{A}|$ for OMQA and $|\mathcal{D}|$ in the database setting. The sizes of all other inputs are treated as fixed constants and so they do not contribute to the complexity.

Combined complexity corresponds to the 'classical' way of measuring complexity, in which we consider all of the inputs to the decision problem and treat them equally. If we show that a problem is in polynomial time for combined complexity, then this is a good indication that the problem can be efficiently solved in practice. However, a problem that is intractable in combined complexity may nonetheless be prove feasible on typical inputs. Indeed, database query evaluation has been proven intractable in combined complexity for all of the commonly considered query languages, yet modern database systems are able to answer most user queries instantaneously. The key observation is that the queries encountered in practice are typically quite small, and their size is negligible when compared to the size of the (typically very large) database, and so the real predictor of performance is how querying algorithms scale with respect to the size of the database. For this reason, data complexity is generally considered the more useful complexity measure for databases. In the setting of ontology-mediated query answering, in addition the query and ABox, we have a TBox whose size can vary widely, from a few dozen axioms up to tens (or even hundreds) of thousands. However, it seems reasonable to assume that in most OMQA applications the ABox will be significantly larger than the TBox, so data complexity is also very relevant in this setting.

Computational complexity [9,172] provides a hierarchy of different complexity classes that can be used to classify problems according to the amount of

---

[8] We typically omit $|\boldsymbol{a}|$ since we have $|\boldsymbol{a}| \leq |q| \cdot |\mathcal{A}|$ (or $|\boldsymbol{a}| \leq |q| \cdot |\mathcal{D}|$).

resources (time, space) that are required in order to solve them. In this paper, we will make use of the following complexity classes, which are ordered according to inclusion with each class being included in those later in the list:

- AC_0: problems that can be solved by a uniform family of circuits of constant depth and polynomial size, with unlimited fan-in AND gates and OR gates.
- NLOGSPACE: problems that can be solved in non-deterministic logarithmic space.
- P: problems that can be solved in polynomial time.
- NP (resp. CONP): problems that can be solved (resp. whose complement can be solved) in non-deterministic polynomial time.
- PSPACE: problems that can be solved in polynomial space.
- EXP: problems that can be solved in single-exponential time.

It is known that AC_0 is strictly contained in the class LOGSPACE of all problems solvable in deterministic logarithmic space, which in particular means that it is a proper subclass of P.

The following theorems summarize what is known about the complexity of evaluating first-order and Datalog queries over databases:

Theorem 1 ([209,210]). *First-order query evaluation is in* AC_0 *in data complexity and* PSPACE*-complete in combined complexity.*

Theorem 2 ([113,209]). *Datalog query evaluation is* P*-complete in data complexity and* EXP*-complete in combined complexity.*

In later sections, we will investigate the complexity of answering different forms of queries over knowledge bases formulated using the Horn DLs introduced in Sect. 2. As we shall see, in contrast to expressive DLs, for which answering even the simplest queries is CONP-hard in data complexity, it is possible to design query answering algorithms for Horn DLs that scale polynomially in the size of the ABox. It is for this reason that we sometimes use the term 'data-tractable' when referring to Horn DLs.

3.5   Techniques for Ontology-Mediated Query Answering

We have seen that in general, ontology-mediated query answering is more complex than database query evaluation, since we must consider all models of a KB rather than the single interpretation associated with a database. Query rewriting and saturation are two techniques that can be used to bridge this gap and enable the use of existing database systems for OMQA. These two techniques underlie most of the OMQA algorithms that have been developed for Horn DLs, including those that will be presented in this chapter.

Query Rewriting. The basic idea behind query rewriting is as follows. In a first step, we rewrite the input query into a new query that contains all the relevant information from the TBox. In a second step, we pass the rewritten query to a database system for evaluation over the ABox, which is treated as a (closed-world) database instance. Query rewriting thus provides a means of reducing the OMQA problem to the more well-studied problem of database query evaluation.

We now formalize the notion of a rewriting of a query. Note that we will use $\mathcal{I}_\mathcal{A}$ to denote the finite interpretation obtained by viewing $\mathcal{A}$ as a database. More precisely: $\Delta^{\mathcal{I}_\mathcal{A}} = \mathsf{Ind}(\mathcal{A})$, $A^{\mathcal{I}_\mathcal{A}} = \{a \mid A(a) \in \mathcal{A}\}$ (for every $A \in \mathsf{N_C}$), $r^{\mathcal{I}_\mathcal{A}} = \{(a,b) \mid r(a,b) \in \mathcal{A}\}$ (for every $r \in \mathsf{N_R}$), and $a^{\mathcal{I}_\mathcal{A}} = a$ (for every $a \in \mathsf{Ind}(\mathcal{A})$).

Definition 4 (Rewriting of a Query). *Let $\mathcal{T}$ be a DL TBox, let Σ be a finite signature, and let q, q' be two queries. We say that q' is a rewriting of q w.r.t. $\mathcal{T}, \Sigma$ just in the case that $\mathsf{cert}(q, (\mathcal{T}, \mathcal{A})) = \mathsf{ans}(q', \mathcal{I}_\mathcal{A})$ for every Σ-ABox $\mathcal{A}$. We call q' a rewriting of q w.r.t. $\mathcal{T}, \Sigma$ relative to consistent ABoxes if $\mathsf{cert}(q, (\mathcal{T}, \mathcal{A})) = \mathsf{ans}(q', \mathcal{I}_\mathcal{A})$ for every Σ-ABox $\mathcal{A}$ such that $(\mathcal{T}, \mathcal{A})$ is satisfiable.*

Remark 8. The signature Σ specifies the concept and role names that can appear in ABoxes of the considered application. To simplify the presentation, we will sometimes omit mention of Σ, when it is unimportant to the discussion at hand.

Example 8. Reconsider the query $q_1 = \mathsf{Dessert}(x)$ and KB $\mathcal{K}_1 = (\mathcal{T}_1, \mathcal{A}_1)$ from Example 7. It can be verified that the query

$$q'_1 = \mathsf{Dessert}(x) \vee \mathsf{Cake}(x) \vee \mathsf{IceCream}(x) \vee \exists y.\mathsf{hasDessert}(y, x)$$

is a rewriting of q_1 w.r.t. $\mathcal{T}_1$. Intuitively, this is because q'_1 captures the four ways to infer, using the axioms in $\mathcal{T}_1$, that a given ABox individual is an instance of the concept $\mathsf{Dessert}$.

If we evaluate q'_1 over $\mathcal{I}_{\mathcal{A}_1}$ (which is identical to $\mathcal{I}_\mathcal{D}$ from Example 6), we obtain $\mathsf{ans}(q'_1, \mathcal{I}_{\mathcal{A}_1}) = \{d_1, d_2, d_3, d_4\}$. Indeed:

- d_1 is an answer to the disjunct $\mathsf{Cake}(x)$, due to the assertion $\mathsf{Cake}(d_1)$
- d_2 is an answer to the disjunct $\mathsf{IceCream}(x)$, due to the assertion $\mathsf{IceCream}(d_2)$
- d_3 is an answer to the disjunct $\mathsf{Dessert}(x)$, due to the assertion $\mathsf{Dessert}(d_3)$
- d_4 is an answer to the disjunct $\exists y.\mathsf{hasDessert}(y, x)$, due to the assertion $\mathsf{hasDessert}(m, d_4)$

We can therefore conclude that $\mathsf{cert}(q_1, \mathcal{K}_1) = \{d_1, d_2, d_3, d_4\}$.   ▲

We can define an analogous notion of rewriting for testing KB satisfiability.

Definition 5. (Rewriting of Unsatisfiability). *Let $\mathcal{T}$ be a DL TBox, let Σ be a finite signature, and let $q_\perp$ be a Boolean query. We call $q_\perp$ a rewriting of unsatisfiability w.r.t. $\mathcal{T}, \Sigma$ if for every Σ-ABox $\mathcal{A}$, we have $\mathsf{cert}(q, (\mathcal{T}, \mathcal{A})) = ()$ iff $(\mathcal{T}, \mathcal{A})$ is unsatisfiable.*

The preceding notions of rewriting can be further specialized by adding to the above definitions the requirement that the query q' (resp. $q_\perp$) be an FO or Datalog query, yielding the notions of *FO rewritings* and *Datalog rewritings*.

In the same way as query answering can be decomposed into satisfiability checking and query answering w.r.t. satisfiable KBs, one can show that it is sufficient to be able to construct rewritings of unsatisfiability and rewritings of queries relative to consistent ABoxes. Indeed, if we have an FO rewriting $q_\perp$ of unsatisfiability w.r.t. $\mathcal{T}, \Sigma$ and an FO rewriting q' of q w.r.t. $\mathcal{T}, \Sigma$ relative to consistent ABoxes, then these can be combined to obtain an FO rewriting of q w.r.t. $\mathcal{T}, \Sigma$ (over arbitrary Σ-ABoxes). Basically, if q has answer variables $x_1, \ldots, x_n$, then the desired rewriting takes the form $q' \vee (q_\perp \wedge q_{ind}^{\Sigma}(x_1) \wedge \ldots \wedge q_{ind}^{\Sigma}(x_n))$, where q_{ind}^{Σ} is a unary query that retrieves all of the individuals that occur in a given Σ-ABox. Using a similar construction, we can show that it is possible to construct a Datalog rewriting of a query by combining a Datalog rewriting of the query relative to consistent ABoxes with a Datalog rewriting of unsatisfiability.

It is important to keep in mind that the existence of a rewriting is not guaranteed: it is possible to find queries and TBoxes for which no FO (resp. Datalog) rewriting exists. Moreover, as the next example illustrates, the existence of a rewriting depends upon the type of rewriting we consider.

Example 9. The query $\mathsf{Spicy}(x)$ has no FO rewriting w.r.t. the TBox

$$\{\exists \mathsf{hasIngredient}.\mathsf{Spicy} \sqsubseteq \mathsf{Spicy}\}.$$

Intuitively, we would like to use the following (infinite) query, which looks for hasIngredient chains that start at x and end at an individual asserted to be Spicy:

$\mathsf{Spicy}(x) \vee \exists x'(\mathsf{hasIngredient}(x, x') \wedge \mathsf{Spicy}(x'))$
$$\vee \exists x'x''(\mathsf{hasIngredient}(x, x') \wedge \mathsf{hasIngredient}(x', x'') \wedge \mathsf{Spicy}(x'')) \vee \ldots$$

It can be proven, using techniques from finite model theory (see the introductory texts [76,145]), that no FO query that is equivalent to this infinite disjunction.

However, this same query and TBox possesses a Datalog rewriting. Indeed, it suffices to take the single-rule Datalog program

$$\Pi = \{\mathsf{Spicy}(x) \leftarrow \mathsf{hasIngredient}(x, y), \mathsf{Spicy}(y)\}$$

and use Spicy as the distinguished relation. In this particular case, the Datalog program is just a translation of the TBox, but this is not the case in general. ▲

Most of the work to date has focused on FO rewritings, since (domain-independent) FO queries can be translated into SQL statements and evaluated using highly optimized relational database management systems. However, Datalog rewritings, which can be passed to Datalog engines for evaluation, are also popular as they are applicable to a wider range of DLs.

Saturation. We have seen that standard database querying algorithms are incomplete for OMQA since they do not take into account the information provided by the TBox. Query rewriting addresses this problem by rewriting the query so as to incorporate the relevant information from the TBox. By contrast, saturation-based approaches to OMQA work by *rendering explicit (some of) the* *implicit information contained in the KB, making it available for query evalua-tion.* In simple cases, saturation involves completing the ABox by adding those assertions that are logically entailed from the KB, and then evaluating the query over the saturated ABox. In more complex cases, we might have to have to enrich the ABox in other ways (perhaps adding new ABox individuals to act as wit-nesses for the existential restrictions), or we may need to combine saturation with query rewriting. Indeed, unlike query rewriting, for which we could for-mulate precise definitions of what constitutes a rewriting, saturation is a more abstract concept that englobes a variety of different approaches whose common-ality is that they enrich the KB with some additional information, which can then be exploited for various reasoning tasks (in our case, query answering). Saturation-based reasoning techniques have been employed in a variety of areas, sometimes under different names: forward chaining, materialization, deductive closure, and consequence-based reasoning.

Example 10. We return to our running example about desserts. By 'applying' the inclusions in the TBox $\mathcal{T}_1$ to the ABox $\mathcal{A}_1$, we obtain a new saturated KB $\mathcal{K}'_1$ with the following additional assertions:

- Dessert(d_1), using Cake(d_1) and Cake $\sqsubseteq$ Dessert
- Dessert(d_2), using IceCream(d_2) and IceCream $\sqsubseteq$ Dessert
- hasCourse(m, d_4), using hasDessert(m, d_4) and hasDessert $\sqsubseteq$ hasCourse
- Menu(m), using hasCourse(m, d_4) and $\exists$hasCourse $\sqsubseteq$ Menu
- Dessert(d_4), using hasDessert(m, d_4) and $\exists$hasDessert$^-$ $\sqsubseteq$ Dessert

Once we have computed $\mathcal{K}'_1$, answering our query Dessert(x) is as simple as reading off the individuals that appear in a Dessert assertion: d_1, d_2, d_3, d_4. We observe that this is the same result as was obtained in Example 8 by means of query rewriting. Note however that the saturation process is performed inde-pendently of the query, so we infer not only those assertions needed to answer the specific query at hand, but also those needed to answer future queries. For example, using the same saturated KB $\mathcal{K}'_1$, we find that m is the unique certain answer to the query Menu(x). ▲

4   Instance Queries

In this section, we begin our exploration of ontology-mediated query answering by considering a very simple type of query that can be used to find all individ-uals that belong to a given concept or role. Up until the mid-2000s, work on querying DL knowledge bases focused almost exclusively on such queries, which are commonly known as instance queries.

Definition 6 (Instance Queries). *An* instance query (IQ) *takes one of the following two forms:*

- $A(x)$ *where* $A \in \mathsf{N_C}$ *(concept instance query)*
- $r(x, y)$ *where* $r \in \mathsf{N_R}$ *(role instance query)*

ALGORITHM ComputeSubsumees

INPUT: DL-Lite$_R$ TBox $\mathcal{T}$, concept $B \in N_C \cup \{\exists R \mid R \in N_R^{\pm}\}$

1. Initialize Subsumees $= \{B\}$ and Examined $= \emptyset$.
2. While Subsumees $\setminus$ Examined $\neq \emptyset$
   (a) Select $D \in$ Subsumees $\setminus$ Examined and add D to Examined.
   (b) For every concept inclusion $C \sqsubseteq D \in \mathcal{T}$
       − If $C \notin$ Subsumees, add C to Subsumees
   (c) For every role inclusion $R \sqsubseteq S \in \mathcal{T}$ such that $D = \exists S$.
       − If $\exists R \notin$ Subsumees, add $\exists R$ to Subsumees
   (d) For every role inclusion $R \sqsubseteq S \in \mathcal{T}$ such that $D = \exists \mathsf{inv}(S)$.
       − If $\exists \mathsf{inv}(R) \notin$ Subsumees, add $\exists \mathsf{inv}(R)$ to Subsumees.
3. Return Subsumees.

Fig. 1. Algorithm for computing subsumees of a given concept in DL-Lite$_R$.

Remark 9. The restriction to concept names in the preceding definition is without loss of generality. Indeed, suppose that we want to find all individuals that belong to C, where C is an arbitrary concept formulated in the DL we are considering. This can be accomplished by taking a fresh concept name A_C, adding the inclusion $C \sqsubseteq A_C$ to the TBox, and using the instance query $A_C(x)$.

In the remainder of this section, we will see how the techniques of query rewriting and saturation introduced in Sect. 3.5 can be applied to the problem of IQ answering (which is more commonly referred to as *instance checking*). We will consider three representative Horn DLs: DL-Lite$_R$, $\mathcal{EL}$, and $\mathcal{ELHI}_\perp$.

4.1 Instance Checking in DL-Lite$_R$ via Query Rewriting

We begin by considering the problem of instance checking over DL-Lite$_R$ knowledge bases. Both query rewriting and saturation-based approaches have been proposed in the literature [52]. We present a procedure based upon rewriting IQs into first-order queries since this is the more commonly used approach for DLs in the DL-Lite family. Moreover, it provides us with a simple setting in which to demonstrate this technique.

As mentioned in Sect. 3.5, to construct an FO-rewriting of an instance query q w.r.t. $\mathcal{T}, \Sigma$, it suffices to construct

− an FO-rewriting of q w.r.t. $\mathcal{T}, \Sigma$ relative to consistent ABoxes, and
− an FO-rewriting of unsatisfiability w.r.t. $\mathcal{T}, \Sigma$.

Indeed, if we have these two rewritings, then they can be straightforwardly combined to obtain an FO-rewriting of q that works for all Σ-ABoxes.

As a first step, we present in Fig. 1 a procedure ComputeSubsumees that takes as input a DL-Lite concept B (that is, either a concept name or an existential concept $\exists R$ with $R \in N_R^{\pm}$) and a DL-Lite$_R$ TBox $\mathcal{T}$ and outputs the set of all DL-Lite concepts C such that $\mathcal{T} \models C \sqsubseteq B$. Such concepts are called the *subsumees*

Algorithm ComputeSubroles
Input: DL-Lite$_R$ TBox $\mathcal{T}$, role $R \in \mathsf{N}_R^{\pm}$

1. Initialize Subroles = $\{R\}$ and Examined = $\emptyset$.
2. While Subroles $\setminus$ Examined $\neq \emptyset$
   (a) Select $S \in$ Subroles $\setminus$ Examined and add S to Examined.
   (b) For every role inclusion $U \sqsubseteq S$ or $\mathsf{inv}(U) \sqsubseteq \mathsf{inv}(S)$ in $\mathcal{T}$
       − If $U \not\subseteq$ Subsumees, add U to Subsumees
3. Return Subroles.

Fig. 2. Algorithm for computing subroles of a given role in DL-Lite$_R$.

of B w.r.t. $\mathcal{T}$, and intuitively they capture all of the different reasons for an individual to be counted as a member of B. The algorithm ComputeSubsumees uses a backward chaining mechanism to iteratively compute the subsumees of B. The set Subsumees is used to store the subsumees that have been identified so far, and Examined keeps track of which concepts in Subsumees have already been examined. When examining a concept D, we add to Subsumees all those concepts that are direct subsumees of D, i.e., those for which we can infer the subsumption relationship using a single inclusion from $\mathcal{T}$.

We illustrate the functioning of ComputeSubsumees on an example.

Example 11. Consider the DL-Lite$_R$ TBox $\mathcal{T}_2$ consisting of the following axioms:

$$\mathsf{ItalianDish} \sqsubseteq \mathsf{Dish} \quad \mathsf{VegDish} \sqsubseteq \mathsf{Dish} \quad \mathsf{Dish} \sqsubseteq \exists\mathsf{hasIngredient}$$

$$\exists\mathsf{hasCourse}^- \sqsubseteq \mathsf{Dish} \quad \mathsf{hasMain} \sqsubseteq \mathsf{hasCourse} \quad \mathsf{hasDessert} \sqsubseteq \mathsf{hasCourse}$$

We run ComputeSubsumees on the input $(\mathcal{T}_2, \mathsf{Dish})$ in order to compute all of the concepts that imply Dish. In Step 1, we initialize Subsumees to $\{\mathsf{Dish}\}$. In the first iteration of the while loop, we have no choice but to select Dish. In Step 2(b), we will add ItalianDish, VegDish, and $\exists\mathsf{hasCourse}^-$ to Subsumees due to the inclusions ItalianDish$\sqsubseteq$Dish, VegDish$\sqsubseteq$Dish, and $\exists\mathsf{hasCourse}^- \sqsubseteq$Dish respectively. Note that we cannot use the inclusion Dish$\sqsubseteq\exists\mathsf{hasIngredient}$ to add $\exists\mathsf{hasIngredient}$, since Dish appears on the left-hand side of the inclusion. Steps 2(c) and 2(d) are inapplicable since Dish is not an existential restriction. We will therefore return to the start of the while loop and select a new unexamined concept from Subsumees. Nothing new will be added to Subsumees when examining ItalianDish and VegDish, since these concepts do not appear on the right-hand side of any inclusions in $\mathcal{T}_2$. However, when we examine $\exists\mathsf{hasCourse}^-$, we will add both hasMain$^-$ and hasDessert$^-$, due to the role inclusions hasMain $\sqsubseteq$ hasCourse and hasDessert$\sqsubseteq$hasCourse (this occurs in Step 2(c)). It can be verified that no further concepts will be added, and so the output of ComputeSubsumees will be

$$\{\mathsf{Dish}, \mathsf{ItalianDish}, \mathsf{VegDish}, \exists\mathsf{hasCourse}^-, \exists\mathsf{hasMain}^-, \exists\mathsf{hasDessert}^-\}.$$

We remark that these concepts capture all of the different ways of inferring that an individual is a member of Dish using the knowledge expressed in $\mathcal{T}_2$.   ▲

Observe that there are at most $3|\mathcal{T}|$ concepts that can be added to Subsumees, since there are at most $|\mathcal{T}|$ concept names appearing in $\mathcal{T}$ and at most $2|\mathcal{T}|$ concepts of the forms $\exists r^{(-)}$ with r a role name occurring in $\mathcal{T}$. As concepts are never removed from Subsumees, and each concept in Subsumees is examined at most once, it follows that ComputeSubsumees runs in polynomial time in $|\mathcal{T}|$. One can further show that on input $(\mathcal{A}, \mathcal{T})$ the algorithm outputs exactly the set of subsumees of A w.r.t. $\mathcal{T}$.

In Fig. 2, we introduce an analogous procedure ComputeSubroles for roles. One can show that the procedure runs in polynomial time in $|\mathcal{T}|$ and a role S belongs to ComputeSubroles$(R, \mathcal{T})$ just in the case that $\mathcal{T} \models S \sqsubseteq R$.

Next, we introduce a function ρ_x that translates concepts into FO queries. The variable x in the subscript of ρ_x indicates that the query should use x as the answer variable. The definition of ρ_x is what one would expect:

- $\rho_x(A) = A(x)$ for $A \in N_C$
- $\rho_x(\exists r) = \exists y. r(x, y)$ for $r \in N_R$
- $\rho_x(\exists r^-) = \exists y. r(y, x)$ for $r \in N_R$

We can similarly introduce a function ρ_{xy} that maps roles to FO queries, using x, y as the first and second distinguished variables:

- $\rho_{xy}(r) = r(x, y)$ for $r \in N_R$
- $\rho_{xy}(r^-) = r(y, x)$ for $r \in N_R$

We now have the necessary machinery to construct the desired FO-rewritings. To obtain a rewriting of $A(x)$ w.r.t. $\mathcal{T}$ relative to consistent ABoxes, we simply take the disjunction of the queries obtained by applying ρ_x to the concepts in ComputeSubsumees$(A, \mathcal{T})$:

$$\text{RewriteIQ}(A, \mathcal{T}) = \bigvee_{C \in \text{ComputeSubsumees}(A, \mathcal{T})} \rho_x(C)$$

The construction is similar if we have a role instance query $r(x, y)$:

$$\text{RewriteIQ}(r, \mathcal{T}) = \bigvee_{S \in \text{ComputeSubsumees}(r, \mathcal{T})} \rho_{x,y}(S)$$

Observe that an individual a belongs to the answer of RewriteIQ$(A, \mathcal{T})$ on $\mathcal{I}_{\mathcal{A}}$ just in the case that there is an assertion in $\mathcal{A}$ that asserts the membership of a in one of the subsumees of A w.r.t. $\mathcal{T}$. Under the assumption that the KB $(\mathcal{T}, \mathcal{A})$ is satisfiable, we can show that the latter statement holds iff a is a certain answer to $A(x)$ over $(\mathcal{T}, \mathcal{A})$. Similar considerations apply to role instance queries.

Theorem 3. *For every finite signature Σ, concept name A (resp. role name r) and DL-Lite$_R$ TBox $\mathcal{T}$, the query RewriteIQ$(A, \mathcal{T})$ (resp. RewriteIQ$(r, \mathcal{T})$) is an FO-rewriting of $A(x)$ (resp. $r(x, y)$) w.r.t. $\mathcal{T}, \Sigma$ relative to consistent ABoxes.*

Remark 10. We can sometimes use the ABox signature Σ to simplify rewritings. Indeed, it is easy to see that the preceding theorem continues to hold if we remove from RewriteIQ$(A, \mathcal{T})$ and RewriteIQ$(r, \mathcal{T})$ all disjuncts that contain a concept or role name that does not belong to Σ.

We continue our previous example to illustrate the rewriting construction.

Example 12. Consider the IQ $q_2 = \mathsf{Dish}(x)$ and the TBox $\mathcal{T}_2$ from Example 11. We have seen that ComputeSubsumees$(\mathsf{Dish}, \mathcal{T}_2)$ contains the following concepts:

$$\mathsf{Dish}, \mathsf{ItalianDish}, \mathsf{VegDish}, \exists\mathsf{hasCourse}^-, \exists\mathsf{hasMain}^-, \exists\mathsf{hasDessert}^-$$

We will therefore obtain the following rewriting of q_2 w.r.t. $\mathcal{T}_2$ relative to consistent ABoxes:

$$\mathsf{RewriteIQ}(\mathsf{Dish}, \mathcal{T}_2) = \mathsf{Dish}(x) \vee \mathsf{ItalianDish}(x) \vee \mathsf{VegDish}(x) \vee \exists y.\mathsf{hasCourse}(y, x)$$
$$\vee \exists y.\mathsf{hasMain}(y, x) \vee \exists y.\mathsf{hasDessert}(y, x)$$

In fact, because $\mathcal{T}_2$ does not contain any inclusions expressing disjointness, we know that every ABox is consistent with $\mathcal{T}_2$, and so the preceding rewriting will give the correct result for all ABoxes. If we evaluate the query RewriteIQ$(\mathsf{Dish}, \mathcal{T}_2)$ over the ABox consisting of the assertions

$$\mathsf{hasMain}(m, d_1) \quad \mathsf{hasDessert}(m, d_2) \quad \mathsf{VegDish}(d_3)$$

then we will obtain the following certain answers:

- d_1, because of the disjunct $\exists y.\mathsf{hasMain}(y, x)$
- d_2, because of the disjunct $\exists y.\mathsf{hasDessert}(y, x)$
- d_3, because of the disjunct $\mathsf{VegDish}(x)$

▲

For unsatisfiability, we proceed in two steps, first showing how to define an FO query that detects violation of a single disjointness constraint, and then showing how these rewritings can be combined to obtain a rewriting of unsatisfiability. For negative concept inclusion $A \sqsubseteq \neg B$, we can use the following Boolean query that checks for the existence of an individual belonging to $A \sqcap B$ by considering all possible ways of choosing a subsumee of A and a subsumee of B:

$$\mathsf{RewriteDisjoint}(A, B, \mathcal{T}) = \bigvee_{\substack{C \in \mathsf{ComputeSubsumees}(A, \mathcal{T}) \\ D \in \mathsf{ComputeSubsumees}(B, \mathcal{T})}} \exists x.(\rho_x(C) \wedge \rho_x(D))$$

For a negative role inclusion $R \sqsubseteq \neg S$, we can define in a similar fashion a Boolean query that checks if there exists a pair of individuals that belongs to both of the roles R and S:

$$\mathsf{RewriteDisjoint}(R, S, \mathcal{T}) = \bigvee_{\substack{U \in \mathsf{ComputeSubroles}(R, \mathcal{T}) \\ V \in \mathsf{ComputeSubroles}(S, \mathcal{T})}} \exists x, y.(\rho_{x,y}(U) \wedge \rho_{x,y}(V))$$

To obtain a rewriting of unsatisfiability w.r.t. $\mathcal{T}$, it then suffices to take the disjunction of the FO queries associated with the negative inclusions in $\mathcal{T}$:

$$\mathsf{RewriteUnsat}(\mathcal{T}) = \bigvee_{G \sqsubseteq \neg H \in \mathcal{T}} \mathsf{RewriteDisjoint}(G, H, \mathcal{T})$$

Indeed, it can be shown that a DL-Lite$_R$ KB $(\mathcal{T}, \mathcal{A})$ is unsatisfiable if and only if one of the negative inclusions in $\mathcal{T}$ is violated.

Theorem 4. *For every finite signature Σ and DL-Lite$_R$ TBox $\mathcal{T}$, the query* $\mathsf{RewriteUnsat}(\mathcal{T})$ *is an FO-rewriting of unsatisfiability w.r.t. $\mathcal{T}, \Sigma$.*

The following example illustrates the construction of a rewriting of unsatisfiability and how such a rewriting can be combined with a rewriting of an IQ relative to consistent ABoxes to obtain a rewriting that works for all ABoxes.

Example 13. We consider a variant $\mathcal{T}_3$ of the preceding TBox that contains two disjointness constraints:

$$\exists \mathsf{hasCourse}^- \sqsubseteq \mathsf{Dish} \quad \mathsf{hasMain} \sqsubseteq \mathsf{hasCourse} \quad \mathsf{hasDessert} \sqsubseteq \mathsf{hasCourse}$$
$$\mathsf{hasMain} \sqsubseteq \neg\mathsf{hasDessert} \quad \mathsf{Dish} \sqsubseteq \neg\exists\mathsf{hasCourse}$$

For the first negative inclusion $\mathsf{hasMain} \sqsubseteq \neg\mathsf{hasDessert}$, we obtain the following FO query:

$$\mathsf{RewriteDisjoint}(\mathsf{hasMain}, \mathsf{hasDessert}, \mathcal{T}_3) = \exists x, y\, \mathsf{hasMain}(x, y) \wedge \mathsf{hasDessert}(x, y)$$

since $\mathsf{hasMain}$ and $\mathsf{hasDessert}$ do not have any subroles (aside from themselves). For the second negative inclusion $\mathsf{Dish} \sqsubseteq \neg\exists\mathsf{hasCourse}$, each of the concepts Dish and $\exists\mathsf{hasCourse}$ has multiple subsumees:

$$\mathsf{ComputeSubsumees}(\mathsf{Dish}, \mathcal{T}_3) = \{\mathsf{Dish}, \exists\mathsf{hasCourse}^-, \exists\mathsf{hasMain}^-, \exists\mathsf{hasDessert}^-\}$$
$$\mathsf{ComputeSubsumees}(\exists\mathsf{hasCourse}, \mathcal{T}_3) = \{\exists\mathsf{hasCourse}, \exists\mathsf{hasMain}, \exists\mathsf{hasDessert}\}$$

The FO query $\mathsf{RewriteDisjoint}(\mathsf{Dish}, \exists\mathsf{hasCourse}, \mathcal{T}_3)$ expressing the violation of $\mathsf{Dish} \sqsubseteq \neg\exists\mathsf{hasCourse}$ will contain 12 disjuncts, corresponding to the 4 choices of a subsumee of Dish and the 3 choices for $\exists\mathsf{hasCourse}$:

$$\bigvee_{\substack{\{\mathsf{hasCourse}, \\ r \in\ \mathsf{hasMain}, \\ \mathsf{hasDessert}\}}} \exists x.(\mathsf{Dish}(x) \vee \exists y.r(x, y)) \vee \bigvee_{\substack{\{\mathsf{hasCourse}, \\ r,s \in\ \mathsf{hasMain}, \\ \mathsf{hasDessert}\}}} \exists x.(\exists y.r(y, x) \wedge \exists y.s(x, y))$$

Combining the preceding FO queries yields the following rewriting of unsatisfiability w.r.t. $\mathcal{T}_3$:

$$\mathsf{RewriteUnsat}(\mathcal{T}) = \mathsf{RewriteDisjoint}(\mathsf{hasMain}, \mathsf{hasDessert}, \mathcal{T})$$
$$\vee\ \mathsf{RewriteDisjoint}(\mathsf{Dish}, \exists\mathsf{hasCourse}, \mathcal{T})$$

In order to construct an FO-rewriting of $\mathsf{Dish}(x)$ w.r.t. $\mathcal{T}_3$, we will need to compute $\mathsf{RewriteIQ}(\mathsf{Dish}, \mathcal{T}_3)$, which can be done as in Example 12. We will also need to construct a query that returns all individuals that appear in some ABox assertion. The definition of this query will depend on the ABox signature Σ. If we take $\Sigma = \mathsf{sig}(\mathcal{T}_3)$, then we could use the following query:

$$q_{\mathsf{ind}}^{\Sigma}(x) = \mathsf{Dish}(x) \vee \exists y.\mathsf{hasCourse}(x, y) \vee \exists y.\mathsf{hasMain}(x, y) \vee \exists y.\mathsf{hasDessert}(x, y)$$
$$\vee \exists y.\mathsf{hasCourse}(y, x) \vee \exists y.\mathsf{hasMain}(y, x) \vee \exists y.\mathsf{hasDessert}(y, x)$$

By combining these queries, we obtain a rewriting of $q_2 = \mathsf{Dish}(x)$ w.r.t. $\mathcal{T}_3, \mathsf{sig}(\mathcal{T}_3)$:

$$\mathsf{RewriteIQ}(\mathsf{Dish}, \mathcal{T}_3) \vee (\mathsf{RewriteUnsat}(\mathcal{T}_3) \wedge q_{\mathsf{ind}}^{\Sigma})$$

Now let us consider what happens when we evaluate the preceding query over a $\mathsf{sig}(\mathcal{T}_3)$-ABox $\mathcal{A}$. When $(\mathcal{T}_3, \mathcal{A})$ is satisfiable, $\mathsf{RewriteUnsat}(\mathcal{T}_3)$ evaluates to false over $\mathcal{I}_\mathcal{A}$, and so we must satisfy the first disjunct $\mathsf{RewriteIQ}(\mathsf{Dish}, \mathcal{T}_3)$. If $(\mathcal{T}_3, \mathcal{A})$ is unsatisfiable, then $\mathsf{RewriteUnsat}(\mathcal{T}_3)$ evaluates to true and q_{ind} will retrieve all of the individuals that appear in $\mathcal{A}$.   ▲

We have shown that for every IQ q, DL-Lite$_R$ TBox $\mathcal{T}$, and ABox signature Σ, it is possible to construct an FO rewriting of q w.r.t. $\mathcal{T}, \Sigma$, and thus we can reduce instance checking to FO query evaluation over databases. Importantly, this reduction is independent of the ABox, which means that the instance checking problem has the same low data complexity as the evaluation of FO queries over databases.

Theorem 5 (Follows from Results in [52], see also [10]). *In DL-Lite$_R$, satisfiability and instance checking are in* AC_0 *for data complexity.*

Regarding combined complexity, it is possible to obtain a P upper bound by observing that the rewriting procedure runs in polynomial time in $|\mathcal{T}|$ and produces an FO query that, because of its restricted syntax, can be answered in polynomial time in $|\mathcal{A}|$ (recall that when we analyze the complexity of query answering, we consider the decision problem of testing whether a given tuple is a (certain) answer). This upper bound can be improved to NLogSpace by employing a non-deterministic logarithmic space procedure that guesses a single disjunct in the rewriting of the IQ and verifies that the input tuple satisfies this disjunct. An alternative proof of NLogSpace membership proceeds by reducing instance checking in DL-Lite$_R$ to the satisfiablity problem of first-order Krom formulas, which is known to be complete for NLogSpace [10].

Theorem 6 ([10]). *In DL-Lite$_R$, satisfiability and instance checking are both* NLogSpace-*complete for combined complexity.*

We remark that the preceding complexity results hold not only for DL-Lite$_R$ but also for several other DL-Lite dialects (like DL-Lite$_F$ and DL-Lite$_A$) and can be shown using similar techniques (see [10,52] for more details).

4.2 Saturation-Based Procedure for Instance Checking in $\mathcal{EL}$

We will next consider the problem of instance checking in $\mathcal{EL}$, which is the basic member of the $\mathcal{EL}$ family of Horn DLs. Unlike DL-Lite$_R$, the first-order query rewriting approach cannot be used in general to handle $\mathcal{EL}$ KBs, since there exist pairs of IQs and TBoxes for which no FO rewriting exists (a concrete example was provided in Example 9). Instead, we will show how instance checking can be performed using a simple saturation-based approach. As we shall in the next subsection, this approach can be extended to handle more expressive Horn DLs.

To simplify the presentation of the saturation procedure, we will assume that the considered $\mathcal{EL}$ KBs have been normalized, that is, they only contain TBox inclusions of the following forms:

$$A_1 \sqcap \ldots \sqcap A_n \sqsubseteq B \quad A \sqsubseteq \exists r.B \quad \exists r.A \sqsubseteq B$$

where $A_{(i)}, B \in \mathsf{N_C} \cup \{\top\}$, $r \in \mathsf{N_R}$, and $n \geq 1$. As mentioned in Sect. 2, this assumption is without loss of generality since every $\mathcal{EL}$ KB $\mathcal{K}$ can be transformed into a normalized KB $\mathcal{K}'$ that has the same logical consequences as $\mathcal{K}$ over the signature of $\mathcal{K}$. This transformation can be performed in polynomial time and will not impact the complexity results obtained in this subsection.

In Table 3, we present a set of five *saturation (or inference) rules* that can be used to infer new inclusions and assertions from a given $\mathcal{EL}$ knowledge base. These rules essentially correspond to a subset of the rules proposed in [19] for reasoning in an extension of $\mathcal{EL}$ called $\mathcal{EL}^{++}$, but use a syntax that is closer to that found in recent works on consequence-based reasoning in DLs. Each of the rules in Table 3 acts as a template that can be instantiated using different concept and role names to obtain a *rule instantiation* of the form

$$\frac{\alpha_1, \ldots, \alpha_n}{\beta}$$

where $\alpha_1, \ldots, \alpha_n, \beta$ are TBox inclusions or ABox assertions. We call $\alpha_1 \ldots \alpha_n$ the *premises* of the rule instantiation and β its *conclusion*. A rule instantiation ρ is said to be *applicable* to a KB $\mathcal{K}$ if $\mathcal{K}$ contains all of the premises of ρ but does not contain ρ's conclusion. If ρ is applicable to $\mathcal{K}$, then applying it means adding the conclusion of ρ to $\mathcal{K}$.

Example 14. Consider the knowledge base $\mathcal{K}_2$ that comprises the inclusions:

PenneArrabiata $\sqsubseteq$ Dish   PenneArrabiata $\sqsubseteq$ Spicy   Spicy $\sqcap$ Dish $\sqsubseteq$ SpicyDish

The following instantiation of rule **T1** is applicable to $\mathcal{K}_2$:

$$\frac{\text{PenneArrabiata} \sqsubseteq \text{Spicy} \quad \text{PenneArrabiata} \sqsubseteq \text{Dish} \quad \text{Spicy} \sqcap \text{Dish} \sqsubseteq \text{SpicyDish}}{\text{PenneArrabiata} \sqsubseteq \text{SpicyDish}}$$

To apply this rule instantiation, we add PenneArrabiata $\sqsubseteq$ SpicyDish to $\mathcal{K}_2$.   ▲

Table 3. Saturation rules for $\mathcal{EL}$. Here $r \in \mathsf{N_R}$ and $A, B, D, E \in \mathsf{N_C} \cup \{\top\}$.

$$\frac{A \sqsubseteq B_i \ (1 \le i \le n) \quad B_1 \sqcap \ldots \sqcap B_n \sqsubseteq D}{A \sqsubseteq D} \ \text{T1} \qquad \frac{A \sqsubseteq B \quad B \sqsubseteq \exists r.D}{A \sqsubseteq \exists r.D} \ \text{T2}$$

$$\frac{A \sqsubseteq \exists r.B \quad B \sqsubseteq D \quad \exists r.D \sqsubseteq E}{A \sqsubseteq E} \ \text{T3}$$

$$\frac{A_1 \sqcap \ldots \sqcap A_n \sqsubseteq B \quad A_i(a) \ (1 \le i \le n)}{B(a)} \ \text{A1} \qquad \frac{\exists r.B \sqsubseteq A \quad r(a,b) \quad B(b)}{A(a)} \ \text{A2}$$

Note that in what follows, we will slightly abuse terminology and speak simply of rules and rule applications, rather than (applications of) rule instantiations.

By inspecting the rules in Table 3, we immediately observe that because of the syntactic restrictions on the conclusions of the saturation rules, there are only finitely many axioms and assertions that can be produced over a given finite signature. It follows that an exhaustive application of the saturation rules to a KB is guaranteed to terminate and produce a finite (saturated) KB. Moreover, the result of the saturation process does not depend on the order in which the rules are applied, so we make speak of *the* saturation of a KB.

The following example illustrates the computation of the saturation of a KB.

Example 15. Consider the $\mathcal{EL}$ KB $\mathcal{K}_3$ whose TBox contains the inclusions

$$\text{PenneArrabiata} \sqsubseteq \exists \text{hasIngredient.ArrabiataSauce} \tag{13}$$
$$\text{PenneArrabiata} \sqsubseteq \text{PastaDish} \tag{14}$$
$$\text{PastaDish} \sqsubseteq \text{Dish} \tag{15}$$
$$\text{PastaDish} \sqsubseteq \exists \text{hasIngredient.Pasta} \tag{16}$$
$$\text{ArrabiataSauce} \sqsubseteq \exists \text{hasIngredient.Peperoncino} \tag{17}$$
$$\text{Peperoncino} \sqsubseteq \text{Spicy} \tag{18}$$
$$\exists \text{hasIngredient.Spicy} \sqsubseteq \text{Spicy} \tag{19}$$
$$\text{Spicy} \sqcap \text{Dish} \sqsubseteq \text{SpicyDish} \tag{20}$$

and whose ABox consists of the single assertion

$$\text{PenneArrabiata}(p). \tag{21}$$

If we apply the saturation rules from Table 3, then we obtain the new axioms and assertions listed below. Note that we indicate on the right the rule that was applied, followed by the axioms and/or assertions used as premises.

$$\text{ArrabiataSauce} \sqsubseteq \text{Spicy} \qquad \textbf{T3} : (17), (18), (19) \tag{22}$$
$$\text{PenneArrabiata} \sqsubseteq \text{Spicy} \qquad \textbf{T3} : (13), (22), (19) \tag{23}$$

PenneArrabiata $\sqsubseteq$ Dish	**T1** : $(14), (15)$	(24)
PenneArrabiata $\sqsubseteq \exists$hasIngredient.Pasta	**T2** : $(14), (16)$	(25)
PenneArrabiata $\sqsubseteq$ SpicyDish	**T1** : $(23), (24), (20)$	(26)
Spicy(p)	**A1** : $(23), (21)$	(27)
Dish(p)	**A1** : $(24), (21)$	(28)
SpicyDish(p)	**A1** : $(28), (27)$	(29)

It can be verified that nothing further can be inferred using the rules.   ▲

In addition to ensuring finite termination, the saturation rules from Table 3 possess two other important properties. First, they are *sound*, that is, they only allow us to derive axioms and assertions that are logical consequences. Secondly, they are *complete for instance checking*, by which we mean that allow us to derive all entailed ABox assertions. These properties can be established by adapting proofs of similar results in [19].

Theorem 7. *Let $\mathcal{K}$ be an $\mathcal{EL}$ knowledge base, and let $\mathcal{K}'$ be obtained by exhaustively applying the rules in Table 3 to $\mathcal{K} \cup \{A \sqsubseteq A, A \sqsubseteq \top \mid A \in \mathsf{N_C} \cap \mathsf{sig}(\mathcal{K})\} \cup \{\top \sqsubseteq \top\} \cup \{\top(a) \mid a \in \mathsf{Ind}(\mathcal{A})\}$ up to saturation. Then for every ABox assertion α, we have $\mathcal{K} \models \alpha$ iff $\alpha \in \mathcal{K}'$.*

Remark 11. To ensure completeness, before running the saturation rules, we first add to the KB some trivially entailed inclusions (of the forms $A \sqsubseteq A$, $A \sqsubseteq \top$) and assertions[9] (of the form $\top(a)$). Alternatively, we could introduce saturation rules with empty premises that generate these inclusions and assertions. In practice, one could simply allow these inclusions and assertions to be used as premises during the saturation process, without adding them.

Remark 12. The rules in Table 3 do not allow us to generate *all* entailed concept inclusions, and indeed, this is a good thing since there can be infinitely many (non-equivalent) concept inclusions that are entailed from a given KB. However, we can show that these rules are sufficient to obtain all entailed concept inclusions between concept names (we say that the rule calculus is *complete for classification*).

By Theorem 7, we can perform instance checking by exhaustively applying the saturation rules to the KB, and then checking if the resulting saturated KB contains the desired assertion.

Example 16. Reconsider the KB $\mathcal{K}_3$ and its saturation from Example 15. The individual p is a certain answer to the IQ SpicyDish(x) w.r.t. $\mathcal{K}_3$ since the assertion SpicyDish(p) is present in the saturation of $\mathcal{K}_3$. However, p is not a certain answer to Peperoncino(x) w.r.t. $\mathcal{K}_3$, since Peperoncino(p) was not derived.   ▲

---

[9] In this section, it will prove convenient to allow ABox assertions using the atomic concepts $\top$ and $\bot$, in addition to concept names. Refer to Sect. 2 for discussion.

A closer inspection reveals that the saturation procedure runs in polynomial time in $|\mathcal{K}|$. Indeed, at each iteration, we must produce at least one new concept inclusion or ABox assertion of one of the following forms:

$$A \sqsubseteq B \qquad A \sqsubseteq \exists r.B \qquad A(a) \qquad r(a,b)$$

which is built using only the individuals, concept names and role names from $\mathcal{K}$, and there are only polynomially many such axioms and assertions. We therefore obtain a P upper bound on the combined complexity of instance checking in $\mathcal{EL}$. This result was first established in [19], and a matching P lower bound for data complexity was provided in [59].

Theorem 8 ([19,59]). *Instance checking in $\mathcal{EL}$ is P-complete for both the data and combined complexity measures.*

4.3   Instance Checking in $\mathcal{ELHI}_\perp$

In this final subsection on instance checking, we move to a richer Horn DL, $\mathcal{ELHI}_\perp$, which integrates constructors from DL-Lite$_R$ and $\mathcal{EL}$. We will present a saturation procedure for $\mathcal{ELHI}_\perp$ that is similar in spirit to our $\mathcal{EL}$ saturation procedure but contains additional rules to handle the new constructors. This saturation procedure will provide a method of performing satisfiability and instance checking over $\mathcal{ELHI}_\perp$ KBs. Moreover, we shall see that inclusions obtained by saturating the TBox can be used to built Datalog rewritings of satisfiability and instance queries. The $\mathcal{ELHI}_\perp$ saturation rules will resurface again in Sect. 5, where they will be used to construct universal models.

As in the preceding subsection, we will assume that the input $\mathcal{ELHI}_\perp$ KB is in normal form, i.e., it contains only TBox inclusions of the forms

$$A_1 \sqcap \ldots \sqcap A_n \sqsubseteq D \quad A \sqsubseteq \exists R.B \quad \exists R.A \sqsubseteq B \quad R \sqsubseteq S$$

where $A_{(i)}, B \in \mathsf{N_C} \cup \{\top\}$, $D \in \mathsf{N_C} \cup \{\top, \perp\}$, $R, S \in \mathsf{N_R^\pm}$, and $n \geq 1$.

The saturation rules for $\mathcal{ELHI}_\perp$ are displayed in Table 4. They have been adapted from the saturation calculus Horn-$\mathcal{SHIQ}$ from [81] (itself adapted from an earlier calculus from [117]). Rules **T4** and rule **T5** handle role inclusions and the $\perp$ concept respectively. Rules **T7** is a more elaborate version of the $\mathcal{EL}$ rule **T3**, adapted to handle the presence of role inclusions and inverse roles. Note that due to the presence of inverse roles, it is necessary to allow conjunctions in existential concepts. Rule **T6** provides a means of introducing new concepts into such conjunctions. To understand rule **T8**, it is helpful to recall that $\exists \mathsf{inv}(S).A \sqsubseteq B$ can be equivalently expressed as $A \sqsubseteq \forall S.B$. The rule adds A as a condition on the right-hand side, which allows B to be added to the existential on the left-hand side of the inclusion. Finally, we introduce three additional ABox saturation rules. Rule **A3** is like **A2** except that is concerns inverse roles, and rules **A4-A5** are used to infer new role assertions using derived role inclusions.

The notions of rule instantiation, applicable rule, and rule application are essentially the same as for $\mathcal{EL}$. Note however that when working with axioms

Table 4. Saturation rules for $\mathcal{ELHI}_\perp$. Here $r \in \mathsf{N_R}$, $R, S \in \mathsf{N_R^\pm}$, $A, B \in \mathsf{N_C} \cup \{\top, \perp\}$, and M and $N^{(\prime)}$ are conjunctions of concepts from $\mathsf{N_C} \cup \{\top, \perp\}$.

$$\frac{\{A \sqsubseteq B_i\}_{i=1}^n \quad B_1 \sqcap \ldots \sqcap B_n \sqsubseteq D}{A \sqsubseteq D} \text{ T1} \qquad \frac{R \sqsubseteq S \quad S \sqsubseteq T}{R \sqsubseteq T} \text{ T4} \qquad \frac{M \sqsubseteq \exists R.(N \sqcap \perp)}{M \sqsubseteq \perp} \text{ T5}$$

$$\frac{M \sqsubseteq \exists R.(N \sqcap N') \quad N \sqsubseteq A}{M \sqsubseteq \exists R.(N \sqcap N' \sqcap A)} \text{ T6} \qquad \frac{M \sqsubseteq \exists R.(N \sqcap A) \quad \exists S.A \sqsubseteq B \quad R \sqsubseteq S}{M \sqsubseteq B} \text{ T7}$$

$$\frac{M \sqsubseteq \exists R.N \quad \exists \mathsf{inv}(S).A \sqsubseteq B \quad R \sqsubseteq S}{M \sqcap A \sqsubseteq \exists R.(N \sqcap B)} \text{ T8}$$

$$\frac{A_1 \sqcap \ldots \sqcap A_n \sqsubseteq B \quad A_i(a) \ (1 \leq i \leq n)}{B(a)} \text{ A1} \qquad \frac{\exists r.B \sqsubseteq A \quad r(a,b) \quad B(b)}{A(a)} \text{ A2}$$

$$\frac{\exists r^-.B \sqsubseteq A \quad r(b,a) \quad B(b)}{A(a)} \text{ A3} \qquad \frac{r \sqsubseteq s \quad r(a,b)}{s(a,b)} \text{ A4} \qquad \frac{r \sqsubseteq s^- \quad r(a,b)}{s(b,a)} \text{ A5}$$

containing conjunctions, we will *treat conjunctions as sets*. That is, we will assume that there are no repeated conjuncts, and we will not pay attention to the order of conjuncts. Thus, if a rule instantiation contains a premise $A \sqsubseteq \exists R.(B \sqcap C \sqcap D)$, and the KB contains the equivalent (but syntactically distinct) inclusion $A \sqsubseteq \exists R.(D \sqcap B \sqcap C)$, then we will consider that the premise is present in the KB when deciding whether the rule instantiation is applicable. Likewise, if a rule instantiation has $D \sqsubseteq \exists R.(A \sqcap B)$ as a conclusion, and the KB already contains $D \sqsubseteq \exists R.(B \sqcap A)$, then the rule instantiation will not be considered applicable.

We are now ready to describe the saturation procedure. Given an $\mathcal{ELHI}_\perp$ knowledge base $\mathcal{K} = (\mathcal{T}, \mathcal{A})$, we first enrich the KB with inclusions and assertions that are trivially entailed:

$$\mathcal{T}' = \mathcal{T} \cup \{A \sqsubseteq A, A \sqsubseteq \top \mid A \in (\mathsf{N_C} \cap \mathsf{sig}(\mathcal{K})) \cup \{\top\}\}$$
$$\cup \{\mathsf{inv}(R) \sqsubseteq \mathsf{inv}(S) \mid S \sqsubseteq R \in \mathcal{T}\}$$
$$\mathcal{A}' = \mathcal{A} \cup \{\top(a) \mid a \in \mathsf{Ind}(\mathcal{A})\}$$

We then exhaustively apply the rules in Table 4 to $(\mathcal{T}', \mathcal{A}')$ until nothing new can be derived (finite termination is guaranteed due to the restricted syntax of the inclusions in rule conclusions). We will denote the resulting KB by $\mathsf{saturate}(\mathcal{K})$. If we instead apply the rules only to $\mathcal{T}'$, then we will use $\mathsf{saturate}(()\mathcal{T})$ to denote the resulting TBox.

The next theorem resumes the key properties of $\mathsf{saturate}(\mathcal{K})$. It can be proven by adapting the proofs of similar results for Horn-$\mathcal{SHIQ}$ [81].

Theorem 9. *For every $\mathcal{ELHI}_\perp$ knowledge base $\mathcal{K}$, we have:*

1. $\mathcal{K} \models \alpha$ *for every* $\alpha \in \mathsf{saturate}(\mathcal{K})$.
2. *If $\mathcal{K}$ is unsatisfiable, then* $\perp(a) \in \mathsf{saturate}(\mathcal{K})$ *for some* $a \in \mathsf{Ind}(\mathcal{K})$.
3. *If $\mathcal{K}$ is satisfiable and $\mathcal{K} \models \alpha$ with α an ABox assertion, then* $\alpha \in \mathsf{saturate}(\mathcal{K})$.

By the preceding theorem, to determine whether a given KB is satisfiable, it suffices to compute $\mathsf{saturate}(\mathcal{K})$ and check whether it contains an assertion of the form $\perp(a)$. Instance checking is also trivial once $\mathsf{saturate}(\mathcal{K})$ has been computed: to test whether $\mathcal{K} \models \alpha$, with $\mathcal{K}$ a satisfiable KB and α an ABox assertion, we merely need to check whether α appears in $\mathsf{saturate}(\mathcal{K})$.

Example 17. Let $\mathcal{K}_4$ be the $\mathcal{ELHI}_\perp$ KB consisting of the TBox $\mathcal{T}_4$:

$$\exists\mathsf{contains}^-.\mathsf{VegFriendly} \sqsubseteq \mathsf{VegFriendly} \tag{30}$$

$$\mathsf{hasIngredient} \sqsubseteq \mathsf{contains} \tag{31}$$

$$\mathsf{Meat} \sqcap \mathsf{VegFriendly} \sqsubseteq \perp \tag{32}$$

$$\mathsf{BologneseSauce} \sqsubseteq \exists\mathsf{hasIngredient}.\mathsf{Meat} \tag{33}$$

and the ABox whose assertions are:

$$\mathsf{VegFriendly}(d) \tag{34}$$

$$\mathsf{hasIngredient}(d, b) \tag{35}$$

$$\mathsf{BologneseSauce}(b) \tag{36}$$

We observe that $\mathcal{K}_4$ is unsatisfiable. Indeed, the inclusion $\exists\mathsf{contains}^-.\mathsf{VegFriendly} \sqsubseteq \mathsf{VegFriendly}$ and assertions $\mathsf{VegFriendly}(d)$ and $\mathsf{hasIngredient}(d, b)$ together imply that b is $\mathsf{VegFriendly}$. We also know that b has an ingredient of type Meat, due to $\mathsf{BologneseSauce}(b)$ and $\mathsf{BologneseSauce} \sqsubseteq \exists\mathsf{hasIngredient}.\mathsf{Meat}$. Since $\mathsf{hasIngredient}$ is a subrole of $\mathsf{contains}$, it follows that b contains this unnamed ingredient. We can therefore use inclusion (30) to conclude that this ingredient is $\mathsf{VegFriendly}$. This contradicts the disjointness constraint $\mathsf{Meat} \sqcap \mathsf{VegFriendly} \sqsubseteq \perp$ which states that it is not possible to belong to both Meat and $\mathsf{VegFriendly}$.

We now show how the unsatisfiability of $\mathcal{K}_4$ can be discovered by means of the saturation rules from Table 4. To begin, we use rule **T8** and the inclusions (33), (30), and (31) to derive

$$\mathsf{BologneseSauce} \sqcap \mathsf{VegFriendly} \sqsubseteq \exists\mathsf{hasIngredient}.(\mathsf{Meat} \sqcap \mathsf{VegFriendly}) \tag{37}$$

Next, we can apply rule **T6** to the preceding inclusion and (32) to infer

$$\mathsf{BologneseSauce} \sqcap \mathsf{VegFriendly} \sqsubseteq \exists\mathsf{hasIngredient}.(\mathsf{Meat} \sqcap \mathsf{VegFriendly} \sqcap \perp) \tag{38}$$

Then, using the preceding inclusion and rule **T5**, we obtain

$$\mathsf{BologneseSauce} \sqcap \mathsf{VegFriendly} \sqsubseteq \perp \tag{39}$$

Finally, by applying the ABox saturation rules, we reach a contradiction:

$$\text{contains}(d, b) \qquad \textbf{A4} : (31), (35) \qquad\qquad (40)$$
$$\text{VegFriendly}(b) \qquad \textbf{A3} : (31), (40) \qquad\qquad (41)$$
$$\bot(b) \qquad \textbf{A1} : (15), (39) \qquad\qquad (42)$$

Since $\bot(b)$ has been derived, we can conclude that $\mathcal{K}_4$ is unsatisfiable. ▲

A simple examination of the rules in Table 4 reveals that all derived axioms and assertions take one of the following forms:

$$R \sqsubseteq S \qquad M \sqsubseteq A \qquad M \sqsubseteq \exists R.N \qquad A(a) \qquad r(a, b)$$

where $r \in \mathsf{N_R}$, $R, S \in \mathsf{N_R^{\pm}}$, $A \in \mathsf{N_C} \cup \{\top, \bot\}$, M, N are conjunctions of concepts from $\mathsf{N_C} \cup \{\top, \bot\}$, and all individual names, concept names, and role names appear in $\mathcal{K}$. As the number of distinct (non-equivalent) axioms and assertions of these forms is at most single-exponential in the size of $\mathcal{K}$, it follows that $\mathsf{saturate}(\mathcal{K})$ can be computed in single-exponential time in $|\mathcal{K}|$, which yields an EXP upper bound for satisfiability and instance checking. This upper bound, which can be derived from EXP upper bounds for non-Horn DLs (see e.g., [71]), cannot be further improved. Indeed, matching EXP lower bounds follow from the EXP-hardness of subsumption in $\mathcal{ELI}$ [20].

Theorem 10. *In $\mathcal{ELHI}_\bot$, satisfiability and instance checking are EXP-complete in combined complexity.*

Observe that the TBox saturation rules do not depend on the ABox saturation rules, so it is possible to first fully saturate the TBox, and then in a second step, apply the ABox rules. We further remark that the ABox saturation rules can be viewed as Datalog rules which use concept names, role names, and the special concepts $\top$ and $\bot$ as predicate symbols. Formally, we can associate with each $\mathcal{ELHI}_\bot$ TBox $\mathcal{T}$ and ABox signature Σ the Datalog program $\Pi(\mathcal{T}, \Sigma)$ defined as follows:

$$
\begin{aligned}
\Pi(\mathcal{T}, \Sigma) = &\{B(x) \leftarrow A_1(x), \ldots, A_n(x) \mid A_1 \sqcap \ldots \sqcap A_n \sqsubseteq B \in \mathsf{saturate}(\mathcal{T})\} \cup \\
&\{B(x) \leftarrow A(y), r(x, y) \mid \exists r.A \sqsubseteq B \in \mathcal{T}\} \cup \\
&\{B(y) \leftarrow A(x), r(x, y) \mid \exists r^-.A \sqsubseteq B \in \mathcal{T}\} \cup \\
&\{s(x, y) \leftarrow r(x, y) \mid r \sqsubseteq s \in \mathsf{saturate}(\mathcal{T}), s \in \mathsf{N_R}\} \cup \\
&\{s(y, x) \leftarrow r(x, y) \mid r \sqsubseteq s^- \in \mathsf{saturate}(\mathcal{T}), s \in \mathsf{N_R}\} \cup \\
&\{\top(x) \leftarrow A(x) \mid A \in \mathsf{N_C} \cap \Sigma\} \cup \\
&\{\top(x) \leftarrow r(x, y) \mid r \in \mathsf{N_R} \cap \Sigma\} \cup \\
&\{\top(x) \leftarrow r(y, x) \mid r \in \mathsf{N_R} \cap \Sigma\}
\end{aligned}
$$

Note that first five sets of Datalog rules making up $\Pi(\mathcal{T}, \Sigma)$ are in one-to-one correspondence with the five ABox saturation rules **A1-A5**, with rules in the i-th line of the definition of $\Pi(\mathcal{T}, \Sigma)$ corresponding the ABox saturation rule **Ai** (for $1 \leq i \leq 5$). The last three sets of Datalog rules merely serve to populate $\top$ with all of the individuals in the ABox.

Example 18. Consider again the TBox $\mathcal{T}_4$ from Example 17, and let $\Sigma = \text{sig}(\mathcal{T}_4)$. The Datalog program $\Pi(\mathcal{T}, \Sigma)$ associated with $\mathcal{T}_4$ and Σ contains the rules:

$$\bot(x) \leftarrow \text{Meat}(x), \text{VegFriendly}(x)$$
$$\bot(x) \leftarrow \text{BologneseSauce}(x), \text{VegFriendly}(x)$$
$$\text{VegFriendly}(y) \leftarrow \text{VegFriendly}(x), \text{hasIngredient}(x, y)$$
$$\text{contains}(x, y) \leftarrow \text{hasIngredient}(x, y)$$

each corresponding to an inclusion from $\text{saturate}(\mathcal{T}_4)$. The program additionally contains rules for populating $\top$ (one rule for each concept name in $\mathcal{T}_4$, and two for each role name) and rules corresponding to the translations of trivial inclusions like $\text{Meat} \sqsubseteq \text{Meat}$ and $\text{Meat} \sqsubseteq \top$ (these latter rules could simply be omitted). ▲

The following theorem, which is a consequence of Theorem 9, resumes the important properties of the Datalog program $\Pi(\mathcal{T}, \Sigma)$.

Theorem 11. *For every finite signature Σ and $\mathcal{ELHI}_\bot$ KB $\mathcal{K} = (\mathcal{T}, \mathcal{A})$ with $\text{sig}(\mathcal{A}) \subseteq \Sigma$:*

1. *$\mathcal{K}$ is unsatisfiable iff $\text{ans}((\Pi(\mathcal{T}, \Sigma), \bot), \mathcal{I}_\mathcal{A}) \neq \emptyset$;*
2. *If $\mathcal{K}$ is satisfiable, then for all $A \in \mathsf{N_C}$, $r \in \mathsf{N_R}$, and $a, b \in \text{Ind}(\mathcal{A})$:*
   - *$\mathcal{K} \models A(a)$ iff $a \in \text{ans}((\Pi(\mathcal{T}, \Sigma), A), \mathcal{I}_\mathcal{A})$;*
   - *$\mathcal{K} \models r(a, b)$ iff $(a, b) \in \text{ans}((\Pi(\mathcal{T}, \Sigma), r), \mathcal{I}_\mathcal{A})$.*

It follows from the first statement of the preceding theorem that the Datalog query $(\Pi(\mathcal{T}, \Sigma) \cup \{Q_\bot \leftarrow \bot(x)\}, Q_\bot)$ is a rewriting of unsatisfiability w.r.t. $\mathcal{T}, \Sigma$. The second statement asserts that $(\Pi(\mathcal{T}, \Sigma), A)$ (resp. $(\Pi(\mathcal{T}, \Sigma), r)$) is a Datalog rewriting of the IQ $A(x)$ (resp. $r(x, y)$) w.r.t. $\mathcal{T}, \Sigma$ relative to consistent ABoxes. As discussed in Sect. 3.5, these rewritings can be combined together in order to obtain Datalog rewritings that hold for all ABoxes.

Since the construction of the Datalog program $\Pi(\mathcal{T}, \Sigma)$ is independent of the ABox (and polynomial w.r.t. $|\Sigma|$), and Datalog query evaluation is P-complete in data complexity, we obtain a P upper bound on the data complexity of instance checking and satisfiability in $\mathcal{ELHI}_\bot$: This positive result, which was first established in [111] for Horn-$\mathcal{SHIQ}$, is the best that we could hope for given that instance checking (resp. satisfiability) is already P-hard in the sublogic $\mathcal{EL}$ (resp. $\mathcal{EL}_\bot$).

Theorem 12 ([111]). *In $\mathcal{ELHI}_\bot$, satisfiability and instance checking are P-complete in data complexity.*

5   (Unions of) Conjunctive Queries

Instance queries are rather limited as a query language, as they do not allow us to express the natural selections and joins over relations that are common in standard database query languages. For this reason, the majority of works on

OMQA in the last decade have adopted *conjunctive queries (CQs)* as the basic query language.

CQs are a special class of first-order queries which allow only for conjunctions of positive atoms and existential quantification. CQs capture the plain *select-project-join* fragment of relational algebra and SQL, as well as the *basic graph patterns* that lie at the heart of SPARQL [106], which is the standard query language for OWL and RDF. It has been documented that a large percentage of queries posed to industrial database systems fall into this fragment. By taking disjunctions of such queries, sharing the same free variables, we obtain *unions of CQs*, another prominent query language. CQs and UCQs play a central role in traditional databases, and they are the query languages of choice in areas like data integration and data exchange [6,142].

Definition 7 ((Unions of) Conjunctive Queries). *A conjunctive query (CQ) is a first-order query $q(\boldsymbol{x})$ of the form*

$$\exists \boldsymbol{y}.P_1(\boldsymbol{t_1}) \wedge \cdots \wedge P_n(\boldsymbol{t_n})$$

where every variable contained in some $\boldsymbol{t_i}$ is contained in either $\boldsymbol{x}$ or $\boldsymbol{y}$. Recall that the free variables $\boldsymbol{x}$ are called the answer variables of q, and that the arity of the query is the length of the tuple $\boldsymbol{x}$.

A union of CQs (UCQ) is a first-order query $q(\boldsymbol{x})$ of the form

$$q_1(\boldsymbol{x}) \vee \cdots \vee q_n(\boldsymbol{x})$$

where all the $q_i(\boldsymbol{x})$ are CQs with the same tuple $\boldsymbol{x}$ of answer variables.

Let $q(\boldsymbol{x}) = \exists \boldsymbol{y}.\varphi(\boldsymbol{x}, \boldsymbol{y})$ be a CQ. Recall that $\mathsf{ans}(q, \mathcal{I}) = \{\boldsymbol{e} = (e_1, \ldots, e_n) \in (\Delta^{\mathcal{I}})^n \mid \mathcal{I} \models \exists \boldsymbol{y}.\varphi[\boldsymbol{x} \mapsto \boldsymbol{e}]\}$. Since the variables in $\boldsymbol{y}$ are existentially quantified, we have that $\mathcal{I} \models \exists \boldsymbol{y}.\varphi[\boldsymbol{x} \mapsto \boldsymbol{e}]$ just in the case that there exists a variable assignment π that extends $(x_1, \ldots, x_n) \mapsto (e_1, \ldots, e_n)$ by additionally mapping the variables in $\boldsymbol{y}$ to objects in $\Delta^{\mathcal{I}}$ in such a way that $\mathcal{I} \models \varphi[\pi]$. We call such a mapping π a *match for q in $\mathcal{I}$*.

Remark 13. A popular alternative syntax for CQs and UCQs is to write them as Datalog rules. A CQ corresponds to a single Datalog rule

$$q(\boldsymbol{x}) = \exists \boldsymbol{y}.P_1(\boldsymbol{t_1}) \wedge \cdots \wedge P_n(\boldsymbol{t_n}) \quad \rightsquigarrow \quad q(\boldsymbol{x}) \leftarrow P_1(\boldsymbol{t_1}), \ldots, P_n(\boldsymbol{t_n})$$

while a UCQ is written as a set of rules with the same head predicate:

$$
\begin{aligned}
q(\boldsymbol{x}) = \ & \exists \boldsymbol{y_1}.P_1^1(\boldsymbol{t_1^1}) \wedge \cdots \wedge P_{n_1}^1(\boldsymbol{t_{n_1}^1}) & & q(\boldsymbol{x}) \leftarrow P_1^1(\boldsymbol{t_1^1}), \ldots, P_{n_1}^1(\boldsymbol{t_{n_1}^1}) \\
& \vee \exists \boldsymbol{y_2}.P_1^2(\boldsymbol{t_1^2}) \wedge \cdots \wedge P_{n_2}^2(\boldsymbol{t_{n_2}^2}) & & q(\boldsymbol{x}) \leftarrow P_1^2(\boldsymbol{t_1^2}), \ldots, P_n^2(\boldsymbol{t_n^2}) \\
& \quad \vdots & \rightsquigarrow & \quad \vdots \\
& \vee \exists \boldsymbol{y_\ell}.P_1^\ell(\boldsymbol{t_1^\ell}) \quad \cdots \quad P_{n_\ell}^\ell(\boldsymbol{t_{n_\ell}^\ell}) & & q(\boldsymbol{x}) \leftarrow P_1^\ell(\boldsymbol{t_1^\ell}), \ldots, P_{n_\ell}^\ell(\boldsymbol{t_{n_\ell}^\ell})
\end{aligned}
$$

We now illustrate some queries that can be expressed as CQs or UCQs.

Example 19. Consider the following queries:

$$q_3(y, x) = \exists z.\mathsf{serves}(x, y) \wedge \mathsf{hasIngredient}(y, z) \wedge \mathsf{Spicy}(z)$$

$$q_4(y, x) = q_1(x, y) \vee$$
$$\exists z, z'.\mathsf{serves}(x, y) \wedge \mathsf{hasIngredient}(y, z) \wedge \mathsf{hasIngredient}(z, z'), \mathsf{Spicy}(z')$$

The first query is a CQ that retrieves dishes y that contain a spicy ingredient, together with the establishment x where they are served. The query q_4 is a UCQ that finds pairs of y and x as in q_3, but it also retrieves the pair y, x if y has an ingredient that in turn contains a spicy ingredient. ▲

While some very restricted forms of (U)CQs can be expressed as instance queries by defining the query as a concept in the TBox, the arbitrary use of variables in CQs makes them a strict generalization of IQs.

We discuss in this section how to answer UCQs over $\mathcal{ELHI}_\bot$ knowledge bases. We assume in what follows that we are always given a satisfiable $\mathcal{K}$ as an input, since query answering over unsatisfiable knowledge bases is trivial, and we can test for satisfiability in advance using the procedure discussed in Sect. 4.3 (which has no higher complexity than any of the procedures described below).

5.1   Canonical Model Construction

As a preliminary step, we will show how to define a universal model of a given satisfiable $\mathcal{ELHI}_\bot$ KB using the saturated TBox obtained by applying the rules in Sect. 4.3. This universal model will play a central role in the query answering techniques developed in this and the following section.

Given a satisfiable $\mathcal{ELHI}_\bot$ KB $\mathcal{K} = (\mathcal{T}, \mathcal{A})$, we consider the interpretation $\mathcal{I}_{\mathcal{T},\mathcal{A}}$ (alternatively denoted $\mathcal{I}_\mathcal{K}$) defined as follows. The domain $\Delta^{\mathcal{I}_{\mathcal{T},\mathcal{A}}}$ consists of sequences of the form $aR_1M_1 \ldots R_nM_n$ ($n \geq 0$), where $a \in \mathsf{Ind}(\mathcal{A})$, and for every $i \geq 1$, $R_i \in \mathsf{N}_\mathsf{R}^\pm$ and M_i is a conjunction of concepts from $\mathsf{N}_\mathsf{C} \cup \{\top\}$. More precisely, $\Delta^{\mathcal{I}_{\mathcal{T},\mathcal{A}}}$ consists of all sequences $aR_1M_1 \ldots R_nM_n$ that satisfy:

- If $n \geq 1$, then there exists $B_1 \sqcap \ldots \sqcap B_m \sqsubseteq \exists R_1.M_1 \in \mathsf{saturate}(\mathcal{T})$ such that $B_j(a) \in \mathsf{saturate}(\mathcal{K})$ for every $1 \leq j \leq m$.
- For every $1 \leq i < n$, $M_i \sqsubseteq \exists R_{i+1}.M_{i+1} \in \mathsf{saturate}(\mathcal{T})$.

To complete the definition of $\mathcal{I}_{\mathcal{T},\mathcal{A}}$, we must fix the interpretation of the individual names, concept names, and role names from $\mathcal{K}$. This is done as follows[10]:

$$a^{\mathcal{I}_{\mathcal{T},\mathcal{A}}} = a$$

$$A^{\mathcal{I}_{\mathcal{T},\mathcal{A}}} = \{a \in \mathsf{Ind}(\mathcal{A}) \mid A(a) \in \mathsf{saturate}(\mathcal{K})\} \cup$$
$$\{e \in \Delta^{\mathcal{I}_{\mathcal{T},\mathcal{A}}} \setminus \mathsf{Ind}(\mathcal{A}) \mid e = e'RM \text{ and } A \in M\}$$

$$r^{\mathcal{I}_{\mathcal{T},\mathcal{A}}} = \{(a, b) \mid r(a, b) \in \mathsf{saturate}(\mathcal{K})\} \cup$$
$$\{(e_1, e_2) \mid e_2 = e_1 S M \text{ and } S \sqsubseteq r \in \mathsf{saturate}(\mathcal{T})\} \cup$$
$$\{(e_2, e_1) \mid e_2 = e_1 S M \text{ and } S \sqsubseteq r^- \in \mathsf{saturate}(\mathcal{T})\}$$

---

[10] Recall that we treat conjunctions of concepts as sets. Abusing notation, we use $A \in M$ to mean that A is a conjunct of M.

It is easy to show that $\mathcal{I}_{\mathcal{K}}$ is a model of $\mathcal{K}$, and we will henceforth refer to it as the *canonical model* of $\mathcal{K}$.

Note that the domain of $\mathcal{I}_{\mathcal{K}}$ contains the individuals in $\mathcal{A}$, and additional objects whose existence if implied by the axioms in saturate$(\mathcal{T})$ of the form $M \sqsubseteq \exists R.N$. The latter objects are called *anonymous* and defined in such a way that if $aR_1M_1 \ldots R_nM_n$ is in $\Delta^{\mathcal{I}_{\mathcal{K}}}$, then so is $aR_1M_1 \ldots R_{n-1}M_{n-1}$. Hence these objects naturally form tree-like structures rooted at the individuals. Moreover, if we take the undirected graph that has the domain of $\mathcal{I}_{\mathcal{K}}$ as nodes and an (undirected) edge between two objects e, e' whenever $(e, e) \in r^{\mathcal{I}_{\mathcal{K}}}$ for some $r \in \mathsf{N_R}$, then we obtain a structure that can be viewed as comprising different parts:

- the restriction to the individuals, which is an arbitrary graph sometimes called the *core* of $\mathcal{I}_{\mathcal{K}}$,
- a set of potentially infinite trees of anonymous objects, each of which is rooted at one of the individuals in the core, as we have discussed

For this reason, $\mathcal{I}_{\mathcal{K}}$ is often associated with a forest and it is given names such as a *(pseudo-) forest model*, see e.g. [57,58,89,90]. This forest-like structure is a useful property that is exploited by many algorithms, and in particular by the ones we discuss in this chapter.

We now illustrate the construction of canonical models on a simple example:

Example 20. Consider the KB $\mathcal{K}_5$ whose TBox $\mathcal{T}_5$ contains the following axioms:

$$\mathsf{PenneArrabiata} \sqsubseteq \exists\mathsf{hasIngredient.Penne}$$
$$\mathsf{Penne} \sqsubseteq \mathsf{Pasta}$$
$$\mathsf{PenneArrabiata} \sqsubseteq \exists\mathsf{hasIngredient.ArrabiataSauce}$$
$$\mathsf{ArrabiataSauce} \sqsubseteq \exists\mathsf{hasIngredient.Peperoncino}$$
$$\mathsf{Peperoncino} \sqsubseteq \mathsf{Spicy}$$
$$\mathsf{PizzaCalabrese} \sqsubseteq \exists\mathsf{hasIngredient.Nduja}$$
$$\mathsf{Nduja} \sqsubseteq \mathsf{Spicy}$$

and whose ABox is as follows:

$$\mathsf{serves}(r, b) \quad \mathsf{serves}(r, p) \quad \mathsf{PenneArrabiata}(b) \quad \mathsf{PizzaCalabrese}(p)$$

Note that saturate$(\mathcal{T}_5)$ contains, additionally to the axioms above, the following axioms that result from applications of **T6**:

$$\mathsf{PenneArrabiata} \sqsubseteq \exists\mathsf{hasIngredient.}(\mathsf{Penne} \sqcap \mathsf{Pasta})$$
$$\mathsf{ArrabiataSauce} \sqsubseteq \exists\mathsf{hasIngredient.}(\mathsf{Peperoncino} \sqcap \mathsf{Spicy})$$
$$\mathsf{PizzaCalabrese} \sqsubseteq \exists\mathsf{hasIngredient.}(\mathsf{Nduja} \sqcap \mathsf{Spicy})$$

The canonical model $\mathcal{I}_{\mathcal{K}_5}$ of this knowledge base is depicted in Fig. 3. For readability, we use the following abbreviations for the anonymous objects:

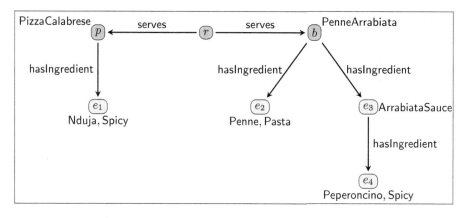

Fig. 3. Canonical model $\mathcal{I}_{\mathcal{K}_5}$ of the knowledge base $\mathcal{K}_5$ in Example 20. We use blue for ABox individuals and yellow for anonymous objects.

$e_1 = p$ hasIngredient (Nduja $\sqcap$ Spicy)
$e_2 = b$ hasIngredient (Penne $\sqcap$ Pasta)
$e_3 = b$ hasIngredient ArrabiataSauce
$e_4 = b$ hasIngredient ArrabiataSauce hasIngredient (Peperoncino $\sqcap$ Spicy)   ▲

The crucial property of $\mathcal{I}_{\mathcal{K}}$ is that it is a *universal* model of $\mathcal{K}$, that is, it is 'contained' in every model of $\mathcal{K}$. For each model $\mathcal{I}$ of $\mathcal{K}$, we can define a *homomorphism* from $\mathcal{I}_{\mathcal{K}}$ to $\mathcal{I}$, which is a function $h : \Delta^{\mathcal{I}_{\mathcal{K}}} \to \Delta^{\mathcal{I}}$ such that

- $h(a^{\mathcal{I}_{\mathcal{K}}}) = a^{\mathcal{I}}$ for each individual a in $\mathcal{K}$,
- $e \in A^{\mathcal{I}_{\mathcal{K}}}$ implies $h(e) \in A^{\mathcal{I}}$ for every concept name A, and
- $(e, e') \in r^{\mathcal{I}_{\mathcal{K}}}$ implies $(h(e), h(e')) \in r^{\mathcal{I}}$ for every role name r.

It is not hard to see that matches of CQs are preserved under homomorphisms:

Fact 1. *Let q be a CQ, and h a homomorphism from an interpretation $\mathcal{I}$ to an interpretation $\mathcal{J}$. If π is a match for q in $\mathcal{I}$, then the mapping $h \circ \pi$ obtained by composing π with h is a match for q in $\mathcal{J}$.*

The importance of this property lies in the fact that, for an arbitrary CQ or UCQ q, every answer to q in $\mathcal{I}_{\mathcal{K}}$ is an answer to q in every model of $\mathcal{K}$. Since the converse also holds (an answer to q in every model is clearly also an answer to q in the particular model $\mathcal{I}_{\mathcal{K}}$), the certain answers to q over $\mathcal{K}$ coincide with the answers to q over $\mathcal{I}_{\mathcal{K}}$.

Theorem 13. *Let $\mathcal{K}$ be a satisfiable $\mathcal{ELHI}_{\perp}$ knowledge base, let $q(\boldsymbol{x}) = q_1(\boldsymbol{x}) \vee \ldots \vee q_n(\boldsymbol{x})$ be a UCQ, and let $\boldsymbol{a}$ be a tuple of individuals of the same arity as $\boldsymbol{x}$. Then $\boldsymbol{a} \in \mathsf{cert}(q, \mathcal{K})$ iff $\boldsymbol{a} \in \mathsf{ans}(q, \mathcal{I}_{\mathcal{K}})$ iff $\boldsymbol{a} \in \mathsf{ans}(q_i, \mathcal{I}_{\mathcal{K}})$ for some $1 \leq i \leq n$.*

This result has been shown even for significantly more expressive query languages than UCQs (for example, positive first-order queries and Datalog queries), and it allows us to focus on the simpler problem of evaluating a CQ over the canonical model only, instead of considering the possibly infinitely many models that a knowledge base may possess.

Example 21. Let $\mathcal{K}_5$ and $\mathcal{T}_5$ be the knowledge base and TBox from Example 20, and recall the queries q_3 and q_4 from Example 19. The match with $x \mapsto r$, $y \mapsto p$ and $z \mapsto e_1$ shows that $(p, r) \in \mathsf{ans}(q_3, \mathcal{I}_{\mathcal{K}_5})$, and there are no further answers, hence $\mathsf{ans}(q_1, \mathcal{I}_{\mathcal{K}_5}) = \{(p, r)\}$. For q_4, we also have $(p, r) \in \mathsf{ans}(q_4, \mathcal{I}_{\mathcal{K}_5})$, but in this case, we additionally get $(b, r) \in \mathsf{ans}(q_4, \mathcal{I}_{\mathcal{K}_5})$, as witnessed by the assignment $x \mapsto r$, $y \mapsto b$, $z \mapsto e_3$ and $z' \mapsto e_4$, which is a match for the second disjunct. Hence $\mathsf{ans}(q_4, \mathcal{I}_{\mathcal{K}_5}) = \{(p, r), (b, r)\}$. We therefore obtain the following certain answers over $\mathcal{K}_5$:

$$\mathsf{cert}(q_3, \mathcal{K}_5) = \{(p, r)\} \qquad \mathsf{cert}(q_4, \mathcal{K}_5) = \{(p, r), (b, r)\}.$$

▲

5.2   Conjunctive Query Answering in $\mathcal{ELHI}_\perp$

By Theorem 13, to design a procedure for answering UCQs over $\mathcal{ELHI}_\perp$ KBs, it is sufficient to focus on the problem of testing whether $\boldsymbol{a} \in \mathsf{ans}(q, \mathcal{I}_{\mathcal{K}})$ for a given tuple $\boldsymbol{a}$, KB $\mathcal{K}$ and CQ $q(\boldsymbol{x})$. By definition, $\boldsymbol{a} \in \mathsf{ans}(q, \mathcal{I}_{\mathcal{K}})$ iff $\boldsymbol{a}$ is the image of $\boldsymbol{x}$ under some match π. In relational databases, a standard way to determine the existence of such a match is take an assignment that maps $\boldsymbol{x}$ to $\boldsymbol{a}$, extend it non-deterministically by assigning an individual in the database to each existentially quantified variable, and finally to test whether the guessed assignment π is a match, that is, whether $A(\pi(x))$ and $R(\pi(x), \pi(y))$ are present in the database for every query atom $A(x)$ or $R(x, y)$.

In the presence of ontologies, the situation is more complicated. First, we have seen that an assertion may hold because it is implied by $\mathcal{K}$, without syntactically occurring in the ABox $\mathcal{A}$. Hence, in the simple algorithm outlined in the preceding paragraph, we would need to replace the syntactic containment of assertions in the database by an instance check $\mathcal{K} \models A(\pi(x))$ or $\mathcal{K} \models A(\pi(x))$, which can be carried out using the procedure described in Sect. 4.3. However, even with this adaptation, the resulting procedure would not be complete. A second and more challenging problem is that when guessing a variable assignment, it is not enough to map every existentially quantified variable to an individual, as we may need to consider mappings to anonymous objects in $\Delta^{\mathcal{I}_{\mathcal{K}}}$ in order to find the desired match. For instance, in the previous example, we saw that we needed to map $z \mapsto e_1$ to obtain $(p, r) \in \mathsf{ans}(q_3, \mathcal{I}_{\mathcal{K}_5})$ and that we have to map $z \mapsto e_3$ and $z \mapsto e_4$ to get $(b, r) \in \mathsf{ans}(q_4, \mathcal{I}_{\mathcal{K}_5})$. There can be infinitely many anonymous objects in $\mathcal{I}_{\mathcal{K}}$, and we do not know in advance which of them may occur in the image of the match. Hence there are infinitely many different matches that may need to be considered, and it is not apparent how to devise an effective procedure over this infinite search space.

We tackle this problem next. One possible solution would be to characterize a finite set O of anonymous objects from $\Delta^{\mathcal{I}_{\mathcal{K}}}$ and show that whenever there exists a match for a CQ in $\mathcal{I}_{\mathcal{K}}$, there exists a match that ranges over the named individuals and O only. Some existing techniques implicitly rely on a characterization of this set O, but only for specific combinations of a query q and a TBox $\mathcal{T}$, see e.g., [80, 148, 164].

Here we take a different approach and present an algorithm [81] that rewrites the query in such a way that we do not need to consider mappings to the anonymous objects, but we can instead restrict our attention to matches to named individuals. More specifically, given a CQ $q(\boldsymbol{x})$, we construct a UCQ $\mathsf{rew}_\mathcal{T}(q)$ (with the same answer variables $\boldsymbol{x}$) with the property that $\boldsymbol{a} \in \mathsf{ans}(q, \mathcal{I}_\mathcal{K})$ iff there is a disjunct q' in $\mathsf{rew}_\mathcal{T}(q)$ and a match π for q' in $\mathcal{I}_\mathcal{K}$ such that $\pi(\boldsymbol{x}) = \boldsymbol{a}$ and the range of π contains only named individuals.

The intuition underlying the rewriting procedure is as follows. Suppose q has an existential variable x, and there is a match π for q in $\mathcal{I}_\mathcal{K}$ such that $\pi(x)$ is an anonymous object in the tree part of $\mathcal{I}_\mathcal{K}$, and it has no descendant in the image of π. Then for all atoms $R(y, x)$ or $R(x, y)$ of q, the 'neighbor' variable y must be mapped to the parent p of $\pi(x)$ in $\mathcal{I}_\mathcal{K}$. A rewriting step chooses such a variable x, together with an existential axiom $M \sqsubseteq \exists S.N$ from $\mathsf{saturate}(\mathcal{T})$ such that all atoms of q involving x are satisfied provided the parent p is an instance of M. Then the algorithm can 'clip off' x, eliminating all query atoms involving it, and adding instead fresh atoms to ensure that the parent p satisfies M. The resulting query q' has a match π' that is similar to π, but crucially, the length of the longest path occurring in the image of π' is strictly shorter than for π. By repeating this procedure, we can clip off all variables matched in the tree part to obtain shorter and shorter matches, until we end up with a set of queries such that, if they have a match in $\mathcal{I}_\mathcal{K}$, then they have a match whose range contains only ABox individuals.

Definition 8. *For a CQ q and a $\mathcal{ELHI}_\perp$ TBox $\mathcal{T}$, we write $q \to_\mathcal{T} q'$ if q' can be obtained from q by applying the following steps:*

(S1) Select in q an arbitrary existentially quantified variable x such that there are no atoms of the form $R(x,x)$ in q.

(S2) Replace each role atom of the form $R(x,y)$ in q, where y and R are arbitrary, by the atom $\mathsf{inv}(R)(y,x)$.

(S3) Let $V_p = \{y \mid R(y,x) \in q \text{ for some } R\}$, and select some $M \sqsubseteq \exists S.N \in \mathsf{saturate}(\mathcal{T})$ such that

    (a) $S \sqsubseteq R \in \mathsf{saturate}(\mathcal{T})$ for every $R(y,x) \in q$, and

    (b) $\{A \mid A(x) \in q\} \subseteq N$.

(S4) Drop from q every atom that contains x.

(S5) Select a variable $y \in V_p$ and replace every occurrence of $y' \in V_p$ in q by y.

(S6) Add the atoms $\{A(y) \mid A \in M\}$ to q.

We write $q \to_\mathcal{T}^* q'$ if $q = q_0$ and $q' = q_n$ for some finite rewrite sequence $q_0 \to_\mathcal{T} q_1 \cdots \to_\mathcal{T} q_n$, $n \geq 0$. Furthermore, we let $\mathsf{rew}_\mathcal{T}(q) = \{q' \mid q \to_\mathcal{T}^* q'\}$.

In (S1) we guess an existentially quantified variable x (we exclude variables appearing in self-loops as such variables cannot be mapped to anonymous objects). For convenience, in (S2), we invert all atoms of the form $R(x,y)$, so that x always appears in the second position of role atoms. In (S3), we let V_p be the set of all 'neighbor' variables y of x for which there is an atom $R(y,x)$ in q;

intuitively, every such variable y must be mapped to the parent p of $\pi(x)$. We also select a TBox inclusion that ensures the existence of a suitable child $\pi(x)$, under the assumption that the left-hand side of the inclusion is satisfied at p. Then we can clip off x in (S4), merge all variables of V_p in (S5), and add to q new atoms that enforce satisfaction of the concepts appearing on the left-hand side of the selected axiom in (S6).

Example 22. Consider the second disjunct of q_4, that is, the following CQ:

$$q_5(y, x) = \exists z, z'.\mathsf{serves}(x, y) \wedge \mathsf{hasIngredient}(y, z) \wedge \mathsf{hasIngredient}(z, z') \wedge \mathsf{Spicy}(z')$$

Recall that $(b, r) \in \mathsf{ans}(q_5, \mathcal{I}_\mathcal{K})$, as witnessed by the match $\pi(x) = r$, $\pi(y) = b$, $\pi(z) = e_3$, and $\pi(z') = e_4$. In our running example, a possible rewriting step for q_5 could select in (S1) the variable z' (which intuitively means that we guess that $\pi(z')$ is a leaf in the image of q_5 under some match, as is the case for the match π). Then there is nothing to do in (S2), and in (S3) we see that $V_p = \{z\}$ is the only variable that has to be mapped to the parent of $\pi(z')$. We need to select some axiom $M \sqsubseteq \exists S.N \in \mathsf{saturate}(\mathcal{T}_5)$ that ensures the satisfaction of all atoms involving z', that is, of $\mathsf{hasIngredient}(z, z')$ and $\mathsf{Spicy}(z')$. We see that $\mathsf{ArrabiataSauce} \sqsubseteq \exists \mathsf{hasIngredient.Spicy}$ is such an axiom, so in (S4) and (S6), we drop the atoms $\mathsf{hasIngredient}(z, z')$ and $\mathsf{Spicy}(z')$ and replace them by $\mathsf{ArrabiataSauce}(z)$ (we may skip (S5) since $|V_p| = 1$). Summing up, after one rewriting step we get:

$$q_5'(y, x) = \exists z.\mathsf{serves}(x, y) \wedge \mathsf{hasIngredient}(y, z) \wedge \mathsf{ArrabiataSauce}(z)$$

Note that every match of q_5' can be extended to a match of q_5, hence the rewriting procedure does not introduce any incorrect answers. The motivation for introducing q_5' is that the image of a match of q_5' goes one step less deep into the anonymous part of the canonical model than the corresponding match for q_5. In a second rewriting step, we again choose to eliminate z, and we get that $V_p = \{y\}$. We select in (S3) the axiom $\mathsf{PenneArrabiata} \sqsubseteq \exists \mathsf{hasIngredient.ArrabiataSauce}$, since mapping y to an instance of $\mathsf{PenneArrabiata}$ suffices to make the atoms that involve z (namely, $\mathsf{hasIngredient}(y, z)$ and $\mathsf{ArrabiataSauce}(z)$) true. We can then replace these atoms by $\mathsf{PenneArrabiata}(y)$ to obtain

$$q_5''(y, x) = \mathsf{serves}(x, y) \wedge \mathsf{PenneArrabiata}(y)$$

Now we have obtained a query q_5'' that has a match $(\pi(x) = r, \pi(y) = b)$ where all variables are mapped to individuals. Moreover, by virtue of the rewriting process, we know that the match for q_5'' implies the existence of a corresponding match for q_5, and so we have $(b, r) \in \mathsf{ans}(q_5, \mathcal{I}_{\mathcal{K}_5})$.   ▲

The rewriting procedure that we have just presented is a slightly simplified version of the one defined in [81] for Horn-$\mathcal{SHIQ}$, and the results in that paper imply the following theorem.

Theorem 14. *Let $\mathcal{K} = (\mathcal{T}, \mathcal{A})$ be a satisfiable $\mathcal{ELHI}_\perp$ knowledge base, and let $q(\boldsymbol{x})$ be a CQ. Then $\boldsymbol{a} \in \mathsf{cert}(q, \mathcal{K})$ iff there is some $q' \in \mathsf{rew}_\mathcal{T}(q)$ and an assignment π from the variables in q' to $\mathsf{Ind}(\mathcal{A})$ such that $\pi(\boldsymbol{x}) = \boldsymbol{a}$ and π is a match for q in $\mathcal{I_K}$.*

Importantly, since $\mathsf{Ind}(\mathcal{A})$ is bounded, for each $q' \in \mathsf{rew}_\mathcal{T}(q)$, there are only a bounded number of candidate assignments π (in fact, single-exponentially many). We need to check whether one of these candidate matches π is indeed a match, that is, all of its atoms are satisfied under π. We can test each candidate assignment in turn, using the instance checking algorithms from Sect. 4.3 to decide whether a given query atom is satisfied under a given assignment. By Theorem 14, the approach we have just described yields a terminating, sound, and complete decision procedure for CQ answering in $\mathcal{ELHI}_\perp$.

The procedure also has an optimal worst-case combined and data complexity. For combined complexity, we know that computing $\mathsf{saturate}(\mathcal{T})$ is feasible in single exponential time. The cardinality of the set of rewritten queries $\mathsf{rew}_\mathcal{T}(q)$ is single exponential in $|\mathcal{T}|$ and $|q|$, since it only contains queries whose variables are a subset of the variables in q, and concept and role names that appear in $\mathcal{T}$. Moreover, the set $\mathsf{rew}_\mathcal{T}(q)$ can be computed in single exponential time. Once $\mathsf{rew}_\mathcal{T}(q)$ has been computed, we can consider the single-exponentially many candidate assignments of the variables for each $q' \in \mathsf{rew}_\mathcal{T}(q)$, and for each such assignment, we need to do a number of instance checks that is linear in the size of q'; by Theorem 12, instance checking can be performed in single exponential time. Since already consistency and instance checking in $\mathcal{ELI}$ are hard for single exponential time [19], the resulting Exp bound is optimal.

As for data complexity, we note that $\mathsf{rew}_\mathcal{T}(q)$ can be computed in constant time for a fixed $\mathcal{T}$ and q, and the number of candidate assignments π is polynomial in the size of the ABox. Since instance checking is in P regarding data complexity, we obtain:

Theorem 15. *CQ answering in $\mathcal{ELHI}_\perp$ and Horn-$\mathcal{SHIQ}$ is Exp-complete in combined complexity and P-complete in data complexity.*

We remark that the same bounds hold for Horn-$\mathcal{SHIQ}$, which is in fact the logic for which this rewriting procedure was developed.

With minor adaptations, we can use the same technique to obtain optimal bounds for $\mathcal{ELH}$ and DL-Lite$_\mathcal{R}$. For combined complexity, we can devise an algorithm that runs in non-deterministic polynomial time. First, we compute $\mathsf{saturate}(\mathcal{T})$ in polynomial time. Then we can non-deterministically guess and build the right $q' \in \mathsf{rew}_\mathcal{T}(q)$, guess a candidate assignment π, and check in polynomial time if it is a match. Indeed, to determine whether an assignment is a match, we must perform a polynomial number of instance checks, and each check can be done in polynomial time for $\mathcal{ELH}$ and DL-Lite$_\mathcal{R}$. This NP bound is optimal, since CQ answering is already NP-hard over an ABox alone, seen as a database, and with no TBox. For data complexity, instance checking in $\mathcal{EL}$ is hard for P, and we can easily obtain a matching upper bound for $\mathcal{ELH}$: the set $\mathsf{rew}_\mathcal{T}(q)$ can be obtained in polynomial time, there are only polynomially candidate assignments for the rewritten queries, and testing for a match only needs a polynomial number of polynomial-time instance checks. In DL-Lite$_\mathcal{R}$, we will see that our techniques can be used to obtain an FO rewriting, yielding membership in AC_0. These bounds are summarized in the next theorem.

Theorem 16. *CQ answering in $\mathcal{ELH}$ and DL-Lite$_\mathcal{R}$ is NP-complete in combined complexity. For $\mathcal{ELH}$ the data complexity is P-complete, and for DL-Lite$_\mathcal{R}$ the data complexity is in AC_0.*

We note that the results in this theorem are anterior to [81]. The upper bounds for DL-Lite$_\mathcal{R}$ follow from the seminal papers on the DL-Lite family and the original PerfectRef query rewriting algorithm [50,52], and the upper bounds for CQ answering in $\mathcal{EL}$ were first established in [133,134,186]. In Sect. 8, we will give a brief overview of subsequent work aimed at developing, optimizing, and implementing efficient CQ answering algorithms for these and related logics.

We close this subsection by considering different possible ways of translating Theorem 14 into a concrete query answering algorithm.

A Datalog Rewriting Approach for CQs in $\mathcal{ELHI}_\perp$. A first option is to define a Datalog rewriting. Indeed, since $\mathsf{rew}_\mathcal{T}(q)$ is a UCQ, it can be viewed as a set Π_rew of Datalog rules that all use the same head predicate Q. By Theorem 14, (Π_rew, Q) will give the correct answer to q if evaluated over the enriched ABox consisting of all assertions that are entailed from the KB. To obtain this completed ABox, we may exploit the Datalog program $\Pi(\mathcal{T}, \Sigma)$ from Sect. 4.3, which has the property that for every Σ-ABox $\mathcal{A}$ and every concept or role assertion $P(t)$, $\mathcal{T}, \mathcal{A} \models P(t)$ iff $t \in \mathsf{ans}(\mathcal{I}_\mathcal{A}, (\Pi(\mathcal{T}, \Sigma), P))$. It follows that the query $(\Pi(\mathcal{T}, \Sigma) \cup \Pi_\mathsf{rew}, Q)$ is a Datalog rewriting of q w.r.t. $\mathcal{T}, \Sigma$ relative to consistent ABoxes.

A Combined Approach for CQs in $\mathcal{ELHI}_\perp$. Another possibility is to use Theorem 14 as the basis of a *combined* approach in the spirit of [152] that uses both saturation and rewriting. As $\mathsf{saturate}(\mathcal{K})$ contains all the assertions entailed by $\mathcal{T}$ and $\mathcal{A}$, it suffices to pose the UCQ $\mathsf{rew}_\mathcal{T}(q)$ over (the interpretation corresponding to) the assertions in $\mathsf{saturate}(\mathcal{K})$ viewed as a database. Compared to the pure Datalog rewriting approach, the combined approach has the advantage that we can use standard relational database systems, which are more mature than Datalog engines. Its main drawback is that the saturated version of the ABox needs to be recomputed whenever the KB is modified (see Sect. 8 for further discussion of combined approaches to OMQA).

An FO Rewriting Approach for CQs in DL-Lite$_\mathcal{R}$. We can also use the rewritten set of queries as the basis of an FO rewriting approach for DL-Lite$_\mathcal{R}$. We know that to determine whether $a \in \mathsf{cert}(q, \mathcal{K})$, we only need to decide whether there is some $q' \in \mathsf{rew}_\mathcal{T}(q)$ and an assignment π from the variables in q' to $\mathsf{Ind}(\mathcal{A})$ such that $\mathcal{T}, \mathcal{A} \models P(\pi(t))$ for each atom $P(t)$ in q. We can exploit our rewriting algorithm for instance checking in DL-Lite$_\mathcal{R}$ (Sect. 4.1), and replace in the queries $q' \in \mathsf{rew}_\mathcal{T}(q)$ each atom $A(t)$ by $\mathsf{RewriteIQ}(A, \mathcal{T})$ and each atom $r(t, t')$ by $\mathsf{RewriteIQ}(r, \mathcal{T})$. The result of this replacement is a (positive)

FO query[11] q_{rew} that is a rewriting of q w.r.t. $\mathcal{T}$ relative to consistent ABoxes. As discussed in Sects. 3 and 4, the latter rewriting can be combined with an FO rewriting of unsatisfiability to obtain an FO rewriting of q w.r.t. $\mathcal{T}$ that works for all ABoxes over the given signature. Since the data complexity of answering FO queries over relational databases is in $\mathsf{AC_0}$, this yields the remaining upper bound in Theorem 16.

5.3 Related Results and Discussion

We close this section with a short discussion of other results that are related to answering CQs and other positive fragments of FO queries in the presence of (both Horn and non-Horn) DL ontologies.

Other Results on CQ Answering in Horn DLs. For members of the $\mathcal{EL}$ family, including $\mathcal{EL}^{++}$ and some other fragments not contained in $\mathcal{ELHI}_\perp$, the first complexity results for CQ answering were established in [133,134,186]. An important result common to the three works was that CQ answering is undecidable for $\mathcal{EL}^{++}$. Both [186], [134] present fragments that are NP-complete for combined complexity, while [133] focused on data complexity. A PSPACE upper bound for a fragment of regular $\mathcal{EL}^{++}$ was obtained in [135]. More recently, a tight NP upper bound was shown for the fragment of regular $\mathcal{ELRO}^+$ that restricts complex role assumptions to transitivity axioms [202], and a tight PSPACE upper bound was obtained for (full) regular $\mathcal{ELRO}^+$ that corresponds to OWL 2 EL [201,203].

For more expressive Horn DLs, like Horn-$\mathcal{SHIQ}$, there are fewer results. The query rewriting technique we have discussed in this section was proposed in [81] for Horn-$\mathcal{SHIQ}$, and it shares core ideas with previous algorithms for $\mathcal{EL}$ [186] and DL-Lite [188]. The complexity bounds for Horn-$\mathcal{SHIQ}$ had been obtained already in [78], but with a different algorithm less suited for implementation. Recent work has considered the more expressive Horn logics Horn-$\mathcal{SHOIQ}$ and Horn-$\mathcal{SROIQ}$ and generalizations of CQs with a limited form of recursion [166]; we will discuss this in Sect. 6.4.

Unions of Conjunctive Queries and Positive Existential Queries. In this section, we have mainly focused on CQs, but by Theorem 13, we know that the obtained results extend to UCQs. In fact, the universal model property also applies to *positive existential queries (PEQs)*, a class of FO queries that generalize CQs by allowing arbitrary combinations of conjunctions and disjunctions of atoms. Since every positive FO formula can be put into disjunctive normal form (i.e., rewritten as a disjunction of conjunctions), PEQs have the same expressive power as UCQs, although they can be exponentially more succinct. The complexity results for (U)CQ answering in Horn DLs can be easily transferred to

---

[11] If desired, we could use standard equivalence-preserving transformations to turn q_{rew} into an equivalent UCQ.

PEQs. The core idea is that to when checking whether a candidate assignment is a match for the query, one also considers a choice of a subset of the query atoms whose satisfaction leads to the PEQ being satisfied. If we consider data complexity, enumerating all possible choices of subsets of query atoms requires only constant time. If we consider combined complexity, then CQ answering is already NP-hard, so an additional step that non-deterministically guesses a suitable 'good' subset of query atoms causes no further increase in complexity.

Results for Non-Horn DLs. Recall that for DLs that are capable of expressing disjunction, a universal model does not exist in general, so to decide whether a given tuple is an answer to a UCQ $\bigvee_i q_i$, we need to verify that in every model $\mathcal{I}$ of the KB $\mathcal{K}$, we have $\boldsymbol{a} \in \mathsf{ans}(q_i, \mathcal{I})$ for some q_i. The loss of a universal model has a major impact on the complexity of query answering. Data complexity becomes coNP-complete-hard [164,193], and for combined complexity, query answering typically becomes harder by one exponential. Over the last decade, 2Exp upper bounds for answering CQs or extensions thereof have been obtained for many expressive DLs for which satisfiability and entailment are Exp-complete, such as $\mathcal{SHIQ}$ [56,89], $\mathcal{SHOQ}$ [90], $\mathcal{ZIQ}$, $\mathcal{ZOQ}$, and $\mathcal{ZOI}$ [57]. These bounds apply for PEQs as well, and they are tight for CQs in every DL that contains $\mathcal{ALCI}$ [147] or $\mathcal{SH}$ [80]. For all DLs between $\mathcal{ALC}$ and $\mathcal{ALCHQ}$, the succinctness gap between PEQs and UCQs makes a difference: UCQs can be answered in single-exponential time [147,167], but PEQs need double-exponential time in the worst case [169].

The results above have been obtained using a variety of techniques, such as automata [57,58], resolution [158,176], or modified tableaux [144,164]. In most other cases, query answering algorithms can be viewed as comprising two main steps. In the first step, partial assignments from the query variables to the individuals occurring in the ABox are used to generate an exponential number of new query answering problems that can be answered over restricted tree-like interpretations. In a second stage, queries over tree-shaped interpretations are answered using techniques like *rolling-up* [54,89,110] that encodes the queries into concepts, or *knot* [79,82] and *domino* [78] techniques that break all possible interpretations into small structures.

The loss of the universal model property is particularly problematic for DLs that simultaneously support inverse roles, nominals, and number restrictions, like $\mathcal{ALCOIQ}$ and its extensions, since these logics also lack the forest-like models that other logics enjoy. This makes the query answering problem so challenging that it has still not been successfully solved. Answering CQs is known to be hard for N2Exp for $\mathcal{ALCOIQ}$ (in fact, for the slightly weaker $\mathcal{ALCOIF}$) [91], and decidable for $\mathcal{ALCHOIQ}$ [191], but no elementary upper bounds on its complexity have been established. For $\mathcal{SHOIQ}$, decidability of CQs remains open, although UCQs are known to be undecidable in the closely related logic that extends $\mathcal{ALCOIQ}$ with a transitive closure operator on roles [165].

6   Navigational Queries

The last decade has seen a huge growth of applications that store and query data that has a relatively simple structure, but that is highly connected and does not comply to a fixed, rigid relational schema. This includes, for example, applications in which the data stems from the so-called web of linked data, or from social, biological, and chemical networks. While CQs and UCQs are the predominant query languages for relational databases, they are widely considered to be insufficient for this kind of applications, since they cannot express even basic reachability queries or retrieve pairs of objects that are connected by a path with certain features. Instead, for querying this kind of data, one is interested in so-called 'navigational' query languages.

The most basic navigational query language is *regular path queries (RPQs)*, which allow one to find all pairs of objects that are connected by a chain of roles (binary relations, in the database setting) that comply with a given regular language. In two-way RPQs (2RPQs), the vocabulary of the regular language comprises both roles and their inverses. We note that 2RPQs lie at the heart of XPath [69], which is the standard query language for querying XML documents, and are also present in SPARQL 1.1 [106], where they go by the name of *property paths*. By combining (2)RPQs and CQs, we obtain *conjunctive (2)RPQs*, allowing one to search for patterns that conjunctively combine regular paths.

Within the database community, there have been considerable research efforts devoted to studying the properties of these navigational query languages, developing query answering algorithms for them, and extending these languages with yet more features to meet the needs of applications. In the past few years, the DL research community has also begun to explore the use of navigational query languages for OMQA. This chapter provides an overview of this recent and ongoing line of research.

6.1   Regular Path Queries and Their Extensions

We start by formally defining the language of C2RPQs. They are syntactically very similar to CQs, but the atoms of the form $R(t, t')$ are generalized to $L(t, t')$, where L is a regular language over the alphabet of role names and their inverses. Intuitively, a pair of objects satisfies such an atom if they are connected via a chain of roles whose label belongs to L. The language L can be represented either by regular expressions or non-deterministic finite state automata (NFAs); the latter representation is known to be exponentially more succinct [77]. We note that the complexity results we mention in this chapter were shown for regular expressions in the case of lower bounds, and NFA for upper bounds, hence they all hold independently of the representation.

Definition 9. *Recall that* $\mathsf{N}_\mathsf{R}^\pm$ *contains all role names and their inverses. A conjunctive two-way regular path query (C2RPQ)* $q(\boldsymbol{x}) = \exists \boldsymbol{y}.\varphi$ *where* $\boldsymbol{x}$ *and* $\boldsymbol{y}$ *are tuples of variables, and* φ *is a conjunction of atoms of the forms:*

(i) $A(t)$*, where* $A \in \mathsf{N}_\mathsf{C}$ *and* $t \in \mathsf{N}_\mathsf{I} \cup \boldsymbol{x} \cup \boldsymbol{y}$*, and*

(ii) $L(t, t')$, where L is (an NFA or regular expression defining) a regular language over $\mathsf{N}_\mathsf{R}^\pm \cup \{A? \mid A \in \mathsf{N}_\mathsf{C}\}$, and $t, t' \in \mathsf{N}_\mathsf{I} \cup \boldsymbol{x} \cup \boldsymbol{y}$.

Conjunctive (one-way) regular path queries (CRPQs) are obtained by disallowing symbols from $\mathsf{N}_\mathsf{R}^\pm \setminus \mathsf{N}_\mathsf{R}$ in atoms of type (ii). Two-way regular path queries (2RPQs) consist of a single atom of type (ii) such that t and t' are both answer variables. Regular path queries (RPQs) are 2RPQs that do not use any roles from $\mathsf{N}_\mathsf{R}^\pm \setminus \mathsf{N}_\mathsf{R}$.

To define the semantics of C2RPQs, we proceed as for CQs by defining a notion of match. As a first step, we must specify how the atoms of the form $L(t, t')$ should be interpreted.

A *path* from e_0 to e_n in interpretation $\mathcal{I}$ is a sequence $e_0 u_1 e_1 u_2 \ldots u_n e_n$ with $n \geq 0$ such that every e_i is an element from $\Delta^\mathcal{I}$, every u_i is a symbol from $\mathsf{N}_\mathsf{R}^\pm \cup \{A? \mid A \in \mathsf{N}_\mathsf{C}\}$, and for every $1 \leq i \leq n$:

- If $u_i = A?$, then $e_{i-1} = e_i \in A^\mathcal{I}$;
- If $u_i = R \in \mathsf{N}_\mathsf{R}^\pm$, then $(e_{i-1}, e_i) \in R^\mathcal{I}$.

The *label* $\lambda(p)$ of path $p = e_0 u_1 e_1 u_2 \ldots u_n e_n$ is the word $u_1 u_2 \ldots u_n$. Note that if $p = e_0$, then we define $\lambda(p)$ to be ε. For every language L over $\mathsf{N}_\mathsf{R}^\pm \cup \{A? \mid A \in \mathsf{N}_\mathsf{C}\}$, the semantics of L w.r.t. interpretation $\mathcal{I}$ is defined as follows:

$$L^\mathcal{I} = \{(e_0, e_n) \mid \text{there is some path } p \text{ from } e_0 \text{ to } e_n \text{ with } \lambda(p) \in L\}$$

A *match* for a C2RPQ q in an interpretation $\mathcal{I}$ is a mapping π from the terms in q to elements in $\Delta^\mathcal{I}$ such that

- $\pi(c) = c^\mathcal{I}$ for each $c \in \mathsf{N}_\mathsf{I}$,
- $\pi(t) \in A^\mathcal{I}$ for each atom $A(t)$ in q, and
- $(\pi(t), \pi(t')) \in L^\mathcal{I}$ for each $L(t, t')$ in q.

Finally, using this notion of match, we can define what it means for a tuple to be an *answer* to a C2RPQ $q(\boldsymbol{x})$ in interpretation $\mathcal{I}$:

$$\mathsf{ans}(q, \mathcal{I}) = \{e \mid e = \pi(\boldsymbol{x}) \text{ for some match } \pi \text{ for } q \text{ in } \mathcal{I}\}$$

We will again be interested in the certain answers, that is, the tuples of individuals $\boldsymbol{a}$ for which $\boldsymbol{a}^\mathcal{I} \in \mathsf{ans}(q, \mathcal{I})$ for every model $\mathcal{I}$ of the KB. Importantly, C2RPQs share with CQs the property of being preserved under homomorphisms, the certain answers to a C2RPQ q over an $\mathcal{ELHI}_\perp$ KB $\mathcal{K}$ coincide with the answers to q in the canonical model $\mathcal{I}_\mathcal{K}$ of $\mathcal{K}$.

Example 23. The following CRPQ is similar to the CQ q_3 and the UCQ q_4 in Example 19: it retrieves dishes y that contain a spicy ingredient, together with the location x where they are served. However, unlike q_3 and q_4, this query can find the spicy component no matter how many hasIngredient steps away it is.

$$q_6(y, x) = \exists z.\mathsf{serves}(x, y) \wedge \mathsf{hasIngredient}^*\mathsf{Spicy}?(y, z)$$

The following one-atom CRPQ can express the infinite FO query of Example 9:

$$q_7(x) = \exists y.\mathsf{hasIngredient}^*\mathsf{Spicy?}(x, y)$$

In fact, it is also possible to compute the answers to this query using a (non-conjunctive) 2RPQ. Since 2RPQs do not support existential variables, we cannot use $\mathsf{hasIngredient}^*\mathsf{Spicy?}(x, y)$ since it will only allow us to retrieve the values of x whose spicy component y happens to be an ABox individual, which need not be the case in general. To make sure that all x with an spicy component are found, we can use the following slightly modified query q_8:

$$q_8(x, y) = \mathsf{hasIngredient}^*\mathsf{Spicy?}\Sigma^*(x, y)$$

where $\Sigma = \mathsf{N}_\mathsf{R}^\pm \cap \mathsf{sig}(\mathcal{K})$. Observe that the language Σ^* allows us to reach some ABox individual starting from any element in $\mathcal{I}_\mathcal{K}$. It follows that whenever there is a match π for q_7, possibly mapping y to an anonymous object, there will be a match π' for q_8 such that $\pi(x) = \pi'(x)$ and $\pi'(x) \in \mathsf{Ind}(\mathcal{A})$. Thus, the query q_7 is equivalent to the projection of q_8 onto its first component, or more formally, $\mathsf{cert}(q_7, \mathcal{K}) = \{a \mid (a, b) \in \mathsf{cert}(q_8, \mathcal{K}) \text{for some} b\}$, for every knowledge base $\mathcal{K}$. ▲

We note that C(2)RPQs are strictly more expressive than CQs. Indeed, every CQ is also a C2RPQ, but there exist RPQs (like $\mathsf{Spicy}^*(x, y)$) that cannot be expressed as a CQ (nor as an FO query). The language of Datalog queries is in turn strictly more expressive than C2RPQs. It is not hard to show that every C2RPQ can equivalently expressed as a Datalog query. In fact, C2RPQs fall inside the *linear* fragment of Datalog that restricts the use of recursion by allowing at most one recursive predicate in each rule body[12].

C2RPQs are in general better behaved computationally than full Datalog. Take for example the fundamental analysis task of query containment, which consists in deciding whether the answer to one query is always contained in the answer to another query over every possible database. Query containment of Datalog queries is known to be undecidable [198], while this problem has been shown decidable even for extensions of C2RPQs [44,55,84,180] and in the presence of constraints [61,99]. Moreover, as we shall see in Sect. 7, Datalog query answering over DL knowledge bases is undecidable even for very simple DLs [144]. In contrast, C2RPQs are decidable even for very expressive DLs [57].

The increased expressiveness of C2RPQs, and in particular their ability to express simple recursive queries like reachability, together with their good computational properties, make them a very appealing query language for OMQA. They are especially relevant when querying KBs formulated in lightweight DLs, since the query language can compensate for limited expressivity of the DL (e.g., inability to propagate information over roles in DL-Lite$_R$, lack of inverses in $\mathcal{EL}$).

---

[12] A predicate is called *recursive* if it occurs in a cycle in the dependency graph of the Datalog program, whose nodes are the program's predicates and which contains an edge between two predicates whenever there is a rule that contains one of the predicates in the body and the other in the head.

Example 24. The query $q_7 = \exists y.\mathsf{Spicy}^*(x,y)$ can be seen as a C2RPQ rewriting of the query $\mathsf{Spicy}(x)$ w.r.t. the TBox $\mathcal{T} = \{\exists\mathsf{hasIngredient}.\mathsf{Spicy}\sqsubseteq\mathsf{Spicy}\}$. There is no DL-Lite$_\mathcal{R}$ TBox equivalent to this TBox, and the desired meaning of $\mathsf{Spicy}(x)$ is not captured by any FO query over DL-Lite.   ▲

6.2   Answering 2RPQs

In this section, we present an algorithm for answering 2RPQs in $\mathcal{ELHI}_\perp$. In 2RPQs, there are no existentially qualified variables, hence it is enough to consider matches to the named individuals. A straightforward algorithm for evaluating a 2RPQ $L(x,y)$ would first guess a pair of individuals (a,b), and then check whether there is a path between a and b whose label complies with L. However, checking the existence of such a path is still challenging: although this chain starts and ends in the 'core' of the canonical model, it need not be fully contained in it. Indeed, a path between two individuals in $\mathcal{I}_\mathcal{K}$ may still need to go (possibly quite deep) into the anonymous part and come back out in order to satisfy the regular expressions in the query, as we illustrate next.

Example 25. Reconsider KB $\mathcal{K}_5$ from Example 20. The mapping $\pi(x) = \pi(y) = p$ is a match for q_8, hence $(p,p) \in \mathsf{ans}(q_8, \mathcal{I}_{\mathcal{K}_5})$. However, the fact that there is a $\mathsf{hasIngredient}^*\mathsf{Spicy}?\Sigma^*$-labelled path from p to p is only witnessed by the path of the form

$$p \;\mathsf{hasIngredient}\; e_1 \;\mathsf{Spicy}?\; e_1 \;\mathsf{hasIngredient}^-\; p$$

or by longer paths that have this one as a suffix. Similarly, all paths witnessing that $\pi(x) = \pi(y) = b$ is a match for q_8 (and hence $(b,b) \in \mathsf{ans}(q_8, \mathcal{I}_{\mathcal{K}_5})$) need to go two steps into the anonymous part and pass by e_4. That is, we need to navigate the path

$$p \;\mathsf{hasIngredient}\; e_3 \;\mathsf{hasIngredient}\; e_4 \;\mathsf{Spicy}?\; e_4 \;\mathsf{hasIngredient}^-\, e_3 \;\mathsf{hasIngredient}^-\, p$$

in order to satisfy the regular expression.   ▲

To describe how to address this problem, let us first suppose that the regular language in the 2RPQ is given by an NFA α (as mentioned earlier, this is without loss of generality, since regular expressions are easily translated into NFAs). Our strategy for deciding the existence of a suitable path is to define a relation Loop_α that stores all possible 'loops' through the anonymous part of $\mathcal{I}_\mathcal{K}$ that can be used to partially satisfy α. That is, we store every path that starts and ends at a given individual a and takes the query automaton α from state s to state s'. Intuitively, if such a loop exists at the individual a, then we may 'jump' directly from (a,s) to (a,s') when looking for a path between two individuals, and in this way we can avoid navigating the anonymous part in our algorithm.

An important observation that we can draw from the construction of the canonical model is that the conjunction of concept names that an object satisfies uniquely determines everything that occurs 'below it' in the anonymous part.

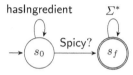

Fig. 4. NFA α_8 for the regular expression hasIngredient*Spicy?Σ^* from query q_8.

Hence, the relevant loops from a state s to a state s' can be characterized in terms of the conjunctions of concepts that enforce them. We thus define Loop_α as a relation that associates with each pair of states s, s' from α a set of conjunctions M of concept names, in such a way that the following holds:

(†) $M \in \mathsf{Loop}_\alpha[s, s']$ iff for every individual a, we have that $a \in M^{\mathcal{I}_\mathcal{K}}$ implies that there exists a path $p = e_0 u_1 e_1 u_2 \ldots u_n e_n$ in $\mathcal{I}_\mathcal{K}$ such that $e_0 = e_n = a$, e_i is of the form $a \cdot w$ for $0 < i < n$, and $\lambda(p) \in L(\alpha_{s,s'})$, where $\alpha_{s,s'}$ obtained from α by making s the starting state and s' the unique final state.

Example 26. In Fig. 4, we display an NFA α_8 representing the (regular language corresponding to the) regular expression hasIngredient*Spicy?Σ^* from the query q_8. Apart from the trivial loops (that is, paths of length 0 from an individual and state to itself), we have that:

- PizzaCalabrese $\in \mathsf{Loop}_{\alpha_8}(s_0, s_f)$, since from any object e that belongs to PizzaCalabrese we can walk one hasIngredient step to an instance e' of Nduja, which is also Spicy (such an object e' exists in the canonical model due to inclusion PizzaCalabrese $\sqsubseteq \exists$hasIngredient.(Nduja $\sqcap$ Spicy) in saturate($\mathcal{T}_5$)). Since the object e' satisfies Spicy, we can move to s_f while staying at e', and then we can take a hasIngredient$^-$ step back to the original e, while staying in the final state s_f.
- PenneArrabiata $\in \mathsf{Loop}_{\alpha_8}(s_0, s_f)$, since from any object e that is of type PenneArrabiata, we can walk one hasIngredient step to an instance e' of ArrabiataSauce, and then take a second hasIngredient step to an instance e'' of Peperoncino, which is also Spicy (again, the existence of e' and e'' is ensured by corresponding axioms in saturate($\mathcal{T}_5$)). Since e'' satisfies Spicy, we can move to s_f while staying at e', and then we can take a hasIngredient$^-$ step back to e', and another one to e, while remaining in final state s_f. ▲

A possible way to test whether $M \in \mathsf{Loop}_\alpha[s, s']$ is to explicitly compute the full table Loop_α. This can be done inductively using the following rules[13], obtained by adapting existing constructions[14] for $\mathcal{ELH}$ and DL-Lite$_\mathcal{R}$ to $\mathcal{ELHI}_\perp$.

(L1) For every $s \in S$: $\mathsf{Loop}_\alpha[s, s] = \mathsf{N_C}$.
(L2) If $M_1 \in \mathsf{Loop}_\alpha[s_1, s_2]$ and $M_2 \in \mathsf{Loop}_\alpha[s_2, s_3]$, then $M_1 \sqcap M_2 \in \mathsf{Loop}_\alpha[s_1, s_3]$.

---

[13] As earlier, we treat conjunctions of concepts as sets, ignoring order and repetitions.
[14] We note that for $\mathcal{ELH}$ and DL-Lite$_\mathcal{R}$, the construction is simpler as we only need to store concept names, rather than conjunctions of concept names.

(L3) If $\{C_1, \ldots, C_n\} \subseteq \mathsf{N_C}$, $\mathcal{T} \models C_1 \sqcap \cdots \sqcap C_n \sqsubseteq A$, and $(s_1, A?, s_2) \in \delta$, then $C_1 \sqcap \cdots \sqcap C_n \in \mathsf{Loop}_\alpha[s_1, s_2]$.

(L4) If $\{C_1, \ldots, C_n\} \subseteq \mathsf{N_C}$, $\mathcal{T} \models C_1 \sqcap \cdots \sqcap C_n \sqsubseteq \exists R.D$, $\mathcal{T} \models R \sqsubseteq R'$, $\mathcal{T} \models R \sqsubseteq R''$, $(s_1, R', s_2) \in \delta$, $D \in \mathsf{Loop}_\alpha[s_2, s_3]$, and $(s_3, R''^-, s_4) \in \delta$, then $C_1 \sqcap \cdots \sqcap C_n \in \mathsf{Loop}_\alpha[s_1, s_4]$.

The resulting table is exactly the desired relation described by (†), see [32] for a formal proof of the analogous results for $\mathcal{ELH}$ and DL-Lite$_{\mathcal{R}}$. Instead of building the full table, another possibility is to add a set of axioms that reduce testing $M \in \mathsf{Loop}_\alpha[s, s']$ to an entailment test in $\mathcal{ELHI}_\perp$. The latter alternative has been used for $\mathcal{ELHI}_\perp$ [27], but for a more involved notion of loop designed for an extension of C2RPQs.

Now that we have a means of determining which loops through the anonymous part are available from a given ABox individual, we are ready to present the evaluation algorithm EvalAtom in Fig. 5. It takes as input an NFA $\alpha = (S, \Sigma, \delta, s_0, F)$, an $\mathcal{ELHI}_\perp$ KB $\mathcal{K} = (\mathcal{T}, \mathcal{A})$, and a pair of individuals (a, b) from $\mathcal{A}$, and it decides whether $(a, b) \in \mathsf{cert}(\alpha(x, y), \mathcal{K})$. First, there is an initial consistency check in Step 1 to determine whether the input KB is satisfiable (this step can be skipped for $\mathcal{ELHI}$ KBs, which are always satisfiable). If the KB is shown to be unsatisfiable, then the query trivially holds, so the algorithm outputs yes. Otherwise, we initialize current with the pair (a, s_0) and count to 0. We also compute the maximum value max of the counter, which corresponds to the longest length of path that needs to be considered. At every iteration of the while loop (Step 3), we start with a single pair (c, s) stored in current and then proceed to guess a new pair (d, s') together with either a transition of the form (s, σ, s'), or a conjunction of concept names $M \in \mathsf{Loop}_\alpha[s, s']$. The first option corresponds to taking a step in the ABox, whereas the second corresponds to a shortcut through the anonymous part. In the first case, the idea is that we would like to append σd to the path guessed so far, but to do so, we must ensure that the conditions of paths are satisfied. This is the purpose of the entailment checks in Step 2(c). If we choose the second option, then we must check that the concept names in the selected conjunction M are entailed at the current individual. In both cases, if the applicable check succeeds, then we place (d, s') in current and increment count. We exit the while loop once we have reached the maximum counter value or the pair in count takes the form (b, s_f) with s_f a final state. In the latter case, we have managed to guess a path with the required properties, and so the algorithm returns yes.

Example 27. We describe a successful run of the algorithm EvalAtom on input α_8 from q_8, the KB $\mathcal{K}_5$ from Example 20, and the pair (p, p). We start with current $= (p, s_0)$. In the first iteration, in Step 3(b) we guess (p, s_f) and PizzaCalabrese $\in \mathsf{Loop}_\alpha[s_0, s_f]$. Then in Step 3(d) we verify that $p = p$ and $\mathcal{K}_5 \models$ PizzaCalabrese(p). Since we now have a pair (p, s_f) and s_f is a final state of α_8, we exit the while loop and in Step 4, we return yes. This is correct, since $(p, p) \in \mathsf{cert}(q_8, \mathcal{K}_5)$. ▲

ALGORITHM EvalAtom

INPUT: NFA $\alpha = (S, \Sigma, \delta, s_0, F)$ with $\Sigma \subseteq N_R^\pm \cup \{A? \mid A \in N_C\}$, $\mathcal{ELHI}_\perp$ KB $(\mathcal{T}, \mathcal{A})$, $(a, b) \in \mathsf{Ind}(\mathcal{A}) \times \mathsf{Ind}(\mathcal{A})$

1. Test whether $(\mathcal{T}, \mathcal{A})$ is satisfiable, output **yes** if not.
2. Initialize current $= (a, s_0)$ and count $= 0$. Set max $= |\mathcal{A}| \cdot |S| + 1$.
3. While count $<$ max and current $\notin \{(b, s_f) \mid s_f \in F\}$
   (a) Let current $= (c, s)$.
   (b) Guess a pair $(d, s') \in \mathsf{Ind}(\mathcal{A}) \times S$ and either $(s, \sigma, s') \in \delta$ or $M \in \mathsf{Loop}_\alpha[s, s']$.
   (c) If (s, σ, s') was guessed
       - If $\sigma \in N_R^\pm$, then verify that $\mathcal{T}, \mathcal{A} \models \sigma(c, d)$, and return **no** if not.
       - If $\sigma = A?$, then verify that $c = d$ and $\mathcal{T}, \mathcal{A} \models A(c)$, and return **no** if not.
   (d) If M was guessed, then verify that $c = d$ and that $\mathcal{T}, \mathcal{A} \models B(c)$ for every concept name $B \in M$, and return **no** if not.
   (e) Set current $= (d, s')$ and increment count.
4. If current $= (b, s_f)$ for some $s_f \in F$, return **yes**. Else return **no**.

Fig. 5. Non-deterministic algorithm for 2RPQ answering in $\mathcal{ELHI}_\perp$.

The correctness of this algorithm was proved for DL-Lite$_\mathcal{R}$ and $\mathcal{ELH}$ in [32], and the result can also be extended to $\mathcal{ELHI}_\perp$:

Proposition 1. *For every 2RPQ $q = \alpha(x, y)$, $\mathcal{ELHI}_\perp$ KB $\mathcal{K} = (\mathcal{T}, \mathcal{A})$, and pair of individuals (a, b) from $\mathsf{Ind}(\mathcal{A})$: $(a, b) \in \mathsf{cert}(q, \mathcal{K})$ if and only if there is some execution of $\mathsf{EvalAtom}(\alpha, \mathcal{K}, (a, b))$ that returns* **yes**.

The algorithm EvalAtom needs to make calls to procedures that decide satisfiability, instance checking, and membership of a conjunction of concept names in the Loop$_\alpha$ table. We have discussed that for $\mathcal{ELHI}_\perp$, satisfiability and instance checking are feasible in Exp in combined complexity. Computing the Loop$_\alpha$ table takes polynomially many iterations in the size of α and $\mathcal{T}$, and each iteration may need to do some subsumption tests (for (L3) and (L4)), which require at most single exponential time. Hence, testing for loops can also be achieved using no more than single exponential time. Thus, we can view EvalAtom as a non-deterministic polynomial-time procedure that makes external calls to Exp procedures. Since $\mathrm{NP}^{\mathrm{Exp}} = \mathrm{Exp}$, we obtain an Exp upper bound for 2RPQ answering in $\mathcal{ELHI}_\perp$. To obtain a matching hardness result, we recall that instance checking is Exp-hard for $\mathcal{ELHI}_\perp$, and observe that instance checking can be reduced to answering a simple 2RPQ given by a regular expression of the form R or $A?$. Thus, 2RPQ answering is Exp-complete in combined complexity. For data complexity, we observe that computing the Loop$_\alpha$ table can be done independently of the ABox $\mathcal{A}$, hence it takes only constant time in $|\mathcal{A}|$ to test whether $B \in \mathsf{Loop}_\alpha[s, s']$. Since in data complexity, satisfiability and entailment in $\mathcal{ELHI}_\perp$ are P-complete, we obtain a tight P upper bound for answering 2RPQs.

Since the complexity of EvalAtom is dominated by the complexity of entailment and instance checking, we can obtain better upper bounds for 2RPQ answering in sublogics of $\mathcal{ELHI}_\perp$ that are not hard for EXP. Indeed, both combined and data complexity drop to P-complete for $\mathcal{ELH}$ [19], and thus 2RPQ answering has the same complexity as subsumption and instance checking in $\mathcal{ELH}$. For DL-Lite$_\mathcal{R}$, satisfiability, subsumption and instance checking are known to feasible in NLOGSPACE in combined complexity and in $AC_0 \subsetneq$ LOGSPACE in data complexity [52]. We do not obtain the same upper bounds for 2RPQ answering, but we can use these facts to argue that EvalAtom gives us P and NLOGSPACE upper bounds in combined in data complexity, respectively; both bounds are known to be tight [32].

Theorem 17 ([32]). *For $\mathcal{ELHI}_\perp$, 2RPQ answering is* EXP-*complete in combined complexity and* P-*complete in data complexity. For DL-Lite$_\mathcal{R}$ and $\mathcal{ELH}$, the combined complexity drops to* P-*complete. In data complexity, the problem is* NLOGSPACE-*complete for DL-Lite$_\mathcal{R}$, and* P *complete for $\mathcal{ELH}$.*

6.3   Extending the Approach to C2RPQs

Recall that 2RPQs are single-atom queries that do not contain quantified variables. The latter restriction turns out to be inessential, as the complexity results for 2RPQs hold also for single-atom queries with quantified variables. This can be easily shown for queries of the form $\exists x.\,\alpha(x,t)$ (with t a term), $\exists x.\,\alpha(t,x)$ (with t a term), and $\exists x,y.\,\alpha(x,y)$ (with $x \neq y$). Indeed, $q(x) = \exists y.\alpha(t,y)$ can be replaced by the 2RPQ $q'(t,y) = \alpha'(t,y)$, where $L(\alpha') = L(\alpha) \cdot \Gamma^*$, where $\Gamma = \mathsf{N}_\mathsf{R}^\pm \cap \mathrm{sig}(\mathcal{K})$, and then the answers to q are obtained by projecting the answers of q' to the first position. Likewise, $\exists x.\alpha(x,t)$ can be answered by taking a 2RPQ with regular language $\Gamma^* \cdot L(\alpha)$ and $\exists x,y.\alpha(x,y)$ by using $\Gamma^* \cdot L(\alpha) \cdot \Gamma^*$. Single-atom queries of the form $\exists x.\alpha(x,x)$ also have the same complexity, but showing this requires a more intricate proof [32].

Using a similar approach, one can show that the upper bounds in Theorem 17 hold even for the more general class of C2RPQs where every existentially quantified variable occurs in at most one role atom, that is, C2RPQs with no existential join variables, since they can be answered by combining the answers to a linear number of one-atom C2RPQs.

For arbitrary C2RPQs, which may have existential join variables, we require a more complex algorithm that combines the ideas discussed in Sect. 5.2 with the loop computation from the present section. Such an algorithm has been proposed in [32] for DL-Lite$_\mathcal{R}$ and $\mathcal{ELH}$, and in [27] for handling an extension of C2RPQs over $\mathcal{ELHI}_\perp$ KBs. The basic idea is to rewrite the input C2RPQ into a set of C2RPQs for which we only need to consider matches that map all variables to ABox individuals. This may be accomplished using rewriting procedure that is quite similar in spirit to the one we described for CQs, but considerably more involved since we need to take into account possible 'loops' that go deeper into the anonymous part than the image of the query variables. By combining this extended rewriting procedure with the 2RPQ answering algorithm described in this section, the following complexity results can be shown:

Theorem 18 ([27,32]). *C2RPQ answering is*

1. NLogSpace-*complete in data complexity for DL-Lite$_\mathcal{R}$,*
2. P-*complete in data complexity for $\mathcal{ELH}$ and $\mathcal{ELHI}_\perp$,*
3. PSpace-*complete in combined complexity for DL-Lite$_\mathcal{R}$ and $\mathcal{ELH}$, and*
4. Exp-*complete in combined complexity for $\mathcal{ELHI}_\perp$.*

6.4   Results for Other DLs

The Exp upper bound in combined complexity for C2RPQs has been shown even for the significantly more expressive Horn-$\mathcal{SHOIQ}$ [166], which is in close correspondence with the Horn fragment of the expressive profiles of OWL. However, the technique employed there is quite different. In a nutshell, it considers all the (exponentially many) different ways of breaking the query into parts that are matched at the core, and parts that are matched in the trees. Answering the latter reduces to C2RPQ answering in the simpler Horn-$\mathcal{SHIQ}$. The authors use automata on infinite trees for this purpose, but the technique we have described could also be used: although presented for lightweight DLs [32], it is based on the earlier algorithm for Horn-$\mathcal{SHIQ}$ and extends easily to the latter. For the parts that are matched at the core, the authors use an explicit, step-by-step computation of all the possible relevant paths between ABox individuals, possibly passing by the anonymous part. This is somehow similar in spirit to the loop computation we have discussed, but necessarily more involved, since the relevant paths in Horn-$\mathcal{SHOIQ}$ are significantly more complex than simple loops (mainly due to the almost complete loss of the forest-like structure of the canonical models) and uses a Horn-$\mathcal{SHIQ}$ C2RPQ answering algorithm as an oracle. The results of [166] can be lifted to P2RPQs (defined analogously to PEQs) and cover also Horn-$\mathcal{SROIQ}$, which is even more expressive than Horn-$\mathcal{SHOIQ}$ and underlies OWL 2, the newest version of OWL [170]. However, for the latter DL, C2RPQ and P2RPQ answering are 2Exp-complete in combined complexity. If we consider data complexity, P2RPQ answering in all Horn logics between $\mathcal{EL}$ and Horn-$\mathcal{SROIQ}$ is complete for P, and all the algorithms we have mentioned run in polynomial time in the size of the ABox.

  In non-Horn DLs, the complexity picture is very similar to CQs: the lack of universal models raises the data complexity to coNP-hard [193], and the combined complexity to 2Exp-complete, for every DL between $\mathcal{ALC}$ and the highly expressive $\mathcal{ZIQ}$, $\mathcal{ZOQ}$ and $\mathcal{ZOI}$ [57,58]. The main difference with the (U)CQ setting is that even restricted classes of C2RPQs are 2Exp-hard for $\mathcal{ALC}$ [169] (by contrast, CQ answering in $\mathcal{ALCHQ}$ is in Exp), and that C2RPQs are undecidable already for $\mathcal{ALCOIF}$.

6.5   Navigational Queries Beyond (C)(2)RPQs

There has been considerable interest in recent years in extending (C)(2)RPQs with additional features that are considered important for applications. In particular, a useful XPath construct that is missing in C2RPQs is the possibility of using *test operators*, also known as *nesting*, to express sophisticated conditions along navigation paths. One simple way to introduce nesting into (C)(2)RPQs is to replace regular expression by so-called *nested regular expressions (NREs)*, in which one can use $\langle \rho \rangle$ to enforce the existence of an outgoing path that satisfies ρ, where ρ may itself be an NRE. For example, one could use ⟨awarded MichelinStar?⟩ to test whether a restaurant has been awarded a Michelin star and the NRE (hasWorkedAt Restaurant? ⟨awarded MichelinStar?⟩ hasWorkedAt⁻)* to find chefs that are connected via a sequence of chefs such that every pair of adjacent chefs has worked at the same Michelin-starred restaurant. NREs were initially introduced for the purpose of defining nSPARQL, a navigational extension of SPARQL [174]. Subsequent investigations into the use of NREs for querying graph databases revealed them to have desirable computational properties [22, 23].

The query answering problem for (C)N2RPQs (defined using NREs) in the presence of DL ontologies was recently investigated in [27]. In that work, the authors show that, for a wide range of DLs, adding nesting to (C)2RPQs does not increase the worst-case data complexity of query answering. For expressive DLs, this can be shown by reducing CN2RPQs to plain C2RPQs, by introducing new concepts in the TBox that capture the nested expressions. For $\mathcal{ELHI}_\perp$ and its sublogics, one can use a more sophisticated version of the rewriting and loop procedures mentioned in Sect. 6.3. However, the news is not all positive as it was further shown that adding nesting leads to EXP-hardness in combined complexity, even for (non-conjunctive) 2NRPQs and the lightweight DLs DL-Lite and $\mathcal{EL}$. This negative result contrasts sharply with the tractable data complexity for the same setting but without nesting (cf. Theorem 17).

The preceding results have been complemented by three other recent works [43, 132, 203]. In [203], the authors consider the problem of answering (a slight extension[15] of) CNRPQs over OWL 2 EL knowledge bases. With regards to combined complexity, they establish a PSPACE upper bound for CNRPQs and a P upper bound for NRPQs, thereby demonstrating that it is the combination of nesting and inverses that leads to EXP-hardness. In [132], the authors investigate a variety of different XPath-inspired query languages, whose most expressive member essentially corresponds to N2RPQs extended with negation over unary and binary expressions. It is shown that negation over binary expressions immediately leads to undecidability, and the query answering problem for the path-positive fragment (allowing only unary negation) is CONP-complete in data complexity and EXP-complete in combined complexity for both DL-Lite$_R$ and $\mathcal{EL}$ (the EXP upper bound is shown for $\mathcal{ELHI}_\perp$). Finally, in [43], the authors compare three different approaches to extending C2RPQs with nesting, with PFO+TC1 (positive FO queries with transitive closure on binary predicates) being the most expressive language. They establish a general decidability result for PFO+TC1 queries that holds for all DLs satisfying a quasi-forest model property, and for the DL $\mathcal{S}$, they show $(k+2)$-EXPTIME-hardness for queries with k levels of nesting of the transitive closure operator.

---

[15] The query languages considered in [132, 203] also allow unary tests to be combined using conjunctive and disjunction. A similar construct was considered in [31].

The issue of defining interesting path query languages that support nesting remains an active area of research in the database community, and there have been several recent proposals, including: regular queries [180], guarded regular queries [33], nested monadically defined queries [192], and the more general family of nested flag-and-check queries [44]. Beyond nesting and negation, (C)2RPQs have also been extended with path variables and regular relations [21].

7   Undecidability of Answering FO and Datalog Queries

We have seen in the preceding sections how various restricted forms of first-order and Datalog queries can be answered over Horn DL knowledge bases. Moreover, the procedures that we have devised run in polynomial time in the size of the ABox, making them suitable for applications involving large amounts of data. It is natural to wonder whether these nice computational properties extend to more expressive query languages, and in particular, to the classes of (full) first-order and Datalog queries defined in Sect. 3.2. Unfortunately, we will shall see that the answer is negative: not only do we lose tractability, but we even *lose decidability*. It is for this reason that full first-order and Datalog queries are not considered suitable query languages for OMQA.

7.1   First-Order Queries

Because of the open-world semantics of DL knowledge bases, it is possible to reduce the validity problem for first-order sentences to the problem of answering Boolean FO queries over empty DL KBs. As the FO validity problem is undecidable, we obtain the following result.

Theorem 19. *First-order query answering is undecidable in every DL.*

The preceding theorem is quite discouraging, but it still leaves open the possibility that there may exist other natural classes of FO queries that are more expressive than (U)CQs, yet remain decidable in the presence of DL ontologies. Of particular interest are the *extensions of (U)CQs with negation or inequalities*, which have been extensively studied in the database setting. These query languages are formally defined as follows.

Definition 10 (Conjunctive Queries with Safe Negation). *A conjunctive query with safe negation ($CQ^{\neg s}$) is an FO query of the form $q(\boldsymbol{x}) = \exists \boldsymbol{y}\, \varphi$ where φ is a conjunction of (positive) atoms and negated atoms using variables in $\boldsymbol{x} \cup \boldsymbol{y}$ and such that every variable occurs in at least one positive atom.*

Remark 14. The requirement that every variable occurs in some positive atom is made to ensure domain independence. Dropping this condition would mean allowing queries like $\neg\mathsf{Spicy}(x)$ that are not domain independent.

Example 28. The following CQ$^{\neg s}$ finds menus whose main course is not spicy.

$$\exists y \; \mathsf{Menu}(x) \wedge \mathsf{hasMain}(x, y) \wedge \neg\mathsf{Spicy}(y)$$

This query will return all individuals m such that in every model of the KB, m belongs to Menu and has an hasMain-successor that does *not* belong to Spicy. ▲

Definition 11 (Conjunctive Queries with Inequalities). *A* conjunctive query with inequalities *(CQ$^{\neq}$) is an FO query $q(\boldsymbol{x}) = \exists \boldsymbol{y} \; \varphi$ where φ is a conjunction of atoms and inequalities $t_1 \neq t_2$ whose variables are contained in $\boldsymbol{x} \cup \boldsymbol{y}$.*

Example 29. The following CQ$^{\neq}$ could be used to to find menus that contain at least three courses:

$$\exists y_1 y_2 y_3 \; \mathsf{Menu}(x) \wedge \mathsf{hasCourse}(x, y_1) \wedge \mathsf{hasCourse}(x, y_2) \wedge \mathsf{hasCourse}(x, y_3)$$
$$\wedge \; y_1 \neq y_2 \wedge y_1 \neq y_3 \wedge y_2 \neq y_3$$

Observe that this query could be captured using the concept $\mathsf{Menu} \sqcap \; \geq$ 3hasCourse in DLs that allow for conjunction and unqualified number restrictions. In effect, by allowing inequalities in the language, we are able to express some limited form of number restrictions.

We could also use inequalities to find two menus offered by the same establishment that contain different dessert courses:

$$\exists y_1 y_2 z_1 z_2 \; \mathsf{offers}(x, y_1) \wedge \mathsf{Menu}(y_1) \wedge \mathsf{hasDessert}(y_1, z_1) \wedge$$
$$\mathsf{offers}(x, y_2) \wedge \mathsf{Menu}(y_2) \wedge \mathsf{hasDessert}(y_2, z_2) \wedge z_1 \neq z_2$$

This query is not expressible as a DL concept. ▲

Analogously to how we defined UCQs, we can define UCQ$^{\neg s}$s (resp. UCQ$^{\neq}$s) as disjunctions of CQ$^{\neg s}$s (resp. CQ$^{\neq}$s) that have the same answer variables.

The complexity and decidability of (unions of) CQ$^{\neg s}$ and CQ$^{\neq}$ was first investigated in [185], but it is only more recently that some key questions, such as the decidability of answering CQ$^{\neg s}$s and CQ$^{\neq}$s in DL-Lite$_R$, have been resolved [101]. While some open questions remain, the results obtained so far paint a decidedly negative picture:

Theorem 20. *The following problems are undecidable:*

- *CQ$^{\neg s}$ answering in DL-Lite$_R$[101]*
- *UCQ$^{\neq}$ answering in $\mathcal{EL}_\perp$ [185]*
- *CQ$^{\neq}$ answering in DL-Lite$_R$[101]*
- *CQ$^{\neq}$ answering in $\mathcal{EL}_\perp$ [122]*

We will not explain how the preceding decidability resuls are obtained, but merely note that in contrast to the query languages from the preceding sections, the answers to CQ$^{\neq}$s and CQ$^{\neg s}$s are not preserved under homomorphisms, and thus we are not able to use the universal model for query answering.

One solution that has been proposed in response to the undecidability of FO query answering is to adopt an alternative *epistemic semantics* [51]. The idea is to start with a standard DL query language $\mathcal{Q}$ (like IQs or CQs) and to introduce *epistemic atoms* of the form $\mathbf{K}q$ ($q \in \mathcal{Q}$), which are interpreted as the certain answers to q. These epistemic atoms can then be combined using the Boolean connectives and first-order logic quantifiers. To answer such a query, one may proceed by first computing the certain answers to the queries appearing in the epistemic atoms, storing the results in a database, and then evaluating a first-order query over this database. It follows that the query answering problem for the epistemic query language with embedded $\mathcal{Q}$-queries is decidable (resp. P in data complexity) in a DL $\mathcal{L}$ whenever $\mathcal{Q}$ answering in $\mathcal{L}$ is decidable (resp. P in data complexity).

Example 30. The epistemic query $\exists y \, \mathbf{K}\mathsf{Menu}(x) \wedge \mathbf{K}\mathsf{hasMain}(x, y) \wedge \neg\mathbf{K}\mathsf{Spicy}(y)$ returns all menus m that have a main dish d that is *not known to be spicy*, or more formally, d is not a certain answer to $\mathsf{Spicy}(x)$. Note that this is quite different from *knowing* that the main dish d is *not spicy* (and such a distinction may be relevant when choosing a menu!).

7.2 Datalog Queries

From the early days of description logic research, there has been significant interest in combining DLs with Datalog rules. Unfortunately, the combination of DLs and rules often leads to undecidability:

Theorem 21 ([144]). *Datalog query answering is undecidable in every DL that can express (directly or indirectly) an inclusion of the form $A \sqsubseteq \exists r.A$.*

Since $A \sqsubseteq \exists r.A$ is directly expressible in $\mathcal{EL}$ and can be simulated using the pair of DL-Lite inclusions $A \sqsubseteq \exists r$, $\exists r^- \sqsubseteq A$, we have the following:

Corollary 1. *Datalog query answering is undecidable in DL-Lite and $\mathcal{EL}$.*

It is worth noting that Datalog queries are preserved under homomorphisms, and thus, one can in principle evaluate a Datalog query over the (potentially infinite) universal model of a Horn DL knowledge base. However, running a Datalog program over the universal model leads to a new interpretation in which the domain elements may be arbitrarily connected, thus lacking the forest structure upon which many query answering techniques rely. For some restricted forms of Datalog queries, like the navigational queries from Sect. 6, it is still possible to develop techniques that exploit the forest structure of the universal model, but for general Datalog queries, the ability to arbitrarily connect unnamed objects leads to undecidability.

One simple way of regaining decidability is to enforce that Datalog rules be only applied to ABox individuals, rather than unnamed objects. This can be formalized using the notion of *(weak) DL-safety* [160,184], which requires that every variable in a rule (head) occurs in a body atom whose relation does not appear in the TBox. DL-safe and weak DL-safe Datalog are considerably less expressive as query languages over DL KBs than unrestricted Datalog, but can nevertheless express some queries that are not captured by other decidable query languages we have considered. Using similar techniques to those presented in Sect. 5 for CQ answering in $\mathcal{ELHI}_\perp$, it was shown in [81] that the complexity of answering weak DL-safe Datalog queries over Horn-$\mathcal{SHIQ}$ KBs is Exp-complete in combined complexity and P-complete in data complexity.

8   Recent and Ongoing Research in OMQA

In this section we provide an overview of recent work on OMQA and areas of ongoing research. Although we try to include many directions in which there are interesting developments going on, it is not a complete survey, and the discussion should not be considered exhaustive.

8.1   OMQA in DL-Lite

In the mid-2000's, Calvanese et al. [50,52] introduced PerfectRef (for 'perfect reformulation'), the first query rewriting algorithm for DL-Lite, which was implemented in the QUONTO system [2]. The PerfectRef algorithm produces a UCQ-rewriting of the input CQ and TBox by interleaving *rewriting steps*, in which a query atom is rewritten by 'applying' a TBox inclusion in the backwards direction (e.g., rewriting Menu(x) into $\exists y.$hasCourse(x,y) using $\exists$hasCourse $\sqsubseteq$ Menu), and *reduction steps*, in which unifiable atoms are merged (such unifications are essential to the completeness of the rewriting mechanism). The PerfectRef algorithm paved the way by showing how OMQA could be reduced to database query evaluation, but experiments showed that the UCQ-rewritings generated by PerfectRef were often extremely large (containing on the order of tens of thousands of CQs), making it very costly, and sometimes impossible, to compute and evaluate them. This spurred a whole line of research devoted to the design, implementation, and optimization of query rewriting algorithms. The RQR algorithm, proposed by Perez-Urbina, Motik and Horrocks and implemented in the REQUIEM system [175], achieved significantly better performance by transforming the input DL-Lite$_\mathcal{R}$ TBox and query into a set of first-order clauses and then applying a resolution procedure to compute a rewriting. The use of function symbols to handle existential axioms and the native support for axioms of the form $A \sqsubseteq \exists R.B$ (instead of having to simulate them via role inclusions, cf. Example 2) makes RQR more goal-oriented and allows it to avoid some unnecessary or redundant intermediate results. Further improvements were obtained by the RAPID system of Chortaras, Trivela and Stamou [67] which by virtue of its more sophisticated resolution strategy and additional optimizations is able to substantially reduce the number of 'useless' inferences.

It should be noted that both REQUIEM and (the initial version of) RAPID generate UCQ-rewritings and thus are limited by the potentially huge size of the minimal UCQ-rewriting (the same holds for other UCQ-based rewriting approaches [95,124,211]). Indeed, it is not hard to see that the smallest

UCQ-rewriting of a query may be exponentially large: take for instance the CQ $A_1(x) \wedge A_2(x) \wedge \ldots \wedge A_n(x)$ and the TBox $\{B_i^j \sqsubseteq A_i \mid 1 \leq i \leq n, 1 \leq i \leq m\}$, whose minimal UCQ-rewriting is a disjunction of $(m+1)^n$ CQs, corresponding to the $(m+1)^n$ different ways of choosing, for each $1 \leq i \leq n$, one of the concepts $A_i, B_i^1, \ldots, B_i^m$. This exponential blowup is commonly observed in practice due to the fact that real-world ontologies typically contain complex hierarchies of concepts, and thus there are often several choices of how to rewrite a given atom. Observe however that such choices can be compactly representing by adopting an alternative representation, e.g., the preceding CQ admits a short rewriting as a positive existential query $(\bigvee_{i=1}^{n}(A_i(x) \vee B_i^1(x) \vee \ldots \vee B_i^m(x)))$ or a *non-recursive Datalog* (NDL) program $(\{Q(x) \leftarrow Q_1(x), \ldots, Q_n(x)\} \cup \{Q_i(x) \leftarrow A_i(x), Q_i(x) \leftarrow B_i^j(x) \mid 1 \leq i \leq n, 1 \leq j \leq m\})$. This suggests that much more substantial gains in performance can be obtained by dropping the UCQ representation of rewritings in favour of more succinct query languages. This idea was first explored by Rosati and Almatelli whose PRESTO system [188] produces NDL-rewritings. An experimental evaluation showed it to significantly outperform the UCQ-based rewriting approaches; similar performances were obtained by RAPID$_d$, a variant of RAPID that outputs NDL-rewritings [68]. The *tree witness rewriting* of Kikot et al. [119], which is utilized by the ONTOP system [181], provides another example of an NDL-rewriting approach. An experimental comparison showed it to be the most efficient among the considered NDL approaches and also confirmed the superiority of NDL-based rewriting algorithms over UCQ-based ones. We note in passing that in addition to NDL-rewritings, there have been some recent works producing different types of PE-rewritings, such as semi-conjunctive queries (SCQs) [206] and joins of unions of conjunctive queries (JUCQs) [45,46]. In the latter work, different decompositions of the original query into subqueries give rise to a space of different JUCQ-rewritings, and a cost function is used to estimate the cost of executing a particular rewriting and to select the most efficient one.

Some further optimizations have been developed that are not applicable in every setting, but can lead to dramatic improvements in performance when they can be used. First, if one has control over the way that data is stored, then one may store concepts as integer values and assign these values in such a way that identifying the set of individuals satisfying a given concept can be achieved by posing simple range queries over the database. This technique, known as *semantic indexing*, has been shown to be very effective, and it is exploited by the UCQ-based QUEST rewriting engine of Rodriguez-Muro and Calvanese [182] and has been more recently used in combination with the aforementioned tree witness rewriting within the ONTOP system [181]. Another important type of optimization involves the use of so-called *ABox dependencies* (also known as *extensional constraints*), which are TBox inclusions that hold in the interpretation (database) associated with the ABox. Intuitively, if we know that the ABox satisfies the TBox inclusion $A \sqsubseteq B$, then it is useless to rewrite the atom $B(x)$ into $A(x)$, since whenever the ABox contains $A(a)$, it must also contain $B(a)$. In the QUEST system, the TBox is simplified by removing inclusions that are made redundant by the constraints, and this simplified TBox is used during query rewriting. Further optimizations based upon exploiting extensional constraints, as well as disjointness and functionality axioms, were developed by Rosati and implemented in the PREXTO system [183]. We should mention that both QUEST and PREXTO produce UCQs, but the rewritings they generate can be significantly smaller than those of other UCQ-based systems, since they only need to work for ABoxes satisfying the constraints, rather than for arbitrary ABoxes.

The *combined approach* of Kontchakov et al. [126] represents an entirely different approach to achieving efficient answering in DL-Lite. The basic idea is to saturate the ABox using the TBox axioms, and then to evaluate the query over the saturated ABox. More precisely, one computes, in an offline phase, a finite first-order interpretation (i.e., a relational database) that corresponds to a compact representation of the canonical model of the KB (recall that we cannot in general compute the full canonical model, as it may be infinite). During the construction of this interpretation, new ABox individuals are introduced to serve as witnesses for the existential restrictions in the TBox axioms. However, to ensure finiteness, instead of generating several (possibly infinitely many) witnesses for the same inclusion (as in the canonical model construction), we will 'reuse' the same witnessing individual. If we now evaluate the input CQ over this new saturated interpretation, then we will be sure to obtain all of the certain answers, but we may also obtain some false answers due to the reuse of witnesses. There are two ways of addressing this issue. The first possibility (adopted in [126]) is to *rewrite* the CQ in order to block spurious answers and to evaluate the rewritten query over the saturated interpretation. If the TBox is formulated in the basic dialect DL-Lite$_{core}$, then the rewriting step results in a polynomial-size FO-query. However, for DL-Lite$_R$, the rewritten query may be exponentially large. Thus, an alternative approach, proposed in a subsequent work [149] and implemented in the COMBO system, consists in evaluating the original query over the saturated interpretation to get a superset of the certain answers, and then applying an external polynomial-time filtering procedure to weed out the spurious answers. An experimental evaluation comparing COMBO with RAPID and PRESTO showed it to be comparable to these systems in simpler settings, but much more robust to increases in the size of the data or the complexity of the concept hierarchy induced by the TBox.

We note that none of the preceding rewriting algorithms for DL-Lite$_R$ is guaranteed to terminate in polynomial time. While UCQ-based rewritings are necessarily exponential in the worst case, it is natural to wonder whether polynomial rewritings can be achieved by adopting the more succinct PE, NDL, and FO representations. A first negative result was obtained by Kikot et al. [118] who proved the impossibility of generating an FO-rewriting in polynomial time (unless P = NP) but left open the existence of polysize rewritings. In a series of subsequent works [29, 120, 121], the preceding authors, joined by Bienvenu and Podolskii, established tight connections between the size of rewritings of CQs w.r.t. DL-Lite$_R$ TBoxes and the circuit complexity of certain Boolean functions, which allowed them to pinpoint the worst-case size of PE-, NDL-, and FO-rewritings under various restrictions on the TBox and the input query. In general, the news is bad: even if we assume that the ABox has been saturated (i.e., we perform query answering over the core of the canonical model), PE- and NDL-rewritings can be exponentially large, and a superpolynomial lower bound on the size of FO-rewritings holds under the widely-held complexity-theoretic assumption that NP $\nsubseteq$ P/poly [120]. For PE-rewritings, this negative result cannot be easily escaped: the exponential lower bound applies even if the query is tree-shaped [120] or if the TBox has depth 2 (i.e., it can only produce canonical models whose elements are at most two 'steps' away from the ABox) [121], and a superpolynomial lower bound has recently been shown for the very restricted setting in which the input query is a linear CQ and the TBox has depth 2 [29]. In the case of NDL-rewritings, the picture is brighter: polysize NDL-rewritings always exist for tree-shaped queries with a bounded number of leaves (and arbitrary DL-Lite$_R$ TBoxes), and for bounded treewidth queries paired with bounded depth ontologies [29]. Moreover, an analysis of the combined complexity shows that CQ answering is tractable for these classes of queries and TBoxes, suggesting that it may be possible to define NDL-rewritings that can be both generated and evaluated in polynomial time (as was done in [34] for tree-shaped CQs in DL-Lite$_{core}$). We should point out that the aforementioned negative results on the size of rewritings concern so-called *pure* rewritings, which do not use any constants other than those given in the query. Indeed, Gottlob and Schwentick [98] showed that if one admits existential quantification over two special constants (assumed to be present in every ABox), then polynomial-size NDL-rewritings exist for all CQs and DL-Lite$_R$ TBoxes, although it is unclear whether the obtained rewritings (which encode non-deterministic guesses using the special constants) can be successfully used in practice (see [93] for further discussion).

8.2   OMQA Beyond DL-Lite

We next review the OMQA algorithms and systems that have been proposed for $\mathcal{EL}$ and its Horn extensions. A Datalog rewriting for $\mathcal{ELH}$ was defined by Rosati [186] and used to establish P data complexity of CQ answering in that logic. Pérez-Urbina et al. [176] subsequently proposed a resolution-based Datalog rewriting algorithm for the much more expressive $\mathcal{ELHIO}^{\perp}$. The algorithm has been implemented in the previously mentioned REQUIEM system; it returns a UCQ-rewriting when the input ontology is in DL-Lite$_R$ and otherwise outputs a Datalog rewriting. The KYRIE system [156] of Mora and Corcho is based upon the same resolution procedure as REQUIEM, but it includes several additional optimizations that significantly improve the running time. A new version, KYRIE2, integrates optimizations based upon extensional constraints from the PREXTO system (see earlier). The first practical algorithm for CQ answering in Horn-$\mathcal{SHIQ}$, based upon Datalog rewriting, was proposed by Eiter et al. [81] and implemented in the CLIPPER system. We presented the main ideas underlying this algorithm in Sect. 5. The resolution-based RAPID system, first developed for DL-Lite$_R$, has been extended first to $\mathcal{ELHI}$ [207], and very recently to Horn-$\mathcal{SHIQ}$ [208]. It is highly optimized and outperforms CLIPPER, making it currently the most efficient approach available to handle all of Horn-$\mathcal{SHIQ}$. As noted in Sect. 5, CQ answering algorithms have been proposed for the even more expressive Horn-$\mathcal{SHOIQ}$ and Horn-$\mathcal{SROIQ}$ [166], but at the time of writing, there are no implemented systems targeting these DLs.

A highly influential line of work was initiated by Lutz et al. [146] who introduced the *combined approach*, which we have already discussed for DL-Lite but was in fact first developed to handle $\mathcal{EL}$ and its extensions. In that work, they introduce the notion of *combined FO-rewritability*, which generalizes FO-rewritability by allowing a query-independent polynomial-time preprocessing step in which one builds an FO-interpretation from the ABox and TBox, followed by an ABox-independent query rewriting step that generates an FO-query whose evaluation of the interpretation yields the certain answers. As we have seen, the first step corresponds to compiling the TBox into the ABox and yields a finite representation of the canonical model, whereas the second step serves to block unsound answers that can result from approximating the possibly infinite canonical model with a finite interpretation (alternatively, one may replace the query rewriting step by a filtering step that identifies and discards the spurious answers). The interest of the combined approach is that it provides a means of exploiting relational database technology, while being applicable to a much wider range of DLs than (plain) FO-rewritability. In particular, the original paper by Lutz et al. showed that the approach could be applied to $\mathcal{ELH}_{\bot}^{dr}$ (which extends $\mathcal{ELH}_{\bot}$ with domain and range restrictions), for which CQ answering is P-hard in data complexity, thus preventing the use of plain FO-rewriting. For this logic, the query rewriting step involves only very simple modifications of the query and is guaranteed to terminate in polynomial time. Stefanoni et al. [201,202] subsequently showed how the technique could be adapted to handle first nominals, then transitive roles. In both works, the saturation step is handled by means of a Datalog program, and following [149], filtering is used in place of rewriting to eliminate unsound answers. Very recently, Feier et al. [83] have further extended the combined approach to RSA, which is a fragment of Horn-$\mathcal{SHOIQ}$ that was introduced in [64] as a way of capturing the three OWL 2 profiles while retaining PTIME combined complexity for basic reasoning tasks (satisfiability and instance checking). Both the saturation and filtering steps are specified declaratively by means of a logic program with function symbols and stratified negation, and the answers are obtained by computing the minimal model of this program using a logic programming system (note however that one could equally well store the saturated interpretation as a database and leverage relational technology to perform the querying phase). Experiments conducted on prototype implementations of the preceding algorithms show the combined approach to be highly effective. The principal drawback is that the saturated interpretation can be costly to compute, and it needs to be kept up to date, which may be problematic in applications in which the data changes frequently.

Another approach to using relational database systems to support OMQA with non-FO-rewritable ontology languages relies upon the observation is that while FO-rewritings need not exist for all CQs and all Horn DL ontologies, it is still possible that for particular query-ontology pairs, an FO-rewriting does exist (and hence relational technology can be used to answer such queries). Thus, an interesting and potentially quite useful research direction is to develop methods for identify the cases where FO-rewriting is possible and to produce such rewritings when they exist. A first step in this direction was made by Bienvenu et al. [30], who established decidability and complexity results for FO-rewritability of IQs in Horn DLs, showing the problem to be PSPACE-complete for $\mathcal{EL}$ TBoxes and the full ABox signature and EXP-complete for $\mathcal{ELHI}$ and for $\mathcal{EL}$ if one may restrict the ABox signature (note that even if FO-rewritings do not exist for arbitrary ABoxes, they might exist for ABoxes formulated in a restricted signature). While these results were quite positive (similar problems in databases are known to be undecidable), the automata-based decision procedures used to show the upper bounds were ill-suited for implementation. Combining these theoretical results with an existing backward-chaining rewriting procedure [124], Hansen et al. recently proposed a practical algorithm for testing FO-rewritability of IQs w.r.t. ontologies formulated in $\mathcal{ELH}^{dr}$. The algorithm has been implemented in the GRIND system, and experimental results on real-world ontologies are very encouraging: the vast majority of IQs do possess FO-rewritings, and the computed rewritings (represented as NDL programs) are typically quite small. The challenge in future work will be to see whether it is possible to extend this approach to more expressive Horn DLs and more expressive queries (in particular, CQs).

8.3   Querying Existing Relational Data Using Mappings

Throughout this chapter, we have assumed that the data is given as a set of ABox assertions, which may be stored as relational tables, Datalog facts, or RDF triples, but which only involve unary and binary relations (concepts and roles). However, in many applications, one is interested in using ontologies to query *existing* relational data, which typically involves relations of arity greater than two. In order to be able to apply the preceding techniques to arbitrary relational databases, it is necessary to provide a *mapping* that specifies the semantic relationship between the database relations and the concepts and roles in the considered DL vocabulary. Formally, a mapping is a finite set of *mapping assertions*, each taking the form $\varphi \rightarrow \psi$ where φ is an query formulated using the database relations and ψ is a query in the DL vocabulary. *Global-as-view (GLAV)* mappings, in which φ is a CQ and ψ is a single atom (without quantifiers), are the most commonly considered. Given a relational database and a GLAV mapping, we obtain the corresponding ABox by applying the mapping assertions (viewed as rules) to the database, and the objective is to compute the certain answers over the KB consisting of this ABox and the TBox. The term *ontology-based data access* (OBDA for short) was originally coined to refer to this problem, but in recent years the term has taken on a more general meaning and is often used when speaking of the simpler OMQA setting without mappings.

Observe that by computing the ABox induced by the database and mappings, we end up with an OMQA problem, to which we can apply all of the techniques discussed in this chapter. However, it is often preferable to work with so-called *virtual ABoxes*, meaning that we use the mappings to define the ABox, but do not actually produce it. Indeed, if we work with DL-Lite ontologies and utilize an FO-rewriting approach, then we can proceed in three steps: (i) perform query rewriting as usual to obtain an FO-query that is guaranteed to give the right answers if it were evaluated over the (virtual) ABox, (ii) *unfold* the rewriting using the mapping assertions to obtain an FO-query over the database signature, and (iii) evaluate the resulting FO-query over the original relational database. This approach was first elaborated by Poggi et al. and implemented in the MASTRO system [178]. Experience using this system in a real-world application with the Italian Ministry of Economy and Finance showed that the mapping unfolding phase yielded extremely large queries, which in many cases could not be handled by the database system. An analysis of the obtained queries revealed that they contained a lot of redundancies and could be significantly simplified by exploiting the containment relationships between the database queries appearing in the mapping assertions. This idea has been formalized in the PerfectMap algorithm [177], which has been incorporated into the MASTRO system and experimentally validated on the aforementioned application. Mappings are also supported by the ONTOP system [181]. In this approach, the TBox is integrated into the mapping in such a way that applying the mapping assertions directly generates all inferable assertions (i.e., the new mapping produces the core of the canonical model), and the tree witness rewriting is used to handle query matches that involve anonymous individuals. The FO-query obtained by unfolding the rewritten query using the modified mapping is simplified using *semantic query optimization*, which exploits the integrity constraints satisfied by the underlying database. Experiments with ONTOP have shown that the resulting queries are typically of reasonable size and can be efficiently evaluated by relational database systems.

8.4   Inconsistency-Tolerant Query Answering

While it may be reasonable to assume that the TBox has been properly debugged, the ABox is typically much larger and subject to more frequent modifications, making errors in the data almost inevitable. Such errors may render the KB inconsistent, making standard query algorithms next to useless (since when the KB is inconsistent, every tuple is trivially returned as an answer). Appropriate mechanisms for dealing with inconsistent data are thus crucial to the successful use of OMQA in practice. Ideally, one would restore consistency by identifying and correcting the errors, but when this is not possible, a sensible strategy is to adopt an *inconsistency-tolerant semantics* which allows reasonable answers to be obtained despite the inconsistencies. The most well-known, and arguably the most natural, such semantics is the *AR semantics* [138], which was inspired by earlier work on consistent query answering in relational databases (see [24] for a survey). The semantics is based upon the notion of a *repair*, defined as an inclusion-maximal subset of the data that is consistent with the ontology. Repairs correspond to the different ways of achieving consistency while retaining as much of the original data as possible. Query answering under AR semantics amounts to computing those answers that hold in every repair.

Two other natural repair-based semantics are the *brave semantics* [35], which only requires that an answer holds in *some* repair, and the more cautious *IAR semantics* [138], which corresponds to evaluating the query over the intersection of the repairs.

The complexity of answering queries under the AR semantics has been thoroughly investigated for a range of DLs [25,35,138,187]. The results are rather discouraging: the problem is coNP-hard in data complexity already for instance queries in DL-Lite [138] and for conjunctive queries in any DL that can express disjointness of atomic concepts [25]. The IAR and brave semantics, which can be seen respectively as providing under- and over-approximations of the set of answers w.r.t. AR semantics, are more computationally well-behaved: for DL-Lite$_R$, both semantics can be computed using first-order query rewriting [35,139], and thus has the same low complexity as CQ answering under classical semantics. Generalizing the IAR and brave semantics, Bienvenu and Rosati [35] introduced two parameterized families of inconsistency-tolerant semantics, called k-defeater and k-support semantics, that approximate the AR semantics from above and from below, respectively, and converge to the AR semantics in the limit. They established a general tractability result that applies to all known first-order rewritable languages, in particular many dialects of DL-Lite.

When information on the reliability of different facts is available, it is natural to use this information to identify *preferred repairs*, and to use the latter as the basis of inconsistency-tolerant query answering. A weight-based version of the AR semantics was first considered in the work of Du et al. [73]. More recently, Bienvenu et al. [26] studied the complexity of CQ answering in DL-Lite$_R$ under variants of the AR and IAR semantics based upon several different notions of preferred repairs, in which preferences are captured by cardinality, weights, or priority levels.

In terms of implementations, there are currently two systems for CQ answering over inconsistent DL-Lite KBs: the QUID system [189] implements the IAR semantics, using either query rewriting or ABox cleaning, and the CQAPRI system [26] implements the AR, IAR and brave semantics, using tractable methods to obtain the answers under IAR and brave semantics and calls to a SAT solver to identify the answers holding under AR semantics (the system can also exploit preferences in the form of priority levels). For expressive DLs, Du et al. [73] have implemented a SAT-based algorithm for answering ground CQs (i.e., conjunctions of IQs) in $\mathcal{SHIQ}$ under weight-based AR semantics.

8.5   Temporal Query Answering

Time plays a central role in many application domains, and data is usually time-dependent: new contracts are signed, projects conclude, students graduate, menus change, etc. It is thus not surprising that the study of extensions of classical DLs that can model and reason about time is almost as old as DLs themselves, dating back to the early 1990s [194]. There are many different approaches to incorporating time into DLs, allowing for different design choices, which lead to a variety of temporal DLs with different computational properties. A prominent approach to construct temporal DLs is to combine DLs with dynamic formalisms, such as classical temporal logics like LTL and CTL; logics of time intervals [105], or action logics [11], and provide a two-dimensional semantics. For specific such combinations, there are other design choices to be made, like deciding to choose to which components of the DL syntax (concepts, roles, ABoxes) temporal operators are applied to. There is a vast amount of literature on temporal DLs; we refer to [12,13,87,154] for surveys. Most work so far, however, focuses on the so-called 'standard' reasoning tasks, like satisfiability testing and concept subsumption. Following the steps of the research on classical DLs, the study of temporal DLs based on the lightweight DLs of the $\mathcal{EL}$ and DL-Lite families has become a very active area of research and with much progress in the last few years [15,16,102,103].

Recently, the study of temporal OMQA is also receiving increasing interest. A general framework for answering temporal queries over temporal data in the presence of classical ontologies was proposed in [104], considering queries with temporal operators over time-stamped databases, but with a *global* TBox (axioms hold at all moments of time) formulated in classical (non-temporal) DLs. For variations of this basic setting, decidability and tight complexity bounds for query answering have been obtained for expressive DLs between $\mathcal{ALC}$ and $\mathcal{SHQ}$ [18], and most recently for the $\mathcal{EL}$ family [40]. Borgwardt et al. have shown that in this setting query rewritability is preserved: the rewritability of the underlying (non-temporal) query language can be lifted to the temporal one [39], implying positive decidability results for OMQA in some Horn DLs.

A major limitation of these approaches is that they only consider global, atemporal TBoxes, and hence they do not allow for the highly desirable conceptual modeling of temporal properties; needed, e.g, in applications related to data streams from sensor networks [14]. This can be supported by allowing for temporal operators to occur as regular concept constructors, which may also appear in TBoxes. Unfortunately, this extension makes query answering harder; in particular, the unrestricted use of temporal operators results in the loss of FO-rewritability for CQs over the DL-Lite family [16]. Positive results for FO-rewritability were obtained in [16] by restricting the set of available temporal operators and the occurrences of temporal concepts in the ontologies. Under these restrictions, rewriting into two-sorted FO with an order relation is indeed possible. The most recent work of these authors [14] carries out a detailed investigation of the limits of rewritability in the presence of more general forms of temporal TBoxes (e.g., more temporal operators are allowed) using as target rewriting languages two-sorted FO with an order relation and addition, as well as monadic second order logic with an order relation.

8.6 Reasoning Support for Building and Maintaining OMQA Systems

In order to use OMQA in a given application, one first requires an ontology that defines the terminology and the semantic relationships between the terms. As developing an ontology is difficult and time-consuming, it is important to provide tools to aid ontology engineers in this task. For ontology debugging, the key reasoning service is *axiom pinpointing* [114,195], in which the problem is to generate minimal subsets of the KB that explain a given (surprising or undesirable) consequence; such subsets are often called *justifications*. For $\mathcal{ELH}$ TBoxes, justifications correspond to minimal models of propositional Horn formulas and can computed using SAT solvers [196]. In DL-Lite, the problem is simpler: all justifications of a TBox axiom can be enumerated in polynomial delay [173].

If suitable reference ontologies are available for the application area, then rather than starting from scratch, one may begin by extracting the relevant portions of existing ontologies. This is known as *module extraction* and has been the subject of a number of works in recent years, see e.g. [100,127,129,204]. In the OMQA setting, one is typically interesting in modules that preserve answers to CQs. This can be formalized using the notion of *query inseparability* [123], in which two TBoxes $\mathcal{T}_1, \mathcal{T}_2$ are said to be Σ-query inseparable just in the case that they return the same answers to all queries formulated in the signature Σ for all Σ-ABoxes (a notion of query inseparability for KBs can be defined similarly [41]). Deciding query inseparability is a difficult task: the problem is EXP-complete for both $\mathcal{EL}$ [153] and DL-Lite$_R$ TBoxes [41]. Despite these discouraging results, Konev et al. [123] have shown that, by employing polynomial-time incomplete algorithms, it is possible to use query inseparability as the basis for practical module extraction in DL-Lite$_R$. Beyond module extraction, query inseparability can be used to analyze the effects of importing an ontology into another or of refining an ontology by adding additional axioms [153].

Another relevant reasoning service is *emptiness testing* [17], which comes in two flavours: *query emptiness* and *predicate emptiness*. The former is relevant when developing OMQA systems that propose a fixed set of predefined queries, as it allows one to detect whether a given query provides an empty answer over all ABoxes formulated in a given vocabulary, a serious modeling error. Predicate emptiness tests whether every query using a given predicate (concept or role) returns an empty answer (again for ABoxes over the specified signature). It can be used to identify the set of concept and role names that can be meaningfully used in queries (and thus should be included in the query formulation interface), and it can also serve as the basis for module extraction. The complexity of emptiness testing has been investigated for a range of DLs. In $\mathcal{EL}$, both forms of emptiness testing are tractable and amenable to efficient implementation.

If we are building a full-fledged OBDA system with mappings to link the ontology to a relational database (see Sect. 8.3), then it is also important to provide support for constructing, debugging, and maintaining mappings. The problem of mapping debugging was first investigated by Lembo et al. [140,141] who provided algorithms and complexity results for detecting inconsistencies and redundancies in mapping assertions. More recently, Bienvenu and Rosati [36] have initiated an investigation into query-based comparison of OBDA specifications (i.e., mapping-TBox pairs), in which two specifications are deemed equivalent if they give the same answers to the considered query or class of queries for all possible data sources. Such comparisons could be used, e.g., to simplify the specification or to determine whether changes to the ontology and/or mappings may impact query results.

8.7   Improving the Usability of OMQA Systems

In order for OMQA to be widely adopted in practice, it is essential that OMQA systems be easily usable by end users. In particular, it should be possible for users without any prior experience with ontologies to formulate queries that capture their information needs. This has motivated research into user-friendly interfaces that aid users in formulating their queries.

A pioneering project in this direction is Quelo [85], which provides a controlled natural language interface for users to interactively construct a query, starting from a very simple query (which is simply phrased as 'I am looking for something'), and adding additional constraints or modifying previously added ones. To support the edits of the user, the interface uses reasoning to retrieve, for example, which are the relevant constraints (concept and role names) that can be added or removed from the query at a given stage. The resulting query corresponds to a tree-shaped CQ, that can be then written as a complex DL concept and answered using existing reasoning engines.

Later projects providing similar functionalities are the Faceted Search interface of Arenas et al. [8], and the Optique *virtual query formulation system (VQS)* [200]. Unlike Quelo, they do not aim at supporting natural language query formulation. Instead, the former one provides faceted search facilities in which the user can interactively click and unclick several options to retrieve the desired information. Optique VQS was developed within the Optique project,[16] and it aims at providing an easy-to-use graphical interface that allows end users to easily build complex queries.

In addition to aiding users in formulating their queries, it is also important to help them understand the query results. As mentioned earlier, the problem of explanation has already been extensively studied in the DL community for the purposes of ontology debugging [38,107,108,114,155,173,195,196]. These works have focused on explaining entailed TBox axioms (or possibly ABox assertions), but not answers to conjunctive queries. To the best of our knowledge, the first work to explicitly consider explanation in the OMQA setting was that of Borgida et al. [37], who proposed a proof-theoretic approach to explaining positive answers to CQs over DL-Lite$_A$ KBs. The approach outputs a single proof, involving both TBox axioms and ABox assertions, generated by 'tracing back' the relevant part of the rewritten query, with minimality criteria being used to select a 'simplest' proof. The problem of explaining negative query answers over DL-Lite$_A$ KBs (that is, why is a given tuple *not* a certain answer?) has been investigated by Calvanese et al. ([62]). Formally, the explanations for $\mathsf{ans} \notin \mathsf{cert}(q, (\mathcal{T}, \mathcal{A}))$ correspond to (minimal) sets $\mathcal{A}'$ of ABox

---

[16] http://optique-project.eu/.

assertions such that ans $\in$ cert$(q, (\mathcal{T}, \mathcal{A} \cup \mathcal{A}'))$. Practical algorithms for computing such explanations were proposed by Du et al., first for consistent KBs [74] and then for inconsistent KBs [75]. Explanations of positive and negative query answers under the brave, AR, and IAR semantics (discussed in Sect. 8.4) have been explored by Bienvenu et al. [42].

8.8   OMQA with Closed Predicates

As discussed in Sect. 6, ABoxes are interpreted under the open world semantics, while databases are given a closed world semantics. However, there are many applications where the open world semantics of DLs is too weak and it does not allow us to do all the desired inferences. For example, suppose the data to be queried by an application contains the students enrolled in an specific course, which are extracted from a database that is known to be complete. Then this information should be considered complete (even if other parts of the data are not), and query answering algorithms should exploit this to exclude irrelevant models and infer more query answers.

Combining open and closed world reasoning in DLs is not a new topic [47], but it has received renewed attention in recent years [86, 150, 197]. A way of achieving partial closed world reasoning is to consider DBoxes [197], which syntactically look just like ABox, but semantically, they are interpreted like a database: the instances of the concepts and roles in a DBox are given exactly by the assertions it contains, and the *unique name assumption* is made for the *active domain* of the individuals occurring in it. More recent approaches enrich the knowledge base by specifying a set of concepts and roles that are to be interpreted as *closed predicates* [150]. In this way, some ABox assertions are interpreted under closed semantics, as in DBoxes, while others are considered open, as in ABoxes.

Most works on reasoning with closed predicates focus on studying the data complexity of query answering. Unfortunately, the problem is NP-hard even for the core fragments of DL-Lite [86]. The authors of this work established a matching upper bound for DL-Lite with functionality (the interaction of the latter with the closed predicates and inverse roles makes the problem particularly challenging. An in-depth analysis of the reasons for NP-hardness, as well as criteria that tractability for specific TBoxes have been studied by Lutz et al. [150]). In more recent work [151], the same authors study further the problem of classifying specific pairs of a TBox and a query by their data complexity and, among other contributions, identify some FO-rewritable cases. The combined complexity had not been studied until very recently [162], but it has now been shown that query answering is at least coNExp hard for any extension of $\mathcal{EL}$, and in most cases 2Exp complete. Some of these complexity bounds are not hard to infer from the standard open world setting, using ideas that had already been exploited by Franconi et al. [86] to show that query answering in $\mathcal{ALCIF}$ with closed predicates is equivalent to standard query answering in $\mathcal{ALCOIF}$, whose complexity is a long standing open problem.

8.9   Aggregates

Aggregate functions like *max, min, count, sum* and *avgr* are among the most common and most frequently used features of popular query languages, including SQL. In the context of OMQA, they have received surprisingly little attention. This is mostly due to the fact that the certain answer semantics is not very suitable for aggregates, and it is not always clear what their expected meaning should be under the open-world semantics. For example, if a knowledge base only states that Mary teaches a course, then we can build models where she teaches n courses for every n, and there are no certain answers to the query 'How many courses does Mary teach?'. This is in fact the semantics given to these kind of queries in the first work OMQA with aggregates [60], where the authors adopt an *epistemic* semantics where aggregation is only done over the data that coincides in all models. A more recent work revisiting this topic gives a stronger semantics for *count* and *count distinct* that in the example above would allow us to infer a lower bound of one course as an answer [131]. It does not consider other aggregate functions. Moreover, the proposed semantics is rather costly: already for DL-Lite deciding if a number is in the answer is hard for coNP in data complexity and for the second level of the polynomial hierarchy in combined complexity. In DL-Lite$_\mathcal{R}$, the combined complexity is even coNExp hard.

8.10   Bridging the Gap with SPARQL

SPARQL is the standard language for querying RDF datasets [179]. The core of the SPARQL language are the so-called *basic graph patterns (BGPs)*, which essentially correspond to CQs. SPARQL also provides additional constructs to build complex queries from BGPs. Some of these constructors, like union, have a natural counterpart in FO queries and the languages we have discussed in this chapter. Others do not directly correspond to FO connectives but are still expressible in FO. In fact, it has been shown that SPARQL, as a query language, is equivalent to relational algebra, and hence to domain-independent FO queries [4]. This implies, unfortunately, that full SPARQL is undecidable if we use it as query language in our OMQA setting. In practice, SPARQL is often used as a query language for query answering in the presence of ontologies, but with a somewhat different semantics defined in the so-called *entailment regimes*, see [88] and its references. We note that SPARQL supports aggregate functions in queries, which we have discussed above. There is a newer version of the SPARQL standard, SPARQL 1.1, [106], and one of its core features is to add the co-called *property paths*, that basically correspond to regular expressions as in C2RPQs.

Optional Operator. A useful feature of SPARQL is the OPTIONAL operator. In the query languages we have discussed, query answers always take the form of a relation (that is, a set of tuples of individuals) of a fixed arity. Using OPTIONAL, one can define queries where binding some of the variables is optional, and obtain as answers tuples of different arities, where the optional variables are matched if possible, but left unassigned otherwise. For example, we can retrieve pairs of dishes and restaurants where they are served, and optionally retrieve also their price if it is available. This can be very useful in the presence of incomplete information, hence it would be a good feature to add to CQs, C2RPQs, or the other query languages for OMQA that we have discussed. Unfortunately, the presence of OPTIONAL makes queries non-monotonic. This means that, unlike CQs and other *positive* fragments of FO queries, they are not preserved under homomorphisms. Hence there is no analogous to Theorem 13 and we cannot rely on the existence of a universal model for answering these queries. The query answering algorithm that we discussed in Sect. 5 has been extended to a family of well-behaved CQs with OPTIONAL [3]. Other recent works also aim at giving a suitable semantics to fragments of SPARQL in the presence of ontologies, and devising query answering algorithms [7,130].

Meta-Modeling and Meta-Querying. Standard DLs and the query languages usually used for OMQA do not have meta-modeling and meta-querying functionalities. Intuitively, in meta-querying, queries can ask for properties of concepts and roles using variables that are bound to such objects (instead of binding variables to individuals only). Meta-modeling can be seen as a generalization of this, where one can use concept and roles as predicate arguments already in the knowledge base. This allows to assert properties of concept and roles, and to ask for such properties in queries. Meta-modeling was considered in the early days of DLs, but nowadays it is not supported in standard DLs. Meta-modeling and meta-querying are both popular in the in the semantic web, and they are supported by RDF and SPARQL.

There have been a few extensions of DLs with meta-modeling functionalities [70,72,92,157,171], which are obtained by introducing features from higher-order logics. It has been shown that, under certain conditions, these higher-order extensions of DLs do not increase the worst-case complexity of reasoning [72]. However, it has also been observed that even when the straightforward adaptation of reasoning algorithms to the setting of higher-order DLs does not increase their worst-case complexity, it can make them less practicable, and improved algorithms for CQ answering in the higher-order version of DL-Lite$_\mathcal{R}$ have been proposed [143].

8.11 Extending the Applicability of Horn DL Techniques

As we have discussed, non-Horn DLs require significantly more involved query answering algorithms that the ones presented in this chapter, and they usually have a higher computational complexity. Even for traditional reasoning tasks that have the same worst case complexity in the Horn and the non-Horn case (e.g., satisfiability in $\mathcal{SHIQ}$ vs. Horn-$\mathcal{SHIQ}$, which are both Exp-complete), the techniques for Horn logics are in general more amenable to implementation and more efficient in practice. For this reason, some researchers have recently aimed at understanding when reasoning in a non Horn DL can be efficiently reduced to reasoning in a Horn one [63,65]. In [115,116] the authors follow a similar idea, but instead of rewriting into a Horn ontology, they rewrite into Datalog, for which efficient off-the-shelf reasoners are available. Unfortunately, most of these results apply only to satisfiability and instance queries, and only [116] presents some results for CQs.

Datalog has also been exploited to achieve scalable query answering in non-Horn logics. For example, the authors of [212] first use a Datalog reasoner to approximate the answers both from below and from above. That is, they obtain a sound, possibly incomplete set of answers (lower bound), and a complete, possible unsound set of answers (upper bound). Importantly, both computations can be done efficiently by reducing them to the evaluation of suitable Datalog programs. If the upper and lower bounds coincide, then running an expensive exact algorithm becomes unnecessary. If they are different, then the difference gives the set of potential answers for which an exact algorithm is necessary. Moreover, even where expensive exact algorithms are needed, it is possible to exploit the candidate answers to optimize the algorithm and reduce the search space.

We also note that there have been a few works aiming at applying FO- and Datalog-rewriting to non-Horn DLs. The problem of deciding existence of an FO- or Datalog-rewriting of IQs for DLs between $\mathcal{ALC}$ and $\mathcal{SHI}$ was shown in [28] to be NExptime-complete by establishing a tight connection between OMQA with expressive DLs and non-uniform constraint satisfaction problems.

8.12   Rule-Based Ontology Languages

In this chapter, we have only discussed ontologies expressed in DLs. Another important and closely related alternative is to express domain knowledge using rules. Indeed, in the absence of existential quantification, most of the Horn DLs we have discussed in this chapter could be expressed as Datalog rules. Expressive rule languages that extend Datalog with existentially quantified variables in rule heads have been devised with the explicit purpose of expressing DLs, and ontological knowledge in general. Since Datalog with existential quantification is well known to be undecidable, these extensions must be done in a cautious and controlled way, and restrictions must be imposed, such as certain acyclicity conditions or allowing only *guarded* quantification. The resulting families of languages are known under the names of *existential rules* or Datalog$^{\pm}$, and they can be seen as generalizations of DLs to predicates of arbitrary arity, rather than only unary and binary. For an overview of those fields and their main results, we refer the reader to recent tutorials in this series of Summer Schools [96,161], and to the Datalog$^{\pm}$ tutorial in this volume. Here we only point out that there is a large and very active research community studying the OMQA problem in the presence of existential rules and Datalog$^{\pm}$, and that they share much of the research agenda of OMQA with DLs we have discussed here. In fact, several of the results and techniques we have discussed here have been extended to that setting, including a vast amount of work on query rewriting, see e.g., [95,124,125,206] and references therein. Also the combined approach has been extended to existential rules [94]. The saturation approach discussed in Sect. 4 has been adapted, and combined with a technique similar in spirit to the rewriting in Sect. 5 to reduce the OMQA problem for existential rules to plain Datalog reasoning [97].

Table 5. The complexity of OMQA. All results are completeness results, unless stated otherwise. For references, please refer to the sections of the tutorial on the corresponding query languages.

	IQs		CQs		2RPQs		C2RPQs	
	Data complexity	Combined complexity	Data complexity	Combined complexity	Data complexity	Combined complexity	Data complexity	Combined complexity
DL-Lite DL-Lite$_R$	in AC$_0$	NLogSpace	in AC$_0$	NP	NLogSpace	P	NLogSpace	PSpace
$\mathcal{EL}, \mathcal{ELH}$	P	P	P	NP	P	P	P	PSpace
$\mathcal{ELI}, \mathcal{ELHI}_\perp$, Horn-$\mathcal{SHOIQ}$	P	Exp	P	Exp	P	Exp	P	Exp
$\mathcal{ALC}, \mathcal{ALCHQ}$	coNP	Exp	coNP	Exp	coNP	Exp	coNP-hard	2Exp
$\mathcal{ALCI}, \mathcal{SH}, \mathcal{SHIQ}$	coNP	Exp	coNP	2Exp	coNP	Exp	coNP-hard	2Exp
$\mathcal{SHOIQ}$	coNP-hard	coNExp	coNP-hard	coN2Exp-hard[a]	coNP-hard	coNExp	coNP-hard	coN2Exp-hard[b]

[a] Decidability if only simple roles occur in follows from [191], but no complexity upper bounds are known.
[b] Decidability remains open.

9   Concluding Remarks

In this chapter we have given an introduction to the OMQA problem, an active area of ongoing research. By allowing to exploit semantic knowledge when querying data, OMQA opens many new perspectives for modern information systems. However, taking into account this additional knowledge raises significant computational challenges. We have discussed some algorithmic techniques, based on the key ideas of query rewriting and saturation, which allow us to overcome these challenges and effectively answer different kinds of queries. We have focused on the so-called *Horn* DLs that allow for query answering in time that is polynomially bounded in the input data, and briefly discussed the main results for more expressive DLs. Table 5 summarizes some of the main complexity results for the OMQA problem, for different DLs and query languages.

We have also surveyed many recent results and current research directions. The current OMQA/OBDA technologies are mature enough to be deployed in all kinds of application areas. They have been successfully applied in many challenging real life applications, including investment risk analysis, configuration and data management of mobile telecommunication data [49], and management of public debt data [5]. The large ongoing project Optique is applying these technologies in the energy sector, supporting diagnosis engineers at power plants service centers, and experts in oil exploration. Another large ongoing project called EPNet[17] uses OBDA to help access and manage data about food transportation in the Roman empire. These projects witness the versatility and potential of exploiting ontological knowledge when querying data.

While there has been much progress in the last years, many open questions remain, and there are many more challenges to be overcome. Readers interested in keeping up with the latest results and research trends in OMQA can refer to the Informal Proceedings of the International Workshop on Description Logics, the annual meeting point of the DL research community. The proceedings are published in the free, open-access CEUR Workshop Proceedings series (http://ceur-ws.org/), and a historic archive of the workshop editions with links to the proceedings can be found on the Description Logics website (http://dl.kr.org/workshops/).

References

1. Abiteboul, S., Hull, R., Vianu, V.: Foundations of Databases. Addison Wesley Publ. Co., Reading (1995)
2. Acciarri, A., Calvanese, D., De Giacomo, G., Lembo, D., Lenzerini, M., Palmieri, M., Rosati, R.: QuOnto: querying ontologies. In: Proceedings of the 20th National Conference on Artificial Intelligence (AAAI 2005), pp. 1670–1671 (2005)
3. Ahmetaj, S., Fischl, W., Pichler, R., Šimkus, M., Skritek, S.: Towards reconciling SPARQL and certain answers. In: Proceedings of the 24th International Conference on World Wide Web, WWW 2015, Florence, Italy, 18–22 May 2015, pp. 23–33 (2015)

---

[17] http://www.roman-ep.net.

4. Angles, R., Gutierrez, C.: The expressive power of SPARQL. In: Sheth, A.P., Staab, S., Dean, M., Paolucci, M., Maynard, D., Finin, T., Thirunarayan, K. (eds.) ISWC 2008. LNCS, vol. 5318, pp. 114–129. Springer, Heidelberg (2008)
5. Antonioli, N., Castanò, F., Coletta, S., Grossi, S., Lembo, D., Lenzerini, M., Poggi, A., Virardi, E., Castracane, P.: Ontology-based data management for the Italian Public Debt. In: Proceedings of 8th International Conference Formal Ontology in Information Systems (FOIS 2014). Frontiers in Artificial Intelligence and Applications, vol. 267, pp. 372–385. IOS Press (2014)
6. Arenas, M., Barceló, P., Libkin, L., Murlak, F.: Foundations of Data Exchange. Cambridge University Press, Cambridge (2014)
7. Arenas, M., Gottlob, G., Pieris, A.: Expressive languages for querying the semantic web. In: Proceedings of the 33rd ACM SIGACT SIGMOD SIGART Symposium on Principles of Database Systems (PODS 2014), pp. 14–26. ACM, New York (2014)
8. Arenas, M., Grau, B.C., Kharlamov, E., Marciuška, S., Zheleznyakov, D.: Faceted search over ontology-enhanced RDF data. In: Proceedings of the 23rd ACM International Conference on Information and Knowledge Management (CIKM), pp. 939–948 (2014)
9. Arora, S., Barak, B.: Computational Complexity - A Modern Approach. Cambridge University Press, Cambridge (2009)
10. Artale, A., Calvanese, D., Kontchakov, R., Zakharyaschev, M.: The DL-Lite family and relations. J. Artif. Intell. Res. (JAIR) **36**, 1–69 (2009)
11. Artale, A., Franconi, E.: A temporal description logic for reasoning about actions and plans. J. Artif. Intel. Res. **9**, 463–506 (1998)
12. Artale, A., Franconi, E.: Temporal description logics. In: Fisher, M., Gabbay, D., Vila, L. (eds.) Handbook of Time and Temporal Reasoning in Artificial Intelligence. MIT Press, Cambridge (2001)
13. Artale, A., Franconi, E.: Temporal description logics. In: Fisher, M., Gabbay, D., Vila, L. (eds.) Handbook of Temporal Reasoning in Artificial Intelligence. Foundations of Artificial Intelligence, pp. 375–388. Elsevier, Amsterdam (2005)
14. Artale, A., Kontchakov, R., Kovtunova, A., Ryzhikov, V., Wolter, F., Zakharyaschev, M.: First-order rewritability of ontology-mediated temporal queries. In: Proceedings of the 24th International Joint Conference on Artificial Intelligence (IJCAI 2015) (2015)
15. Artale, A., Kontchakov, R., Ryzhikov, V., Zakharyaschev, M.: A cookbook for temporal conceptual data modelling with description logics. ACM Trans. Comput. Logic **15**(3), 25:1–25:50 (2014)
16. Artale, A., Kontchakov, R., Wolter, F., Zakharyaschev, M.: Temporal description logic for ontology-based data access. In: Proceedings of the 23rd International Joint Conference on Artificial Intelligence (IJCAI 2013) (2013)
17. Baader, F., Bienvenu, M., Lutz, C., Wolter, F.: Query and predicate emptiness in description logics. In: Proceedings of the 12th International Conference on the Principles of Knowledge Representation and Reasoning (KR 2010) (2010)
18. Baader, F., Borgwardt, S., Lippmann, M.: Temporal query entailment in the description logic $\mathcal{SHQ}$. Sci. Serv. Agents World Wide Web, Web Seman. (2014, in press). doi:10.1016/j.websem.2014.11.008
19. Baader, F., Brandt, S., Lutz, C.: Pushing the $\mathcal{EL}$ envelope. In: Proceedings of the 19th International Joint Conference on Artificial Intelligence (IJCAI 2005) (2005)
20. Baader, F., Brandt, S., Lutz, C.: Pushing the $\mathcal{EL}$ envelope further. In: Proceedings of the 5th International Workshop on OWL: Experiences and Directions (OWLED 2008) (2008)

21. Barceló, P., Libkin, L., Lin, A.W., Wood, P.T.: Expressive languages for path queries over graph-structured data. ACM Trans. Database Syst. **37**(4), 31 (2012)
22. Barceló, P., Pérez, J., Reutter, J.L.: Relative expressiveness of nested regular expressions. In: Proceedings of AMW 2012. CEUR Workshop Proceedings, vol. 866, pp. 180–195 (2012)
23. Barceló Baeza, P.: Querying graph databases. In: Proceedings of the 32nd ACM SIGACT SIGMOD SIGART Symposium on Principles of Database Systems (PODS 2013), pp. 175–188 (2013)
24. Bertossi, L.E.: Database Repairing and Consistent Query Answering. Synthesis Lectures on Data Management. Morgan and Claypool Publishers, San Rafael (2011)
25. Bienvenu, M.: On the complexity of consistent query answering in the presence of simple ontologies. In: Proceedings of the 26th AAAI Conference on Artificial Intelligence (AAAI 2012) (2012)
26. Bienvenu, M., Bourgaux, C., Goasdoué, F.: Querying inconsistent description logic knowledge bases under preferred repair semantics. In: Proceedings of the 28th AAAI Conference on Artificial Intelligence (AAAI 2014) (2014)
27. Bienvenu, M., Calvanese, D., Ortiz, M., Šimkus, M.: Nested regular path queries in description logics. In: Proceedings of the 14th International Conference on the Principles of Knowledge Representation and Reasoning (KR 2014) (2014)
28. Bienvenu, M., ten Cate, B., Lutz, C., Wolter, F.: Ontology-based data access: a study through disjunctive datalog, CSP, and MMSNP. ACM Trans. Database Syst. **39**(4), 33:1–33:44 (2014)
29. Bienvenu, M., Kikot, S., Podolskii, V.V.: Tree-like queries in OWL 2 QL: succinctness and complexity results. In: Proceedings of the 30th Annual ACM/IEEE Symposium on Logic in Computer Science (LICS 2015). IEEE (2015)
30. Bienvenu, M., Lutz, C., Wolter, F.: First-order rewritability of atomic queries in horn description logics. In: Proceedings of the 23rd International Joint Conference on Artificial Intelligence (IJCAI 2013). IJCAI/AAAI (2013)
31. Bienvenu, M., Ortiz, M., Šimkus, M.: Answering expressive path queries over lightweight DL knowledge bases. In: Proceedings of the 25th International Workshop on Description Logic (DL 2012) (2012)
32. Bienvenu, M., Ortiz, M., Šimkus, M.: Conjunctive regular path queries in lightweight description logics. In: Proceedings of the 23rd International Joint Conference on Artificial Intelligence (IJCAI 2013) (2013)
33. Bienvenu, M., Ortiz, M., Šimkus, M.: Navigational queries based on frontier-guarded datalog: preliminary results. In: Proceedings of the Ninth Alberto Mendelzon International Workshop on Foundations of Data Management (AMW 2015) (2015)
34. Bienvenu, M., Ortiz, M., Šimkus, M., Xiao, G.: Tractable queries for lightweight description logics. In: Proceedings of the 23rd International Joint Conference on Artificial Intelligence (IJCAI 2013). AAAI Press (2013)
35. Bienvenu, M., Rosati, R.: Tractable approximations of consistent query answering for robust ontology-based data access. In: Proceedings of the 23rd International Joint Conference on Artificial Intelligence (IJCAI 2013) (2013)
36. Bienvenu, M., Rosati, R.: Query-based comparison of OBDA specifications. In: Proceedings of the 29th International Workshop on Description Logic (DL 2015) (2015)
37. Borgida, A., Calvanese, D., Rodriguez-Muro, M.: Explanation in the DL-Lite family of description logics. In: Meersman, R., Tari, Z. (eds.) OTM 2008, Part II. LNCS, vol. 5332, pp. 1440–1457. Springer, Heidelberg (2008)

38. Borgida, A., Franconi, E., Horrocks, I.: Explaining ALC subsumption. In: Proceedings of ECAI (2000)
39. Borgwardt, S., Lippmann, M., Thost, V.: Temporalizing rewritable query languages over knowledge bases. Sci. Serv. Agents World Wide Web, Web Seman. (2014, in press). doi:10.1016/j.websem.2014.11.007
40. Borgwardt, S., Thost, V.: Temporal query answering in the description logic $\mathcal{EL}$. In: Proceedings of the 24th International Joint Conference on Artificial Intelligence (IJCAI 2015) (2015)
41. Botoeva, E., Kontchakov, R., Ryzhikov, V., Wolter, F., Zakharyaschev, M.: Query inseparability for description logic knowledge bases. In: Proceedings of the 14th International Conference on the Principles of Knowledge Representation and Reasoning (KR 2014) (2014)
42. Bourgaux, C., Bienvenu, M., Goasdoué, F.: Explaining query answers under inconsistency-tolerant semantics over description logic knowledge bases (extended abstract). In: Proceedings of the 29th International Workshop on Description Logic (DL 2015) (2015)
43. Bourhis, P., Krötzsch, M., Rudolph, S.: How to best nest regular path queries. In: Proceedings of the 27th International Workshop on Description Logic (DL 2014), vol. 1193, pp. 404–415. CEUR-WS.org (2014)
44. Bourhis, P., Krötzsch, M., Rudolph, S.: Query containment for highly expressive datalog fragments. CoRR abs/1406.7801 (2014). http://arxiv.org/abs/1406.7801
45. Bursztyn, D., Goasdoué, F., Manolescu, I.: Efficient query answering in DL-Lite through FOL reformulation. In: Proceedings of the 29th International Workshop on Description Logic (DL 2015) (2015)
46. Bursztyn, D., Goasdoué, F., Manolescu, I.: Optimizing reformulation-based query answering in RDF. In: Proceedings of the 18th International Conference on Extending Database Technology (EDBT), pp. 265–276 (2015)
47. Cadoli, M., Donini, F.M., Schaerf, M.: Closed world reasoning in hybrid systems. In: Proceedings of the 5th International Symposium on Methodologies for Intelligent Systems (ISMIS 1990), pp. 474–481. North-Holland Publ. Co. (1990)
48. Calvanese, D., De Giacomo, G., Lembo, D., Lenzerini, M., Poggi, A., Rodriguez-Muro, M., Rosati, R.: Ontologies and databases: the DL-Lite approach. In: Tessaris, S., Franconi, E., Eiter, T., Gutierrez, C., Handschuh, S., Rousset, M.-C., Schmidt, R.A. (eds.) Reasoning Web. LNCS, vol. 5689, pp. 255–356. Springer, Heidelberg (2009)
49. Calvanese, D., De Giacomo, G., Lembo, D., Lenzerini, M., Poggi, A., Rodriguez-Muro, M., Rosati, R., Ruzzi, M., Savo, D.F.: The MASTRO system for ontology-based data access. Seman. Web 2(1), 43–53 (2011)
50. Calvanese, D., De Giacomo, G., Lembo, D., Lenzerini, M., Rosati, R.: DL-Lite: tractable description logics for ontologies. In: Proceedings of the 20th National Conference on Artificial Intelligence (AAAI 2005), pp. 602–607 (2005)
51. Calvanese, D., De Giacomo, G., Lembo, D., Lenzerini, M., Rosati, R.: EQL-Lite: effective first-order query processing in description logics. In: Proceedings of the 20th International Joint Conference on Artificial Intelligence (IJCAI 2007), pp. 274–279 (2007)
52. Calvanese, D., De Giacomo, G., Lembo, D., Lenzerini, M., Rosati, R.: Tractable reasoning and efficient query answering in description logics: the DL-Lite family. J. Autom. Reason. 39(3), 385–429 (2007)

53. Calvanese, D., De Giacomo, G., Lenzerini, M.: On the decidability of query containment under constraints. In: Proceedings of the 17th ACM SIGACT SIGMOD SIGART Symposium on Principles of Database Systems (PODS 1998), pp. 149–158 (1998)

54. Calvanese, D., De Giacomo, G., Lenzerini, M.: Conjunctive query containment and answering under description logics constraints. ACM Trans. Comput. Logic **9**(3), 22.1–22.31 (2008)

55. Calvanese, D., De Giacomo, G., Lenzerini, M., Vardi, M.Y.: Containment of conjunctive regular path queries with inverse. In: Proceedings of the 7th International Conference on the Principles of Knowledge Representation and Reasoning (KR 2000), pp. 176–185 (2000)

56. Calvanese, D., Eiter, T., Ortiz, M.: Answering regular path queries in expressive description logics: an automata-theoretic approach. In: Proceedings of the 22nd AAAI Conference on Artificial Intelligence (AAAI 2007), pp. 391–396 (2007)

57. Calvanese, D., Eiter, T., Ortiz, M.: Regular path queries in expressive description logics with nominals. In: Proceedings of the 21st International Joint Conference on Artificial Intelligence (IJCAI 2009), pp. 714–720 (2009)

58. Calvanese, D., Eiter, T., Ortiz, M.: Answering regular path queries in expressive description logics via alternating tree-automata. Inf. Comput. **237**, 12–55 (2014)

59. Calvanese, D., Giacomo, G.D., Lembo, D., Lenzerini, M., Rosati, R.: Data complexity of query answering in description logics. In: Proceedings of the 10th International Conference on the Principles of Knowledge Representation and Reasoning (KR 2006), pp. 260–270. AAAI Press (2006)

60. Calvanese, D., Kharlamov, E., Nutt, W., Thorne, C.: Aggregate queries over ontologies. In: Proceedings of the 2nd International Workshop on Ontologies and Information Systems for the Semantic Web, ONISW 2008, Napa Valley, California, USA, 30 October 2008, pp. 97–104 (2008)

61. Calvanese, D., Ortiz, M., Šimkus, M.: Containment of regular path queries under description logic constraints. In: Proceedings of the 22nd International Joint Conference on Artificial Intelligence (IJCAI 2011) (2011)

62. Calvanese, D., Ortiz, M., Šimkus, M., Stefanoni, G.: Reasoning about explanations for negative query answers in DL-Lite. J. Artif. Intell. Res. (JAIR) **48**, 635–669 (2013)

63. Carral, D., Feier, C., Cuenca Grau, B., Hitzler, P., Horrocks, I.: *EL*-ifying ontologies. In: Demri, S., Kapur, D., Weidenbach, C. (eds.) IJCAR 2014. LNCS, vol. 8562, pp. 464–479. Springer, Heidelberg (2014)

64. Carral, D., Feier, C., Grau, B.C., Hitzler, P., Horrocks, I.: Pushing the boundaries of tractable ontology reasoning. In: Mika, P., Tudorache, T., Bernstein, A., Welty, C., Knoblock, C., Vrandečić, D., Groth, P., Noy, N., Janowicz, K., Goble, C. (eds.) ISWC 2014, Part II. LNCS, vol. 8797, pp. 148–163. Springer, Heidelberg (2014)

65. Carral, D., Feier, C., Romero, A.A., Grau, B.C., Hitzler, P., Horrocks, I.: Is your ontology as hard as you think? Rewriting ontologies into simpler DLs. In: Informal Proceedings of the 27th International Workshop on Description Logics, Vienna, Austria, 17–20 July 2014. CEUR Workshop Proceedings, vol. 1193, pp. 128–140. CEUR-WS.org (2014)

66. Ceri, S., Gottlob, G., Tanca, L.: Logic Programming and Databases. Springer, Berlin (Germany) (1990)

67. Chortaras, A., Trivela, D., Stamou, G.: Optimized query rewriting for OWL 2 QL. In: Bjørner, N., Sofronie-Stokkermans, V. (eds.) CADE 2011. LNCS, vol. 6803, pp. 192–206. Springer, Heidelberg (2011)

68. Chortaras, A., Trivela, D., Stamou, G.B.: Goal-oriented query rewriting for OWL 2 QL. In: Proceedings of the 24th International Workshop on Description Logics (DL) (2011)
69. Clark, J., DeRose, S.: XML path language (XPath) version 1.0. W3C recommendation, World Wide Web consortium (1999)
70. Colucci, S., Noia, T.D., Sciascio, E.D., Donini, F.M., Ragone, A.: Second-order description logics: semantics, motivation, and a calculus. In: Proceedings of the 23rd International Workshop on Description Logic (DL 2010). CEUR Workshop Proceedings, vol. 573. CEUR-WS.org (2010)
71. De Giacomo, G., Lenzerini, M.: Boosting the correspondence between description logics and propositional dynamic logics. In: Proceedings of the 12th National Conference on Artificial Intelligence (AAAI 1994), pp. 205–212 (1994)
72. De Giacomo, G., Lenzerini, M., Rosati, R.: Higher-order description logics for domain metamodeling. In: Proceedings of the 25th AAAI Conference on Artificial Intelligence (AAAI 2011) (2011)
73. Du, J., Qi, G., Shen, Y.D.: Weight-based consistent query answering over inconsistent $\mathcal{SHIQ}$ knowledge bases. Knowl. Inf. Syst. **34**(2), 335–371 (2013)
74. Du, J., Wang, K., Shen, Y.: A tractable approach to ABox abduction over description logic ontologies. In: Proceedings of the 28th AAAI Conference on Artificial Intelligence (AAAI 2014) (2014)
75. Du, J., Wang, K., Shen, Y.: Towards tractable and practical ABox abduction over inconsistent description logic ontologies. In: Proceedings of the 29th AAAI Conference on Artificial Intelligence (AAAI 2015) (2015)
76. Ebbinghaus, H.D., Flum, J.: Finite Model Theory, 2nd edn. Springer, Heidelberg (1999)
77. Ehrenfeucht, A., Zeiger, P.: Complexity measures for regular expressions. In: Proceedings of the Sixth Annual ACM Symposium on Theory of Computing (STOC 1974) (1974)
78. Eiter, T., Gottlob, G., Ortiz, M., Šimkus, M.: Query Answering in the Description Logic Horn-$\mathcal{SHIQ}$. In: Hölldobler, S., Lutz, C., Wansing, H. (eds.) JELIA 2008. LNCS (LNAI), vol. 5293, pp. 166–179. Springer, Heidelberg (2008)
79. Eiter, T., Lutz, C., Ortiz, M., Šimkus, M.: Query answering in description logics: the knots approach. In: Ono, H., Kanazawa, M., de Queiroz, R. (eds.) WoLLIC 2009. LNCS, vol. 5514, pp. 26–36. Springer, Heidelberg (2009)
80. Eiter, T., Lutz, C., Ortiz, M., Šimkus, M.: Query answering in description logics with transitive roles. In: Proceedings of the 21st International Joint Conference on Artificial Intelligence (IJCAI 2009), pp. 759–764 (2009)
81. Eiter, T., Ortiz, M., Simkus, M., Tran, T., Xiao, G.: Query rewriting for Horn-SHIQ plus rules. In: Proceedings of the 26th AAAI Conference on Artificial Intelligence (AAAI 2012). AAAI Press (2012)
82. Eiter, T., Ortiz, M., Šimkus, M.: Conjunctive query answering in the description logic SH using knots. J. Comput. Syst. Sci. **78**(1), 47–85 (2012)
83. Feier, C., Carral, D., Stefanoni, G., Grau, B.C., Horrocks, I.: The combined approach to query answering beyond the OWL 2 profiles. In: Proceedings of the 24th International Joint Conference on Artificial Intelligence (IJCAI 2015) (2015)
84. Florescu, D., Levy, A., Suciu, D.: Query containment for conjunctive queries with regular expressions. In: Proceedings of the 17th ACM SIGACT SIGMOD SIGART Symposium on Principles of Database Systems (PODS 1998), pp. 139–148 (1998)
85. Franconi, E., Guagliardo, P., Trevisan, M., Tessaris, S.: Quelo: an ontology-driven query interface. In: Proceedings of the 24th International Workshop on Description Logics (DL) (2011)

86. Franconi, E., Ibáñez-García, Y.A., Seylan, I.: Query answering with DBoxes is hard. Electr. Notes Theor. Comput. Sci. **278**, 71–84 (2011)
87. Gabbay, D., Kurusz, A., Wolter, F., Zakharyaschev, M.: Many-dimensional Modal Logics: Theory and Applications. Elsevier Science Publishers, Amsterdam (2003)
88. Glimm, B.: Using SPARQL with RDFS and OWL entailment. In: Polleres, A., d'Amato, C., Arenas, M., Handschuh, S., Kroner, P., Ossowski, S., Patel-Schneider, P. (eds.) Reasoning Web 2011. LNCS, vol. 6848, pp. 137–201. Springer, Heidelberg (2011)
89. Glimm, B., Horrocks, I., Lutz, C., Sattler, U.: Conjunctive query answering for the description logic $\mathcal{SHIQ}$. J. Artif. Intell. Res. **31**, 151–198 (2008)
90. Glimm, B., Horrocks, I., Sattler, U.: Unions of conjunctive queries in SHOQ. In: Proceedings of the 11th International Conference on the Principles of Knowledge Representation and Reasoning (KR 2008), pp. 252–262. AAAI Press/MIT Press (2008)
91. Glimm, B., Kazakov, Y., Lutz, C.: Status QIO: an update. In: Proceedings of the 22nd International Workshop on Description Logic (DL 2009). CEUR Workshop Proceedings, vol. 745 (2011)
92. Glimm, B., Rudolph, S., Völker, J.: Integrated metamodeling and diagnosis in OWL 2. In: Patel-Schneider, P.F., Pan, Y., Hitzler, P., Mika, P., Zhang, L., Pan, J.Z., Horrocks, I., Glimm, B. (eds.) ISWC 2010, Part I. LNCS, vol. 6496, pp. 257–272. Springer, Heidelberg (2010)
93. Gottlob, G., Kikot, S., Kontchakov, R., Podolskii, V., Schwentick, T., Zakharyaschev, M.: The price of query rewriting in ontology-based data access. Artif. Intell. **213**, 42–59 (2014)
94. Gottlob, G., Manna, M., Pieris, A.: Polynomial combined rewritings for existential rules. In: Proceedings of the 14th International Conference on the Principles of Knowledge Representation and Reasoning (KR 2014) (2014)
95. Gottlob, G., Orsi, G., Pieris, A.: Ontological queries: rewriting and optimization. In: IEEE 27th International Conference on Data Engineering 2011 (ICDE), April 2011, pp. 2–13 (2011)
96. Gottlob, G., Orsi, G., Pieris, A., Šimkus, M.: Datalog and its extensions for semantic web databases. In: Eiter, T., Krennwallner, T. (eds.) Reasoning Web 2012. LNCS, vol. 7487, pp. 54–77. Springer, Heidelberg (2012)
97. Gottlob, G., Rudolph, S., Šimkus, M.: Expressiveness of guarded existential rule languages. In: Proceedings of the 33rd ACM SIGACT SIGMOD SIGART Symposium on Principles of Database Systems (PODS 2014), pp. 27–38. ACM, New York (2014)
98. Gottlob, G., Schwentick, T.: Rewriting ontological queries into small nonrecursive datalog programs. In: Rosati, R., Rudolph, S., Zakharyaschev, M. (eds.) Description Logics. CEUR Workshop Proceedings, vol. 745. CEUR-WS.org (2011)
99. Grahne, G., Thomo, A.: Query containment and rewriting using views for regular path queries under constraints. In: Proceedings of the 22nd ACM SIGACT SIGMOD SIGART Symposium on Principles of Database Systems (PODS 2003), pp. 111–122 (2003)
100. Grau, B.C., Horrocks, I., Kazakov, Y., Sattler, U.: Modular reuse of ontologies: theory and practice. J. Artif. Intell. Res. (JAIR) **31**, 273–318 (2008)
101. Gutiérrez-Basulto, V., Ibañez-García, Y., Kontchakov, R., Kostylev, E.V.: Conjunctive queries with negation over DL-Lite: a closer look. In: Faber, W., Lembo, D. (eds.) RR 2013. LNCS, vol. 7994, pp. 109–122. Springer, Heidelberg (2013)

102. Gutiérrez-Basulto, V., Jung, J.C., Schneider, T.: Lightweight description logics and branching time: a troublesome marriage. In: Proceedings of the 14th International Conference on the Principles of Knowledge Representation and Reasoning (KR 2014) (2014)

103. Gutierrez-Basulto, V., Jung, J.C., Schneider, T.: Lightweight temporal description logics with rigid roles and restricted TBoxes. In: Proceedings of the 24th International Joint Conference on Artificial Intelligence (IJCAI 2015) (2015)

104. Gutiérrez-Basulto, V., Klarman, S.: Towards a unifying approach to representing and querying temporal data in description logics. In: Krötzsch, M., Straccia, U. (eds.) RR 2012. LNCS, vol. 7497, pp. 90–105. Springer, Heidelberg (2012)

105. Halpern, J.Y., Shoham, Y.: A propositional modal logic of time intervals. J. ACM **38**, 935–962 (1991)

106. Harris, S., Seaborne, A.: SPARQL 1.1 query language. W3C recommendation (2013). Available at http://www.w3.org/TR/sparql11-query/

107. Horridge, M., Bail, S., Parsia, B., Sattler, U.: The cognitive complexity of OWL justifications. In: Aroyo, L., Welty, C., Alani, H., Taylor, J., Bernstein, A., Kagal, L., Noy, N., Blomqvist, E. (eds.) ISWC 2011, Part I. LNCS, vol. 7031, pp. 241–256. Springer, Heidelberg (2011)

108. Horridge, M., Parsia, B., Sattler, U.: Extracting justifications from BioPortal ontologies. In: Cudré-Mauroux, P., Heflin, J., Sirin, E., Tudorache, T., Euzenat, J., Hauswirth, M., Parreira, J.X., Hendler, J., Schreiber, G., Bernstein, A., Blomqvist, E. (eds.) ISWC 2012, Part II. LNCS, vol. 7650, pp. 287–299. Springer, Heidelberg (2012)

109. Horrocks, I., Kutz, O., Sattler, U.: The irresistible $\mathcal{SRIQ}$. In: Proceedings of the 1st International Workshop on OWL: Experiences and Directions (OWLED 2005) (2005)

110. Horrocks, I., Tessaris, S.: A conjunctive query language for description logic ABoxes. In: Proceedings of the 17th National Conference on Artificial Intelligence (AAAI 2000), pp. 399–404 (2000)

111. Hustadt, U., Motik, B., Sattler, U.: Data complexity of reasoning in very expressive description logics. In: Proceedings of the 19th International Joint Conference on Artificial Intelligence (IJCAI 2005), pp. 466–471 (2005)

112. Imielinski, T., Lipski Jr, W.: Incomplete information in relational databases. J. ACM **31**(4), 761–791 (1984)

113. Immerman, N.: Relational queries computable in polynomial time. Inf. Control **68**, 86–104 (1986)

114. Kalyanpur, A., Parsia, B., Sirin, E., Hendler, J.A.: Debugging unsatisfiable classes in OWL ontologies. J. Web Seman. **3**(4), 268–293 (2005)

115. Kaminski, M., Grau, B.C.: Computing Horn rewritings of description logics ontologies. In: Proceedings of the 24th International Joint Conference on Artificial Intelligence (IJCAI 2015) (2015). http://arxiv.org/abs/1504.05150

116. Kaminski, M., Nenov, Y., Cuenca Grau, B.: Computing datalog rewritings for disjunctive datalog programs and description logic ontologies. In: Kontchakov, R., Mugnier, M.-L. (eds.) RR 2014. LNCS, vol. 8741, pp. 76–91. Springer, Heidelberg (2014)

117. Kazakov, Y.: Consequence-driven reasoning for horn SHIQ ontologies. In: Proceedings of the 21st International Joint Conference on Artificial Intelligence (IJCAI 2009), pp. 2040–2045 (2009)

118. Kikot, S., Kontchakov, R., Zakharyaschev, M.: On (In)Tractability of OBDA with OWL 2 QL. In: Proceedings of the 24th International Workshop on Description Logic (DL 2011). CEUR Workshop Proceedings, vol. 745. CEUR-WS.org (2011)

119. Kikot, S., Kontchakov, R., Zakharyaschev, M.: Conjunctive query answering with OWL 2 QL. In: Proceedings of the 13th International Conference on the Principles of Knowledge Representation and Reasoning (KR 2012), pp. 275–285. AAAI Press (2012)

120. Kikot, S., Kontchakov, R., Podolskii, V., Zakharyaschev, M.: Exponential lower bounds and separation for query rewriting. In: Czumaj, A., Mehlhorn, K., Pitts, A., Wattenhofer, R. (eds.) ICALP 2012, Part II. LNCS, vol. 7392, pp. 263–274. Springer, Heidelberg (2012)

121. Kikot, S., Kontchakov, R., Podolskii, V.V., Zakharyaschev, M.: On the succinctness of query rewriting over OWL 2 QL ontologies with shallow chases. In: Proceedings of the 29th Annual ACM/IEEE Symposium on Logic in Computer Science (LICS 2014). ACM Press (2014)

122. Klenke, T.: Über die Entscheidbarkeit von Konjunktiv Anfragen mit Ungleichheit in der Beschreibungslogik $\mathcal{EL}$. Master's thesis, Universität Bremen (2010)

123. Konev, B., Kontchakov, R., Ludwig, M., Schneider, T., Wolter, F., Zakharyaschev, M.: Conjunctive query inseparability of OWL 2 QL TBoxes. In: Proceedings of the 29th AAAI Conference on Artificial Intelligence (AAAI 2015) (2011)

124. König, M., Leclère, M., Mugnier, M.-L., Thomazo, M.: A sound and complete backward chaining algorithm for existential rules. In: Krötzsch, M., Straccia, U. (eds.) RR 2012. LNCS, vol. 7497, pp. 122–138. Springer, Heidelberg (2012)

125. König, M., Leclère, M., Mugnier, M.L.: Query rewriting for existential rules with compiled preorder. In: Proceedings of the 24th International Joint Conference on Artificial Intelligence (IJCAI 2015) (2015)

126. Kontchakov, R., Lutz, C., Toman, D., Wolter, F., Zakharyaschev, M.: The combined approach to ontology-based data access. In: Proceedings of the 22nd International Joint Conference on Artificial Intelligence (IJCAI 2011), pp. 2656–2661. IJCAI/AAAI (2011)

127. Kontchakov, R., Pulina, L., Sattler, U., Schneider, T., Selmer, P., Wolter, F., Zakharyaschev, M.: Minimal module extraction from DL-Lite ontologies using QBF solvers. In: Proceedings of the 21st International Joint Conference on Artificial Intelligence (IJCAI 2009), pp. 836–841 (2009)

128. Kontchakov, R., Rodríguez-Muro, M., Zakharyaschev, M.: Ontology-based data access with databases: a short course. In: Rudolph, S., Gottlob, G., Horrocks, I., van Harmelen, F. (eds.) Reasoning Weg 2013. LNCS, vol. 8067, pp. 194–229. Springer, Heidelberg (2013)

129. Kontchakov, R., Wolter, F., Zakharyaschev, M.: Logic-based ontology comparison and module extraction, with an application to DL-Lite. Artif. Intell. **174**(15), 1093–1141 (2010)

130. Kostylev, E.V., Cuenca Grau, B.: On the semantics of SPARQL queries with optional matching under entailment regimes. In: Mika, P., Tudorache, T., Bernstein, A., Welty, C., Knoblock, C., Vrandečić, D., Groth, P., Noy, N., Janowicz, K., Goble, C. (eds.) ISWC 2014, Part II. LNCS, vol. 8797, pp. 374–389. Springer, Heidelberg (2014)

131. Kostylev, E.V., Reutter, J.L.: Answering counting aggregate queries over ontologies of the DL-Lite family. In: Proceedings of the 27th AAAI Conference on Artificial Intelligence (AAAI 2013) (2013)

132. Kostylev, E.V., Reutter, J.L., Vrgoc, D.: XPath for DL ontologies. In: Proceedings of the 29th AAAI Conference on Artificial Intelligence (AAAI 2015) (2015)

133. Krisnadhi, A., Lutz, C.: Data complexity in the $\mathcal{EL}$ family of description logics. In: Dershowitz, N., Voronkov, A. (eds.) LPAR 2007. LNCS (LNAI), vol. 4790, pp. 333–347. Springer, Heidelberg (2007)

134. Krötzsch, M., Rudolph, S.: Conjunctive queries for $\mathcal{EL}$ with composition of roles. In: Proceedings of the 20th International Workshop on Description Logic (DL 2007) (2007)

135. Krötzsch, M., Rudolph, S., Hitzler, P.: Conjunctive queries for a tractable fragment of OWL 1.1. In: Aberer, K., Choi, K.-S., Noy, N., Allemang, D., Lee, K.-I., Nixon, L.J.B., Golbeck, J., Mika, P., Maynard, D., Mizoguchi, R., Schreiber, G., Cudré-Mauroux, P. (eds.) ASWC 2007 and ISWC 2007. LNCS, vol. 4825, pp. 310–323. Springer, Heidelberg (2007)

136. Krötzsch, M., Rudolph, S., Hitzler, P.: Complexities of Horn description logics. ACM Trans. Comput. Logic **14**(1), 2:1–2:36 (2013)

137. Krotzsch, M., Simancik, F., Horrocks, I.: Description logics. IEEE Intell. Syst. **29**(1), 12–19 (2014)

138. Lembo, D., Lenzerini, M., Rosati, R., Ruzzi, M., Savo, D.F.: Inconsistency-tolerant semantics for description logics. In: Hitzler, P., Lukasiewicz, T. (eds.) RR 2010. LNCS, vol. 6333, pp. 103–117. Springer, Heidelberg (2010)

139. Lembo, D., Lenzerini, M., Rosati, R., Ruzzi, M., Savo, D.F.: Query rewriting for inconsistent DL-Lite ontologies. In: Rudolph, S., Gutierrez, C. (eds.) RR 2011. LNCS, vol. 6902, pp. 155–169. Springer, Heidelberg (2011)

140. Lembo, D., Mora, J., Rosati, R., Savo, D.F., Thorstensen, E.: Towards mapping analysis in ontology-based data access. In: Kontchakov, R., Mugnier, M.-L. (eds.) RR 2014. LNCS, vol. 8741, pp. 108–123. Springer, Heidelberg (2014)

141. Lembo, D., Mora, J., Rosati, R., Savo, D.F., Thorstensen, E.: Mapping analysis in ontology-based data access: algorithms and complexity. In: Proceedings of the 29th International Workshop on Description Logic (DL 2015) (2015)

142. Lenzerini, M.: Data integration: a theoretical perspective. In: Proceedings of the 21st ACM SIGACT SIGMOD SIGART Symposium on Principles of Database Systems (PODS 2002), pp. 233–246 (2002)

143. Lenzerini, M., Lepore, L., Poggi, A.: Making metaquerying practical for Hi(DL-Lite$_R$) knowledge bases. In: Meersman, R., Panetto, H., Dillon, T., Missikoff, M., Liu, L., Pastor, O., Cuzzocrea, A., Sellis, T. (eds.) OTM 2014. LNCS, vol. 8841, pp. 580–596. Springer, Heidelberg (2014)

144. Levy, A.Y., Rousset, M.C.: Combining Horn rules and description logics in CARIN. Artif. Intell. **104**(1–2), 165–209 (1998)

145. Libkin, L.: Elements of Finite Model Theory. Springer, Heidelberg (2004)

146. Lutz, C., Toman, D., Wolter, F.: Conjunctive query answering in the description logic $\mathcal{EL}$ using a relational database system. In: Proceedings of the 21st International Joint Conference on Artificial Intelligence (IJCAI 2009), pp. 2070–2075. AAAI Press (2009)

147. Lutz, C.: The complexity of conjunctive query answering in expressive description logics. In: Armando, A., Baumgartner, P., Dowek, G. (eds.) IJCAR 2008. LNCS (LNAI), vol. 5195, pp. 179–193. Springer, Heidelberg (2008)

148. Lutz, C.: Two upper bounds for conjunctive query answering in SHIQ. In: Proceedings of the 22nd International Workshop on Description Logic (DL 2008). CEUR Workshop Proceedings, vol. 353. CEUR-WS.org (2008)

149. Lutz, C., Seylan, I., Toman, D., Wolter, F.: The combined approach to OBDA: taming role hierarchies using filters. In: Alani, H., Kagal, L., Fokoue, A., Groth, P., Biemann, C., Parreira, J.X., Aroyo, L., Noy, N., Welty, C., Janowicz, K. (eds.) ISWC 2013, Part I. LNCS, vol. 8218, pp. 314–330. Springer, Heidelberg (2013)

150. Lutz, C., Seylan, I., Wolter, F.: Ontology-based data access with closed predicates is inherently intractable (sometimes). In: Proceedings of the 23rd International Joint Conference on Artificial Intelligence (IJCAI 2013). IJCAI/AAAI (2013)

151. Lutz, C., Seylan, I., Wolter, F.: Ontology-mediated queries with closed predicates. In: Proceedings of the 24th International Joint Conference on Artificial Intelligence (IJCAI 2015) (2015)

152. Lutz, C., Toman, D., Wolter, F.: Conjunctive query answering in the description logic $\mathcal{EL}$ using a relational database system. In: Proceedings of the 21st International Joint Conference on Artificial Intelligence (IJCAI 2009), pp. 2070–2075 (2009)

153. Lutz, C., Wolter, F.: Deciding inseparability and conservative extensions in the description logic $\mathcal{EL}$. J. Symb. Comput. **45**(2), 194–228 (2010)

154. Lutz, C., Wolter, F., Zakharyaschev, M.: Temporal description logics: a survey. In: Proceedings 15th International Symposium on Temporal Representation and Reasoning (TIME 2008), pp. 3–14. IEEE Computer Society (2008)

155. McGuinness, D.L., Borgida, A.: Explaining subsumption in description logics. In: Proceedings of the 14th International Joint Conference on Artificial Intelligence (IJCAI 1995) (1995)

156. Mora, J., Corcho, Ó.: Engineering optimisations in query rewriting for OBDA. In: Proceedings of the 9th International Conference on Semantic Systems (I-SEMANTICS), pp. 41–48 (2013)

157. Motik, B.: On the properties of metamodeling in OWL. In: Gil, Y., Motta, E., Benjamins, V.R., Musen, M.A. (eds.) ISWC 2005. LNCS, vol. 3729, pp. 548–562. Springer, Heidelberg (2005)

158. Motik, B.: Reasoning in description logics using resolution and deductive databases. Ph.D. thesis, Univesität Karlsruhe (TH), Karlsruhe, Germany, January 2006

159. Motik, B., Cuenca Grau, B., Horrocks, I., Wu, Z., Fokoue, A., Lutz, C.: OWL 2 web ontology language profiles. W3C recommendation (2012). Available at http://www.w3.org/TR/owl2-profiles/

160. Motik, B., Sattler, U., Studer, R.: Query answering for OWL-DL with rules. In: McIlraith, S.A., Plexousakis, D., van Harmelen, F. (eds.) ISWC 2004. LNCS, vol. 3298, pp. 549–563. Springer, Heidelberg (2004)

161. Mugnier, M.-L., Thomazo, M.: An introduction to ontology-based query answering with existential rules. In: Koubarakis, M., Stamou, G., Stoilos, G., Horrocks, I., Kolaitis, P., Lausen, G., Weikum, G. (eds.) Reasoning Web. LNCS, vol. 8714, pp. 245–278. Springer, Heidelberg (2014)

162. Ngo, N., Ortiz, M., Šimkus, M.: The combined complexity of reasoning with closed predicates in description logics. In: Proceedings of the 29th International Workshop on Description Logic (DL 2015) (2015)

163. Ortiz, M.: Ontology based query answering: the story so far. In: Proceedings of the Seventh Alberto Mendelzon International Workshop on Foundations of Data Management (AMW 2013) (2013)

164. Ortiz, M., Calvanese, D., Eiter, T.: Data complexity of query answering in expressive description logics via Tableaux. J. Autom. Reason. **41**(1), 61–98 (2008)

165. Ortiz, M., Rudolph, S., Šimkus, M.: Query answering is undecidable in DLs with regular expressions, inverses, nominals, and counting. Technical report, INFSYS RR-1843-10-03, Institut für Informationssysteme, Technische Universität Wien, A-1040 Vienna, Austria, April 2010

166. Ortiz, M., Rudolph, S., Šimkus, M.: Query answering in the Horn fragments of the description logics SHOIQ and SROIQ. In: Proceedings of the 22nd International Joint Conference on Artificial Intelligence (IJCAI 2011), pp. 1039–1044. IJCAI/AAAI (2011)

167. Ortiz, M., Šimkus, M., Eiter, T.: Worst-case optimal conjunctive query answering for an expressive description logic without inverses. In: Proceedings of the 23rd AAAI Conference on Artificial Intelligence (AAAI 2008), pp. 504–510. AAAI Press (2008)

168. Ortiz, M., Šimkus, M.: Reasoning and query answering in description logics. In: Eiter, T., Krennwallner, T. (eds.) Reasoning Web 2012. LNCS, vol. 7487, pp. 1–53. Springer, Heidelberg (2012)

169. Ortiz, M., Šimkus, M.: Revisiting the hardness of query answering in expressive description logics. In: Kontchakov, R., Mugnier, M.-L. (eds.) RR 2014. LNCS, vol. 8741, pp. 216–223. Springer, Heidelberg (2014)

170. OWL working group, W.: OWL 2 web ontology language: document overview. W3C recommendation, 27 October 2009. Available at http://www.w3.org/TR/owl2-overview/

171. Pan, J.Z., Horrocks, I.: OWL FA: a metamodeling extension of OWL DL. In: Proceedings of the 15th International Conference on World Wide Web, WWW 2006, pp. 1065–1066. ACM, New York (2006)

172. Papadimitriou, C.H.: Computational Complexity. Addison Wesley Publ. Co., Boston (1994)

173. Peñaloza, R., Sertkaya, B.: Complexity of axiom pinpointing in the DL-Lite family of description logics. In: Proceedings of ECAI (2010)

174. Pérez, J., Arenas, M., Gutierrez, C.: nSPARQL: a navigational language for RDF. J. Web Seman. 8(4), 255–270 (2010)

175. Pérez-Urbina, H., Horrocks, I., Motik, B.: Efficient query answering for OWL 2. In: Bernstein, A., Karger, D.R., Heath, T., Feigenbaum, L., Maynard, D., Motta, E., Thirunarayan, K. (eds.) ISWC 2009. LNCS, vol. 5823, pp. 489–504. Springer, Heidelberg (2009)

176. Pérez-Urbina, H., Motik, B., Horrocks, I.: Tractable query answering and rewriting under description logic constraints. J. Appl. Logic 8(2), 186–209 (2010)

177. Pinto, F.D., Lembo, D., Lenzerini, M., Mancini, R., Poggi, A., Rosati, R., Ruzzi, M., Savo, D.F.: Optimizing query rewriting in ontology-based data access. In: Proceedings of the 16th International Conference on Extending Database Technology (EDBT), pp. 561–572 (2013)

178. Poggi, A., Lembo, D., Calvanese, D., De Giacomo, G., Lenzerini, M., Rosati, R.: Linking data to ontologies. J. Data Seman. 10, 133–173 (2008)

179. Prud'hommeaux, E., Seaborne, A.: SPARQL query language for RDF. W3C recommendation (2008). http://www.w3.org/TR/rdf-sparql-query/

180. Reutter, J., Romero, M., Vardi, M.Y.: Regular queries on graph databases. In: Proceedings of ICDT 2015 (2015)

181. Rodríguez-Muro, M., Kontchakov, R., Zakharyaschev, M.: Ontology-based data access: Ontop of databases. In: Alani, H., Kagal, L., Fokoue, A., Groth, P., Biemann, C., Parreira, J.X., Aroyo, L., Noy, N., Welty, C., Janowicz, K. (eds.) ISWC 2013, Part I. LNCS, vol. 8218, pp. 558–573. Springer, Heidelberg (2013)

182. Rodriguez-Muro, M., Calvanese, D.: High performance query answering over DL-Lite ontologies. In: Brewka, G., Eiter, T., McIlraith, S.A. (eds.) Proceedings of the 13th International Conference on the Principles of Knowledge Representation and Reasoning (KR 2012). AAAI Press, Menlo Park, CA (2012)

183. Rosati, R.: Prexto: query rewriting under extensional constraints in DL-Lite. In: Simperl, E., Cimiano, P., Polleres, A., Corcho, O., Presutti, V. (eds.) ESWC 2012. LNCS, vol. 7295, pp. 360–374. Springer, Heidelberg (2012)

184. Rosati, R.: DL+log: tight integration of description logics and disjunctive datalog. In: Proceedings of the 10th International Conference on the Principles of Knowledge Representation and Reasoning (KR 2006), pp. 68–98 (2006)

185. Rosati, R.: The limits of querying ontologies. In: Schwentick, T., Suciu, D. (eds.) ICDT 2007. LNCS, vol. 4353, pp. 164–178. Springer, Heidelberg (2006)

186. Rosati, R.: On conjunctive query answering in $\mathcal{EL}$. In: Proceedings of the 20th International Workshop on Description Logic (DL 2007) (2007)

187. Rosati, R.: On the complexity of dealing with inconsistency in description logic ontologies. In: Proceedings of the 22nd International Joint Conference on Artificial Intelligence (IJCAI 2011) (2011)

188. Rosati, R., Almatelli, A.: Improving query answering over DL-Lite ontologies. In: Proceedings of the 12th International Conference on the Principles of Knowledge Representation and Reasoning (KR 2010) (2010)

189. Rosati, R., Ruzzi, M., Graziosi, M., Masotti, G.: Evaluation of techniques for inconsistency handling in OWL 2 QL ontologies. In: Cudré-Mauroux, P., Heflin, J., Sirin, E., Tudorache, T., Euzenat, J., Hauswirth, M., Parreira, J.X., Hendler, J., Schreiber, G., Bernstein, A., Blomqvist, E. (eds.) ISWC 2012, Part II. LNCS, vol. 7650, pp. 337–349. Springer, Heidelberg (2012)

190. Rudolph, S.: Foundations of description logics. In: Polleres, A., d'Amato, C., Arenas, M., Handschuh, S., Kroner, P., Ossowski, S., Patel-Schneider, P. (eds.) Reasoning Web 2011. LNCS, vol. 6848, pp. 76–136. Springer, Heidelberg (2011)

191. Rudolph, S., Glimm, B.: Nominals, inverses, counting, and conjunctive queries or: why infinity is your friend!. J. Artif. Intell. Res. **39**, 429–481 (2010)

192. Rudolph, S., Krötzsch, M.: Flag & check: data access with monadically defined queries. In: Proceedings of the 32nd ACM SIGACT SIGMOD SIGART Symposium on Principles of Database Systems (PODS 2013), pp. 151–162. ACM (2013)

193. Schaerf, A.: Reasoning with individuals in concept languages. In: Torasso, P. (ed.) AI*IA 1993. LNCS, vol. 728, pp. 108–119. Springer, Heidelberg (1993)

194. Schild, K.: Combining terminological logics with tense logic. In: Damas, L.M.M., Filgueiras, M. (eds.) EPIA 1993. LNCS, vol. 727, pp. 105–120. Springer, Heidelberg (1993)

195. Schlobach, S., Cornet, R.: Non-standard reasoning services for the debugging of description logic terminologies. In: Proceedings of the 18th International Joint Conference on Artificial Intelligence (IJCAI 2003) (2003)

196. Sebastiani, R., Vescovi, M.: Axiom pinpointing in lightweight description logics via Horn-SAT encoding and conflict analysis. In: Schmidt, R.A. (ed.) CADE-22. LNCS, vol. 5663, pp. 84–99. Springer, Heidelberg (2009)

197. Seylan, I., Franconi, E., de Bruijn, J.: Effective query rewriting with ontologies over DBoxes. In: Proceedings of the 21st International Joint Conference on Artificial Intelligence (IJCAI 2009), pp. 923–925 (2009)

198. Shmueli, O.: Decidability and expressiveness aspects of logic queries. In: Proceedings of the 6th ACM SIGACT SIGMOD SIGART Symposium on Principles of Database Systems (PODS 1987), pp. 237–249 (1987)

199. Sioutos, N., de Coronado, S., Haber, M., Hartel, F., Shaiu, W., Wright, L.: NCI thesaurus: a semantic model integrating cancer-related clinical and molecular information. J. Biomed. Inf. **40**(1), 30–43 (2006)

200. Soylu, A., Kharlamov, E., Zheleznyakov, D., Jiménez-Ruiz, E., Giese, M., Horrocks, I.: OptiqueVQS: visual query formulation for OBDA. In: Informal Proceedings of the 27th International Workshop on Description Logics (DL), pp. 725–728 (2014)

201. Stefanoni, G., Motik, B.: Answering conjunctive queries over EL knowledge bases with transitive and reflexive roles. In: Proceedings of the 29th AAAI Conference on Artificial Intelligence (AAAI 2015), pp. 1611–1617. AAAI Press (2015)

202. Stefanoni, G., Motik, B., Horrocks, I.: Introducing nominals to the combined query answering approaches for EL. In: Proceedings of the 22nd AAAI Conference on Artificial Intelligence (AAAI 2007). AAAI Press (2013)

203. Stefanoni, G., Motik, B., Krötzsch, M., Rudolph, S.: The complexity of answering conjunctive and navigational queries over OWL 2 EL knowledge bases. J. Artif. Intell. Res. (JAIR) **51**, 645–705 (2014)

204. Stuckenschmidt, H., Parent, C., Spaccapietra, S. (eds.): Modular Ontologies: Concepts, Theories and Techniques for Knowledge Modularization. Lecture Notes in Computer Science, vol. 5445. Springer, Heidelberg (2009)

205. Ashburner, M., Ball, C.A., Blake, J.A., Botstein, D., Butler, H., Cherry, J.M., Davis, A.P., Dolinski, K., Dwight, S.S., Eppig, J.T., Harris, M.A., Hill, D.P., Issel-Tarver, L., Kasarskis, A., Lewis, S., Matese, J.C., Richardson, J.E., Ringwald, M., Rubin, G.M., Sherlock, G.: Gene ontology: tool for the unification of biology. Nat. Genet. **25**, 25–29 (2000)

206. Thomazo, M.: Compact rewritings for existential rules. In: Proceedings of the 23rd International Joint Conference on Artificial Intelligence (IJCAI 2013) (2013)

207. Trivela, D., Stoilos, G., Chortaras, A., Stamou, G.: Optimising resolution-based rewriting algorithms for OWL ontologies. J. Web Seman. (2015, to appear)

208. Trivela, D., Stoilos, G., Chortaras, A., Stamou, G.: Query rewriting in Horn-$\mathcal{SHIQ}$ (extended abstract). In: Proceedings of the 29th International Workshop on Description Logic (DL 2015) (2015)

209. Vardi, M.Y.: The complexity of relational query languages. In: Proceedings of the 14th ACM SIGACT Symposium on Theory of Computing (STOC 1982), pp. 137–146 (1982)

210. Vardi, M.Y.: On the complexity of bounded-variable queries. In: Proceedings of the 14th ACM SIGACT SIGMOD SIGART Symposium on Principles of Database Systems (PODS 1995), pp. 266–276 (1995)

211. Venetis, T., Stoilos, G., Stamou, G.B.: Query extensions and incremental query rewriting for OWL 2 QL ontologies. J. Data Seman. **3**(1), 1–23 (2014)

212. Zhou, Y., Nenov, Y., Cuenca Grau, B., Horrocks, I.: Pay-as-you-go OWL query answering using a triple store. In: Proceedings of the 28th Conference on Artificial Intelligence (AAAI 2014), pp. 1142–1148 (2014)

Answer Set Programming: A Tour from the Basics to Advanced Development Tools and Industrial Applications

Nicola Leone and Francesco Ricca[⊠]

Department of Mathematics and Computer Science, University of Calabria,
Rende, Italy
{leone,ricca}@mat.unical.it

Abstract. Answer Set Programming (ASP) is a powerful rule-based language for knowledge representation and reasoning that has been developed in the field of logic programming and nonmonotonic reasoning. After more than twenty years from the introduction of ASP, the theoretical properties of the language are well understood and the solving technology has become mature for practical applications. In this paper, we first present the basics of the ASP language, and we then concentrate on its usage for knowledge representation and reasoning in real-world contexts. In particular, we report on the development of some industry-level applications with the ASP system DLV, and we illustrate two advanced development tools for ASP, namely ASPIDE and JDLV, which speed-up and simplify the implementation of applications.

1 Introduction

Answer Set Programming (ASP) [11,19,30] is a powerful rule-based language for knowledge representation and reasoning that has been developed in the field of logic programming and nonmonotonic reasoning. ASP features disjunction in rule heads, non monotonic negation in rule bodies [30], aggregate atoms [16] for concise modeling of complex combinatorial problems, and weak constraints [12] for the declarative encoding of optimization problems.

Computational problems, even of high complexity [19], can be solved in ASP by specifying a logic program, i.e., a set of logic rules, such that its answer sets correspond to solutions, and then, using an answer set solver to find such solutions [34,38].

After more than twenty years from the introduction of ASP, the theoretical properties of the language are well understood and the solving technology has become mature [13] for practical applications. The high knowledge-modeling power of ASP made it suitable for solving a variety of complex problems arising in scientific applications [13] from several areas ranging from Artificial Intelligence [2,4,5,10,25,27,39], to Knowledge Management [3,6] and Databases [7,9, 32,35].

© Springer International Publishing Switzerland 2015
W. Faber and A. Paschke (Eds.): Reasoning Web 2015, LNCS 9203, pp. 308–326, 2015.
DOI: 10.1007/978-3-319-21768-0_10

Recently, an ASP system, namely the DLV system [33], has undergone an industrial exploitation by a spin-off company called DLVSYSTEM l.t.d., favouring the interest of some industries in ASP and DLV, which has led to its successful usage in a number of industry-level applications [31]. A key advantage of DLV for applications development is its endowment with powerful development tools [22,24], supporting the activities of researchers and implementors.

In this paper, after a brief introduction to the ASP standard language, we illustrate its usage for advanced Knowledge Representation and Reasoning by presenting a number of industry-level real-world applications of ASP, that we have implemented by using the DLV system and its accompanying tools. Namely:

– A platform employed by the call-centers of Italia Telecom, which automatically classifies the incoming calls for optimal routing. The platform works in real-time and deals with a very large number of parallel calls.
– A tool for the automatic generation of the teams of employees [42] that has been employed in the sea port of Gioia Tauro for intelligent resource allocation.
– A mediator system for e-tourism [41], where ASP is used to single out, in a short time, the travel solution that best matches the user profile.
– A tool for travel agents for the intelligent allotment of touristic packages. Basically, the system selects from service-suppliers blocks of touristic packages to be pre-booked for the next season in such a way that the expected earnings are maximized, and a number of preference criteria are satisfied.
– An ASP-based platform for data cleaning [44] that is part of a business intelligence suite developed for analyzing and cleaning-up the distributed archives of the Italian Healthcare System storing data on tumor diseases.

Moreover, we illustrate two advanced development tools for ASP, namely ASPIDE [24] and JDLV [22], that have played a crucial role for the successful usage of DLV in the above mentioned applications. ASPIDE is an extensible integrated development environment for ASP, which integrates powerful editing tools with a collection of development tools for program testing and rewriting, database access, solver execution configuration and output-handling. JDLV is a plug-in for Eclipse, supporting a hybrid language that transparently enables a bilateral interaction between ASP and Java. The development tools support researchers and software developers and simplify the integration of ASP in mature widely-adopted development platforms based on imperative and object-oriented programming languages.

2   Answer Set Programming

In this section we overview the language of ASP, and we recall a methodology for solving complex problems with ASP. More detailed descriptions and a more formal account of ASP, including the features of the language employed in this paper, can be found in [12,21,28,30], whereas a nice introduction to ASP can be found in [3]. Hereafter, we assume the reader is familiar with logic programming conventions.

2.1 Syntax

Following a convention dating back to Prolog, strings starting with uppercase letters denote logical variables, while strings starting with lower case letters denote constants. Also *terms*, *atoms* and *literals* are defined as usual.

A *disjunctiverule* (*rule*, for short) r is a construct

$$a_1 \mid \cdots \mid a_n \; :- \; b_1, \cdots, b_k, \; \text{not} \; b_{k+1}, \cdots, \text{not} \; b_m. \tag{1}$$

where $a_1, \cdots, a_n, b_1, \cdots, b_m$ are atoms and $n \geq 0$, $m \geq k \geq 0$. The disjunction $a_1 \mid \cdots \mid a_n$ is called the *head* of r, while the conjunction $b_1, ..., b_k, \text{not} \; b_{k+1}, ..., \text{not} \; b_m$ is referred to as the *body* of r. Here not denotes default negation. A rule without head (i.e. $n = 0$) is usually referred to as an *integrity constraint*. A rule having precisely one head atom (i.e. $n = 1$) is called a *normal rule*. If the body is empty (i.e. $k = m = 0$), it is called a fact, and in this case the ":–" sign is usually omitted. An *ASP program* P is a finite set of rules.

In ASP, rules in programs are usually required to be safe. A rule is *safe* if each variable in that rule also appears in at least one positive literal in the body of that rule. An ASP program is safe, if each of its rules is safe, and in the following we will only consider safe programs. A term (an atom, a rule, a program, etc.) is called *ground*, if no variable appears in it.

Optimization problems are modeled in ASP using *weak constraints* [12]. A weak constraint ω is of the form:

$$:\sim b_1, \ldots, b_k, \text{not} \; b_{k+1}, \ldots, \text{not} \; b_m.[w@l]$$

where w and l are the weight and level of ω. (Intuitively, $[w@l]$ is read "as weight w at level l", where weight is the "cost" of violating the condition in the body of w, whereas levels can be specified for defining a priority among preference criteria). An ASP program with weak constraints is $\Pi = \langle P, W \rangle$, where P is a program and W is a set of weak constraints.

2.2 Semantics

Let P be an ASP program. The *Herbrand universe* U_P and the *Herbrand base* B_P of P are defined as usual (see e.g., [3]). The ground instantiation G_P of P is the set of all the ground instances of rules of P that can be obtained by substituting variables with constants from U_P.

An *interpretation* I for P is a subset I of B_P. A ground literal ℓ (resp., $\text{not} \; \ell$) is true w.r.t. I if $\ell \in I$ (resp., $\ell \notin I$), and false (resp., true) otherwise. An aggregate atom is true w.r.t. I if the evaluation of its aggregate function (i.e., the result of the application of f on the multiset S) with respect to I satisfies the guard; otherwise, it is false.

A ground rule r is *satisfied* by I if at least one atom in the head is true w.r.t. I whenever all conjuncts of the body of r are true w.r.t. I.

A model is an interpretation that satisfies all the rules of a program. Given a ground program G_P and an interpretation I, the *reduct* [20] of G_P w.r.t. I is the subset G_P^I of G_P obtained by deleting from G_P the rules in which a body literal is false w.r.t. I. An interpretation I for P is an *answer set* (or stable model [30]) for P if I is a minimal model (under subset inclusion) of G_P^I (i.e., I is a minimal model for G_P^I) [20].

Given a program with weak constraints $\Pi = \langle P, W \rangle$, the semantics of Π extends from the basic case defined above. Thus, let $G_\Pi = \langle G_P, G_W \rangle$ be the instantiation of Π; a constraint $\omega \in G_W$ is violated by an interpretation I if all the literals in ω are true w.r.t. I. An *optimum answer set* O for Π is an answer set of G_P that minimizes the sum of the weights of the violated weak constraints in G_W as a prioritized way.

2.3 Programming Methodology

ASP has been exploited in several domains, ranging from classical deductive databases to artificial intelligence. ASP can be used to encode problems in a declarative fashion; indeed, the power of disjunctive rules allows for expressing problems which are more complex than NP, and the (optional) separation of a fixed, non-ground program from an input database allows one to obtain uniform solutions over varying instances. More in detail, many problems of comparatively high computational complexity can be solved in a natural manner by following a "Guess&Check" programming methodology, originally introduced in [18] and refined in [33]. The idea behind this method can be summarized as follows: a database of facts is used to specify an instance of the problem, while a set of (usually disjunctive) rules, called "guessing part", is used to define the search space; solutions are then identified in the search space by another (optional) set of rules, called "checking part", which impose some admissibility constraint. To grasp the intuition behind the role of both the guessing and checking parts, consider the well-known NP-complete problem 3-COLORING: given an undirected graph $G = (V, E)$, assign each vertex one of three colors -say, red, green, or blue- such that adjacent vertices always have distinct colors. 3-COLORING can be encoded in ASP as follows:

```
%Fact database specifying an instance
vertex(v).        ∀v ∈ V;        edge(i,j).        ∀(i, j) ∈ E

%Uniform non-ground program solving the problem
col(X,red) | col(X,green) | col(X,blue) :− vertex(X).      % guessing part
:− edge(X,Y), col(X,C), col(Y,C).                          % checking part
```

The first two lines introduce suitable facts, representing the input graph G, the third line contains a rule stating that each vertex needs to have exactly one color. The last line contains a rule that acts as an integrity constraint since it disallows situations in which two connected vertices are associated with the same color.

3 Applications

In this section we briefly describe a number of real-world applications based on ASP. These applications were implemented by using the DLV system. DLV is the first ASP system which is undergoing an industrial exploitation by a spin-off company called DLVSYSTEM l.t.d. The usage of ASP in real context outlined several advantages from a Software Engineering viewpoint of using such a powerful and expressive framework. In particular the main qualities of ASP are flexibility, readability, extensibility, ease of maintenance. A lesson learned by developing real world applications is that ASP allows one to develop complex features at a lower (implementation) price than in traditional imperative languages. Indeed, the possibility of modifying complex reasoning task by editing text files, and testing it "on-site" together with the customer has been often a great advantage of the ASP-based development.

3.1 Routing and Classification of Call-Center Customers

Contact centers are used by many organizations to provide remote assistance to a variety of services. Their front-ends are flooded by a huge number of telephone calls every day. In this scenario the ability of routing automatically customers to the most appropriate service brings a two-fold advantage: improved quality of service and reduction of costs.

Exeura s.r.l, a spin-off company of the University of Calabria, developed a platform for customer profiling for phone calls routing based on ASP that is called zLog (http://www.exeura.eu/en/archives/solution/customer-profiling).

The key idea is to classify customer profiles and try to anticipate their actual needs for creating a personalized experience of customer care service. Contact center operators can define customer categories, but it is very likely that these employees may not have the competence for defining categories with a traditional programming language. Thus, the definition of customer categories is done by using an user-friendly user interface (see Fig. 1) that allows to create and modify categories to be added to the call routing system in real time. Categories definition criteria include customer behavioral aspects, such as recent history of contacts (e.g., telephone calls to the contact center, messages sent to customer assistance, etc.) or basic customer demographics (e.g., age, residence, etc. the latter useful, for instance, in case of natural disasters), or type of contract. When a customer calls the contact center, he/she is automatically assigned to a category (based on his/her profile) and then routed to an appropriate human operator or automatic responder. The customer categories specified trough the user interface are then automatically translated into ASP rules and fed as input to DLV together with the factual data extracted from the databases storing defined customer classes.

The zLog platform has been deployed in a production system handling Telecom Italia contact centers. Every day, over one million telephone calls asking for diagnostic services reach the contact centers of Telecom Italia. The needs are optimizing the operators assignment process, in order to reduce the average call response times, and improve customer support quality. The zLog platform can detect customer category in less than 100 ms (starting from his/her telephone number) and manage over 400 calls/sec. As a result, zLog enables huge time savings for over one million daily calls.

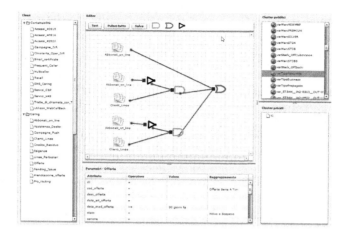

Fig. 1. Example of call center customer's class defined via the zLog user interface (Color figure online).

We now report an example of ASP program defining a customer class extracted from a real-world scenario that is also depicted in Fig. 1. The (simplified) set of rules generated by zLog corresponding to the specification of Fig. 1 is the following:

varTipoAbbonato(CLI) : − OR1(CLI).

OR1(CLI) : − AND1(CLI).   OR1(CLI) : − AND2(CLI).
OR1(CLI) : − Abbonati_on_line1(CLI).

AND1(CLI) : − Clienti_Linee(CLI, ...), not Abbonati_on_line2(CLI).
AND2(CLI) : − Clienti_Linee1(CLI), not Abbonati_on_line2(CLI).

Abbonati_on_line1(CLI) : − Abbonati_on_line(CLI, ..., ESITO_OPSC, ESITO_TGDS, ...),
      ESITO_OPSC = "2", ESITO_TGDS = "0".

Abbonati_on_line2(CLI) : − Abbonati_on_line(CLI, ..., ESITO_OPSC, ESITO_TGDS, ...),
      DatiOPSC(ESITO_OPSC).

DatiOPSC(codifica: "11"). DatiOPSC(codifica: "12"). DatiOPSC(codifica: "13").

Clienti_Linee1(CLI) : − Clienti_Linee(CLI, ..., TIPO_CLIENTE, STATO, ...),
      TIPO_CLIENTE = "ABB", STATO = "A".

Here it is easy to recognize that the above rules mimic the structure of the expression composed by using AND, OR, NOT operands in the graphical user interface. In particular it is defined the customer class labeled "varTipoAbbonato" (translated in English "kind of customer") outlined in blue in Fig. 1. In this specification data is extracted from other customer classes, namely "Clienti_Linee", and "Abbonati_Online" representing customers that own a traditional telephone line and subscribed a contract via the Internet portal of the company, respectively. These are filtered according to some criteria on class attributes (only the relevant ones are reported shown in the program snippet) that are specified trough a specific panel of the user interface. In this case it corresponds to those that have a permanent contract (they are called "clienti in abbonamento" in Italian), but the device they are using is not known. The new class "varTipoAbbonato" is then computed applying the rules generated according to the graphical representation. zLog then exploits DLV in order to quickly compute the new class of customers.

3.2   Workforce-Management in the International Seaport of Gioia Tauro

The problem we dealt with in this application is a form of *workforce management* problem [37]. It amounts to computing a suitable allocation of the available personnel of the seaport such that cargo ships mooring in the port are properly handled. To accomplish this task several constraints have to be satisfied. An appropriate number of employees, providing several different skills, is required depending on the size and the load of cargo ships. Moreover, the way an employee is selected and the specific role she will play in the team (each employee is able to cover several roles according to her skills) are subject to many conditions (e.g., fair distribution of the working load, turnover of the heavy/dangerous roles, employees' contract rules, etc.). To cope with this crucial problem DLV has been exploited for developing a team builder. First of all we modeled the input as follows: The employees and their skills by predicate *hasSkill(employee, skillName)*. The specification of a shift for which a team needs to be allocated, by predicate *shift(id, date, duration)*. The number of employees necessary for a certain skill on the shift, by *neededEmployee (shift, skill, num)*. Weekly statistics specifying, for each employee, both the number of worked hours per skill and the last allocation date by predicate *wstat(employee, skill, hours, lastTime)*. Employees excluded due to a management decision by *excluded(shift, employee)*. Absent employees by predicate *absent(day, employee)*, and total amount of working hours in the week per employees by predicate *workedHours(employee,weekHours)*. A simplified version of the program computing teams is the following:

(r) assign(E,Sh,Sk) | nAssign(E,Sh,Sk) :− hasSkill(E,Sk),
             employee(E,_),shift(Sh,Day,Dur), not absent(Day,E),
                      not excluded(Sh,E), neededEmployee(Sh,Sk,_),
                      workedHours(E,Wh), Wh + Dur $\leq$ 36.

(c_1) :− shift(Sh,_,_), neededEmployee(Sh,Sk,EmpNum),
                   #count{E : assign(E,Sh,Sk)} $\neq$ EmpNum.

(c_2) :− assign(E,Sh,Sk1), assign(E,Sh,Sk2), Sk1 $\neq$ Sk2.

(c_3) :− wstats(E1,Sk,_,LastTime1), wstats(E2,Sk,_,LastTime2),
               LastTime1 > LastTime2, assign(E1,Sh,Sk),
               not assign(E2,Sh,Sk).

(c_4) :− workedHours(E1,Wh1), workedHours(E2,Wh2), threshold(Tr),
               Wh1 + Tr < Wh2, assign(E1,Sh,Sk),
               not assign(E2,Sh,Sk).

(r') workedHours(E,Wh) :− hasSkill(E,_),
                   #count{H,E : wstats(E,_,H,_)} = Wh.

The disjunctive rule r generates the search space by guessing the assignment of a number of available employees to the shift in the appropriate roles. Absent or excluded employees, together with employees exceeding the maximum number of weekly working hours are automatically discarded. Then, admissible solutions are selected by means of constraints: c_1 discards assignments with a wrong number of employees for some skill; c_2 avoids that an employee covers two roles in the same shift; c_3 implements the turnover of roles; and c_4 guarantees a fair distribution of the workload. Finally, rule r' computes the total number of worked hours per employee. Note that, only the kernel part of the employed logic program is reported here (in a simplified form), and many other constraints were developed, tuned and tested.

The final user interface allows to modify manually computed teams, and the system is able to verify whether the manually-modified team still satisfies the constraints. In case of errors, causes are outlined and suggestions for fixing a problem are proposed. E.g., if no plan can be generated, then the system suggests the user to relax some constraints. In this application, the pure declarative nature of the language allowed for refining and tuning both problem specifications and ASP programs while interacting with the stakeholders of the seaport. The system, developed by Exeura s.r.l, has been adopted by the company ICO BLG operating automobile logistics in the seaport of Gioia Tauro.

3.3   Advanced Tools for the Tourism Industry

We now overview two applications of ASP to problems arising in the tourism industry. The first application is an intelligent advisor that select the most promising offers for customers of a travel agency. The second is a tool for the travel agent that helps in selecting blocks of touristic packages to pre-book during the allotment phase.

Intelligent Touristic Advisor. In [41] it is described a service based on ASP that has been integrated into an e-tourism portal. The idea is to devise a tool that helps both employees and customers of a travel agency in finding the best possible travel solution in a short time. It can be seen as a "mediator" system finding the best match between the offers of the tour operators and the requests of the tourists. A knowledge base has been specified by analyzing the touristic domain in cooperation with the staff of a real touristic agency, which models the key entities that describe the process of organizing and selling a complete holiday package. In particular, all the required information, such as geographic information, kind of holiday, transportation means, etc. is stored in the knowledge base. Moreover, the mere geographic information is, then, enriched by other information that is usually exploited by travel agency employees for selecting a travel destination. For instance, one might suggest avoiding sea holidays in winter; whereas, one should be recommended a visit to Sicily in summer. Also user preferences are stored, so to exploit the knowledge about users to personalize holiday package search. Then DLV has been used to develop several search modules that simplify the task of selecting the holiday packages that best fit the customer needs. As an example we report a (simplified) logic program that creates a selection of holiday packages:

```
%detect possible and suggested places
possiblePlace(Place) :− askFor(TripKind,_), PlaceOffer(Place, TripKind).
suggestPlace(Place) :− possiblePlace(Place), askFor(_,Period),
                       suggestedPeriod(Place, Period),
                       not BadPeriod(Place, Period).
```

```
%select packages that the user is possibly interested in
possibleOffer(O) :− TouristicOffer(O, Place), possiblePlace(Place).
```

The first two rules select: possible places (i.e., the ones that offer the kind of holiday as input); and places to be suggested (because they offer the required kind of holiday in the specified period). Finally, the remaining rule searches in the available holiday packages the ones which offer an holiday that matches the original input (possible offer). This is one of the several reasoning modules that have been devised for implementing the intelligent search, for more details we refer the reader to [41].

Automatic Allotment. In the travel industry it is common for tour operators to pre-book from service suppliers blocks of touristic packages, which are called allotments in jargon. Basically, given a set of requirements on the properties of packages to be bought, budget limits, and an offer of packages from several suppliers, the problem from the perspective of the travel agent is to select a set of offers to be brought (or pre-booked) for the next season so that the expected earnings are maximized [15]. Despite allotment is one of the most commonly-used supplying practices in the tourism industry, the final selection of packages offered by travel suppliers is often done in small travel agencies more or less manually. Thus we developed an ASP-based tool for assisting tour operators in the allotment process. We now illustrates a simplified version of the ASP program which solves the allotment problem. In particular, the following disjunctive rule guesses a quantity to buy for each required package limiting the search space to available package tours which are requested and their selling price is in the requested range as follows:

$$buy(P, Q) \mid nBuy(P, Q) :− availablePackages(P, \_, D, T, SP, PP, \_, AvQ),$$
$$requiredPackages(D, T, MinP, MaxP, ReqQ),$$
$$0 \leq Q \leq ReqQ, Q \leq AvQ, MinP \leq SP \leq MaxP.$$

The following constraint ensures only one quantity the same package is selected:

$$:− \#count\{Q, P : buy(P, Q) \} > 1, availablePackages(P, \_, \_, \_, \_, \_, \_, \_).$$

Here a special aggregate atom count is used see [16]. An other constraint enforces a critical requirement on the budget, i.e. the sum of prices of selected package tours must not exceed a limited budget:

$$:− \#sum\{ PP*Q, P : buy(P, Q),$$
$$availablePackages(P, S, \_, \_, SP, PP, \_, \_) \} > B, budget(B).$$

then earnings are maximized by using a weak constraint [12]:

$$:\sim \text{ discountPrices(P, SP, PP), buy(P, Q), E} = \text{(SP-PP)*Q. [-E]}$$

Intuitively, when a stock of package tours is bought the violation of this constraint is associated with a cost depending on the earnings obtained by buying those packages. The weight of weak constraint is negative since weak constraints expresses the minimization of the cost associated to a solution. Travel agencies might specify a number of additional optional preference criteria that were encoded also by means of weak constraints. The ASP program is included as an advanced reasoning service of the e-tourism platform developed under the iTravelPlus project by the Tour Operator Top Class s.r.l. and the University of Calabria.

3.4   Business Intelligence Platform for Cleaning Medical Archives

The approach described in the following addresses multi-source data cleaning for syntactic and semantic anomaly detection with ASP [44]. The idea is to define of an automatic procedure for generating logic programs able to identify and, whenever possible, correct errors within the data. Then, an automatically-generated logic program is embedded in a business intelligence work-flow (including data extraction, integration, manipulation and transformation) developed with Pentaho Kettle. The ASP-based solution has been implemented in a Penthao plugin called DLVCleaner. The proposed approach should be considered complementary to the existing ones, and capable to provide simplified and flexible specification of the logic of the data cleaning task. In the following we report a brief description of a real use case employing ASP for data cleaning. We refer the reader to [44] for more details on the DLV Cleaner. ASP was used to clean data from several tumor registries of the Calabria region. We first provide some background information about this scenario (from [44]). Currently no law obliges hospitals and clinics in Italy to collect and archive data on diagnosis and treatment of tumors. Then, various organizations autonomously collect such information in tumor registries. Currently, 34 tumor registries are active in Italy, covering overall almost 25 % of the population. The registry used in our use case considers information related to several local healthcare centers from the Calabria Region. Data are collected from many different sources, including public hospitals, healthcare centers, family doctors, etc. Collected information include the kind of diagnosed cancer, personal data of the patient, current clinical conditions, past and current treatments, disease evolution, etc. All such information are extremely important to analyze causes and evolutions of cancer diseases, in order to study proper treatments, prevention policies, and to schedule sanitary budgets. Overall, we considered more than 200 tables as sources of data. Almost all of this information should be inter-linked by the identity of the patient. However, different registries used different schemas and standards to represent data; and such an information is often imprecise in local sources, since in many cases data are loaded manually. Thus these often contain errors or incomplete information. As a consequence, the proper identification of each mentioned patient through a subset of its attributes

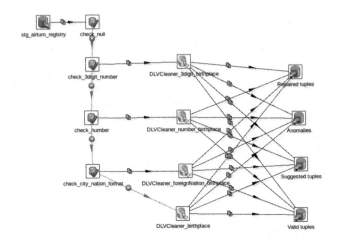

Fig. 2. Example of a Kettle workflow using the DLVCleaner plugin (from [44]).

is a difficult and fundamental task. The entire dataset has been cleaned applying several cleaning workflows embedding several instances of DLVCleaner (in Fig. 2) is reported a picture of a workflow configured for cleaning patient information). Each data flow is sent to a specifically configured DLVCleaner instance which, based on stream classifications rules specified in ASP outputs results onto one of four tables, namely *valid tuples*, *corrected tuples*, *suggested tuples*, and *anomalies*. As an example, the *DLVCleaner_3digit_birthplace* instance in Fig. 2 embeds a transformation in which the birthplace is mapped onto the *nationality* attribute of the reference dictionary, whereas in *DLVCleaner_number_birthplace* the birthplace is mapped onto the *ISTAT code* dictionary attribute. Analogously, in *DLVCleaner_birthplace* the pair *(city - nation)* is handled by a matching function that first tokenizes the string, singling out the city name, and then matches it to the *city name* dictionary attribute. In order to detect potential corrections, the most proper comparison function is applied, depending on data format; as an example, for the three-digit birthplaces, we used the Hamming distance whereas for city names we used the Levenshtein distance. Setting up the workflow shown in Fig. 2 takes only few minutes and it is possible to follow a try-and-error approach. Clearly, the cleaning step for birthplaces shown above is only one small step in a more complete workflow dealing with the overall database.

To give an idea of the size of the data involved in the described use case, the input table was composed of 1.000.000 tuples collecting records from 155 municipalities, whereas the dictionary stored about 15.000 tuples. From the application of the transformation shown in Fig. 2 it was obtained that almost 50 % of input tuples were wrong. 72 % of wrong tuples have been automatically corrected, whereas 24 % had multiple corrections. Only 2 % of input tuples have been detected as wrong and not repairable.

3.5 Other Applications

The exploitation of DLV for developing applications is not limited to the examples reported in this section. Actually, DLV is at the basis of several other advanced applications of which it is worth mentioning data integration sys-tems [32,35], web data extraction [26], and computation of minimum cardinality diagnoses [25]. Moreover, the Polish company Rodan Systems S.A. has exploited DLV in a tool for the detection of price manipulations and unauthorized use of confidential information, which is used by the Polish Securities and Exchange Commission. The company Exeura s.r.l. developed systems exploiting DLV for implementing specific modules in e-Government, e-Medicine and tele-assistance systems.

4   Development Tools

The real-world applications of DLV that we described in previous sections have demonstrated that ASP can be used to implement real-world applications. Nonetheless developers need specialized tools that make easier the develop-ment of applications, and that support the integration of different tools in the same environment. DLV is well-suited for applications development also thanks to the endowment of powerful development tools [22,24], supporting the activities of researchers and implementors. Indeed, we endowed DLV with effective programming-tools, which are conceived to ease the usage and the integration of ASP-based technologies in the existing environments tailored for imperative/object-oriented programming languages. In the following we intro-duce two advanced development tools for developing ASP-based applications, namely *ASPIDE* and JDLV .

4.1   IDE for ASP

ASPIDE [24] is a complete IDE for ASP programs, which integrates an advanced editing tool with a collection of user-friendly graphical tools for program com-position and execution. The user interface of *ASPIDE* is depicted in Fig. 3. In the upper part of the interface a toolbar allows the user to quickly access some common operations. In the center of the interface there is the main editing area where it is possible to open several files organized in a tabbed panel. The left part of the interface is dedicated to the workspace explorer, which list projects, and to the error console, which organizes errors and warnings according to the project and files where they are localized. On the right, there are the outline panel and the template panel. The layout of the IDE is customizable, indeed the user can rearrange components the way he/she likes best.

 In the following we overview the main features that are available in *ASPIDE*.

Advanced Editor. The system allows for organizing logic programs in projects à la Eclipse, which are collected in a workspace. Projects collect either different parts of an encoding or several equivalent encodings solving the same problem. *ASPIDE* supports a number of file editors and can be extended to support virtu-ally any kind of input files by user-defined plugins (which are described below). The main editor for ASP programs offers, besides the basic functionalities, such as code line numbering, find/replace, undo/redo, copy/paste, also:

- *Text coloring.* The editor performs keyword outlining (such as ":–" and "not") and dynamic highlighting of predicate names, variables, strings, and comments.
- *Automatic completion.* The system is able to complete (on request) predicate names, as well as variable names. Predicate names are both learned while writing, and extracted from the files belonging to the same project; variables are suggested by taking into account the rule we are currently writing.
- *Refactoring.* The refactoring tool allows to modify programs in a guided way. For instance, variable renaming in a rule is done by considering bindings of variables; custom refactorings can applied by selecting rules and applying some functionality offered by a user-defined plugin.
- *Dynamic code checking and errors highlighting.* Programs are parsed while writing, and both errors or possible warnings are immediately outlined.
- *Quick fixes.* The editor suggests quick fixes to reported errors or warnings, and applies them (on request) by automatically changing the affected part of code.
- *Code templates.* ASPIDE provides support for assisted writing of rules (guessing patterns, etc.), as well as automated writing of entire subprograms (e.g., transitive closure rules) by means of code templates, which can be instantiated while writing.
- *Program Outline.* ASPIDE creates an outline view which graphically represents program elements. Each item in the outline can be used to quickly access the corresponding line of code (a very useful feature when dealing with long files).
- *Visual editor.* The users can *draw* logic programs by exploiting a full graphical environment that offers a QBE-like tool for building logic rules. The user can switch from the text editor to the visual one (and vice versa) thanks to a reverse-rengineering mechanism from text to graphical format.

Fig. 3. The user interface of *ASPIDE*.

Dependency Graph. *ASPIDE* creates automatically a graphical representation of several variants of the (non-ground) dependency graphs associated with a project, and can be used for analyzing rule dependencies and browsing the program.

Debugger and Profiler. *ASPIDE* embeds the debugging tool *spock* [8], and provides a graphical user interface that wraps the above mentioned tool. Regarding the profiler, *ASPIDE* fully embeds the graphical interface presented in [14].

Unit Testing. In software engineering, the task of testing and validating programs is a crucial part of the life-cycle of software development process and a test conceived for verifying the behavior of a specific part of a program is called unit testing. The testing feature consists on a unit testing framework for logic programs in the style of JUnit. The developer can specify rules by composing one or several units, specify one or more inputs and assert a number of conditions on both expected outputs and the expected behavior of sub-programs. For an exhaustive description the testing language and the graphical tool we refer the reader to [23].

Interaction with Databases. *ASPIDE* simplifies access to external databases by a graphical tool connecting to DBMSs via JDBC. The database management feature of *ASPIDE* supports the creation of both *#import/#export* directives of DLV, and fully-graphical composition of TYP files [43]. Imported sources are emphasized also in the program editor by exploiting a specific color indicating the corresponding predicates. Database oriented applications can be run by setting DLV^{DB} as engine in a run configuration. A data integration scenario [32] can be implemented by exploiting these features.

Configuration of the Execution. The execution of ASP programs is fully customizable by using the RunConfiguration Dialog that allows one to set the system executable, setup invocation options and input files. A number of shortcuts and drop down menus allows one for a quick execution of single files or selection of files within a project.

Results Window. The results are presented to the user in a comfortable view combining tabular representation of predicates and a tree-like representation of answer sets. Further output extensions can be added by means of output plugins. Two examples are the ARVis comparator of answer sets [1] and the answer set visualizer IDPDraw [45].

User-Defined Plugins. An important feature of *ASPIDE* is the possibility to extend it with user defined plugins. Developers can create libraries for extending *ASPIDE* with: (*i*) new input formats, (*ii*) program rewritings, and even (*iii*) customizing the visualization/format of results. An input plugin can take care of input files that appear in *ASPIDE* as a logic program, and an output

Fig. 4. The JDLV Eclipse plugin.

plugin can handle the external conversion of the computed results. A rewriting plugin may encode a procedure that can be applied to rules in the editor (e.g., disjunctive rule shifting can be applied on the fly by selecting rules in the editor and applying the mentioned rewriting). An SDK available from the *ASPIDE* web site allows one to develop new plugins.

System Availability. *ASPIDE* is written in Java and is available for all the major operating systems, including Linux, Mac OS and Windows. It can be downloaded from the system website http://www.mat.unical.it/ricca/aspide.

4.2   Combining Java and ASP

JDLV is a plug-in for the Eclipse platform [17], offering a seamless integration of ASP-based technologies within the most popular development environment for Java. JDLV is based on *JASP* [22], a hybrid language that transparently supports a bilateral interaction between (disjunctive) ASP and Java. A key ingredient of *JASP* is the mapping between (collections of) Java objects and ASP facts. In *JASP*, Java Objects are mapped to logic facts (and vice versa) by adopting a structural mapping strategy. *JASP* exploits the same ideas of modern Object-Relational Mapping (ORM) frameworks, such as Hibernate and TopLink, where objects are saved/loaded from/to relational databases. *JASP* supports both a default mapping strategy, which fits the most common programmers' requirements, and custom ORM specifications that comply with the Java Persistence API (JPA) [40] to suit enterprise application development standards. The $\mathcal{JASP}$ code is very natural and intuitive for a programmer skilled in both ASP and Java.

In Fig. 4 is depicted the a simple $\mathcal{JASP}$ program open in the JDLV plugin that will serve as a running example. A monolithic block of plain ASP code (called *module*) is embedded in the Java method, which is executed "in-place", i.e., the solving process is triggered at the end of the module specification. In particular the program in Fig. 4 defines the method *compute3Coloring()*, that contains a module to computes a 3-coloring of the given graph. Intuitively, the ASP program is enclosed within special tags ($< \# \ldots \# >$), and when *compute3Coloring()* is invoked, Java objects are transformed into logic facts, by applying an ORM strategy as specified in the module parameters. In the example Java variables *arcs* and *nodes* are mapped to corresponding predicates *arc* and *node*, respectively, whereas the local variable *res* is mapped as output variable to the predicate *col*. In this example, each string x in *nodes* is transformed in unary facts *node(x)*; similarly, each instance of *Arc* in the variable *arcs* produces a binary fact, e.g., *arc(from,to)*. These facts are input of the logic program, which is evaluated "in-place". If no 3-coloring exists, the variable *res* is set to *null*; otherwise, when the first answer set is computed, for each fact *col* contained in the solution a new object of the class *Colored* is created and added to *res*, which, in turn, is returned by the method. Here the $\mathcal{JASP}$'s default ORM strategy is applied to map one object per logic fact, which compound keys, i.e., keys made of all basic attributes, and *embedded values* for one to one associations, which naturally fits the usual way of representing information in ASP, e.g., in the example, one fact models one node. Such a mapping is inverted to obtain Java objects from logic facts, and ensures the safe creation of new Java objects without requiring value invention in logic programs. Although this strategy poses (very few) restrictions such as non-recursive type definition (e.g., tree-like structures are not admitted in $\mathcal{JASP}$-core), based on our experience, it is sufficient to handle common use cases. On the other hand, as we show in the following, full $\mathcal{JASP}$ language allows for custom ORM strategies specified by JPA [40] annotations. It is now clear that, $\mathcal{JASP}$ directly extends the syntax of Java such that $\mathcal{JASP}$ module statements are allowed in Java *block statements*. Concerning the syntax allowed within modules, $\mathcal{JASP}$ is compliant with the language of DLV, and also supports a number of advanced features that are mentioned in the following.

The language also features a number of additional features that further ease the development of programs, such as incremental modules, non positional notation, and database access. We refer the reader to [22] for a full account of the $\mathcal{JASP}$ language.

System Availability. JDLV is available in form of an Eclipse platform [17] plugin from http://www.dlvsystem.com/dlvsystem/index.php/JDLV. JDLV includes *Jdlvc*, a compiler to generate plain Java classes from $\mathcal{JASP}$ files. The *Jdlvc* compiler produces plain Java classes which manage the generation of logic programs and control statements for the underlying solver DLV.

5   Conclusion

In this paper we have introduced ASP, and we have described some industry-level applications of the ASP system DLV. These applications confirmed the applicability of ASP-based technologies for solving complex real-world applications. Moreover, it is worth observing that the DLV system is well-suited for applications development also thanks to the endowment of powerful development tools. In particular, we described two of them conceived for developing ASP-based applications, namely *ASPIDE* and JDLV . *ASPIDE* is an integrated development environment, supporting the entire life-cycle of logic programs development; JDLV is an implementation of $\mathcal{JASP}$, a new programming framework integrating ASP with Java.

References

1. Ambroz, T., Charwat, G., Jusits, A., Wallner, J.P., Woltran, S.: ARVis: visualizing relations between answer sets. In: Cabalar, P., Son, T.C. (eds.) LPNMR 2013. LNCS, vol. 8148, pp. 73–78. Springer, Heidelberg (2013)
2. Balduccini, M., Gelfond, M., Watson, R., Nogueira, M.: The USA-Advisor: a case study in answer set planning. In: Eiter, T., Faber, W., Truszczyński, M. (eds.) LPNMR 2001. LNCS (LNAI), vol. 2173, pp. 439–442. Springer, Heidelberg (2001)
3. Baral, C.: Knowledge Representation Reasoning and Declarative Problem Solving. CUP, New York (2003)
4. Baral, C., Gelfond, M.: Reasoning agents in dynamic domains. In: Minker, J. (ed.) Logic-Based Artificial Intelligence, pp. 257–279. Kluwer, USA (2000)
5. Baral, C., Uyan, C.: Declarative specification and solution of combinatorial auctions using logic programming. In: Eiter, T., Faber, W., Truszczyński, M. (eds.) LPNMR 2001. LNCS (LNAI), vol. 2173, pp. 186–199. Springer, Heidelberg (2001)
6. Bardadym, V.A.: Computer-aided school and university timetabling: the new wave. In: Burke, E.K., Ross, P. (eds.) PATAT 1995. LNCS, vol. 1153, pp. 22–45. Springer, Heidelberg (1996)
7. Bertossi, L., Hunter, A., Schaub, T. (eds.): Inconsistency Tolerance. LNCS, vol. 3300. Springer, Heidelberg (2005)
8. Brain, M., Gebser, M., Pührer, J., Schaub, T., Tompits, H., Woltran, S.: That is illogical captain. the debugging support tool spock for answer-set programs: system description. In: Vos, M.D., Schaub, T., (eds.) SEA 2007 (2007)
9. Bravo, L., Bertossi, L.: Logic programming for consistently querying data integration systems. In: IJCAI-2003, pp. 10–15 (2003)
10. Brewka, G., Coradeschi, S., Perini, A., Traverso, P. (eds.): ECAI 2006, 29 - September 1, 2006, Riva del Garda, Italy, Including PAIS 2006, FAIS, vol. 141. IOS Press (2006)
11. Brewka, G., Eiter, T., Truszczynski, M.: Answer set programming at a glance. Commun. ACM **54**(12), 92–103 (2011)
12. Buccafurri, F., Leone, N., Rullo, P.: Enhancing disjunctive datalog by constraints. IEEE TKDE **12**(5), 845–860 (2000)
13. Calimeri, F., Ianni, G., Ricca, F.: The third open answer set programming competition. TPLP **14**(1), 117–135 (2014)
14. Calimeri, F., Leone, N., Ricca, F., Veltri, P.: A visual tracer for DLV. In: Proceedings of SEA 2009, Potsdam, Germany, September 2009

15. Castellani, M., Mussoni, M.: An economic analysis of tourism contracts: allotment and free sale*. In: Matia, Á., Nijkamp, P., Neto, P. (eds.) Advances in Modern Tourism Research, pp. 51–85. Physica-Verlag, Heidelberg (2007)
16. Dell'Armi, T., Faber, W., Ielpa, G., Leone, N., Pfeifer, G.: Aggregate functions in disjunctive logic programming: semantics, complexity, and implementation in DLV. In: IJCAI 2003, Acapulco, Mexico, pp. 847–852, August 2003
17. Eclipse: Eclipse (2001). http://www.eclipse.org/
18. Eiter, T., Faber, W., Leone, N., Pfeifer, G.: Declarative problem-solving using the DLV system. In: Minker, J. (ed.) Logic-Based Artificial Intelligence, pp. 79–103. Kluwer, USA (2000)
19. Eiter, T., Gottlob, G., Mannila, H.: Disjunctive datalog. ACM TODS **22**(3), 364–418 (1997)
20. Faber, W., Leone, N., Pfeifer, G.: Recursive aggregates in disjunctive logic programs: semantics and complexity. In: Alferes, J.J., Leite, J. (eds.) JELIA 2004. LNCS (LNAI), vol. 3229, pp. 200–212. Springer, Heidelberg (2004)
21. Faber, W., Leone, N., Pfeifer, G.: Semantics and complexity of recursive aggregates in answer set programming. AI **175**(1), 278–298 (2011). Special Issue: John McCarthy's Legacy
22. Febbraro, O., Grasso, G., Leone, N., Ricca, F.: JASP: a framework for integrating answer set programming with Java. In: Proceedings of KR2012. AAAI Press (2012)
23. Febbraro, O., Leone, N., Reale, K., Ricca, F.: Unit testing in aspide. CoRR abs/1108.5434
24. Febbraro, O., Reale, K., Ricca, F.: ASPIDE: integrated development environment for answer set programming. In: Delgrande, J.P., Faber, W. (eds.) LPNMR 2011. LNCS (LNAI), vol. 6645, pp. 317–330. Springer, Heidelberg (2011)
25. Friedrich, G., Ivanchenko, V.: Diagnosis from first principles for workflow executions. Technical report, Alpen Adria University, Applied Informatics, Klagenfurt, Austria (2008). http://proserver3-iwas.uni-klu.ac.at/download_area/Technical-Reports/technical_report_2008_02.pdf
26. Furche, T., Gottlob, G., Grasso, G., Guo, X., Orsi, G., Schallhart, C.: Opal: automated form understanding for the deep web. In: WWW (2012)
27. Garro, A., Palopoli, L., Ricca, F.: Exploiting agents in e-learning and skills management context. AI Commun. **19**(2), 137–154 (2006)
28. Gelfond, M., Leone, N.: Logic programming and knowledge representation - the A-Prolog perspective. AI **138**(1–2), 3–38 (2002)
29. Gelfond, M., Lifschitz, V.: The stable model semantics for logic programming. In: Kowalski, R.A., Bowen, K.A. (eds.) ICLP/SLP 1988, pp. 1070–1080. MIT Press, Cambridge (1988)
30. Gelfond, M., Lifschitz, V.: Classical negation in logic programs and disjunctive databases. NGC **9**, 365–385 (1991)
31. Grasso, G., Leone, N., Manna, M., Ricca, F.: Logic Programming, Knowledge Representation, and Nonmonotonic Reasoning: Essays in Honor of M. Gelfond. LNAI, vol. 6565. Springer, Heidelberg (2011)
32. Leone, N., Gottlob, G., Rosati, R., Eiter, T., Faber, W., Fink, M., Greco, G., Ianni, G., Kałka, E., Lembo, D., Lenzerini, M., Lio, V., Nowicki, B., Ruzzi, M., Staniszkis, W., Terracina, G.: The INFOMIX system for advanced integration of incomplete and inconsistent data. In: SIGMOD 2005, pp. 915–917. ACM Press, June 2005
33. Leone, N., Pfeifer, G., Faber, W., Eiter, T., Gottlob, G., Perri, S., Scarcello, F.: The DLV system for knowledge representation and reasoning. ACM TOCL **7**(3), 499–562 (2006)

34. Lifschitz, V.: Answer set planning. In: Schreye, D.D. (ed.) ICLP 1999, pp. 23–37. The MIT Press, Las Cruces (1999)

35. Manna, M., Ricca, F., Terracina, G.: Consistent query answering via ASP from different perspectives: theory and practice. TPLP **13**(2), 227–252 (2013)

36. Marek, V.W., Truszczyński, M.: Stable models and an alternative logic programming paradigm. CoRR cs.LO/9809032 (1998)

37. Naveh, Y., Richter, Y., Altshuler, Y., Gresh, D.L., Connors, D.P.: Workforce optimization: identification and assignment of professional workers using constraint programming. IBM J. Res. Dev. **51**(3.4), 263–279 (2007)

38. Niemelä, I.: Logic programs with stable model semantics as a constraint programming paradigm. In: Proceedings of the Workshop on Computational Aspects of Nonmonotonic Reasoning, Trento, Italy, pp. 72–79 (1998)

39. Nogueira, M., Balduccini, M., Gelfond, M., Watson, R., Barry, M.: An A-Prolog decision support system for the space shuttle. In: Ramakrishnan, I.V. (ed.) PADL 2001. LNCS, vol. 1990, pp. 169–183. Springer, Heidelberg (2001)

40. Oracle: JSR 317: JavaTM Persistence 2.0 (2009). http://jcp.org/en/jsr/detail?id=317

41. Ricca, F., Dimasi, A., Grasso, G., Ielpa, S.M., Iiritano, S., Manna, M., Leone, N.: A logic-based system for e-Tourism. FI **105**(1–2), 35–55 (2010)

42. Ricca, F., Grasso, G., Alviano, M., Manna, M., Lio, V., Iiritano, S., Leone, N.: Team-building with answer set programming in the gioia-tauro seaport. TPLP. CUP **12**(3), 361–381 (2012). CUP

43. Terracina, G., Leone, N., Lio, V., Panetta, C.: Experimenting with recursive queries in database and logic programming systems. TPLP **8**, 129–165 (2008)

44. Terracina, G., Martello, A., Leone, N.: Logic-based techniques for data cleaning: an application to the italian national healthcare system. In: Cabalar, P., Son, T.C. (eds.) LPNMR 2013. LNCS, vol. 8148, pp. 524–529. Springer, Heidelberg (2013)

45. Wittocx, J.: IDPDraw, a tool used for visualizing answer sets (since 2009). http://dtai.cs.kuleuven.be/krr/software/visualisation

The TPTP World – Infrastructure for Automated Reasoning

Geoff Sutcliffe[⊠]

University of Miami, Coral Gables, USA
geoff@cs.miami.edu

The TPTP World is a well established infrastructure that supports research, development, and deployment of Automated Theorem Proving (ATP) systems for classical logics. The TPTP World includes the TPTP problem library, the TSTP solution library, standards for writing ATP problems and reporting ATP solutions, tools and services for processing ATP problems and solutions, and it supports the CADE ATP System Competition (CASC). The TPTP World infrastructure has been deployed in a range of applications, in both academia and industry. The web page http://www.tptp.org provides access to all components.

The TPTP Problem Library: The Thousands of Problems for Theorem Provers (TPTP) problem library [5] is the original core component of the TPTP World, and is commonly referred to as "the TPTP". The TPTP problem library supplies the ATP community with a comprehensive library of the test problems that are available today, in order to provide an overview and a simple, unambiguous reference mechanism, to support the testing and evaluation of ATP systems, and to help ensure that performance results accurately reflect capabilities of the ATP systems being considered. The TPTP contains test problems in a broad range of domains, including logic, mathematics, computer science, science and engineering, social sciences, and arts & humanities. Since its first release in 1993, many researchers have used the TPTP as an appropriate and convenient basis for ATP system evaluation. Over the years the TPTP has also increasingly been used as a conduit for ATP users to provide samples of their problems to ATP system developers — users have found that contributing samples of their problems to the TPTP exposes the problems to the developers, who then improve their systems' performances on the problems, which completes a cycle to provide the users with more effective tools.

The TSTP Solution Library: The Thousands of Solutions from Theorem Provers (TSTP) solution library is the "flip side" of the TPTP – a corpus of ATP systems' solutions to TPTP problems. A major use of the TSTP is for ATP system developers to examine solutions to problems, and thus understand how they can be solved, leading to improvements to their own systems. The TSTP is also the basis for the TPTP problem ratings [9], which provide a well-defined measure of how difficult the problems are for ATP systems, and how effective the ATP systems are for different types of problems. Over time, decreasing ratings for individual problems have provided an indication of progress in the field [7]. The analysis done for problem ratings also provides ratings for ATP systems.

© Springer International Publishing Switzerland 2015
W. Faber and A. Paschke (Eds.): Reasoning Web 2015, LNCS 9203, pp. 327–329, 2015.
DOI: 10.1007/978-3-319-21768-0

The TPTP Language: One of the keys to the success of the TPTP World is the consistent use of the TPTP language for writing both problems and solutions [8], which enables convenient communication between different systems and researchers. The language shares many features with Prolog, so that with a few operator definitions, units of TPTP data can be read and written using single read/1 and writeq/1 calls. The TPTP language is defined using an extended BNF that is easy to translate into lex/yacc/flex/bison input, so that construction of parsers (in languages other than Prolog) is a reasonably easy task [12]. The TPTP Process Instruction (TPI) language [6] provides commands that can be used in conjunction with the TPTP logical language, allowing users to easily input, output, and organize logical formulae, and to control the execution of ATP systems. In conjunction with the TPTP language, the TPTP World uses the SZS[1] ontologies [4] to record what is known or has been established about a TPTP problem. The ontologies are used to precisely specify the semantic relationship between the axioms and conjecture of a problem, and to specify the nature of formulae output by ATP systems and tools. The SZS standard also recommends the precise way in which the ontology values should be presented, in order to facilitate easy processing.

The TPTP Tools and Services: The TPTP World includes tools, programming libraries, and online services that are used to support the application and deployment of ATP systems. SystemOnTPTP [2] is a utility that allows an ATP problem or solution to be easily and quickly submitted in various ways to a range of ATP systems and tools. The utility uses a suite of currently available ATP systems and tools, whose properties (input format, reporting of result status, etc.) are stored in a simple text database. It is available online, and as a standalone utility. GDV [3] is a tool that verifies TPTP format derivations. Structural checks verify that inferences have been done correctly in the context of the derivation, and semantic checks verify the expected semantic relationship between the parents and inferred formula of each inference step. AGInTRater [1] is a tool that that measures the "interestingness" of formulae in TPTP format derivations, e.g., obviousness estimates the difficulty of proving a formula, complexity estimates the effort required to understand a formula, and surprisingness measures new relationships between symbols in a formula. IDV [11] is a tool that provides an interactive interface for viewing TPTP format derivations. The rendering of a derivation DAG uses shapes, colors, and tags to provide information about the derivation, and the user can interact with the rendering in various ways. A particularly novel feature of IDV is its ability to provide a synopsis of a derivation by using the AGInTRater to identify interesting lemmas.

This TPTP World Tutorial: This tutorial provides a practical introduction to the TPTP World. Attendees will be led through the various online components, shown how to use the online tools to process ATP problems, encouraged to download and use the libraries and tools on their own computers, and instructed on robust techniques for automated reasoning in the TPTP World.

---

[1] SZS is an acronym from the initials of the original authors' family names [10].

References

1. Puzis, Y., Gao, Y., Sutcliffe, G.: Automated generation of interesting theorems. In: Sutcliffe, G., Goebel, R. (eds.) Proceedings of the 19th International FLAIRS Conference, pp. 49–54. AAAI Press (2006)
2. Sutcliffe, G.: System description: SystemOnTPTP. In: McAllester, D. (ed.) CADE-17. LNCS (LNAI), vol. 1831, pp. 406–410. Springer, Heidelberg (2000)
3. Sutcliffe, G.: Semantic derivation verification. Int. J. Artif. Intell. Tools **15**(6), 1053–1070 (2006)
4. Sutcliffe, G.: The SZS ontologies for automated reasoning software. In: Sutcliffe, G., Rudnicki, P., Schmidt, R., Konev, B., Schulz, S. (eds.) Proceedings of the LPAR Workshops: Knowledge Exchange: Automated Provers and Proof Assistants, and The 7th International Workshop on the Implementation of Logics. CEUR Workshop Proceedings, vol. 418, pp. 38–49 (2008)
5. Sutcliffe, G.: The TPTP problem library and associated infrastructure: The FOF and CNF Parts, v3.5.0. J. Autom. Reason. **43**(4), 337–362 (2009)
6. Sutcliffe, G.: The TPTP process instruction language, with applications. In: Benzmüller, C., Woltzenlogel Paleo, B. (eds.) Proceedings of the 11th Workshop on User Interfaces for Theorem Provers. Electronic Proceedings in Theoretical Computer Science, vol. 167, p. 1 (2014)
7. Sutcliffe, G., Fuchs, M., Suttner, C.: Progress in automated theorem proving, 1997–1999. In: Hoos, H., Stützle, T. (eds.) Proceedings of the IJCAI 2001 Workshop on Empirical Methods in Artificial Intelligence, pp. 53–60 (2001)
8. Sutcliffe, G., Schulz, S., Claessen, K., Van Gelder, A.: Using the TPTP language for writing derivations and finite interpretations. In: Furbach, U., Shankar, N. (eds.) IJCAR 2006. LNCS (LNAI), vol. 4130, pp. 67–81. Springer, Heidelberg (2006)
9. Sutcliffe, G., Suttner, C.B.: Evaluating general purpose automated theorem proving systems. Artif. Intell. **131**(1-2), 39–54 (2001)
10. Sutcliffe, G., Zimmer, J., Schulz, S.: TSTP data-exchange formats for automated theorem proving tools. In: Zhang, W., Sorge, V. (eds.) Distributed Constraint Problem Solving and Reasoning in Multi-Agent Systems. Frontiers in Artificial Intelligence and Applications, vol. 112, pp. 201–215. IOS Press (2004)
11. Trac, S., Puzis, Y., Sutcliffe, G.: An interactive derivation viewer. In: Autexier, S., Benzmüller, C. (eds.) Proceedings of the 7th Workshop on User Interfaces for Theorem Provers, 3rd International Joint Conference on Automated Reasoning. Electronic Notes in Theoretical Computer Science, vol. 174, pp. 109–123 (2006)
12. Van Gelder, A., Sutcliffe, G.: Extending the TPTP language to higher-order logic with automated parser generation. In: Furbach, U., Shankar, N. (eds.) IJCAR 2006. LNCS (LNAI), vol. 4130, pp. 156–161. Springer, Heidelberg (2006)

Towards Embedded Answer Set Solving

Torsten Schaub

University of Potsdam, Potsdam, Germany

This tutorial introduces advanced problem solving techniques addressing the growing range of applications of Answer Set Programming (ASP; [1]) in practice [2]; its particular focus lies on recent techniques needed for embedding ASP in complex software environments.

The tutorial starts with an introduction to the essential formal concepts of ASP [3], needed for understanding its semantics and solving technology. In fact, ASP solving rests on two major components: A grounder turning specifications in ASP's modeling language into propositional logic programs [4] and a solver computing a requested number of answer sets of the program [5]. We illustrate ASP's grounding techniques and describe the major algorithms used in the ASP grounder `gringo` 4. This is accompanied with an introduction to the new ASP language standard [6]. The remainder of the tutorial is dedicated to using ASP in conjunction with Python for modeling complex reasoning scenarios. This involves an introduction to the API of `clingo` 4, an ASP system extending `clasp` and `gringo` with control capacities expressible in Python (and Lua). See [7] for details. We illustrate this by developing a sample board game [8] and sketch more sophisticated usages in robotics [9] and preference handling [10].

All involved ASP systems, documentation, lecture slides, videos, and further resources are freely available from http://potassco.sourceforge.net.

References

1. Brewka, G., Eiter, T., Truszczynski, M.: Answer set programming at a glance. Commun. ACM **54**(12), 92–103 (2011)
2. Gebser, M., Kaminski, R., Kaufmann, B., Schaub, T.: Answer Set Solving in Practice. Synthesis Lectures on Artificial Intelligence and Machine Learning. Morgan and Claypool Publishers (2012)
3. Gelfond, M., Lifschitz, V.: Logic programs with classical negation. In: Warren, D., Szeredi, P. (eds.) Proceedings of the Seventh International Conference on Logic Programming (ICLP 1990), pp. 579–597. MIT Press (1990)
4. Gebser, M., Harrison, A., Kaminski, R., Lifschitz, V., Schaub, T.: Abstract gringo. http://www.cs.utexas.edu/users/vl/papers/AG.pdf
5. Gebser, M., Kaufmann, B., Schaub, T.: Conflict-driven answer set solving: From theory to practice. Artif. Intell. **187-188**, 52–89 (2012)
6. Calimeri, F., Faber, W., Gebser, M., Ianni, G., Kaminski, R., Krennwallner, T., Leone, N., Ricca, F., Schaub, T.: ASP-Core-2: Input language format (2012). https://www.mat.unical.it/aspcomp2013/files/ASP-CORE-2.0.pdf
7. Gebser, M., Kaminski, R., Kaufmann, B., Lindauer, M., Ostrowski, M., Romero, J., Schaub, T., Thiele, S.: Potassco User Guide. Institute for Informatics, University of Potsdam. 2nd edn. (2015)

© Springer International Publishing Switzerland 2015
W. Faber and A. Paschke (Eds.): Reasoning Web 2015, LNCS 9203, pp. 330–331, 2015.
DOI: 10.1007/978-3-319-21768-0

8. Gebser, M., Kaminski, R., Obermeier, P., Schaub, T.: Ricochet robots reloaded: a case-study in multi-shot asp solving. In: Eiter, T., Strass, H., Truszczyński, M., Woltran, S. (eds.) Advances in Knowledge Representation, Logic Programming, and Abstract Argumentation. LNCS (LNAI), vol. 9060, pp. 17–32. Springer, Heidelberg (2015)

9. Andres, B., Obermeier, P., Sabuncu, O., Schaub, T., Rajaratnam, D.: ROSoClingo: A ROS package for ASP-based robot control. In: Proceedings of Combined Robot Motion Planning and AI Planning for Practical Applications (RSS-CP13) (2013). http://arxiv.org/abs/1307.7398

10. Brewka, G., Delgrande, J., Romero, J., Schaub, T.: asprin: customizing answer set preferences without a headache. In: Bonet, B., Koenig, S. (eds.) Proceedings of the Twenty-Ninth National Conference on Artificial Intelligence (AAAI 2015). AAAI Press (2015)

Author Index

Printed in the United States
By Bookmasters